FARM JOURNAL'S

Homemade Pies, Cookies & Bread

FARM JOURNAL'S

Homemade Pies, Cookies & Bread

by the Food Editors of *Farm Journal*

Greenwich House
Distributed by Crown Publishers, Inc.
New York

This 1983 edition is published by Greenwich House,
a division of Arlington House, Inc.,
distributed by Crown Publishers, Inc. by arrangement
with Doubleday & Company, Inc.

Manufactured in the United States of America

This book was originally published in 3 volumes as
Complete Pie Cookbook, Homemade Cookies, and
Homemade Bread.

Library of Congress Cataloging in Publication Data
Main entry under title:

Farm journal's homemade pies, cookies, and bread.

  Originally published in three volumes as: Complete pie
cookbook, Homemade cookies, and Homemade bread.
  Includes index.
  1. Pastry.   2. Cookies.   3. Bread.   I. Farm journal
(Philadelphia, Pa. : 1956)   II. Title: Homemade pies,
cookies, and bread.
TX773.F3313   1983   641.8′65   83-11674

ISBN: 0-517-415232
h g f e d c b a

CONTENTS

PIES

COOKIES

BREAD

Pies

ALL ABOUT PIES

We invite you to the largest showing of American pies ever presented between the covers of one book. You'll find tested recipes for almost every pie you ever heard of, and for others so new they've never been made outside our Test Kitchens. We've also included pies so old-fashioned you've probably never seen written-down recipes for them—treasures of your heritage.

Pie is America's top dessert. It appeared on New World tables almost from the start—long before the Stars and Stripes flew from a flagpole or the Fourth of July was an extraordinary day. The early pies had more crust than filling—thrifty ingenious pioneer wives stretched scarce ingredients in this way. But pies caught on at once, and each generation of women has widened the variety, improved quality and invented new recipes. Pie has kept in step with the times and new ingredients.

Fruit pies lead the array in our biggest chapter. Recipes using 28 different kinds of fruits and berries—those that grow wild along roadside fence rows or in the woods, those scientifically cultivated, as well as some fruits imported from other countries, all in Chapter 3.

Delicate, velvety custard and cream pies, rich with fresh country eggs, milk and cream, follow. Then the beauty queens—a whole chapter of those refrigerator and ice cream specials (Chapter 5). They are desserts made ahead and held in the controlled, low temperatures of up-to-date refrigerators and freezers until serving time. You'll find some spectacular ones that will bring praise from your guests.

Homey deep-dish pies, the serve-in-bowl desserts practical for every day, are long on fruit and short on pastry. They've always been the farm woman's favorite way to salvage fruit that might otherwise be wasted when the orchard yields a bumper crop. Today, they're good calorie savers, too. You ladle their colorful juices over the servings and set a pitcher of "pour cream" on the table (each individual can be guided by his calorie conscience). Country cobblers—maybe you call them family pies—are a variation of the deep-dish pies. They're so easy to make and ideal for serving a hungry family, especially with unexpected drop-in guests.

3

You'll find samples of the old-time cake pies (cake baked in pie shells) in our Cookbook. Not merely in memory of Grandfather who ate them with such enthusiasm, but also for the hostess who wants something unusual and good for her coffee party.

New fast-fix pies, modern as space travel, make a bow in this book. The cream pies which use modern packaged ingredients in a new way will delight you on busy days. Our Frozen Strawberry Pie is another example. You whip it up with the electric mixer, put it in the freezer and forget about it until you need a luscious dessert in a hurry. Then all you have to do is bring it out, cut the pieces and take it to the table. Like many country specials, the recipe makes two pies.

Tarts and turnovers, the dainty pastries for receptions, teas and parties, are attractive and appetizing served from a tray (Chapter 7). Also among the hostess specials in this book are the toppings (Chapter 9) that touch pies with glamour and make them excitingly different.

No section of our Cookbook holds more surprises than the two chapters (Chapters 10 and 11) of hearty, main-dish pies. Their great variety is impressive, their taste rewarding. Grandmother's Sunday-best and church-supper chicken pies and such new inventions as meaty chicken pieces topped with crunchy, brown popover crust get equal billing.

Many kinds of crusts—rice, potato, biscuit, pastry and corn pone—contribute to the wonderful flavors and texture contrasts of these main dishes. Frozen mashed-potato pie shells and toppings, developed in FARM JOURNAL'S Test Kitchens, will help you bake compliment-winning main dishes on short notice and with small effort. And the vegetable pies in this book are a mother's answer on how to get the children to eat most everything that grows in the garden.

You may wonder why so many apple, cherry and pumpkin pies are featured in our showing. Our reason is simple: They are the pies most often named as favorites. We asked members of our Family Test Group, farm women in all states, to name their families' favorite pies. They listed them in this order: apple, cherry, pumpkin, lemon, chocolate, pecan and coconut —a vote that tallies with other surveys. We felt duty bound to offer you both the traditional versions and creative new ways with these seven wonders of our pie world!

Pioneer Pies—Why Were They Round?

The history of pies fascinates most women. So find an easy chair or prop yourself up in bed—you'll enjoy the next few pages particularly. The creativity of pioneer homemakers, who were as eager as you are to prepare food to please family and friends, will inspire you.

Why were the first pies round instead of square or oblong, for instance? What happened in the New World that shaped pies for centuries to come? Sparse food supplies had much to do with it. Colonial women used round pans literally to cut corners and stretch the ingredients. For the same reason they baked shallow pies. When the orchards and berry patches they planted on cleared, fertile land started to supplement the fruits of the wilderness and "garden sass" became plentiful, truly American pies, plump and juicy, came from ovens. Rhubarb, a New World garden plant, was called pieplant to designate its major use. Increasingly generous amounts of filling were held or wrapped in crisp, golden pastry made with three available staples: flour, lard and water.

Pastry itself was originated on the other side of the Atlantic by the Greeks during their Golden Age. The Romans, sampling the delicacy, carried home recipes for making it—a prize of victory when they conquered Greece. It spread throughout Europe, via the Roman roads, where every country adapted the recipes to their customs and foods. American women followed suit. When they experimented in their colonial kitchens, they came up with different pastries than they had made in their former homes.

Gradually regional pies developed—pumpkin (a native vegetable) in New England, chess and pecan in the South and "nervous pies," or quivering custards teamed with fruits, in Pennsylvania Dutch kitchens. For pies were important taste pleasures in pioneer life. Once, when a sailing ship bringing molasses to Connecticut colony was delayed on the high seas, the Thanksgiving celebration was postponed until the homemakers could have molasses to make pumpkin pies. So it's not surprising that Thanksgiving dinner isn't complete in New England today without pumpkin pie.

Early homemakers were limited by the foods grown on their farms. They of course had to "make do" as much as possible with what they could produce. In contrast, we now draw on the wide world for pie ingredients—chocolate, vanilla, bananas, pineapple and coconut, for example. In our devotion to creamy chocolate pies we sometimes think we are the great chocolate fans of all time. Far from it! The ancient Aztec Indians in Mexico loved the chocolate taste. They prized the native evergreen trees with their clusters of pale pink blossoms that produced the football-shaped pods from which chocolate is made. They even paid their taxes with chocolate —the same as money to them. These ancient Mexicans also revered their "climbing orchid" with its green-yellow flowers—one flower in about a thousand produces a vanilla bean from which the fragrant flavoring is extracted to this very day.

When pioneers traveled inland by waterway and in covered wagons, cherished pie recipes went along. But soon new pies also were created in log cabins and frontier homes—Hoosier Cream Pie, for one (Chapter 4). This is the pie in which the ingredients for the filling were mixed right in pastry-lined pans by fingers so deft that they did not tear the tender pastry.

So from pioneer beginnings to this very day pie recipes have multiplied, and keep multiplying. There is nothing static about pie recipes. Women continually adapt them to changing conditions and ingredients. Trained home economists in test kitchens of research and business perfect techniques and ingredients, too.

Chiffon pies, served originally in a restaurant located by the railroad tracks in Marshalltown, Iowa, are typical of the evolution that takes place. Chiffon pies retain many of the characteristics of their forerunners, the fluff pies, which are still enjoyed (see recipes for Lemon Fluff and Fluffy Pineapple Pies in Chapter 4). Their fluffiness derives from beaten egg whites folded into the filling, as does that of chiffon pies. But it's the addition of gelatin that transformed the old fluff pies into the gorgeous chiffons, and the refrigerator makes them practical.

Pies Are Party Fare

Because pies were enjoyed so much, they became a part of neighborhood festivities from the start. Pie-eating contests were highlights at gatherings like county fairs. The champion—the man who could eat the most pie—was the envy of his neighbors, many of whom secretly wished for a greater capacity for their pie favorites.

Young women, as recently as a generation ago, practiced to bake pretty pies of exceptional quality for pie-supper auctions in one-room country schoolhouses. They toted these pies in boxes they had covered with pastel colored tissue or crepe paper or wallpaper scraps and decorated with paper flowers made by their nimble and artistic fingers. The auctioneer was a clever fellow who used all the showman's tricks. He hinted who baked the pie he held, removing the lid of the box just enough to give the tantalized young beaux a glimpse of the treat within.

Pies went along in carriages and spring wagons to all-day picnics in the grove and showed up at family reunions in quantity and variety. They pleased and satisfied the hungry threshing crews in the steam engine era. The men always had a choice: "Raisin? Apple? Do try this berry!"

No wonder pie baking stimulated a friendly, competitive spirit in country kitchens. Women vied with one another, as they do today, to see who could bake the best to take to church suppers, bake sales and other social gatherings. We guarantee that the tested, unusual recipes in this Cookbook will win prizes and praises.

Pies Stimulate Baking Contests

Today baking contests, sponsored by food manufacturers, thrive on a national scale, enlisting the interest, efforts and imagination of thousands of homemakers. The 4-H Club baking demonstrations, judged by home economics experts coast-to-coast, who hand out the blue, red and white ribbons, promote good baking among future homemakers. The Cherry Pie Baking Contest for girls, formerly national, still is held in some regions. And home-baked pies are entered year after year in state and county fairs to win coveted prizes and recognition for the women who make them.

Pies Capture Hearts

Pies have won their way into our culture—and our sentiments. You've heard a doting grandmother call a grandchild, "Sweetie Pie," an expression of endearment. Husbands and wives use the same affectionate term. The lonely cowboy, returning from a long day in the saddle to the brightest spot on the cattle spread, the chuck wagon, called it the pie box.

Now, the chuck wagon is likely to be a pickup truck, complete with a bottled-gas stove, refrigerator and running water. The dishpan still is the "wreck pan" in which the workers at roundups stack their dishes after a meal. Canned goods are "airtights," sweet syrups are "lick," knives and forks are "artillery." But the bread is usually the commercial loaf. Not the pies, though! They are baked on the spot. A New Mexico roundup helper puts it this way: "Freshly baked pies are the men's favorite dessert. We demand them. And we hope for luck—occasional servings of fresh peach and berry pies."

Some young men still refer to their homes as "the pie house"—a tribute to their mothers' baking skills. One homemaker says: "I've wiped away more than one tear over a letter from my son, far away in military service, when he writes, 'What wouldn't I give for a piece of your chocolate pie!' To cheer myself up, I start planning all the pies I'm going to bake when my boy comes home." And some FARM JOURNAL readers tell us they bake birthday pies for their husbands by request. These men prefer to have lighted candles on pies rather than cakes.

Pies Like Mother Used to Make

It's one of our national traits to hold on to the best of the old that's practical under present conditions and to accept the best of the new with enthusiasm, like chiffon and ice cream pies. Almost all women at one time feel the urge to bake an old-fashioned pie whose appeal has been proved through the generations. Frequently the spur is the husband with a yen for a wonderful pie his mother used to make. Some old baking techniques worth holding on to (although more work than most women would put into everyday pie) are the maneuvers with crust.

New England, most food historians agree, was the cradle of American pies. The tricks with crust which women there used were not glamorous; they created good eating, not beauty. Indeed they were as free of adornment as a Puritan hat. Take-off crusts, for example. Some homemakers still make apple pies (and peach) this way. They place the apples in the pastry-lined pan and gently lay the crust on top, but do not seal it to the undercrust. After baking the pie, they carefully lift off the top crust, add the sugar and spices and return the pastry lid to the pie. Champions of this old-fashioned pie insist that the fruit sweetened after baking has an unusually fresh-from-the-orchard taste. (For peaches, they usually combine

½ cup sugar with the fruit before baking and pour a cool, delicate custard instead of sugar and spices, into the finished pie.)

Old-time pour-through crusts have a somewhat larger band of loyal supporters (see Dutch-Style Apple Pie, Chapter 3). The apple pie, for instance, is made in the standard way, except that the steam vents in the top crust are cut larger. About 5 minutes before the pie is done, early-day homemakers would take it from the oven and pour ½ cup heavy cream (for a nine-inch pie) through the vents, then finish the baking. A similar custom, with some ardent admirers, is performed with baked apple pie. Just before serving, the cook cuts around the pie with a small sharp knife, through the crust, near the fluted edge. She lifts the cut-out circle and pours the cream into the pie, places the crust back on the pie, cuts and serves it.

Bake an Old-Fashioned Pie

There are times when a truly old-fashioned pie becomes a great conversation piece. You'll find some in this Cookbook—2-Crust Lemon, Shoofly, Lemon Whey, Brown-Butter Butterscotch and Marlborough, to name a few. For the butterscotch pie (Chapter 4), you brown the butter and then add dark brown sugar. Requires close skillet watching to avoid scorching the butter, but it has its own taste that some people rave over. Certainly it's not as foolproof as the recipe for Butterscotch Cream Pie in the same chapter, one of our own Test Kitchen specials.

Try the historic Marlborough Pie (Chapter 3), a glorification of everyday apple pie, that is thickened with eggs; lemon juice and grated peel point up the flavors. This pie is still served in New England, and during the Thursday-through-Sunday Thanksgiving holiday it shares honors with pumpkin, mince and cranberry pies. Sometimes slivers (small triangles) of the four pies are served together to make the proper traditional meal ending at this season.

Pies for Calorie Counters

Perhaps the greatest compliment to pies is the way the dessert holds its own in a weight-conscious age—proof that they're too good to give up. True, some of the exceptionally rich treats have been abandoned. Hoosier

Cream Pie, for instance, the old-fashioned pie previously mentioned. Its filling contained only pure cream, sugar, flavoring and a little flour for thickening. Apple-Pork Pie (Chapter 6) is disappearing even from farm tables. Part of its decline can be attributed to the changing farm scene. Now that farm animals usually are slaughtered, processed and the meat frozen in locker plants, there's rarely the former excess of salt pork that must be used. So naturally, apple pie with salt pork, cut in pieces the size of small peas, combined with the fruit and baked in pastry, would be baked less frequently, regardless of its calorie content. (Good, though!)

The excellent cooks of this country have, however, found ways to reduce calories, either in a meal they'll end with pie, or in the pie itself. You'll find lower-calorie pies scattered throughout this Cookbook. And in Chapter 2 there are special recipes for crusts that contain minimum amounts of fat.

We serve more single-crust pies today—one gesture to weight control. We often substitute whipped dry milk and packaged whip mix for whipped cream. Frequently we cut pies in smaller pieces—especially the rich ones. You'll notice that the recipes in this Cookbook give pan sizes, but rarely suggest the number of servings. How a woman divides a pie is an individual matter controlled by the rest of the meal, the family's appetite and degree of weight consciousness.

No Matter How You Cut It

All country homemakers know that, traditionally, an eight-inch pie cuts 4 to 6 wedges, a nine-inch, 6 and a ten-inch, 8. Frequently, if the pie is not being served to men who do hard physical labor, women cut more wedges. Or they cut the pieces of uneven size, the larger ones for grownups, the smaller for the children. And for preschool youngsters, often only the filling, baked in custard cups instead of in pastry, is served.

You can easily cut a pie in 5 pieces of equal size if that arrangement fits your family. Here's the way to do it. Start at the center of the pie and cut a straight line to the edge of the pie. From the center above the line, cut a V. You then will have a capital Y, the upper part making a wedge. Divide the 2 remaining large pieces in half. You will have pieces the same size. Practice with pencil and paper before you use a knife on a pie, to make certain the V is the right width. Of course, you can cut a narrower V if you wish to cut 1 wedge smaller than the other 4.

When our recipe indicates that an eight- or nine-inch pie makes more than 6 servings, that's our way of saying the pie is extremely rich.

Freezers Revolutionize Pie Storage

Home food freezers have practically banished seasons for pies—like pumpkin in autumn, cherry at cherry-picking time and dewberry and boysenberry when the berries are ripe in the patch. Even the wild fruits—blueberries, blackberries, huckleberries, raspberries, elderberries, mulberries and the West's service berries (pronounced sarvis)—are frozen when ripe for year-round pie baking. Colorado mountain ranchwomen often complain that bears get more than their share of the raspberry crop, Minnesota women that bears are too fond of blueberries. So we still have our frontiers where wild animals interfere with pie baking!

Freezers also have changed the pattern of storing pies. Less than a century ago, pie safes with pierced tin panels were standard equipment in Pennsylvania Dutch and other farm kitchens. The perforations in the tin formed decorative designs, which partly explains why these safes today are antique-fanciers' prizes. The tiny openings provided ventilation for the rows of pies on the shelves waiting for hungry people, and also gave protection from flies in an age when windows were unscreened and fly sprays were unknown.

New England homemakers often baked from 50 to 100 mince pies in November, stacked them in covered stone crocks and stored them in the woodshed or some other service room attached to the rear of the house. The pies were protected by a roof. And so was the homemaker; she did not have to step out in the snow and cold to bring them, when needed, to the kitchen to thaw and warm on the shelves of the pie cupboard in the fireplace chimney. (In Boston, this was after mince pies "came back." Originally they were baked in manger-shaped pans at Christmastime, with the shape of the pies symbolic of the Christ child's manger and the spices of the gifts of the Three Wise Men. The Puritans considered these pies idolatrous and abolished not only the pies by law, but also the outward celebration aspects of Christmas.)

Today's farm homemakers usually bake at least a couple of extra pies while they have the rolling pin out and the ingredients handy. A member of FARM JOURNAL's Family Test Group says: "I seldom bake one pie at a time. Ordinarily, I make 4 to 6 and the same number of crusts and put them in the freezer. I make these pies in assorted sizes so that I can select the one that best fits the number of people to be served."

Modern Pie-making Bees

It's not too unusual for two or more farm women to spend a day together in one of their kitchens making pies to freeze when a fruit is plentiful. They socialize while they work—a new kind of get-together, replacing the quilting bee. (Some homemakers prefer to fix and freeze pie fillings instead of the finished pie. This Cookbook gives the directions.)

Cars become pie wagons as visiting neighbors take their share of the pies home to their freezers. Convenient pie carriers, plastic and metal, simplify toting one or two pies to community suppers, bake sales and other places. Compare the ease of this system with the Southern custom of horse-and-buggy days, when women stacked transparent pies (a form of chess pie) and fastened them together by spreading on a cooked frosting so they could be carried safely in a basket to all-day picnics once so popular.

What's Your Pie Appeal?

How attractive are your shut, open and bar pies, as Grandmother classified the pies she baked? (We refer to them as 2-crust, 1-crust and open-face pies.) Many of today's cooks are not the top-crust artists their mothers and grandmothers were. If you want to fix pies with fancy tops and pretty edges, read the suggestions in Chapter 2. Perhaps we also can take a few lessons from old-time Dutch or German women in Pennsylvania, Virginia, Connecticut and North Carolina, who excelled in creating beautiful pies (extra good) with tools commonplace in their kitchens—the 4-tined fork, for instance.

One of their homespun tricks was to run a fork in one direction over the top of an unbaked 2-crust pie, then the other direction. The lines formed a plaid. In baking, the surface at different levels took on variegated shades of brown—most attractive and it cost no more. Or they would cut a design (steam vents) in the top crust with a sharp knife—through the pastry in some places, not quite through in others. With a thin knife blade, they carefully lifted the cut edges (in places where the cut was not through the crust) to ruffle during the baking. Again uneven browning made the pie top intriguing.

Take a thimble from your sewing basket. Wash and use it for a pattern, as your grandmothers did, to cut steam vents and a Coin Edge (Chapter 2). Today there are tiny cookie and canapé cutters of many shapes that make interesting steam vents and trims for pie edges. And some homemakers paint pastry cutouts with egg-yolk paint—a few drops of food color added to egg yolk—and bake them separately from the 1-crust pie. They arrange them over the baked pie.

Hearty Main-Dish Pies

While the major part of this book features dessert pies, the last two chapters are filled with tempting meat, chicken, fish, sea food, cheese and vegetable pies. Many of these main-dish pies are outstanding enough to serve on special occasions. All of them are simply delicious. Explore these pages and use the recipes to give your meals a pleasing change, your meat platters a rest. Interestingly enough, main-course pies have not caught on in America the way dessert pies have. But in Europe they are great favorites. We think our recipes will make fans out of you and your family.

Try a cheese pie some evening. Or shrimp pie. Treat your family to Brunswick Chicken Pie. Or make the crusty chicken pie with the light meat on one side, the dark on the other. Notice the tantalizing effect the fragrance has on everyone around the table when the serving spoon cuts through the flaky crust into the steaming gravy and chicken. Guaranteed to fascinate guests! Serve updated Shepherd's Pie with pride—there are farmers who say no better way of serving leftover roast beef or lamb, mashed potatoes and brown gravy has ever been invented. You'll wonder why main-dish pies could be neglected.

Perfect Pies Every Time

Never were pies so good as they are today. Research has improved and standardized ingredients and techniques. For instance, you'll observe that many of the pies in this Cookbook are baked at a constant temperature—

no adjusting of the oven regulator during baking is necessary. And top-notch ingredients are universally available. (Especially has rancid fat become rare in home kitchens!)

But the best part of all is that any woman who wants to bake perfect pies can realize her ambition—quickly. All she need do is follow the recipes and directions in this Cookbook. If she does this, the old expression "easy as pie" will come true for her.

Every neighborhood has a few women experienced in cooking who are locally famous for their crusts and pies. Some beginners (often brides) believe these homemakers are born with special talents in baking. They don't realize how many of them learned by the discouraging "trial and error" method no longer necessary with up-to-date recipes and directions. What suggestions do these wonderful home bakers have for new cooks?

Universally, their first tip is: Use a light hand with pastry. The next one: roll the dough lightly from the center in all directions to make a circle, lifting the rolling pin near the edges to avoid splitting the pastry or getting it too thin. Lift the pastry to the pie pan gently—as carefully as you'd handle a full-blown rose—and avoid stretching it. Bend your right index finger (if you're right-handed) and fit the pastry into the pan. One expert pie maker, remembering her first pies, sympathetically adds: "Don't despair if you tear the pastry. Pinch the edges together or put on a pastry patch so the juices can't run away. But do avoid a repeat of the mishap when you bake the next pie."

First Things First—Pastry

Turn the pages of this Cookbook—cooking adventure and success are that near. For with pie, it's pastry first, and the next chapter is all about pastry. Master the making of pie crusts and you've won more than half of the victory in achieving perfect pies. When you're proud of the traditional and oil pastry you make, branch out and try some of the marvelous specialties in this chapter—like cheese, orange, egg, cornmeal and peanut pastry. And when you're making a lemon pie, do use the pastry designed especially for pies made with sunny, citrus fruit. Make many kinds of crusts, not only those with graham cracker crumbs. Use those made with coconut, cereals, nuts, cookie dough and pretzels, for instance, and the light, crunchy-crisp meringues.

From the chapter on pie crusts turn the pages of this book to plump and juicy fruit pies; delicate, browned-topped custards; flavorful cream pies and the make-ahead beauties; refrigerator and ice cream pies. Continue your recipe tour to deep-dish fruit and cake pies, homey cobblers, apples and peaches baked in flaky dumpling jackets, party-pretty tarts and dainty turnovers. You'll want to stop long enough to get acquainted with the appealing fast-fix pies if ever you're short on time for cooking. Your dessert journey ends with glamorous, sweet pie toppings that offer new flavor blends and a new look. By this time, we believe you'll have a long list of pies you'll want to bake soon.

But keep reading and get acquainted with the main-dish pies. You'll find their succulent tastes a big help in putting new zip and surprise in your meals.

Round Out a Square Meal

"Cutting the pie" has come to mean dividing something good. And that's exactly what we are doing with this Cookbook—sharing with you favorite pie recipes from farm women in all parts of the country and from our own Test Kitchens. We hope you will enjoy making and serving many of these luscious pies. You can do so with complete confidence that your family will compliment you on your baking skill and guests will beg for your recipes.

Remember that pies please men. Since men are the great pie eaters and promoters, let's give a rancher friend the last word—his definition of his favorite dessert: "A triangle of pie is the best way ever discovered to round out a square meal."

PIE CRUSTS OF ALL KINDS

Pie crust is one of the great kitchen discoveries of all time. Women who transform flour, salt, fat and water into flaky, fork-tender, golden pastry are magicians in their way. They pull gorgeous pies from ovens rather than colored-silk handkerchiefs from hats. Think of the pleasure they bring—velvet-smooth pumpkin pies for Thanksgiving reunions, juicy cherry pies for February parties and plump apple pies for friendly Sunday dinners.

Country women know you can't have a good pie without a good crust. What some homemakers don't appreciate is the way you can introduce tasty variety in pies by using different crusts. This chapter has two important purposes—to help you make perfect pies every time and to encourage you to experiment with the many kinds of pie crusts we give you.

You'll first find basic pastry, both that made with solid vegetable shortening or lard, and with salad oil. Perfecting these basics is the initial step in successful pie making. There also are recipes for Electric-Mixer Pastry, Homemade Pie Crust Mixes, special crusts for tarts and turnovers, one particularly luscious with butter, Beginner's Pastry (the paste method) and a short-cut version that you mix in the pie pan.

Then we have the specialty crusts, mentioned in Chapter 1—everything from fancy pastry to crumb, cereal, coconut and crispy-firm meringue pie shells, large and individual sizes, for angel pies. Biscuit Toppers for Main-Dish Pies (the recipe also makes wonderful hot biscuits) with nine variations are included. At the chapter end you'll find our Pie Clinic, which gives you the reasons your pies may fall short of perfection and answers your pastry questions.

Many suggestions for making pretty pies and fancy edges are described. You'll enjoy using these dress-up ideas for pies to tote to church and community suppers and bake sales.

Perfect Pastry for Country Pies

Country cooks need no introduction to perfect pastry; they know a good pie crust when they see, cut and taste it. The top of the pie is light-golden to golden in the center, the brown deepening slightly toward the edges. It has what our grandmothers called "bloom," a soft luster rather than a dull look.

The surface of the baked crust is a little blistery or irregular, although pastry made with hot water or oil usually is smoother (it also is more mealy than pastry made with lard or other shortening). The crust is thin. It's delicately crisp and flaky, easy to cut, fork-tender and not crumbly; it holds its shape when cut.

Blandness in taste is characteristic and desirable—the filling provides heightened flavors. The taste depends primarily on just the right amount of salt and on the kind of fat used. It's important, of course, to use high-quality fat, free of rancidity.

In this chapter's recipes, use all-purpose flour unless another kind is listed. If you use flour that does not require sifting, follow package directions. Or use the special pastry recipe we give for instant-type flour.

There's no mystery about pastry making. All you need do to achieve success is to be loyal to the recipe you are following in this chapter.

Do not improvise. Heed the technique suggested and *do not change the ingredients*—their proportions are balanced. Just one warning—be careful when adding water. If you add too much, you'll have to increase the flour to take care of it and the ratio of fat to flour is upset. This is one of the common causes of inferior pie crusts.

When it comes to making *attractive* pies, every woman is largely on her own. We do give you tips for pretty pie tops and fancy edges, which may help. Be an observing pie scout—look at the pies you see at parties, church suppers, bake sales and other places. Notice why some of them are especially attractive. Don't be afraid to copy some of the ideas you see.

Do serve your pies the day you bake them unless you are freezing them or making one by a recipe that specifies otherwise. It's the fresh-baked quality that won first place among desserts for pies on the farms and eventually in the entire United States. Their supremacy constantly is challenged by other desserts, but never successfully. Country cooks have had much to do with keeping pie the top-ranking American dessert—a tribute to the women on farms and ranches.

Basic Pastry-making Tools

Standard measuring spoons and cup

Mixing bowl (large enough to hold all ingredients with ample room for measuring)

Pastry blender, 2 table knives or an electric mixer at low speed (to cut shortening or lard into flour)

Fork (to combine water with flour-shortening mixture)

Evenly floured pastry cloth or board or waxed paper (for rolling pastry)

Rolling pin that rolls easily (floured stockinette cover helps prevent sticking when pastry is not rolled between sheets of waxed paper)

Pie pans of size (check by measuring top inside diameter) recommended in recipe (members of FARM JOURNAL's Family Test Group have more 9" pans, but many kitchens have 8" and 10" pans)

Pie pans that absorb and distribute heat evenly, such as glass or dull aluminum (shiny pans reflect heat and interfere with browning)

Pie server (wedge-shaped spatula)

Flaky Pastry

This is the traditional or standard pie crust. Make it with solid fats, except butter and margarine. Measure shortening or lard in nested measuring cups. Press it into the cup to avoid air pockets and level it off with a knife or spatula.

FLAKY PASTRY FOR 2-CRUST PIE

(Traditional Method)

2   c. sifted flour
1   tsp. salt
¾   c. vegetable shortening or ⅔ c. lard
4   to 5 tblsp. cold water

• Combine flour and salt in mixing bowl. Cut in shortening with pastry blender or with two knives until mixture is the consistency of coarse cornmeal or tiny peas.

• Sprinkle on cold water, 1 tblsp. at a time, tossing mixture lightly and stirring with fork. Add water each time to the driest part of mixture. The dough should be just moist enough to hold together when pressed gently with a fork. It should not be sticky.

• Shape dough in smooth ball with hands, and roll. Or if you are not ready to make the pie, wrap it in waxed paper and refrigerate 30 minutes or until ready to fill and bake pie.

• Makes crust for 1 (8" or 9") 2-crust pie, 2 (8" or 9") pie shells, 8 or 9 (4") tart shells, 1 (9" or 10") pie with latticed top or topping for 2 (8" or 9") deep-dish pies.

To Make 2-Crust Pie

• Divide dough in half and shape in 2 flat balls, smoothing edges so there are no breaks.

Bottom Crust: Press 1 dough ball in flat circle with hands on lightly floured surface. Roll it lightly with short strokes from center in all directions to ⅛″ thickness, making a 10″ to 11″ circle. Fold rolled dough in half and ease it loosely into pie pan with fold in center. Unfold and fit into pan, using care not to stretch dough. Gently press out air pockets with finger tips. Make certain there are no openings for juices to escape.

• Trim edge even with pie pan. Then roll top crust.

Top Crust: Roll second ball of dough like the first one (for bottom crust). Put filling in pastry-lined pan. Fold pastry circle in half; lift it to the top of the pie with fold in center. Gently unfold over top of pie. Trim with scissors to ½″ beyond edge of pie. Fold top edge under bottom crust and press gently with fingers to seal and to make an upright edge. Crimp edge as desired.

• Cut vents in top crust or prick with fork to allow steam to escape. (Or cut vents before placing pastry on top of pie.) Bake as pie recipe directs.

Lattice Pie Tops Display Filling

Country women especially like to top their pies with a pastry lattice when the filling is colorful—cherries, for instance. For the same reason, this peek-a-boo topping is traditional for cranberry pies in Cape Cod communities.

Many farm women roll pastry slightly thicker than usual for a lattice top. That's because the strips are easier to handle.

There are several ways to make the lattice. Here are a few of the favorites, including the new Wedge Lattice, developed in our Test Kitchens.

LATTICE PIE TOP: Line pie pan with pastry as described, leaving 1″ overhang. Cut rolled pastry for top crust in strips ½″ wide. Add filling to pastry-lined pan. Moisten rim of pie with water and lay half of the strips over the pie about 1″ apart. Repeat with remaining strips, placing them in opposite direction in diamond or square pattern. Trim strips even with pie edge. Turn bottom crust's overhang up over rim and ends of strips. Press firmly all around to seal strips to rim. Flute edge as desired.

FANCY LATTICE TOP: Twist strips of pastry placed over pie to make the lattice; cut strips with rippled pastry wheel to give a pretty edge.

WOVEN LATTICE TOP: Lay half the pastry strips 1″ apart over the filled pie. Weave the first cross strip through the center. Add another cross strip, first folding back every other strip to help in weaving crosswise strips over and under. Continue weaving until lattice is complete. Fold lower crust over pastry strips, press firmly around the edge to seal strips to the rim. Flute edge as desired. You may find it easier to weave lattice on waxed paper, lifting it on to pie.

SPIRAL TOPPING: Cut pastry strips ¾" wide and fasten them together by moistening ends with water and pressing with fingers. Twist strip and swirl in spiral from pie's center, covering pie's filling.

WEDGE LATTICE: Cut long strips of pastry ½" wide. Place on top of pie in the same number of wedge shapes as you plan to cut pieces of pie (see color photo elsewhere in book), keep sides of wedges inside lines where you will cut serving pieces. Use more pastry strips to make smaller V shapes inside the larger wedges, trimming off excess pastry. Press ends to moistened pastry on pan edge. Fold pastry overhang to cover ends of pastry strips and seal. Finish with decorative edge.

method. Shape 1 smooth ball of dough. Makes enough for 1 (8" or 9") pie shell or top crust for 1½ qt. casserole.

To Make Pie Shell

Unbaked: On lightly floured surface roll Pastry for 1-Crust Pie. Roll it lightly from the center out in all directions to ⅛" thickness, making a 10" to 11" circle. Fold rolled dough in half and ease it loosely into pie pan, with fold in center. Gently press out air pockets with finger tips and make certain there are no openings for juices to escape.
• Fold under edge of crust and press into an upright rim. Crimp edge as desired. Refrigerate until ready to fill.

Baked: Make pie shell as directed for Unbaked Pie Shell, pricking entire surface evenly and closely (¼" to ½" apart) with a 4-tined fork. Refrigerate ½ hour. Meanwhile, preheat oven. Bake pie shell in very hot oven (450° F.) from 10 to 15 minutes, or until browned the way you like it. Cool before filling.

FLAKY PASTRY FOR 1-CRUST PIE

(*Traditional Method*)

1	c. sifted flour
½	tsp. salt
⅓	c. plus 1 tblsp. vegetable shortening or ⅓ c. lard
2	to 2½ tblsp. cold water

• Combine ingredients as directed for Pastry for 2-Crust Pie, traditional

PASTRY FOR (10") 2-CRUST PIE

(*Traditional Method*)

3	c. sifted flour
1½	tsp. salt
1	c. plus 2 tblsp. vegetable shortening or 1 c. lard
6	tblsp. water

• Combine as directed in recipe for Flaky Pastry for 2-Crust Pie.

GOOD IDEA: Draw a circle on waxed paper to use for a guide in rolling pastry. Make the circle about 1½″ to 2″ larger than your pie-pan diameter.

HOMEMADE PASTRY MIX

With Lard:
7   c. sifted flour
4   tsp. salt
2   c. lard

With Vegetable Shortening:
6   c. sifted flour
1   tblsp. salt
1   (1 lb.) can vegetable shortening (about 2⅓ c.)

· Mix flour and salt in large bowl. Cut in lard or shortening until mixture resembles coarse meal. Cover and store mix made with lard in refrigerator. It will keep about a month. Store mix made with vegetable shortening in a cool place. It does not require refrigeration. Makes from 8 to 9 cups.

How to Use Pastry Mix

To Make a 1-Crust Pie: Use 2 to 4 tblsp. cold water and:
1¼   c. mix for 8″ pie
1½   c. mix for 9″ pie
1¾   c. mix for 10″ pie

To Make a 2-Crust Pie: Use 4 to 6 tblsp. cold water and:
2   to 2¼ c. mix for 8″ pie
2¼   to 2½ c. mix for 9″ pie
2½   to 2¾ c. mix for 10″ pie

· Measure mix into bowl. Sprinkle on water, a small amount at a time, mixing quickly and evenly with fork until dough just holds together in a ball. Use no more water than necessary.
· Proceed as with traditional pastry.

GOOD IDEA: Spread a sheet of aluminum foil directly on bottom of oven under a 2-Crust fruit pie to catch runaway juices. When so placed, it will not deflect the heat from the pie.

GOOD IDEAS FROM OUR TEST KITCHENS

Home economists in FARM JOURNAL's Test Kitchens prefer to use ice water instead of cold water in pastry making. They recommend that beginners put the water in a salt shaker to sprinkle over the flour-shortening mixture. This helps to add the water evenly.

They like to cut two thirds of the shortening or lard into the flour until it resembles cornmeal, then to cut in the remaining third until the particles are the size of small peas.

Pastry with Instant-Type Flour

There are two methods of making pastry with instant-type flour. The ingredients for both are combined with the electric mixer. Follow directions carefully and accurately.

METHOD NUMBER ONE

PASTRY FOR 2-CRUST PIE

1¾   c. instant-type flour
1   tsp. salt
¾   c. vegetable shortening
¼   c. cold water

· Measure flour and salt into electric mixer's small bowl. Stir to mix. Add shortening and mix at low speed about

1 minute, scraping bowl constantly. Add water and continue mixing until all flour is moistened, about 1 minute. Scrape bowl constantly. (You may need to add 1 to 2 tsp. more water, but be careful not to add too much.) Shape in smooth ball with hands.
• Follow directions for making 2-Crust Pie from Flaky Pastry.
• Makes 1 (8″ or 9″) 2-crust pie.

Note: You can use ½ c. plus 2 tblsp. lard instead of vegetable shortening.

PASTRY FOR 1-CRUST PIE

1   c. instant-type flour
½   tsp. salt
⅓   c. plus 1 tblsp. vegetable shortening
2   tblsp. cold water

• Combine as for Pastry for 2-Crust Pie. Shape in smooth ball of dough. Makes 1 (8″ or 9″) pie shell.

Note: You can use ⅓ c. lard instead of the vegetable shortening.

METHOD NUMBER TWO
PASTRY FOR 2-CRUST PIE

⅓   c. plus 1 tblsp. cold water
¾   c. shortening
2   c. instant-type flour
1   tsp. salt

• Measure all ingredients into electric mixer's bowl. Mix on lowest speed until dough begins to form, 15 to 30 sec-

onds. Shape in firm, smooth ball with hands. Follow directions for 2-Crust Pie from Flaky Pastry.
• Makes 1 (8″ or 9″) 2-crust pie.

PASTRY FOR 1-CRUST PIE

¼   c. water
½   c. shortening
1 ¼   c. instant-type flour
½   tsp. salt

• Combine as for pastry for 2-Crust Pie. Shape in firm, smooth ball.
• Makes 1 (8″ or 9″) pie shell.

ELECTRIC-MIXER PASTRY

Blending is done with mixer—no cutting of shortening into flour and salt

2-Crust 8″ or 9″ Pie
⅔   c. vegetable shortening
1 ¾   c. flour
1   tsp. salt
¼   c. cold water

1-Crust 8″ or 9″ Pie
¼   c. vegetable shortening
¾   c. flour
½   tsp. salt
2   tblsp. cold water

• Place shortening, flour and salt in mixer bowl. Blend at low speed about ½ minute or until mixture is consistency of coarse cornmeal.
• Add all water at one time and mix on low speed about 15 seconds, or until dough clings together. Shape dough in ball. It should feel moist. Follow directions for crusts mixed by traditional method.

Freezing Pastry

Busy farm women sometimes find it easier to make pies and tarts if they have the frozen pastry shells on hand. Other homemakers prefer to freeze pastry dough to thaw and shape when they're ready to use it. Here are directions to follow:

BAKED PIE AND TART SHELLS: Freeze without wrapping. When frozen, wrap with sheet freezer material and seal or place in freezer bags.

To use, unwrap and heat in moderate oven (375°F.) about 10 minutes. If more convenient, let thaw, unwrapped, at room temperature.

UNBAKED PIE AND TART SHELLS: Freeze without wrapping. Stack when frozen, placing crumpled waxed paper between them for easier separation. Package or place in freezer bags, and return to freezer.

To use, unwrap and bake in very hot oven (450°F.) 5 minutes. Then prick with 4-tined fork and continue baking until browned, about 15 minutes.

UNBAKED PASTRY: Roll it before or after freezing. If rolled, stack the circles with 2 or 3 sheets of waxed paper between them. Freeze and then package or place in freezer bags. Wrap unrolled pastry dough in freezer paper or plastic wrapping and place in freezer.

To use frozen pastry, unwrap and let it thaw at room temperature; then proceed as if it had just been made.

Note: The recommended storage time for unbaked pie and tart shells and pastry is 2 months; for baked pie and tart shells and pastry, 4 to 6 months.

Pie Crusts Made with Oil

The pastry dough is tender. Be sure to roll it between sheets of waxed paper. One advantage of using oil is that it's easy to measure.

PASTRY FOR 2-CRUST PIE

(*With Oil*)

2   c. sifted flour
1   tsp. salt
½   c. cooking or salad oil
3   tblsp. cold water

• Sift flour and salt into mixing bowl. Add oil, mix well with fork. Sprinkle cold water over mixture and mix well.

• With hands press mixture into a smooth ball. (If mix is too dry, add 1 to 2 tblsp. more oil, a little at a time and then shape ball.) Divide ball in half and flatten both parts slightly. Makes 1 (8″ or 9″) 2-crust pie or 2 (8″ or 9″) pie shells.

PASTRY FOR 1-CRUST PIE

(*With Oil*)

1⅓   c. sifted flour
½   tsp. salt
⅓   c. cooking or salad oil
2   tblsp. cold water

• Combine ingredients as directed for Pastry for 2-Crust Pie with cooking oil. Make 1 smooth ball of dough. (If mixture is too dry, add 1 to 2 tblsp. more oil, a little at a time.) Makes 1 (8″ or 9″) pie shell.

To Make 2-Crust Pie
(With Oil)

Bottom Crust: Wipe countertop or board with a damp cloth so waxed paper will not slip. Roll out 1 dough ball to circle between 2 (12″) square sheets waxed paper to edge of paper. Peel off top sheet of paper and gently invert pastry over pie plate; peel off paper. (The pastry is tender. If it tears, press edges together or lightly press a patch over it.)
• Fit pastry carefully into pie pan, using care not to stretch. Trim evenly with edge of pan.

Top Crust: Roll out remaining dough ball between two sheets of waxed paper as directed for Bottom Crust. Peel off top paper. Add filling to pastry-lined pan. Arrange rolled pastry over filled pie and peel off paper. Cut vents for steam to escape. Trim crust ½″ beyond edge of pie pan; fold top crust under bottom crust. Flute edge. Bake as pie recipe directs.

To Make Pie Shell
(Oil Pastry)

Unbaked Pie Shell: Wipe countertop or board with a damp cloth so paper will not slip. Roll out pastry between 2 (12″) sheets waxed paper to edge of paper. Peel off top sheet of paper and gently invert pastry over pie pan; peel off paper. Fit pastry into pie pan, pressing gently with finger tips toward center of pan.
• Trim crust ½″ beyond edge of pie pan, fold under edge of crust and crimp to make upright rim. Refrigerate until ready to fill and bake.

Baked Pie Shell: Make pie shell as directed for Unbaked Pie Shell, only prick entire surface evenly with 4-tined fork. Refrigerate ½ hour. Meanwhile, preheat oven. Bake pie shell in very hot oven (450°F.), 10 to 15 minutes, until browned. Cool before filling.

GOOD IDEA: Roll pastry between waxed paper to the desired size. Chill in waxed paper while you fix the pie filling. You'll find the paper will peel off easily from the pastry. This is one way to avoid rolling too much flour into the dough.

Pastry with Less Fat

If someone in the family is counting calories, or if you're cutting down on fat in your diet, we have two recipes for satisfactory pastry with less than the usual amount of fat. Follow mixing directions closely—they were worked out by U. S. Department of Agriculture scientists. Do not try to freeze either of the recipes. The low-oil pastry and pastry made with less than ⅓ c. shortening to 1 c. flour do not freeze satisfactorily.

SOLID-FAT PASTRY

Breaking the solid fat into fine particles and sprinkling in water distributes them evenly—makes for flakiness

2 c. sifted flour
¾ tsp. salt
½ c. lard or vegetable shortening (room temperature)
3 tblsp. water

• Sift flour and salt together into mixing bowl. Using an electric mixer on lowest speed, blend lard into dry ingredients for 2 minutes, then sprinkle in the water gradually while blending 1 minute. Or, cut in fat with pastry blender or two knives until finely distributed. The dough will look dry and crumbly, but will shape into a ball. Roll out between sheets of waxed paper. Makes 1 (8″ or 9″) 2-crust pie.

OIL PASTRY

Even distribution of oil and water makes melt-in-the-mouth pastry

½ c. minus 1 tblsp. cooking or salad oil
¼ c. water
2 c. sifted flour
¾ tsp. salt

• Shake together oil and water (both at room temperature).
• Sift dry ingredients together into mixing bowl; sprinkle with water-oil mixture while blending with electric mixer at lowest speed for 3 minutes. Or, stir it in with a fork. Dough will seem dry but it can be molded easily by hand. Shape it into ball, flatten slightly, roll out between sheets of waxed paper. Makes 1 (8″ or 9″) 2-crust pie.

Pretty Tops for Country Pies

Country cooks have many last-minute, quick, glamorous touches for 2-crust pies. They use the ingredients in their kitchens and obtain attractive results. Here are the favorites of FARM JOURNAL readers and of our food staff.

SPARKLE TOPS: With fingers, moisten top crust with cold water and sprinkle evenly with a little sugar.

SHINY TOPS: Brush top pastry crust lightly with beaten egg or egg yolk, cream, milk, undiluted evaporated milk or melted butter, margarine, shortening or salad oil. Sprinkle with sugar, if desired.

DECORATIVE VENTS: Use tiny cookie cutters or cut around homemade patterns with sharp knife to make steam vents in the shape of the fruit in the pie—cherries, apples or a cluster of grapes, for instance.

INITIAL TOPS: Farm women frequently cut initials with a knife or prick them with a fork for steam vents —A for apple, B for blueberry or C for cherry. These steam vents are especially helpful at bake sales because they indicate the kind of pie at a glance.

Fancy Pie Edges

FLUTES: Trim pastry ½" beyond rim and fold under to make double rim. Make a stand-up rim. Place left index finger inside pastry rim. With right thumb and index finger on outside of rim, press pastry into V shapes ½" apart. Pinch flutes to make points, if desired. For 1- or 2-crust pies.

SCALLOPS: Form like flutes but do not make points. Flatten each flute with a 4-tined fork. For 2-crust pies.

FORK TRIM: Make a high-standing rim. With 4-tined fork, press pastry to rim at ½" intervals. For 1- or 2-crust pies.

ROPE: Turn overhang under and make a stand-up rim. Press right thumb into pastry at an angle. Press pastry between right thumb and knuckle of index finger. Repeat around the pie. For 1- or 2-crust pies.

COIN: Trim overhang even with pie pan. Cut circles the size of pennies from pastry scraps with toy cookie cutter, thimble or bottle cap. Moisten rim with cold water and place circles on rim, overlapping them slightly. Press lightly to rim. For 1-crust pies.

FLUTED COIN: Fold under overhang; make stand-up rim; flute pastry. From extra pastry, cut rounds of dough to size that will fit the indentations of fluting; moisten outside edges of fluting and press into each flute a round of dough standing on edge. (See Cream Pies photo.)

CORNUCOPIA: Leave ¾" overhang, cut with scissors in sawtooth design, making "teeth" that are 1" wide at pan edge; roll from one angled side of each to make cornucopia that rests on pan edge.

BEAN CUTTER: Fold under overhang; use cutter for French-style green beans to press design all around edge. (See photo of unusual pie shells.)

WREATH: Fold under overhang; make stand-up rim. Snip pastry with scissors at ¼" intervals. Lay cut pieces alternately toward pie and away from pie.

SAWTOOTH: Cut pastry overhang with scissors in sawtooth design; moisten rim and fold the triangles of pastry up on rim, pointing to center of pie; press down. (See Lemon Pies photo.)

LOOPED: Trim pastry even with pan edge; cut extra strip of pastry same width as pan edge; mold pastry strip over pencil held at right angles to pan edge to make loop; press bottom of loop to seal; keep pastry moistened to seal strip to edge. (See Lemon Pie photo.)

RUFFLE: Fold overhang over pastry on pan edge loosely; press left index finger under fold of pastry, press right index finger firmly next to lifted portion.

BUTTON: Fold under overhang; use handle end of measuring spoon to press design into edge (hole in end of handle makes button design).

FLUTED FORK: Fold under overhang; make 1″ wide flutes that rest on pan edge, with ¼″ flute between them that stands up and points to pan center. Press floured 4-tined fork into each wide flute. (See Rhubarb Pie photo.)

QUARTER-MOON: Trim pastry even with pan edge; cut long strip of pastry same width as pan edge and press down onto moistened pastry on pan edge; with inverted ½-teaspoon measuring spoon, press design of two semicircles (one inside the other) around edge. (See photo of unusual pie shells.)

Pastry Shells for Miniature Pies

Take your pick of the following methods we suggest for shaping tart shells—the plain and the fancy. Then turn to the tart and turnover recipes in Chapter 7. Once you've read them, you'll start planning an excuse to bake the tiny pies and show them off!

TART SHELLS FROM BASIC PASTRY (FROM 2-CRUST PIE RECIPE)

• Divide pastry into 5 parts. Roll out each part to make 4½″ to 5″ circles.

In Tart Pans: Fit pastry circles into 3½″ tart pans, pressing them evenly over bottoms and sides of pans, removing air bubbles. Let them extend about ½″ beyond pans' edges, turn under and flute. Prick well on bottoms and sides with 4-tined fork. Refrigerate 30 minutes.

On Muffin-Cup Pans or Custard Cups: Fit pastry circles over backs of inverted 3½″ muffin-cup pans. Make pleats so pastry will fit snugly. Prick entire surface with 4-tined fork. Or fit pastry over inverted custard cups, prick well and set on baking sheet. Refrigerate 30 minutes before baking.

Muffin-Cup-Pan Measurements: Regardless of the size of your muffin-cup pans, you can bake tart shells on them. With a string, measure one of the inverted cups down one side, across the bottom and up on the other side. Cut the string this length. Find a bowl, saucer or small plate in the kitchen that has the same diameter as the string. Or cut a cardboard this size. Use for a pattern to cut the rolled pastry in circles. Fit pastry rounds on alternate muffin cups—6 on a pan with 12 cups. Pleat pastry to fit snugly.

With Aluminum Foil: Cut circles of heavy-duty aluminum foil same size as pastry circles (use small saucer as pattern, trimming around it with knife). Lay pastry on them. Shape tart shells by bringing the foil and pastry up and pinching to make flutes or scallops. Or shape as desired. Set shaped tarts on baking sheet and chill 30 minutes.

• *To Bake Tart Shells:* Meanwhile preheat oven to 450°F. Bake tart shells 10 to 12 minutes or until golden. Cool on wire racks. Then carefully remove from pans, custard cups or foil. Fill as desired. Makes 10 tarts. (By rolling pastry thinner, 12 tarts; thicker, 8 tarts.)

VARIATIONS

BUTTER-RICH TART SHELLS: Divide pastry for 2-crust pie in half. Roll first half ⅛″ thick and dot with 3 tblsp. firm butter (if too hard or soft, butter breaks through). Fold pastry from two sides to meet in center. Press with fingers to seal. Fold other two ends to center and seal. Wrap in waxed paper and chill. Repeat with other half of pastry. When ready to use, roll out, cut in circles and bake like Tart Shells from Basic Pastry for 2-Crust Pie.

PETAL TART SHELLS: You will need 6 (2¼″) circles of pastry for each tart shell. (Cut circles with cookie cutter if you have the right size.) Place 1 circle in bottom of each 2¾″ muffin-cup pan or 6 oz. custard cup. Moisten edge of circle with cold water. Press remaining 5 pastry circles to sides and bottom of the cup, overlapping them slightly and pressing firmly to sides and bottom. Prick entire surface with 4-tined fork and bake like Tart Shells.

FLOWER TART SHELLS: Cut pastry in 4″ or 5″ squares instead of circles. Fit a square in each 3″ muffin-cup pans, letting corners stand up. Prick entire surface with 4-tined fork and press pastry firmly to sides and bottoms of pans. Bake like Tart Shells.

TINY TART SHELLS: Use 1¼″ muffin-cup pans. Cut rolled pastry with 1¾″ cookie cutter or use cardboard circle as pattern and cut around it with knife. Prick, chill and bake like Tart Shells

from Basic Pastry for 2-Crust Pies. Use Cheese Pastry for variety. Makes about 60 tart shells, 1- or 2-bite or canapé size.

READY-TO-GO PASTRY: Prick entire surface of the pastry circles with 4-tined fork. Stack them with waxed paper between. Wrap in aluminum foil or freezer wrap and freeze. To use, preheat oven to 450°F. Remove pastry from freezer and lay rounds over inverted muffin-cup pans or custard cups set on baking sheet. Let thaw just enough so you can pleat it. Bake 10 to 12 minutes or until tart shells are golden. Cool, remove from pans or cups and fill as desired.

Note: Packaged pie-crust mix may be used to make tart shells.

TART SHELLS MADE WITH BUTTER

½   c. soft butter or margarine
¼   c. sugar
¼   tsp. salt
1   egg yolk
1 ½ c. sifted flour
2   tblsp. milk

• Combine butter, sugar and salt in medium bowl and beat until light. Beat in egg yolk.
• Beat in flour and then milk (on low speed if using electric mixer).
• Shape into ball, wrap in waxed paper and refrigerate at least 1 hour.
• Divide chilled dough in 8 equal parts and pat each part into 3¾″ tart pans or muffin-cup pans. Set tart pans on large baking sheet. Refrigerate 30 minutes.
• Prick over entire surface of tart shells with 4-tined fork. Bake in mod-

erate oven (375°F.) about 20 minutes, or until golden.

• Partially cool in pans (about 10 minutes); remove from pans and complete cooling. Fill as desired. Makes 8.

VARIATIONS

LEMON TART SHELLS: Substitute 2 tblsp. lemon juice for milk and add 1 tsp. grated lemon peel.

ORANGE TART SHELLS: Substitute 2 tblsp. orange juice for milk and add 2 tsp. grated orange peel.

NUT TART SHELLS: Add ½ c. finely chopped walnuts with the flour.

COCONUT TART SHELLS: Add ½ c. flaked coconut with the flour.

GOOD IDEAS FROM OUR TEST KITCHENS

Home economists in FARM JOURNAL's Test Kitchens, who bake many tarts, find it is easier to prick the pastry after rolling than after it is fitted in or on inverted muffin-cup pans or shaped in foil. They prick it either before or after cutting.

They also roll out pastry scraps, trimmed from 8" and 9" pies, cut them in circles for tarts and freeze for later use. It's a thrifty trick. And you'll be surprised how soon you have enough circles to make all the tart shells you need for a party or a meal.

BASIC PUFF PASTRY

The most elegant pastry of all—extra-rich and extra-flaky

1   lb. butter, chilled thoroughly
4¼ c. sifted flour

1   c. ice water
2   tblsp. lemon juice

• Cut ½ lb. butter into flour in large mixing bowl, using pastry blender or two knives, until mixture is crumbly and pale yellow. Add ice water and lemon juice all at once; stir with fork until mixture is moistened completely and pastry is stiff. Shape in a ball, wrap in waxed paper, foil or plastic wrap. Chill at least 30 minutes.

• Roll out on a well-floured pastry cloth into an 18" × 12" rectangle, ¼" thick. Roll pastry straight, lifting rolling pin at edge of pastry so pastry will be of even thickness.

• Slice remaining ½ lb. chilled butter into thin, even pats. Arrange pats over two thirds of pastry, making a 12" × 12" square.

• Fold uncovered third of pastry over the middle third. Then fold butter-covered pastry end over the top. Now fold pastry in thirds, crosswise, to make a block. There are 9 layers of pastry with butter between each.

• Roll out again to an 18" × 12" rectangle. Fold again as above. Chill 30 minutes.

• Continue rolling, folding and chilling 3 more times. Before each rolling, pastry will be stiff. First pound with rolling pin to flatten, using care to keep thickness uniform.

• After last folding, chill pastry 30 minutes before using. You can wrap in waxed paper and refrigerate or freezer-wrap and store in freezer for use within a month.

• Use to make: Elegant French Pastries (Chapter 7).

PATTY SHELLS

Professional-looking, crisp, golden main-dish or dessert pastry holders

½ recipe Basic Puff Pastry

• Chill 2 baking sheets.
• Roll pastry on lightly floured surface to make a rectangle ¼" thick. Cut 10 rounds with 3" plain or fluted cookie cutter.
• Rinse chilled baking sheets with cold water. Place rounds 3" apart on baking sheets. You can reroll trimmings of pastry to make two more rounds.
• Press 2" cookie cutter into each pastry round, cutting only halfway through. Refrigerate 30 minutes.
• Bake, one sheet at a time, in very hot oven (450°F.) 15 minutes. Reduce temperature to 350° and bake until lightly browned, about 15 minutes.
• With sharp knife, cut around center circles and carefully remove tops; place tops on baking sheet. Scoop out any uncooked pastry in centers and discard. Return shells and tops to oven and continue baking 5 minutes.
• Repeat with remaining pastry circles on second baking sheet. Use at once, or freeze.
• Serve filled with creamed chicken or shellfish; replace pastry tops. Or use the tops as the base for canapés. Makes 12 patty shells.

Note: Shells also may be used for desserts. Fill with Pastry Cream (recipe in Chapter 7) and garnish with berries or fruit.

Specialty Pie Crusts

Several recipes from farm women are featured in this section. Try them to find out why they are such favorites —and to treat your family and friends to something different. Many good country cooks like to include egg, vinegar and lemon juice and other special ingredients in their pastry. It's wise to use recipes designed especially for such additions.

SHORT-CUT PASTRY FOR FRUIT PIES

You skip the rolling pin—mix pastry in pie pan. Use this for fruit pies

2   c. sifted flour
2   tsp. sugar
1 ¼ tsp. salt
⅔   c. cooking or salad oil
3   tblsp. milk

• Combine flour, sugar and salt; sift into an 8" or 9" pie pan.
• Whip oil and milk together with a fork and pour over flour mixture.
• Mix with fork until all flour is moistened. Save out about one third of dough to top pie.
• Press remaining dough evenly in pie pan, covering bottom and sides. Crimp the edges. Add the fruit filling. Crumble reserved dough over filling to make top crust. Bake as fruit-pie recipe directs.

BEGINNER'S PASTRY

(Paste Method)

2   c. sifted flour
1   tsp. salt
⅔   c. vegetable shortening
4   tblsp. cold water

• Mix flour and salt in a bowl. Cut in shortening with pastry blender until mixture is like coarse meal. Combine ⅓ c. of this mixture with the water; add to the remaining flour-shortening mixture. Mix with fork and then with fingers just until dough holds together and will shape into a ball. Divide dough in two parts. Follow directions for rolling, etc., given with Flaky Pastry for 2-Crust Pie. Makes 1 (8″ or 9″) 2-crust pie.

HOT-WATER PASTRY

¾   c. vegetable shortening
¼   c. boiling water
1   tblsp. milk
2   c. sifted flour
1   tsp. salt

• Put shortening in medium bowl. Add water and milk; break up shortening with a 4-tined fork. Tilt bowl and beat with fork in quick, cross-the-bowl strokes until mixture is smooth and thick like whipped cream and holds soft peaks when fork is lifted.
• Sift flour and salt onto shortening. With vigorous, round-the-bowl strokes, stir quickly, forming dough that clings together and cleans bowl. Pick up dough and work into a smooth, flat round. Then divide in half and form in two balls. Roll out, following directions given in Flaky Pastry for 2-Crust Pie. Makes enough for 1 (8″ or 9″) 2-crust pie.

EGG PASTRY

2   c. sifted flour
1   tsp. salt
⅔   c. vegetable shortening
1   egg, slightly beaten
2   tblsp. cold water
2   tsp. lemon juice

• Sift flour with salt into mixing bowl. Cut in shortening until particles are the size of small peas.
• Combine egg, water and lemon juice. Sprinkle over dry ingredients, tossing and stirring with fork until mixture is moist enough to hold together. (You may need to add a few more drops of water.)
• Divide in half; shape in two flat balls. Roll. Makes 1 (8″ or 9″) 2-crust pie.

COUNTRY TEAROOM PASTRY

4   c. sifted flour
1   tblsp. sugar
1½   tsp. salt
1½   c. lard
1   egg
1   tblsp. vinegar
½   c. cold water

• Blend flour, sugar and salt. Cut in lard until particles are the size of peas.
• Beat egg, blend in vinegar and water. Sprinkle over flour mixture, a tablespoonful at a time, tossing with fork to mix. Gather dough together with fingers so it cleans the bowl. Chill before rolling. Makes 2 (9″) 2-crust pies and 1 (9″) pie shell.

Note: This is the pastry used by a Wisconsin woman in the tearoom she operates in her home. (Also see Egg Yolk Pastry, Chapter 3.)

CREAM CHEESE PASTRY

½   c. butter
1   (3 oz.) pkg. cream cheese
1   c. sifted flour
⅛   tsp. salt

• Cream butter and cheese, beating until smooth. Combine flour and salt and add half at a time to cheese mixture. Mix thoroughly.
• Shape in ball, wrap in waxed paper and chill until pastry will roll and handle easily. (Or shape in 2″ rolls, wrap, refrigerate overnight and slice in about 18 circles.) Roll, cut in 2″ circles and bake in (2″) muffin-cup pans in very hot oven (450°F.) about 12 minutes, or until lightly browned. Cool before filling. Makes 18 (2″) tart shells.

CHEESE PASTRY

Marvelous for apple and many kinds of pies—see recipes in this Cookbook

1⅔   c. sifted flour
½   tsp. salt
1   c. grated sharp natural Cheddar cheese
½   c. vegetable shortening
4   to 6 tblsp. cold water

• Sift flour with salt into medium bowl. Add cheese and toss with a fork to mix thoroughly with flour. Cut in shortening until mixture resembles small peas.
• Sprinkle water over pastry mixture, 1 tblsp. at a time, until dough will hold together. Shape into a ball with hands, wrap in waxed paper and refrigerate until ready to use. Divide in halves, flatten each half with hand. Make bottom and top crusts as directed in Flaky Pastry for 2-Crust Pie. Makes pastry for 1 (8″ or 9″) 2-crust pie.

CHEESE PIE SHELL: Follow recipe for Cheese Pastry but reduce flour to 1 c. and use ¼ tsp. salt, ½ c. grated Cheddar cheese, ¼ c. shortening and 2 to 3 tblsp. water. Proceed as with Baked Pie Shell made with Flaky Pastry. Makes 1 (8″ or 9″) pie shell or top crust for 1½ qt. casserole.

VARIATION

• Use grated process Cheddar or American cheese instead of sharp Cheddar cheese.

CALIFORNIA ORANGE PASTRY

3   c. sifted flour
1   tsp. salt
1   c. vegetable shortening
6   to 8 tblsp. orange juice

• Sift together flour and salt. Cut in shortening until mixture resembles cornmeal.
• Add orange juice, a small amount at a time, tossing lightly with fork until dough is moist enough to hold together. Shape into ball and roll or refrigerate. Pastry, wrapped in waxed paper, may be kept in refrigerator several days. Makes 1 (8″ or 9″) 2-crust pie and 2 (8″ or 9″) pie shells.

Note: Another way to introduce orange flavor to pastry is to add 1 tblsp. grated orange peel and 1 tsp. sugar to the flour for a 1-crust pie before cutting in shortening.

PEANUT PIE SHELL

Fascinating flavor blend with cream, chocolate and butterscotch pies

1   c. sifted flour
½   tsp. baking powder
½   tsp. salt
⅓   c. vegetable shortening
¼   c. crushed salted peanuts
3   to 4 tblsp. cold water

• Sift flour, baking powder and salt into mixing bowl. Cut in shortening with knives, or blend with pastry blender until mixture resembles coarse cornmeal. Add peanuts.
• Sprinkle cold water over mixture, a little at a time, stirring with fork until dough is just moist enough to hold together and form a ball.
• Roll out on lightly floured surface to a circle 1½" larger than an 8" or 9" pie pan inverted over it. Fit loosely into pan and flute edges. Prick over entire surface with a 4-tined fork.
• Bake in hot oven (425°F.) 12 to 15 minutes. Cool.

CHOCOLATE CANDY PIE SHELL

Try this for chiffon-pie fillings

1   (12 oz.) pkg. semisweet choc-
      late pieces
2   tblsp. vegetable shortening
2   tblsp. sifted confectioners sugar

• Form pie shell by pressing 12"-square heavy-duty aluminum foil in 9" pie pan. Cut off excess at rim. Carefully remove foil pie shell. Sprinkle in chocolate pieces and place on baking sheet in very slow oven (250°F.) for 5 minutes. Remove and set aluminum shell in pie pan. Add shortening and blend with back of spoon. Add confectioners sugar; blend. Spread mixture evenly on bottom and sides of foil shell. Chill until well set.
• Carefully remove foil and return chocolate liner to pie pan. Fill with chiffon-pie filling.

Note: Pie shell is crispy hard like coating on chocolate bonbons. It will soften some for easier cutting if allowed to stand at room temperature 20 minutes.

CHOCOLATE PIE SHELL

1   c. sifted flour
½   tsp. salt
3   tblsp. sugar
3   tblsp. cocoa
⅓   c. vegetable shortening
¼   tsp. vanilla
3   to 4 tblsp. cold water

• Sift flour with salt, sugar and cocoa into bowl. Cut in shortening until particles of mixture resemble small peas in size. Blend in vanilla.
• Sprinkle water over cocoa mixture, stirring lightly with fork, until dough is moist enough to hold together. Shape into ball.
• Roll between two sheets of waxed paper to ⅛" thickness. Gently peel off top paper. Cut dough in circle 1½" to 2" larger than an 8" or 9" pie pan inverted over it. Fit dough loosely into pan, remove paper and pat out all air pockets. Fold edge to make a standing rim and flute as desired. Prick generously with a 4-tined fork.
• Bake in hot oven (400°F.) 8 to 10

minutes. Cool and fill as desired. Makes 8" or 9" pie shell.

Note: Cut scraps of leftover rolled dough with fancy cookie cutters, place on baking sheet and bake in hot oven (400°F.). Use to garnish top of pie.

PASTRY FOR LEMON PIES

It accents that wonderful lemon taste

1 ½ c. sifted flour
1 ½ tsp. sugar
½ tsp. salt
½ c. vegetable shortening
1 tblsp. lemon juice
2 tblsp. cold water

• Sift together flour, sugar and salt. Take out 2 tblsp. of shortening. Cut remaining shortening with two knives or blend with pastry blender into flour mixture until mixture resembles coarse meal. Cut in the 2 tblsp. shortening in pieces the size of large peas. Add lemon juice and cold water gradually, mixing lightly with fork. Form into ball.
• Roll out on lightly floured pastry cloth to ⅛" thickness. Cut in circle 1½" larger than inverted 9" pie pan. Fit loosely in pan; pat out air bubbles; turn edge under and flute. Prick sides and bottom with fork.
• Bake in very hot oven (450°F.) 10 to 12 minutes. Cool. Makes 1 (9") pie shell.

SESAME SEED CRUST: Toast ⅓ c. sesame seeds in moderate oven (375°F.) 12 to 15 minutes, or until light golden brown. Add to pastry for a 1-crust pie after cutting in shortening.

Graham Cracker Crusts

Graham cracker crumbs, finely rolled, are available in packages. Each (13¾ oz.) package will make 3 (9") pies. Or you can make the crumbs in a jiffy by blending the crackers in an electric blender. If you crush and roll the crackers, place them in a plastic bag or between sheets of waxed paper before using the rolling pin.

Baking gives a firmer and more crunchy crust, but the unbaked type is satisfactory for chiffon and other light and fluffy pie fillings.

BAKED GRAHAM CRACKER CRUST

1 ⅓ c. graham cracker crumbs (16 to 18)

¼ c. sugar
¼ c. soft butter or margarine
¼ tsp. nutmeg or cinnamon (optional)

• In medium mixing bowl combine graham cracker crumbs, sugar, butter and nutmeg; blend until crumbly. Save out ⅓ c. crumbs to sprinkle on top of pie, if desired. Press remaining crumbs evenly on bottom and sides of 9" pie pan, making a small rim.
• Bake in moderate oven (375°F.) 8 minutes, or until edges are lightly browned. Cool on wire rack and fill as pie recipe directs.

UNBAKED GRAHAM CRACKER CRUMB CRUST: Use the same ingredients as for the baked crust; do not make rim on pie shell. Chill about 1 hour, or until set before filling.

VARIATIONS

WALNUT GRAHAM CRACKER CRUST: Reduce crumbs to 1 c. and add ½ c. finely chopped walnuts. Follow directions for Baked Graham Cracker Crumb Crust. (You can use finely chopped pecans, almonds or Brazil nuts instead of walnuts.)

CHOCOLATE GRAHAM CRACKER CRUST: Reduce crumbs to 1 c. and add 2 squares unsweetened chocolate, grated. Follow recipe for Baked Graham Cracker Crumb Crust.

Wafer and Cereal Crusts

An excellent way to introduce change in crumb crusts is to use wafers or cereals instead of graham cracker crumbs. Here are a few good examples.

CHOCOLATE WAFER CRUMB CRUST: Mix 1⅓ c. fine chocolate wafer crumbs, about 18 (2¾″) wafers, with 3 tblsp. soft butter or margarine until crumbly. Press on bottom and sides of 8″ or 9″ pie pan, saving out 3 tblsp. crumbs to sprinkle on top of pie, if desired. Bake in moderate oven (375°F.) 8 minutes.

VANILLA WAFER CRUMB CRUST: Mix 1⅓ c. fine vanilla wafer crumbs, about 24 (2″) wafers, with ¼ c. soft butter or margarine until crumbly. Press on bottom and sides of 8″ or 9″ pie pan, reserving 3 tblsp. mixture to sprinkle on top of pie, if desired. Bake in moderate oven (375°F.) 8 minutes, or until edge is lightly browned.

GINGERSNAP CRUMB CRUST: Mix 1⅓ c. fine gingersnap crumbs, about 20 (2″) gingersnaps, with 6 tblsp. soft butter or margarine until crumbly. Press mixture on bottom and sides of 8″ or 9″ pie pan, reserving 3 tblsp. crumbs to sprinkle on top of pie, if desired. Bake in moderate oven (375°F.) 8 minutes.

PRETZEL CRUMB CRUST

¾ c. coarsely crushed pretzel sticks
¼ c. soft butter or margarine
3 tblsp. sugar

• Combine ingredients in medium mixing bowl. Press into bottom and on sides of 9″ pie pan. Refrigerate until ready to fill as pie recipe directs.

CORN FLAKE CRUMB CRUST: Mix 1⅓ c. corn flake crumbs (3 c. corn flakes) with 2 tblsp. sugar and ¼ c. soft butter until mixture is crumbly. Press on bottom and sides of 8″ or 9″ pie pan, saving out 3 tblsp. crumbs to sprinkle on top of pie, if desired. Bake in moderate oven (375°F.) 8 minutes. (Packaged corn flake crumbs are available.)

VARIATION

RICE CEREAL CRUMB CRUST: Follow directions for Corn Flake Crumb

Crust, substituting rice cereal flakes for corn flakes.

WALNUT-CEREAL CRUST

1   c. uncooked rolled oats (quick cooking)
3   tblsp. brown sugar
⅛   tsp. salt

⅔   c. chopped walnuts
⅓   c. melted butter or margarine

• Spread rolled oats in large, shallow pan. Toast in moderate oven (350°F.) 10 minutes.
• Combine with sugar, salt, nuts and melted butter. Press on bottom and sides of 9″ pie pan. Chill while you prepare filling.

Nut and Coconut Crusts

Nuts, finely ground, are delicious substitutes for graham cracker crumbs in pie crusts. If you add the finely ground nuts to a beaten egg white and line the pie pan with the mixture, you get a "chewy" crust that's a favorite of many people. Here are recipes for these crusts, along with several for coconut pie shells. Crunchy coconut crusts are wonderful for chiffon-pie fillings and for holding balls or scoops of ice cream. Add the ice cream just before serving and cut at the table. And do vary the coconut crusts using some of the recipes that follow.

NUT BROWN PASTRY

1   c. finely ground blanched almonds, filberts, Brazil nuts, pecans, peanuts or walnuts
2½   tblsp. sugar

• Blend nuts and sugar, mixing well. Press firmly with spoon on bottom and sides of 8″ or 9″ pie pan. Do not make rim. Bake in hot oven (400°F.) 6 to 8 minutes. Cool.

NUT MERINGUE CRUST: To 1½ c. finely ground Brazil nuts, pecans or walnuts (put through food chopper using medium blade), add ¼ c. sugar and ⅛ tsp. salt. Beat 1 egg white until soft peaks form; add nut mixture. Line bottom of greased 9″ pie pan with circle of waxed paper, cut to fit. Press nut mixture over bottom and sides of pan, not on rim. Bake in moderate oven (375°F.) until lightly browned, about 12 to 15 minutes. Remove from oven and loosen crust around edges with spatula; let cool on rack in pan about 10 minutes. Lift out crust with care, removing waxed paper. Cool thoroughly, then return to pan, before filling.

UNBAKED COCONUT CRUST

1½   c. packaged grated coconut
½   c. confectioners sugar
3   tblsp. melted butter

• Combine fine grated coconut with confectioners sugar. Gradually stir in butter. Press evenly over bottom and sides of an oiled 8″ or 9″ pie pan. Refrigerate until firm, about 1 hour.

TOASTED COCONUT CRUST

2   c. flaked coconut
¼   c. butter or margarine   *more*

• Place coconut and butter, mixed together, in 9″ pie pan. Toast in moderate oven (300°F.) 15 to 20 minutes, stirring occasionally, until golden brown. Press over bottom and sides of pie pan. Cool before filling.

SHORT-CUT TOASTED COCONUT CRUST

2 c. moist toasted coconut (1 7 oz. pkg.)
¼ c. melted butter or margarine

• Combine coconut and butter. Press evenly over sides and bottom of an oiled 8″ or 9″ pie pan. Chill until firm, about 1 hour. Crust may be frozen.

CHOCONUT PIE SHELL

A chocolate-flavored nut crust

1 c. sifted flour
2 oz. sweet cooking chocolate, grated or ground
¼ tsp. salt
¼ c. vegetable shortening
3 tblsp. milk
½ tsp. vanilla
¼ c. finely chopped pecans

• Stir together flour, grated chocolate and salt. Cut in shortening with two knives or blend with pastry blender until mixture resembles coarse meal. Combine milk and vanilla; add gradually to dry mixture, tossing lightly with a fork. Form into ball.

• Roll out on lightly floured pastry cloth to ⅛″ thickness. Cut in circle 1½″ larger than inverted 9″ pie pan. Fit loosely in pan; pat out air bubbles; turn edge under and flute.

• Sprinkle with chopped pecans and press gently into pastry. Prick sides and bottom with a fork.

•˙ Bake in hot oven (400°F.) 10 to 12 minutes. Makes 1 (9″) pie shell.

MARSHMALLOW-COCONUT CRUST

¼ c. butter or margarine
1 c. marshmallow creme
½ c. flaked coconut
¼ tsp. vanilla
1½ c. crushed bite-size rice cereal

• Butter a 9″ pie pan. Heat and stir marshmallow creme and butter over hot water. Add coconut, vanilla and rice cereal crumbs. Press on bottom and sides of pie pan. Chill.

Cookie-Type Pie Shells

When a recipe calls for a baked pie shell, a sweet, rich crust may be made with cookie dough. Many superior farm cooks have favorite refrigerator cookie recipes they enjoy using to make pie shells for chiffon and other fluffy, light pie fillings. You can roll the thoroughly chilled dough and fit it, like pastry, into the pie pan. Or you can shape the dough in the traditional roll, chill and then slice it ⅛″ thick.

Cover the bottom and sides of the lightly greased pie pan with overlapping slices. It takes about 30 to 33 slices for an 8″ pie pan. The overlapping cookies on the sides of the pie pan will make an attractive scalloped edge. Chill for at least 15 minutes, prick the entire surface with a 4-tined fork and bake in a moderate oven (375°F.) until lightly browned, about 10 minutes.

We give you two recipes for these crusts, one you pat into the pie pan and one that you roll and fit into the pan. Packaged refrigerator cookies, available in supermarkets, also may be used (Hawaiian Pineapple Pie, Chapter 8).

COOKIE PIE SHELL

1   c. sifted flour
½   c. butter (room temperature)
Grated peel of ½ lemon
⅛   tsp. salt
2   tblsp. sugar
1   egg yolk, slightly beaten
Ice water

• Combine flour, butter, lemon peel and salt in medium bowl. Blend in sugar.
• Add egg yolk and just enough water to make particles adhere. Shape into ball, wrap in waxed paper and refrigerate 1 hour or longer.
• Roll out dough on a lightly floured surface and fit into a 9″ pie pan, making pie shell. Chill at least 15 minutes.
• Prick entire surface of pie shell and bake in hot oven (400°F.) until light-golden, 15 to 20 minutes. Cool thoroughly on wire rack.

VARIATION

ORANGE COOKIE PIE SHELL: Substitute grated peel of ½ orange for lemon peel.

RICH COOKIE CRUST

1   c. sifted flour
¼   c. sugar
1   tsp. grated orange or lemon
     peel
½   c. butter
1   egg yolk, slightly beaten
¼   tsp. vanilla

• Combine flour, sugar and lemon peel in bowl. Cut in butter until mixture resembles coarse meal. Stir in egg yolk and vanilla and mix with hands until blended.
• Pat evenly into a 9″ pie pan. Make a small edge on pie shell. Prick with fork.
• Bake in hot oven (400°F.) until a light brown, about 10 minutes. Cool on rack before filling.

Glamorous Meringue Crusts

Meringues make dramatic crusts for special-occasion pies and tarts. Rarely are variations made in the basic recipe, which follows, but good country cooks, especially in the South, frequently add pecans. They fold ½ c. finely ground nuts into the meringue just before spreading it into the pie pan.

Meringue pie shells are perfect for holding fresh strawberries, raspberries or sliced peaches, lightly sweetened, and whipped cream or ice cream. During the seasons when fresh fruits are unavailable, custard-type fillings are favorites. Not for flavor alone, although it's important, but also because custard-filled meringues are make-ahead desserts. Most homemakers prefer to chill them overnight, adding the whipped-cream topping shortly before serving time.

PERFECT PUFFY MERINGUE
FOR PIE AND TART SHELLS

Here are the rules to follow for success every time.
• Choose a cool, dry day to make meringue shells, if possible. Humidity often softens meringues.
• Be sure your tools are dry and clean. It takes only a tiny speck of fat to ruin meringues.
• Use egg whites at room temperature. Take eggs from the refrigerator, separate and let whites stand at least 1 hour before beating.
• Let your electric mixer do the work —save your arm. The beating takes from 25 to 30 minutes. The sugar must be completely dissolved or the meringue will weep. To test, rub a little of the meringue between the fingers. It should feel smooth. If grainy, continue beating until it feels smooth.
• Cool before filling.

BASIC MERINGUE PIE SHELL

3   egg whites (room temperature)
1/4 tsp. cream of tartar
1/8 tsp. salt
3/4 c. sugar

• Combine egg whites, cream of tartar and salt. Beat until frothy. Gradually add sugar and beat until stiff glossy peaks form. Meringue should be shiny and moist and all sugar dissolved.
• Spread over bottom and sides of a well-greased 9″ pie pan. Build up sides. (You can make fancy edge with cake decorator, if desired.)
• Bake in very slow oven (275°F.) 1 hour, or until light brown and crisp

to touch. Let cool in pan away from drafts. Spoon in filling and chill.

Note: Don't be disturbed if the meringue pie shell falls and cracks in the center—it usually does.

MERINGUE TART SHELLS

3   egg whites (room temperature)
1/4 tsp. cream of tartar
1/4 tsp. salt
1/2 tsp. vanilla
3/4 c. sugar

• Combine egg whites, cream of tartar, salt and vanilla in large mixer bowl. Beat until very soft peaks form when beater is lifted slowly. Beat in sugar, 2 tblsp. at a time, beating after each addition. Continue beating until stiff peaks form. The meringue should be glossy and moist.
• Line baking sheets with heavy brown paper. Drop spoonfuls of meringue on paper to make 8 mounds of even size, 3″ apart. With back of spoon hollow out each mound to make tart shell.
• Bake in very slow oven (275°F.) 1 hour. Turn off oven heat and let shells remain in oven, with door closed, until cold.
• At serving time, fill with ice cream and top with berries, cut-up fruit or butterscotch, chocolate or other sauce. Or fill with berries or fresh fruit and top with whipped cream.
• To store Meringue Tart Shells for a few days, loosely wrap them, when cool, in waxed paper. Keep in a cool, dry place, such as a cupboard. Do not put in airtight containers or meringues will soften.

DO'S FOR BAKING PIES

• Follow package directions when using commercial pie crust mixes.
• Use the ingredients specified in all pastry recipes—don't substitute or change.
• Use cold water unless otherwise specified. It helps make flaky pastry.
• Measure accurately—it's important.
• Use pan size recommended by recipe so your filling will fit.
• Check pie-pan size by measuring top inside diameter.
• Use pans that are not shiny, such as glass or dull aluminum that do not reflect heat away from pie during baking.
• Use pie tape or a narrow strip of foil to cover pie edge if it gets too brown when baking.
• Cool baked pies on a wire cooling rack to let air circulate under and prevent sogginess.

PIE CRUST CLINIC

If you're troubled with pie crust problems, all you need to do is follow the recipes in this chapter. But if you wonder why your crust sometimes goes wrong, here are some answers. They show how important it is to follow recipe directions carefully.

WHAT MAKES PIE CRUST . . .

Tough?
1. Use of too little fat or too much flour
2. Failure to blend flour, fat and water enough

3. Handling or rerolling dough too much
4. Incorrect proportion of ingredients —too much flour and too little fat
5. Too much water

Crumbly?
1. Too much fat or too little water
2. Insufficient blending of flour, fat and water
3. Use of self-rising flour without special recipe

Shrink and lose its shape?
1. Stretching of dough when fitting it into pie pan or when fluting edge
2. Rolling dough to uneven thickness, too much rerolling or patching
3. Not pricking dough enough when baking pie shell

Soggy?
1. Underbaking—too short baking time or too low oven temperature
2. Using shiny pie pans that reflect heat so crust does not bake thoroughly
3. Placing pie pan on aluminum foil or baking sheet, deflecting oven heat from pie
4. Pricking, a break or tear in bottom crust of 2-crust pie or filled 1-crust pie
5. Allowing filled 2-crust pie to stand too long before baking

Fail to brown?
1. Same reasons as for soggy crusts
2. Too little fat or oil
3. Too much liquid
4. Overmixing or overhandling of dough
5. Too much flour used when rolling dough
6. Rolling crust too thin

Brown unevenly?
1. Rolling dough to uneven thickness or shaping it unevenly
2. Edge too high
3. Not enough filling for 2-crust pie
4. Pie baked too high or too low in oven
5. Pie placed too close to oven wall or pies baked too close together
6. Oven shelf that is not level

Stick to bottom of pan?
1. Filling boils over
2. Break in crust allowing juice from filling to leak

Have an unpleasant flavor?
1. Raw taste from underbaking
2. Scorched taste from overbaking
3. Bitter or rancid fat or oil
4. Too much or too little salt

COMMON PASTRY QUESTIONS

Q. Why does my pie dough handle differently at times?

A. Temperature, humidity and atmospheric conditions affect it. In hot, humid weather the dough often is soft; when the humidity is low, it may be dry. Chill soft dough. Add a few drops of cold water to dry doughs (use caution—it's easy to add too much).

Q. When do you put the filling in the crust for best results?

A. Follow the pie recipe when adding filling to a baked pie shell. Fill 1-crust pie just before baking; a 2-crust pie after the top crust is rolled and ready to be transferred to top of pie.

Q. Why does my pie dough sometimes crack around the edges when rolled?

A. Either the dough is too dry or it was not mixed sufficiently after water was added. The edges also may not have been smoothed after ball of dough was flattened before rolling.

Q. Why does my 2-crust fruit pie sometimes boil over?

A. Too much filling or insufficient thickening of filling, top and bottom crust edges not sealed completely or inadequate vents cut in top of crust for escape of steam or vents cut too near edge of pie, overbaking, oven shelf not level or uneven thickness of top crust.

Q. What makes my pie shells shrink?

A. Stretching pastry, when putting it in the pan, is one cause. (Unfold pastry in pan and ease it gently and loosely into pan. Press out air bubbles lightly with finger tips and then fit pastry into pan with bent index finger.)

Use of too much shortening or lard in proportion to flour encourages shrinkage.

Baking pie shells in an oven at too low temperature results in shrinkage. The oven temperature generally recommended is 450°F., but some home economists prefer to use a higher one, 475°F.

Good Idea: To prevent a pastry shell from shrinking during baking, a farm woman says she places a foil pan of the same size in the pie pan containing the pastry. She bakes the pie shell in a very hot oven (450°F.) 8 minutes, then removes foil pan and continues the baking until pastry is browned, about 7 minutes.

COBBLER CRUSTS

Look in Chapter 6 for cobbler toppings. You'll see several made with pastry, others with biscuit dough. Here are examples of recipes you'll find:

Cobbler Topping
Orange Biscuit Topping
Batter Topping
Biscuit Lattice

Biscuit Toppers for Main-Dish Pies

BAKING POWDER BISCUITS

(*Basic Recipe*)

2   c. sifted flour
3   tsp. baking powder
1   tsp. salt
6   tblsp. shortening
⅔ to ¾ c. milk

• Sift flour, baking powder and salt into bowl. Cut in shortening with pastry blender or two knives until mixture resembles cornmeal.
• Make a well in center of flour mixture and pour in ½ c. milk. Mix lightly and quickly with fork. Add more milk, just enough to make dough moist enough to leave the sides of the bowl and to cling to the fork in a ball. Turn on a lightly floured surface.
• Knead dough gently 6 or 8 times. Lightly roll from center in all directions, lifting rolling pin at edges. Roll ⅛" to ¼" thick. Cut as desired for topping main-dish pies. Place on hot pie filling and bake as directed in pie recipe.

VARIATIONS

DROP BISCUITS: Increase milk to 1 c. and drop from spoon on hot pie filling and bake as in basic recipe.

EXTRA-RICH BISCUITS: Increase shortening to ½ c.

CHEESE: Add ½ c. grated sharp Cheddar cheese to sifted dry ingredients.

BUTTERMILK: Reduce baking powder to 2 tsp. and add ¼ tsp. baking soda. Substitute buttermilk for sweet milk.

ONION: Sauté ¼ c. finely chopped onions in 2 tblsp. butter or margarine until light golden brown. Add to sifted dry ingredients with milk.

CURRY: Add ¼ to ½ tsp. curry powder to sifted dry ingredients (for chicken pies).

CARAWAY: Add 1 to 2 tsp. caraway seeds to sifted dry ingredients (for pork pies).

HERB: Add ¼ c. chopped fresh parsley or chives to sifted dry ingredients.

SAGE: Add ¼ tsp. dry mustard and ½ tsp. crumbled dried sage to sifted dry ingredients (for chicken and pork).

CHEESE-HERB: Add ½ c. grated sharp Cheddar cheese and 1 tsp. caraway or celery seeds to dry ingredients (for beef, pork and chicken pies).

Note: To make hot biscuits to serve as bread, roll dough ½″ to ¾″ thick for fluffy biscuits, ⅛″ for crusty, thin biscuits. Makes about 18 (2″) biscuits.

Frozen Mashed Potatoes to Hold Pie Fillings and to Top Pies

If the men who eat at your table are meat-and-potato fans, you'll welcome the new method of successfully freezing mashed potatoes developed in FARM JOURNAL's Test Kitchens. You can use them to top main-dish pies or to make nestlike shells to hold chicken, meat, vegetable, fish and other hearty fillings.

There's one important precaution to heed: Shape the potatoes ready for use before freezing. Thawing softens potatoes and makes them mushy.

A convenient way to stock your freezer is to cook and mash double the amount of potatoes when you are getting a meal. Use one half, freeze the other. You can store frozen mashed potatoes up to 2 months. Here is the basic recipe with some suggestions of what to do with it. You'll find many more ways to make pies with frozen potatoes once you start keeping the shells or nests and the topping in your freezer.

BASIC MASHED POTATOES

Play it smart and keep a supply in your freezer to use at busy seasons

4   lbs. boiling potatoes
1   c. milk (amount varies with moisture in potatoes)
¼   c. butter or margarine
1½ tsp. salt

• Peel potatoes. Boil until soft; drain. Press potatoes through ricer, or mash.
• Heat milk, butter and salt together. Gradually whip into potatoes; whip until smooth and fluffy. Makes 2 pie shells for 1½ qt. casserole.

POTATO PIE SHELLS

• Line 1½ qt. casserole with aluminum foil. Spoon half of hot Basic Mashed Potatoes into casserole. Shape into nestlike pie shell, building up sides to top of casserole. Remove from casserole with foil to hold shape of potato mixture. Repeat with remaining half of potatoes. Cool; freeze until firm. Remove from freezer; package, seal and label. Return to freezer.

To Use: Remove wrap from frozen Potato Pie Shell. Place in casserole in which it originally was shaped. Drizzle with 2 tblsp. melted butter or margarine. Cover and bake in hot oven (400°F.) 30 minutes. Uncover and bake 30 minutes. Fill with hot filling for chicken or meat pie and serve.

PIMIENTO-POTATO PIE SHELLS: Add ½ c. chopped pimiento to hot Basic Mashed Potatoes. Shape, freeze, bake and fill like Potato Pie Shells.

CHEESE-POTATO PIE SHELLS: Add ½ c. grated Cheddar cheese to hot Basic Mashed Potatoes. Shape, freeze and bake like Potato Pie Shells.

POTATO PIE TOPPING

SNOWCAPS: Add 2 egg yolks to Basic Mashed Potatoes; whip until blended. Spoon hot potatoes in mounds on baking sheet. Cool; freeze until firm. Remove from baking sheet; place in plastic bags. Seal, label and return to freezer.

To Use: Place frozen Snowcaps on top of hot meat-pie mixture. Bake in moderate oven (375°F.) 30 minutes, or until potatoes brown lightly. Use them to convert the thickened beef-vegetable stew into a main-dish pie. (See Hamburger-Potato Pie, Chapter 10.) Makes 24 Snowcaps.

Dessert Pies

FRUIT PIES

You don't need a calendar to tell you when a new pie season is about to start. When the wiry willows brighten to yellow-green and the light lingers in the evening sky, country cooks know that before too long there will be fresh fruit in their yards and gardens. Already they can visualize the plump strawberries glistening under shiny glazes in flaky pastry or teamed up with pink rhubarb in a luscious beauty, colorful Latticed Strawberry-Rhubarb Pie, pictured on this Cookbook's jacket. Other berries, cherries, currants, peaches, pears, plums and grapes follow, to the joy of pie bakers—and pie eaters.

Later in the year when, with little warning, sugar maples turn flame-colored and orchards glow with the deep red and blush-gold of apples, farm women concentrate their talents on the greatest of all American pies . . . apple. Often the season's nuts and fresh cider add their flavors to apple pie (for tasty examples, see Apple-Pecan and Apple Strip Pies).

Children used to keep track of the seasons by visiting Grandmother's kitchen to see, smell and taste the pies she was baking. The old rhythm is less obvious today. With improved canned, frozen and dried fruits widely available and transportation and storage methods greatly improved, fresh-tasting fruit pies come from home ovens the year around. And country women capture the elusive flavors of ripe fruit when it is plentiful by making pies and fillings and freezing them.

On the farm, the bounty of fresh fruits encourages their lavish use in summer. Twenty-six different kinds show up in our recipes. Fruit pies are a logical answer to the busy woman's eternal question: What can I fix for dessert that will glorify my otherwise ordinary meal?

Not to be overlooked is the fact that most men will vote a fruit pie their favorite dessert! We predict that after reading through the pages of this chapter you will get out your rolling pin and go on a pie-baking spree. Good luck and good pies!

Perfect Pies Have Flaky Crusts

Even if your family and neighbors consider you the best pie baker in the country, do read the preceding chapter, Pie Crusts of All Kinds, before you make any of the fruit pie recipes in this chapter. Remember that no pie is better than its pastry. And much of the success with pie crusts depends on you—because the ingredients are really quite simple. It's how you handle them that counts.

You will find a wide variety of pastry recipes. Some of them are new; you'll want to give them a try. (And when you don't have time to make pie crust, don't forget you can buy the mix in packages or frozen rolled pastry.)

You will notice that many of our pies are baked at one temperature, so you won't have to change the regulator setting once the pie is in the oven. Do look at your pie occasionally, though, especially the first time you use a recipe, to make certain that it doesn't brown too much. Remember that the higher the crimped edges of the rim are, the more quickly they brown. Here are suggestions for baking pies with tops browned just the way you like them.

Top-Crust Pointers

Some good pastry makers fold the rolled pastry for the top crust in quarters, cut vents near the center and lift it to the top of the pie. Other pie bakers prefer to cut their own designs (vents) in the pastry and then roll the pastry around the rolling pin and unroll it over the pie. Another school of farm cooks find it easier to avoid stretching the pastry when they cut the vents or prick the top crust after it is adjusted on the pie. Take your choice of methods, but REMEMBER TO CUT VENTS, plain or decorative, or to prick the top crust to allow steam to escape.

To keep pie edges from getting too brown while baking, cover them with 1½" strips of aluminum foil. Remove the foil about 15 minutes before end of baking time so edge will brown lightly. Another good way to protect the pie edges is to cut a circle of aluminum foil 1½" larger than the pie pan. Then cut out center of foil circle so only pie edges will be covered by the ring. Keep a few of these foil rings ready for quick and easy use.

Thickening Fruit Pies

The juiciness of fruit varies from one variety and from one season to another—and from different areas in the same season. Our measurement is for average juiciness. You may want to add a little more or less thickening (flour, cornstarch, quick-cooking tapioca) than the amount specified in the filling recipes. Then, too, you may like your pie fillings a little thicker or thinner than some other cooks. The accepted rule for a fruit filling is that it should be juicy, but not "runny."

Apple Pie—the Top Farm Favorite

To a farmer, an apple tree covered with blossoms is a lovely sight. He may watch the birds shake a shower of the petals to the earth and rejoice in trees glistening after an early morning rain. But you can bet he also has thoughts of a juicy wedge of apple pie. We predict that any of the apple pie recipes in this Cookbook will bring you his compliments. Try them all to find his very favorite!

For who can decide which apple pie is best? Members of FARM JOURNAL'S Family Test Group voted the traditional Old-Fashioned Apple Pie their families' first love, but there were bountiful praises of others. Open-Face Apple Pie won the second most votes, and nutmeg fans were excited and enthusiastic about Country Apple Pie. Then there's Apple-Pecan Pie . . . but why attempt to select the champions from the many pies we share with you? They all deserve blue ribbons!

Try the different recipes and find out for yourself which pies are best liked at your house. Maybe your final decision will be like that of one farmer who says: "Makes little difference what dessert my wife fixes—so long as it's apple pie."

OLD-FASHIONED APPLE PIE

First choice of all farm pies, it's juicy, plump and luscious

Pastry for 2-crust pie
¾   to 1 c. sugar
2   tblsp. flour
½   to 1 tsp. cinnamon
⅛   tsp. nutmeg
¼   tsp. salt
6   to 7 c. sliced peeled apples (2 to 2½ lbs.)
2   tblsp. butter or margarine

• Combine sugar, flour, cinnamon, nutmeg and salt. Mix lightly through apples (sliced ¼" thick). Heap in pastry-lined 9" pie pan. Dot with butter. Adjust top crust and flute edges; cut vents.
• Bake in hot oven (425°F.) 50 to 60 minutes, or until crust is browned and apples are tender.

Note: Amount of sugar you will need varies with tartness of apples.

VARIATIONS

DUTCH-STYLE APPLE PIE: Cut large vents in top crust and omit butter. Five minutes before baking time is up, remove pie from oven and pour ½ c.

heavy cream into pie through vents. Return to oven and complete baking.

CINNAMON APPLE PIE: Omit cinnamon and nutmeg and add 3 tblsp. red cinnamon candies (red hots) to sugar. Use a lattice pastry top if desired.

CRUMB APPLE PIE: Use ¾ c. sugar. Omit pastry top crust; instead, sprinkle filling with crumbs made by mixing ½ c. butter, ½ c. light brown sugar, firmly packed, and 1 c. flour. Bake in hot oven (400°F.) 45 to 55 minutes. Serve warm with ice cream or pass a pitcher of cream for pouring over pie.

SPEEDY APPLE PIE: Substitute 2 (1 lb. 4 oz.) cans sliced apples for the fresh apples.

GREEN APPLE PIE: Add ½ c. more sugar. Omit spices completely, or reduce amounts. If apples are very juicy, add 2 tblsp. more flour.

APPLE-PECAN PIE

You'll like what the nuts do to apple pie—both in flavor and texture

Unbaked 9" pie shell
¼   c. chopped pecans
6   c. sliced peeled apples
1   c. sugar
2   tsp. flour
½   tsp. cinnamon
¼   tsp. nutmeg
Spicy Pecan Topping

• Sprinkle chopped pecans in bottom of pie shell. Combine apples, sugar, flour, cinnamon and nutmeg. Turn into pie shell and spread topping (see recipe) over apple mixture.
• Bake in hot oven (425°F.) 40 to 45 minutes, or until apples are tender and pie top is a rich brown.

SPICY PECAN TOPPING: Mix ¼ c. butter or margarine, ½ c. brown sugar, ⅓ c. flour and ½ tsp. cinnamon until completely blended. Stir in ¼ c. chopped pecans.

OPEN-FACE APPLE PIE

Farmers voted this the best 1-crust apple pie—with ice cream on top!

Unbaked 9" pie shell
1   c. sliced peeled apples
5   c. quartered peeled apples
1⅓   c. sugar
3   tblsp. flour
¾   tsp. salt
⅓   c. light cream
¼   tsp. cinnamon

• Thinly slice 1 apple and lay across bottom of pie shell. Arrange quartered apples to fill the shell, overlapping pieces, rounded side up. (Cut apples in eighths if they are not quick-cooking.)
• Combine sugar, flour and salt; add cream, mixing well. Sprinkle top with cinnamon.
• Bake in moderate oven (375°F.) 1½ to 2 hours, or until apples are tender. Cover top with aluminum foil (tucking corners under edge of pie

COUNTRY APPLE PIE

Nutmeg and lemon flavors blend in this pie that tastes wonderful

Pastry for 2-crust pie
½ c. heavy cream
2 tblsp. quick-cooking tapioca
1 c. sugar
¼ tsp. salt
½ tsp. nutmeg
¼ tsp. cinnamon
2 tsp. lemon juice
5 c. sliced peeled apples
2 tblsp. butter or margarine

• Combine cream, tapioca, sugar, salt, spices and lemon juice in bowl.
• Add thinly sliced apples and toss to mix. Spoon half of mixture into pastry-lined 9″ pie pan. Fill around edges and pack well. Dot with butter. Add remaining apples. Adjust top crust and flute edges; cut vents. Brush top lightly with milk.
• Bake in hot oven (400°F.) 50 to 60 minutes, or until apples are tender and crust is golden brown.

APPLE STRIP PIE

When cider presses are busy, make this unforgettable autumn pie

Pastry for 2-crust pie
3 c. grated peeled apples
½ c. sugar
½ tsp. cinnamon
¼ tsp. nutmeg
⅛ tsp. salt
2 tsp. grated lemon peel
1 tblsp. lemon juice
3 tblsp. butter or margarine

3 tblsp. flour
1 c. apple cider
½ c. raisins
1 egg white
1 tsp. water
Cinnamon Nut Topping

• Combine apples, sugar, cinnamon, nutmeg, salt, lemon peel and juice.
• Melt butter in saucepan; add flour and blend. Add cider and cook over medium heat, stirring constantly, until mixture comes to a boil. Add apple mixture and raisins. Bring to a boil and cool.
• Line a 9″ pie pan with pastry. Beat together egg white and water. Brush part of mixture over pie shell. Turn apple mixture into pie shell. Roll out remaining pastry and cut in three (1½″) strips. Lay across top of pie, leaving space between; brush strips with remaining egg white.
• Sprinkle topping between strips.
• Bake in moderate oven (350°F.) until crust is brown and filling is bubbly, 40 to 50 minutes.

CINNAMON NUT TOPPING: Combine ¼ c. chopped pecans with 1 tblsp. sugar and ¼ tsp. cinnamon.

APPLE-CHEESE PIE

Cheese bakes in pie and unites with apples in this tasty dessert

Pastry for 2-crust pie
5 c. sliced peeled tart apples (about 2 lbs.)
½ tsp. grated lemon peel
2 tsp. lemon juice
¾ c. sugar
2 tblsp. flour   *more*

⅛ tsp. salt
½ tsp. cinnamon
¼ tsp. nutmeg
1 tblsp. butter or margarine
4 thin slices sharp process cheese
      (¼ lb.)
Cream to brush top

• Combine apples, sliced ¼" thick, with lemon peel and juice.
• Combine sugar, flour, salt, cinnamon and nutmeg. Sprinkle 2 tblsp. mixture over bottom of pastry-lined 8" pie pan.
• Toss apples in remainder of sugar mixture. Turn into pie shell. Dot with butter. Lay slices of cheese over apples, leaving space for steam to escape. Adjust top crust; flute edges, cut vents and brush on cream.
• Bake in hot oven (400°F.) about 40 minutes, or until apples are tender and crust is golden.

APPLE PIE GLACÉ

Spiral of apple slices under apricot glaze makes this a festive pie

Unbaked 9" pie shell
7 large apples
½ c. water
½ c. plus 1 tblsp. sugar
5 tblsp. butter or margarine
1 tblsp. lemon juice
½ tsp. cinnamon
¼ tsp. nutmeg
⅛ tsp. salt
2 small apples
¼ c. apricot jam
1 tblsp. hot water

• Peel and quarter large apples; cook with water and ½ c. sugar until soft

(about 35 minutes). Put through sieve; add butter, lemon juice, spices and salt. Pour into pie shell.
• Peel small apples; slice thinly lengthwise. Arrange in spiral starting at center of pie; sprinkle with 1 tblsp. sugar.
• Bake in hot oven (400°F.) 35 minutes, until apples on top are tender and the pastry is golden. Melt jam in hot water; pour over top.

FROSTED BIG APPLE PIE

Jumbo apple pie for treating a crowd —have a pot of coffee ready to pour

Egg Yolk Pastry
4 tsp. lemon juice
5 lbs. peeled, thinly sliced, tart
      apples (about 12 to 15 c.)
¾ c. granulated sugar
¾ c. brown sugar, firmly packed
1 tsp. cinnamon
¼ tsp. salt
½ tsp. nutmeg
Confectioners sugar frosting

• Roll out half the pastry into rectangle and use to line 15½" × 10½" jelly-roll pan. Sprinkle lemon juice on apples. Place half the apples in bottom of pastry-lined sheet.
• Combine remaining ingredients, except apples and frosting. Sprinkle half the mixture over apples in pan. Spread remaining apple slices on top and sprinkle with remaining sugar-spice mixture.
• Top with remaining pastry, rolled out; seal and crimp edges. Brush with milk and sprinkle with a little sugar. (Cut vents or prick with fork as for all 2-crust fruit pies.)

sprinkle with remaining sugar-spice mixture.

• Top with remaining pastry, rolled out; seal and crimp edges. Brush with milk and sprinkle with a little sugar. (Cut vents or prick with fork as for all 2-crust fruit pies.)

• Bake in hot oven (400°F.) 50 minutes. When cool, drizzle with confectioners sugar mixed with milk to make a thin icing. Cut in squares to serve. Makes 24 servings.

EGG YOLK PASTRY

5   c. sifted flour
4   tsp. sugar
½   tsp. salt
½   tsp. baking powder
1 ½ c. lard
2   egg yolks
Cold water

• Combine dry ingredients; cut in lard. Beat egg yolks slightly in measuring cup with fork and blend in enough cold water to make a scant cupful.

• Roll out like any pastry. Makes pastry for 1 Frosted Big Apple Pie or 3 (2-crust) 9″ pies.

APPLE MOLASSES PIE

Good way to salvage windfall apples —pie has that brown-sugar butter taste

Pastry for 2-crust pie
¾   c. light molasses
¼   c. water
1   tblsp. lemon juice
½   tsp. salt
6   c. sliced peeled apples
¼   c. melted butter or margarine
¼   c. flour

• Combine molasses, water, lemon juice and salt and bring to a boil.

• Add apples, cook until tender and remove from syrup.

• Blend butter and flour and add to hot syrup gradually, stirring constantly. Cook until thick and smooth. Fold apples lightly into syrup. Cool slightly. Turn into pastry-lined 9″ pie pan, top with pastry lattice.

• Bake in hot oven (425°F.) 30 minutes.

Men Praise This Two-Fruit Pie

The Massachusetts homemaker who shares the recipe for Apple-Cranberry Pie which follows, likes to bake it in autumn when harvesting is in full swing in the local cranberry bogs and juicy apples are fresh from orchards. She prefers Baldwin and McIntosh apples if they're available. Jonathans are a splendid choice, but any good cooking apple will fill the bill.

This New England pie baker brushes the tops of the unbaked pies with milk and sprinkles on a little sugar. "One time I made 25 of these pies for a men's dinner," she says. "I served them with cheese slices and the pies really made a hit."

Try this recipe yourself any day during Indian summer when you want to end a meal with something special.

HARVEST APPLE-CRANBERRY PIE

It's a bit tart—to sweeten, top with scoops of vanilla ice cream

Pastry for 2-crust pie
¾ c. sugar
3 tblsp. cornstarch
¼ tsp. salt
¾ c. light corn syrup
¼ c. water
1 ½ c. raw cranberries
2 tsp. grated orange peel
1 ½ c. chopped peeled apples
2 tblsp. butter or margarine

• Mix sugar, cornstarch and salt in saucepan; gradually add corn syrup and water. Cook, stirring constantly, until mixture thickens slightly.
• Add cranberries and continue cooking until skins break. Add orange peel; cool.
• Add apples to cranberry mixture and turn into pastry-lined 9″ pie pan. Dot with butter. Adjust top crust and flute edges; cut vents.
• Bake in hot oven (425°F.) 40 to 50 minutes.

APPLE-APRICOT PIE

Apricots provide the tart flavor that makes this apple pie unusual

Pastry for 2-crust pie
½ c. sugar
1 tblsp. flour
½ tsp. cinnamon
¼ tsp. salt
4 c. sliced peeled apples (about 5 medium)
1 c. coarsely chopped, drained, canned apricots

• Combine sugar, flour, cinnamon and salt. Toss apples and apricots with sugar mixture.
• Turn into pastry-lined 9″ pie pan; adjust top crust and flute edges; cut vents.
• Bake in hot oven (400°F.) until apples are tender and pie is golden, about 40 minutes.

FROSTED APPLE-RAISIN PIE

A FARM JOURNAL *5-star recipe—from our* COUNTRY COOKBOOK

Pastry for 2-crust pie
¾ c. sugar
2 tblsp. flour
⅛ tsp. salt
½ tsp. cinnamon
6 c. sliced peeled tart apples
½ c. seedless raisins
2 tblsp. orange juice
3 tblsp. butter or margarine
Orange Frosting

• Combine sugar, flour, salt and cinnamon; mix with apples and raisins; place in pastry-lined 9″ pie pan. Sprinkle with orange juice; dot with butter. Adjust top crust and flute edges; cut vents.
• Bake in hot oven (400°F.) about 40 minutes, or until crust is browned and apples are tender.
• Spread Orange Frosting over hot pie.

ORANGE FROSTING: Mix 1 c. confectioners sugar, 3 tblsp. strained orange juice and 1 tsp. grated orange peel.

Apples, Blackberries Join Flavors

About the time yellow-green, summer apples are coming into their own, lustrous, black-purple blackberries ripen. The wild berries, available in many parts of the country, have superb flavor and relatively small seeds. Gather them; put up with stained fingers and thorn pricks—it's worth it. Combine them with early apples for a pie that can't be surpassed.

Summer apples are juicy, tart and fast-cooking—ideal for pies. They make superior applesauce, too, but brown too quickly when cut for salads and they're too tart to eat out of hand. But don't weep over these shortcomings . . . they make superior pies.

BLACKBERRY-APPLE PIE

Use either wild or cultivated berries

Pastry for 2-crust pie
- 3 c. fresh blackberries
- 1 c. thin, peeled green apple slices
- 2½ to 3 tblsp. quick-cooking tapioca
- 1 c. sugar
- ½ tsp. cinnamon
- 2 tblsp. butter or margarine

• Pick over and wash berries in cold water. Lift out and drain. In large bowl, combine berries, apples, tapioca, sugar and cinnamon, mixing well.
• Turn into pastry-lined 9″ pie pan. Dot with butter and adjust top crust and flute edges; cut vents.

• Bake in hot oven (425°F.) until crust is golden brown and juices start to bubble up in vents, 40 to 50 minutes.

Note: For a change use Cheese Pastry (see Chapter 2).

SWISS APPLE-CHERRY PIE

This pie's double popularity is no mystery—it combines two tasty fruits

Pastry for 2-crust pie
- 1¼ c. sugar
- ¼ c. flour
- 1 tsp. cinnamon
- ¼ tsp. nutmeg
- 5 medium apples, thinly sliced and peeled (3½ c.)
- 1 (1 lb. 4 oz.) can tart cherries, drained
- 2 tblsp. butter

• Combine sugar, flour, cinnamon and nutmeg. Divide mixture in four parts.
• Arrange one third of apple slices over bottom of pastry-lined 9″ pie pan. Sprinkle with one fourth of sugar-spice mixture. Cover with half of the cherries; sprinkle on second fourth of sugar-spice mixture. Repeat, using all of sugar-spice mixture, apples and cherries. Dot with butter. Adjust top crust; flute edges and cut vents.
• Bake in hot oven (400°F.) 50 minutes, or until pastry is browned and filling is bubbly in vents.

Note: For an interesting pie top, sprinkle with 1 tsp. sugar and ⅛ tsp. cinnamon before baking pie.

Try Hawaiian Apple Pie

Hawaiian cooks are famed for dishes made with coconut, which grows in the Islands. So you'd expect them to add coconut to apple pie, but you'll be surprised how wonderful the combination of the two tastes when baked in pastry. Here's a recipe from the palm-fringed shores of our fiftieth state worthy of adoption across country.

COCONUT-CRUNCH APPLE PIE

A 2-layer, 1-crust pie—crisp coconut tops the juicy, spiced apples

Pastry for 1-crust pie
 1   c. granulated sugar
 ¼   c. brown sugar, firmly packed
 2   tblsp. flour
 ½   tsp. cinnamon
 5   c. sliced peeled apples
 2   tblsp. butter or margarine
 2   c. shredded coconut
 1   egg, beaten
 ¼   c. milk
 ½   tsp. salt

• Combine ½ c. white sugar, the brown sugar, flour and cinnamon. Place half the apples in pastry-lined 9″ pie pan; sprinkle with half the sugar-spice mixture. Repeat. Dot with butter.
• Cut two layers of aluminum foil in a circle to cover filling only. Bake, foil-covered, in moderate oven (375°F.) 30 minutes.

• Combine coconut, egg, the remaining ½ c. sugar, milk and salt.
• Remove pie from oven and lift off foil. Spread coconut mixture on top. Return to oven and bake 30 minutes longer.

BUTTERSCOTCH APPLE PIE

Introduce this new apple pie to your family—they'll ask for a repeat

Unbaked 9″ pie shell
 5   c. sliced peeled apples
 1   (6 oz.) pkg. butterscotch morsels
Cinnamon
 ¼   c. sugar
 ¼   c. flour
 1   tsp. salt
 ½   c. light cream

• Combine apples and butterscotch morsels; put into pastry shell. Sprinkle generously with cinnamon.
• Combine sugar, flour and salt; then add cream. Drizzle over apples so that slices are coated.
• Place pie in large paper bag; fasten bag securely. Bake in moderate oven (375°F.) about 70 minutes.
• Remove from bag at once. Cool.

APPLE-DATE PIE

Cherries are scattered like garnets in filling to show through lattice

Pastry for 2-crust pie
 4   c. peeled and diced tart apples
 ½   c. dates, cut into pieces

½ c. maraschino cherries, cut into quarters
½ c. coarsely chopped walnuts
¾ c. sugar
¼ c. flour
¼ tsp. salt
¼ c. light cream
¼ c. lemon juice

• Combine apples, dates, cherries and nuts; put into pastry-lined 9″ pie pan.
• Combine sugar, flour and salt. Add cream, mix well. Add lemon juice. Pour cream mixture over fruit. Top with lattice design of strips made from remaining pastry.
• Place pie in large paper bag. Close and fasten bag. Bake in hot oven (400°F.) 60 minutes (pie will brown, bag keeps steam around pie). Remove from oven; remove pie from bag at once.

APPLE-GRAPEFRUIT PIE

Grapefruit fans like the tart taste

Baked 9″ pie shell
5 apples peeled (3 c. thin slices)
2½ c. sweetened grapefruit juice (canned)
3½ tblsp. cornstarch
⅔ c. sugar
¼ tsp. salt
Sweetened whipped cream

• Cook apple slices in grapefruit juice until tender. Remove apples from juice.
• Mix cornstarch, sugar and salt; add to juice and cook about 10 minutes, or until thickened and clear. Cool.
• Place apples in pie shell. Pour thickened juice over them.
• Serve with sweetened whipped cream.

STREUSEL APPLE-MINCE PIE

Version of mince pie men brag about

Unbaked 9″ pie shell
2 c. prepared mincemeat
3 c. sliced peeled apples
½ c. sugar
1 tblsp. lemon juice
Brown Sugar Streusel

• Spoon mincemeat into pie shell. Combine apples, sugar and lemon juice. Spread over mincemeat.
• Sprinkle Brown Sugar Streusel over apples.
• Bake in hot oven (425°F.) until apples are tender and pie browned the way you like it, about 45 minutes.

BROWN SUGAR STREUSEL: Blend ½ c. flour and ½ c. brown sugar. Cut in ¼ c. butter or margarine until well mixed.

MARLBOROUGH PIE

Rich yellow pie has sharp lemon taste but texture of apples—cuts like jelly

Unbaked 9″ pie shell
1 c. unsweetened applesauce
3 tblsp. lemon juice
½ tsp. lemon peel
1 c. sugar
4 eggs, slightly beaten
2 tblsp. butter, melted
½ tsp. salt

• Chill pie shell while preparing filling.
• Combine applesauce, lemon juice and peel, sugar, eggs, butter and salt. Blend thoroughly and pour into pastry-lined pie pan.   *more*

• Bake in very hot oven (450°F.) 15 minutes; reduce heat to 350°F. and bake 10 to 15 minutes longer, or until silver knife inserted halfway between center and edge of pie comes out clean. Cool on rack.

Note: New England homemakers steam peeled and cored apples and put them through food mill or sieve to make sauce.

ROSY CRAB APPLE PIE

A FARM JOURNAL *5-star recipe—from our* FREEZING & CANNING COOKBOOK

Pastry for 2-crust pie
 1 c. sugar
 1 tblsp. flour
 ¼ tsp. salt
 6 c. finely chopped unpeeled crab apples
 1 tsp. vanilla
 1 ½ tblsp. lemon juice
 ⅓ c. water
 1 ½ tblsp. butter

• Combine sugar, flour and salt; toss together with apples.
• Pour apple mixture into pastry-lined 9″ pie pan. Sprinkle with mixture of vanilla, lemon juice and water. Dot with butter. Adjust top crust and flute edges; cut vents.
• Bake in hot oven (400°F.) 50 minutes, or until filling is tender and crust is browned.

Note: If you wish to freeze pie, steam apple bits in colander over boiling water 1 to 2 minutes before mixing filling and cool quickly. This will preserve color.

APRICOT-STRAWBERRY PIE

Wonderful served slightly warm with a topknot of vanilla ice cream

Pastry for 2-crust pie
 4 c. pitted quartered fresh apricots
 1 c. crushed fresh strawberries
 1 c. sugar
 1 tblsp. lemon juice
 2 tblsp. quick-cooking tapioca
 ⅛ tsp. salt
 2 tblsp. butter or margarine

• Combine apricots, strawberries, sugar, lemon juice, tapioca and salt in mixing bowl. Pour into pastry-lined 9″ pie pan. Dot with butter. Adjust top crust, cut steam vents and flute edges.
• Bake in hot oven (425°F.) about 35 to 45 minutes, or until crust is browned and juices start to bubble in vents. Cool on rack.

Note: The natural sweetness of apricots dictates the amount of sugar to use. Fully ripe fruit requires less than the firm apricots usually available in markets in areas where the fruit is not grown, the kind used in testing this recipe.

Summer's Best—Berry Pies

Early summer mornings, when the air's still dewy, farm children gather ripe, juicy berries for Mother's superb pies. Step into the farm kitchen mid-morning and a taunting fragrance greets you. Visit and sip coffee for a half hour and you'll see sugar-sprinkled pies with color-bright juice bubbling in the vents being carried from oven to cooling racks on the counter. You'll want to accept that invitation to linger longer for dinner—fresh berry pie for dessert!

We'll give you several berry pie recipes, but we'll start with a plus: basic directions that will insure your success with fresh berry pies.

Tips for Success with 2-Crust Fresh Berry Pies

BERRIES: You can use blueberries, blackberries, boysenberries, gooseberries, loganberries, raspberries, strawberries, etc. If the strawberries are large, cut them in half.

Pick over and wash berries, removing stems and hulls. Combine 1⅓ c. sugar and ⅓ c. flour. Add 4 c. ripe berries and toss gently to mix. Pour mixture into pastry-lined 9″ pie pan. Dot with 2 tblsp. butter or margarine. Adjust top crust, cut vents or prick with 4-tined fork, seal and flute edges to make a high-standing rim.

Bake in hot oven (425°F.) until crust is golden, about 35 to 45 minutes. Serve faintly warm.

SUGAR: The amount of sugar you need depends on the ripeness and tartness of the berries—also on how sweet you like your pies. Sometimes 1 c. is adequate, but if berries are very tart or not fully ripe, you may need as much as 2 c. but 1⅓ c. is the average amount.

SPICE: A few country cooks like to add a touch of spice to berry pies, usually ½ tsp. cinnamon or ¼ tsp. cloves or nutmeg.

LEMON JUICE: Most pie bakers add from 1 to 2 tblsp. lemon juice to berry pie fillings. They find it brings out the best flavors. Its addition is optional, of course.

SUGAR-SPARKLE TOPS: It's standard procedure in country kitchens to brush the top crust of berry pie with milk or cream and sprinkle on 1 tsp. sugar before baking.

FAVORITE TOPPING: Vanilla ice cream on faintly warm pie can't be beat.

Note: Some cooks prefer a thinner pie with runaway juices under firm control. They use 3 c. berries, ⅔ to 1 c. sugar, 2 tblsp. cornstarch or 4 tblsp. flour and 1½ tblsp. butter.

FARM KITCHEN IDEA: A Kansas homemaker's first choice is pie made with half blackberries and half red raspberries. Do try the combination— serve the pie faintly warm with scoops of ice cream on top.

COUNTRY KITCHEN IDEA: Make larger than usual vents in top crust of blueberry pie. Omit butter. Five minutes before pie is baked, remove from oven and pour ½ c. heavy cream into pie through vents. Return to oven to complete baking.

Country Blueberry Pies

Many farm women prefer wild blueberries to the prettier, larger cultivated fruit with softer seeds. They hold that domesticating the berry tamed its flavor, too! Both have their champions—both make excellent pies.

If you live where you can pick your own, use the berries soon after taking them from the bush. We especially recommend our 1-Crust Double-Good Blueberry and Lemon-Blueberry Pies. The first, a New England special, is a half-and-half pie—contains both raw and cooked berries. In the second, grated lemon peel enhances the berry taste. The recipe comes from a Wisconsin farm kitchen in which the pie shows up on the dinner table the year around. Frozen berries do the honors when fresh ones are unseasonal.

Blueberries freeze successfully. It's easy to fix them. Just wash the stemmed fruit in cold water, the colder the better. Lift out and drain. Package and freeze without sweetening and use like fresh berries.

DOUBLE-GOOD BLUEBERRY PIE

Secret of the pie's popularity is its remarkably fresh berry taste

Baked 9" pie shell
¾ c. sugar

3   tblsp. cornstarch
⅛ tsp. salt
¼ c. water
4   c. blueberries
1   tblsp. butter
1   tblsp. lemon juice
Whipped cream (optional)

• Combine sugar, cornstarch and salt in saucepan. Add water and 2 c. blueberries; cook over medium heat, stirring constantly, until mixture comes to a boil and is thickened and clear. (Mixture will be quite thick.)

• Remove from heat and stir in butter and lemon juice. Cool.

• Place remaining 2 c. raw blueberries in pie shell. Top with cooked berry mixture. Chill. Serve garnished with whipped cream.

LEMON-BLUEBERRY PIE

Money-making pie—a favorite in a successful farm-home tearoom

Pastry for 2-crust pie
4   c. frozen blueberries or 2 (10 oz.) pkgs.
1   c. sugar
⅓ c. flour

1 tsp. grated lemon peel
⅛ tsp. salt
2 tblsp. butter

• Combine berries, sugar, flour, lemon peel and salt. Place in pastry-lined 9″ pie pan. Dot with butter. Adjust top crust and flute edges; cut vents.
• Bake in hot oven (425°F.) 40 to 50 minutes, or until crust is lightly browned and juice bubbles through steam vents.

BLUEBERRY-LEMON SPONGE PIE

Blueberries combine with lemon sponge in a delectable 2-layer pie

Baked 9″ pie shell

Blueberry Layer:
2 c. fresh blueberries
¾ c. sugar
2 tblsp. flour
⅛ tsp. salt
2 egg yolks, well beaten
¼ c. orange juice

Sponge Layer:
½ c. sugar
2 tblsp. flour
⅛ tsp. salt
½ c. cold water
1 egg yolk, slightly beaten
1 tblsp. lemon juice
1 tsp. grated lemon peel
3 egg whites

Blueberry Layer: Heat berries in heavy saucepan over low heat. Blend dry ingredients and add to egg yolks. Add orange juice and beat until smooth. Pour over berries and cook over low heat until thick, stirring constantly. Pour into pie shell.

Sponge Layer: Add blended ¼ c. sugar, flour, salt and cold water to egg yolk; blend and cook over low heat until thick, stirring constantly. Remove from heat; add lemon juice and peel.
• Beat egg whites until soft peaks form; add remaining ¼ c. sugar gradually, beating until mixture is stiff and glossy. Fold cooked lemon mixture into meringue. Pile onto blueberry layer, making sure it touches crust all around.
• Bake in slow oven (325°F.) 35 minutes, or until lightly browned.

Elderberry Pie

Creamy, white blossoms on elderberry bushes start daydreams of summer pies. Elderberry is a pioneer pie that never has gone out of style. The edible blue or black berries have a tart flavor of their own, which country cooks frequently point up with a touch of vinegar or lemon juice. Some pie bakers prefer to combine elderberries with other fruits—apples, gooseberries, cherries, for instance.

Elderberries, like blueberries, freeze successfully without sweetening. During seasons when bucketfuls of berries may be picked free as all outdoors, some cooks put packages of elderberries in their freezers for around-the-year pie baking. They use the frozen berries like fresh ones.

One rule of country cooking is to serve elderberry pie hot from the oven. Frequently a pitcher of sweetened pour cream is passed—a traditional custom. Today, with vanilla ice cream kept on hand in many farm freezers, it also often tops elderberry pie at serving time.

Whenever you talk elderberry pies with farm women, you discover that almost every good cook has tricks of her own. An Iowa homemaker likes to combine 1 part elderberries with 3 parts gooseberries or tart cherries in pies. Then she omits the vinegar or lemon juice and adds a trifle less sugar than when she bakes either a plain gooseberry or cherry pie.

A Kentucky homemaker says: "When I bake apple pies, I often scatter from ½ to 1 cup stemmed elderberries among the apples, sprinkle on a little lemon juice and add a lattice top to show off the beautiful color of the filling. One taste brings compliments—the second bite, requests for my recipe! I always suggest that everyone make her favorite apple pie, adding the ½ or 1 cup of elderberries for a special touch."

The amount of thickening—tapioca, cornstarch or flour—required varies somewhat with the season—depending on the juiciness of the berries. Our recipe suggests the amount usually needed, but you may have to make some adjustment from one year to another.

PIONEER ELDERBERRY PIE

A dessert that makes the search for elderberries along fence rows pay off

Pastry for 2-crust pie
3 ½ c. washed, stemmed elderberries
1 tblsp. vinegar or lemon juice
1 c. sugar
¼ tsp. salt
⅓ c. flour
1 tblsp. butter or margarine

• Spread elderberries in pastry-lined 9″ pie pan. Sprinkle with vinegar.
• Combine sugar, salt and flour; sprinkle over berries. Dot with butter.
• Adjust top crust and flute edges; cut vents. Bake in hot oven (400°F.) 35 to 45 minutes, or until juices show in vents and crust is golden brown.

Note: A farm kitchen trick—use a wide-tooth comb to strip elderberries from their stems.

ELDERBERRY-APPLE PIE

An old-time FARM JOURNAL *favorite*

Unbaked 9″ pie shell
2 c. elderberries
1 ½ c. chopped peeled tart apples
1 c. sugar
⅛ tsp. salt
3 tblsp. quick-cooking tapioca
2 tblsp. butter

• Wash and stem elderberries. (Hold berries in palm of hand and pull stems off with wire egg beater, the kind shaped like tennis racquet.)

• Combine elderberries, apples, sugar, salt and tapioca, crushing berries with spoon.
• Spoon mixture into pie shell; dot with butter; top with pastry lattice.
• Bake in hot oven (400°F.) 35 to 40 minutes, or until apples are tender and crust is golden.

Gather Mulberries for Pies

The recipe for mulberry pie properly starts: "Select a sunny summer day when the breezes are light. Stand on the shady side of the mulberry tree and fill your pail with the knobby, long, glistening berries. Do a little bird watching while you work." Or if you are of a different berry-picking school: "Spread a worn sheet on the emerald grass beneath the tree, shake the branches lightly and run from the shower of juicy, warm, sweet berries that plop down. Get your exercise bending over to pick up berries."

Certainly mulberries are one of the easiest berries to transfer directly from tree to pail. There's no stooping, kneeling or squatting the way there is when you are picking strawberries, raspberries and blackberries, for instance.

Bake a wonderful country pie that day—a pie most city people never are fortunate enough to see or taste. Combine the sweet mulberries with a tart fruit, like gooseberries, or rhubarb. The sweet-tart blend is extra-delicious. We give you a recipe for the berry-rhubarb team that makes one of the most economical farm fruit pies—and one of the best.

MULBERRY PIE

Enjoy this summer pie every month—freeze berries and rhubarb to make it

Pastry for 2-crust pie
2   c. mulberries
1   c. finely sliced rhubarb
1   c. sugar
4   tblsp. flour
2   tblsp. butter or margarine

• Combine mulberries and rhubarb in medium bowl.
• Combine sugar and flour. Sprinkle about ⅓ of mixture in bottom of pastry-lined 9″ pie pan. Turn mulberries and rhubarb into pie pan and add remaining sugar-flour mixture. Dot with butter. Adjust top crust, cut steam vents and flute edges.
• Bake in hot oven (425°F.) 40 to 50 minutes, or until crust is browned and juices bubble in vents.

Two-Berry Pie—Popular with Men

Among popular fruit pies in the Pacific Northwest are the luscious cranberry-blueberry specials. A Washington farm homemaker says: "We have a cranberry bog and my favorite Cranberry-Blueberry Pie recipe comes in handy during the harvest season when I cook for a crew of men. They all seem to enjoy this dessert best. For company, I often put a lattice top on this pie—sometimes spoon vanilla ice cream on top.

"We have enough blueberry bushes to yield fruit for fresh berry pies, and to freeze to combine with fresh cranberries and pastry."

If you want to bake a pie with both blueberries (frozen) and cranberries, follow our famous recipe for Burgundy Berry Pie, which also originated in a Washington country kitchen.

CRANBERRY-BLUEBERRY PIE

Latticed pastry top will display rich color of luscious fruit filling

Pastry for 2-crust pie
2   c. fresh cranberries
2   c. frozen, unsweetened blueberries
1 ½ c. sugar
⅓   c. flour
⅛   tsp. salt
2   tblsp. butter or margarine

• Put cranberries through food chopper. Combine with frozen blueberries, sugar, flour and salt. Place in pastry-lined 9″ pie pan. Dot with butter. Adjust top crust and flute edges; cut vents.
• Bake in hot oven (425°F.) 45 to 50 minutes or until crust is golden.

CRANBERRY-RAISIN PIE

Colorful Cape Cod pie that's perfect with turkey, chicken and pork

Pastry for 2-crust pie
3   c. fresh cranberries

2   tblsp. flour
2   c. sugar
¼   tsp. salt
⅔   c. boiling water
1   c. seedless raisins
2   tsp. grated lemon peel
2   tblsp. butter or margarine

• Remove stems from cranberries.
• Combine flour, sugar and salt in saucepan. Stir in cranberries, water, raisins and lemon peel. Cover and cook until cranberries start to pop. Remove from heat and add butter. Cool until lukewarm.
• Pour filling into pastry-lined 9″ pie pan. Arrange lattice of pastry strips on top (see Chapter 2).
• Bake in hot oven (425°F.) 40 to 50 minutes, or until juices bubble in lattice openings and crust is browned.

BURGUNDY BERRY PIE

A FARM JOURNAL *5-star recipe—from our* FREEZING & CANNING COOKBOOK

Baked 9″ pie shell and cutouts
1 ¼ c. sugar
5   tblsp. cornstarch
⅛   tsp. salt
2   tblsp. water
1 ½ c. frozen whole cranberries, unsweetened
2   c. frozen blueberries, unsweetened

• Combine sugar, cornstarch and salt in heavy saucepan; stir in water and cook over very low heat until mixture melts and comes to a full boil. Add cranberries; cook gently until soft. Remove from heat, and add frozen blueberries. Cool.

• Pour into cooled pastry shell and top with pastry cutouts.

Note: To make pastry cutouts, cut rolled pastry for top crust in fancy shapes with cookie cutter. Brush with water and sprinkle with sugar. Bake on baking sheet in very hot oven (450°F.) a few minutes, or until lightly browned. Cool. Place on pie, one cutout per wedge.

CRANBERRY RELISH PIE

Fine with chicken dinners—make it with frozen cranberries in summer

Pastry for 2-crust pie
2 ½ c. ground fresh cranberries
1 c.   ground unpeeled apple (about 2 medium)
½ c. ground orange pulp and peel (1 small)
½ c. chopped nuts
1 ½ c. sugar
2 tblsp. flour
½ tsp. cinnamon
¼ tsp. nutmeg
2 tblsp. butter

• Combine cranberries, apple, orange, nuts, sugar, flour, cinnamon and nutmeg. Place in pastry-lined 9″ pie pan. Dot with butter.
• Adjust latticed top crust; flute edges. Bake in hot oven (425°F.) until pastry is browned and juice begins to bubble through openings in lattice, 40 to 50 minutes.

FRESH GOOSEBERRY PIE

Old-time favorite with as big-time popularity as in pioneer days

Almond Pastry for 2-crust pie
3 c. fresh gooseberries

1 ½ c. sugar
3 tblsp. quick-cooking tapioca
⅛ tsp. salt
2 tblsp. butter or margarine

• Crush ¾ c. gooseberries and add to sugar, tapioca and salt. Stir in remainder of berries. Cook and stir until mixture thickens.
• Turn into pastry-lined 9″ pie pan. Dot with butter. Adjust top crust and flute edges; cut vents. Brush with milk.
• Bake in hot oven (425°F.) 35 to 45 minutes, or until crust is golden. Serve slightly warm.

ALMOND PASTRY: Before adding water to blended flour and shortening in making pastry for a 2-crust pie, add 1 tsp. almond extract. Also good for peach and cherry pies.

RASPBERRY GLACÉ PIE

"My company special," says the Minnesota woman who shares her recipe

Baked 9″ pie shell
1 qt. red raspberries
1 c. water
1 c. sugar
3 tblsp. cornstarch
Few drops red food color
2 tsp. lemon juice
1 (3 oz.) pkg. cream cheese (room temperature)
1 tblsp. milk
Whipped cream (optional)

• Wash berries gently in cold water, lift out and spread on paper toweling to drain thoroughly.   *more*

• Place 1 c. berries and ⅔ c. water in saucepan; simmer 3 minutes. Run through strainer to remove seeds.

• Blend sugar, cornstarch and remaining ⅓ c. water. Add to cooked raspberries and cook until mixture is thick and translucent, stirring constantly. Remove from heat, add food color and lemon juice. Cool.

• Combine cream cheese with milk and spread evenly over bottom of pie shell. Pour remaining berries into pie shell, reserving a few of the prettiest ones for garnishing. Spread cooled, cooked berry mixture over berries. Chill until firm, at least 2 hours. Serve garnished with whipped cream and whole berries.

STRAWBERRY GLACÉ PIE

Hostess idea—substitute individual tart shells for the big pie shell

Baked 9" pie shell
1 ½ qts. strawberries
 1 c. sugar
 3 tblsp. cornstarch
 ½ c. water
 1 tblsp. butter or margarine
 1 c. heavy cream, whipped
 2 tblsp. sifted confectioners sugar

• Hull, wash in cold water and thoroughly drain berries. Crush enough (with potato masher) to make 1 c.

• Combine sugar and cornstarch. Add crushed berries and water. Cook over medium heat, stirring constantly, until mixture comes to a boil. Continue cooking and stirring over low heat 2 minutes. The mixture will be thickened and translucent. Remove from heat and stir in butter. Cool.

• Place whole berries in pie shell, reserving a few choice ones for garnishing. Pour cooked mixture over berries and chill at least 2 hours.

• Serve topped with whipped cream, confectioners sugar added. Garnish with remaining strawberries.

VARIATION

STRAWBERRY CHEESE GLACÉ PIE: Combine 1 (3 oz.) pkg. cream cheese (room temperature) with 1 tblsp. milk and spread over bottom of pie shell before adding berries.

STRAWBERRY FESTIVAL PIE

Crunchy topped, red-bright filling—a beauty that tastes as good as it looks

Baked 9" pie shell
 3 tblsp. cornstarch
 ¾ c. sugar
 ¼ c. water
 4 c. strawberries
Few drops red food color
Toasted Oat Topping
Whipped cream (optional)

• Combine cornstarch and ½ c. sugar in saucepan; blend in water. Add 2 c. berries and cook, stirring constantly, until thickened and translucent (mixture will be very thick).

• Remove from heat, add food color, remaining ¼ c. sugar and 2 c. berries. Chill.

• Turn strawberry mixture into pie shell and scatter Toasted Oat Topping over pie. Serve with whipped cream if you like.

TOASTED OAT TOPPING: Combine 1 c. quick-cooking rolled oats, ¼ c. brown sugar and ¼ c. melted butter or margarine. Spread in shallow pan. Toast in moderate oven (350°F.) 10 minutes. Toss lightly with a fork.

STRAWBERRY-APRICOT PIE

These fruits ripen at the same time in California's Santa Clara Valley where this pie is a favorite

Baked 9" pie shell
12   fresh unpeeled apricots, pitted and halved
¾   c. water
½   c. sugar
2   tblsp. cornstarch
½   tsp. salt
2   tblsp. lemon juice
1   qt. ripe strawberries, sliced
1   c. heavy cream, whipped

• Combine apricots and ¾ c. water in saucepan. Bring to a boil and remove from heat at once. Drain, saving liquid. Measure liquid into cup and add water to make ¾ c.
• Purée apricots in blender with a little of the measured liquid, or by putting through sieve or food mill. Return puréed apricots and cooking liquid to saucepan; bring to a boil.
• Combine sugar, cornstarch and salt, mixing thoroughly. Stir into apricot purée. Continue cooking and stirring until mixture thickens and becomes clear. Stir in lemon juice. Cool.
• Fill pie shell with berries; cover with apricot glaze. Top with whipped cream.

STRAWBERRY CREAM PIE

Pie filling contains both cooked and uncooked berries—extra-good flavor

Baked 9" pie shell
1   qt. hulled strawberries
3   tblsp. cornstarch
1   c. sugar
2   tblsp. lemon juice
⅛   tsp. salt
Whipped cream

• Crush half of berries with potato masher or fork; stir in cornstarch, sugar, lemon juice and salt. Cook over medium heat until mixture is thickened and clear. Cool.
• Cut remaining 2 c. berries in halves, saving out 6 whole berries; fold into the cooked mixture. Pour into pie shell and chill.
• To serve, garnish with puffs of whipped cream and a few choice berries.

STRAWBERRY-CANTALOUPE PIE

Cool-looking, colorful, tempting and refreshing with luscious flavor blend

Baked 9" pie shell
1   (3 oz.) pkg. cream cheese
1   tblsp. milk
1   c. ripe strawberries
½   c. water
½   c. sugar
2   tblsp. cornstarch
⅛   tsp. salt
1   tblsp. butter
1   tsp. finely grated lemon peel

more

Red food color
3 c. fresh cantaloupe balls, drained

• Spread cream cheese, softened with milk, over bottom of cool pie shell.
• Crush strawberries slightly and combine with water; simmer 5 minutes and press through sieve. Discard seeds.
• Blend sugar, cornstarch and salt; stir into strawberry mixture. Cook over medium heat, stirring constantly until mixture comes to a boil. Continue cooking and stirring over low heat 2 minutes. The mixture will be thickened and translucent. Remove from heat and stir in butter and lemon peel. Add a few drops of red color. Cool until lukewarm.
• Place cantaloupe balls in pie shell on top of cheese; spoon strawberry glaze over them. Let glaze set before serving.

STRAWBERRY-PINEAPPLE PIE

Competes with strawberry shortcake for blue ribbons—try it for a change

Pastry for 2-crust pie
1   c. sugar
4   tblsp. cornstarch
½   tsp. salt
4   c. fresh strawberries, sliced
½   c. drained crushed pineapple (canned)
2   tblsp. butter
Whipped cream (optional)

• Combine sugar, cornstarch and salt. Stir in strawberries and pineapple. Turn into pastry-lined 9″ pie pan. Dot with butter. Adjust top crust (use latticed top for greatest appeal); flute edges. Brush top of pie with milk.
• Bake in hot oven (400°F.) 40 to 50 minutes. Cool on rack before serving. Garnish with fluffs of whipped cream and choice, ripe berries.

Red Cherry Orchard Pie

If you have a cherry tree, the chances are you race with the birds to see who will get the juicy, red fruit. Country homemakers refuse to let their feathered friends win—a determination that has their families' approval. Cherry pie is one of the royal American desserts—it competes with apple pie for top honors. Here's our best recipe for the classic, a simple, unadorned one. For who always wants to try to improve on the bright cherry flavor and color?

FRESH CHERRY PIE

Every forkful of our best cherry pie brings delight—an easy one to make

Pastry for 2-crust pie
1 ⅓   c. sugar
⅓   c. flour
⅛   tsp. salt
3   drops almond extract (optional)
4   c. pitted tart cherries
2   tblsp. butter or margarine

• Combine sugar, flour and salt. Add almond extract to cherries and toss with sugar-flour mixture to mix thoroughly. Turn into pastry-lined 9″ pie pan. Adjust lattice top; flute edges.
• Bake in hot oven (425°F.) about 40 minutes. If edges brown too much, cover loosely with strip of aluminum foil.

Note: Use 1½ c. sugar if you do not like a cherry pie on the tart side.

CRISSCROSS CHERRY PIE

A FARM JOURNAL *5-star recipe—from our* COUNTRY COOKBOOK

Rich Pastry
2 (1 lb.) cans pitted tart cherries (water pack)
2½ tblsp. quick-cooking tapioca
¼ tsp. salt
¼ tsp. almond extract
1 tsp. lemon juice
4 drops red food color
1¼ c. sugar
1 tblsp. butter or margarine

• Drain cherries. Measure ⅓ c. liquid into mixing bowl. Add tapioca, salt, almond extract, lemon juice and food color, then cherries and 1 c. sugar. Mix and let stand while making pastry.
• Fit pastry into bottom of 9″ pie pan. Trim ½″ beyond outer rim of pan. Fill with cherry mixture. Dot with butter. Sprinkle with remaining sugar. Moisten rim with water. Adjust latticed top; flute edges. (To keep high rim from browning faster than crisscross strips, circle pie with a stand-up foil collar. Fold foil over rim and leave on during entire baking.)

• Bake in hot oven (425°F.) 40 to 45 minutes. Serve warm.

RICH PASTRY

2¼ c. sifted flour
1 tsp. salt
1 tblsp. sugar
¾ c. vegetable shortening
1 egg yolk
1 tblsp. lemon juice
¼ c. milk

• Sift flour with salt and sugar. Cut in shortening until mixture resembles coarse cornmeal.
• Beat egg yolk and lemon juice. Blend in milk. Add to dry ingredients, tossing with fork into a soft dough.
• Divide dough in half. Form each into ball. Flatten each on lightly floured surface. Roll to about ⅛″ thickness. Use half for bottom crust. Cut second half into 18 strips with sharp knife or pastry wheel. Interlace 14 strips, pressing ends against moistened rim and folding lower crust up over them. Moisten rim again and circle it with remaining 4 strips. Press down firmly.

CHERRY PIE GLACÉ

Dessert they'll praise—open-face pie filled with shiny, red cherries

Unbaked 9″ pie shell
4 c. pitted fresh tart cherries
1 c. sugar
⅛ tsp. salt
¼ c. flour
1 tblsp. lemon juice
2 tblsp. butter or margarine
Cinnamon Jelly Glaze
Whipped cream (optional)   *more*

• Combine cherries, sugar, salt, flour and lemon juice. Pour into pie shell. Dot with butter.

• Bake in moderate oven (375°F.) 40 minutes. Cool on rack.

• Spoon Cinnamon Jelly Glaze over cherries. To serve, garnish with spoonfuls of whipped cream.

CINNAMON JELLY GLAZE: Melt ¾ c. red currant or other tart jelly over hot water. Add ¼ tsp. cinnamon.

VARIATIONS

CHERRY PIE GLACÉ WITH CANNED FRUIT: Substitute 2 (1 lb. 4 oz.) cans tart cherries, well drained, for fresh pitted cherries.

CHERRY PIE GLACÉ WITH FROZEN FRUIT: Substitute 2 (1 lb.) cans frozen tart cherries (packed in syrup), thawed and well drained, for fresh pitted cherries. Reduce sugar from 1 c. to ½ c.

REGAL CHERRY PIE

Crust and filling bake separately—good way to curb runaway juices

Crust:
1 ¾ c. sifted flour
¼ tsp. salt
1 tsp. baking powder
1 tblsp. sugar
¾ c. butter or shortening
3 egg yolks, slightly beaten
1 tblsp. water

Filling:
2 (1 lb. 4 oz.) cans tart cherries, drained
1 c. sugar
¼ c. cornstarch
½ c. cherry juice
1 tsp. almond extract
Few drops red food color
Meringue (3 egg whites)

Crust: Sift together flour, salt, baking powder and sugar. Cut in butter. Add egg yolks mixed with water. Stir until dough clings together.

• Press mixture into a 10″ pie pan, lining bottom and sides evenly. Bake in moderate oven (375°F.) 15 minutes.

Filling: Combine cherries, sugar, cornstarch and cherry juice. Cook until thickened. Stir in almond extract and food color. Cool; turn into cool baked pie shell.

• Spoon meringue over pie (see Perfect Meringue for Topping Pies, Chapter 9).

• Bake in moderate oven (350°F.) 12 to 15 minutes, or until meringue is browned. Cool. Makes 8 servings.

CHERRY-MINCEMEAT PIE

No need to get in a pie rut—bake a double-good cherry-mincemeat treat

Pastry for 2-crust pie
1 (1 lb. 4 oz.) can pitted tart cherries
½ c. sugar
Few drops red food color
2 c. prepared mincemeat
3 tblsp. flour
⅛ tsp. salt
1 egg, beaten

• Drain cherries (you should have 2 c.).
• Combine cherries and the sugar. Let stand while you make pastry.
• Combine cherry mixture, food color, mincemeat, flour, salt and egg. Pour into a pastry-lined 9″ pie pan. Top with a lattice crust.
• Bake in hot oven (425°F.) 35 to 40 minutes.

CHERRY-WALNUT PIE

No wonder it's a holiday favorite—so festive, colorful, delicious

Crust:
1   c. flour
2   tblsp. confectioners sugar
½   c. butter or margarine

Filling:
2   eggs, slightly beaten
1   c. sugar
¼   c. flour

½   tsp. baking powder
1   c. chopped walnuts
¾   c. flaked coconut
1   (5 oz.) jar maraschino cherries
Whipped cream

Crust: Combine flour, sugar and butter in small bowl. Use mixer at low speed and mix only until dough forms. Press dough, with fingers, in bottom and sides of 9″ pie pan. Bake 10 minutes in moderate oven (350°F.). Cool.
Filling: Beat eggs and add sugar gradually. Stir in flour and baking powder, sifted together. Stir in walnuts, coconut, cherries and cherry juice, saving out some nuts, cherries and coconut for garnishing. Spread in cooled pie shell, mounding slightly in center.
• Bake in moderate oven (350°F.) 30 to 35 minutes. Spread with whipped cream and top with reserved nuts, cherries and coconut. Makes 8 servings.

Change-of-Pace Cherry Pie

Cherry pies take the spotlight in February—thanks to George Washington and the month's many parties. Why not surprise your family and friends by baking a pie with canned *sweet* cherries? They have a distinctive flavor and an appealing deep-red color. And you can buy them pitted if you don't have your own canned fruit. Here's a country-style pie to make ahead and refrigerate a few hours—one bound to be praised.

SWEET CHERRY PIE

Bake this pie once and you'll make it again and again—ever so good

Baked 9″ pie shell
2   (1 lb.) cans pitted dark sweet cherries
⅔   c. sugar
3   tblsp. cornstarch
⅛   tsp. salt
1   tblsp. butter   *more*

2   tblsp. lemon juice
1   (3 oz.) pkg. cream cheese
Whipped cream (optional)

• Drain cherries, reserving juice. Combine sugar, cornstarch and salt in saucepan. Add 1 c. cherry juice. Cook, stirring constantly, over medium heat until mixture comes to a boil. Continue cooking and stirring 2 minutes. Add cherries and cook 2 minutes.
• Remove from heat; add butter and lemon juice, stirring until butter melts. Cool.
• Let cream cheese stand at room temperature to soften. Spread over bottom of pie shell. Pour cooled cherry mixture into pie shell. Chill several hours. Serve garnished with whipped cream.

CHERRY MACAROON PIE

An exquisite party pie worth its cost in ingredients and in time

Macaroon Crust:
1   c. sifted flour
½   tsp. salt
1   tsp. granulated sugar
⅓   c. shortening
½   c. crushed macaroon cookie
      crumbs (8 two-inch cookies)
1   egg yolk, slightly beaten
4   tblsp. cold water

Filling:
1   (8 oz.) pkg. cream cheese
      (room temperature)
½   c. dairy sour cream
⅓   c. brown sugar, firmly packed
1   tsp. cinnamon
1   (1 lb. 4 oz.) can pitted tart
      cherries

½   c. sugar
⅛   tsp. salt
2½   tblsp. cornstarch
⅛   tsp. almond extract
Few drops red food color
1   (3½ oz.) can flaked coconut
Meringue (3 egg whites)

Crust: Sift together flour, salt and sugar. Cut in shortening until mixture resembles small peas. Blend in macaroon crumbs. Combine egg yolk and water; gradually sprinkle over crumbs, tossing with fork. (You may need a few more drops of water to make dough workable.)
• Form dough into ball, flatten and roll on a lightly floured surface to make a 10½″ circle. Fit dough into 9″ pie pan. Flute edge and prick well with 4-tined fork.
• Bake in hot oven (400°F.) 15 minutes. Cool.
Filling: Combine cream cheese, sour cream, brown sugar and cinnamon. Spread on bottom of cool pie shell.
• Drain cherries, saving juice. Add enough water to juice to make 1 c.
• Combine sugar, salt and cornstarch. Slowly stir in cherry juice. Cook, stirring constantly, until thick and clear. Remove from heat, add almond extract and a few drops of food color; add cherries and coconut, mixing well. Spoon mixture into pie shell. Top with meringue (see Perfect Meringue for Topping Pies, Chapter 9) and bake in moderate oven (350°F.) until tipped with gold, 12 to 15 minutes. Cool away from drafts.

Note: For an especially pretty pie, sprinkle meringue with ¼ c. flaked coconut before baking.

Red and Green Currant Pie

Country cooks are skillful in using the fruits of the woods and field—currants, for instance. Some pie bakers choose red-ripe fruit, but most of them prefer currants that are either half ripe or mostly green with a few berries starting to blush or turn color.

You may be able to buy or grow red currants if you live where the wild fruit is not available. (Most of the commercial production goes to the producers of that marvelous spread, currant jelly.) In the majority of neighborhoods fresh currants are becoming a rare treat. Their season is short, so farm homemakers lose no time in making pies when currants are ripe.

Our grandmothers' recipes for currant pie always started: "Take a scant quart of currants." If you use 4 cups of berries in a 9" pie pan, you may end up with part of the juice in the oven instead of in the pie. Modern recipes almost always call for 3 cups of fruit.

The unwritten farm-kitchen rule is to bake green currants between two pie crusts, the ripe with a latticed top to display the attractive color. If you haven't baked a currant pie and decide to make the adventure, you'll wonder why you never baked this dessert before. Almost incomparable!

FRESH CURRANT PIE

Just tart enough, very juicy; the filling has gorgeous color

Pastry for 2-crust pie
  3   c. washed, stemmed currants
  1 ½ c. sugar
  3   tblsp. quick-cooking tapioca
  ½   tsp. salt
  1   tblsp. butter or margarine

• Drain currants. Place in a bowl and crush lightly with spoon.
• Combine sugar, tapioca and salt. Add to currants and stir gently to mix.
• Turn into pastry-lined 9" pie pan; dot with butter. Adjust top crust; flute edges and cut vents.
• Bake in hot oven (425°F.) until crust is golden and the juices are bubbly, 35 to 45 minutes.

Concord Grape Pie—Extra-Delicious

It's a fragrant, tantalizing moment in the farm kitchen when grape pie comes from the oven bubbling with sweet-tart juices. Everybody wants to have dinner at once!

Today's homemakers extend the short Concord grape pie season by fixing, packaging and freezing a few pie fillings ready to add to pastry. They bake a pie or two during the holiday season or between Thanksgiving and Christmas to bring a welcome remembrance of summer to meals. The frozen filling holds its flavor three to four months.

Many women feel that the superlative taste of this old-fashioned dessert pleases their families and friends enough to justify labor and time costs. It does take a little time to slip the skins from the blue-black grapes, to heat the pulp, strain out the seeds and reunite pulp and skins before you can fix the filling.

Unfortunately, these juicy, winy native American grapes aren't grown across the nation. They are available in largest amounts in the Northeast, upper Midwest and the Middle Atlantic States.

But pie bakers on Western ranches and other places where fresh Concords are not available do not deprive their tables entirely of the rich, fruity flavor combined with tender, flaky pastry. They use frozen grape juice concentrate or bottled juice to make their pies (see Chapter 5).

Concord grape cobblers are another wonderful farm dessert. See our recipe in Chapter 6.

STREUSEL CONCORD GRAPE PIE

You can bake this filling in 2 crusts if you prefer pastry to streusel

Unbaked 9″ pie shell
4½ c. Concord grapes
1   c. sugar
¼ c. flour
2   tsp. lemon juice
⅛ tsp. salt
Oat Streusel

• Wash grapes and remove skins by pinching at end opposite stem. Reserve skins.
• Place pulp in saucepan and bring to a boil; cook a few minutes until pulp is soft. Put through strainer or food mill, while pulp is hot, to remove seeds.
• Mix strained pulp with skins. Stir in sugar, flour, lemon juice and salt.
• Place grape mixture in pastry-lined pie pan. Sprinkle on Oat Streusel.
• Bake in hot oven (425°F.) 35 to 40 minutes.

OAT STREUSEL: Combine ½ c. quick-cooking rolled oats, ½ c. brown sugar and ¼ c. flour. Cut in ¼ c. butter or margarine to distribute evenly.

Seedless Grapes—Pie-Fancier's Joy

Here's a pie that captures the honeylike sweetness of the yellow-green grapes—and the enthusiasm of all tasters. Thompson seedless grapes, developed less than a century ago in California by William Thompson, are still grown most extensively in the Golden State's vineyards. More than half the world's seedless raisins are made from them. Although the grapes have been developed to a larger size in recent years, they have retained their pleasing flavor.

If you live where you can get the immature Thompson seedless grapes, you can fashion a pie with them using your recipe for gooseberry pie. Just substitute the unripe grapes for the berries, suggests an Arizona ranch cook.

The ripe grapes are greenish-white to pale-gold color; they are sweet and have tender skins. That's the kind we used in the recipe that follows. There's no worry about stray seeds in this grape pie!

GREEN GRAPE-APPLE PIE

Grapes blend their honey sweetness with tart, juicy summer apples

Pastry for 2-crust pie
2   c. seedless green grapes

3   c. sliced peeled apples
1   c. sugar
3   tblsp. quick-cooking tapioca
¼   tsp. ground cardamon
¼   tsp. cinnamon
¼   tsp. salt
2   tblsp. butter

• Combine grapes, apples, sugar, tapioca, spices and salt. Turn into pastry-lined 9" pie pan. Dot with butter.
• Adjust top crust; flute edges and cut vents. Bake in hot oven (425°F.) 50 to 60 minutes.

Big Red Grapes—the Tokays

Never had Tokay pie? You've missed something! When the firm, compact clusters of brilliant-red Tokay or Flame Tokay grapes are ripe, surprise your family and company by making a pie with them. It's a fine way to introduce a change of pace in your autumn meals.

RED GRAPE PIE

They'll ask what it's made of and beg for your recipe

Pastry for 2-crust pie
5   c. seeded, cut-up Tokay grapes
⅔   c. sugar

1   tsp. grated lemon peel
1   tsp. lemon juice
2½ to 3 tblsp. quick-cooking tapioca
2   tblsp. butter or margarine
2   tsp. sugar
⅛   tsp. cinnamon

• Combine grapes, ⅔ c. sugar, lemon peel and juice and tapioca. Place in pastry-lined 9" pie pan. Dot with butter.
• Adjust top crust, flute edges and cut vents; sprinkle with mixture of 2 tsp. sugar and cinnamon. Bake in hot oven (425°F.) 45 to 50 minutes.

Peach Pies for Summer Suppers

"Peach pie is a reward tired and hungry men who have worked late in the field trying to finish a job really appreciate," one farm woman says. "A cool evening and a peach pie are country joys to sample together."

Here are some of the best peach pies that farm women across the country bake. Take your pick and give your family a taste treat.

OLD-FASHIONED PEACH PIE

One of summer's best treats. For a pretty pie, use a latticed pastry top

Pastry for 2-crust pie
¾ c. sugar
3   tblsp. flour
¼   tsp. cinnamon or nutmeg
⅛   tsp. salt
5   c. sliced fresh peaches
1   tsp. lemon juice
⅛   tsp. almond extract (optional)
2   tblsp. butter or margarine

• Combine sugar, flour, cinnamon and salt. Add to peaches; sprinkle on lemon juice and almond extract.
• Pour into a pastry-lined 9″ pie pan. Dot with butter.
• Adjust top crust, flute edges and cut steam vents.
• Bake in hot oven (425°F.) 40 to 45 minutes, or until peaches are tender and crust is browned.

BROWN SUGAR PIE

Give this old-time pie a new twist—top servings with lemon sherbet

Pastry for 2-crust pie
½   c. granulated sugar
¼   c. brown sugar, firmly packed
3   tblsp. flour
¼   to ½ tsp. cinnamon
⅛   tsp. salt
5   c. sliced peeled fresh peaches
1   tblsp. lemon juice (optional)
¼   tsp. almond extract (optional)
2   tblsp. butter or margarine

• Combine sugars, flour, cinnamon and salt.

• Sprinkle peaches with lemon juice and almond extract.
• Add sugar-flour mixture to peaches and mix gently. Turn into pastry-lined 9″ pie pan. Dot with butter. Adjust top crust and flute edges; cut vents. (Use lattice top, if desired.)
• Bake in hot oven (425°F.) about 35 to 45 minutes, or until juices start to bubble in vents and crust is golden. Serve slightly warm with ice cream, if desired.

VARIATION

PEACH-BLUEBERRY PIE: Spread 2 c. blueberries in pastry-lined pan. Sprinkle with half the sugar-flour mixture and half the lemon juice. Top with 2½ c. sliced fresh peaches. Sprinkle with remaining sugar-flour mixture and lemon juice. Omit almond extract. Dot with butter. Add top crust and bake like Brown Sugar Pie.

PEACH CREAM PIE

A new version of peaches and cream

Unbaked 9″ pie shell
1   qt. sliced peeled peaches
½   c. sugar
½   tsp. cinnamon
1   egg
2   tblsp. cream
Lemon Crumb Topping

• Arrange peaches in pastry-lined pie pan; sprinkle with sugar and cinnamon. Beat together egg and cream; pour over peaches. Sprinkle Lemon Crumb Topping over peaches.
• Bake in hot oven (425°F.) until lightly browned, 35 to 40 minutes.

LEMON CRUMB TOPPING: Combine ¼ c. brown sugar, ½ c. flour and 1 tsp. grated lemon peel. Cut in ¼ c. butter or margarine until mixture is crumbly.

CHEESE-TOP PEACH PIE

Sour cream and cheese enhance flavor

Unbaked 9" pie shell
1 c. sugar
3 tblsp. flour
⅛ tsp. salt
½ tsp. cinnamon
5 c. sliced fresh peaches
½ c. dairy sour cream
½ c. grated Cheddar cheese

• Chill pie shell 30 minutes.
• Meanwhile, combine sugar, flour, salt and cinnamon. Sprinkle about 2 tblsp. of this mixture over bottom of chilled pie shell.
• In large mixing bowl, lightly toss together sliced peaches and remainder of sugar mixture.
• Pour peach mixture into pie shell. Dot with sour cream and sprinkle with grated cheese.
• Bake in hot oven (425°F.) 35 to 40 minutes.

SOUR CREAM PEACH PIE

Summer's treat—peaches and cream under spicy, sparkly pastry cover

Pastry for 2-crust pie
4 c. sliced peeled peaches (7 to 8 medium)
1 c. sugar
5 tblsp. flour
⅛ tsp. salt
½ c. dairy sour cream
¼ tsp. cinnamon
¼ tsp. nutmeg

• Spread peaches in pastry-lined 9" pie pan. Combine sugar (reserving 2 tblsp.), flour, salt and sour cream. Spread over peaches. Adjust top crust and flute edges; cut vents.
• Mix remaining 2 tblsp. sugar, cinnamon and nutmeg. Sprinkle over top.
• Bake in hot oven (400°F.) about 40 minutes or until peaches are tender and crust is browned.

VARIATION

SOUR CREAM PEACH PIE WITH CANNED FRUIT: Substitute 2 (1 lb.) cans sliced peaches for fresh peaches. Drain canned peaches; you should have 3 c. after draining.

OPEN-FACE PEACH PIE

Rich, shortbreadlike crust holds ripe peaches in spicy custard

Crust:
2 c. flour
¼ tsp. baking powder
½ tsp. salt
2 tblsp. sugar
½ c. butter or margarine
1 egg white, beaten

Filling:
5 medium-size freestone peaches
¾ c. sugar
½ tsp. cinnamon
¼ tsp. nutmeg
3 egg yolks, beaten
⅔ c. heavy cream   *more*

Crust: Combine flour, baking powder, salt and 2 tblsp. sugar in a bowl. Cut in butter until mixture resembles coarse crumbs. Pat evenly on sides and bottom of a 10″ pie pan. Brush bottom of crust with beaten egg white and chill while you fix the filling.

Filling: Peel, halve and pit peaches. Arrange cut side up in crust.

• Combine ¾ c. sugar and spices and sprinkle evenly over fruit.

• Bake in hot oven (400°F.) 15 minutes.

• Blend egg yolks with cream; pour over fruit, letting some of mixture run into center of peaches. Continue baking until filling is set, about 30 minutes. Cool at least 1 hour before serving. Makes 8 servings.

Note: If you do not have a 10″ pie pan, bake this pie in an 8″ square pan. And if you're not calorie conscious, top servings with vanilla ice cream.

PEACHY PRALINE PIE

Pecans and brown sugar give this summer Dixie pie superb flavor

Unbaked 9″ pie shell
 ¾ c. granulated sugar
 3 tblsp. flour
 4 c. sliced peeled peaches
 1 ½ tsp. lemon juice
 ⅓ c. brown sugar, firmly packed
 ¼ c. flour
 ½ c. chopped pecans
 3 tblsp. butter or margarine

• Combine granulated sugar and 3 tblsp. flour in large bowl. Add peaches and the lemon juice.

• Combine brown sugar, ¼ c. flour and pecans in small bowl. Mix in butter until mixture is crumbly. Sprinkle one third of pecan mixture over bottom of pie shell; cover with the peach mixture and sprinkle remaining pecan mixture over peaches.

• Bake in hot oven (400°F.) until peaches are tender, about 40 minutes.

ALL-SEASON PEACH PIE

A FARM JOURNAL *5-star recipe—great favorite at Maine church suppers*

Unbaked 9″ pie shell
 2 (1 lb.) cans peach halves, well drained
 ⅓ c. sugar
 3 tblsp. cornstarch
 ¾ tsp. nutmeg
 ¼ tsp. salt
 ¾ c. heavy cream
 ¾ tsp. vanilla
Whipped cream

• Arrange peach halves, cut side up, in pie shell.

• Combine sugar, cornstarch, ½ tsp. nutmeg, salt, cream and vanilla. Pour over peaches in shell; sprinkle with remaining nutmeg.

• Bake in hot oven (400°F.) 40 minutes, or until peaches are tender. Serve with whipped cream.

Note: Extra-good made with fresh peaches. Use ½ c. instead of ⅓ c. sugar.

Peaches off the Cupboard Shelf

Home-canned peaches on the shelf and your own pie-crust mix nearby in the kitchen! No wonder country cooks are famed for their baking talents. They keep the ingredients handy for turning out golden-topped pies in a hurry. They appreciate that a marvelous dessert, like Butterscotch Peach Pie, is the best answer to the menu maker's age-old question: What dessert can I fix that will make an otherwise commonplace meal something special? This old-fashioned, sugar-sprinkled pie is a farm favorite. Do try it.

BUTTERSCOTCH PEACH PIE

Butter, brown sugar and peaches make this homey pie a praiseworthy treat

Pastry for 2-crust pie
3 ½ c. home-canned peaches, drained
½ c. brown sugar, firmly packed
2 tblsp. flour
⅛ tsp. salt
½ c. syrup from canned peaches
¼ c. butter or margarine
2 tsp. lemon juice
¼ to ½ tsp. almond extract
1 tsp. granulated sugar

• Place peaches in pastry-lined 9" pie pan.
• Combine sugar, flour, salt and peach syrup; add butter. Cook until thick, stirring. Remove from heat; add lemon juice and almond extract. Pour over peaches. Adjust top crust; flute edges and cut vents. Sprinkle with granulated sugar.
• Bake in hot oven (425°F.) 30 minutes. Cool on rack.

Note: You can use 1 (1 lb. 13 oz.) can peaches if you do not have a supply of home-canned fruit.

PEACH MARSHMALLOW PIE

Sweet sauce brings out fruit flavor in this country kitchen pie

Pastry for 2-crust pie
¼ c. sugar
1 ½ tblsp. quick-cooking tapioca
¼ tsp. salt
1 tblsp. lemon juice
¼ tsp. almond extract
1 (1 lb. 13 oz.) can sliced peaches, drained
⅓ c. peach juice
2 tblsp. butter or margarine
Marshmallow Sauce

• Mix sugar, tapioca and salt. Add lemon juice, almond extract, peach juice and drained peaches (2 c.). Let stand 15 minutes.
• Pour into pastry-lined 8" pie pan. Dot with butter. Adjust top crust; flute edges and cut vents.
• Bake in hot oven (425°F.) about 45 minutes, or until crust is browned and juices start to bubble in vents.
• Serve with Marshmallow Sauce.

MARSHMALLOW SAUCE: Measure ½ c. marshmallow creme into small bowl. Beat in 1 tblsp. milk with fork until smooth. Serve to pour over pie.

CHAMPION PEACH PIE

Top winner in a national bake-off

Crust:
1   (1 lb. 13 oz.) can peach slices
2   c. sifted flour
1   tsp. salt
⅔ c. vegetable shortening

Filling:
½ c. sugar
2   tblsp. cornstarch
2   tblsp. corn syrup
2   tsp. pumpkin pie spice
2   tsp. vanilla
2   tblsp. butter

Topping:
2   eggs, slightly beaten
⅓ c. sugar
1   (3 oz.) pkg. cream cheese
½ c. dairy sour cream
1   tblsp. lemon juice

Crust: Drain peaches; reserve juice. Combine flour with salt in mixing bowl and cut in shortening until mixture is the size of small peas. Sprinkle 6 to 7 tblsp. peach juice, a little at a time, over mixture, tossing and stirring lightly with fork. Add juice to driest particles, pushing lumps to side, until dough is just moist enough to hold together. Roll out half of dough on floured surface to a circle 1½″ larger than inverted 9″ pie pan. Fit loosely into pan.

Filling: Combine reserved peach slices, sugar, cornstarch, corn syrup, pumpkin pie spice and vanilla. Place in pastry-lined pie pan. Dot with butter.

Topping: Combine eggs, sugar and 2 tblsp. reserved peach juice in small saucepan. Cook over low heat, stirring constantly, until mixture thickens. Soften cream cheese in small mixing bowl.

• Blend in sour cream and lemon juice. Gradually add hot mixture, beating constantly until smooth. Spread on peach filling.

• Adjust top crust, flute edges and cut vents. Brush with peach juice.

• Bake in hot oven (425°F.) for 10 minutes; reduce heat to 350°F. and continue baking 30 to 35 minutes until golden brown. (Cover edge with foil the last 20 minutes.)

Sample This Nectarine Pie

If you grow or can get nectarines, they make elegant summer pies. There are many kinds of nectarines, as there are peaches, but most of them produce extra-special pies with a peachy flavor. Some California cooks, including the one who sent us the recipe, believe nectarines have more flavor and aroma than peaches. Our recipe testers agreed the fruit makes really good "peach" pies!

NECTARINE PIE

Nectarines retain good color and texture when baked in pies

Pastry for 2-crust pie
5   c. sliced peeled and pitted nectarines
1   tsp. lemon juice
1   c. sugar
⅓   c. flour
¼   tsp. mace
⅛   tsp. salt

¼   tsp. grated lemon peel
1½ tblsp. butter or margarine

• Combine nectarines, lemon juice, sugar, flour, mace, salt and lemon peel. Place in pastry-lined 9″ pie pan. Dot with butter.
• Adjust top crust and flute edges; cut steam vents. Bake in hot oven (425°F.) about 45 minutes or until crust is browned and juice begins to bubble through the slits.

Plum-Delicious Pie

By the time school bells ring in September, silver-dusted purple Italian plums, grown extensively in Idaho, appear on fruit counters. Pies made with "blue plums," as farm women commonly call them, end many autumn meals in fine fashion.

A spicy, buttery crumb topping complements the tart-sweet fruit flavor of this juicy Purple Plum Pie, the favorite recipe of an Iowa homemaker, who bakes it in a heavy paper bag from her grocery store. The bag catches any runaway juices that bubble over and prevents the edges and top of the pie from browning too much. Also, she doesn't have to watch the pie as it bakes.

PURPLE PLUM PIE

Best faintly warm with nippy cheese slices or scoops of ice cream

Unbaked 9″ pie shell
4   c. sliced, pitted purple plums
½   c. sugar

¼   c. flour
¼   tsp. salt
¼   tsp. cinnamon
1   tblsp. lemon juice
Spicy Topping

• Remove pits and cut plums in quarters. Combine with sugar, flour, salt and cinnamon. Turn into pie shell and sprinkle with lemon juice. Add Spicy Topping.
• Place pie in heavy brown paper bag from supermarket. Be sure bag is large enough to cover pie loosely. Fold over open end twice to close, and fasten with paper clips. Set on baking sheet in hot oven (425°F.); bake 1 hour. Remove from oven, let rest a few minutes before removing pie from paper bag. Partially cool on rack.

SPICY TOPPING: Combine ½ c. flour, ½ c. sugar, ¼ tsp. cinnamon and ¼ tsp. nutmeg. Cut in ¼ c. butter or margarine until mixture resembles coarse crumbs. Sprinkle over plums, mounding crumbs up in center of pie.

FRESH PLUM PIE

Use sweet, blue-to-purple prune plums to make this open-face pie

Press-in-Pan Pastry:
1 ½   c. sifted flour
¼   tsp. baking powder
½   c. soft butter
1   egg
⅓   c. sugar
⅛   tsp. salt

Filling:
1 ½   lbs. fresh prune plums, quartered and pitted
2   tblsp. granulated sugar
1   tsp. grated orange peel
½   tsp. cinnamon
1   tblsp. butter
3   tblsp. confectioners sugar

Pastry: Sift flour and baking powder into bowl; blend in butter until mixture is smooth.
• Beat egg until frothy; gradually add sugar and salt, beating until egg thickens. Add to flour mixture, stirring until smooth.
• Turn dough into greased 9″ pie pan and press evenly over sides and bottom of pan, but do not make rim. Refrigerate.
Filling: Circle plums in pastry-lined pie pan to make rows. Sprinkle with granulated sugar, orange peel, cinnamon and dots of butter.
• Bake in hot oven (400°F.) 15 minutes; reduce heat to 350°F. and bake about 45 minutes longer, or until plums are tender. Remove from oven and sift confectioners sugar over pie. Cool on rack. Serve slightly warm with a scoop of vanilla ice cream, if desired, or garnish with whipped cream.

FRESH PINEAPPLE PIE

Excellent way to point up the fruit's natural tart-sweet, fresh flavor

Pastry for 2-crust pie
1   medium pineapple
2   eggs, slightly beaten
1 ½   c. sugar
2   tblsp. flour
1   tblsp. grated lemon peel
1   tblsp. lemon juice
⅛   tsp. salt

• Cut peeled and cored pineapple in bite-size chunks. You should have about 3 c. fruit.
• Place eggs in bowl and beat in sugar, flour, lemon peel and juice and salt. Turn into pastry-lined 9″ pie pan. Adjust top crust (or use lattice top); flute edges and cut vents.
• Bake in hot oven (425°F.) 45 minutes, or until crust is lightly browned.

PINEAPPLE-APRICOT PIE

Combination of fruits that complement each other, with ginger top

Crumb Pie Shell:
1 ½   c. sifted flour
3   tblsp. confectioners sugar
¾   c. butter or margarine
½   c. granulated sugar
½   tsp. ginger

Filling:
1   (11 oz.) pkg. dried apricots (about 2 c.)
2   c. water
½   c. sugar
2   tblsp. flour
1   (1 lb. 4 oz.) can crushed pineapple
⅛   tsp. salt

Shell: Sift flour and confectioners sugar into mixing bowl. Cut in butter until mixture resembles coarse crumbs. Remove 1 c. crumbs; mix with ½ c. granulated sugar and ginger; set aside. Pat remaining crumbs in bottom and on sides of 9″ pie pan. Bake in hot oven (425°F.) about 8 minutes, or until lightly browned. Cool.

Filling: Cook apricots, cut in pieces, in 2 c. water over low heat until very tender, stirring occasionally. Add a little more water during cooking, if necessary. Apricot mixture should be thick when cooked. Remove from heat; add sugar, flour, pineapple and salt.

• Spoon pineapple-apricot mixture in pie shell; sprinkle rest of ginger crumbs on top. Broil at least 5″ to 9″ from heat until crumbs are browned, watching carefully (crumbs brown very fast). Partially cool before cutting.

• Combine cornstarch and ¼ c. brown sugar in saucepan. Add lemon juice and pineapple syrup mixture; cook, stirring constantly, until mixture is thick and clear. Remove from heat and add 2 tblsp. butter, stirring until it melts. Add pineapple.

• While preheating oven to 425°F., place remaining 4 tblsp. butter in bottom of 9″ pie pan; place in oven until butter is melted. Sprinkle with remaining ½ c. brown sugar and 1 tblsp. water. Arrange pecan halves, rounded side down, around bottom and sides of pie pan. Carefully line pan with pastry. Spoon in pineapple mixture.

• Adjust top crust, flute edges; cut vents. Place pie on square of foil in oven to catch drippings.

• Bake in hot oven (425°F.) 25 minutes. Turn out, upside down, on serving plate immediately. Cool on rack before cutting. Serve with ice cream or whipped cream, if desired.

PINEAPPLE UPSIDE-DOWN PIE

New, nut-topped pie makes its own luscious caramel sauce while it bakes

Pastry for 2-crust pie
1   (1 lb. 4½ oz.) can pineapple
    tidbits
Water
3   tblsp. cornstarch
¾   c. brown sugar, firmly packed
2   tblsp. lemon juice
6   tblsp. butter
½   c. pecan halves

• Drain pineapple. Add water to pineapple syrup to make 1¼ c.

SPRINGTIME "PINE-APPLE" PIE

Candy spices the filling and gives color —a becoming blush of spring

Pastry for 2-crust pie
1   (8¾ oz.) can crushed pineapple (1 c.)
¼   c. red cinnamon candies (red hots)
¼   c. brown sugar, firmly packed
⅔   c. granulated sugar
½   tsp. salt
2   tblsp. quick-cooking tapioca
3   c. thinly sliced peeled apples
2   tblsp. butter   *more*

• Combine pineapple and red hots, cook over low heat until candies melt.
• Combine sugars, salt, tapioca and apples. Let stand 15 minutes.
• Combine pineapple and apple mixtures, turn into pastry-lined 9" pie pan.

• Adjust top crust and flute edges; cut vents. Bake in hot oven (425°F.) 40 to 50 minutes, or until filling is tender and crust golden. Partially cool on rack.

Winter-Pear Pies

Now that juicy, meaty fresh pears are available the winter through, you can bake pear pies from late summer, when the Bartletts are ripe in many places, until May. Try using Bosc pears, the fruit with a rich russet exterior and tender, buttery, sugar-sweet flesh, or the Anjou variety, the pear shaped like a huge teardrop. The Anjou is green, but turns a creamy-yellow when ripe, is fine-grained and has a delicate spicy flavor. It is available from October through April, the Bosc from September through January. Either kind will make a perfect Ginger Pear Pie.

1   tsp. grated lemon peel
3   tblsp. lemon juice
¾   c. milk

• Combine ¼ c. sugar, 1 tblsp. flour, ginger and salt. Sprinkle in pie shell.
• Peel and core pears, slice thinly and lay slices over sugar-flour mixture.
• Cream butter; add remaining ½ c. sugar and 1 tblsp. flour. Add egg yolks, lemon peel and juice. Beat thoroughly.
• Add milk and mix.
• Beat egg whites until stiff. Fold into lemon mixture. Pour over pears.
• Bake in hot oven (425°F.) 10 minutes; reduce heat to 350°F. and bake 30 minutes.

GINGER PEAR PIE

Elegant!   Lemon-and-ginger-flavored fresh pear slices enveloped in pastry

Unbaked 9" pie shell
¾   c. sugar
2   tblsp. flour
¾   tsp. ginger
¼   tsp. salt
3   ripe winter pears
2   tblsp. soft butter
2   eggs, separated

PEAR-APPLE PIE

A pie you'll bake again and again— unusual but makes new friends quickly

Unbaked 9" pie shell
3   c. thinly sliced peeled Anjou pears
3   c. thinly sliced peeled apples
¾   c. sugar
3   tblsp. flour
½   tsp. cinnamon
¼   tsp. salt

Topping:
½ c. brown sugar, firmly packed
¼ c. flour
½ c. finely chopped pecans
¼ c. butter

• Combine pears, apples, sugar, flour, cinnamon and salt. Place in pie shell. Topping: Combine brown sugar, flour, pecans and butter. Sprinkle over top of pie.
• Fold a 14" circle of foil loosely over top and around sides of pie. Bake in hot oven (425°F.) 40 minutes. Remove foil and continue baking 20 minutes.

FRENCH PEAR PIE

Spices, orange and lemon flavors and ripe, juicy pears blend deliciously

Unbaked 9" pie shell
5 large Bartlett pears
3 tblsp. frozen orange juice concentrate
½ tsp. grated lemon peel
¾ c. flour
½ c. sugar
⅛ tsp. salt
1 tsp. cinnamon
½ tsp. ginger
⅓ c. butter or margarine

• Peel, core and slice pears thinly. Toss lightly with undiluted orange juice concentrate and lemon peel. Arrange in pie shell.
• Mix together remaining ingredients until crumbly. Sprinkle evenly over pears, being careful to cover all.
• Bake in hot oven (400°F.) 40 minutes, or until fruit is tender.

OPEN-FACE PEAR PIE

Use fully ripened Bartlett pears to make this unusual, interesting pie

Unbaked 9" pastry shell
4 medium-size pears
Juice of ½ lemon
¼ c. butter or margarine
1 c. sugar
¼ c. flour
3 eggs
1 tsp. vanilla
⅛ tsp. salt
⅛ tsp. mace
Whipped cream (optional)

• Peel, halve and core pears. Brush with lemon juice. Place pears cut side down in pie shell with narrow ends toward center.
• Cream together butter and sugar. Beat in flour, eggs, vanilla and salt. Pour over pears. Sprinkle lightly with mace.
• Bake in moderate oven (350°F.) 45 minutes or until filling is set and lightly browned. Cool on cakerack 1 hour or longer before cutting. Top with whipped cream. Serve the same day you bake the pie—pear filling may darken if you keep pie overnight.

PEAR ANISE PIE

Serve thin slices of Parmesan cheese with this gourmet pie

Pastry for 2-crust pie
5 c. sliced peeled Anjou pears (6 medium)
⅔ c. granulated sugar
4 tblsp. cornstarch
1½ tsp. whole anise seed   *more*

2 tsp. grated lemon peel
Lemon juice
2 tblsp. butter or margarine
½ c. confectioners sugar

• Combine pears, sugar, cornstarch, anise seed and lemon peel. Mix gently. Place in pastry-lined 9″ pie pan.
• Sprinkle pie filling with 1½ tsp. lemon juice. Dot with butter. Adjust top crust and flute edges; cut vents.
• Bake in hot oven (400°F.) until pears are tender and crust is lightly browned, about 40 minutes.
• While pie is hot, brush with glaze made by mixing confectioners sugar with enough lemon juice for spreading consistency (about 2½ tsp.). Cool.

CRUNCH TOP PEAR PIE

Luscious flavor—oranges and pears, deftly spiced, sweetened crunchy top

Unbaked 9″ pie shell
6 sliced peeled and cored large winter pears
½ c. granulated sugar
1 orange
½ c. brown sugar, firmly packed
½ c. flour
½ tsp. cinnamon
¼ tsp. ginger
¼ tsp. mace
⅓ c. butter
1 c. heavy cream, whipped

• Gently mix pears with sugar, 2 tsp. grated orange peel and 3 tblsp. orange juice. Arrange in pie shell.
• Combine brown sugar, flour and spices. Cut in butter until mixture is crumbly. Sprinkle over pears.

• Bake in hot oven (400°F.) until pears are tender, about 45 minutes. Partially cool. Serve warm with whipped cream.

Note: For a tasty topping, sweeten whipped cream lightly and flavor it with 1 tsp. vanilla. When it is on the pie, scatter on a little grated orange peel.

SUMMER PEAR PIE

Cheese pastry and faintly spiced pears —an unsurpassable flavor team

Cheese Pastry for 2-crust pie (Chapter 2)
2 tblsp. lemon juice
4 c. sliced peeled Bartlett pears
⅓ c. granulated sugar
⅓ c. brown sugar, firmly packed
2 tblsp. cornstarch
¼ tsp. salt
¼ tsp. mace
2 tblsp. butter or margarine

• Sprinkle lemon juice over pears.
• Combine sugars, cornstarch, salt and mace.
• Place half of pears in pastry-lined 9″ pie pan.
• Sprinkle with half the sugar mixture. Add remaining pears; sprinkle with remaining sugar mixture. Dot with butter. Adjust top crust; flute edges and cut vents.
• Bake in hot oven (425°F.) 35 to 40 minutes, or until pears are tender, crust is browned and juices bubble in vents.

Pies from Country-Cupboard Fruits

Grandmother had her snow cupboard—a well-chosen cache of foods to meet emergencies. Like awakening on a winter morning to find the roads had vanished in the night's blizzard!

Among the choice contents of her kitchen warehouse were dried fruits—raisins, prunes and apricots, to name a few. With sugar and flour in bins and plenty of home-rendered lard on hand, she had the makings for unforgettable winter pies. Her family rejoiced at her cleverness in outwitting the swirling snow.

Farm life changes and, nowadays, with highways and country roads cleared of snow promptly and freezers filled with many good things to eat, even severe storms rarely are much of a problem. But the habit of keeping generous supplies of dried (as well as canned) fruits hasn't changed. There's a good reason why—farm people like the wonderful pies made with dried fruit. They're really tasty!

Raisin pies, according to the number of recipes shared by FARM JOURNAL readers, are a prime favorite. We give you samples of the different kinds—those made with seedless, seeded, and golden or light raisins, along with one in which the raisins are put through a food chopper. Don't miss the 5-star recipe offered in this chapter to meet repeated requests for it—Frosted Apple-Raisin Pie.

Look at all the raisin pie recipes in this chapter. You'll find the traditional one in which vinegar supplies the classic tart taste. And you'll notice new touches for old-time pies, like walnuts and citrus fruits. And recipes for new unusual ones. There are also many pies in this book in which raisins team with other fruits—cranberries and apples, for instance.

You'll also find our famous recipes for homemade mincemeats, rich with raisins, and for pies made with commercially prepared mincemeat to save the cook's time.

Don't overlook the elegant prune and dried apricot pies. We'll be surprised if you don't agree that Prune Crumble Pie is a gourmet dessert to serve on special occasions. You will notice that a Montana ranchwoman combines dried fruits for a wonderful pie filling.

We hope you will agree with our taste testers when you eat our dried fruit pies. They repeatedly gave these desserts a score of "Excellent" or "Outstanding."

VIENNESE APRICOT PIE

A gourmet pie to serve to fastidious guests who are expert cooks

Unbaked 10″ pie shell
2   eggs, slightly beaten
2   c. dairy sour cream
1 ½ c. sugar
¼   c. flour
½   tsp. salt
4   drops almond extract
1 ½ c. dried apricots
Crumbly Topping   *more*

• Combine eggs, sour cream, sugar, flour, salt and almond extract; beat with rotary beater until blended. Stir in apricots, cooked, drained and cut in small pieces.

• Pour mixture into pie shell. Bake in hot oven (400°F.) 25 minutes. Remove from oven and sprinkle with Crumbly Topping. Return to oven and continue baking 20 to 25 minutes, or until filling is set. Cool to room temperature or chill before serving. Makes 8 servings.

CRUMBLY TOPPING: Combine ½ c. light brown sugar and ⅓ c. flour, mixing well. Cut in ¼ c. butter or margarine until mixture resembles coarse crumbs.

FRESNO RAISIN-NUT PIE

Spices accent raisin flavor, fluffy meringue topping provides eye appeal

Baked 8″ pie shell
  ¾ c. sugar
  2 tblsp. cornstarch
  ¼ tsp. salt
  ½ tsp. cinnamon
  ½ tsp. cloves
  2 eggs, separated
  1 c. dairy sour cream
  1 c. seedless raisins
1 ½ tsp. lemon juice
  ½ c. chopped walnuts
Meringue (2 egg whites)

• Combine sugar, cornstarch, salt and spices. Blend in egg yolks. Add sour cream, raisins and lemon juice. Cook over moderate heat, stirring constantly, until mixture thickens. Cool. Stir in walnuts. Pour into pie shell. Top with meringue (see Perfect Meringue for Topping Pies, Chapter 9).

• Bake in moderate oven (350°F.) about 15 minutes, or until meringue is browned.

RAISIN CREAM PIE

Country cook's trick—put raisins through food chopper for rich flavor

Pastry for 2-crust pie
  3 c. seedless raisins
  ½ c. sugar
1 ½ c. light cream
  ¼ tsp. salt
  2 tblsp. lemon juice

• Rinse raisins in warm water; drain thoroughly. Put through food chopper, using medium blade.

• Add sugar, cream and salt. Heat, stirring constantly, until sugar is dissolved and mixture thickens. Remove from heat and stir in lemon juice.

• Pour into pastry-lined 9″ pie pan. Adjust top crust; flute edges, cut vents.

• Bake in hot oven (425°F.) until lightly browned, 30 to 35 minutes.

HOMESTEAD RAISIN PIE

Like Grandmother used to make— GOOD! Be sure to try this

Baked 9″ pie shell
1 ⅓ c. seeded raisins (muscat)
  2 c. water
  3 eggs, separated
  1 c. sugar
  2 tblsp. vinegar
  2 tblsp. flour
  2 tblsp. butter
Meringue (3 egg whites)

• Add raisins to water in saucepan and simmer 5 minutes. Beat egg yolks,

sugar, vinegar and flour until light and creamy. Slowly add to raisins. Cook, stirring constantly, until filling is thick, 4 to 5 minutes. Remove from heat, stir in butter and cool until lukewarm.
• Pour raisin mixture into pie shell and top with meringue (see Perfect Meringue for Topping Pies, Chapter 9).
• Bake in moderate oven (350°F.) until meringue browns, 12 to 15 minutes. Cool away from drafts.

Vineyard-Country Favorite

Here's a pie that cuts like a charm, suggestive of a rich chess pie, but accented with raisins. It's one of the many unusual raisin pie recipes in the much-thumbed collections of farm women.

HARVEST FESTIVAL RAISIN PIE

Pie full of suntanned raisins made a hit at a California harvest festival

Unbaked 9" pie shell
2 c. seedless raisins
1 c. water
½ c. butter or margarine
¾ c. sugar
1 tblsp. flour
2 eggs, separated
¾ c. broken walnuts

• Simmer raisins in water 10 minutes. Remove from heat and stir in butter, sugar, flour and beaten egg yolks. Return to heat; cook, stirring constantly, until mixture is slightly thickened. Cool briefly and stir in nuts. Fold in stiffly beaten egg whites.
• Spoon into pie shell, mounding slightly in center.
• Bake in slow oven (325°F.) 55 minutes.

GOLDEN RAISIN PIE

Sour cream raisin meringue pie with medley of spices and orange undertone

Baked 8" pie shell
¼ c. sugar
1½ tblsp. cornstarch
½ tsp. salt
½ tsp. ginger
½ tsp. cinnamon
⅛ tsp. cloves
⅛ tsp. nutmeg
½ c. light corn syrup
3 egg yolks, beaten
1 c. dairy sour cream
1 c. light raisins
1 tblsp. grated orange peel
Meringue (3 egg whites)

• Mix sugar, cornstarch, salt and spices in top of double boiler. Stir in corn syrup, egg yolks, sour cream, raisins and orange peel.
• Cook over hot water, stirring, until smooth and thick, about 15 to 18 minutes. Pour into cool pie shell.
• Top with meringue (see Perfect Meringue for Topping Pies, Chapter 9) while filling is hot.
• Bake in moderate oven (350°F.) until brown, 12 to 15 minutes.

Good Country Idea: When the California ranch cook bakes raisin pies containing either orange juice or grated peel, she often adds a little red and yellow food color to the filling for deepening the tawniness.

MINCEMEAT PIE

Top warm pie with vanilla ice cream

Pastry for 2-crust pie
1   (1 lb. 12 oz.) jar prepared mincemeat (2½ c.)
1   c. diced apples
½   c. raisins
⅓   c. grape or orange juice
¼   tsp. grated lemon peel

• Combine mincemeat, apples, raisins, grape juice and lemon peel in bowl. Pour into 9″ pie pan lined with pastry. Adjust top crust, cut steam vents and flute edges.
• Bake in hot oven (425°F.) 40 to 45 minutes or until pastry is golden.

VARIATION

Christmas Mincemeat Pie: Add 2 tblsp. thinly sliced candied cherries and 2 tblsp. chopped walnuts to mincemeat pie filling.

FRUIT AND NUT MINCE PIE

Wintertime ranch favorite in Montana —recipe makes two marvelous pies

Pastry for 2 (2-crust) pies
1   c. dried apricots
1   c. dried prunes

1   c. raisins
Juice of 1 medium orange
½   tsp. cinnamon
¼   tsp. nutmeg
¼   tsp. cloves
1   c. sugar
¼   c. chopped walnuts
¼   c. shredded almonds

• Pour boiling water over apricots and prunes. Drain; cover with cold water and let stand 3 hours. Drain, reserving water, and cut fruits in small pieces. Cook in water in which fruits soaked until ¾ c. liquid remains. Remove from heat.
• Add other ingredients to apricot-prune mixture. Divide in half. Pour each half into pastry-lined 8″ pie pan. Adjust top crusts; flute edges and cut vents.
• Bake in hot oven (400°F.) until crust is browned, about 30 minutes.

Note: For a sparkly top crust, brush pie tops with milk and sprinkle lightly with sugar before baking.

MINCEFRUIT PIE FILLING

Here's a filling for pies to keep on your cupboard shelf ready-to-go

4   lbs. pears
3   lbs. apples
4   medium oranges
2   (15 oz.) pkgs. seedless raisins
5   c. sugar
1   tblsp. salt
4   tsp. cinnamon
1   tsp. cloves

• Cut unpeeled pears, apples and oranges in quarters. Remove cores and seeds. Run through food chopper, using medium blade.

• Add remaining ingredients; stir to combine. Bring to a boil over medium heat. Simmer until thick, about 1 hour. Stir frequently.

• Pack at once in hot pint jars. Adjust lids. Process in boiling-water bath (212°F.) 25 minutes.

• Remove jars from canner and complete seals unless closures are self-sealing type. Makes 8 pints, or about enough for 4 (9″) pies.

MINCEFRUIT PASTRY SQUARES

Just the pie to serve a crowd; pieces also carry successfully in lunches

2 ½ c. sifted flour
1   tblsp. sugar
1   tsp. salt
1   c. lard
1   egg, separated
Milk
3   c. Mincefruit Pie Filling
1   c. confectioners sugar
2   tblsp. lemon juice

• Sift together flour, sugar and salt; cut in lard with pastry blender or two knives, until like coarse meal.

• Put egg yolk into measuring cup and add milk to make ½ c. Add to lard mixture; mix just enough so dough shapes into a ball. Roll out half to 15″ × 11″ rectangle; transfer to baking sheet. Spread Mincefruit Pie Filling evenly over dough to within ¾″ of edges.

• Roll out other half of dough for top crust; place over filling; pinch edges together, cut vents.

• Beat egg white until stiff; spread on top crust. Bake in hot oven (400°F.) 25 to 30 minutes.

• Mix confectioners sugar and lemon juice. Drizzle over top of crust while hot. Makes 16 servings.

CHEESE CRUMBLE PRUNE PIE

Prunes have exciting fresh plumlike taste in this cheese-crumb pie shell

1 ½ c. flour
¾   c. brown sugar, firmly packed
½   tsp. salt
¾   c. butter
1 ½ c. (6 oz.) shredded mild Cheddar cheese
2   c. coarsely cut cooked prunes

• Combine flour, sugar and salt in a mixing bowl. With pastry blender or two knives, cut in butter and cheese until particles are fine. Press two thirds of the crumb mixture over bottom and sides of 8″ pie pan to form a shell. Fill with prunes. Spread remaining crumbs over prunes.

• Bake in moderate oven (350°F.) 25 minutes, or until crumbs are golden brown. Place on rack and cool slightly. Cut into slender wedges and serve warm. Makes 10 servings.

CALIFORNIA PRUNE PIE

Four-seasons pie—as tempting and rewarding in June as in January

Baked 9″ pie shell
2   c. cooked prunes
1   orange, peeled and diced (⅓ c.)
½   c. brown sugar, firmly packed
¼   tsp. salt
2   tblsp. cornstarch   *more*

1   c. liquid from prunes
1   tblsp. grated orange peel
2   tblsp. butter
2   tblsp. granulated sugar
1   c. heavy cream, whipped
Orange sections
Walnut halves

• Drain cooked prunes, reserving 1 c. liquid, pit and measure. Remove all white inner peel when peeling orange.
• Combine sugar, salt and cornstarch. Add prune liquid and bring to a boil, stirring constantly. Cook until thick. Add prunes, orange, orange peel and butter; cook 10 minutes, stirring occasionally. Cool.
• Pour into pie shell. Refrigerate until mealtime. To serve, add 2 tblsp. sugar to whipped cream and spread on pie. To dress up pie, garnish with orange sections and a few walnut halves.

PRUNE MERINGUE PIE

One look, one delicious taste—this old-fashioned pie is a great success

Baked 8″ pie shell
1   c. sugar

¼   c. cornstarch
¼   tsp. salt
1   c. boiling water
2   eggs, separated
3   tblsp. lemon juice
2   tsp. grated lemon peel
2   tblsp. butter or margarine
1   c. cooked pitted prunes, drained
Meringue (2 egg whites)

• Combine sugar, cornstarch and salt. Stir in boiling water. Cook over direct heat until mixture thickens and boils, stirring constantly.
• Place in double boiler and cook 10 minutes. Beat egg yolks slightly; gradually beat in hot mixture until half of it has been added. Pour quickly into mixture in double boiler; cook 5 minutes, stirring constantly.
• Remove from hot water and blend in lemon juice and peel and butter. Cool.
• Arrange prunes in cool pie shell.
• Pour lemon mixture over prunes. Top with meringue (see Perfect Meringue for Topping Pies, Chapter 9).
• Bake in moderate oven (350°F.) 12 to 15 minutes, or until browned. Cool.

Dates Are Grand in Pies

Fresh dates are widely available today. Women who are expert pie bakers make excellent use of them. They keep the fruit in their freezers for around-the-year use. The dates you use should be soft if pies are to be at their best. If the fruit has become dry or hard, steam it for a few minutes. The moisture has a marvelous softening effect.

CHEESE-DATE PIE

Cottage cheese imparts its flavor to this tasty country-kitchen pie

Baked 9″ Graham Cracker Crumb Crust (Chapter 2)
2   c. creamed cottage cheese
2   eggs
⅓   c. sugar

¼ c. dairy sour or sweet cream
2 tblsp. flour
1 tsp. grated lemon peel
1 tblsp. lemon juice
1 c. chopped dates
4 tblsp. chopped walnuts

• Beat cottage cheese in electric mixer until smooth. Add eggs, one at a time, beating until well blended. Add sugar, cream, flour, lemon peel and juice and blend thoroughly. Mix in dates.
• Pour into cool crust and sprinkle with nuts. Bake in slow oven (300°F.) until set, about 1 hour.

FRESH DATE-NUT PIE

Rich, but not so sweet as some date pies—lemon peel adds subtle touch

Unbaked 9″ pie shell
3 eggs
½ c. sugar
1 c. dark corn syrup
¼ c. melted butter
1 ½ tsp. vanilla
¼ tsp. salt
1 c. finely cut fresh dates
¾ c. chopped walnuts
1 ½ tsp. grated lemon peel
1 c. heavy cream, whipped

• Beat eggs until thick and light; gradually beat in sugar. Beat in corn syrup, butter, vanilla and salt. Fold in dates, walnuts and lemon peel. Turn into pie shell.
• Bake in moderate oven (375°F.) 30 minutes, or until filling is set and browned. Cool. Top each serving with whipped cream. Makes 8 servings.

BUTTERMILK DATE PIE

Buttermilk adds just the right touch of tartness to the sweet fruit filling

Baked 9″ pie shell
1 c. sugar
¼ c. cornstarch
½ tsp. nutmeg
½ tsp. cinnamon
¼ tsp. salt
2 ½ c. buttermilk
2 egg yolks, beaten
1 c. chopped dates
Meringue (2 egg whites)

• Combine sugar, cornstarch, spices and salt in saucepan; blend thoroughly. Gradually stir in buttermilk and egg yolks. Add dates. Cook over medium heat, stirring constantly until mixture boils and thickens. Cool slightly. Pour into pie shell. Top with meringue and brown (see Perfect Meringue for Topping Pies, Chapter 9). Or chill pie thoroughly and serve topped with whipped cream.

CALIFORNIA DATE PIE

For a really rich version, omit the meringue and spoon on whipped cream with a little Date Butter added

Unbaked 9″ pie shell
3 eggs, separated
1 ½ c. Date Butter
1 tsp. grated lemon peel
2 c. milk
Meringue (3 egg whites)

• Beat egg yolks, add Date Butter, beating until well blended.
• Stir in lemon peel and milk.   *more*

• Pour into pie shell. Bake in hot oven (400°F.) 15 minutes; reduce temperature to 350°F. and bake 25 minutes, or until set.
• Spoon meringue over pie (see Perfect Meringue for Topping Pies, Chapter 9).
• Bake in moderate oven (350°F.) 12 to 15 minutes.

DATE BUTTER

2 (7 oz.) pkgs. pitted dates
¾ c. water

• Chop or cut up dates. Add water.
• Cover; cook over medium heat until mixture boils; reduce heat, cook about 10 minutes, or until dates are mushy. Stir occasionally. Makes about 1¾ cups.

ORANGE-DATE PIE

This rich, delicious pie serves 8

Unbaked 9" pie shell
½   c. butter or margarine
1¼ c. sugar
4   eggs, separated
1   c. chopped dates
1   c. flaked coconut (or chopped nuts)
1   tblsp. grated orange peel
2   tblsp. frozen orange juice concentrate, undiluted

• Cream butter and sugar; add egg yolks, one at a time, beating well after each. Add dates, coconut, orange peel and juice.
• Beat egg whites until stiff but not dry. Fold into filling. Turn into pie shell. Bake in slow oven (300°F.) 1 hour. Cool before serving.

Garden Is Pie Baker's Friend

Many farm women eagerly watch their gardens in spring for the first tender, strawberry-pink rhubarb stalks. And in autumn, when trees are tinted red by summer's afterglow and the pleasing warmth of country kitchens invites baking, they pick tomatoes green to cheat Jack Frost. And to make pies! Both of these tart vegetables make excellent pie fillings. Surrounded by flaky pastry, they behave like fruits and actually rival them in flavor. For this reason they're at home in the company of pies made with the gifts of orchards and berry patches.

We include some of our best rhubarb and green tomato pie recipes in this collection of dessert fruit pies. You will find several other vegetable pies in this Cookbook; pumpkin, for instance. Also in main-dish pies, Chapter 11.

FRESH RHUBARB PIE

This rosy rhubarb pie has a fascinating, though subtle, orange taste

Pastry for 2-crust pie
1⅓ c. sugar
⅓   c. flour
½   tsp. grated orange peel
⅛   tsp. salt
4   c. (½" pieces) rhubarb
2   tblsp. butter

- Combine sugar, flour, orange peel and salt. Add to pink rhubarb.
- Place in pastry-lined 9" pie pan and dot with butter.
- Adjust top crust (lattice top is attractive) and flute edges to make high-standing rim, cut vents.
- Bake in hot oven (425°F.) 40 to 50 minutes, or until juice begins to bubble through vents and crust is golden brown. Partially cool.

Note: If your rhubarb is not the pink variety, add a few drops of red food color to filling. To eliminate peeling rhubarb, use tender, young stalks. The amount of sugar varies with the tartness of the rhubarb—from 1⅓ c. to 2 c. Usually rhubarb is less tart early in the season.

VARIATIONS

SPICED RHUBARB PIE: Omit the grated orange peel and add ¼ tsp. nutmeg.

PINEAPPLE-RHUBARB PIE: Substitute 1 c. drained crushed pineapple (canned) for 1 c. rhubarb.

GLAZED STRAWBERRY-RHUBARB PIE

Luscious spring dessert: Serve pie warm with sour cream spread on top

Pastry for 2-crust pie
1 ¼ c. sugar
⅛ tsp. salt
⅓ c. flour
2 c. fresh strawberries

2   c. (1" pieces) fresh rhubarb
2   tblsp. butter or margarine
1   tblsp. sugar

- Combine 1 ¼ c. sugar, salt and flour.
- Arrange half of strawberries and rhubarb in pastry-lined 9" pie pan. Sprinkle with half of sugar mixture. Repeat with remaining fruit and sugar mixture; dot with butter.
- Adjust top crust and flute edges. Brush top of pie with cold water and sprinkle on 1 tblsp. sugar. Cut steam vents.
- Bake in hot oven (425°F.) 40 to 50 minutes or until rhubarb is tender and crust is browned.

VARIATION

LATTICED STRAWBERRY-RHUBARB PIE: Use a lattice top to show off the beauty of this spring pie. See its picture on the jacket of this Cookbook.

Quick Oven-to-Table Pie

You'll never find a more tasty and satisfying jonquil-time dessert than this homey, last-minute pie. It will make practically any meal a success. Good idea to finish baking the pie while everyone is enjoying the main course (put it in the oven about 10 minutes before you sit down to eat). Just before serving, make the sweet, caramel-tasting syrup that contrasts so delightfully with the crisp, hot crust and cold ice cream.

RHUBARB POPOVER PIE

Spring comes to the table in this superb flavor-texture combination

2 eggs
¾ c. milk
¾ c. flour
½ tsp. salt
¼ c. butter
1 ½ c. (¾" slices) fresh cut-up rhubarb
½ c. drained pineapple chunks (canned)
Brown Sugar Syrup
1 pt. vanilla ice cream

• Beat eggs and milk; add flour and salt and beat until smooth.
• Put butter in a 9" pie pan and heat in oven until it bubbles. Immediately pour in batter. Combine and drop rhubarb and pineapple in center of batter, within about 2" of pan edges.
• Bake in hot oven (425°F.) 25 minutes, or until batter is puffed and brown. Immediately cut in 6 wedges for serving, topping each with a big spoonful of warm Brown Sugar Syrup and a small scoop of ice cream. Serve at once.

BROWN SUGAR SYRUP: Melt ⅓ c. butter. Stir in 1 c. brown sugar, firmly packed, making a thick syrup. Serve at once.

VARIATION

RHUBARB POPOVER PIE: Omit pineapple in Rhubarb Popover Pie.

HONEYED RHUBARB PIE

A FARM JOURNAL 5-star recipe

Pastry for 2-crust pie
4 c. (½" pieces) rhubarb
1 ¼ c. sugar
6 tblsp. flour
¼ tsp. salt
2 tsp. grated lemon peel
⅓ c. strained honey
4 to 5 drops red food color
2 tblsp. butter or margarine

• Combine rhubarb, sugar, flour, salt and lemon peel; mix well. Blend in honey and food color. Let stand several minutes.
• Spoon rhubarb mixture into pastry-lined 9" pie pan; dot with butter. Adjust top crust and flute edges; cut vents. (For sparkling top, brush with milk and sprinkle with sugar.)
• Bake in hot oven (400°F.) 50 to 60 minutes.

RHUBARB-APPLE PIE

Rhubarb adds refreshing flavor to canned apples in this homey pie

Pastry for 2-crust pie
1 (1 lb. 4 oz.) can sliced apples
2 c. (½" pieces) rhubarb
1 c. sugar
¼ tsp. salt
½ tsp. cinnamon
3 tblsp. quick-cooking tapioca
2 tblsp. butter or margarine

• Combine apples and their syrup, with rhubarb, sugar, salt, cinnamon and tapioca; mix well. Turn into pastry-lined 9" pie pan. Dot with butter. Cover with lattice pastry top.

• Bake in hot oven (425°F.) about 50 minutes, or until filling starts to bubble and crust is golden.

SPICED RHUBARB-STRAWBERRY PIE

Pink of perfection in springtime pies —pastry lattice shows bright filling

Pastry for 2-crust pie
- 3   c. cut-up rhubarb (1 lb.)
- 1   pt. strawberries, cut in halves
- ¾   c. sugar
- 4   tblsp. flour
- ⅛   tsp. salt
- ¼   tsp. pumpkin pie spice or mace
- 2   tblsp. butter or margarine

• Combine rhubarb, cut in ¾″ pieces, and strawberries in bowl. Sprinkle on sugar, flour, salt and pumpkin pie spice; mix gently. Turn into pastry-lined 9″ pie pan; dot with butter. Adjust lattice pastry top, flute edges.
• Bake in hot oven (400°F.) 40 minutes, or until crust is browned and juices bubble. Cool on rack.

RHUBARB-ORANGE PIE

Orange and rhubarb flavors taste as good together as peaches and cream

Pastry for 2-crust pie
- 2   eggs
- 1 ¾   c. sugar
- ¼   c. flour
- ⅛   tsp. nutmeg or mace
- ¼   c. orange juice
- 4   c. cut-up rhubarb (1 ½ lbs.)

• Beat eggs in large bowl; add sugar, flour, nutmeg and orange juice; stir in rhubarb. Turn into pastry-lined 9″ pie pan. Adjust top crust; flute edges and cut vents.
• Bake in hot oven (425°F.) 50 minutes, or until crust is browned and juices bubble in vents. Cool.

Note: Recipe was tested with early hothouse rhubarb, which sometimes is less juicy than stalks grown in outdoor gardens.

PARTY RHUBARB PIE

Definitely a special-occasion pie—it suggests spring even if it is snowing

Unbaked 9″ pie shell
- 2   (1 lb.) pkgs. frozen rhubarb in syrup
- 3   tblsp. flour
- 1   c. sugar
- 4   (3 oz.) pkgs. cream cheese
- 2   eggs
- 1   c. dairy sour cream

• Thaw and drain rhubarb. You should have 1 qt. fruit. Blend with flour and ½ c. sugar. Turn into pie shell; bake in hot oven (425°F.) 15 minutes.
• Meanwhile, blend together cream cheese, eggs and remaining ½ c. sugar. Remove pie from oven and spread cheese mixture over top of rhubarb filling. Return to oven and bake in moderate oven (350°F.) 30 minutes. Cool. Spread sour cream over top. Refrigerate until ready to serve.

Note: You will have about 1 c. pretty, pink rhubarb juice which you won't use in this recipe. But do use it for part of the liquid in making gelatin salads or desserts. Or combine with orange juice and chill for a refreshing breakfast starter.

Green Tomato Pies

One of the joys of having a garden is that you can gather green tomatoes for cooking. Spicy pies made with them have a distinctive flavor of their own. No wonder they're farm favorites! Many country women bake them with immature tomatoes on the vines at frost time. But some gourmet cooks like to pick a few of the mature full-size green tomatoes earlier in the season for a couple of special pies.

Mature tomatoes turn color quickly, however. Once they are in the kitchen, use them promptly—or at least refrigerate them. Also use immature green tomatoes soon after you bring them to the house. They rarely ripen, but often rot, especially if left standing at room temperature.

Many FARM JOURNAL readers have told us they like to use our recipe for Green Tomato Mincemeat in autumn when they have lots of tomatoes. We'll give you this famous recipe, too.

Green tomatoes combined with peeled apple slices make one of the tastiest of all country pies. (And you can substitute apples for the green tomatoes in the following recipe for a *good* apple pie!) Try our recipes and see if you don't agree.

GREEN TOMATO-APPLE PIE

Once you try it, we predict you'll have it several times every year

Pastry for 2-crust pie
2   c. skinned, quartered and thinly sliced green tomatoes
3   c. thin, peeled apple slices
⅔   c. brown sugar, firmly packed
⅓   c. granulated sugar
2   to 3 tblsp. flour
½   tsp. cinnamon
⅛   tsp. salt
2   tblsp. butter

• To peel green tomatoes easily, place in boiling water. Let stand 2 to 3 minutes, or until skins can be slipped off.
• Combine tomatoes, apples, sugars, flour, cinnamon and salt. Place in a pastry-lined 9″ pie pan. Dot with butter.
• Adjust top crust and flute edges; cut steam vents. Bake in hot oven (425°F.) 50 to 60 minutes.

SLICED GREEN TOMATO PIE

A gardener's dessert-time special

Pastry for 2-crust pie
4   c. peeled, thinly sliced green tomatoes
1¼ c. sugar
½   tsp. cinnamon
½   tsp. nutmeg
¼   tsp. salt
4   to 5 tblsp. flour
2   tblsp. lemon juice

• To peel tomatoes easily, immerse in boiling water until skins will slip off (about 3 minutes).
• Blend together sugar, cinnamon, nutmeg, salt, flour and lemon juice in bowl. Toss with green tomatoes.

• Place in pastry-lined 9″ pie pan. Adjust top crust and flute edges; cut vents.

• Bake in hot oven (425°F.) until tomatoes are soft and crust is lightly browned, about 50 to 60 minutes.

Country-Good Homemade Mincemeat

When a big kettle of simmering mincemeat fills the kitchen with its tantalizing aroma, everyone in the house starts looking forward to plump winter pies. One of our readers says: "Almost always someone in our family, sniffing the spicy fragrance of cooking mincemeat, asks if we have to wait until Thanksgiving and Christmas to have pie made with it. My answer comes a few days later when I carry the season's first mincemeat pie to the table. It's one of the best ways to please my family and to round out an otherwise light meal."

We are reprinting in this chapter a popular and balanced collection of mincemeat recipes from our FREEZING & CANNING COOKBOOK. All five of them have their ardent champions. Pear-growers' wives perfected the pear version, ranchwomen in the Mountain West laud the venison special and Midwestern gardeners vote for the Green Tomato Mincemeat, for instance.

Canning directions accompany each recipe, but you can freeze mincemeat if you prefer and have freezer space. Don't forget the commercial mincemeats available in food markets—they are such a help for busy cooks. (You'll also find recipes using them in this book.) Regardless of what kind of mincemeat pie you bake, do serve it slightly warm, with a topping of soft vanilla ice cream for special.

GREEN TOMATO MINCEMEAT

Decidedly different—on the tart side

6   lbs. green tomatoes
2   lbs. tart apples
2   c. raisins
4   c. brown sugar, firmly packed
2   c. strong coffee
1   lemon (grated peel and juice)
2   tsp. grated orange peel
½   c. vinegar
1   tsp. salt
1   tsp. nutmeg
1   tsp. allspice

• Core and quarter tomatoes and apples; put through food chopper with raisins.
• Combine all ingredients in large saucepan. Simmer 2 hours, stirring frequently.
• Pack at once in hot pint jars. Adjust lids. Process in boiling-water bath (212°F.) 25 minutes.
• Remove jars from canner and complete seals unless closures are self-sealing type. Makes about 10 pints.

BLUE RIBBON MINCEMEAT

Cider gives this fascinating flavor

6   c. ground beef
12   c. chopped apples
6   c. seedless raisins   *more*

1   c. cider
1   tblsp. cinnamon
1   tblsp. allspice
1   tblsp. nutmeg
3 ½   c. sugar

• Cook beef thoroughly, but do not brown.
• Put meat and apples through food chopper, using medium blade.
• Combine all ingredients in large kettle. Simmer 30 minutes.
• Pack at once in hot pint jars. Adjust lids. Process in pressure canner 60 minutes at 10 pounds pressure (240°F.).
• Remove jars from canner and complete seals unless closures are self-sealing type. Makes 8 pints.

STATE-OF-THE-UNION MINCEMEAT

California-style, fruited mincemeat

3   lbs. lean beef
1   qt. water
1   c. chopped dates
1   c. washed suet, finely chopped
3 ½   lbs. apples
1   lb. seedless raisins
1   lb. white raisins
4   c. orange marmalade
2   qts. cider
2   tblsp. cinnamon
1   tsp. cloves
1   tsp. nutmeg
3   tblsp. salt

• Simmer beef in water until tender (add more water if needed). Drain. Trim away bone and gristle. Put meat through food chopper, using medium blade.

• Combine all ingredients in large kettle. Mix well. Bring to a boil; reduce heat and simmer 1½ hours, stirring often.
• Pour at once into hot pint jars. Adjust lids. Process in pressure canner 60 minutes at 10 pounds pressure (240°F.).
• Remove jars from canner and complete seals unless closures are self-sealing type. Makes about 10 pints. Store in cool, dark place.

Note: Takes time to make, but this recipe, adapted by a California homemaker from the Alaska favorite, is rich in blended fruit flavors.

VENISON MINCEMEAT

Hunters vote for that venison taste

4   lbs. venison "trim" meat with bones
Water
¾   lb. beef suet
3   lbs. apples, peeled and quartered
2   lbs. seedless raisins
1   (15 oz.) pkg. seeded raisins
1   (12 oz.) pkg. currants
1   tblsp. salt
1   tblsp. cinnamon
1   tblsp. ginger
1   tblsp. cloves
1   tblsp. nutmeg
1   tsp. allspice
1   tsp. mace (optional)
2   qts. cider, grape or other fruit juice
1   lb. brown sugar

• Trim fat from venison. Cover with water; simmer until meat is tender.

Refrigerate venison in cooking liquid overnight. Remove all fat from top of liquid. Separate meat from bones and put meat through food chopper—using coarse blade. (There should be enough ground venison to make at least 2 qts.)
• Put suet and apples through food chopper.
• Combine all ingredients in large kettle. Simmer 2 hours to plump fruit and blend flavors. Stir often to prevent sticking.
• Pack at once in hot pint jars. Adjust lids. Process in pressure canner at 10 pounds pressure (240°F.) 60 minutes.
• Remove jars from canner and complete seals unless closures are self-sealing type. Makes about 11 pints.

Note: You can freeze mincemeat. Recommended storage time: 3 months.

OLD-TIME PEAR MINCEMEAT

Good way to salvage pear-crop windfalls or the less choice fruit

7   lbs. ripe Bartlett pears
1   lemon
2   (1 lb.) pkgs. seedless raisins
6¾ c. sugar
1   c. vinegar
1   tblsp. cloves
1   tblsp. cinnamon

1   tblsp. nutmeg
1   tblsp. allspice
1   tsp. ginger

• Core and quarter pears.
• Cut lemon into quarters, removing seeds.
• Put pears, lemon and raisins through food chopper.
• Combine remaining ingredients in large kettle. Add chopped-fruit mixture. Bring to a boil over medium heat; simmer 40 minutes.
• Pack at once in hot pint jars. Adjust lids. Process in boiling water bath (212°F.) 25 minutes.
• Remove jars from canner and complete seals unless closures are self-sealing type. Makes 9 pints.

BASIC HOMEMADE MINCEMEAT PIE

• You will need 4 c. homemade mincemeat for a 9″ pie. Dot the filling with 1 tblsp. butter, adjust top crust, cut vents and flute edges. Brush top with light cream, if desired. (It's a good idea to cover pie edges with 1½″ strip of aluminum foil the first half hour of baking to prevent excessive browning.)
• Bake in hot oven (425°F.) 40 to 45 minutes, or until pastry is golden. Partially cool on rack before serving.

Freezing Fruit Pies

You can freeze baked or unbaked 2-crust fruit pies successfully. Many people believe frozen unbaked pies have a fresher fruit taste and a crisper crust than pies baked before freezing.

But busy farm homemakers sometimes find it more convenient and time saving to bake and then freeze their pies. Follow the system that works best for you.

If you freeze apple or peach pies, pretreat the fruit to prevent darkening. Add 1 tblsp. lemon juice (or ¼ tsp. ascorbic acid, mixed with 1 tblsp. water) to peaches for a pie. Steam apple slices 3 to 5 minutes. Or use a commercial color protector, following label directions. Good pie bakers like to coat sweet cherries and berries with the sugar-flour mixture before adding them to a pie for freezing.

UNBAKED PIE: Freeze pie and then wrap. You can place pie in tin, aluminum or special paper pie pan designed for the freezer. Cover with a second pan to protect pie top. Tape top pan in place and insert pie in plastic bag or wrap in freezer wrapping; seal, label, date and return to freezer.

To serve pie, unwrap, cut vents if not cut before freezing and bake on lower shelf of hot oven (425°F.) 10 to 20 minutes longer than regular time for unfrozen pie. If rims of pie brown too quickly, cover with 1½" strips of aluminum foil.

BAKED PIE: Remove pie from oven when only lightly browned. It will finish browning when reheated for serving. Cool, then freeze without wrapping. Package frozen pie like frozen unbaked pie.

To serve, partially thaw in original wrap at room temperature, about 30 minutes. Unwrap and place on lower shelf of moderate oven (375°F.) 30 minutes, or until warm, and the juices in center are bubbling.

To Freeze Fruit-Pie Fillings

Many farm women find it more convenient to freeze pie fillings, when fresh fruit is plentiful, than finished pies. The fillings take less time and are economical of freezer space.

Here are the basic directions:
• Combine 1 qt. of any of the following ripe fruits—blueberries, pitted cherries, sliced strawberries, peaches, apples or pears—with ¾ to 1 c. sugar, depending on tartness, 3 tblsp. quick-cooking tapioca, ¼ tsp. salt and 1 to 2 tblsp. lemon juice. Before adding sugar, stir ¼ to ½ tsp. ascorbic acid into fruit that darkens. (Or use commercial color protector as directed on label.)
• Line 8" pie pan with heavy-duty aluminum foil, several layers of saran or freezer wrap. Let lining extend 6" beyond rim of pie pan. Add pie filling

and cover loosely with lining. Freeze. When frozen firm, wrap with lining to cover completely and seal with freezer tape. Label, date and return to freezer.
• To make pie with frozen filling, unwrap, but do not thaw. Place in pastry-lined 9" pie pan. Dot with 1½ tblsp. butter or margarine. Adjust top crust, cut vents and flute edges. Bake in hot oven (425°F.) about 1 hour, or until juices in vents boil with thick bubbles that do not burst.

Here are two FARM JOURNAL filling recipes that have many boosters among farm women who freeze them. The combination of cornstarch and tapioca thickens the fruit mixture just right. The recipes were first printed in our FREEZING & CANNING COOKBOOK.

APPLE-CRANBERRY PIE FILLING

Almost magic—making pie with autumn fruit favorites when lilacs bloom

3   c. sliced peeled apples
2   c. fresh cranberries
1 ¾ c. sugar
¼   c. flour
1   tsp. cinnamon
1 ½ tsp. melted butter

• Combine all ingredients. Arrange in a foil-lined 8″ pie pan. Cover loosely with aluminum foil and freeze. Remove frozen filling from pan, wrap, seal, label, date and return to freezer. Recommended storage time: up to 3 months.
• To make pie, place unwrapped, unthawed filling in pastry-lined 9″ pie pan. Top with pastry strip lattice.
• Bake in hot oven (425°F.) 1 hour and 10 minutes.

PEACH PIE FILLING

Let it snow! You can treat your guests with fresh-tasting peach pie

4   qts. sliced peeled peaches (9 lbs.)
1   tsp. ascorbic acid
1   gal. water
3 ½ c. sugar
½   c. plus 2 tblsp. quick-cooking tapioca
¼   c. lemon juice
1   tsp. salt

• Place peaches in large container. Dissolve ascorbic acid in water and pour over peaches. Drain.
• Combine peaches, sugar, tapioca, lemon juice and salt.

• Line 4 (8″) pie pans with heavy-duty aluminum foil, letting it extend 5″ beyond rim. Divide filling evenly between pans. Makes fillings for 4 (9″) pies.
To Freeze: Fold foil loosely over fillings; freeze. Remove from freezer, turn filling from pans and wrap snugly with foil. Return to freezer. Recommended storage time: 6 months.
To Bake: Remove foil from frozen pie filling and place it, unthawed, in a pastry-lined 9″ pie pan. Dot with butter and, if you like, sprinkle on ¼ tsp. nutmeg or cinnamon. Add top crust; seal and flute edges. Cut slits in top crust with kitchen scissors or knife.
• Bake in hot oven (425°F.) 1 hour and 10 minutes, or until syrup boils with heavy bubbles that do not burst.

COUNTRY BLUEBERRY PIE

Brings summer flavor to winter meals

Pastry for 2-crust pie
3   c. frozen blueberries (unsweetened)
Blueberry juice
Water
¾   c. sugar
2   tblsp. quick-cooking tapioca
1 ½ tblsp. cornstarch
1   tsp. lemon juice

• Thaw berries until most of free ice has disappeared. Drain off juice, measure and add water to make ½ c. liquid; stir into mixture of sugar, tapioca and cornstarch in saucepan. Heat rapidly until thickening is complete. Boiling is not necessary. Set aside to cool.
• Add berries and lemon juice to cooled, thickened juice. Pour filling

into pastry-lined 9″ pie pan. Cut steam vents and adjust top crust; flute edges.
• Bake in hot oven (425°F.) 30 minutes, or until nicely browned. For a brown undercrust, bake on lowest oven shelf.

PERFECT CHERRY PIE

It deserves its name—try it and see

Pastry for 2-crust pie
3   c. pitted tart frozen cherries
1   c. tart cherry juice
3   tblsp. sugar
2   tblsp. quick-cooking tapioca
1 ⅔ tblsp. cornstarch (5 tsp.)
⅛   tsp. almond extract

• Thaw cherries until most of the free ice has disappeared. Drain off the juice; measure and stir it into mixture of sugar, tapioca and cornstarch in saucepan. Heat rapidly until thickening is complete. Boiling is not necessary. Set aside to cool.
• Add cherries and extract to cooled, thickened juice. Pour filling into pastry-lined 9″ pie pan. Cut vents and adjust top crust; flute edges.
• Bake in hot oven (425°F.) 30 to 35 minutes, or until nicely browned. For a brown undercrust, bake on lowest oven shelf.

Note: Proportions of sugar, tapioca and cornstarch are based on 5 parts cherries frozen with 1 part sugar.

DOUBLE CHERRY PIE

Doubly good—two kinds of cherries

Pastry for 2-crust pie
2   c. pitted tart frozen cherries
1   c. pitted dark sweet frozen cherries

⅔   c. tart cherry juice
⅓   c. sweet cherry juice
¼   c. sugar
2 ⅓ tblsp. quick-cooking tapioca
1 ½ tsp. cornstarch
1   tsp. lemon juice

• Thaw cherries until most of the free ice has disappeared. Drain off juices, measure and stir into mixture of sugar, tapioca and cornstarch in saucepan. Heat rapidly until thickening is complete. Boiling is not necessary. Set aside to cool.
• Add cherries and lemon juice to cooled, thickened juice. Pour filling into pastry-lined 9″ pie pan. Cut vents and adjust top crust; flute edges.
• Bake in hot oven (425°F.) 30 to 35 minutes, or until nicely browned. For a brown undercrust, bake on lowest oven shelf.

Note: Proportions of sugar, tapioca and cornstarch are based on 5 parts cherries frozen with 1 part sugar.

GOLDEN PEACH PIE

Sweet perfection in peach pie

Pastry for 2-crust pie
3   c. frozen sliced peaches
1   c. peach juice
1 ½ tblsp. brown sugar
1 ½ tblsp. granulated sugar
2 ⅓ tblsp. quick-cooking tapioca
1 ½ tblsp. cornstarch
⅛   tsp. cinnamon
1   tsp. lemon juice

• Thaw peaches until most of free ice has disappeared. Drain off the juice, measure and stir it into mixture of sugars, tapioca, cornstarch and cinnamon in saucepan. Heat rapidly until thickening is complete. Boiling is not necessary. Set aside to cool.

• Add peaches and lemon juice to cooled, thickened juice. Pour filling into pastry-lined 9″ pie pan. Cut vents and adjust top crust; flute edges.

• Bake in hot oven (425°F.) 30 minutes, or until nicely browned. For a brown undercrust, bake on lowest oven shelf.

Note: Proportions of sugar, tapioca and cornstarch are based on 5 parts peaches frozen with 1 part sugar.

PEACH-STRAWBERRY PIE

A jewel of a pie in color and taste

Pastry for 2-crust pie
1 ½ c. frozen sliced peaches
1 ½ c. frozen strawberries
½ c. peach juice
½ c. strawberry juice
3 tblsp. sugar
2 ½ tblsp. quick-cooking tapioca
1 ½ tblsp. cornstarch
1 tsp. lemon juice

• Thaw fruit until most of free ice has disappeared. Drain off the juices and measure, then stir into mixture of sugar, tapioca and cornstarch in saucepan. Heat rapidly until thickening is complete. Boiling is not necessary. Set aside to cool.

• Add fruit and lemon juice to cooled, thickened juice. Pour filling into pastry-lined 9″ pie pan. Cut vents and adjust top crust; flute edges.

• Bake in hot oven (425°F.) 30 to 35 minutes, or until nicely browned. For a brown undercrust, bake on lowest oven shelf.

Note: Proportions of sugar, tapioca and cornstarch are based on 5 parts peaches frozen with 1 part sugar; 4 parts strawberries frozen with 1 part sugar.

VARIATION

PEACH-BLUEBERRY PIE: Substitute blueberries for strawberries. If blueberries were frozen unsweetened, use ⅓ c. sugar; add water to the combined fruit juices to make 1 c. liquid.

WONDERFUL STRAWBERRY PIE

Top with ice cream for extra festivity

Pastry for 2-crust pie
2 ⅔ c. frozen strawberries
1 ⅓ c. strawberry juice
3 tblsp. sugar
2 ½ tblsp. quick-cooking tapioca
1 ½ tblsp. cornstarch
1 tsp. lemon juice

• Thaw berries until most of free ice has disappeared. Drain off the juice; measure and stir it into mixture of sugar, tapioca and cornstarch in saucepan. Heat rapidly until thickening is complete. Boiling is not necessary. Set aside to cool.

• Add berries and lemon juice to cooled, thickened juice. Pour filling into pastry-lined 9″ pie pan. Cut vents and adjust top crust; flute edges.

• Bake in hot oven (425°F.) 30 minutes, or until nicely browned. For a brown undercrust, bake on lowest oven shelf.

Note: Proportions of sugar, tapioca and cornstarch are based on 4 parts strawberries frozen with 1 part sugar.

CUSTARD AND CREAM PIES

Forks never will cut into creamier and more velvety pies than those made by recipes in this chapter. Here are the really great country pies, royally rich with fresh farm produce—eggs, milk and cream. They are 1-crust versions (with an occasional surprise 2-crust), often graced with tall meringues and other decorative toppings.

True custard pies are made with eggs, milk and sugar, baked with the crust. Cream pies have a custard-type cooked filling, thickened with flour or cornstarch, turned into a baked pie shell. Both kinds are delicious and have their fans.

Pumpkin pies head this family of pies. They're as important as turkey and cranberry sauce for family reunions at Thanksgiving time. You'll want to bake our Pumpkin Pecan Pie with its smooth, spicy filling and crunchy Caramelized Pecan Topping.

Next in popularity, and always the beauty queens, are lemon meringue pies. We have, besides the favorite old versions, some exciting new ones. Black Bottom Lemon Pie, with chocolate painted on its golden pastry shell, is unforgettable in good looks and in its delightful blending of flavors, for instance.

Honorable mention must go to the basic Vanilla Cream Pie recipe, perfected in our Test Kitchens, and to the array of glamorous pies made with it. All are superior.

You'll find hostess-special chocolate pies in this and in Chapter 5.

Do try the coconut pies, made with recipes from country kitchens where they, like holly and mistletoe, are a part of Christmas holiday festivities. Southern chess pie and its cousins, the pecan and other nut pies, make their bow in this chapter. Just turn the pages and you'll find more than a year's supply of marvelous country pies for church suppers and company feasts.

P Stands for Pumpkin . . . and Pie

When ripe pumpkins lie like harvest moons in fields, glow in orange heaps at roadside stands and in winking jack-o'-lanterns, it's time to get out the rolling pin and bake a pie. Pumpkin pie is one of the great autumn dessert glories in country places—and a must for Thanksgiving dinner.

FARM JOURNAL readers say that the pie no longer is a seasonal treat. By using commercially canned pumpkin, a staple in kitchen cupboards, you can have pumpkin pie the calendar around. Some women make their own pumpkin purée and freeze it. Here are the directions they pass along:

Don't let pumpkins freeze before cooking them. The belief that this improves the flavor is a myth. Instead, freezing injures the keeping qualities of raw pumpkins.

So, to freeze pumpkin, prepare it as you would for immediate use. Select sound pumpkins of bright color, heavy for their size. Cut them in halves, remove seeds and strings and arrange cut side up on baking sheets or in shallow pans. Bake in a hot oven (400°F.) until tender, about 1 hour.

Scoop out the pulp and put through a strainer or food mill. Or use your blender if you have one. Pour ⅓ c. water into blender bowl and add 2 c. cut-up, cooked pumpkin. Blend until smooth. Repeat until all pumpkin is blended. Then cook the purée in a shallow pan, stirring constantly, until it is very thick. The boiling evaporates the water added in blending. Use the purée as you do canned pumpkin.

To freeze it, pack in airtight containers, allowing 1″ head space. A pound of pumpkin makes about ¾ c. purée.

The USDA (U. S. Department of Agriculture) has successfully turned pure pumpkin purée into powder, which can be used in pie fillings.

Popular Pumpkin Pies

Pumpkin pie is so popular that every neighborhood has several prize recipes. But all good pumpkin pies have mellow fillings, smooth to the tongue and enriched with eggs and cream or evaporated milk. A blend of spices points up the flavor. (Spice mixes for pumpkin pies are also available.) A shell of tender, flaky pie crust that melts in the mouth is essential to set off the filling.

An Indiana farm cook, who is a pie baker of recognized ability, says there is greater variety in the color and taste of pumpkin pies at bake sales and club and church suppers than other kinds of pies. No two are exactly alike. This indicates the remarkable talent country women have in adding their own touches of genius—aside from the choice of spices, the addition of brown or maple sugar, honey, nuts, grated orange peel, peanut butter, etc.

Taste testers gave our Pecan-Pumpkin Pie excellent ratings, including the comment: "The best pumpkin pie I've ever eaten." You can bypass the caramelized topping if you prefer a whipped-cream trim.

TAWNY PUMPKIN PIE

A FARM JOURNAL *5-star special from our* COUNTRY COOKBOOK

Unbaked 9" pie shell
1 ¼ c. cooked or canned pumpkin
¾ c. sugar
½ tsp. salt
¼ tsp. ginger
1 tsp. cinnamon
1 tsp. flour
2 eggs, slightly beaten
1 c. evaporated milk
2 tblsp. water
½ tsp. vanilla

• Combine pumpkin, sugar, salt, spices and flour in mixing bowl.
• Add eggs; mix well. Add evaporated milk, water and vanilla; mix. Pour into pie shell.
• Bake in hot oven (400°F.) 45 to 50 minutes, or until knife inserted near center comes out clean.

PUMPKIN PECAN PIE

Filling is a mellow golden brown, rich like an old gold coin

Unbaked 9" pie shell
2 eggs, slightly beaten
1 (1 lb.) can pumpkin (2 c.)
¾ c. sugar
½ tsp. salt

1 tsp. cinnamon
½ tsp. ginger
¼ tsp. cloves
1 ⅔ c. light cream or evaporated milk
Caramelized Pecan Topping

• Blend together eggs and pumpkin. Stir in sugar, salt, cinnamon, ginger and cloves. Blend in cream.
• Turn into pie shell. Bake in hot oven (400°F.) 45 to 55 minutes or until knife inserted halfway between center and edge of pie comes out clean. Cool completely on rack.

CARAMELIZED PECAN TOPPING: Combine 3 tblsp. soft butter or margarine, ⅔ c. brown sugar and ⅔ c. coarsely chopped pecans. Gently drop by spoonfuls over cooled pie to cover top. Broil 5" below heat until mixture begins to bubble, about 3 minutes. Watch carefully. (If cooked too long, top will turn syrupy.) Cool on rack.

HONEYED PUMPKIN PIE

Be sure to flute pie-shell edges high to hold the generous filling

Unbaked 9" pie shell, edges fluted high
1 (1 lb.) can pumpkin (2 c.)
½ tsp. ginger
½ tsp. cinnamon
1 tsp. salt
4 eggs, slightly beaten
1 c. honey
½ c. milk
½ c. heavy cream

• In large bowl blend together pumpkin, ginger, cinnamon and salt. Beat in eggs, honey, milk and cream. Pour into pie shell.

• Bake in hot oven (400°F.) until knife inserted 1″ from edge of pie comes out clean, about 50 to 55 minutes. (The filling will set as pie cools.)

GOOD IDEA: Make your pumpkin pie the usual way but use 1 tsp. vanilla and a few drops of lemon extract instead of spices. The pie is a pretty color and the flavor pleases people who do not care for spicy foods.

APPLE BUTTER-PUMPKIN PIE

Mighty good, mighty filling. Serve faintly warm (doesn't weep when cut)

Unbaked 9″ pie shell
1 c. apple butter
1 c. cooked or canned pumpkin
½ c. brown sugar, firmly packed
½ tsp. salt
¾ tsp. cinnamon
¾ tsp. nutmeg
⅛ tsp. ginger
3 eggs, slightly beaten
¾ c. evaporated milk

• Combine apple butter, pumpkin, sugar, salt and spices. Add eggs; mix well. Add milk gradually; mix.

• Pour into pie shell. Bake in hot oven (425°F.) about 40 minutes.

FROSTED PUMPKIN PIE

Decorate spicy, snowy-topped pie with walnuts or bright corn candy

Unbaked 9″ pie shell

Filling:
1 ¾ c. pumpkin
1 ¾ c. milk

3 eggs
⅔ c. brown sugar, firmly packed
2 tblsp. granulated sugar
1 ¼ tsp. cinnamon
½ tsp. ginger
½ tsp. nutmeg
½ tsp. salt
¼ tsp. cloves

Frosting:
½ c. shortening or butter
2 ½ tblsp. flour
¼ tsp. salt
½ c. milk
3 c. sifted confectioners sugar
½ tsp. vanilla

Filling: Measure ingredients in large bowl. Beat until smooth with rotary beater. Pour into pie shell. (Have pastry a little thicker than ⅛″ so it will be crisper.)

• Bake in hot oven (425°F.) 45 to 55 minutes, until a silver knife inserted 1″ from edge of pie comes out clean. The filling may look soft, but it will set later. Let pie cool. Spread with frosting.

Frosting: Melt shortening in saucepan; remove from heat; blend in flour and salt. Slowly stir in milk. Return to heat; cook and stir until mixture has boiled 1 minute. (The frosting may look curdled at this stage.)

• Add confectioners sugar and vanilla. Stir until creamy. (Set pan in ice water to hasten setting of frosting.)

• Spread frosting on cooled pie. Decorate top with walnuts or raisins.

PUMPKIN-MINCEMEAT PIE

Two holiday favorites baked together

Unbaked 9" pie shell
1   egg, slightly beaten
1   c. canned or cooked pumpkin
⅓   c. sugar
¼   tsp. salt
½   tsp. cinnamon
¼   tsp. nutmeg
¼   tsp. ginger
⅛   tsp. cloves

¾   c. undiluted evaporated milk
2   c. prepared mincemeat

• Combine and blend together egg, pumpkin, sugar, salt, spices and evaporated (not condensed) milk.
• Pour mincemeat into bottom of pie shell, spreading evenly. Spoon pumpkin mixture over mincemeat layer.
• Bake in hot oven (400°F.) 45 to 50 minutes or until knife inserted halfway between edge and center of pie comes out clean.

Squash Pie—Delicate and Delicious

When the yard and fields are white and more snow is falling, most farm women depend on their imagination and cooking skills to fix meals that bring cheer to everyone at the dinner table. "At our house," says a New Hampshire homemaker, "we often celebrate by having our favorite squash pie for dessert. And while our forks are busy, someone, thinking of more pies next year, almost always suggests that we plant more squash in our garden."

New England country kitchens were the birthplace of these smooth, satiny custard pies. Now cooks in all areas, especially if they grow squash, make pies with it. The Butternut, with its yellow-orange flesh, is the top-ranking autumn variety. Buttercups and Blue Hubbards assume a pie role, come December. When there's freezer space, pie bakers like to cook, mash, package and freeze each variety at its flavor peak—and certainly no later than early January, when squash in home storage often need to be sal-

vaged. Then they can make the pies throughout winter and spring.

Squash pies resemble their cousins, pumpkin pies, in appearance and taste. But some New England cooks insist that you use only white sugar in squash and always some brown sugar in pumpkin pies. And they say cloves are taboo in squash-pie fillings. Thus, the custard is milder in taste than the pumpkin and you get more of the vegetable's flavor. Here's the recipe named by a country cook in honor of a snowstorm, but you'll like it equally well when autumn leaves are brilliant or jonquils are blooming by the front porch. It's a winner.

SNOWSTORM SQUASH PIE

Delicate custard in crisp pastry is the vegetable gardener's tasty reward

Unbaked 9" pie shell
1 ¾ c. strained, mashed, cooked
        squash
1   c. sugar
1   tsp. salt   *more*

1   tsp. cinnamon
½   tsp. nutmeg
½   tsp. ginger
3   eggs
1 ½   c. milk
1   tblsp. butter or margarine,
      melted

• Combine squash, sugar, salt and spices.

• Blend in eggs, milk and butter. Pour into pie shell.
• Bake in hot oven (400°F.) 50 minutes, or until silver knife inserted in filling 1″ from pie's edge comes out clean. Cool. Serve slightly warm or cold.

Potato Pies Made with Sweets

When we asked our readers for their treasured pie recipes, the mail brought us directions for several intriguing sweet potato pies from southern kitchens. Every pie baker labeled her contribution just plain Potato Pie. That's because people, south of the Mason and Dixon line, refer to the sweets as potatoes, the whites as Irish potatoes.

The sweet potatoes used in southern recipes were the varieties with a light reddish or coppery skin and a rather moist, bright, orange-yellow interior. You'll notice that in one of the recipes sliced potatoes bake in a pastry envelope. Quite a welcome discovery for northern women who commonly use only the puréed or mashed potatoes in pie. Requests come to FARM JOURNAL kitchens every year from northern readers wanting the recipe for a wonderful sliced sweet potato pie they enjoyed on a trip in the South—usually in Virginia or Kentucky.

Farm women have been making pies with this vegetable (it's a rich source of vitamins A and C) for many years. Sweet potatoes were grown commercially in Virginia as long ago as the mid-1600s. Our collection of sweet potato pie recipes that follows includes the great favorites of the countryside, updated.

During the harvest season this vegetable has a truly fresh taste. To prolong this superior fall flavor, some homemakers cook and freeze sweet potatoes then, for winter and spring pies. You can either bake or cook the unpeeled vegetable in salted water just until tender, then cool, peel, purée it and package and freeze. Dried sweet potato flakes also have been developed by research and are available for convenient use the year around.

SWEET POTATO CUSTARD PIE

Velvety custard with a fascinating, subtle flavor all its own

Unbaked 9″ pie shell
2   eggs, slightly beaten
¼   c. sugar
½   tsp. salt
¼   tsp. nutmeg
¼   tsp. cinnamon

1   tsp. grated orange peel
1 ¾ c. milk
2 ½ c. peeled and grated raw sweet
         potato, lightly packed
1   tblsp. melted butter or marga-
         rine

• Combine eggs, sugar, salt, nutmeg, cinnamon, orange peel and milk. Add sweet potatoes, grated just before adding to egg-milk mixture. Stir in butter.
• Pour into pie shell; bake in hot oven (400°F.) until a silver knife inserted in filling 1" from edge of pie comes out clean, about 45 to 50 minutes. Serve slightly warm or cold.

SLICED SWEET POTATO PIE

Flaky pastry envelops rich, spicy, orange-colored filling—it's luscious!

Pastry for 2-crust pie
1 ½ lbs. sweet potatoes (4 medium)
1   c. light brown sugar
½   tsp. cinnamon
⅛   tsp. nutmeg
½   tsp. ginger
¼   tsp. salt
6   tblsp. butter or margarine
½   c. heavy cream

• Boil sweet potatoes until half-cooked, 15 to 20 minutes. Peel and slice thinly.
• Mix sugar, spices and salt.
• Place a layer of sweet potatoes in pastry-lined 9" pie pan, sprinkle with some of the sugar-spice mixture and dot with a little butter. Continue until all ingredients are used, dotting top with butter. Add cream. Adjust top crust; flute edges and cut vents.
• Bake in hot oven (425°F.) 30 to

40 minutes. If potatoes are still not tender, reduce temperature to 350°F. and continue baking until they are done.

PURÉED SWEET POTATO PIE

For a special occasion, top pie with whipped cream, sprinkle with walnuts

Unbaked 9" pie shell
2   c. sweet potato purée
2   eggs, slightly beaten
¾   c. sugar
½   tsp. salt
½   tsp. ginger
½   tsp. nutmeg
1   tsp. vanilla
1 ⅔ c. light cream or evaporated
         milk
½   c. butter or margarine, melted

• Bake sweet potatoes until tender, peel and mash. Make sure all lumps are removed, straining if necessary.
• Mix all ingredients together and pour into pie shell. Bake in hot oven (400°F.) 50 minutes or until a silver knife inserted in filling 1" from edge of pie comes out clean.

GRATED SWEET POTATO PIE

Blindfold them and most people think they're eating extra-good pumpkin pie

Unbaked 8" pie shell
½   c. brown sugar
¼   tsp. salt
¼   tsp. cinnamon
¼   tsp. nutmeg
⅛   tsp. cloves (optional)
1   c. milk
2   eggs, slightly beaten   *more*

1 ½ c. finely grated, raw sweet potatoes, lightly packed
1 tsp. lemon juice
1 tblsp. butter or margarine,
  melted

• Combine brown sugar, salt, cinnamon, nutmeg and cloves. Stir in milk
and eggs. Add sweet potatoes, grated

just before using, lemon juice and
butter.
• Pour into pie shell and bake in hot
oven (425°F.) until a silver knife inserted in filling 1″ from edge of pie
comes out clean, about 45 to 50 minutes. (Filling in center may still look
soft but it will set later.) Serve slightly
warm or cold.

Custard Pies at Their Country Best

If you live south of the Mason and
Dixon line, you probably call them
Egg Custard Pies; north of it, just
plain Custard Pie. By either name
they're famous, country-kitchen desserts. A sprinkling of nutmeg traditionally tops the pie. Some cooks grate
whole nutmegs to give their pies a
gourmet touch.

Women know that the perfect custard pie is an achievement. This is because the filling requires a low baking
temperature; the crust, if it's to be
flaky, a high temperature. One way to
surmount the difficulty is to bake the
custard and the crust separately at the
ideal temperatures for each and then
combine them (see our Best-Ever
Custard Pie).

The cardinal rule to heed is to avoid
overcooking, which produces a watery
or "weeping" custard. Test the filling
for doneness with a silver knife, when
specified in the recipes.

When you are in a hurry, try our

quick pies, Speedy Custard and Easy
Lemon Custard. One stays in the oven
about 15 minutes and the other, half
an hour. Both are surprisingly good,
considering the baking time required.

Cool all custard pies 30 minutes on
wire racks and then refrigerate until
mealtime. But you'll find the crust will
taste better if pie is taken from refrigerator and left at room temperature
while the main dinner course is eaten.
This is true of all refrigerator pies.

BEST-EVER CUSTARD PIE

Guarantee: a crisp undercrust

Baked 9″ pie shell
½   c. sugar
½   tsp. salt
2 ½ c. milk, scalded
1   tsp. vanilla
4   eggs, slightly beaten
½   tsp. nutmeg

• Add sugar, salt, warm milk and vanilla to eggs. Pour into buttered 9" pie pan. Sprinkle with nutmeg. Set in shallow pan containing water (water should reach halfway up sides of pie pan). Bake in moderate oven (350°F.) until silver knife inserted halfway between edge and center of custard comes out clean, 30 to 35 minutes. The center of custard may look a little soft, but it will set later. (Over-baking will make the custard pie watery.) Remove from oven and cool on rack at room temperature until luke-warm.
• Carefully loosen custard around edge of pan with small spatula and gently shake pan to loosen custard completely. Tilt the custard over the cooled pie shell, holding the edge of custard directly above far edge of shell. Slip the custard into the pie shell, pulling the pan back to you until all the custard is in the shell. Let custard settle in place.

CHOCOLATE-FROSTED CUSTARD PIE: When Best-Ever Custard Pie is cold, spread on your favorite chocolate frosting made with confectioners sugar. Or mix ½ c. sifted confectioners sugar with ⅛ tsp. salt and 2 tblsp. cream until smooth. Blend in 1 square unsweetened chocolate, melted, and 2 tblsp. melted butter.

VARIATIONS

COCONUT CUSTARD PIE: Omit nutmeg and add 1 c. flaked coconut to the custard. Sprinkle a little coconut on top and bake. Or sprinkle 1 c. flaked or shredded coconut over bottom of pie shell just before adding custard.

RICH CUSTARD PIE: Use 1½ c. milk and 1 c. heavy cream instead of 2½ c. milk. For a sweeter pie, use ⅔ c. sugar instead of ½ c. in custard filling.

MAPLE NUT CUSTARD PIE: Drizzle a little maple-blended syrup over top of cold custard pie and sprinkle with chopped walnuts or almonds.

COUNTRY-KITCHEN CUSTARD PIE

This filling, smooth as velvet, is rich in eggs, milk and cream

Unbaked 9" pie shell
4   eggs
⅔   c. sugar
¼   tsp. salt
1½ c. milk, scalded
1   c. light cream, scalded
1   tsp. vanilla
½   tsp. nutmeg

• Chill pie shell thoroughly.
• Beat eggs slightly; then beat in remaining ingredients, except nutmeg. Pour into well-chilled pie shell with high fluted edge. Sprinkle on nutmeg.
• Bake in hot oven (400°F.) until silver knife inserted 1" from edge of pie comes out clean, 25 to 35 minutes. (Baking too long makes a watery custard pie.) Cool on rack 30 minutes and refrigerate until ready to serve.

SPEEDY CUSTARD PIE

Bakes quickly, in about 15 minutes

Unbaked 9" pie shell
4   eggs, slightly beaten
½   c. sugar
¼   tsp. salt   *more*

1 ½ tsp. vanilla
2 ½ c. milk, scalded
Nutmeg

• Thoroughly mix eggs, sugar, salt and vanilla; slowly stir in scalded milk. Pour at once into pie shell. Dust lightly with nutmeg.
• Bake in very hot oven (475°F.) 5 minutes, then at 425°F. for 10 minutes, or until knife inserted halfway between center and edge of pie comes out clean. Serve cool or chilled.

EASY LEMON CUSTARD PIE

Busy country pie baker's delight

Unbaked 8″ pie shell
¾ c. sugar
¾ c. water
⅓ c. lemon juice
1 tsp. grated lemon peel
¼ tsp. salt
3 eggs
Nutmeg

• Chill pie shell.
• Combine sugar, water, lemon juice and peel, salt and eggs in mixing bowl. Beat at medium speed 7 to 8 minutes.
• Place pie shell on oven rack. Pour egg mixture into it. Bake in hot oven (425°F.) 20 minutes. Reduce temperature to 250°F. (very slow) and continue baking 10 minutes. Remove from oven and sprinkle with nutmeg. Cool before serving.

BUTTERMILK PIE IN CORNMEAL PASTRY

One of our best Southern pies

Unbaked Cornmeal Pie Shell
3 eggs, separated
1 c. sugar
1 tblsp. butter
¼ c. flour
2 c. buttermilk
¼ tsp. grated lemon peel
2 tblsp. lemon juice
Meringue (3 egg whites)

• Beat yolks, adding sugar gradually.
• Cut butter into flour; add buttermilk, lemon peel and juice. Fold in yolks.
• Pour into 9″ Cornmeal Pie Shell.
• Bake in hot oven (425°F.) 10 minutes; reduce temperature to 350°F. and bake 20 to 25 minutes. Cool.
• Pile meringue lightly over cooled filling (see Perfect Meringue for Topping Pies, Chapter 9). Bake in moderate oven (350°F.) 12 to 15 minutes.

CORNMEAL PIE SHELL: Sift together 1 c. sifted flour and ½ tsp. salt; stir in ½ c. cornmeal. Cut in ½ c. shortening until mixture resembles fine crumbs. Stir in ⅓ c. grated Cheddar cheese; sprinkle ¼ c. water over mixture gradually, mixing lightly with fork. Shape into ball; flatten on lightly floured surface. Roll to about ⅛″ thickness. Line 9″ pie pan; trim and flute edge. Fill and bake as directed.

Creamiest Cream Pies in the Country

Farm women make the world's best cream pies. For two reasons: they almost always have the necessary ingredients in their kitchens, and they have lots of practice—the pies taste so wonderful that they're favorites.

A Colorado ranchwoman says she bakes cream pies for church sales because they are spoken for by the time she delivers them. Her husband sums up his regard for the dessert by saying: "My definition for good is different from Webster's. To me, good is the kind of cream pie my wife bakes."

If your cream pies must wait a few hours before serving, cool them on wire racks for 30 minutes and then refrigerate. It is important to keep them refrigerated until serving time. Return leftovers promptly to refrigerator. These precautions guard against danger of food poisoning, which exists to a larger extent in milk-egg mixtures than in other foods, especially in hot and humid weather.

Cream Filling Pointers

Use a heavy saucepan and stir the filling constantly while it cooks, to prevent scorching.

Do not undercook the filling or it will have a raw, starchy taste.

If you have trouble with lumping, try the paste method of adding cornstarch (see basic recipe for Vanilla Cream Pie).

BROWN-BUTTER BUTTERSCOTCH PIE

For a real treat, sprinkle chopped toasted nuts on whipped cream top

Baked 9" pie shell
6 tblsp. butter
1 c. dark brown sugar
1 c. boiling water
3 tblsp. cornstarch
2 tblsp. flour
½ tsp. salt

1 ⅔ c. milk
3 egg yolks, slightly beaten
1 tsp. vanilla
Whipped cream

• Melt butter in heavy skillet over low heat. Watch carefully. When golden brown, add brown sugar; cook, stirring constantly, until mixture comes to a boil. Stir in water and remove from heat.
• In saucepan mix cornstarch, flour and salt. Blend in milk, stirring until smooth. Stir in brown-sugar mixture. Cook over medium heat, stirring constantly, until mixture comes to a boil. Boil 1 minute longer. Remove from heat.
• Stir a little of hot mixture into egg yolks; then blend into hot mixture. Boil 1 minute. Remove from heat. Add vanilla. Cool, stirring occasionally.
• Pour into cool pie shell and chill.
• To serve, spread top with whipped cream.

Note: If you prefer to top pie with meringue made with 3 egg whites (see Perfect Meringue for Topping Pies, Chapter 9), you need not cool filling before pouring it into pie shell.

VANILLA CREAM PIE

A FARM JOURNAL *5-star basic recipe*

Baked 8" pie shell
½ c. sugar
3 tblsp. flour
1 tblsp. cornstarch
¼ tsp. salt
1 ½ c. milk
3 egg yolks, slightly beaten
1 tblsp. butter or margarine
1 tsp. vanilla   *more*

• Combine sugar, flour, cornstarch and salt in top of double boiler. Mix with wooden spoon. Blend in milk gradually, then add egg yolks. Add butter.

• Place over rapidly boiling water so pan is touching water. Cook until thick and smooth, about 7 minutes, stirring constantly. Scrape down sides of pan frequently.

• Remove from heat. Add vanilla. Stir until smooth and blended, scraping sides of pan well. Pour hot filling into pie shell.

Note: Quantities may be doubled and filling cooked for 2 (8″) pies at the same time.

VARIATIONS

CHOCOLATE CREAM PIE: Melt 1½ squares unsweetened chocolate in milk in top of double boiler. Set aside to cool. Then proceed as directed for Vanilla Cream Pie filling, using the chocolate-milk mixture and increasing sugar from ½ to ¾ c. Especially good topped with Coconut Macaroon Topping (Chapter 9).

BUTTERSCOTCH CREAM PIE: Substitute ¾ c. brown sugar for granulated sugar and increase butter to 2 tblsp. Proceed as directed for Vanilla Cream Pie.

BLACK BOTTOM PIE: Add 2 tsp. unflavored gelatin to dry ingredients. Cook filling as directed in recipe for Vanilla Cream Pie. Add ½ c. hot filling to ½ c. semisweet chocolate pieces; stir until they melt and mixture is smooth. Spread chocolate mixture in bottom of baked 9″ pie shell. Cover and set remaining filling aside. Add ¼ tsp. salt to 3 egg whites; beat until frothy. Gradually add 3 tblsp. sugar, beating until stiff peaks form. With beater, beat half of this meringue into cream filling until mixture is smooth. Fold remaining half of meringue into mixture. Spread on chocolate layer in pie shell. Chill pie several hours before serving.

CHERRY CREAM PIE: Add 2 tsp. unflavored gelatin to dry ingredients and cook filling as directed for Vanilla Cream Pie. Remove from heat; cover and set aside. Add ¼ tsp. salt to 3 egg whites; beat until frothy. Gradually add 3 tblsp. sugar, beating until stiff peaks form. Beat half of meringue into cream filling until mixture is smooth. Fold remaining half of meringue into mixture. Spread 1 c. commercially canned or homemade cherry pie filling on bottom of baked 9″ pie shell. Cover with cream filling. Chill several hours before serving.

STRAWBERRY SPONGE CREAM PIE: Drain 1 (10 oz.) pkg. partially thawed frozen strawberries. If necessary, add water to make ½ c. juice. Combine 2 tblsp. cornstarch and 1 tblsp. sugar in small saucepan; slowly add juice, stirring to make smooth paste. Cook over low heat, stirring constantly until mixture is thick and clear. Remove from heat and stir in strawberries. Set aside. Prepare filling for Vanilla Cream Pie, reducing flour to 2 tblsp. and egg yolks to 2. Pour into baked 9″ pie shell. Beat egg whites at high speed until frothy. Gradually add 3 tblsp. sugar, beating at high speed until very stiff peaks form. Fold thickened fruit into egg whites. Spread evenly on hot cream filling, sealing to crust all around. Bake in moderate oven (350°F.) about 30 minutes. Cool before serving.

RASPBERRY CREAM PIE: Follow directions for Strawberry Sponge Cream Pie, substituting raspberries for strawberries.

BLUEBERRY CREAM PIE: Follow directions for Strawberry Sponge Cream Pie, substituting blueberries for strawberries. Add 1 tsp. lemon juice to berries.

VINEGAR PIE

Ranch-kitchen pie—truly delicious

Baked 9" pie shell
3 egg yolks, beaten
1 c. sugar
¼ tsp. salt
1 ¾ c. boiling water
¼ c. cider vinegar
¼ c. cornstarch
¼ c. cold water
1 tsp. lemon extract
Meringue (3 egg whites)

• Place egg yolks in top of double boiler; add sugar and salt. Gradually add boiling water, stirring constantly. Add vinegar and cornstarch dissolved in cold water. Cook over boiling water until thick and smooth, about 12 minutes.
• Remove from heat. Add lemon extract. Stir until filling is smooth and blended, scraping sides of pan.
• Pour hot filling into pie shell. Top lukewarm filling with meringue (see Perfect Meringue for Topping Pies, Chapter 9), spreading to edges and sealing to crust. Bake in moderate oven (350°F.) 12 to 15 minutes, or until meringue is lightly browned.

Elegant Pie for Special Occasions

The good Utah cook, who shares her recipe for this superb, company dessert, says: "When you cut the pie, little, tempting dribbles of caramel sauce follow the knife. Tiny rivulets of the caramel run down the sides of the wedges on the tall and handsome filling. Guests are impatient to taste."

CELESTIAL VANILLA PIE

This high pie has unusual, delicate fluffy filling with caramel on top

Baked 9" pie shell
4 ½ tblsp. cornstarch
1 c. sugar
1 ½ c. boiling water
½ tsp. salt
3 egg whites
1 ½ tsp. vanilla
Caramel Sauce
½ c. heavy cream, whipped
½ square unsweetened chocolate, coarsely grated

• Combine cornstarch and ¾ c. sugar in saucepan. Add boiling water, stirring constantly; continue to cook and stir until thick and clear, 10 to 12 minutes.
• Add salt to egg whites and beat until stiff. Add 3 tblsp. of remaining sugar and vanilla, beating until egg whites are creamy. *more*

• Pour hot cornstarch mixture over egg whites, beating constantly. Cool slightly and pour into pie shell, heaping filling high. Chill at least 2 hours.
• Just before serving, spoon thin Caramel Sauce over filling in pie to cover; then top with whipped cream sweetened with remaining 1 tblsp. sugar. Sprinkle with grated chocolate.

CARAMEL SAUCE: Melt 2 tblsp. butter in small saucepan. Add 1¼ c. firmly packed brown sugar and 2 tblsp. dark corn syrup. Stir and cook over medium heat 1 minute. Remove from heat and add ½ c. light cream or top milk. Cook and stir until sugar is dissolved, then simmer 1 minute longer. Remove from heat and add ½ tsp. vanilla. Cool. Dilute with cream if necessary; the caramel sauce should be fairly thin. Makes 1 cup.

Heirloom American Pie

Most people today prefer updated cream pies, in which cooked filling is put in already baked pie shells—pies certain to have crisp, flaky crusts. Here's a pioneer pie, however, created in farm kitchens along the Wabash River during covered-wagon days. This baked cream pie enjoyed great prestige in the prairie states.

It's an heirloom recipe used today almost entirely by homemakers who learned to like it at their grandmothers' tables. We include the recipe primarily for its historic interest, a reminder of what pies were like a century ago. . . . Also for women who've searched for the recipe for a rich, cream pie their grandmothers used to make by mixing the filling in an unbaked pastry shell. (Their way of cutting down on dishwashing!)

HOOSIER CREAM PIE

Shallow, rich pie from frontier days

Unbaked 8″ pie shell
½   c. brown sugar
½   c. granulated sugar
2   tblsp. flour
2   c. light cream
½   tsp. vanilla

• Combine sugars and flour, mixing well. Stir in cream and vanilla. Pour into thoroughly chilled pie shell.
• Bake in hot oven (400°F.) until silver knife inserted halfway between center and edge of pie comes out clean, about 25 to 30 minutes. Cool on rack and refrigerate until serving time.

Cream Pie Filling that Freezes

If you've tried freezing cream pies you may have been disappointed. The fillings often separate, or become grainy or spongy.

Home economists at Texas Technological College worked on this problem, trying different thickeners. They found that fillings thickened with cornstarch, plus a small amount of gelatin, freeze and store successfully for 1 month with no changes in texture.

They had best results when they froze the filling and the baked pastry shells separately. To serve, they recommend putting the frozen filling in the baked shell, spreading it with meringue, then browning. (Egg whites left over from filling may also be frozen and used for meringue.) By changing the layer that goes over the frozen filling, you can serve delicious pies of different flavors. Here's the recipe the Texas home economists developed to freeze successfully:

CREAM PIE FOR FREEZING

Makes 3 pie fillings—saves time

2   tsp. unflavored gelatin
6   c. milk
2   c. sugar
9   tblsp. cornstarch
½   tsp. salt
6   egg yolks, beaten
6   tblsp. butter or margarine
3   tsp. vanilla

• Soften gelatin in ¼ c. milk.
• Scald remaining milk. Add the combined sugar, cornstarch and salt; continue heating rapidly until boiling, stirring constantly.
• Stir about ½ c. of the hot mixture into egg yolks; pour back into saucepan; simmer 5 minutes more.
• Stir in gelatin mixture; add butter and vanilla. Pour into three 8" pie pans; freeze. (Frozen filling will be right diameter to fit 9" shell.)
• Remove from pan, wrap in moistureproof freezer material; return to freezer.

To Bake: Place unthawed filling in baked 9" pastry shell. You may cover it with a fruit or coconut layer (see variations), then top with meringue, making sure it touches crust all around. Bake in moderate oven (375°F.) about 10 to 12 minutes. (For best results, avoid heating the filling completely through.) Cool.

MERINGUE: Beat 3 egg whites (fresh or thawed frozen) with ¼ tsp. cream of tartar until frothy; beat in 6 tblsp. sugar, a little at a time. Beat until meringue stands in firm peaks. Spread on frozen filling at once.

PASTRY FOR FREEZING: Recipes using ⅓ c. shortening to each cup of flour are recommended by the Texas home economists at Texas Technological College. Pastry made with less fat did not freeze as well; neither was oil pastry at its best when frozen.

VARIATIONS

BANANA CREAM PIE: Slice 2 ripe bananas over frozen filling; sprinkle with 1 tblsp. confectioners sugar. Cover with meringue and bake.

STRAWBERRY OR PEACH CREAM PIE: Arrange 1½ c. sliced strawberries or peaches over frozen filling; sprinkle with 3 tblsp. confectioners sugar; cover with meringue and bake.

COCONUT CREAM PIE: Sprinkle 1½ c. flaked coconut over frozen filling; cover with meringue and bake.

FRENCH STRAWBERRY PIE

Glossy glazed berries on top hide the surprise, a rich custard layer

Baked 9″ pie shell
⅓ c. sugar
3½ tblsp. cornstarch
6 egg yolks, slightly beaten
2 c. milk, scalded
1 tsp. vanilla
1 (12 oz.) jar currant jelly
1 pt. fresh strawberries

• Combine sugar, cornstarch and egg yolks in saucepan. Gradually stir in the milk, while bringing to a boil. Cook, stirring constantly, 1 minute.
• Remove from heat and add vanilla. Cool and chill.
• Melt the currant jelly over heat. Cool until it is about ready to set. Brush the inside of pie shell with part of the jelly. Spoon in custard filling.
• Arrange stemmed, washed and drained strawberries, pointed ends up, on top of pie. Spoon remaining currant jelly over berries to glaze them. Chill a few hours before serving.

Beautiful Lemon Pies

Lemon pies of many kinds come to country tables. With their buttercup-yellow, tart-sweet filling and white, gold-tipped meringue, they're tempting at meal's end. Many farmers consider such a pie the perfect finish for a fish dinner, but the tart flavor also pleasantly rounds out a dinner with poultry or meat on the platter.

Notice our method of thickening Best-Ever Lemon Meringue and Vanilla Cream Pies with cornstarch blended with water to make a smooth paste, added to the boiling mixture. Give it a trial—you'll have gratifying results.

BEST-EVER LEMON MERINGUE PIE

A FARM JOURNAL 5-star special

Baked 9″ pie shell
1½ c. sugar
1½ c. water
½ tsp. salt
½ c. cornstarch
⅓ c. water
4 egg yolks, slightly beaten
½ c. lemon juice
3 tblsp. butter
1 tsp. grated lemon peel
4 egg whites
¼ tsp. salt
½ c. sugar

• Combine sugar, 1½ c. water and salt in saucepan; heat to boiling.
• Mix cornstarch and ⅓ c. water to make smooth paste; add to boiling mixture gradually, stirring constantly; cook until thick and clear. Remove from heat.
• Combine egg yolks and lemon juice; stir into thickened mixture. Return to heat and cook, stirring constantly, until mixture bubbles again. Remove from heat. Stir in butter and lemon peel. Cover and cool until lukewarm.
• For meringue, add salt to egg

whites; beat until frothy. Gradually add ½ c. sugar, beating until glossy peaks are formed. Stir 2 rounded tblsp. of meringue into lukewarm filling.

• Pour filling into cool pie shell. Pile remaining meringue on top and spread lightly over filling, spreading evenly to edge of crust.

• Bake in slow oven (325°F.) about 15 minutes, or until lightly browned. Cool on rack at least 1 hour before cutting.

Good Idea: Store extra grated lemon and orange peel in a tightly covered small jar, placed in refrigerator. It stays fresh a long time and saves getting out the grater when you need a small amount of peel.

BLACK BOTTOM LEMON PIE

Brand-new taste thrill—chocolate and lemon—you've no idea how good it is

Baked 9" pie shell
2   oz. semisweet chocolate
4   eggs, separated
¼   c. lemon juice
3   tblsp. water
1   tsp. lemon peel
1   c. sugar

• Melt chocolate over hot water. Spread evenly over bottom of cool pie shell.

• In top of double boiler, beat egg yolks until thick and lemon-colored. Add lemon juice and water, mixing well. Then stir in lemon peel and ½ c. sugar. Cook over hot (not boiling) water, stirring constantly, until thick,

about 12 minutes. Remove from hot water.

• Beat egg whites until frothy. Add remaining ½ c. sugar gradually, beating constantly until stiff, glossy peaks form. Fold half of this mixture into egg-yolk mixture. Pour over chocolate in pie shell.

• Spoon remaining egg-white mixture into pastry tube and make a lattice design on top of filling.

• Bake in slow oven (325°F.) 10 to 15 minutes, or until lightly browned. Cool on wire rack.

LEMON MERINGUE PIE SUPREME

Our best lemon pie for freezing from our Freezing & Canning Cookbook

Baked 9" pie shell
7   tblsp. cornstarch
1 ½ c. sugar
¼   tsp. salt
1 ½ c. hot water
3   egg yolks, beaten
2   tblsp. butter or margarine
1   tsp. grated lemon peel
½   c. fresh lemon juice
Meringue (3 egg whites)

• Mix cornstarch, sugar and salt in saucepan; gradually stir in hot water. Cook over direct heat, stirring constantly, until thick and clear, about 10 minutes.

• Remove from heat. Stir ½ c. hot mixture into yolks; stir this back into hot mixture. Cook over low heat; stirring constantly, 2 to 3 minutes. Remove from heat; stir in butter. Add lemon peel and juice, stirring until smooth. Cool. Pour into pie shell.

more

• Spread meringue on filling, making sure it touches inner edge of crust all around pie (see Perfect Meringue for Topping Pies, Chapter 9).
• Bake in moderate oven (350°F.) 15 minutes, or until delicately browned. Cool on wire racks.
• Place in freezer. When frozen, slip into plastic bag or wrap in moisture-vaporproof freezer material. Seal, label, date and return to freezer.
Recommended storage time: up to 1 month.
• To serve, remove from freezer 2 to 3 hours before serving.

A Pie to Remember

If you had the pleasure of visiting a grandmother who baked pies almost every day of the week, you'll need no introduction to Lemon Whey Pie. Old-time country cooks had the remarkable knack of using the foods in their kitchens—of avoiding waste. They salvaged the whey, left when making cottage cheese, in several dishes to extend the then scarce and more expensive lemon juice. And of all their whey concoctions, the meringue pie made with the clear, tart, yellow whey was the best.

The pie our recipe produces is a first cousin of lemon meringue pie. They look alike and have somewhat the same delicate taste, although whey imparts an indescribable fullness of flavor that appeals especially to some country people.

If you ever make fresh cottage cheese in your kitchen and have the whey, you may want to bake the pie the way old-fashioned cooks did with a pastry pie shell. Or you may prefer to pour the filling into a baked and cooled graham cracker crust. Broil the meringue-topped pie about 10" below the heat until the snowy peaks are tinged with gold. Be sure to cool Lemon Whey Pie away from drafts and then chill it before serving. At mealtime, grandmothers hurried to their beds of mint to get a few sprigs to garnish the tops of these pies—a trick you may want to follow if mint grows in your garden.

LEMON WHEY PIE

An old-fashioned FARM JOURNAL *favorite from* COUNTRY COOKBOOK

Baked 8" pie shell
1 ½ c. whey
1   c. sugar
3 ⅓ tblsp. cornstarch
2   eggs, separated
1 ½ tblsp. butter
½   tsp. salt
¼   c. lemon juice
1   tsp. grated lemon peel
Meringue (2 egg whites)

• Bring 1 c. whey to a boil. Mix sugar and cornstarch and add to remaining cold whey to make a smooth paste. Combine mixture with hot whey and cook until thick, stirring constantly.
• Combine thickened mixture with slightly beaten egg yolks, butter, salt, lemon juice and peel.
• Cook 2 minutes. Pour into pie shell.
• Top with meringue (see Perfect Me-

ringue for Topping Pies, Chapter 9) and bake in moderate oven (350°F.) 12 to 15 minutes. Cool away from drafts.

LEMON CHEESE PIE

Cheerful-looking, like sunshine in winter—lemon tang is refreshing

Crust:

1	c. sifted flour
½	tsp. salt
⅓	c. shortening
1	egg, slightly beaten
1	tblsp. lemon juice
1	tsp. grated lemon peel

Filling:

1 ¼	c. sugar
¼	c. cornstarch
1	c. water
1	tsp. grated lemon peel
⅓	c. lemon juice
2	eggs, separated
½	c. softened cream cheese (4 oz.)

Crust: Sift flour with salt; cut in shortening until mixture resembles coarse cornmeal. Combine egg with lemon juice and peel; sprinkle over flour mixture and mix lightly with fork until dough holds together. Roll out and fit into a 9″ pie pan; flute edge and prick over entire surface with a 4-tined fork. Bake in hot oven (400°F.) until pie shell is golden brown, about 12 minutes. Cool.

Filling: Combine 1 c. sugar with cornstarch; add water, lemon peel and juice, and egg yolks, slightly beaten. Stir until smooth. Cook, stirring constantly, until mixture thickens. Remove from heat and blend in cream cheese. Cool thoroughly.

• Beat egg whites until soft peaks form. Gradually add remaining ¼ c. sugar, beating until stiff peaks form. Slowly fold into lemon mixture. Turn into pie shell and chill thoroughly. Makes 6 or 8 servings.

Cut This Pie at the Table

Some pies are so pretty it's a shame to cut them in the kitchen. Lemon Fluff Pie is a wonderful example. Fluffy, gold-tipped meringue forms a collar around edge of pie, framing the pale-yellow filling in the center. Carry the dessert to the table and let everyone feast on its beauty while you cut the wedges. You'll enjoy watching the expressions of anticipation everyone has when your knife gets busy—the eager waiting to get into the act.

LEMON FLUFF PIE

Filling is light as a sunny cloud and it's just tart enough to please

Baked 9″ pie shell	
4	eggs
Grated peel of 1 lemon	
¼	c. fresh lemon juice
3	tblsp. water
1	c. sugar

• Separate eggs, putting whites in mixing bowl and yolks in top of double boiler.

• Beat yolks until thick, gradually stir in lemon peel and juice, water and ½ c. sugar. Cook over hot water until thickened, stirring constantly. Remove from hot water.

• Beat egg whites until stiff; beat in remaining ½ c. sugar (1 tblsp. at a time). Continue beating until whites are glossy and pile well.

• Fold half the whites into warm yolk mixture; when evenly blended, empty into pie shell, smoothing surface.

• Spoon remaining meringue to make a crown around edge of pie (make sure it touches crust).

• Bake in slow oven (325°F.) long enough to brown meringue lightly, about 15 minutes.

Mother-Daughter Lime Pies

A Midwestern farm woman, who went to Florida on vacation, returned home with a treasured recipe for Key West Lime Pie. She bakes the pie several times a year and says: "It tastes as good in our farm home as it did in its native, tropical setting. I think mine is even more attractive because I add a few drops of food color to tint the filling a pretty lime green."

She shared the prized recipe with her daughter, the mother of several young children, who bakes the pie for "occasions." But, ordinarily, she fixes a Short-Cut Lime Pie, with a no-cook filling. She says: "It's so much quicker and easier to make than Mother's kind."

Both recipes follow—they're typical of other recipes for traditional and short-cut versions that you'll find for other pies in this Cookbook. Around our Test Kitchens we often refer to them as Mother-Daughter recipes.

KEY WEST LIME PIE

Tropical pie has refreshing, tangy taste; a cool, lime-green filling

Baked 9″ pie shell
⅓   c. cornstarch
1 ½   c. sugar
¼   tsp. salt
1 ½   c. water
3   egg yolks, beaten
¼   c. fresh lime juice
1   tblsp. grated lime peel
Few drops green food color
Meringue (3 egg whites)

• Combine cornstarch, sugar and salt in saucepan; gradually add water, stirring until smooth. Bring to a boil over medium heat, stirring constantly, and boil 1 minute.

• Remove from heat and quickly add one half the hot mixture to the egg yolks, mixing well. Return to the hot mixture, blending thoroughly.

• Bring the mixture to a boil, stirring, over medium heat. Boil 1 minute longer.

• Remove from heat; stir in lime juice and peel and food color to make filling a delicate green. Pour into cool pie shell at once. Completely cover with meringue (see Perfect Meringue for Topping Pies, Chapter 9).

• Bake in moderate oven (350°F.) 12 to 15 minutes, or until meringue is golden. Cool on wire rack away from drafts, at least 1 hour before cutting.

SHORT-CUT LIME PIE

You can fix it in the morning and chill it to serve in the evening

Baked 8" pie shell
1 (15 oz.) can sweetened condensed milk
1 tsp. grated lime peel
⅓ c. lime juice
1 drop green food color
2 egg yolks
Meringue (2 egg whites)

• Combine sweetened condensed milk (not evaporated milk), lime peel and juice and food color; blend until smooth and thick. Stir in egg yolks and blend well.

• Pour into pastry shell and top with meringue (see Perfect Meringue for Topping Pies, Chapter 9).

• Bake in moderate oven (350°F.) 12 to 15 minutes, or until lightly browned. Cool away from drafts 2 to 3 hours before cutting.

SATINY FRESH COCONUT PIE

This special-occasion pie is worth the time and effort required to make

Baked 9" pie shell
1 c. sugar
½ c. cornstarch
¼ tsp. salt
3 c. milk, scalded
3 egg yolks, beaten
1½ tsp. vanilla
2 c. grated fresh coconut
1 c. heavy cream, whipped

• Combine sugar, cornstarch and salt in saucepan. Gradually add milk, stirring until mixture is smooth. Bring to a boil over medium heat, stirring constantly. Boil, stirring, 2 minutes. Remove from heat.

• Stir half of hot mixture into egg yolks; combine with rest of hot milk mixture in saucepan. Cook, stirring, over low heat until mixture boils and is thick enough to mound from spoon, about 5 minutes.

• Turn into bowl. Add vanilla and 1 c. coconut. Place waxed paper directly on filling and refrigerate at least 1 hour. Spread in pie shell and refrigerate at least 3 hours.

• To serve, spread with whipped cream and sprinkle with remaining coconut.

Note: Grate coconut by hand or cut coconut meat in small cubes and add, ¼ to ½ c. at a time, in blender bowl. Blend until fine.

FLAKED COCONUT PIE: Follow directions for Fresh Coconut Pie, substituting 2 (3½ oz.) cans flaked coconut for fresh coconut.

FRESH GRATED COCONUT PIE

Never-fail recipe for your party—custard is made with packaged mix

Partially baked 10″ pie shell
2   (3 ¼ oz.) pkgs. vanilla pudding mix
⅔   c. sugar
⅛   tsp. salt
2   eggs, well beaten
2 ½ c. milk
1   c. coconut milk
2   tblsp. butter
4   c. finely grated fresh coconut
1   tsp. almond extract
2   tblsp. sugar

• Combine pudding mix, ⅔ c. sugar and salt in top of double boiler. Stir in eggs, milk and coconut milk. Cook over boiling water until very thick. Add butter and 3 c. coconut; cook about 5 minutes longer. Remove from heat; add almond extract.
• Pour into warm pie shell, baked 4 to 5 minutes in very hot oven (450°F.). Reduce oven temperature to 425°.
• Sprinkle top of pie with remaining coconut mixed with 2 tblsp. sugar.
• Bake 20 minutes.

COCONUT PIE

Nutmeg makes the difference in this unusual, marvelous, all-coconut pie

Unbaked 9″ pie shell
4   egg whites
1   tsp. nutmeg
⅛   tsp. salt
2   tsp. vanilla extract
2   c. sifted confectioners sugar

1 ½ c. flaked coconut
2   c. milk, scalded
2   tblsp. butter or margarine

• In top of double boiler, combine 2 egg whites, nutmeg, salt, vanilla, sugar, coconut, milk and butter. Stir over hot (not boiling) water 5 minutes, or until mixture has slightly thickened (do not overcook). Remove from heat; cool to room temperature.
• Beat remaining 2 egg whites *only* until they stand in soft, stiff peaks (do not beat too stiff). Fold into cooled coconut mixture. Empty into pie shell.
• Bake in very hot oven (450°F.) 10 minutes; reduce heat to moderate (350°F.) and bake 30 to 40 minutes longer, or until filling is firm in center. Serve cold.

COCONUT MACAROON PIE

Country cupboards always have makings for this favorite, all-season pie

Unbaked 9″ pie shell
¼   c. chopped pecans (optional)
2   eggs, slightly beaten
½   c. water
1 ½ c. sugar
¼   c. flour
¼   tsp. salt
1   (3 ½ oz.) can flaked coconut (1 ⅓ c.)
½   c. butter or margarine, melted (1 stick)

• Sprinkle pecans over bottom of pie shell. Combine remaining ingredients; pour into pie shell.
• Bake in slow oven (325°F.) until golden brown, and almost set, about 45 minutes. Cool.

Fluffy Pineapple Pie

You may wander any place in this world in search of a beautiful, extra-delicious dessert to spring on guests, but you'll have a hard time surpassing this meringue pie. The secret is folding part of the meringue into the sunny-yellow, pineapple-scented and -flavored custard filling. It's a gorgeous tall pie, guaranteed to bring compliments to the cook.

FLUFFY PINEAPPLE PIE

Enchanting in appearance and taste

Baked 9" pie shell
1 ⅓ c. sugar
⅓ c. cornstarch
1 ⅔ c. canned pineapple juice
5 eggs, separated
2 tblsp. butter or margarine
½ tsp. salt
½ tsp. cream of tartar

• Blend ¾ c. sugar, cornstarch and pineapple juice together. Cook, stirring, until mixture begins to thicken. Continue cooking over low heat, stirring often, until mixture is clear and very thick, about 10 minutes. Blend a little of the hot mixture into egg yolks, well beaten. Return to hot pineapple mixture and cook 2 to 3 minutes longer. Remove from heat. Beat in butter. Cool.
• Beat egg whites, salt and cream of tartar until soft peaks form when beater is lifted. Gradually beat in remaining sugar until stiff peaks form.

• Gently fold about half the meringue mixture into cooled pineapple custard. Turn into pie shell.
• Swirl remaining meringue over top of pie, completely covering filling.
• Bake in moderate oven (350°F.) until lightly browned, about 15 minutes. Cool completely before cutting.

BANANA MERINGUE PIE

Pie cuts best if cooled 4 hours

Baked 9" pie shell
⅓ c. sifted flour
⅔ c. sugar
¼ tsp. salt
2 c. milk, scalded
3 eggs, separated
¼ c. butter or margarine
1 tsp. vanilla
3 medium bananas
Meringue (3 egg whites)

• Combine flour, sugar and salt in saucepan. Blend scalded milk in slowly. Cook, stirring constantly, over medium heat until mixture thickens and boils. Continue cooking and stirring 1 minute.
• Remove from heat and add a little hot mixture to beaten egg yolks. Quickly stir into mixture in saucepan. Return to medium heat and cook, stirring constantly, 3 minutes or until it thickens again and mounds slightly.
• Remove from heat and add butter and vanilla, stirring until butter is melted. Cool while you make meringue (see Perfect Meringues for Topping Pies, Chapter 9).   *more*

• Slice peeled firm bananas into pie shell, making an even layer. Pour luke-warm filling over bananas. Spoon meringue over filling and spread over top, making sure it touches inner edges of crust all around.

• Bake in moderate oven (350°F.) until peaks of meringue are golden brown, about 12 minutes.

GRAPEFRUIT CUSTARD PIE

Top of pie bakes to rich red-orange— filling is tasty and sweet-tart

Unbaked 9" pie shell
1   c. sugar
2 ½ tblsp. flour
1 ½ tblsp. soft butter or margarine
⅛   tsp. salt
3   eggs, separated
1   medium grapefruit
1   tsp. grated orange peel
1   c. light cream

• Combine sugar, flour, butter and salt in bowl; add egg yolks and mix thoroughly.

• Ream grapefruit; do not strain juice. You should have about 1 c. juice and pulp.

• Stir grapefruit juice into sugar mixture; add orange peel and light cream, mixing well.

• Beat egg whites until they form soft peaks when beater is lifted; fold into grapefruit mixture. Pour into pie shell.

• Bake in moderate oven (350°F.) until filling is set and browned on top, about 45 to 50 minutes. Cool on rack.

RHUBARB CUSTARD PIE

Tangy rhubarb in rich creamy custard is an early spring farm-style treat

Unbaked 9" pie shell
Filling:
1 ½ lbs. rhubarb (about 4 c.)
¾   c. sugar
2   tblsp. flour
1   tblsp. lemon juice
⅛   tsp. salt

Topping:
3   eggs
1   c. heavy cream
2   tblsp. butter or margarine, melted
¼   tsp. nutmeg
2   tblsp. sugar

Filling: In bowl, combine rhubarb, cut in ¼" slices, sugar, flour, lemon juice and salt. Toss to mix and turn into pie shell. Bake in hot oven (400°F.) 20 minutes.

Topping: Beat eggs slightly in bowl; stir in cream, butter and nutmeg to blend. Pour over hot rhubarb in pie shell.

• Bake 10 minutes; sprinkle with sugar. Bake 10 minutes more, or until pie's top is browned. Cool on rack before cutting.

RHUBARB-ORANGE CUSTARD PIE

One of FARM JOURNAL's *best recipes*

Pastry for 1-crust pie
3   eggs, separated
1 ¼ c. sugar
¼   c. soft butter or margarine
3   tblsp. frozen orange juice concentrate

¼ c. flour
¼ tsp. salt
2½ c. rhubarb, cut in ½" pieces
⅓ c. chopped pecans

• Beat egg whites until stiff; add ¼ c. sugar gradually, beating well after each addition.
• Add butter and juice concentrate to egg yolks; beat thoroughly. Add remaining 1 c. sugar, flour and salt; beat well.
• Add rhubarb to yolk mixture; stir well. Gently fold in meringue. Pour into pastry-lined 9" pie pan (make high-fluted rim); sprinkle with nuts.
• Bake in hot oven (400°F.) 40 to 50 minutes. Cool.

CUSTARD CRUNCH MINCE PIE

Excellent variation for mincemeat

Unbaked 9" pie shell
1 c. sugar
2 tblsp. flour
⅛ tsp. salt
3 eggs, slightly beaten
¼ c. butter or margarine, melted
½ c. chopped walnuts
1 c. prepared mincemeat

• Blend dry ingredients and slowly add to eggs. Add remaining ingredients; mix well.

• Pour into pastry and bake in hot oven (400°F.) 15 minutes. Reduce heat to 325°F. and bake 30 minutes.

QUINCE CUSTARD PIE

An old-time FARM JOURNAL *favorite from our* COUNTRY COOKBOOK

Unbaked 9" pie shell
2 large ripe quinces
½ c. sugar
1 tsp. lemon juice
¼ tsp. nutmeg
¼ tsp. cinnamon
2 tblsp. melted butter or margarine
3 eggs, separated
1 c. milk, scalded
Meringue (3 egg whites)

• Peel and quarter quinces. Cook, covered, in small amount of water, until tender; drain. Put through food mill (should yield 1 c.). Add sugar, lemon juice, nutmeg, cinnamon and butter.
• Beat egg yolks until thick; add milk. Add to quince mixture. Pour into pie shell.
• Bake in hot oven (400°F.) until custard sets, about 50 minutes.
• Top with meringue (see Perfect Meringue for Topping Pies, Chapter 9) and bake in moderate oven (350°F.) 12 to 15 minutes. Cool away from drafts.

Out-of-the-Cupboard Pie

If you have canned apricots and pears on your cupboard shelves, here's a fascinating pie you can bake for a refreshing surprise some frosty day.

The farm woman who shares the recipe calls it a Winter Pie. The sour cream custard is creamy and the fruit juicy and tasty.

APRICOT-PEAR PIE

Apricot halves in the lemon-yellow custard look like small harvest moons

Unbaked 9" pie shell
1 ½ c. drained apricot halves (1 lb. can)
1 ½ c. drained pear halves (1 lb. can)
¾ c. sugar
1 tblsp. flour
2 tblsp. butter or margarine
3 eggs
1 c. dairy sour cream
3 tblsp. lemon juice
2 tsp. grated lemon peel
Mace

• Arrange fruits (thoroughly drained) in bottom of pie shell, saving out 6 apricot halves.
• Combine sugar, flour and butter in bowl; blend in unbeaten eggs, beating well. Add sour cream, lemon juice and peel. Blend well.
• Pour over fruit in pie shell. Arrange apricot halves, cut side down and evenly spaced, on filling. Sprinkle lightly with mace.
• Bake in hot oven (400°F.) 30 minutes.

Chess and Nut Pies

Chess pies, of English descent, came first to plantation kitchens. Later, clever cooks came up with pecan pies. The appeal of the rich nut desserts is so great that women all over the country learned to make them, using the nuts that were most available in their neighborhoods—Missouri's Black-Walnut Pie, for instance. Usually, the pies are puffed up when taken from the oven, but the filling falls as it cools and has a jellylike consistency.

Peanuts are not nuts, but their name and the marvelous, inexpensive pies you can make with them (Farmer's Peanut Pie, to name one) entitles them to space in this Cookbook. The same goes for Oatmeal Pie, which some cooks call mock-nut pie. The oatmeal, when baked, has a texture and flavor that suggests nuts.

A farm-kitchen rule is never to package or store peanuts with other nuts. If you do, all the nuts will take on the peanut flavor.

Tree nuts are especially easy to freeze. Just see that they are clean. Wash them quickly and drain. Then crack the shells and remove the nuts. Pack them tightly in frozen-food containers or polyethylene bags of fairly heavy strength. They will keep up to a year stored at 0°F.

HEIRLOOM CHESS PIE

Southern-origin pie rich with farm foods—now it's enjoyed everywhere

Unbaked 9" pie shell
¼ c. butter
½ c. granulated sugar
1 c. brown sugar, firmly packed
⅛ tsp. salt
3 eggs
1 tsp. vanilla

2   tblsp. flour
½   c. cream
1   c. chopped pecans

• Cream butter. Add sugars and salt; cream thoroughly. Add eggs, one at a time, beating well after each addition. Stir in remaining ingredients.
• Pour mixture into pie shell.
• Bake in moderate oven (375°F.) until a silver knife inserted halfway between edge and center of filling comes out clean, about 40 to 50 minutes. Do not overbake. Serve slightly warm or cold.

PINEAPPLE CHESS PIE

Luxurious pie—butter, eggs and sour cream blend with pineapple in filling

Pastry for 1-crust pie
1   (13½ oz.) can pineapple chunks
1   tblsp. flour
½   c. butter
½   c. granulated sugar
½   c. brown sugar, firmly packed
2   tsp. vanilla
¼   tsp. salt
3   eggs
½   c. dairy sour cream
Whipped cream (optional)

• Line 9" pie pan with pastry, fluting edge. Prebake in hot oven (425°F.) 5 minutes. Remove from oven.
• Drain pineapple well; sprinkle with flour.
• Cream butter with sugars, vanilla and salt until fluffy. Beat in eggs, one at a time, until mixture is smooth. Stir in sour cream and pineapple. Filling may separate slightly, but it becomes smooth during baking.
• Turn into pie shell, mounding in center. Brown in slow oven (325°F.) 50 to 60 minutes. Remove from oven and cool thoroughly.
• When ready to serve, garnish pie with rim of whipped cream.

LEMON CHESS PIE

Shimmery and golden inside, nut brown on top—a state fair prizewinner

Unbaked 9" pie shell
2   c. sugar
1   tblsp. flour
1   tblsp. cornmeal
4   eggs
¼   c. butter, melted
¼   c. milk
4   tblsp. grated lemon peel
¼   c. lemon juice

• Combine sugar, flour and cornmeal in large bowl. Toss lightly with fork to mix. Add eggs, butter, milk, lemon peel and lemon juice. Beat with rotary or electric beater until smooth and thoroughly blended. Pour into pie shell.
• Bake in moderate oven (375°F.) 35 to 45 minutes, or until top is golden brown. Cut pie while warm.

Note: A thin layer of the filling originally was baked in tart shells. It's a strong-flavored sweet filling, and should be shallow. A topping of unsweetened whipped cream takes away some of the potency of the filling.

RAISIN CHESS PIE

California ranch cook adds raisins to chess pie with tasty results—try it

Unbaked 9″ pie shell
½ c. butter or margarine
1 c. sugar
¼ tsp. salt
3 eggs
1 c. chopped walnuts
1 c. chopped raisins
1 tsp. vanilla

• Cream butter, sugar and salt thoroughly. Add eggs, one at a time, beating well after each addition.
• Blend in walnuts, raisins and vanilla. Turn into pastry-lined pie pan.
• Bake in moderate oven (375°F.) 10 minutes. Reduce heat to 325°F. and bake 30 to 35 minutes longer.

Walnut Pie—Missouri Style

Missouri, especially in Ozark country, has more than its share of fabulous pie bakers. Anyone who lives or visits the beautiful hill section, knows how extra-good the nut pies are when made with native black walnuts. A farm homemaker in the "show me" state sent this recipe which produces a pie you'll be proud to serve and everyone will be delighted to eat.

BLACK-WALNUT PIE

So rich you can cut pie in 8 servings; so delicious no one will want you to

Unbaked 9″ pie shell
½ c. granulated sugar
½ c. brown sugar
1 c. light corn syrup
3 tblsp. butter or margarine
3 eggs, slightly beaten
1 c. chopped black walnuts
1 tblsp. granulated sugar
1 tblsp. flour

• Combine ½ c. granulated sugar, brown sugar and corn syrup in saucepan. Heat just to boiling. Remove from heat and add butter. Stir until butter melts.
• Gradually stir hot mixture into eggs. Stir in black walnuts.
• Combine 1 tblsp. sugar and flour. Sprinkle evenly over bottom of pastry-lined pie pan. Turn walnut mixture into pastry.
• Bake in moderate oven (350°F.) until top is browned, 45 to 50 minutes.

RAISIN BLACK-WALNUT PIE

Best seller in a Home Demonstration Club's booth at a Virginia county fair

Unbaked 9″ pie shell
3 eggs, beaten
¾ c. light brown sugar
¼ c. soft butter or margarine
1 c. dark corn syrup
½ c. crushed black walnuts
1 tsp. vanilla
1 c. seedless raisins

• Combine eggs, sugar and butter, beating until thick and fluffy. Add corn syrup; beat until fluffy. Add walnuts and vanilla; add raisins, beating gently.

• Turn into pie shell. Bake in moderate oven (375°F.) until firm in the center, 30 to 40 minutes.

BLENDER PECAN PIE

The easiest pecan pie to make and one of the best—a good freezer

Unbaked 8" pie shell
2   eggs
⅔   c. sugar
½   tsp. salt
½   c. light corn syrup
2   tblsp. butter or margarine, melted

1   tsp. vanilla
1   c. pecans
12 pecan halves

• Put eggs, sugar, salt, corn syrup, butter and vanilla in blender bowl and blend well.
• Add 1 c. pecans and blend just enough to chop nuts coarsely.
• Pour into pie shell. Place pecan halves on top.
• Bake in hot oven (425°F.) 15 minutes; reduce heat to 350°F. and continue baking until top is lightly browned, about 30 minutes.

Holiday Pie Has Sales Appeal

Here's a pie with a good sales record. For 25 years, it's been much in demand at the USDA cafeteria bake shop, especially during winter's holly season. Workers in the government offices like to buy these pies every year to tote home for holiday entertaining. The bakers have to hustle to fill all the orders.

One characteristic of the USDA Pecan Pie is that the luscious filling makes a fairly shallow layer. Washingtonians prefer it this way. They say it's too rich for a deep filling.

We begged the recipe for you. If you carry this pie to a church or other community supper or serve it to the family and friends, you'll get compliments on it. You can bake it in a 9" pie pan, if you wish, and use the surplus filling in two small tarts.

USDA PECAN PIE

You can make this your bake-sale special. It has sales appeal

Unbaked 10" pie shell
4   eggs
1   c. sugar
⅛   tsp. salt
1 ½ c. dark corn syrup
2   tblsp. plus 1 tsp. melted butter
1   tsp. vanilla
1   c. pecan halves

• Preheat oven to 350°F.
• Beat eggs just until blended, but not frothy. Add sugar, salt and corn syrup. Add cooled melted butter and vanilla, mixing just enough to blend.
• Spread nuts in bottom of pie shell. Pour in filling.   *more*

• Place pie in oven. Reduce heat to 325°F., at once. Bake 50 to 60 minutes. Makes 8 to 10 servings.

PECAN PUFF PIE

This puffy-topped, chocolate-nut pie deserves a place of honor in meals

Baked 9″ pie shell

Chocolate Filling:
1 (6 oz.) pkg. semisweet chocolate pieces
½ c. evaporated milk or light cream
½ tsp. vanilla

Pecan Meringue:
½ c. sifted flour
½ tsp. salt
4 egg whites
1 c. light brown sugar, firmly packed
1 c. chopped pecans
3 tblsp. melted butter or margarine
1 tsp. vanilla
½ c. pecan halves

Chocolate Filling: Place chocolate pieces in top of double boiler. Melt over hot water.
• Add evaporated milk and vanilla. Blend thoroughly.
• Spread in a layer over bottom of pie shell and fill with Pecan Meringue.
Pecan Meringue: Sift flour; measure; sift again with salt.
• Beat egg whites until they form soft peaks.
• Gradually add brown sugar, beating until it holds firm peaks.
• Fold in flour, chopped pecans, butter and vanilla.

• Spread over chocolate layer. Arrange pecan halves around edge of pie to make a wreath.
• Bake in slow oven (325°F.) 50 to 60 minutes. Cool. Serve with whipped cream or ice cream.

OATMEAL PIE

Many who eat this think it's pecan pie, it's so rich and luscious

Unbaked 9″ pie shell
¼ c. butter or margarine
½ c. sugar
½ tsp. cinnamon
½ tsp. cloves
¼ tsp. salt
1 c. dark corn syrup
3 eggs
1 c. quick-cooking rolled oats

• Cream together butter and sugar. Add cinnamon, cloves and salt. Stir in syrup.
• Add eggs, one at a time, stirring after each addition until blended. Stir in rolled oats.
• Pour into pie shell and bake in moderate oven (350°F.) about 1 hour, or until knife inserted in center of pie comes out clean.

Note: During baking, the oatmeal forms a chewy, "nutty" crust on top —pie is rich, delicately spiced.

ORANGE PECAN PIE

Orange flavor doesn't shout—just sings —in this rich plantation pie

Unbaked 9″ pie shell
1 c. sugar
1 tsp. salt

1 tblsp. flour
1 c. dark corn syrup
3 eggs, beaten until foamy
½ c. orange juice
1 tblsp. grated orange peel
1 ½ c. broken pecans

• Combine sugar, salt and flour. Add syrup, eggs, orange juice and peel.
• Stir in pecans and pour into pie shell. Bake in moderate oven (375°F.) 40 to 50 minutes, or until filling is set and pastry is browned.

DATE PECAN PIE

A FARM JOURNAL 5-star recipe

Unbaked 9" pie shell
1 c. dairy sour cream
3 eggs, beaten
1 c. sugar
1 tsp. cinnamon
¼ tsp. salt
¾ c. dates, cut in pieces
½ c. chopped pecans
Whipped cream or ice cream

• Combine sour cream, eggs, sugar and seasonings in a bowl; mix well. Add dates and pecans. (Put dates and nuts through food chopper to save time.) Blend well. Pour into pie shell.
• Bake in moderate oven (375°F.) 30 minutes, or until filling is set and browned. Serve spread with whipped cream or small scoops of vanilla ice cream. Makes 8 servings.

FARMER'S PEANUT PIE

Good-tasting, easy to make, inexpensive dessert men especially enjoy

Unbaked 10" pie shell
4 eggs

¼ tsp. salt
1 c. dark corn syrup
1 c. light corn syrup
2 tblsp. melted butter or margarine
1 c. salted peanuts

• With rotary or electric beater, medium speed, beat together eggs, salt and corn syrups. Add melted butter.
• Sprinkle peanuts over bottom of pie shell. Pour in egg mixture.
• Bake in moderate oven (350°F.) until lightly browned, 45 to 50 minutes. Cool thoroughly before serving. Makes 8 servings.

CHOCOLATE BITTERSWEET PIE

Chocolate favorite—satiny, smooth filling, extra-rich, extra-tasty

Baked 9" pie shell
1 (12 oz.) pkg. semisweet chocolate pieces
¼ c. milk
¼ c. sugar
⅛ tsp. salt
4 eggs, separated
1 tsp. vanilla
Whipped cream

• Combine chocolate, milk, sugar and salt in top of double boiler. Cook over hot water until mixture is blended and smooth. Cool slightly.
• Add egg yolks, one at a time, beating after each addition. Stir in vanilla. Beat egg whites until stiff peaks form. Fold into chocolate mixture, blending well. *more*

• Pour into cool pie shell. Let set at least 2 or 3 hours. To serve, spread with thin layer of whipped cream. Makes 8 to 10 servings.

SANTIAGO CHOCOLATE PIE

Cook's trick—fold nuts and raisins or dates into the whipped-cream topping

Baked 9″ pie shell

Filling:
3   squares unsweetened chocolate
3 ½ c. milk
⅔   c. sifted cake flour
¾   c. sugar
¾   tsp. salt
1   egg or 2 egg yolks
2   tblsp. butter or margarine
1 ½ tsp. vanilla

Topping:
½   c. heavy cream
2   tblsp. sugar
¼   c. chopped raisins or dates
¼   c. broken nuts

Filling: Combine chocolate and milk in top of double boiler. Cook over hot water until chocolate melts. Beat with a rotary beater until smoothly blended.
• Sift flour; measure; sift again with sugar and salt.
• Add a small amount of chocolate mixture, stirring until smooth. Return to double boiler and cook until thickened, stirring constantly. Then cook 10 minutes longer, stirring occasionally.
• Beat the whole egg or egg yolks. Add a little of hot mixture, stirring vigorously. Return to double boiler; cook 2 minutes, stirring constantly.
• Remove from boiling water. Add butter and vanilla. Cool slightly.
• Pour into pie shell. Chill.
Topping: Whip cream until slightly thick. Add sugar and whip until just stiff. Fold in raisins or dates and nuts. Spread over top of filling.

Note: Instead of whipped cream, the pie may be topped with meringue.

Postscript Pies

Here are four 2-crust cream pies signing off a chapter otherwise filled almost entirely with 1-crust specials. They're unusual and taste-rewarding— too good to miss.

DOUBLE CRUST LEMON PIE

Here's an updated version of the sunny lemon pie Mother used to make

Pastry for 2-crust pie
¼   c. cornstarch
¼   c. water
1 ½ c. boiling water
1 ½ c. sugar
2   tblsp. grated lemon peel
1   tblsp. butter or margarine
2   eggs, slightly beaten
¼   c. lemon juice

• Blend cornstarch with ¼ c. water. Add boiling water. Cook and stir over medium heat until mixture comes to a boil and is very thick and clear. Add sugar, lemon peel and butter. Cool.

• Stir in eggs and lemon juice. Turn into pastry-lined 9″ pie pan. Adjust top crust, flute edges and cut vents.
• Bake in moderate oven (375°F.) for 30 minutes, then in hot oven (425°F.) until top of pie is golden, 5 to 10 minutes. Cool on rack before serving.

DOUBLE SURPRISE LEMON PIE

Unusual—fresh-tasting lemon slices in filling and sugared top crust

Pastry for 2-crust pie
1 ¼ c. sugar
  2 tblsp. flour
  ⅛ tsp. salt
  ¼ c. butter or margarine
  3 eggs
  1 tsp. grated lemon peel
  1 medium lemon
  ½ c. water
  2 tsp. sugar
  ½ tsp. cinnamon

• Combine 1¼ c. sugar, flour and salt. Cream butter until soft and blend with sugar mixture.
• Add 3 well-beaten eggs, reserving 1 tsp. egg white for topping.
• Grate lemon peel; then peel lemon, discarding white membrane. Cut lemon in paper-thin slices (should be ⅓ c.). Add lemon peel and slices and water to sugar mixture. Pour into pastry-lined 8″ pie pan.
• Adjust top crust, flute edges and cut vents. Brush with reserved egg white and sprinkle with mixture of sugar and cinnamon.
• Bake in hot oven (400°F.) 30 to 35 minutes, or until pie is golden.

SQUARE LEMON PIE

Choice combination—coconut pastry and tangy, tart-sweet lemon filling

Coconut Pastry:
  1 c. sifted flour
  1 tsp. baking powder
  1 c. sugar
  ⅛ tsp. salt
  1 c. flaked coconut
  ½ c. butter or margarine

Filling:
  ½ tsp. unflavored gelatin
  2 tblsp. water
  1 lemon, juice and grated peel
  ⅔ c. sugar
  2 eggs, slightly beaten
  1 tblsp. butter or margarine

Pastry: Sift together flour, baking powder, sugar and salt. Mix in coconut. Cut in butter until mixture resembles coarse crumbs.
Filling: Add gelatin to water. Combine lemon juice (there should be ¼ c.), lemon peel (1 tsp.), sugar and eggs in saucepan. Cook over low heat, stirring constantly, until mixture is thick. Remove from heat. Add butter and softened gelatin; stir until gelatin is dissolved. Chill.
• Press half of pastry mixture into a well-greased 9″ square pan. Spread cold lemon filling on top. Then sprinkle reserved half of pastry mixture on top, distributing it evenly.
• Bake in moderate oven (375°F.) until lightly browned, about 25 minutes. Makes 9 servings.

2-Crust Nut Pie Marvel

Call this dessert a pie or tart, which-ever you prefer. It's a joy both to the hostess and to her guests, especially if they're fond of almonds. Different and distinctive. Better have pencils and pa-per ready for your guests—they'll want to copy the recipe for Sugar Custard Pie to make for parties.

SUGAR CUSTARD PIE

Almond fans rave about this unusual pie with its shallow, rich filling

Crust:
- 1   c. sifted flour
- ¼   tsp. salt
- ½   c. butter
- 1   egg

Filling:
- 2   eggs
- 1   c. sugar
- 1   tsp. vanilla
- ¼   tsp. almond extract
- 1   c. sliced blanched almonds, lightly toasted

Crust: Sift flour and salt into mixing bowl. Cut in butter until particles are fine. Beat egg slightly and add to flour-butter mixture. Toss with fork to blend. Gather into ball and knead lightly. Divide into 2 balls, one slightly larger than the other. Chill 15 min-utes.

Filling: Beat eggs for filling until light; gradually add sugar, beating until mix-ture is light and thick. Beat in vanilla and almond extract. Fold in almonds.
• Line 9″ pie pan with larger ball of dough rolled 1½″ larger than pie pan. Turn custard filling into it. Adjust top crust (remaining ball of dough, rolled), flute edges and prick entire surface with 4-tined fork to prevent dough from bulging during baking. (Sprinkle top with a little sugar, about 1 tsp., if desired.)
• Bake in moderate oven (350°F.) un-til golden brown, about 30 minutes. Serve cool or warm. Makes 8 servings.

REFRIGERATOR AND ICE CREAM PIES

Here's a whole chapter of dessert beauties—pie recipes to delight the hostess. You will find great variety when you leaf through the pages—both in the fillings and the crusts. And you will notice that they have one thing in common: They are pies you make ahead and chill before serving.

The refrigerator pie family is large. Chiffon pies with their billows of fluffy filling in crisp crumb, pastry, coconut and other kinds of crusts, are universal favorites. With a can of mandarin oranges in your cupboard, for instance, you can make a gorgeous chiffon pie on short notice—our Golden Nugget Orange Pie. Bavarian pies, with whipped cream folded into their fruity fillings, are among the many refrigerator specials that contain gelatin.

Ice cream pies—so popular on the farm now that home freezers make ice cream available all the time—get special attention in this book. They can be as simple as Strawberry Social Ice Cream Pie or as elaborate as the Alaska pies with ice cream in a crust topped with a tall meringue and frozen for quick browning at mealtime. Do try our Lemon-Layered Alaska Pie and enjoy its enthusiastic reception. Feast your family and friends on the other glamorous lemon pies, including the one made with pink lemonade, which we've nicknamed Fourth of July Pie.

You'll marvel at our fabulous collection of chocolate pies—Chocolate Pie Spectacular, to name one, with flecks of shaved chocolate in the filling and chocolate sauce drizzled on top. And look at the angel pies with their crunchy meringue crusts and fillings out-of-this-world, as angel pies should be. Notice the cheese pies to make in home kitchens—worthy rivals of those made by professional hotel chefs.

Many of these picture pies create a sensation and will make you famous for your desserts. Some of the fanciest take time to make, but can be made at your convenience—hours, and in some instances, days before dinner.

Chiffon Pies—Light as Sea Foam

Chiffon pies need no introduction to farm cooks—they know how beautiful and refreshing the dessert can be. And they have worked out rules for making these pretty pies.

The first step is to dissolve gelatin and sugar in fruit juice or other liquid over heat. The next is to chill the mixture until it mounds slightly when dropped from a spoon. Test frequently. Then it's time to beat egg whites until they form glistening, stiff peaks and fold them into the gelatinized filling. If this mixture mounds, spoon it into the crust; if it doesn't, chill it briefly to the mounding stage. The secret of fluffy chiffon pies is not to let the gelatin mixture get too firm before folding in egg whites (and whipped cream, if it is used). Chill pie until firm before cutting.

Many chiffon pies go to the country table crowned with whipped cream. If you want to freeze a chiffon pie, do not add whipped cream until serving time. Freeze the unwrapped pie until firm and then place it in a freezer bag or enclose it in freezer wrap; label, date and return to freezer. To serve, unwrap pie and let it stand in food compartment of refrigerator from 1 to 1½ hours.

Note: Use egg whites from washed, uncracked eggs for making chiffon pies (and other dishes in which the egg whites are not cooked). Refrigerate the pies immediately after they're made. Heed these precautions to avoid the possibility of salmonellosis, food poisoning caused by food-borne bacteria, sometimes via raw whites from cracked or unclean eggs.

LEMON CHIFFON PIE

Refreshing dessert after a heavy meal

9" Graham Cracker Crumb Crust (Chapter 2)
1 envelope unflavored gelatin
1 c. sugar
⅛ tsp. salt
4 eggs, separated
⅓ c. lemon juice
⅔ c. water
1 tsp. grated lemon peel
½ c. heavy cream, whipped

• Combine gelatin, ½ c. sugar and salt; mix well. Beat egg yolks, lemon juice and water together. Stir into gelatin mixture and cook, stirring constantly, over medium heat about 5 minutes, or until mixture just comes to a boil.

• Remove from heat, stir in lemon peel and chill until mixture is partially set. Stir occasionally while chilling.

• Beat egg whites until soft peaks form; then beat in the remaining ½ c. sugar gradually. Continue beating until stiff peaks form. Fold into lemon mixture.

• Spoon into pie shell. Chill several hours, or until set. At serving time, spread with whipped cream (sweeten lightly with confectioners sugar, if desired) and garnish with shaved chocolate or chocolate candy shot (jimmies).

FRESH RASPBERRY CHIFFON PIE

A pie with cool, billowy filling that refreshes on sultry summer days

Baked 9" pie shell
1 ½ envelopes unflavored gelatin
¼ c. water
4 eggs, separated
1 tblsp. lemon juice
¾ c. sugar
2 pts. fresh raspberries
⅛ tsp. salt
¾ c. heavy cream, whipped

• Soften gelatin in cold water.
• Combine egg yolks, lemon juice and ½ c. sugar in small saucepan. Heat slowly, stirring constantly, until mixture is thickened slightly, and coats the back of a metal spoon. Remove from heat and add softened gelatin to the hot mixture; stir to dissolve.
• Put 1½ pts. raspberries through a sieve to make a purée (you should have 1 c. purée). Stir into gelatin mixture and cool until it mounds slightly when dropped from a spoon. (Do not let it get too firm.)
• Beat egg whites with salt until frothy. Gradually beat in remaining ¼ c. sugar and continue beating until meringue is stiff and shiny, but not dry.
• Fold into raspberry mixture along with whipped cream, reserving about one third of the whipped cream. Pour into pie shell and chill a few hours.
• To serve, decorate with remaining whipped cream and berries.

VARIATION

FROZEN RASPBERRY CHIFFON PIE: Substitute 1 (10 oz.) pkg. frozen raspberries for fresh raspberries.

APPLESAUCE CHIFFON PIE

Something new made with applesauce —pie with light, richly spiced filling

9" Graham Cracker Crumb Crust (Chapter 2)
1 envelope unflavored gelatin
¼ c. water
2 eggs, separated
½ c. sugar
¼ tsp. salt
¼ tsp. nutmeg
⅛ tsp. cinnamon
⅛ tsp. ginger
1 ¼ c. thick applesauce
1 ¼ c. milk
1 tblsp. lemon juice
Whipped cream (optional)

• Soften gelatin in water.
• Beat egg yolks; add 2 tblsp. sugar, salt, nutmeg, cinnamon, ginger, applesauce and milk. Cook over hot water until mixture thickens, about 15 minutes.
• Remove from heat, add gelatin and stir until it dissolves. Cool. Add lemon juice.
• Beat egg whites until frothy; gradually add remaining 6 tblsp. sugar, beating until glistening, stiff peaks form.
• Fold into applesauce mixture and chill until it mounds a little when dropped from a spoon.
• Spoon into pie shell and chill until firm. Serve garnished with whipped cream or, if you prefer, save out some of the crumb mixture when making Graham Cracker Crumb Crust and sprinkle over top of pie.

FARMSTEAD EGGNOG PIE

Festive pie on light side to serve at end of a hearty holiday dinner

Baked 9″ Graham Cracker Crumb
    Crust (Chapter 2)
  1 envelope unflavored gelatin
  ½ c. sugar
  ⅛ tsp. salt
  3 eggs, separated
1 ¼ c. light cream
  1 tsp. vanilla
  ½ tsp. nutmeg
Whipped cream (optional)

• Combine gelatin, ¼ c. sugar and salt.
• Beat egg yolks, stir in cream and gelatin mixture. Cook in double boiler over hot, not boiling, water, stirring constantly, until mixture coats metal spoon (about 12 minutes). Remove from heat, stir in vanilla and cool until mixture mounds when dropped from a spoon. Beat just enough to make smooth.
• Beat egg whites until frothy; gradually add remaining ¼ c. sugar, beating until glossy, stiff peaks form. Fold into gelatin mixture. Pour into crust and sprinkle with nutmeg. Chill until set. Serve topped with whipped cream.

VARIATIONS

STRAWBERRY FLUFF PIE: Fold 1 c. ripe strawberries, sliced, into filling. Garnish pie with whipped cream and berries.

BANANA FLUFF PIE: Line crust with sliced bananas before pouring in the filling.

COCONUT FLUFF PIE: Fold ½ c. flaked coconut and ½ c. heavy cream, whipped, into filling. Omit nutmeg.

EGGNOG PIE GLACÉ: Just before serving, spread top of pie with whipped cream and drizzle on melted currant or other tart, colorful jelly.

ORANGE DREAM PIE

Tawny toasted coconut rings the top of billowy yellow-gold filling

Baked 9″ pie shell
 1 envelope unflavored gelatin
 ¾ c. sugar
 ⅛ tsp. salt
 1 c. hot water
 3 eggs, separated
 1 (6 oz.) can frozen orange juice
    concentrate
 2 tblsp. lemon juice
 3 tblsp. toasted coconut

• Combine gelatin and ½ c. sugar and salt in top of double boiler. Add hot water and stir over boiling water until gelatin is dissolved. Stir gradually into beaten egg yolks. Return to double boiler and cook, stirring constantly, until mixture thickens and coats metal spoon.
• Remove from heat and add orange juice concentrate and lemon juice. Chill until mixture starts to set.
• Beat egg whites until frothy. Add remaining ¼ c. sugar gradually and continue beating until stiff peaks form. Beat orange mixture until stiff peaks form. Fold egg whites into orange mixture. Turn into pie shell; sprinkle coconut around edge of pie for decorative touch. Chill several hours.

Note: Substitute a coconut pie shell (see Chapter 2) for baked pie shell.

3/4 c. sugar
1/8 tsp. salt
1/2 c. heavy cream, whipped
1/4 c. flaked coconut

Gorgeous Mandarin-Orange Pie

This golden pie is a real beauty. The bright pieces of fruit in a sunny yellow custard make it a picture pie. And while this one needs no fancy trim, it's surprising how pompons of whipped cream, sprinkled with shreds or flakes of coconut and garnished with a few orange segments transform the pie into a special-occasion treat.

The small oranges, of Chinese origin, are deep orange in color. Most of the supply in our supermarkets is canned in Japan. Their miniature segments add both flavor and brightness to salads and desserts. They're a beautiful garnish.

Toasted coconut makes an unusual, appealing trim, but the fluffy, white coconut also is attractive. Now that you can buy toasted coconut in packages, it's easy to use. Just keep it in the cupboard near a can of mandarin oranges and you'll have the makings for this marvelous tasting pie at your finger tips.

• To syrup from drained mandarins add enough water to make 1 c.
• Soften gelatin in 1/4 c. cold water.
• Beat egg yolks until light and fluffy; stir in sugar, salt and orange syrup mixture. Cook until thickened, stirring constantly. Add softened gelatin and stir until it is dissolved. Cool.
• Reserve several mandarin segments (at least 6) for garnishing. Cut remaining segments in small pieces and fold gently into custard mixture.
• Beat egg whites until they form soft peaks; fold into fruit-custard mixture. Pour into cool pie shell. Chill until set.
• To serve, top each wedge of pie with a spoonful of whipped cream and at least one reserved mandarin segment. Sprinkle with coconut. You can sweeten whipped cream with 1 tblsp. sugar, if you like.

MANDARIN-APRICOT PIE

Guaranteed to brighten any meal with festive color and tasty flavor blend

2   tblsp. butter or margarine
2   c. flaked coconut
1   (11 oz.) can mandarin oranges, drained
2   c. apricot nectar
1   (6 oz.) pkg. lemon flavor gelatin, or 2 (3 oz.) pkgs.
1/2 c. heavy cream, whipped

• Spread butter evenly on bottom and sides of 9" pie pan. Pat coconut

GOLD NUGGET ORANGE PIE

A light, tall, fluffy and handsome chiffon pie that tastes wonderful

Baked 9" pie shell
1   (11 oz.) can mandarin oranges, drained
1   tblsp. lemon juice
1   envelope unflavored gelatin
1/4 c. cold water
4   eggs, separated

evenly in pan to make a pie shell. Bake in slow oven (300°F.) 15 to 20 minutes, or until coconut is delicately toasted. Cool.

• Meanwhile, measure syrup drained from mandarins. Add it to apricot nectar. Add enough water to make 3 c. Bring juices to a boil and dissolve gelatin in hot mixture. Cool; then chill until mixture starts to thicken. Fold in mandarin segments, reserving a few for garnishing. Pour mixture into cool pie shell and refrigerate until firm.

• To serve, garnish with reserved mandarin segments and dollops of whipped cream.

CHERRY CHIFFON PIE

Pink and pretty—uses canned cherries

Baked 9″ pie shell
2   tsp. unflavored gelatin
2   tblsp. cold water
1   (1 lb. 4 oz.) can tart cherries
4   eggs, separated
¼   tsp. salt
¾   c. sugar
1 ½ tsp. grated lemon peel
Whipped cream (optional)

• Soften gelatin in water. Drain cherries, reserving juice. Beat egg yolks and add juice from cherries (¾ c.), salt and ½ c. sugar. Cook over low heat until thickened, stirring constantly. Stir in softened gelatin and stir until it is dissolved. Cool slightly and add lemon peel and drained cherries (1½ c.).

• Beat egg whites until soft peaks form when beater is lifted. Gradually add remaining ¼ c. sugar, 2 tblsp. at a time, beating thoroughly after each

addition. Beat until stiff peaks form. Fold into gelatin mixture. Pile lightly in pie shell and chill until firm.

• When ready to use, garnish each serving with whipped cream.

SOUR CREAM PUMPKIN PIE

Add excitement to party refreshments with this tasty layered pumpkin pie

Baked 9″ pie shell
1   envelope unflavored gelatin
¼   c. cold water
3   eggs, separated
⅓   c. granulated sugar
1 ¼ c. pumpkin purée, canned or homemade
½   c. dairy sour cream
½   tsp. salt
1   tsp. cinnamon
¼   tsp. cloves
¼   tsp. nutmeg
¼   tsp. ginger
¼   c. granulated sugar
1   c. heavy cream, whipped
1   c. sifted confectioners sugar
1   tsp. vanilla, or ½ tsp. vanilla and ½ tsp. rum extract
½   c. chopped pecans

• Soften gelatin in water.

• Beat egg yolks with ⅓ c. sugar until thick and lemon-colored. Add pumpkin, sour cream, salt and spices. Cook over medium heat, stirring constantly, until mixture comes to a boil. Reduce heat and cook 2 minutes, stirring constantly. Remove from heat and stir in softened gelatin. Stir until gelatin is dissolved. Cool.

• Beat egg whites until frothy; add ¼ c. sugar gradually, beating until

stiff peaks form and sugar is dissolved. Fold into pumpkin mixture.
• To whipped cream, add confectioners sugar and vanilla, mixing well.
• Spoon half of pumpkin mixture into cool pie shell; then spread half of whipped cream mixture on top. Repeat. Sprinkle with pecans. Chill at least 2 hours before serving. Makes 8 servings.

Short-Cut and Traditional Chiffon Pies

In any beauty contest for chiffon pies, color-gay apricot, orange and lime entries would have a good chance of winning prizes. They're lovely to look at when made either by the short-cut or traditional method. And they're refreshing.

Today's clever cooks often have two sets of recipes, one to use when they're busy and minutes are short, the other for traditional "from scratch" when there's less rush. Here are three pies with two recipes for each. The quick versions are from our TIMESAVING COOKBOOK. We reprint them in this chapter along with the traditional recipes so you can make the pie that fits best into the time you have to fix the dessert.

Try each of the six pies and compare them! See whether your family can tell the difference.

TRADITIONAL APRICOT CHIFFON PIE

Filling the color of sunset clouds—reprinted from TIMESAVING COOKBOOK

Baked 9" pie shell
½ lb. dried apricots (1 ½ c.)
1 ½ c. water
1 c. sugar

1 envelope unflavored gelatin
4 egg yolks, slightly beaten
2 tblsp. lemon juice
4 egg whites
½ tsp. cream of tartar
⅛ tsp. salt
¼ tsp. almond extract
Toasted coconut

• Soak apricots in water 1 hour; cook, covered, until tender; drain. Put through food mill or sieve to make 1 c. purée.
• Blend together ½ c. sugar, gelatin, egg yolks, lemon juice and apricot purée; cook until mixture comes to boil. Cool by setting pan in cold water until mixture mounds slightly when dropped from spoon.
• Beat egg whites, cream of tartar and salt until frothy. Gradually add remaining ½ c. sugar and extract; beat until stiff and glossy. Fold into cool apricot mixture. Pile into pie shell, swirling top. Chill several hours. Garnish with drifts of toasted coconut.

VARIATIONS

Make the following as you would Apricot Chiffon Pie, omitting apricots, water and lemon juice: *more*

LIME PIE: Blend ½ c. sugar, gelatin, ⅔ c. water and ⅓ c. lime juice with yolks. Add 1 tblsp. grated lime peel and 3 or 4 drops green food color before cooling. Fold into egg white mixture.

ORANGE PIE: Blend ½ c. sugar, gelatin and 1 c. orange juice with yolks as directed in Lime Pie. Add 1 tblsp. grated orange peel and, if desired, red and yellow food color before cooling, to step up orange color. Fold into egg white mixture. Garnish with shredded orange peel.

SHORT-CUT APRICOT CHIFFON PIE

Double-quick to make and tasty, too

Baked 9″ pie shell
1   (3 oz.) pkg. lemon chiffon pie filling
½   c. boiling water
1   c. apricot nectar
⅛   tsp. almond extract
Red and yellow food color
⅓   c. sugar
Toasted coconut

• Thoroughly dissolve pie filling in water. Beat in nectar, almond extract and 3 drops each of the two food colors (makes orange hue). Add sugar and beat until mixture stands in peaks.
• Pile filling into pie shell; swirl top. Chill until set. Garnish with coconut. (You can buy packaged toasted coconut.)

VARIATIONS

Thoroughly dissolve lemon chiffon pie filling in ½ c. boiling water, and proceed as follows:

SHORT-CUT LIME PIE: Beat in ¼ c. each frozen limeade concentrate and cold water; add 4 drops green food color. Add ⅓ c. sugar; beat until mixture stands in peaks. Spoon filling into pie shell; swirl top. Chill until set.

SHORT-CUT ORANGE PIE: Beat in juice of 1 orange plus cold water to make ½ c.; add 1 tsp. grated orange peel and 3 or 4 drops red food color. Add ⅓ c. sugar; beat until peaks form. Spoon filling into pie shell; swirl top. Chill until set. Garnish with shredded peel from ½ orange.

Lemon Accents Superior Flavors

Country pie bakers have the lemon habit—it's a touch of genius they rely on to produce extra-good eating. They add lemon juice or grated peel—sometimes both—to many pie fillings to enhance flavors. When you are looking at recipes in this book, notice the frequency with which lemon appears in the list of ingredients. Lemons have the remarkable ability of bringing out the best taste in many foods, including other fruits.

It's the reason many farm women keep cans of frozen lemonade concentrate in their freezers. The custard in the two recipes, Lemon Coconut and Fruit Cocktail Pies, owes its marvelous taste to the frozen concentrate. Both pies are handsome. And in both of them the tangy lemon taste glorifies the coconut and canned fruit cocktail.

LEMON COCONUT PIE

Lemon-flavored custard is creamy—smooth, fluffy, delicate and tasty

Baked 9" pie shell
1   envelope unflavored gelatin
½   c. cold water
3   eggs, separated
⅛   tsp. salt
1   (6 oz.) can frozen lemonade concentrate (⅔ c.)
½   c. sugar
1   c. flaked or shredded coconut

• In top of double boiler, soften gelatin in water. Add egg yolks, slightly beaten, and salt. Place over boiling water and cook, stirring constantly, until mixture thickens, about 7 minutes. Remove from heat and stir in unthawed frozen lemonade. Stir until mixture thickens. (The custard usually sets fast and needs no chilling.)
• Beat egg whites to soft peaks; stir in sugar, 2 tblsp. at a time, beating well after each addition. Beat until stiff peaks form. Fold into gelatin mixture; then fold in coconut, reserving a little to sprinkle on top of pie. Drop a spoonful of mixture into pie shell. It should mound. If it doesn't, chill, stirring a few times, until it will mound. Turn into pie shell and chill pie until firm before cutting.

FRUIT COCKTAIL PIE: Omit coconut in Lemon Coconut Pie and add canned fruit cocktail instead. Drain 1 (1 lb.) can fruit cocktail. You will have about 1½ c. fruit. Save out a little of it to make a wreath on top of pie at serving time; fold remainder of fruit cocktail into pie filling.

SILVER CREAM PIE

A different lemon pie—a dessert that makes friends and wins compliments

Baked 9" pie shell
4   eggs, separated
1   c. sugar
1   lemon, juice and grated peel
½   envelope unflavored gelatin (1½ tsp.)
¼   c. cold water
Whipped cream

• Beat egg yolks with ½ c. sugar and lemon juice and peel. Cook in double boiler until thick and creamy, stirring constantly.
• Soften gelatin in water; then stir into hot lemon mixture until it is dissolved. Cool.
• Beat egg whites until frothy, then gradually add remaining ½ c. sugar, beating until stiff; fold in gelatin mixture. Pour into pie shell and chill 2 hours or longer.
• To serve, garnish, if desired, with whipped cream and sprinkle with silver dragées or grated unsweetened chocolate.

DOUBLE-LEMON AMBROSIA PIE

Layer of fluffy white is topped with deeper lemon yellow—a glamorous pie

Coconut Butter Crust:
⅓   c. soft butter
1   egg yolk
1   c. sifted flour
1   (3½ oz.) can flaked coconut (1¼ c.)
more

Filling:

1 ⅓   c. sugar
1 ¼   c. water
½   tsp. salt
⅓   c. cornstarch
¼   c. water
2   eggs, separated
⅓   c. lemon juice
2   tblsp. butter
1   tsp. grated lemon peel
1   envelope unflavored gelatin
¼   c. cold water
1   c. light cream

Crust: Cream butter and egg yolk together. Add flour, mixing thoroughly. Work coconut into dough.
• Pat mixture into 9″ pie pan, bringing up on sides and fluting edge. Chill 30 minutes.
• Bake in moderate oven (350°F.) 25 to 30 minutes, or until light brown.

Filling: Combine sugar, 1¼ c. water and salt in saucepan; heat to boiling. Combine cornstarch and ¼ c. water to make smooth paste; add to boiling mixture gradually, stirring constantly and cooking until thick and clear. Remove from heat.
• Combine slightly beaten egg yolks and lemon juice; add to thickened mixture and stir well. Return to heat and cook, stirring constantly, until mixture bubbles again. Remove from heat. Stir in butter and lemon peel. Take out 1 c. filling and set aside.
• Soften gelatin in ¼ c. water; add to remaining filling, stirring until dissolved. Stir in light cream. Refrigerate until mixture begins to set. Beat until mixture is smooth.

• Beat egg whites to form stiff peaks. Fold into refrigerator-cooled and thickened lemon mixture. Pour into cooled pie shell. Refrigerate until set. Then spread reserved cup of filling over top. Refrigerate until serving time.

LEMON-PLUS PIE

Orange and lemon flavors share honors in this make-ahead treat

Baked 9″ pie shell
1   envelope unflavored gelatin
¼   c. cold water
4   eggs, separated
½   c. lemon juice
3   tblsp. orange juice
¾   c. sugar
¼   tsp. salt
1   tsp. grated lemon peel
⅔   c. sugar
⅔   c. heavy cream

• Soften gelatin in water.
• In top of double boiler, beat egg yolks until thick and lemon-colored. Add juices and mix well. Stir in sugar and salt. Cook over hot (not boiling) water until slightly thickened (about 10 minutes). Remove from heat; stir in lemon peel and gelatin. Chill until mixture begins to set (about 1 hour). Beat until smooth.
• Beat egg whites until frothy. Gradually add ⅔ c. sugar, beating until glossy peaks are formed.
• Whip cream and fold into egg whites. Then fold into thickened lemon mixture. Spoon into cool pie shell. Refrigerate several hours before serving.

PINK LEMONADE PIE

Pink of perfection—this delicious, un-usual refrigerator cream pie

8" Vanilla Wafer Crumb Crust
   (Chapter 2)
1 (6 oz.) can frozen pink lemonade concentrate
¾ c. water
1 envelope unflavored gelatin
¼ c. sugar
1 c. heavy cream
Few drops of red food color
¼ c. vanilla wafer crumbs

• Chill crumb crust.
• Thaw lemonade and combine with ½ c. water.
• Soften gelatin in remaining ¼ c. water; dissolve over hot water.
• Add dissolved gelatin and sugar to lemonade; stir until sugar dissolves. Chill until mixture is thick but not set (about 1 hour).
• Whip thickened gelatin mixture until light and fluffy. Then whip cream and fold into lemon mixture. Add food color to make mixture a delicate pink. Pour into chilled crust. Sprinkle with ¼ c. wafer crumbs. Chill.

PINEAPPLE POSY PIE

Yellow flowers with cherry centers trim this pie that's gay as a festival

9" Graham Cracker Crumb Crust
   (Chapter 2)
1 (6 oz.) can frozen pineapple
   juice concentrate
1 envelope unflavored gelatin
¼ c. cold water
4 egg yolks, beaten until thick and
   creamy

½ c. sugar
¼ tsp. salt
2 tblsp. finely grated orange peel
4 egg whites
¼ c. sugar
⅔ c. heavy cream, whipped

• Thaw pineapple juice and simmer until it is reduced to ½ c. (or until the total is ⅓ less). Cool.
• Soften gelatin in water at least 5 minutes.
• Add egg yolks to pineapple juice; add gelatin and ½ c. sugar. Place in double boiler. Cook 10 minutes, stirring often. Remove from heat. Add salt and orange peel. Mix well and chill until mixture thickens, but do not let it set. It usually takes about 45 minutes.
• Beat egg whites until frothy, then gradually add ¼ c. sugar while continuing to beat. Beat until stiff peaks form. Fold in whipped cream. Fold egg white mixture into pineapple filling and spoon into cool pie shell.
• At serving time, garnish, if desired, with 6 pineapple flowers. To make flower, arrange 5 drained pineapple tidbits around a maraschino cherry.

Note: A coconut pie shell may be used instead of the crumb crust. See recipe for Coconut Pie Shell (Chapter 2).

PINK RHUBARB PIE

For dieting pie eaters—nonfat dry milk substitutes for whipped cream

Baked 9" low-calorie pie shell
   (Chapter 2)   *more*

Filling:
3   c. (½″ cubes) fresh rhubarb (about 1 lb.)
¼   c. water
¼   c. sugar
1   (3 oz.) pkg. strawberry flavor gelatin
¼   c. ice water
¼   c. nonfat dry milk

Topping:
¼   c. ice water
1   tblsp. lemon juice
½   tsp. vanilla
¼   c. nonfat dry milk
Banana

Filling: Combine rhubarb, water and sugar in saucepan; cover and cook about 5 minutes, or until rhubarb is just tender, but a little firm. There should be 2 c. cooked rhubarb.
• Add gelatin to hot rhubarb and stir until it is dissolved. Reserve ¾ c. of this mixture for glaze. Cool at room temperature.
• Chill remaining rhubarb mixture (for filling) until slightly thickened.
• Measure into bowl ¼ c. ice water and sprinkle on ¼ c. nonfat dry milk. Beat with rotary or electric beater until stiff enough to hold peaks. Fold in chilled rhubarb filling. Pour into pie shell.
• Spoon over the pie the ¾ c. gelatin mixture reserved for glaze. It should be cool, but not cold enough to start congealing. Chill pie again until filling is set.
Topping (prepare at serving time): To the ice water, add lemon juice and vanilla. Sprinkle nonfat milk over water mixture. Beat with rotary or electric beater until mixture holds peaks. Spoon over pie and garnish with banana slices.

PEANUT BUTTER PIE

A FARM JOURNAL *5-star recipe favorite from our* COUNTRY COOKBOOK

Baked 9″ pie shell
1   envelope unflavored gelatin
1   c. cold water
3   egg yolks, well beaten
½   c. sugar or light corn syrup
½   tsp. salt
½   c. smooth peanut butter
½   tsp. vanilla
3   egg whites, unbeaten
½   c. heavy cream, whipped (optional)
Peanut halves
Chocolate pieces

• Soften gelatin in ¼ c. water.
• Combine egg yolks, ¼ c. sugar, ¼ c. water and salt in top of double boiler; blend. Add gelatin.
• Place over boiling water; beat constantly with rotary beater until thick and fluffy (about 5 minutes). Cool.
• Place peanut butter in bowl; add remaining ½ c. water gradually; beat until smooth. Add vanilla to egg yolk mixture; blend into peanut butter. Chill until slightly thickened, but still syrupy (10 to 15 minutes).
• Beat egg whites until foamy; add remaining sugar gradually, beating until stiff. Fold into peanut butter mixture. Turn into pie shell. Chill until firm.
• To serve, cover top with thin layer of whipped cream, if desired. (Cream is pretty but does detract a bit from the peanut flavor.) Decorate with "daisies" of peanut halves with chocolate pieces for centers.

Note: Crumb crust may be substituted for baked pastry pie shell.

ORANGE-MINCEMEAT PIE

Keep a baked pie shell in the freezer to make this mincemeat Bavarian pie

Baked 9" pie shell
1   (9 oz.) pkg. mincemeat
½   c. water
1   (3 oz.) pkg. orange flavor gelatin
1   c. hot water
¼   c. chopped walnuts
1   c. heavy cream, whipped

• Crumble mincemeat into a saucepan. Add ½ c. water and cook, stirring, until lumps are broken and mixture comes to a boil. Boil vigorously 1 minute. Cool.
• Dissolve gelatin in hot water. Chill until spoonful of mixture mounds slightly. Fold in mincemeat and walnuts, then whipped cream.
• Pour into pie shell. Chill until firm. (Garnish with additional whipped cream if you wish.)

ORANGE-LIME PIE

An orange and green hostess dessert

2   (9") baked pie shells
1   (3 oz.) pkg. orange flavor gelatin
1   (3 oz.) pkg. lime flavor gelatin
3   c. boiling water
2   envelopes unflavored gelatin
1   c. orange juice
4   (11 oz.) cans mandarin oranges, drained
2   c. heavy cream
4   tblsp. sugar

• Prepare orange and lime gelatins as directed on package, but use only 1½ c. water each. Pour each into an 8" layer cake pan. Chill until firm.
• Sprinkle unflavored gelatin over orange juice to soften. Stir over hot water until dissolved. Chill until partially thickened. Stir cut-up orange segments into gelatin.
• Beat cream until stiff. Fold sugar into whipped cream, and fold into orange juice-gelatin mixture.
• Cut firm orange and lime gelatin into ½" cubes. Fold into whipped cream mixture; then spoon lightly into pie shells. Chill at least 3 hours before cutting, but use within 8 hours. Serve garnished with additional whipped cream, if desired, or with a few orange and green gelatin cubes (reserved). Makes 2 pies.

COFFEE-AND-CREAM PIE

You can garnish this rich pie with toasted almonds instead of coconut

Baked 9" pie shell
2   c. heavy cream
½   c. sugar
3   tblsp. instant coffee powder
⅛   tsp. salt
½   tsp. vanilla
1   envelope unflavored gelatin
¼   c. cold water
½   c. toasted coconut

• Combine heavy cream, sugar, coffee, salt and vanilla in large mixer bowl. Beat until thick.
• Soften gelatin in water; heat over hot water until thoroughly dissolved.
• Gradually add the dissolved gelatin to the cream mixture and continue beating until well blended. Pour into pie shell. Sprinkle coconut over top. Chill at least 1 hour before serving. Makes 8 servings.

APRICOT COCONUT PIE

No fuss to make, mighty good to eat

9" Toasted Coconut Pie Shell (Chapter 2)
1 envelope unflavored gelatin
⅓ c. sugar
⅛ tsp. salt
1 (12 oz.) can apricot nectar (1½ c.)
1 tsp. lemon juice
4 drops almond extract
2 egg whites

• Combine gelatin, sugar and salt. Heat apricot nectar to boiling point. Add to gelatin mixture and stir until gelatin is dissolved. Add lemon juice and almond extract.

• Chill until mixture starts to thicken (consistency of unbeaten egg white). Beat egg whites until soft peaks form, fold into gelatin mixture and beat with rotary beater until mixture mounds when dropped from spoon. Turn into chilled pie shell. Garnish with a little coconut and chill.

RED AND GREEN CHRISTMAS PIE

This showy dessert will say Merry Christmas to all who sit at your table

2 (8") Graham Cracker Crumb Crusts (Chapter 2)
1 (3 oz.) pkg. lime flavor gelatin
2 c. hot water
1 c. sweetened canned grapefruit juice
1 (3 oz.) pkg. cherry flavor gelatin
1 c. orange juice

1 envelope unflavored gelatin
¼ c. cold water
1 c. pineapple juice
½ c. sugar
1 tsp. vanilla
½ c. heavy cream, whipped

• Dissolve lime gelatin in 1 c. hot water; add grapefruit juice. Pour into a shallow pan; chill. Dissolve cherry gelatin in remaining 1 c. hot water; add orange juice. Pour into a shallow pan; chill.

• Soften unflavored gelatin in ¼ c. cold water. Heat pineapple juice to boiling; add softened gelatin and stir until it is dissolved. Chill until mixture thickens (a little thicker than unbeaten egg white). Add sugar and vanilla to whipped cream and fold into pineapple-gelatin mixture.

• Cut lime and cherry gelatins in small cubes with a knife. Fold into pineapple and whipped-cream mixture, saving out a few cubes of both colors.

• Spoon into pie shells. Chill. To serve, garnish with reserved gelatin cubes and, if desired, with whipped cream. Makes 2 pies, 12 to 16 servings.

Note: You can substitute water for the grapefruit and orange juices; the pie will be less fruity in flavor, however.

MERRY CHRISTMAS PIE

A favorite holiday pie of many women who like to bring it to the table, uncut

Baked 9" pie shell
1 envelope unflavored gelatin
1 c. sugar

¼ c. flour
¼ tsp. salt
1 ¾ c. milk
½ c. heavy cream
¾ tsp. vanilla
¼ tsp. almond extract
3 egg whites
1 (3 ½ oz.) can flaked coconut
Maraschino cherries

• Combine gelatin, ½ c. sugar, flour and salt in medium-size saucepan. Gradually stir in milk. Cook over low heat, stirring constantly, until mixture comes to boil. Remove from heat, cool. If mixture becomes too stiff, beat with mixer or rotary beater until smooth.
• Whip cream; fold it, the vanilla and almond extract into cooked mixture.
• Beat egg whites until frothy. Gradually add remaining ½ c. sugar, beating until egg whites are stiff but not dry. Fold egg whites and coconut into gelatin mixture. Turn into pie shell. Chill 3 to 4 hours, or until firm. To serve, decorate with pieces of maraschino cherries.

GRAPE BAVARIAN PIE

A royal Western-ranch version of year-round Concord grape pie

Walnut Crumb Crust
1 envelope unflavored gelatin
¾ c. cold water

1 (6 oz.) can frozen grape juice concentrate
1 c. heavy cream, whipped

• Sprinkle gelatin over water in saucepan. Stir over low heat until gelatin dissolves. Remove from heat.
• Add grape juice concentrate. Stir until it is melted.
• Chill just until gelatin mixture is syrupy, about 5 minutes. Fold gelatin mixture into whipped cream. Pour mixture into crust. Chill until firm.

WALNUT CRUMB CRUST: Mix 1⅓ c. fine graham cracker crumbs, ¼ c. finely chopped walnuts, ½ tsp. each cinnamon, allspice and nutmeg and ¼ c. sugar. Blend in 6 tblsp. soft butter or margarine until mixture is crumbly. Press evenly onto bottom and sides of well-greased 9″ pie pan.

VARIATIONS

• For grape juice, substitute 1 (6 oz.) can frozen fruit juice concentrate—orange, tangerine, lemonade, limeade or cherry-lemon punch.
• For heavy cream, substitute 1 (6 oz.) can evaporated milk, whipped (freeze milk until ice crystals form around edge of bowl before whipping); or 1 (2 oz.) pkg. dessert topping mix, whipped; or ⅓ c. nonfat dry milk whipped with ⅓ c. ice water and 1 tblsp. lemon juice.

Company Pie to Make Ahead

Apple Cider Pie, regardless of where you bake it, will live up to the reputation it enjoys in a Michigan fruit-growing neighborhood where it originated. Orchard people and their friends give the pie a top rating. You can fix it in the morning, put it in the refrigerator and forget it until dinner- or suppertime.

APPLE CIDER PIE

At mealtime decorate with scoops of whipped cream and a few red candies

Baked 9″ pie shell
1 ½ c. apple cider
2 tblsp. red cinnamon candies (red hots)
1 (3 oz.) pkg. lemon flavor gelatin
2 large apples
1 c. heavy cream, whipped

• Heat ¾ c. apple cider (apple juice if cider is not available) with red candies to boiling, stirring until candies are melted. Remove from heat, add gelatin, stirring until it dissolves. Add remaining ¾ c. cider. Chill until mixture thickens slightly.
• Quarter apples; peel, core and grate directly into gelatin. Stir after each apple quarter is grated to coat the apple with gelatin immediately.
• Fold in whipped cream.
• Pour into cooled pie shell. Chill until firm, at least 2 hours.

Exciting Chocolate Pies

You'll find wide variety in our chocolate refrigerator pies. Some of them are fancy enough to show off when you entertain and want to impress your guests. Others are simpler and ideal for family and less pretentious company meals. All are rich, but they're the kind chocolate lovers will rave about.

Do try all of the recipes to find out which ones please you most. In all the pie fillings in this Cookbook that call for unsweetened chocolate, packets of unsweetened liquid chocolate product for baking may be substituted. Just press the creamy mixture into the filling and skip the measuring and melting. The contents of each 1 oz. packet equal 1 square of unsweetened chocolate.

It's a good idea to remove chilled pies from the refrigerator about 20 minutes before serving. Just set them on the counter in the kitchen when you sit down to enjoy the main course.

These chocolate pies are excellent in plain pastry shells or Graham Cracker Crumb Crusts if you can't take time to make some of the more elaborate crusts.

CHOCOLATE PIE SPECTACULAR

A hostess' dream come true

Pecan Crumb Crust:
1 c. fine graham cracker crumbs
½ c. finely chopped pecans
⅓ c. brown sugar, firmly packed
⅓ c. melted shortening

Filling:
1 envelope unflavored gelatin
¼ c. cold milk
⅔ c. sugar
2 eggs, separated
¼ tsp. salt
1 ¼ c. scalded milk
1 tsp. vanilla
1 c. heavy cream, whipped
1 square semisweet chocolate, shaved
Chocolate Topping

Crust: Combine ingredients and press firmly into 9" pie pan. Make even layer on bottom and sides of pan. Bake in slow oven (300°F.) 10 minutes. Cool.

Filling: Soften gelatin in cold milk.

• Combine ⅓ c. sugar, slightly beaten egg yolks, salt and scalded milk. Cook, stirring, over very low heat until mixture coats a metal spoon. Remove from heat, blend in softened gelatin and vanilla.

• Chill until mixture begins to thicken. Beat until light. Beat egg whites until frothy; gradually add remaining ⅓ c. sugar, beating until glossy, firm peaks form. Fold into gelatin mixture. Fold in whipped cream and shaved chocolate. Heap filling into cool Pecan Crumb Crust. Chill until firm. Drizzle on Chocolate Topping. Refrigerate or freeze until serving time. Cut in wedges with sharp knife. Makes 6 to 8 servings.

CHOCOLATE TOPPING: Heat ½ (6 oz.) pkg. semisweet chocolate pieces (½ c.) and 2 tsp. butter or margarine over hot, not boiling, water, until chocolate is just melted. Remove from heat; add 1 tblsp. hot water and stir until smooth. Immediately drizzle over top of pie.

CHOCOLATE MALT PIE

Crunchy nuts on smooth chocolate-malt filling make a distinctive pie

Baked 9" pie shell
½ lb. large marshmallows (32)
½ c. milk
⅛ tsp. salt
½ c. semisweet chocolate pieces, ½ (6 oz.) pkg.

1   c. heavy cream
¼   c. chocolate malted milk powder
1   tsp. vanilla
⅓   c. chopped walnuts

• Combine marshmallows, milk and salt in top of double boiler. Cook over water, stirring constantly, until marshmallows are melted. Remove from heat.

• Add chocolate pieces, stirring until they are melted. Cool.

• Whip cream until stiff. Fold malted milk powder and vanilla into cream. Then fold into marshmallow mixture and pour into pie shell. Sprinkle walnuts over top. Chill several hours before serving.

CHOCOLATE TOFFEE PIE

This elegant, luscious pie topped with fruited Apple Snow—unusual

Toffee Crust

Filling:
1   (6 oz.) pkg. semisweet chocolate pieces
¼   c. water
2   tsp. instant coffee powder
3   egg yolks
⅛   tsp. salt
6   tblsp. sugar
3   egg whites
2   tsp. vanilla

Apple Snow:
1   egg white
⅓   c. sugar
1   tsp. finely grated lemon peel
⅛   tsp. salt
1   large unpeeled apple, freshly grated (1 c.)   *more*

Filling: Combine chocolate and water; melt chocolate over hot, not boiling, water. Add coffee powder and set aside to partially cool.

• Combine egg yolks, salt and 2 tblsp. sugar; beat until thick and lemon-colored. Combine slightly cooled chocolate and egg yolk mixtures, beating constantly. Cook in double boiler, stirring, 3 minutes. Remove from heat and cool 30 minutes.

• Beat egg whites until frothy; gradually add remaining 4 tblsp. sugar and vanilla, beating until glossy, firm peaks form. Fold egg whites into chocolate mixture; spoon into cool Toffee Crust. Chill until set.

Apple Snow: Beat egg white until foamy. Gradually add sugar, beating constantly. Blend in lemon peel and salt. Add apple; beat at least 10 minutes with electric mixer.

• Spread on filling in pie shell; sprinkle on reserved baked crumbs (from crust recipe). Refrigerate until serving time. Serve the same day. Makes 6 to 8 servings. Tint Apple Snow with a few drops of red food color for a most attractive pie.

TOFFEE CRUST

1   c. sifted flour
½   tsp. salt
1   tsp. granulated sugar
⅓   c. shortening
¼   c. brown sugar, firmly packed
¾   c. chopped pecans
1   square unsweetened chocolate, grated
1   tblsp. water
1   tsp. vanilla

• Sift together flour, salt and granulated sugar. Cut in shortening until mixture resembles small peas. Blend in brown sugar, pecans and chocolate. Mix well, reserving 1 tblsp. mixture. Add water and vanilla to remainder of mixture and press into well-greased 8″ pie pan, moistening fingers if necessary, to make pie shell.

• Bake in moderate oven (375°F.) 15 minutes. During last 5 minutes, bake the 1 tblsp. reserved crumb mixture, spread in a pan. Cool crust.

MOCHA PECAN PIE

Light and airy pecan treat for guests

Coffee Nut Crust
1   envelope unflavored gelatin
1   c. cold water
3   tblsp. cocoa
1   c. sugar
2   tsp. instant coffee powder
3   eggs, separated
1   tsp. vanilla
½   tsp. rum extract (optional)
¼   tsp. salt
¾   c. finely chopped pecans
½   c. heavy cream, whipped
Pecan halves for garnish

• Soften gelatin in ¼ c. water.

• Combine in saucepan cocoa, ¾ c. sugar, ¾ c. water and coffee powder, stirring to dissolve sugar. Bring to a boil and cook gently 4 to 5 minutes, stirring constantly. Remove from heat.

• Pour a little of hot mixture over slightly beaten egg yolks, mix and stir into remaining hot mixture. Cook until mixture thickens, about 5 minutes, stirring constantly. Remove from heat. Add vanilla, rum extract and softened gelatin. Stir until gelatin is dissolved. Chill until mixture mounds slightly when dropped from a spoon.

• Combine egg whites and salt and

beat until frothy; add remaining ¼ c. sugar gradually, beating until glossy, stiff peaks form.
• Fold pecans into gelatin mixture; then fold in egg whites. Spoon into cool Coffee Nut Crust. Chill until firm.
• To serve, garnish with spoonfuls of whipped cream arranged around edge of pie, placing a pecan half on each spoonful of whipped cream. Serves 8.

COFFEE NUT CRUST

7 tblsp. shortening
1 tsp. instant coffee powder
3 tblsp. hot water
1 tsp. milk
1 ¼ c. sifted flour
½ tsp. salt
¼ c. finely chopped pecans

• Combine softened shortening, coffee powder dissolved in hot water and milk. Whip with fork until thick and smooth. Combine flour and salt with shortening mixture. Roll between 2 (12") squares waxed paper; peel off top paper and sprinkle with 2 tblsp. finely chopped pecans, leaving 1" border plain. Replace paper and gently roll pecans into dough. Turn pastry over and repeat, using remaining 2 tblsp. pecans. Remove top paper.
• Fit into 9" pie pan, remove paper; flute and prick pastry with fork.
• Bake in very hot oven (450°F.) 12 to 14 minutes. Cool in pan on rack.

MINTED CHOCOLATE PIE

Two-tone party pie you fix ahead—blend of flavors makes it outstanding

Baked 9" pie shell
1 envelope unflavored gelatin
¾ c. sugar
2 c. milk
3 eggs, separated
1 tblsp. cornstarch
½ c. heavy cream, whipped
2 squares unsweetened chocolate, melted
¼ tsp. peppermint extract
Chocolate candy shot (jimmies)

• Combine gelatin and ½ c. sugar in top of double boiler. Gradually stir in milk and cook over boiling water until milk is scalded.
• Beat egg yolks with cornstarch to blend well. Gradually stir half of milk mixture into egg yolks. Return to double boiler and cook over boiling water, stirring constantly, until mixture is thickened. Cool, then chill until mixture starts to set.
• Beat egg whites until frothy. Beat in remaining ¼ c. sugar gradually, beating until stiff peaks form. Beat chilled custard mixture until fluffy. Fold in egg whites, then whipped cream.
• Divide mixture in half. Fold chocolate into one half and mint extract into other half. Spread chocolate filling into pie shell; chill 5 minutes. Top with mint filling. Chill several hours before serving. Garnish top with chocolate shot or shaved chocolate.

CHOCOLATE CHERRY PIE

This pie captures that marvelous taste of chocolate-coated cherries

9" Vanilla Wafer Pie Shell (Chapter 2)
½ c. butter   *more*

¾ c. sugar
1 square unsweetened chocolate, melted and cooled
1 tsp. vanilla
2 eggs
2 tblsp. chopped maraschino cherries
Whipped cream
Maraschino cherries (whole)

• Cream butter and sugar together until smooth. Blend in chocolate and vanilla.
• Add eggs, one at a time, beating 5 minutes after each addition. Stir in chopped cherries.
• Spread into pie shell and chill 3 to 4 hours. Serve topped with whipped cream, garnished with maraschino cherry flowers. Makes 8 servings.

Note: To make cherry flowers, slit cherries from stem end almost to opposite end 8 times, spacing slits evenly.

CHOCOLATE PEPPERMINT-CANDY PIE

A beauty in looks and taste—pretty pink filling frosted with chocolate

Baked 9″ pie shell
1 envelope unflavored gelatin
¼ c. cold water
2 eggs, separated
1¼ c. milk
½ c. crushed peppermint-stick candy
½ c. heavy cream, whipped
Few drops red food color
⅛ tsp. salt
¼ c. sugar
Chocolate Topping

• Soften gelatin in water.
• Combine egg yolks with milk. Cook in top of double boiler or over low heat until mixture coats a metal spoon.
• Add gelatin and candy. Stir until both are dissolved. Chill until slightly thickened.
• Fold in cream and food color.
• Add salt to egg whites. Beat until they hold soft peaks. Add sugar gradually, beating until stiff.
• Fold in pink mixture.
• Pour into baked pie shell; chill until firm.
• Spread with Chocolate Topping.

CHOCOLATE TOPPING

1½ squares unsweetened chocolate
6 tblsp. butter or margarine
6 tblsp. confectioners sugar
1 egg yolk
1 tsp. water
¼ c. pecan halves

• Melt chocolate.
• Cream together butter and sugar. Add chocolate and egg yolk. Add water and mix thoroughly.
• Spread over top of pie. Garnish rim with pecan halves.

Note: Chocolate Topping won't crack if knife is dipped in hot water. Or leave pie at room temperature for 20 minutes before cutting.

TWO-TONE PIE

Black-and-white spectacular pie

Baked 9″ pie shell
1 envelope unflavored gelatin
¼ c. cold water

2   c. milk, scalded
4   eggs, separated
1   c. sugar
2   tblsp. cornstarch
2   squares unsweetened chocolate
2   tsp. vanilla
¼   tsp. cream of tartar

• Soften gelatin in water.
• Add milk to egg yolks and beat with rotary beater.
• Mix ½ c. sugar and cornstarch; add to milk and eggs. Cook in top of double boiler or over low heat until thickened, stirring constantly. Remove from heat. Reserve 1 c. of mixture.

• Add gelatin to remaining mixture and stir until gelatin is dissolved.
• Melt 1½ squares chocolate and add to reserved cup of cream filling. Add 1 tsp. vanilla and beat with rotary beater. Cool. Pour chocolate filling into pie shell and chill.
• Beat egg whites until frothy; add cream of tartar and beat until stiff; add remaining sugar gradually, beating until stiff. When gelatin mixture is slightly thickened, fold in egg whites and remaining vanilla.
• Pour into pie shell, covering the chocolate layer. Chill thoroughly. Grate remaining ½ square chocolate. Sprinkle over top.

Praiseworthy Ice Cream Pies

When man first topped his wedge of pie with ice cream, he discovered one of this country's best dessert combinations. And the cook who first put ice cream into a pie shell and topped it with crushed, red-ripe strawberries or glossy chocolate sauce created a fabulous dessert.

Take your pick of our ice cream pies, fancy or plain, and then, using them as guides, try other combinations. It's difficult to go wrong when you put pastry and ice cream together, but you do need a freezer or a freezing compartment in the refrigerator to insure success.

Precaution: When topping ice cream pies with meringue that's browned quickly in a very hot oven, use especial care to select unbroken eggs, washed clean. (The meringue is not baked long enough to destroy the bacteria that cause salmonellosis, a form of food poisoning.)

LEMON-LAYERED ALASKA PIE

Spectacular dessert for a party—ready to brown quickly at serving time

Baked 9″ pie shell
6   tblsp. butter
1   tsp. grated lemon peel
⅓   c. lemon juice
⅛   tsp. salt
1   c. sugar
2   eggs
2   egg yolks
1   qt. vanilla ice cream
Meringue (3 egg whites)

• Melt butter in top of double boiler. Add lemon peel and juice, salt and sugar. Combine eggs and egg yolks and beat slightly. Stir into butter mixture and cook over boiling water, beating constantly with a wire whisk until thick and smooth. Cool.

• Spread half of ice cream over bottom of cooled pie shell. Freeze firm. Spread half of cooled lemon mixture over ice cream. Freeze firm. Cover with remaining ice cream; freeze firm. Cover with remaining lemon mixture; freeze firm.

• Spread fluffy meringue on pie, completely covering filling (see Perfect Meringue for Topping Pies, Chapter 9). Make certain meringue extends to edges. Pie may be frozen and baked later or baked at once.

• To bake, place pie on board. Put into extremely hot oven (500°F.) 3 to 5 minutes, or until meringue is lightly browned. Serve immediately. Makes 6 servings.

PUMPKIN PIE ALASKA

A showy dessert to serve on special occasions. It's as good as it looks

Unbaked 10″ pie shell
1   egg
3   egg yolks
1 ½ c. dark brown sugar
1   tsp. cinnamon
1   tsp. pumpkin pie spice
½   tsp. salt
¼   tsp. nutmeg
¼   c. maple syrup
1   (1 lb.) can pumpkin (2 c.)
1 ½ c. evaporated milk
1   pt. butter brickle ice cream
Brown Sugar Meringue

• Beat egg and egg yolks slightly. Blend in sugar, spices, maple syrup,

pumpkin and milk. Pour into pie shell. Bake in hot oven (425°F.) 45 minutes. Cool and then chill thoroughly.
• Line 9″ pie pan with waxed paper. Press ice cream evenly into pie pan; return to freezer and freeze until solid.
• At serving time, turn ice cream out on top of pie. Spread Brown Sugar Meringue over top, sealing well at edges. Bake in extremely hot oven (500°F.) until lightly browned, 2 to 3 minutes. Serve at once. Makes 8 servings.

BROWN SUGAR MERINGUE

3   egg whites
¼   tsp. cream of tartar
2   tsp. vanilla
⅓   c. brown sugar

• Combine egg whites and cream of tartar. Beat until soft peaks form. Add vanilla. Gradually add sugar, beating until stiff peaks form.

FROZEN CHERRY MIX

Extends cherries if crop is short—freeze it for use in pies all winter

5   qts. stemmed tart red cherries
2   (1 lb. 4 oz.) cans crushed pineapple, drained
8   c. sugar
8   tsp. ascorbic acid powder
2   tsp. cinnamon
⅛   tsp. cloves
2   (1 ¾ oz.) pkgs. powdered fruit pectin

• Pit cherries, chop coarsely. (Fruit and juice should measure about 12 cups.)

• Drain juice from cherries and reserve.
• Add pineapple to cherries.
• Combine sugar, ascorbic acid powder and spices. Add to cherries and pineapple; mix well. Let stand to dissolve sugar.
• Combine pectin and cherry juice in large saucepan. Heat to a full rolling boil; boil 1 minute, stirring constantly. Add to cherry mixture; stir for 2 minutes. Ladle into containers. Seal. Allow to stand at room temperature until set (about 8 to 10 hours). Freeze. Makes 10 pints.

CHERRY-COCONUT ICE CREAM PIE

A new cherry pie from our Test Kitchens—perfect blend of flavors

1 ⅓ c. flaked coconut
2   tblsp. butter or margarine, melted
¼   c. graham cracker crumbs
2   tblsp. sugar
1   qt. vanilla ice cream
1   c. Frozen Cherry Mix

• Combine coconut and butter; mix well. Add crumbs and sugar, mixing thoroughly. Press firmly on bottom and sides of 8" pie pan. Bake in moderate oven (375°F.) 10 to 12 minutes, or until lightly browned. Cool.
• Soften ice cream and spread in coconut shell. Spread Frozen Cherry Mix over top and freeze.
• Thaw just enough to soften so that pie may be cut in wedges.

PINK PARTY PIE

A FARM JOURNAL *5-star recipe—a favorite in our* TIMESAVING COOKBOOK

Baked 9" Pink Pie Shell
1   qt. strawberry ice cream
1   (10 oz.) pkg. frozen strawberries
Meringue (2 egg whites)
Few drops red food color

• Pile softened ice cream into cool pie shell and spread evenly. Freeze overnight.
• To serve, heat oven to extremely hot (500°F.). Meanwhile, make meringue (see Perfect Meringue for Topping Pies, Chapter 9), tinting it a pretty pink.
• Arrange berries over ice cream and top with meringue, covering filling completely so heat will not melt ice cream.
• Set pie on wooden breadboard in extremely hot oven (500°F.) and bake about 5 minutes, or until lightly browned. Serve immediately.

PINK PIE SHELL: Make pastry (or use pie-crust mix), adding enough red food color (about 4 drops) to the water to make pink crust.

VARIATION

FRESH STRAWBERRY PINK PIE: Substitute fresh for frozen berries. Place 2 c. ripe berries in baked pie shell, cover with 1 pt. vanilla ice cream and then with pink meringue. Brown meringue as directed for Pink Party Pie. Or use 1 c. each frozen strawberries and sliced peaches for an exotic pie.

STRAWBERRY MARSHMALLOW PIE

Pretty pie with strawberry-pink top-knot—a hostess special

Baked 9″ pie shell
16 marshmallows
2 tblsp. strawberry juice
Few drops red food color
2 egg whites
¼ tsp. salt
¼ c. sugar
¾ qt. vanilla ice cream
1 c. fresh strawberries, sliced

• Melt marshmallows in strawberry juice over low heat, folding with spoon until mixture is smooth. Add food color and cool.
• Combine egg whites and salt; beat until frothy. Add sugar gradually and beat until they hold glossy, stiff peaks. Then gently whip in cooled marshmallow mixture.
• Fill pastry pie shell with ice cream, spreading evenly. Cover with strawberries. Top with marshmallow mixture swirled attractively. Hurry to broiler and broil to brown lightly.
• Tuck a few choice unstemmed berries in marshmallow swirls and serve at once.

Note: The country cook who cherishes this recipe and shares it finds it is convenient to spread the slightly softened ice cream in the pie shell, then freeze it until firm.

STRAWBERRY ICE CREAM PIE

One of the best strawberry pies. It's often called Strawberry Parfait Pie

Baked 9″ pie shell
1 (3 oz.) pkg. strawberry flavor gelatin
1 ¼ c. boiling water
1 pt. vanilla ice cream
1 ½ c. sliced fresh strawberries, sweetened to taste (about ¼ c. sugar)
Whipped cream

• Dissolve gelatin in boiling water in 2 qt. saucepan. Add spoonfuls of ice cream gradually, stirring until it is melted. Chill until mixture is thickened, but do not let it set. Fold in strawberries.
• Pour into pie shell and chill until firm, 25 to 35 minutes. Serve garnished with whipped cream and, if desired, a few whole or sliced berries.

VARIATIONS

DOUBLE STRAWBERRY: Use strawberry instead of vanilla ice cream.

FROZEN STRAWBERRY: Use 1 (10 oz.) pkg. frozen strawberry halves, drained, instead of fresh berries and use strawberry juice for part of water. Use vanilla ice cream.

RASPBERRY: Use raspberry flavor gelatin and fresh raspberries, sweetened to taste (about ¼ c. sugar) and vanilla ice cream.

PEACH: Use lemon flavor gelatin, sliced fresh peaches, sweetened to taste (about ¼ c. sugar) and vanilla ice cream. Add ¼ tsp. almond extract.

ORANGE-BANANA: Use orange flavor gelatin, ½ c. sliced bananas, ½ c. drained fresh orange sections, 2 tsp. grated orange peel and vanilla ice cream. Garnish pie with puffs of whipped cream, banana slices and a little diced orange.

MERINGUE: At serving time, omit whipped cream. Top pie with a meringue made with 2 egg whites (Chapter 9). Seal well around pastry edges. Place in preheated broiler for 3 minutes, just long enough to lightly brown meringue. Serve at once.

LEMON: Use lemon flavor gelatin, 1 tsp. grated lemon peel, 3 tblsp. lemon juice and vanilla ice cream. Garnish pie with whipped cream, strips of lemon peel and, if you have them, a few fresh mint leaves.

POPCORN ICE CREAM PIE

Novel party dessert teen-agers like

2   qts. unsalted popped corn
1   c. toasted coconut
1   c. sugar
1   c. light corn syrup
½   c. butter or margarine
¼   c. water
2   tsp. salt
1   tsp. vanilla
1   qt. vanilla ice cream
Chocolate sauce (optional)

• Put popped corn and coconut in large buttered bowl.
• Combine sugar, syrup, butter, water and salt in heavy saucepan. Bring to a boil over medium heat, stirring until sugar melts. Continue cooking until mixture reaches hard crack stage (290° to 295°F.). Remove from heat and stir in vanilla.
• Pour syrup in fine stream over popped corn, stirring until all kernels are evenly coated.
• Divide in half and pat mixture on 2 greased baking sheets or pizza pans to make 2 (10″) rounds. Cool. Mark both circles with knife in wedge-shaped servings.
• Spread one layer with ice cream and top with second layer. Store in freezer. Cut in wedges to serve. Pass chocolate sauce to pour over. Makes 8 servings.

FROSTED ICE CREAM PIE

People of all ages are enchanted with this gala 3-layer frozen pie

9″ Chocolate Wafer Crumb Crust (Chapter 2)
1½ pts. vanilla or peppermint-stick ice cream
Chocolate Frosting

• Fill chilled crust with ice cream, softened at room temperature just enough to spread. Freeze.
• When pie is frozen, quickly spread Chocolate Frosting on top of ice cream and return to freezer for several hours or overnight. Makes 6 servings.

CHOCOLATE FROSTING: In double boiler, over hot, not boiling, water, melt 2 squares unsweetened chocolate. Remove from heat. Gradually beat in ½ c. confectioners sugar and 1 tblsp. hot water. Add 1 egg, beating thoroughly, and 3 tblsp. soft butter or margarine, 1 tblsp. at a time. Beat until smooth.

VARIATIONS

• Use graham cracker or other crumb crusts instead of Chocolate Wafer Crumb Crust.
• Substitute different flavors of ice cream for the vanilla or peppermint stick.

STRAWBERRY SOCIAL PIE

Simple, but oh so good

Baked 9" Graham Cracker Crumb
　　Crust (Chapter 2)
1　qt. strawberry ice cream
1　pt. fresh strawberries
Heavy cream, whipped

• Let ice cream soften slightly at
room temperature. Spread into cool
crumb crust. Place in freezer.
• To serve, cut in wedges and garnish
with ripe strawberries, sweetened, and
whipped cream.

VARIATIONS

PEACH ICE CREAM PIE: Substitute vanilla or peach ice cream for strawberry ice cream. Serve with sliced,
sweetened peaches and whipped
cream. If peaches must stand in refrigerator before serving, add a commercial color protector to them as directed
on label. Or sprinkle with lemon
juice.

PEACH-BLUEBERRY ICE CREAM PIE:
Top crumb crust, filled with peach
ice cream, with blueberries, crushed
lightly and sweetened. Whipped cream
garnish is optional.

BLUEBERRY ICE CREAM PIE: Fill Gingersnap Crumb Crust (Chapter 2)
with vanilla ice cream. Serve topped
with crushed and sweetened blueberries.

GINGER PEACH ICE CREAM PIE: Serve
vanilla ice cream or lemon sherbet in
Gingersnap Crumb Crust (Chapter 2)
and top with sweetened sliced peaches.

Note: Choose your favorite ice cream
and crumb crust for these homey ice
cream pies. Instead of topping with
sweetened fruit or berries, top with a
meringue (3 egg whites and 6 tblsp.
sugar), spreading to edges. Place on
board and brown in extremely hot
oven (500°F.). Serve with chocolate
or other sweet sauce, or freeze for use
later.

Pies with Ice Cream Crusts

Among the recipes that our readers
rate high are the double ice cream
treats—ice cream for the crust and in
the filling. Women tell us they use
these recipes year after year, especially to serve guests.

These desserts originated in the
kitchen of a Kansas farm homemaker
and made their debut in our COUNTRY
COOKBOOK. Their long record of success prompted us to bestow our high-

est honor—they rank among FARM
JOURNAL's 5-star specials. The pies not
only taste remarkably good, but they
also are quite easy to fix. And they're
handy to keep in the freezer to bring
out when you need a wonderful dessert.

Some women tell us they pass a
sweet sauce to pour over the wedges
of pie. And one hostess offers her party
guests a choice of sauces and a variety

of chopped nuts so they can have the fun of dressing up their pie servings. Almost all the farm women who wrote us about these frozen pies said they vary the pie shells by using different kinds of ice cream. So let imagination be your guide!

ICE CREAM PIE SHELL

• Line 8" pie pan with 1 pt. vanilla or favorite ice cream flavor. For a more generous "crust," use 1½ pts. Cut ice cream in ½" slices; lay on bottom of pan to cover. Cut remaining slices in half; arrange around pan to make rim. Fill spots with ice cream where needed. With tip of spoon, smooth "crust." Freeze until firm before adding the filling.

CRANBERRY NUT PIE

The gala, all-around favorite is one of FARM JOURNAL'S *5-star specials*

Ice Cream Pie Shell
2   c. fresh or frozen raw cranberries
1   c. sugar
1   c. heavy cream
½   c. chopped nuts

• Put cranberries through food chopper, using fine blade. (Grind your cranberries frozen—less juicy.) Add sugar; let stand overnight.
• Whip cream. Mix cranberries and nuts. Fold in whipped cream. Pour into Ice Cream Pie Shell. Freeze. To serve, cut in wedges.

CHOCOLATE PEPPERMINT PIE

Use pink-and-white peppermint ice cream shells to hold chocolate filling

2   Pink Peppermint Ice Cream Pie Shells
1   tblsp. cocoa
½   c. sugar
1   (4 oz.) pkg. chocolate pudding mix
1   tsp. vanilla
2   c. heavy cream

• Combine cocoa and sugar. Add to pudding mix and prepare as directed on package. Cool; add vanilla.
• Whip cream and fold into chocolate mixture. Pour into Peppermint Ice Cream Pie Shells. Freeze. To serve, cut in wedges.

BUTTERSCOTCH PECAN PIE

Flavor blend makes this pie memorable

2   Ice Cream Pie Shells
¼   c. brown sugar
1   (4 oz.) pkg. butterscotch pudding or pie filling mix
1   tsp. vanilla
2   c. heavy cream
½   c. chopped pecans

• Add sugar to pudding mix. Prepare as directed on package. Cool; then add vanilla.
• Whip cream. Add nuts to butterscotch mixture. Fold in whipped cream. Pour into Ice Cream Pie Shells. Freeze. To serve, cut in wedges.

VARIATION

• Omit nuts and use butter-pecan ice cream shell.

SPICY PUMPKIN PIE

A frozen pie that's spiced just right

Ice Cream Pie Shell
 1   c. cooked or canned pumpkin
 1   c. sugar
 ¼   tsp. salt
 ¼   tsp. ginger
 1   tsp. cinnamon
 ¼   tsp. nutmeg
 1   c. heavy cream

• Mix together pumpkin, sugar, salt and spices. Cook over low heat 3 minutes. Cool.
• Whip cream; fold into pumpkin mixture. Pour into Ice Cream Pie Shell. Freeze. To serve, cut in wedges.

FROZEN STRAWBERRY VANILLA PIE

Good as strawberries and ice cream

 2   Ice Cream Pie Shells
 1   (10 oz.) pkg. frozen strawberries, sliced (use fresh ones in season)
 2   c. heavy cream
 ¼   c. confectioners sugar
 ½   tsp. vanilla
Red food color

• Partially thaw berries.
• Whip cream; add sugar, vanilla and food color. Fold in strawberries. Pour into Ice Cream Pie Shells. Freeze. To serve, cut in wedges.

SWEET 'N' TART LEMON PIE

Marvelous team: lemon and ice cream

Ice Cream Pie Shell
 3   eggs
 ½   c. sugar
 ¼   tsp. salt
 ¼   c. lemon juice
 1   c. heavy cream

• Beat together 1 whole egg and 2 yolks. Add sugar, salt and lemon juice. Cook over low heat, stirring constantly until thick. Cool.
• Beat egg whites until stiff; then whip cream (no need to wash beaters). Fold cream into lemon mixture. Next, fold in whites. Pour into Ice Cream Pie Shell. Freeze. To serve, cut in wedges.

NO-COOK PIE

When the weather is warm and appetites need tempting, make an All Ice Cream Pie for a supper treat. Here are directions:
• Chill a 9″ pie pan in freezer about 10 minutes. Set a pint carton of chocolate ice cream on the kitchen counter to soften during this 10 minutes. Spoon the slightly softened ice cream smoothly on bottom and sides of chilled pie pan to make pie shell. Return to freezer to freeze firm. Then spread slightly softened strawberry ice cream in chocolate ice cream pie shell. Return to freezer to freeze firm.
• Top the pie with slightly softened vanilla ice cream to make a snowy coverlet. Sprinkle with chopped nuts, if desired. Freeze at least 1 hour before serving. Cut in wedges. If you have chocolate or other sweet dessert sauce in the refrigerator, pass it for pouring over dessert.

Angel Pies Deserve Their Name

Angel pies have crisp, golden meringue crusts and cream or ice cream fillings. They are a glamorous way to use egg whites. Whipped cream and fruits are among the favorite other ingredients. These are elegant desserts not difficult to perfect if recipe directions are followed.

You can freeze the meringue crusts successfully (see Chapter 2).

CHOCOLATE ANGEL PIE

A FARM JOURNAL *5-star special and a favorite from* COUNTRY COOKBOOK

Walnut Meringue Pie Shell
¾ c. semisweet chocolate pieces
¼ c. hot water
1 tsp. vanilla
⅛ tsp. salt
1 c. heavy cream, whipped

• Melt chocolate pieces in double boiler over not, not boiling, water. Add hot water, vanilla and salt. Cook and stir until smooth. Cool.
• Fold in whipped cream and pour into Walnut Meringue Pie Shell. Chill 4 hours or overnight. Spread thin layer of whipped cream over top when serving, if desired.

WALNUT MERINGUE PIE SHELL: Combine 3 egg whites, ⅛ tsp. salt, ¼ tsp. cream of tartar and ½ tsp. vanilla. Beat until soft peaks form. Add ¾ c. sugar gradually, beating until very stiff and sugar is dissolved. Spread over bottom and sides of greased 9″ pie pan. Build up sides. (Use cake decorator for fancy edge.) Sprinkle ⅓ c. chopped pecans or walnuts on bottom of pie shell. Bake in very slow oven (275°F.) 1 hour. Cool.

CHOCOLATE-BAR ANGEL PIE

A most delicious chocolate-almond pie to make a day before your party

9″ Meringue Pie Shell (Chapter 2)
3 (1½ oz.) milk-chocolate almond candy bars
3 tblsp. water
1 tsp. vanilla
1 c. heavy cream, whipped

• Melt candy bars with water; add vanilla and cool. Fold into whipped cream (sweeten whipped cream with sifted confectioners sugar, if desired). Pour into Meringue Pie Shell. Chill 24 hours. Makes 6 to 8 servings.

CHERRY ANGEL PIE

Elegant and fancy-looking dessert for special occasions—tastes scrumptious

10″ Meringue Pie Shell (Chapter 2)
1 (1 lb. 4 oz.) can sweetened frozen cherries, thawed
1 envelope unflavored gelatin
¼ c. cold water
¼ c. confectioners sugar   *more*

½ tsp. vanilla
1 c. heavy cream, whipped
½ c. shredded coconut
¼ c. chopped pecans

• Simmer cherries 5 minutes. Drain and cool. Soften gelatin in cold water. Heat 1 c. cherry juice to boiling. Add softened gelatin and stir until it is dissolved. Remove from heat, cool and chill until mixture thickens to the consistency of syrup. Beat until fluffy.
• Beat confectioners sugar and vanilla into whipped cream. Fold into gelatin mixture. Fold in cherries, coconut and nuts. Spread into cooled Meringue Pie Shell. Chill several hours. Makes 8 servings.

ORANGE ANGEL PIE

Showy dessert to fix ahead for guests

9″ Meringue Pie Shell (Chapter 2)
4   egg yolks
1   whole egg
⅔   c. sugar
¼   c. frozen orange juice concentrate
1   tblsp. lemon juice
1   c. heavy cream, whipped

• Beat egg yolks and whole egg until thick and lemon-colored. Beat in sugar, concentrated orange juice and lemon juice. Cook over simmering water, stirring constantly, until thick. It should be thick enough to mound slightly when dropped from spoon. Chill, stirring several times.
• Fold whipped cream into cold orange mixture. Pile into Meringue Pie Shell. Chill at least 12 hours or overnight. Garnish at serving time, if desired, with spoonfuls of extra cream (½ c.), whipped. Makes 6 to 8 servings.

LEMON ANGEL PIE

Gay as a daisy—meringue holds white-capped billows of lemon filling

9″ Meringue Pie Shell (Chapter 2)
4   egg yolks
½   c. sugar
¼   c. lemon juice
1   tblsp. grated lemon peel
1   c. heavy cream, whipped

• Beat egg yolks until thick and lemon-colored. Gradually beat in sugar. Stir in lemon juice and peel. Cook over simmering water, stirring constantly, until mixture is thick, about 5 to 8 minutes. Mixture should be thick enough to mound slightly when dropped from spoon. Cool.
• Spread cool lemon mixture into Meringue Pie Shell. Top with whipped cream. Chill 12 hours or overnight. Makes 6 to 8 servings.

Soda Cracker Pie Shells

Good country cooks make many pie crusts with graham cracker crumbs. Some of them also use soda and round buttery crackers in egg whites to produce crisp, meringue-type pie crusts. Here are three recipes typical of many cracker desserts made in farm kitchens.

RANCH-STYLE PEACH PIE

Peaches and cream in crisp pie shell

3 egg whites
1 c. sugar
12 soda crackers, crushed (⅓ c.)
½ c. finely chopped pecans
¼ tsp. baking powder
1 tsp. vanilla
2 c. heavy cream
1 (1 lb.) can peach halves

• Beat egg whites until soft peaks form when beater is lifted. Add sugar, 2 tblsp. at a time, beating after each addition. Beat to stiff peaks.
• Fold in crackers, pecans, baking powder and vanilla. Spread on bottom and sides of a greased 9″ pie pan.
• Bake in slow oven (325°F.) 30 minutes. Cool.
• An hour or two before serving, whip cream. Drain peaches and slice very thin. Save out a few peach slices for garnishing. Alternate layers of cream and peaches in pie shell, having top layer of the cream. Place in refrigerator. Just before serving, garnish top of pie with reserved peach slices. Makes 6 to 8 servings.

VARIATION

• Substitute fresh peaches, sliced and lightly sweetened, for the canned fruit.

Note: The Montana ranchwoman who shares this recipe often puts the canned peaches and whipped cream in the crust and refrigerates overnight.

EASY PECAN PIE

Party pie with crisp cracker-nut crust from our Timesaving Cookbook

20 round buttery crackers, crushed
1 c. chopped pecans
1 c. sugar
3 egg whites
1 tsp. vanilla
½ c. heavy cream, whipped
½ c. flaked or shredded coconut

• Combine crackers, pecans and ½ c. sugar.
• Beat egg whites until stiff; gradually beat in remaining sugar and vanilla. Fold into cracker mixture.
• Spread on bottom and sides of greased 9″ pie pan to make pie shell. Bake in slow oven (325°F.) 30 minutes. Cool.
• Fill with whipped cream and sprinkle with coconut just before serving.

VARIATION

Easy Walnut Pie: Substitute walnuts for pecans.

DATE-NUT PIE

Tasty with dates, ice cream and nuts from our Timesaving Cookbook

12 soda crackers, crushed
½ c. chopped walnuts
12 dates, chopped
3 egg whites
½ tsp. baking powder
¾ c. sugar
½ tsp. vanilla
1 pt. vanilla ice cream   *more*

• Combine crackers, nuts and dates. Beat egg whites until frothy; add baking powder. Continue beating, adding sugar gradually, until mixture forms stiff peaks. Beat in vanilla.
• Fold cracker mixture into egg whites. Spread on bottom and sides of greased 9" pie pan to make pie shell.
• Bake in slow oven (325°F.) 25 to 30 minutes. Fill with spoonfuls of vanilla ice cream just before serving.

Country Cheese Pies

Serving slices of cheese with pie is a farm custom of long standing. Now pie fillings containing cheese, usually cream and cottage types, are becoming favorites. Here are recipes for some of them—pies that inspire bouquets to the cook.

OHIO CHEESE PIE

Prediction: This is the best cheese pie you've ever made or tasted

Crust:
2 ½ c. graham cracker crumbs
 ½ c. melted butter or margarine
 1 tsp. cinnamon
 ⅓ c. sugar

Filling:
 1 (12 oz.) carton cottage cheese
 2 (8 oz.) pkgs. cream cheese
1 ½ c. sugar
 4 eggs, beaten
 1 tsp. vanilla
 1 tblsp. lemon peel
 ⅓ c. lemon juice

Topping:
 ½ pt. heavy cream
 1 pt. dairy sour cream
 3 tblsp. sugar

Crust: Combine ingredients, mixing well. Pat into 2 (9") cake pans. Bake 5 minutes in hot oven (400°F.). Cool.
Filling: Sieve cottage cheese. Combine with other ingredients and whip until stiff. Pour into crust-lined pans; bake in moderate oven (350°F.) 30 minutes. Cool.
Topping: Whip heavy cream until very stiff. Combine with sour cream and sugar; spread over top. Chill. Makes 12 servings.

HAWAIIAN CHEESE PIE

Cooling and nourishing summer pie— flute shell high to hold filling

Baked 9" pie shell
 1 (1 lb. 4 oz.) can crushed pineapple
 ½ c. sugar
 ⅛ tsp. salt
 1 envelope unflavored gelatin
 2 eggs, separated
 1 c. cottage cheese
 1 tsp. grated lemon peel
 2 tblsp. lemon juice
 ½ c. heavy cream, whipped
 ⅓ c. flaked coconut

• Drain pineapple, reserving syrup. Combine ¼ c. sugar, salt, gelatin, ¾ c. pineapple syrup and slightly beaten egg yolks. Cook over low heat, stirring constantly, until mixture thickens slightly and coats metal spoon. Remove from heat.

• Press cottage cheese through sieve. Stir cheese, pineapple, lemon peel and juice into gelatin mixture.

• Beat egg whites until frothy. Gradually beat in remaining ¼ c. sugar, beating until stiff peaks form. Fold egg whites and whipped cream into pineapple mixture. Pour into pie shell and garnish with coconut. Chill until firm before serving.

CHOCOLATE CHEESE PIE

Heavenly, but serve small portions to the dieters at your table

9" Chocolate Graham Crust
1   (6 oz.) pkg. semisweet chocolate pieces
1   (8 oz.) pkg. cream cheese, softened
¾   c. light brown sugar
⅛   tsp. salt
1   tsp. vanilla
2   eggs, separated
1   c. heavy cream, whipped

• Melt chocolate over hot (not boiling) water; cool about 10 minutes.

• Blend cream cheese, ½ c. sugar, salt and vanilla. Beat in egg yolks, one at a time. Beat in cooled chocolate. Blend well.

• Beat egg whites until stiff but not dry. Gradually beat in ¼ c. sugar; beat until stiff and glossy.

• Fold chocolate mixture into beaten whites. Fold in whipped cream.

• Pour into chilled crust, reserving ¼ of mixture for decorating. Chill until filling sets slightly. With tapered spoon, drop reserved mixture in mounds over top of pie. Chill overnight. Makes 8 servings.

CHOCOLATE GRAHAM CRUST: Mix thoroughly 1½ c. graham cracker crumbs, ¼ c. brown sugar, ⅛ tsp. nutmeg, ⅓ c. melted butter or margarine and 1 square unsweetened chocolate, melted. Press into 9" pie pan. Chill until firm.

SHORT-CUT CHOCOLATE CHEESE PIE

This dieters' version of the preceding recipe has less filling, fewer calories

9" Chocolate Graham Crust (see preceding recipe)
1   (6 oz.) pkg. semisweet chocolate pieces
1   (3 oz.) pkg. cream cheese, softened
¼   c. light brown sugar
1   (2 oz.) pkg. dessert topping mix

• Melt chocolate over hot (not boiling) water. Remove from heat. Stir in the cheese until it is blended. Stir in sugar.

• Prepare topping mix as directed on package; blend ½ c. into chocolate mixture. Fold in remaining topping.

• Spread filling in crust. Chill overnight. Makes 8 servings.

RASPBERRY-CHEESE PIE

A show-off pie for little effort—fix it several hours ahead

Baked 9" pie shell
1   (3 oz.) pkg. raspberry flavor gelatin
2   tblsp. sugar
1¼ c. hot water   *more*

1 (16 oz.) pkg. frozen raspberries
1 (3 oz.) pkg. cream cheese
2 tblsp. milk
Sweetened whipped cream

• Dissolve gelatin and sugar in hot water. Add unthawed berries and stir to break them up. Gelatin thickens as berries thaw.
• Blend cream cheese with milk. Spread over bottom of cool pie shell.
• Pour partially set gelatin mixture over cheese in pie shell. Refrigerate until set.
• Serve garnished with spoonfuls of whipped cream.

FROZEN ORANGE PIE

Country cook's dream come true: this exciting pie ready in freezer

Baked 10″ Graham Cracker Crumb
Crust (Chapter 2)

4 eggs, separated
¾ c. sugar
1 tblsp. grated orange peel
¼ c. orange juice
1 c. heavy cream, whipped

• Beat egg yolks slightly; combine with sugar, orange peel and juice. Cook over boiling water, stirring constantly, until thickened. Cool.
• Fold stiffly beaten egg whites and whipped cream into the cooled orange mixture. Pour into crust. Chill.
• Freeze pie. Remove from freezer, package in moisture-vaporproof wrapping and return to freezer.
• Let stand at room temperature 10 minutes before serving. Do not thaw completely. Makes 8 servings.

Pie Inspired by Hawaiian Cooks

We've discovered a make-ahead pie that tastes like Grandmother's gingerbread, layered with banana slices and crowned with whipped cream. That means it's really good. You can get the pie ready in the morning and refrigerate it for noontime or evening guests.

The banana and ginger combination is a favorite in Hawaiian homes, where big-leafed banana trees with their bunches of pale-yellow fruit often grow near kitchen doors.

BANANA GINGER PIE

Serve frosty cold with hot coffee

9″ Gingersnap Crumb Crust (Chapter 2)
1 envelope unflavored gelatin
⅔ c. sugar
¾ c. water
1 tsp. grated lemon peel
3 tblsp. lemon juice
3 medium bananas
2 egg whites, unbeaten
Whipped cream

• Mix gelatin and sugar in top of double boiler; add water. Place over boiling water and cook, stirring constantly, until gelatin is dissolved. Remove from heat.

• Add lemon peel and juice and 1 c. mashed bananas (2 bananas) to gelatin mixture and chill until mixture mounds when dropped from a spoon. Add egg whites and beat with rotary beater until mixture begins to hold its shape. (If necessary, chill briefly until mixture mounds when dropped from spoon.) Spoon into crust and chill. At serving time, peel and slice remaining banana; dip slices in lemon juice. Spread top of pie with whipped cream and garnish with banana slices.

STRAWBERRY TORTE PIE

Low-calorie meringue takes whipped cream role in this luscious berry pie

Baked 9″ pie shell
2 (10 oz.) pkgs. frozen strawberries

⅓ c. sugar
1 tblsp. lemon juice
2 tblsp. cornstarch
Few drops red food color
2 egg whites
¼ c. sugar
⅛ tsp. salt

• Thaw berries and drain, reserving juice. To the juice (about 1 c.) add ⅓ c. sugar, lemon juice and cornstarch. Cook over low heat until thickened; add food color to intensify berry color. Cool glaze.

• Beat egg whites until frothy; gradually add ¼ c. sugar, beating until glistening, stiff peaks form. Spoon into cool pie shell, spreading high on sides to make hollow in center.

• Arrange berries spoke fashion in center of lined pie shell. Pour glaze over berries. Chill in refrigerator 1 hour or longer. Makes 8 servings.

Apricot Refrigerator Pie

One forkful of this pie and you'll want to praise the country cook in California's apricot-growing Santa Clara Valley who invented the recipe. If you like dried apricots, here's a dessert that does the golden fruit justice. Be sure to cook the apricots until very tender, evaporating most of the liquid around them. This really great pie deserves care in making. It's easy to fix, but do heed the little details that make for perfection.

APRICOT LAYER PIE

Tart-sweet, extra-delicious pie you can make the day before serving

Crumb Walnut Pie Shell
1 ½ c. dried-apricot purée (1 ½ c. dried apricots)
½ c. granulated sugar
¼ c. soft butter or margarine
1 egg
2 c. sifted confectioners sugar
more

1   c. heavy cream, whipped
2   tblsp. fine graham cracker
    crumbs

• Cook apricots in water to barely cover until very tender, about 1 hour, and drain thoroughly; stir to make a smooth purée. Then stir in granulated sugar. Cool.
• Beat butter until creamy; beat in egg. Gradually add confectioners sugar and beat until smooth. Spoon into Crumb Walnut Pie Shell and spread to make a smooth layer.

• Spoon apricot purée evenly over layer of confectioners sugar mixture.
• Spoon fluffy whipped cream over apricots, completely covering them. Sprinkle on graham cracker crumbs. Refrigerate overnight or at least 4 hours. Makes 8 servings.

CRUMB WALNUT PIE SHELL: Toss 1¼ c. fine graham cracker crumbs, ⅓ c. melted butter and ⅓ c. chopped walnuts together. Press over bottom and sides of 9″ pie pan.

DEEP-DISH AND CAKE PIES, COBBLERS AND DUMPLINGS

You'll feel right at home when you read the recipes in this chapter—they're heirloom desserts, adapted by each generation of new country cooks, and almost every family has inherited a few. We give you a roundup of our readers' and our own favorites.

Deep-dish pies are just right for people who like double the amount of fruit filling and half as much pastry as in the regular 2-crust pie. Try the richly colored Deep Peach-Plum Pie for a summer treat. It's a classic example of wonderful, two-fruit flavor and color blends.

When the purple lilac plumes brush against the garden fence, make our Rhubarb Cobbler. And when leaves of all colors are feathering down and the cranberry harvest is on, make Apple-Cranberry Cobbler—a treat. Wintry weather has its cobblers, too. What dessert could be more heartening on a cold day than our sunny Peach-Apricot Cobbler? Remember that all cobblers are quick desserts. They have biscuit, batter or pastry toppings, and sometimes allow you your choice.

Whole peeled and pitted peaches or cored and peeled apples, baked in pastry, are famous old-time meal endings. Like deep-dish pies and cobblers, dumplings are bowl desserts, often served with cream.

If you've never made or eaten cake baked in a pie shell, you've an exciting experience coming up. Try our delicate, sweet-tart Lemon Cake-Pie. Or serve Blueberry Funny Cake-Pie when you entertain. It's bound to create conversation.

Boston Cream Pie is pie in name only. The 1-layer cake, split and filled with soft custard or whipped cream, is served in wedges like pie. Today's homemakers bake two layers at a time, serving one and freezing the other. If the superlatives of our taste testers mean anything, Superb Boston Cream Pie deserves your attention.

Deep-Dish Pies—Luscious

Among the pleasantries of country kitchens is the serving of freshly baked deep-dish pies—apricot, cherry, peach, boysenberry or whatever fruit is at its seasonal height. Cut through the flaky, crisp crust with your serving spoon and dip into the bubbling, jewel-toned fruit juices and fruit. Ladle the fragrant dessert into individual bowls and take them to the table along with a pitcher of light cream. The family's welcome for your offering will be ample reward for the effort spent.

Even the inexperienced cook excels with these pies. She need not blush over a soggy undercrust. The pastry bakes on top of the filling and gives the juices no opportunity to destroy its golden crispness.

Basic Directions for Deep-Dish Fresh Fruit Pies

• Roll pastry for 1-crust pie into 10" square. Cut several vents or prick with 4-tined fork for the escape of steam during baking.
• Double the filling for a 9" fruit or berry pie. Place filling in 9" square pan. Adjust top crust, fold a little of the edge under and flute just inside edge of pan.
• Bake in a hot oven (425°F.) 40 to 50 minutes, or until lightly browned and the filling starts to bubble through the vents. Serve warm with cream, whipped cream, ice cream or a sauce.

Note: If you use a deep 10" pie pan instead of a square pan, cut rolled pastry in 11" circle. Cut vents and place on top of filling; trim and flute edge, pulling points of fluting over outer rim of pie pan to fasten crust.

Fillings for Deep-Dish Pies

BERRY: Look in Chapter 3 for 2-Crust Fresh Berry Pies. Double the ingredients for filling to make a deep-dish berry pie baked in 9" square pan.

CHERRY: Use 8 c. pitted tart fresh cherries, 2⅔ c. sugar, ⅛ tsp. salt, ⅔ c. flour and 3 tblsp. butter or margarine.

PEACH: Use 8 c. sliced and peeled fresh firm peaches, 2 c. sugar, ⅛ tsp. salt, 2 tblsp. less flour than for Cherry Filling, ½ tsp. cinnamon and 3 tblsp. butter or margarine.

APRICOT: Substitute sliced unpeeled apricots for peaches and follow directions for Peach Filling.

Note: Very tart berries or fruit may require more sugar.

DEEP-DISH APPLE PIE

Country pie to eat with a spoon—it's juicy, mellow and spiced just right

Pastry for 1-crust pie
 1   c. sugar
 ¼   c. flour
 ½   tsp. cinnamon
 ⅛   tsp. nutmeg
 ⅛   tsp. salt
 8   c. sliced peeled apples
 1   tblsp. lemon juice
 2   tblsp. butter or margarine

• Combine sugar (amount of sugar depends on tartness of apples, but you may need 1½ c.), flour, cinnamon, nutmeg and salt in 9″ × 9″ × 2″ pan. Add apples and lemon juice. Stir to combine. Dot with butter and top with pastry, rolled 1″ larger than top of pan. Cut steam vents; trim and flute edge just inside edge of pan. Or pull points of fluting over outer rim of pan to fasten crust.
• Bake in hot oven (425°F.) until apples are tender and crust is browned, about 50 minutes. Serve warm or cool in bowls with light cream or topped with scoops of vanilla ice cream. Or top pie with whipped cream and drizzle with Cinnamon Syrup (recipe follows). Makes 8 servings.

Note: You can bake pie in a 9″ × 12″ × 2″ baking pan. Use 12 c. sliced apples and 2 c. sugar. Fold a little of top pastry edge under and flute just inside edge of pan.

Cinnamon Syrup: In a small saucepan over heat stir constantly ¼ c. each cinnamon candies (red hots) and water until candies dissolve. Partially cool at room temperature to drizzle over pie at serving time.

APPLE-PORK PIE

This old-fashioned succulent apple pie often is called Sunday Supper Pie

Pastry for 1-crust pie
 8   c. sliced peeled apples
20   pieces salt pork (1″ × 1″ × 1″
       cube)
 1   c. sugar
 ½   tsp. cinnamon
 ¼   tsp. nutmeg
 ¼   tsp. salt

• Place apples in 8″ × 8″ × 2″ pan.
• Cut a 1″ cube of salt pork in 5 slices and then cut each slice in 4 pieces.
• Combine pork with sugar, cinnamon, nutmeg and salt. Sprinkle over apples.
• Roll pastry into square ½″ larger than top of pan. Place over apples. Fold pastry under and flute against inside edge of pan. Cut steam vents in top.
• Bake in hot oven (425°F.) 50 minutes, or until apples are tender. (Cover top crust with foil if it starts to brown too much.) Serve warm or cold with cheese. Makes 6 servings.

DEEP-DISH PEACH PIE

Summer's golden special—make it of ripe fruit; serve fresh from oven

Pastry for 1-crust pie
 2   c. sugar
 ½   c. flour   *more*

½ tsp. cinnamon
½ tsp. mace
8 c. sliced peeled fresh peaches
3 tblsp. butter

• Roll pastry into a 10″ square. (Invert pan, before adding filling, over pastry and cut crust in a straight line 1″ beyond edge of pan.)
• Combine sugar, flour, cinnamon and mace. Stir gently into ripe peaches. Pour into a 9″ × 9″ × 2″ pan. Dot with butter.
• Place pastry over peaches. Fold edge of crust under and flute against inside edge of pan. Cut steam vents.
• Bake in hot oven (425°F.) until lightly browned, about 40 to 50 minutes. Serve warm with cream, whipped cream or vanilla ice cream. Serves 9.

PEACH-PLUM PIE

Juicy, deep-dish summer pie; a beauty in color and in taste

Pastry for 1-crust pie
2 c. sliced peeled peaches
2 c. quartered red plums
1 c. sugar
¼ c. flour
½ tsp. cinnamon
2 tblsp. butter or margarine
Cream or ice cream

• Place fruits in an 8″ × 8″ × 2″ pan.
• Combine sugar, flour and cinna-mon; sprinkle over fruits. Dot with butter.
• Roll pastry into a 9″ square; place over filling. Trim off excess pastry to make even around the edge. Fold edge of crust under and press against inside of pan. Cut steam vents.
• Bake in hot oven (425°F.) 35 to 40 minutes. Serve warm with cream or ice cream. Makes 6 servings.

DEEP-DISH PEAR-MINCEMEAT PIE

Bake this juicy pie with cheese crust on a frosty day—enjoy compliments

Cheese Pastry for 1-crust pie (Chapter 2)
4 large pears (3 c. sliced)
¼ c. sugar
1 tblsp. flour
¼ tsp. salt
1½ c. prepared mincemeat
1 tblsp. lemon juice
2 tblsp. butter

• Arrange pear slices in bottom of 8″ × 8″ × 2″ baking dish. Combine sugar, flour and salt; sprinkle over pears. Cover with mincemeat, sprinkle with lemon juice and dot with butter.
• Roll pastry about 1″ larger than top of baking dish. Place pastry on fruit. Fold a little of the pastry under; crimp edges and cut slits.
• Bake in hot oven (425°F.) 35 to 40 minutes. Serve warm. Serves 6.

Cobblers You'll Want to Make

Cobblers are a busy woman's quick and hearty dessert standby. Take any fruit filling and top with soft biscuit dough, pour-on batter or pricked pastry cutouts. Bake the dessert while you get the remainder of the meal.

There's one important rule—have the fruit filling hot when you add topping. Bake at once. Availability of fruits need be the only limit to the kinds of cobblers you make. Use ripe fruit in season, canned and frozen the rest of the time.

Fresh Fruit Cobblers (Basic Directions)

• Mix together in saucepan ⅔ to 1 c. sugar, depending on natural sweetness of fruit or berries, and 1 tblsp. cornstarch. Stir in 1 c. boiling water gradually. Bring to a boil and boil 1 minute.
• Add prepared fresh fruit (include juice) and pour into a 10" × 6" × 2" baking dish or a 1½ qt. casserole. Dot with 1 tblsp. butter or margarine and sprinkle with ½ tsp. cinnamon or ¼ tsp. nutmeg.
• Make soft dough this way: Sift together 1 c. sifted flour, 1 tblsp. sugar, 1½ tsp. baking powder and ½ tsp. salt. Blend in ¼ c. shortening until mixture resembles cornmeal. Stir in ½ c. milk to make a soft dough.
• Drop spoonfuls of dough over hot fruit filling. Bake in hot oven (400°F.) about 30 minutes. Serve in bowls with cobbler juices and cream. Makes 6 servings.

VARIATIONS

BLACKBERRY COBBLER: Use ¾ c. sugar.

BOYSENBERRY COBBLER: Use ¾ c. sugar.

CANNED FRUITS IN COBBLERS: Use 1 (1 lb. 13 oz.) can fruit (2½ c.) instead of fresh fruit. Omit water and use only ½ c. sugar.

SWEET CHERRY COBBLER: Add 2 or 3 drops of almond extract to filling made with pitted sweet cherries.

Note: Slice peeled fresh peaches; pit and cut fresh apricots in halves.

CHERRY COBBLER

Homespun dessert that's a snap to fix

1   (1 lb. 4 oz.) can pitted tart cherries, undrained (2 c.)
½   c. sugar
1   tblsp. quick-cooking tapioca
2   tblsp. butter
⅛   tsp. salt
4   drops almond extract
Cobbler Topping

• Combine cherries, sugar and tapioca. Cook, stirring constantly, until mixture is thick and clear, about 15 minutes. Stir in butter, salt and almond extract.

• Pour hot mixture into 10" × 6" × 1½" baking dish. Add Cobbler Topping at once.

• Bake in hot oven (400°F.) about 20 minutes, or until crust is browned. Serve warm with cream or vanilla ice cream. Makes 6 servings.

Note: If you like more cherry filling, double the recipe, but use the same quantity of Cobbler Topping.

COBBLER TOPPING: Sift together 1 c. flour, 1 tblsp. sugar, 1½ tsp. baking powder and ¼ tsp. salt. Cut in ¼ c. butter or margarine until mixture resembles coarse crumbs. Mix ¼ c. milk and 1 slightly beaten egg. Add all at once to dry ingredients. Stir just to moisten. Drop by spoonfuls on hot cherry mixture. Bake as directed in Cherry Cobbler recipe.

VARIATION

RHUBARB COBBLER: To 4 c. rhubarb, cut in 1" pieces, add 1 c. sugar and 2 tblsp. cornstarch, mixed together. Add 1 tblsp. water and bring to a boil. Cook and stir about a minute. Add 2 tblsp. water. Pour into 8" round baking dish. Dot with 1½ tblsp. butter. Add Cobbler Topping to hot rhubarb filling as directed for Cherry Cobbler, only add 2 tsp. grated orange peel to flour in making topping. Bake in hot oven (400°F.) 20 minutes, or until crust is browned. Serve with cream or vanilla ice cream. Makes 6 servings.

APPLE COBBLER

This juicy cobbler calls for hearty appetites—also cups of hot coffee

1   c. sugar
2   tblsp. cornstarch
⅛   tsp. salt
½   tsp. cinnamon
1   c. water
2   tblsp. butter or margarine
5   c. thinly sliced peeled apples
Orange Biscuit Topping

• Blend sugar, cornstarch, salt and cinnamon in large saucepan. Add water, bring to a boil, stirring constantly. Add butter and apples. Pour into 8" × 12" × 2" baking dish.

• Meanwhile, prepare Orange Biscuit Topping. Arrange biscuits on top of hot apple mixture. Bake in hot oven (400°F.) 20 to 25 minutes, or until apples are tender and biscuits are golden. Serve hot in bowls with whipped cream, vanilla ice cream or Fluffy Orange Sauce (Chapter 9). Makes 6 to 7 servings. (It's a good idea to cover cobbler with foil during first 15 minutes of baking.)

ORANGE BISCUIT TOPPING: Combine 1½ c. prepared biscuit mix and 3 tblsp. sugar. Add ½ c. milk to make soft dough. Roll ½" thick and cut with 3" biscuit cutter. Cut each round in half and arrange on top of cobbler, around edge and in center. Sprinkle tops of biscuits with 2 tblsp. sugar and 1½ tsp. grated orange peel.

APRICOT DUMPLINGS

For a change, combine canned apricots and peaches in these dumplings

Crust:
    2   c. biscuit mix
    2   tblsp. sugar
    ⅔   c. milk

Filling:
    1   (1 lb. 14 oz.) can apricot halves
    2   tblsp. sugar
    2   tsp. grated orange peel
    2   tblsp. butter
Apricot Syrup

Crust: Combine biscuit mix and sugar. Add milk all at once and stir to a soft dough. Beat vigorously 20 strokes. Place on a floured board and knead 8 to 10 times. Roll in a 15″ × 10″ rectangle and cut in 6 (5″) squares. (Dough will be soft.)

Filling: Place 3 drained apricot halves in center of each square. Sprinkle 1 tsp. sugar and a little grated orange peel over apricots on each square; dot with butter. Pull corners of squares over apricots and press seams to seal. Carefully place dumplings, seams up, in baking pan; bake in moderate oven (375°F.) about 25 minutes, or until lightly browned.

• Serve in bowls, spooning Apricot Syrup over each serving. Garnish with any remaining apricots. Pass a pitcher of cream or top with vanilla ice cream. Makes 6 dumplings.

APRICOT SYRUP: Combine syrup drained from apricots with 1 tblsp. honey and ½ tsp. cinnamon. Bring to a boil. Makes about 1 cup.

LEMON-APPLE COBBLER

Early spring dessert—lemon and nutmeg complement apple flavors

Pastry for 1-crust pie
    ½   lemon, grated peel and juice
    ½   c. water
    ¾   c. sugar
    2   tblsp. flour
    ⅛   tsp. salt
    ¼   tsp. nutmeg
    4   c. peeled apple slices
    2   tblsp. butter or margarine

• Simmer lemon juice and peel with water about 5 minutes.
• Combine sugar, flour, salt and nutmeg. Blend into lemon mixture.
• Cook, stirring constantly, until mixture is thickened. Add apples and butter. Pour into a 6″ × 10″ × 2″ pan or 9″ pie pan. Cover top with rolled pastry and flute against pan. Cut steam vents.
• Bake in hot oven (400°F.) until apples are tender and crust is golden, about 35 minutes. Serve in bowls with cream or ice cream. Makes 5 servings.

Note: You may want to bake two of these cobblers if you're feeding hungry people.

APPLE-CRANBERRY COBBLER

Autumn's apples and cranberries are flavor mates in biscuit-topped dish

Filling:
    6   c. sliced peeled apples
    1 ½   c. cranberries
    1 ¼   c. sugar
    3   tblsp. quick-cooking tapioca
    2   tblsp. orange juice   *more*

1   tsp. grated orange peel
¼   tsp. salt
¼   tsp. cinnamon
2   tblsp. butter or margarine,
       melted

Topping:
1   c. biscuit mix
⅓   c. milk
2   tblsp. butter or margarine,
       melted
2   tblsp. sugar

Filling: Combine apples, cranberries, sugar, tapioca, orange juice and peel, salt and cinnamon. Turn into a 2 qt. casserole. Dot with butter.
• Cover and bake in hot oven (425°F.) 30 minutes.
Topping: Combine biscuit mix, milk, butter and sugar. Stir with fork until just moistened. Drop by tablespoonfuls on hot fruit mixture. Bake uncovered until topping is browned the way you like it, 15 to 18 minutes.
• Serve warm in dessert bowls with half-and-half or light cream. Makes 6 servings.

• Preheat oven to hot (400°F.).
• Combine plums, sugar and cornstarch in saucepan. Add water and cook, stirring constantly, until mixture comes to a boil. Remove from heat and stir in butter and cinnamon.
• Pour into greased 1½ qt. casserole. Place in hot oven while you prepare biscuit topping.
• Combine biscuit mix and sugar. Add milk and stir to make a soft dough with fork; beat 20 strokes. Drop by spoonfuls on top of hot plum mixture. Place in hot oven (400°F.) and bake 25 minutes or until biscuit topping is brown and juice is bubbly. Serve warm in bowls, topped with juices from cobbler and ice cream, or pass a bowl of whipped cream. Makes 6 servings.

Note: This recipe was tested with Santa Rosa plums. You can peel this fruit if you wish—dip it in boiling water, when skin cracks remove and peel with knife like a tomato.

RED PLUM COBBLER

Tart-sweet, color-bright fruit makes an especially delicious cobbler

2   c. sliced pitted red plums
1   c. sugar
2   tblsp. cornstarch
1   c. water
1   tblsp. butter
½   tsp. cinnamon
2   c. prepared biscuit mix
2   tblsp. sugar
⅔   c. milk

Springtime Pie in Winter

You don't have to wait to see the first robin of the season to have this refreshing dessert—not if you have frozen rhubarb in your freezer, or can find it in your supermarket. Pink cubes, teamed with juicy, sweet winter pears and rich biscuit topping, make a festive cobbler. Serve it warm in bowls with light cream. This is a dessert your family will ask you to repeat again and again.

PEAR-RHUBARB COBBLER

Red hots nip fruits with cinnamon and make them blush attractively

Filling:
1   (10 oz.) pkg. frozen rhubarb
3   ripe pears, any variety
2   tblsp. water
¼   c. sugar
2   tblsp. cornstarch
¼   tsp. cinnamon
1   tblsp. red cinnamon candies
     (red hots)
⅛   tsp. salt
1 ½ tblsp. butter or margarine

Crust:
1 ¼ c. biscuit mix
1   tblsp. sugar
2   tblsp. melted butter or marga
     rine
½   c. milk

Filling: Thaw package of rhubarb.
• Wash, core and peel pears; cut into ½″ cubes. Add to rhubarb along with water.
• Combine sugar, cornstarch, cinnamon, cinnamon candies (red hots) and salt. Add to fruit.
• Pour into greased 8″ square baking dish. Dot with butter. Cover and bake in hot oven (400°F.) 10 minutes, or until bubbling.
Crust: Combine biscuit mix and sugar; add butter and milk. Mix with a fork.
• Drop by spoonfuls on hot fruit mixture. Sprinkle additional sugar on top.
• Continue baking until biscuit is done, 15 to 20 minutes. Makes 6 servings.

Note: If frozen rhubarb is unsweetened, increase sugar to ⅔ c.

FRESH PEACH COBBLER

A summer version of peaches and cream with Honeyed Cream on top

1 ½ tblsp. cornstarch
¼   to ⅓ c. brown sugar
½   c. water
4   c. sweetened sliced peeled
     peaches
1   tblsp. butter
1   tblsp. lemon juice
Batter Topping
1   tblsp. granulated sugar
Spiced Honeyed Cream

• Mix cornstarch, sugar and water. Add peaches and cook until mixture is thickened, about 15 minutes. Add butter and lemon juice. Pour into an 8″ round baking dish.
• Drop spoonfuls of Batter Topping on top hot peach mixture. Sprinkle with sugar. Bake in hot oven (400°F.) 40 to 50 minutes. Serve warm, in bowls, with Spiced Honeyed Cream (recipe follows). Makes 6 servings.

BATTER TOPPING

½   c. sifted flour
½   c. sugar
½   tsp. baking powder
¼   tsp. salt
2   tblsp. soft butter
1   egg, slightly beaten

• Combine all ingredients and beat with spoon until batter is smooth.
• Drop by spoonfuls on hot peach mixture, spreading evenly. It spreads over peaches during baking.
• Bake as directed in Fresh Peach Cobbler.

SPICED HONEYED CREAM: Beat 1 c. heavy cream until thick. Add 2 tblsp. honey and ½ tsp. cinnamon. Beat to mix. Makes 1⅔ cups.

PEACH-APRICOT COBBLER

Two fruits produce wonderful flavor

Filling:
    1   (1 lb. 13 oz.) can sliced peaches
    1   (8¾ oz.) can apricot halves
    ½   c. sugar
    1   tblsp. cornstarch
    1   tblsp. butter or margarine
    ¼   tsp. cinnamon

Topping:
    1   c. sifted flour
    1   tblsp. sugar
    1½   tsp. baking powder
    ½   tsp. salt
    3   tblsp. shortening
    ½   c. milk

Filling: Drain peaches and apricots, reserving juices. Add enough peach juice to apricot juice to make 1 c.
• Combine sugar and cornstarch in saucepan. Blend in juice and cook over medium heat, stirring constantly, until mixture comes to a boil. Cook 1 minute longer.
• Remove from heat and stir in butter and cinnamon. Add fruits to thickened juice and pour into 1½ qt. casserole. Place in hot oven (400°F.) while you prepare topping.
Topping: Sift together flour, sugar, baking powder and salt. Cut in shortening until mixture resembles coarse crumbs. Stir in milk to make a soft dough.
• Drop by spoonfuls over hot fruit. Bake in hot oven (400°F.) until top is lightly browned, about 30 minutes. Serve warm with cream. Makes 6 servings.

CONCORD GRAPE COBBLER

From our FREEZING & CANNING COOKBOOK—*filling freezes successfully*

Biscuit Lattice
    10   c. stemmed and washed grapes
    2   c. sugar
    2½   tblsp. quick-cooking tapioca
    ¼   tsp. salt
    ⅛   tsp. cinnamon
    2   tblsp. lemon juice
    1   tblsp. butter

• Slip skins from grapes; set aside. Heat pulp to boiling; rub through coarse sieve or food mill to remove seeds. Discard seeds.
• Combine sugar, tapioca, salt and cinnamon. Add lemon juice and grape pulp. Cook until thickened, stirring.
• Remove from heat; add skins; mix.
• Pour into 8" square baking pan. Dot with butter. Add Biscuit Lattice.
• Bake in hot oven (400°F.) about 20 minutes, or until lattice crust is golden. Makes 9 servings. This filling will make 2 (8" or 9") pies.

BISCUIT LATTICE

    1½   c. sifted flour
    2¼   tsp. baking powder

.1   tblsp. sugar
¼   tsp. salt
¼   c. butter or margarine
¼   c. milk
1   egg, slightly beaten

• Sift together dry ingredients.
• Cut in butter. Make well in center; add milk and egg all at once; stir with fork into soft dough. Turn out on lightly floured pastry cloth and knead dough 10 times. Roll dough into 7″ x 9″ rectangle; cut in seven (9″) strips. Place 4 strips on hot filling one way, lattice other 3 strips opposite way. Start with center strip. Bake as directed in recipe for Concord Grape Cobbler.

To Freeze Cobbler Filling: Pour hot filling into 8″ square foil-lined baking pan; cool and freeze.
• Remove block of filling from pan; overwrap and return to freezer. Recommended storage time: 3 to 4 months.
To Serve: Return unthawed filling to pan. Dot with butter. Bake in hot oven (400°F.) about 35 to 40 minutes until bubbling hot, stirring occasionally.
• Remove from oven, cover with Biscuit Lattice; return to oven and bake about 20 minutes. Serve warm.

Dumplings Made with Pie Crust

Pastry and fruit bake together in many forms of fruit desserts. Among the all-time greats are dumplings— tender, juicy fruit in flaky, golden pastry jackets. With farm families, apple dumplings outrank all the rest. We give you two recipes for this treat. In one, you wrap the pastry around the apples, making an especially attractive dessert. You'll find a picture of this kind of dumpling in this book. In the other, you simply lay the pastry over the apples after they're in the baking pan, shaping it around the fruit. Both crusts are exceptionally crisp.

Vanilla ice cream, whipped cream and cream-to-pour are the traditional fruit-dumpling accompaniments. Some farmers say slices of cheese belong with dumplings. And there are country cooks who spice and slightly sweeten the pour cream.

APPLE DUMPLINGS

It's the method of adding pastry jackets that's different—try it

2   c. sifted flour
1   tsp. salt
⅔   c. shortening
⅓   c. cold water
6   medium apples
1   tsp. cinnamon
¼   tsp. nutmeg
1   c. sugar
4   tblsp. butter or margarine
2   tblsp. lemon juice
1   c. hot water

• Combine flour and salt. Cut in shortening until about the size of small peas. Add cold water, a little at a time, mixing with fork until particles form a ball when pressed together. Roll out

on lightly floured board ⅛″ thick. Cut in 6″ circles.
· Peel and core apples; place 2″ apart in greased casserole or 13″ × 9″ × 2″ pan. Combine cinnamon, nutmeg and ½ c. sugar. Divide mixture and put in centers of apples. Dot with 2 tblsp. butter.
· Fit pastry circle over each apple, barely tucking it under. Prick pastry in several places. Bake in very hot oven (450°F.) about 25 minutes. Reduce heat to 350°. Remove from oven.
· Meanwhile, combine remaining ½ c. sugar, lemon juice and remaining 2 tblsp. butter; add hot water. Simmer 5 minutes. Pour over dumplings; return to oven at once and continue baking 15 minutes, or until apples are tender. Serve warm or cold with cream or vanilla ice cream. Makes 6 servings.

Note: No chance of dumplings having a soggy undercrust. There's no pastry under the apples.

APPLE DUMPLINGS DE LUXE

One of FARM JOURNAL'S *best recipes reprinted from* COUNTRY COOKBOOK

Pastry for 2-crust pie
 3 tblsp. butter or margarine
 ¾ tsp. cinnamon
 ¾ tsp. allspice
 ¾ tsp. nutmeg
 ⅓ c. sifted brown sugar
 8 medium apples, peeled and cored
 3 tblsp. orange marmalade
1 ½ c. boiling water
1 ½ c. granulated sugar
 3 tblsp. fruit juice (orange, lemon, pineapple, apricot, etc.)

Red food color (optional)
Cream or Strawberry Hard Sauce

· Make paste of butter, spices and brown sugar.
· Roll out pastry ⅛″ thick; cut into eight (6″) squares. Place apple in center of each; put marmalade (or jelly) in cavity, and spread spicy paste over each apple.
· Moisten edges of pastry; bring points together over apple; seal sides firmly. Roll leftover pastry; cut into "streamers" to lay across tops of dumplings.
· Place in large greased baking dish, about 11″ × 15″; bake in moderate oven (375°F.) 30 minutes.
· While apples are baking, make syrup of water, granulated sugar and fruit juice; simmer to dissolve sugar. Pour over apples; bake 10 to 20 minutes more, basting frequently, to give attractive glaze. A little color may be added to syrup. Serve warm with cream or Strawberry Hard Sauce (Chapter 9). Makes 8 servings.

PEACH DUMPLINGS

Country cook's rule: Chill pastry-wrapped peaches before baking

Pastry for 2-crust pie
 6 medium peaches
 6 tblsp. granulated sugar
 6 tblsp. butter or margarine
Cinnamon or mace
 1 c. brown sugar
 ½ c. water

· Roll pastry in a rectangle about ⅛″ thick. Cut in 6 squares.
· Peel and pit firm, ripe peaches, using care to keep peaches whole. Fill cavity in each peach with 1 tblsp. granulated sugar and 1 tblsp. butter.

Place peaches in center of pastry squares and mold pastry around peaches to cover completely. Dust lightly with cinnamon. Place dumplings in a deep pan. Bake 10 minutes in hot oven (425°F.).

• Meanwhile, combine brown sugar and water; cook, stirring, about 5 minutes. Spoon some of syrup over dumplings. Reduce heat to moderate oven (350°F.) and continue baking, 40 to 50 minutes, basting every 10 minutes with a little of the syrup. Serve cold or warm with pitcher of cream, whipped cream or spoonfuls of vanilla ice cream. Makes 6 servings.

Cakes That Are Called Pies

Baking cake batter in pastry was an Early American custom. And the dividing line between cakes and pies was very thin—Boston Cream Pie, for instance. (Washington Pie is similar but has jelly filling.) Most of these farm desserts originated in New England and Pennsylvania Dutch country kitchens, but the recipes traveled with pioneers seeking their fortunes in the fertile heartlands and on to the Pacific shores.

Many of the old recipes have been abandoned with changes in diet patterns. We are including a few examples of these desserts that still are popular—too delicious to give up. They are adapted to the kinds of meals served in country homes. See if you don't agree that they're worth preserving in our culture.

SUPERB BOSTON CREAM PIE

This French version will make two cakes—freeze one and serve the other

```
3    eggs
1½  c. sugar
1¾  c. sifted cake flour
½   c. water
2    tsp. baking powder
¼    tsp. salt
1    c. heavy cream, whipped
```

• Beat eggs 2 minutes, using electric mixer on medium speed. Add sugar gradually and beat about 3 minutes. Add 1 c. cake flour and beat 1 minute longer. Mix in water with few rotations of beaters.

• Sift remaining ¾ c. cake flour, baking powder and salt together twice. Add to batter; beat 1 minute.

• Grease and flour 2 (9") round layer-cake pans. Divide batter evenly between them.

• Bake in slow oven (325°F.) 30 minutes. Remove from pans; cool thoroughly.

• Split one cake layer in half crosswise and put together with whipped cream. Wrap and refrigerate overnight. Just before serving, dust top with confectioners sugar. Makes 6 to 8 servings.

• Wrap and freeze remaining cake layer. When ready to use, split and fill like first layer.

Note: You will need to double the amount of heavy cream for filling if you serve both the cake layers instead of freezing one for future use.

BOSTON CREAM PIE

A FARM JOURNAL *5-star special from our* COUNTRY COOKBOOK

2   c. sifted cake flour
1 ¼ c. sugar
2 ½ tsp. baking powder
1   tsp. salt
⅓   c. shortening
1   c. milk
1   tsp. vanilla
¼   tsp. almond extract (optional)
1   egg, unbeaten
Custard Cream Filling
Chocolate Icing (optional)

• Sift dry ingredients into mixing bowl. Add shortening, milk, vanilla and almond extract. Beat 2 minutes (mixer at medium speed) or 300 strokes by hand.
• Add egg; beat 2 minutes as before. Pour into two greased 8″ or 9″ round layer pans.
• Bake in moderate oven (350°F.) 25 to 30 minutes. Makes 2 layers. Use one to make Boston Cream Pie; freeze the other.
• Split cooled cake layer in crosswise halves. Spread Custard Cream Filling over lower half. Cover with top half. Dust with confectioners sugar, or spread with Chocolate Icing.

CUSTARD CREAM FILLING

1   c. milk, scalded
½   c. sugar
3   tblsp. cornstarch
⅛   tsp. salt
2   eggs, slightly beaten
1   tblsp. butter or margarine
1   tsp. vanilla

• Gradually add milk to mixture of sugar, cornstarch and salt. Cook slowly, stirring constantly, until mixture thickens (about 10 to 15 minutes).
• Add about ½ c. hot mixture to eggs and blend; carefully combine both mixtures and cook about 3 minutes, stirring constantly.
• Remove from heat; blend in butter and vanilla. Cool. Makes 1¼ cups.

CHOCOLATE ICING

2   tblsp. butter or shortening
2   squares melted chocolate
¼   tsp. salt
½   tsp. vanilla
2 ¼ c. sifted confectioners sugar
¼   to ⅓ c. milk

• Blend together shortening, chocolate, salt and vanilla. Add sugar alternately with milk. Beat until smooth. If thinner glaze is desired, add a little more liquid.

FILLING VARIATIONS

BANANA: Spread Custard Cream Filling between halves of cooled split cake layer. Cover custard with banana slices (1 medium to large banana, sliced and sprinkled with lemon juice) and top with remaining cake.

PINEAPPLE: Combine 1 c. cooled filling with ½ c. drained crushed pineapple just before spreading between split cake. Pineapple may also be added to Coconut Filling.

ORANGE-PINEAPPLE: Add 1 tsp. grated orange peel to pineapple filling.

COCONUT: Add ⅔ c. flaked or cut shredded coconut to custard filling.

WASHINGTON PIE: Bake cake as for Boston Cream Pie. Put cool, split layers together with jelly; sprinkle top generously with confectioners sugar. Serve cut in wedges like pie.

Lemon Pie That's Different

Cooks in Pennsylvania Dutch communities turn out excellent pies that have a close kinship to cakes. Lemon Cake-Pie is one tasty example. Flaky pastry holds the cheerful yellow filling with a lovely, rich red-orange top, the color that develops in browning. Most acceptable dessert for a rather heavy meal. Truly delicate and delicious.

LEMON CAKE-PIE

Three-layered pie—crisp pastry holds custard layer with cakelike topping

Unbaked 9" pie shell
1   c. sugar
1   tblsp. butter
2   eggs, separated
2   tblsp. flour
1   lemon, grated peel and juice
1   c. milk

• Cream together sugar and butter. Beat egg yolks and add to creamed mixture. Add flour, grated lemon peel (2 tsp.) and lemon juice (3 tblsp.) and milk.
• Beat egg whites until stiff, but not dry, peaks form. Fold into lemon mixture. Pour into pie shell.
• Bake in very hot oven (450°F.) 10 minutes; reduce heat to 325°F. and bake 20 minutes longer, or until filling sets and top is browned.

BLUEBERRY FUNNY CAKE-PIE

You can keep the makings for this winter dessert treat in your cupboard

Unbaked 10" pie shell
¼   c. butter
¾   c. sugar
1   egg
1 ¼   c. sifted cake flour
1   tsp. baking powder
½   tsp. salt
½   c. milk
1   tsp. vanilla
Blueberry Sauce
Vanilla ice cream

• Cream butter; add sugar and mix thoroughly. Add egg and mix well. Sift flour with baking powder and salt; add alternately with milk to creamed mixture. Add vanilla.
• Pour batter into pie shell. Gently pour lukewarm Blueberry Sauce over top.
• Bake in moderate oven (375°F.) 35 to 40 minutes, or until cake tests done. Serve warm with vanilla ice cream. Makes 8 servings.

BLUEBERRY SAUCE: Thoroughly drain 1 (15 oz.) can blueberries, saving 1 tblsp. juice. Combine the 1 tblsp. juice with 1 tblsp. lemon juice, ½ c. sugar and blueberries. Heat just until sugar is dissolved. Cool to lukewarm.

OLD-FASHIONED DATE PIE

Rich but delicious winter dessert

1   c. sugar
3   tblsp. flour
2   tsp. baking powder
1   c. pitted chopped dates
1   c. chopped walnuts
2   eggs, beaten
Sweetened whipped cream

• Sift together sugar, 3 tblsp. flour and baking powder.
• Dredge dates and walnuts with remaining 1 tblsp. flour. Add to beaten eggs.
• Fold in sugar mixture. Pour into greased 9″ pie pan.
• Bake in moderate oven (350°F.) 40 to 50 minutes. Cut in wedges and serve warm or cold with sweetened whipped cream. Makes 8 servings.

Shoofly Pie for Coffee Parties

This famous Pennsylvania Dutch molasses pie, sometimes called a molasses cake, has many variations, but there are three important versions. One is dry—gingerbread baked in a pastry shell. It's favored for dunking in coffee. Number two is put together in the pastry with alternate layers of crumbs and a molasses mixture. The third, and the charm, at least for most gourmets, is the pie with what Pennsylvania Dutch cooks call "a moist zone." We give you our recipe for the third type.

Important points to heed in baking this historical pie are (1) use level measurement of shortening, not butter, to avoid a soggy crust, and (2) work fast once you combine the baking soda and hot water so you won't lose the leavening properties before the pie reaches the oven.

SHOOFLY PIE

Originally a breakfast pie—favored now for coffee party refreshments

Pastry for 2-crust pie
2   c. sifted flour
½   c. sugar
½   tsp. baking soda
¼   c. shortening
1   c. light molasses or cane syrup
1   tsp. baking soda
1   c. hot water

• Line 2 (8″) pie pans with pastry; flute edges.
• Combine flour, sugar, ½ tsp. baking soda and shortening and mix to make crumbs. Divide crumbs evenly between 2 pastry-lined pie pans and spread in smooth layers.
• Combine molasses, 1 tsp. baking soda and hot water. Pour over crumbs in pie pans.
• Bake in moderate oven (375°F.) 40 minutes. Makes 10 to 12 servings.

TARTS AND TURNOVERS

Tarts and turnovers show up at parties, picnics and on the company dinner table, but they're equally at home in family meals. And no pies come in greater variety of size, shape and fillings than these miniatures.

Turnovers serve a double purpose. Fill them with meat and they're sandwiches (Ranchers' Beef Turnovers, Chapter 10). Bake fruit mixtures in them, they're dessert. Cut the pastry in circles, fold, they're half-moons; in squares, they're pocketbooks. Try serving Mincemeat, Frosted Mincemeat or Date-Walnut Turnovers with coffee when you entertain at Christmastime. Our man-sized, husband-pleasing Raisin or Apple Turnovers are fine for family dinners. They're mighty popular as lunch-box tuck-ins, too.

As party pickups, tiny tarts make wonderful easy-to-serve—and eat—finger food. What would delight guests more at a tea party than our Honeyed Lemon or Pecan Tarts? And what would please the family more on a snowy day than big, juicy Concord Grape Tarts with that fresh-from-the-vine taste? We tell you how to make tart shells of all sizes.

We're including in this chapter directions for making French Puff Pastry, because it has been the base for fancy party food for many years, all over the world. If you're skeptical of your ability to make French pastries, you'll find that our recipes give exact instructions. They take time, of course, but aren't difficult. A tray of homemade Napoleons, Cream Twists and Butterflies will charm and impress guests.

Many tarts are at their best assembled shortly before serving. With baked pastry shells on hand and fillings ready in the refrigerator, putting them together and adding a garnish is quick, easy and rewarding.

One big reason for the popularity of these self-contained servings of pie is that they are all ready to bring out—no last-minute cutting of pies or difficult transfer of cream-filled wedges. Just the thing for crowds, for receptions or company refreshments.

Pastry for Tarts

While most homemakers think of tarts as party food because they look so festive, they're one of the best ways to salvage leftover pastry scraps. Look in Chapter 2 for directions on how to freeze unbaked and baked tart shells. You also will find, in the same chapter, detailed recipes for making the shells. Read them before using the tart recipes that follow. And try some of the interesting kinds of pastry designed especially for these little pies.

You can vary the size and shape of tarts by shaping the pastry on aluminum foil (Chapter 2). This way you can make the 2- or 3-bite size or pastries large enough to take the place of pieces of pie in a meal.

We also baked some of our tart shells over inverted muffin-cup pans.

The number of tart shells a recipe yields depends primarily on how thick you roll the pastry and the size of muffin-cup pans and pastry-lined foil circles.

Glamorous Fruit Tarts

Fruit-filled tarts are the largest family in the world of small pastries. That's why we start this chapter with recipes that feature the gifts of orchards, berry patches and citrus groves.

We're repeating a suggestion to remind you again of the many exciting surprises you can introduce in tarts with different kinds of crusts. Cheese Pastry and fruit fillings are fast friends. And tart shells shortened with butter have many boosters in the hostess crowd (see Chapter 2). Or do as many women do and use your own make of pie crust, or a packaged mix, and depend on the fillings to provide color brightness and piquant flavors.

APRICOT TARTS

Wonderful way to serve the tawny-orange fresh fruit to summer guests

1 ¼ c. fine graham cracker crumbs
½ c. sugar
½ c. butter
½ tsp. cinnamon
1 ½ c. ripe apricot quarters
2 tsp. lemon juice
⅛ tsp. salt
2 drops almond extract
1 c. heavy cream, whipped

• Mix crumbs with ¼ c. sugar, butter and cinnamon in bowl.
• Arrange 12 paper baking cups in muffin-cup pan. Divide crumb mixture

evenly in them. Press crumbs against bottom and sides of paper cups to make a firm crust. Place in refrigerator until thoroughly chilled.

• Gently mix ripe apricots with lemon juice, salt, almond extract and remaining ¼ c. sugar. Fold into whipped cream. Spoon lightly into crumb crusts. Chill until serving time, or freeze, wrap and return to freezer for use within a week. Let thaw at room temperature about 30 minutes before serving.

CONCORD GRAPE TARTS

They're made with bottled grape juice but have a vineyard-fresh taste

Tart shells (pastry for 2-crust pie)
¼   c. cornstarch
½   c. sugar
¼   tsp. salt
4   egg yolks, beaten
1   (1 pt. 8 oz.) bottle grape juice
     (3 c.)
1 ½ tblsp. butter
1   tblsp. lemon juice
Meringue (4 egg whites)

• Combine cornstarch, sugar and salt in saucepan.
• To egg yolks gradually add grape juice, mixing well and blend into cornstarch-sugar mixture, stirring until smooth. Cook over medium heat, stirring constantly; boil 5 minutes. Remove from heat.
• Stir in butter and lemon juice. Cover and cool.
• Fill baked tart shells; top with meringue (see Perfect Meringue for Topping Pies, Chapter 9), sealing to edges. Bake in moderate oven (350°F.) 12 to 15 minutes. Makes about 12 (3½") tarts.

GOOD COUNTRY-KITCHEN IDEA: "Line cool tart shells with a thin layer of cream cheese," suggests a Georgia homemaker. "I soften the cheese by beating in a little orange or pineapple juice before spreading it. Next, I cover cheese layer with fresh or frozen fruit or berries. Strawberries and peaches are my family's favorites. Then I melt a little jelly and spoon it over the fruit for an attractive glaze. The brighter the jelly is in color, the prettier the tarts are. Sometimes I use apple jelly which I've tinted with a few drops of food color."

Cherry Tarts for Tea Party

When you want a tray of color-bright tarts to serve along with cookies and tea, try these attractive and easy-to-make miniature tart shells filled with red cherries. The Ohio farm woman who sent us the recipe says her young granddaughter is proud of the tarts she makes. They're glamorous enough to give junior cooks the feeling of real accomplishment. You'll find plenty of uses for any leftover cherry pie filling—as topping for ice cream, vanilla and tapioca puddings and slices of unfrosted cake, for instance.

CHERRY TARTS

Pick-up tarts to eat like cookies— they're colorful, delicious, inviting

1   c. flour
½   c. butter or margarine
1   (3 oz.) pkg. cream cheese
Canned cherry pie filling

• Mix flour, butter and cream cheese to make dough. Wrap in waxed paper and refrigerate at least 2 hours, or overnight. (If overnight, let stand at room temperature ½ hour before rolling.)
• Roll to ¼" thickness and cut in 12 circles (about 2½") and 24 rings the same size, using doughnut cutter. Moisten edge of a circle with water and lay one ring on it. Moisten edge of ring and place second ring on top of it. Press edge of tart with a sharp fork. Repeat until all pastry is used.
• Place on baking sheet and bake in very hot oven (450°F.) 7 minutes. Cool.
• Fill tarts with prepared cherry pie filling. Makes 12 tarts.
• For added appeal, top each tart, just before serving, with 1 tsp. sweetened whipped cream.

VARIATION

MINCEMEAT TARTS: Fill cooled tart shells with mincemeat pie filling instead of cherry. Garnish with a little whipped cream.

CHEESE PARTY TARTS

Make them one day and chill; garnish prettily and serve the next day

Crust:
2   c. sifted flour
½   c. sugar
¼   tsp. salt
2   tsp. grated lemon peel
½   tsp. vanilla
1   c. soft butter or margarine
2   egg yolks

Filling:
2   (8 oz.) pkgs. cream cheese
1   (3 oz.) pkg. cream cheese
¾   c. sugar
1½ tblsp. flour
⅛   tsp. salt
½   tsp. grated lemon peel
⅛   tsp. vanilla
2   eggs
1   egg yolk
2   tblsp. light cream

Crust: Combine flour, sugar, salt, lemon peel and vanilla. Cut in butter and egg yolks with pastry blender until well blended.
• Put about ¼ c. mixture in each of 10 well-greased 5 oz. custard cups. Pat mixture evenly into bottom and sides to line cups. (Dip fingers in water to keep them from sticking.)
• Chill at least 1 hour.
Filling: Beat softened cream cheese until light and fluffy. Gradually add mixture of sugar, flour and salt, beating smooth after each addition. Beat in lemon peel and vanilla. Add eggs, one at a time, and egg yolk, beating well after each addition. Beat in cream.
• Spoon into lined custard cups.

• Bake in extremely hot oven (500°F.) 10 minutes. Reduce heat to 350°F. and continue baking until golden brown, 20 to 25 minutes. (There will be cracks in cheese filling.)

• Cool at room temperature. Carefully remove from custard cups and chill thoroughly.

• To serve, top with a little dairy sour cream and a spoonful of colorful jam, jelly or fruit preserves. Or top with fresh or frozen fruit. Makes 10 tarts.

Note: These tarts are suggestive of cheesecake baked in individual pastry shells.

SPEEDY FRUIT TARTS

Warm-from-the-oven family dessert

½   c. soft butter or margarine
2   c. biscuit mix
6   tblsp. boiling water
1   (1 lb. 5 oz.) can raspberry pie
    filling

• Cut butter into biscuit mix. Add boiling water and stir to make a ball.

• Press about 2 tblsp. dough on bottom and sides of 12 muffin-cup pans, forming a shell about ⅛" to ³⁄₁₆" thick. Bake in hot oven (425°F.) 6 minutes.

• Remove from oven and fill each biscuit cup with 2 tblsp. raspberry pie filling. Return to oven and bake 8 minutes longer. Serve warm. Makes 12 tarts.

Note: Substitute cherry, apricot-pineapple and other kinds of canned pie fillings for raspberry.

PRUNE-APRICOT TARTS

Recipe from our COUNTRY COOKBOOK
—too good to leave out of this book

Pastry for 2-crust pie
1 ½   c. dried prunes
1   c. dried apricots
½   c. sugar
½   tsp. salt
1   tsp. cinnamon
½   tsp. nutmeg
¾   c. prune liquid
Orange Cream Dress-Up

• Rinse and drain prunes. Cook in boiling water to cover, about 15 minutes; drain, reserving ¾ c. liquid. Remove pits.

• Rinse and drain apricots; do not cook.

• Chop and combine fruits; add sugar, salt, spices and prune liquid; bring to boil. Simmer until thickened, about 5 minutes.

• Roll out pastry and cut in 5" circles. Place on foil rounds the same size as pastry. Put about 3 tblsp. filling in center of each circle. Moisten edges and pinch together in about 6 or 7 pleats.

• Bake in hot oven (425°F.) 15 to 18 minutes. Top tarts with Orange Cream Dress-Up. Makes about 9 tarts.

ORANGE CREAM DRESS-UP: Whip ½ c. heavy cream; fold in ¼ c. sieved cottage cheese. Add ¼ tsp. grated orange peel. Chill. Spoon on tarts just before serving.

VARIATIONS

PRUNE-APRICOT TURNOVERS: Place the filling on half of each pastry circle, fold over and seal edges by pressing with tines of fork or with handle of teaspoon. Make a few slits in top of turnovers. Follow baking directions for Prune-Apricot Tarts.

These turnovers freeze well. Cool thoroughly, wrap and freeze. To serve, heat in a moderate oven (350°F.). Top with Orange Cream Dress-Up. Makes about 9 turnovers.

PRUNE-APRICOT PIE: Bake filling for Prune-Apricot Tarts in a 2-crust (9") pie.

MINCE TARTLETS

You'll be ready for holiday guests with these tartlets in the freezer

Pastry for 2 (2-crust) pies
1   (1 lb. 6 oz.) can mince pie filling
Sugar

• Divide pastry in fourths. Roll out, one at a time, on lightly floured surface. Cut in circles with 3" cookie cutter.
• Place half the circles on baking sheet. Top each with 1 tblsp. mincemeat. Place other half pastry circles on tops. Seal edges together by pressing with tines of fork. Prick top of each tartlet for steam vent. Sprinkle with sugar.
• Bake in moderate oven (375°F.) until lightly browned, about 30 minutes. Makes 20 to 22 tartlets.

FRUIT-OF-THE-MONTH TARTS

One of our FARM JOURNAL's California readers is praised in her neighborhood for her glamorous way of serving seasonal and drained canned fruits in tart shells. She dips the prepared fruits in melted currant jelly to glaze them. Then she places them in tart shells, spoons whipped cream on top and serves the dessert at once. If the fruit needs to be extended, she first lines the tart shells with vanilla pudding and pie filling, prepared by package directions, or with softened and whipped cream cheese.

Among the favorite fresh fruits for these exotic tarts are: strawberries, blueberries, pitted sweet cherries, grapes, peach halves, chunks of fresh pineapple, thick banana slices, nectarine halves and pears, cut in lengthwise halves and then in two crosswise. Canned apricots and peach halves also are good.

The tarts must be assembled at mealtime. They are not a make-ahead dessert.

SPECIAL SUNDAE TARTS

Like to use your imagination in cooking? If you do, here's your chance to try out some of your ideas. You don't need recipes to make fascinating sundae tarts. All you must have is fruit or berries, ice cream and the spirit of adventure.

Just before mealtime, fill tart shells about three fourths full of prepared fruit. Experiment with sliced strawberries or peaches; lightly sweetened raspberries or blueberries; frozen or drained, canned pineapple chunks; diced bananas dipped in lemon juice or mixed with diced oranges; thick applesauce; rhubarb sauce; cooked and cut-up prunes or dried apricots, or a combination of the two; or frozen strawberries and peaches.

Top the fruit with scoops of ice cream or fluffs of whipped cream and garnish attractively until the tarts look like ice cream sundaes. You can spoon on the ice cream, sweetened, crushed berries, diced peaches or other fruit in the tart shells; or top with chopped maraschino cherries, flaked coconut, chopped nuts or chocolate shavings, for instance.

Try different kinds of ice cream, too. Try peach ice cream on raspberry tarts, peppermint stick on applesauce, strawberry on pineapple, prune and apricot tarts. Pour chocolate sauce on banana tarts. You'll get some wonderfully good flavor and color combinations—and plenty of good eating.

STRAWBERRY CREAM TARTS

French Pastry Cream plus fresh berries make glamorous pastries

Tart shells (pastry for 2-crust pie)
1   recipe Pastry Cream
½   c. currant jelly
1   pt. strawberries

• Spoon Pastry Cream (in this chapter) into baked tart shells, dividing it equally.
• Melt currant jelly over low heat.
• Place four ripe berries, pointed ends up, in each tart shell. Spoon currant jelly over berries. Refrigerate until time to serve. Makes about 12 (3″) tarts.

Note: Assemble the tarts the day you serve them.

STRAWBERRY TARTS

Set out a tray of these delicious beauties at your next buffet supper

Tart shells (pastry for 1-crust pie)
1 ½   pts. fresh strawberries
¼   c. sugar
½   c. currant or red apple jelly
Few drops red food color
½   c. heavy cream, whipped

• Slice half of strawberries (1½ c.). Place in bowl and add sugar. Cut remaining berries in lengthwise halves.
• Stir jelly in small pan over medium heat until it melts. Add food color to deepen color.
• Assemble tarts shortly before serving. Spoon about 3 tblsp. sliced berries into each baked tart shell. Top with berry halves. Spoon on melted jelly and garnish with whipped cream. Makes about 6 (3½″) tarts.

CHOCOLATE CRINKLE CUPS

Party dessert for Junior High set

• Melt 2 tblsp. semisweet chocolate pieces at a time over hot (not boiling) water. As soon as melted, spread chocolate over inside of fluted cupcake papers. Set in muffin pans; freeze at once until firm, about 15 minutes; peel off the paper and return cups to freezer until ready to serve.
• At serving time, fill them with ice cream or sherbet and garnish with fruit. One (6 oz.) pkg. semisweet chocolate pieces makes about 8 crinkle cups.

Note: Junior High cooks will like to make these. Their mothers will enjoy serving them to guests, too.

HONEYED LEMON TARTS

Garnish at serving time with coconut—finger food for your next tea party

Tart shells (pastry for 2-crust pie)
1   c. sugar
¼   c. butter
½   c. lemon juice
1   tblsp. grated lemon peel
2   eggs, beaten

• Combine sugar, butter, lemon juice and peel and eggs. Cook in double boiler over hot water until mixture thickens.
• Pour into baked tart shells. Makes about 20 (2″) tarts.

Note: Filling for Best-Ever Lemon Meringue Pie (Chapter 4) may be served in tart shells. Garnish with whipped cream puffs.

ORANGE SURPRISE TARTS

The surprise is the chocolate liner under the fluffy filling—different

Tart shells (pastry for 2-crust pie)
1   (4 or 5 oz.) milk-chocolate bar
2   tblsp. light cream
3   egg yolks, slightly beaten
¼   c. orange juice
1   tsp. lemon juice
½   c. sugar
⅛   tsp. salt
1   c. heavy cream, whipped
1   tblsp. grated orange peel
Orange segments

• Melt chocolate bar with cream over hot water. Stir until smooth. Cool slightly and spread in tart shells.
• Place egg yolks in double boiler.

Gradually add orange and lemon juices, stirring constantly. Stir in sugar and salt. Cook over hot water, stirring constantly, until mixture thickens. Remove from heat and cool.
• Carefully fold cream, whipped very stiff, and orange peel into orange mixture. Chill. Just before serving, spoon into baked tart shells. Garnish tops with orange segments. Makes about 10 (4″) tarts.

CURRANT COCONUT TARTLETS

Party guests will like these dainty old-fashioned-tasting teatime treats

Pastry (Pecan Tartlets)
⅔   c. currants (dried)
4   tsp. butter
⅔   c. brown sugar, firmly packed
1   small egg, beaten
⅓   tsp. vanilla
⅓   tsp. nutmeg
⅓   c. flaked coconut

• Wash currants and cover with boiling water. Let stand a few minutes. Drain and while still hot, add butter, brown sugar and egg. Stir in remaining ingredients and drop mixture into pastry for Pecan Tartlets in this chapter. (It's a good idea to cover tartlets the first 10 minutes of baking with sheet of aluminum foil.)
• Bake in moderate oven (350°F.) 15 minutes; reduce oven temperature to 250° and continue baking 10 minutes longer. Makes about 3 dozen.

Note: To garnish tartlets, add polka dots of Orange Cheese Topping (Chapter 9) shortly before serving.

Light-as-Chiffon Tarts

You can heap the cloudlike fillings of chiffon pies in tender, flaky tart shells with confidence the dessert will make a glorious meal ending. Many of the fillings are colorful and all of them are attractive garnished at serving time with whipped cream. They contain fewer calories than most tarts, which adds to their high favor with weight-conscious people.

We give you recipes for Strawberry and Pumpkin Chiffon Tarts, but don't stop with them. Turn to Chapter 5 and select other fillings from the recipes for chiffon pies. The filling for a 9" pie is the right amount for 12 (3") tart shells.

STRAWBERRY CHIFFON TARTS

Fresh as spring—and luscious

Tart shells (pastry for 2-crust pie)
1 pt. fresh strawberries
¾ c. sugar
1 envelope unflavored gelatin
¼ c. cold water
½ c. hot water
1 tblsp. lemon juice
⅛ tsp. salt
1 c. heavy cream
2 egg whites
12 strawberries

• Crush 1 pt. berries (you will have 1¼ c.); cover with ½ c. sugar and let stand 30 minutes.
• Soften gelatin in cold water; dissolve in hot water. Cool. Add crushed

berries, lemon juice and salt. Chill until mixture mounds when dropped from spoon. Test frequently while chilling.
• Fold in ½ c. cream, whipped. Beat egg whites until frothy; gradually add remaining ¼ c. sugar, beating until glossy, firm peaks form. Fold into strawberry mixture. Spoon into tart shells and chill until firm.
• To serve, garnish with remaining ½ c. cream, whipped, and whole berries. Makes about 12 (3") tarts.

VARIATION

STRAWBERRY CHIFFON PIE: Spoon filling into 9" Graham Cracker Crumb Crust.

PUMPKIN CHIFFON TARTS

Sweet and spicy holiday dessert

Tart shells (pastry for 2-crust pie)
1 envelope unflavored gelatin
¾ c. light brown sugar, firmly packed
½ tsp. salt
1 tsp. pumpkin pie spice
3 eggs, separated
¾ c. milk
1¼ c. canned pumpkin
⅓ c. granulated sugar
Whipped cream
Amber Caramel Sauce (Chapter 9)

• Combine gelatin, brown sugar, salt and spice in saucepan. Combine egg yolks and milk; stir into gelatin mixture. Cook, stirring constantly, until mixture comes to a boil. Remove from heat; add pumpkin. Chill mixture until it mounds slightly when dropped from spoon. Test frequently for mounding stage.

• Beat egg whites until frothy; add sugar and beat until glossy, stiff peaks form.

• Fold pumpkin mixture into egg whites. Spoon into tart shells. Chill until firm. Serve topped with whipped cream; pass Amber Caramel Sauce to pour over. Makes about 12 (3″) tarts.

VARIATION

PUMPKIN CHIFFON PIE: Spoon filling into a 9″ Graham Cracker Crumb Crust.

RAINBOW TARTS: One farm hostess delighted her guests at a springtime tea party by serving a tray of tarts, colorful as the season's blossoms. For filling tart shells she used Lime, Orange (Chapter 5), Lemon and Strawberry (Chapter 7) Chiffon Pie fillings. The garnishes were tiny fresh mint leaves on the lime, small canned mandarin orange sections, drained, on the orange, coconut on the lemon and ripe strawberries on the strawberry tarts.

Nuts Provide Flavor and Texture

Come with us to another sweet world of party-spirit tarts—a quartet of little pies in which nuts are important. Notice that Individual Chess Pies are rich and luscious with farm foods, eggs and cream, with raisins and lemon juice adding to their tastiness. Some people call them Chess Tarts. By any name, they're indisputably delicious.

Make Pecan Tartlets at your leisure and freeze until needed. Then you'll have refreshments for your party or drop-in guests as quickly as you can make coffee. Heavenly Tarts are miniature Lemon Angel Pies, with no cutting required at serving time.

The filling for Mocha Tarts carries that wonderful blend of chocolate and coffee flavors, with nuts as garnish. Your guests will be talking about how good they are, long after your party.

INDIVIDUAL CHESS PIES

Buttery-rich, nut-raisin filling—delightful contrast to flaky pastry

Tart shells (pastry for 2-crust pie)
½   c. butter or margarine
1   c. sugar
4   eggs, separated
½   c. chopped walnuts or pecans
1   c. chopped raisins
1   tblsp. lemon juice
Meringue (2 egg whites)

• Cream butter; add sugar and mix until light and fluffy. Beat yolks of 2 eggs and 2 whole eggs together and add to sugar-butter mixture. Add nuts and raisins. Stir in lemon juice and cook in double boiler over hot water until thick and dark brown in color, about 15 minutes. Cool.

• Pour into baked tart shells; top with meringue (see Perfect Meringue for Topping Pies, Chapter 9). Brown in moderate oven (350°F.) 12 to 15 minutes. Makes about 8 (4″) tarts.

Note: Serve these rich pies cold, never warm.

PECAN TARTLETS

Delicious serve them like cookies

1   c. butter or margarine
2   (3 oz.) pkgs. cream cheese
2 ½ c. unsifted flour
¾   tsp. salt
1 ½ c. chopped pecans
1   c. brown sugar, firmly packed
2   eggs, slightly beaten
2   tblsp. melted butter or margarine
½   tsp. vanilla
½   c. light corn syrup

• Soften 1 c. butter and cheese. Blend in half the flour at a time and ½ tsp. salt; shape pastry into two 2″ diameter rolls; wrap and chill overnight.
• Slice pastry into 36 portions; press into 2″ muffin-cup pans. Line cups; do not make rims.
• Place half the nuts in lined cups.
• Using a rotary beater, gradually add sugar to eggs. Add melted butter, remaining ¼ tsp. salt and vanilla. Stir in syrup. Pour into tart shells.
• Sprinkle with remaining nuts. Bake in moderate oven (350°F.) about 20 minutes. Makes 3 dozen.

Note: For tiny bite-size tarts, bake in paper bonbon cups. Have pastry at room temperature when you line cups.

HEAVENLY TARTS

You can make these a day ahead

1 ½ c. sugar
¼   tsp. cream of tartar
4   eggs, separated
3   tblsp. lemon juice
1   tblsp. grated lemon peel
1   pt. heavy cream

• Sift together 1 c. sugar and cream of tartar. Beat egg whites until soft peaks form; add sugar mixture gradually and continue beating until very stiff. Spoon in mounds on baking sheet covered with heavy ungreased paper; shape cups (6 to 8) with spoon.
• Bake in very slow oven (275°F.) 1 hour. Remove from paper and cool.
• Beat egg yolks slightly, stir in remaining ½ c. sugar, lemon juice and peel. Cook in top of double boiler until very thick, 8 to 10 minutes. Cool.
• Whip cream, combine half of it with lemon-egg mixture and use to fill meringue shells. Cover with remaining whipped cream. Place in refrigerator for 24 hours. Makes 6 to 8 servings.

MOCHA TARTS

For a special party, omit walnuts and top with chopped pistachio nuts

Tart shells (pastry for 1-crust pie)
½   c. chopped walnuts
1   (4 oz.) pkg. instant chocolate pudding and pie mix
1   tsp. instant coffee powder
¾   c. milk
1   c. dairy sour cream

• Sprinkle ¼ c. walnuts in baked tart shells.   *more*

• Beat together pudding mix, coffee powder and milk until smooth. Fold in sour cream. Spoon into tart shells.

Sprinkle remaining ¼ c. nuts on top. Chill. Makes about 6 (3½″) tarts.

Good Ideas from Our Test Kitchens

TART FILLINGS: Line tart shells with packaged pudding and pie filling mix, softened cream cheese, whipped cream or packaged whip mix. Fill with perfect pieces of fresh, frozen or canned fruits.

BANANA TARTS: Fill tart shells with sieved apricot preserves and top with banana slices. Glaze bananas with some of the preserves, melted over heat.

SHERBET TARTS: Scoop balls of lime sherbet or sherbets of other flavors with melon scoop; place on tray and freeze. Put the firm, colorful sherbet balls in tiny tart shells just before serving.

FRUIT TURNOVERS: Use 3″ squares or circles of pastry and ½ tsp. berry or fruit preserves to make tiny turnovers.

Turnovers Tote Successfully

Turnovers travel well—in lunch boxes, picnic hampers and packages for potluck meals—or wherever you go, taking along food to share with friends. You can bake these individual pies several days or weeks ahead and freeze them. They'll thaw on the way.

You may prefer to freeze turnovers before baking, especially if you're going to serve them at home. To bake frozen turnovers, unwrap, place on a baking sheet and bake on the lower shelf in a hot oven (425°F.) until golden, about 20 to 25 minutes. Serve them as the occasion dictates—sprinkled with sifted confectioners sugar; frosted; faintly warm, with ice cream; with a dessert sauce poured over.

Picnic Cherry Turnovers, for instance, may be sugar-glazed when served out in the yard or in a park, but when you're having them for at-home company, hot Cherry Sauce spooned over them adds color and double-cherry taste. We give you recipes for both Sugar Glaze and Cherry Sauce.

Turnovers are extremely adaptable pies. Farmers almost always will settle for them as a dessert or snack any day and any place if there's plenty of coffee to sip with them.

Notice to cooks: Remember that the critical point in making turnovers is to be certain you have a tight seal around the edges. This will prevent juices from escaping during baking.

DATE AND WALNUT TURNOVERS

Add these dainties to tray of Christmas cookies for a new taste treat

Pastry for 2-crust pie
24 whole fresh dates, pitted
½   c. walnut pieces
2   tblsp. sugar
1   tsp. cinnamon

• Divide pastry in half. Roll each half into a 10″ × 9″ rectangle. Cut into 2½″ × 3″ rectangles.
• Stuff dates with walnuts and wrap each date in pastry rectangle; press edges to seal and tuck the ends under.
• Combine sugar and cinnamon. Dip tops of turnovers in sugar-cinnamon mixture. Bake on baking sheet in hot oven (425°F.) until golden brown, about 12 minutes. Makes 24 turnovers.

PICNIC CHERRY TURNOVERS

Just right for toting to picnics and in lunch boxes—a finger-food pie

Pastry for 2-crust pie
1   (1 lb.) can drained pitted tart
       cherries (about 1 ¾ c.)
½   c. sugar
1   tblsp. quick-cooking tapioca
⅛   tsp. salt
4   drops almond extract
Few drops red food color
1   tblsp. butter or margarine
Sugar Glaze

• Combine cherries, sugar, tapioca and salt in medium saucepan; cook and stir over medium heat until mixture comes to a boil; let simmer about 5 minutes. Remove from heat; add almond extract, food color and butter. Cool.
• Divide pastry dough in half and roll each in a large square. Cut each in 4 (6″) squares. Put about ¼ c. cherry mixture in center of each square of pastry. Moisten edges and fold over each square to make a triangle. Seal edges by pressing with a floured fork. Cut slits in turnovers over filling to permit steam to escape. Place on an ungreased baking sheet.
• Bake in hot oven (425°F.) 12 to 15 minutes, or until light golden brown. Remove from oven and brush, while warm, with Sugar Glaze. Makes 8 (6″) turnovers.

SUGAR GLAZE: Combine ½ c. sifted confectioners sugar, 1 tblsp. water and 1 drop vanilla. Brush on hot turnovers.

VARIATION

• Omit Sugar Glaze and serve warm with Cherry Sauce—makes turnovers rival cherry pie.

CHERRY SAUCE

1   (1 lb.) can pitted tart cherries
⅔   c. sugar
3   tblsp. cornstarch
⅛   tsp. salt
2   tblsp. butter or margarine
Few drops red food color

• Drain cherries, reserving juice. Add water, if needed, to make 1⅓ c. juice.
• Combine sugar, cornstarch and salt in saucepan; gradually stir in cherry

juice. Cook mixture, stirring constantly, over medium heat until it boils and is thickened and clear, about 6 minutes.

• Add butter, stirring until it melts, and a few drops of red food color. Stir ½ c. drained cherries into the sauce. Serve warm over Picnic Cherry Turnovers. Makes about 2 cups.

RAISIN-ORANGE TURNOVERS

Keep a supply in freezer to serve with hot coffee—extra-good flavor team

Pastry for 2-crust pie
1 ¾ c. seedless raisins
1 ¾ c. water
¼ c. orange juice
⅓ c. brown sugar, firmly packed
1 tblsp. quick-cooking tapioca
½ tsp. cinnamon
¼ tsp. salt
1 tblsp. vinegar
1 tblsp. butter
2 tsp. grated orange peel

• Combine raisins, water and orange juice in saucepan. Bring to a boil; boil 5 minutes. Add sugar, tapioca, cinnamon and salt. Cook, stirring, until mixture again comes to a boil. It should be thick. Remove from heat, add vinegar, butter and orange peel. Cool.

• Roll out pastry very thin (less than ⅛" if possible). Cut in 6" circles or 5" squares. Moisten edges with cold water. Place 2 to 3 tblsp. filling on one side of each square or circle of pastry; fold over and seal edges with fork. Make slits with sharp knife in tops of turnovers for escape of steam. Bake in hot oven (425°F.) about 20 minutes. Makes 8 to 10 turnovers.

Note: You can give the turnovers a glistening top with the following Apricot Glaze or plain Sugar Glaze (see Picnic Cherry Turnovers).

APRICOT GLAZE: Combine ¾ c. apricot preserves and ¼ c. water. Stir over medium heat until preserves melt. Put through sieve and spoon over slightly warm Raisin-Orange Turnovers.

Old-Fashioned Half-Moons

Maybe you've never fried pies, but your grandmother, especially if she lived south of the Mason and Dixon line, rated these turnovers from the kettle a great winter dessert. Today's cooks often fry them in the electric skillet. A rather tart fruit filling contrasts delightfully with the sugar-sprinkled, flaky pastry. Serve the turnovers, often called Half-Moons, either hot or cold. And tuck them in a packed lunch for a much appreciated treat.

FRIED PIES

Southern country-kitchen specials

Pastry for 2-crust pie
1 ½ c. cooked dried apricots or prunes, mashed and sweetened to taste

• Roll pastry ⅛" thick. Cut in 5" circles. On each pastry round place about 1 ½ tblsp. fruit mixture. Fold pastry

to make half-moons; press edges together with fork tines to seal. Prick tops in several places.
• Fry turnovers in deep hot fat (375°F.) until light brown, about 3 minutes. Drain on paper towels and sprinkle with sifted confectioners sugar. Makes about 12.

FROSTED MINCEMEAT TURNOVERS

Tasty change from mincemeat pies

Pastry for 2-crust pie
1 c. prepared or homemade mincemeat
¼ c. diced peeled apples
Confectioners Sugar Frosting

• Roll pastry about ⅛" thick and cut in 4½" circles.
• Combine mincemeat and apples. Place about a tablespoon of mixture on each pastry circle. Fold over to make half-moons and seal edges with 4-tined fork. Prick tops.
• Bake in a very hot oven (450°F.) about 15 minutes, or until browned.
• Spread tops while slightly warm with Confectioners Sugar Frosting. Makes 15.

CONFECTIONERS SUGAR FROSTING: Combine ¼ c. soft butter or margarine, ½ tsp. vanilla and 1 c. sifted confectioners sugar. Blend in water, a little at a time, to make frosting of spreading consistency.

APPLE TURNOVERS

Spicy apples in pastry pocketbooks

Pastry for 2-crust 10" pie
4 c. diced peeled apples
⅛ tsp. salt
⅔ c. sugar
½ tsp. cinnamon
¼ tsp. nutmeg
1 tblsp. lemon juice
6 tblsp. soft butter
Milk

• Combine apples, salt, sugar, cinnamon, nutmeg and lemon juice.
• Divide pastry in half and roll one half to make 11" square. Dot with 3 tblsp. butter, fold over and roll out again to make an 18" × 12" rectangle. Cut in 6" squares. Repeat with second half of dough.
• Place about ⅓ c. apple mixture on each square of pastry; fold over and seal edges by pressing with 4-tined fork. Prick tops of turnovers. Brush with milk.
• Bake in hot oven (400°F.) until golden, about 25 to 30 minutes. Serve warm or cold. Top with vanilla ice cream or whipped cream, if desired. Makes 1 dozen.

Note: You can bake half the turnovers and freeze the other half to bake later.

DATE-WALNUT TURNOVERS

Make these dainties to serve with an assortment of holiday cookies

Pastry for 2-crust pie
1 c. finely cut dates
¼ c. chopped walnuts   *more*

⅛ tsp. salt
½ tsp. grated orange peel
¼ c. orange juice
Orange Glaze

• Roll pastry ⅛" thick and cut in 4½" circles.
• Combine dates, walnuts, salt, orange peel and juice; stir to blend. Place about a tablespoon of date mixture on each pastry circle. Fold over, seal edges by pressing with 4-tined fork. Prick tops.

• Bake in very hot oven (450°F.) until browned, about 12 minutes. Cover tops while slightly warm with Orange Glaze. Makes 15.

ORANGE GLAZE: Combine 1 c. sifted confectioners sugar, ⅛ tsp. salt and 1 tsp. grated orange peel in bowl. Blend in 1½ to 2 tblsp. orange juice until mixture has the consistency of a glaze. Spread on turnovers.

Special Tarts from Overseas

Banbury Tarts are raisin turnovers, as English as the hot tea that usually accompanies them. Named for the town northwest of London, where they originated, they're as famous as the town's Banbury Cross of the nursery rhyme. Keep some of these turnovers in your freezer to serve on afternoons when a neighbor stops by for a visit. They are satisfying and encourage good talk.

BANBURY TARTS

You can make the filling ahead and store in refrigerator if convenient

Pastry for 2-crust pie
1½ c. raisins
1 tsp. grated lemon peel
⅛ tsp. salt
¾ c. sugar

1 c. water
4 soda crackers, finely crushed
1 tblsp. butter or margarine
2 tblsp. lemon juice

• Combine raisins, lemon peel, salt, sugar, water and cracker crumbs. Cook slowly, stirring occasionally, until about the consistency of jam (about 30 minutes). Stir in butter and lemon juice. Cool.
• Roll pastry ⅛" thick. Cut in 4" circles, using a bowl, jar lid or cardboard circle for pattern. Place 1 tblsp. raisin mixture in center of each pastry circle. Fold over, moisten edges with cold water, seal edges with 4-tined fork. Prick tops.
• Bake in very hot oven (450°F.) until pastry is lightly browned, about 12 minutes. Serve warm or cold with cheese. Makes 15 to 16.

Elegant French Pastries

Imagine what excitement a woman making French pastries in her kitchen would have created a generation ago! Now you can bake them whenever you please. Just use our recipe for Basic Puff Pastry (Chapter 2). It's a simplified version that gives professional results. You need to have patience, willingness to follow techniques and will power to resist changing the specified ingredients. It's really not difficult, just time consuming.

Busy women don't do the work these special pastries take all at one time. You can freeze the pastry, pre-shaped if you like, and use it any time within a month. Or you can refrigerate pastry, wrapped in aluminum foil, for two or three days before shaping. When you are about ready to entertain, you can bake the pastries, garnish and freeze them for a few days.

We give you recipes for five of the most famous French pastries. And we include a filling recipe, Pastry Cream, also borrowed from the French. It's one of the most delicious tart fillings ever invented. You can make it a day ahead, too; cover and refrigerate, folding in whipped cream when you fill the tarts.

Notice our recipe for Strawberry Cream Tarts, also in this chapter. In this delicacy, an exquisite color picture, we combine Pastry Cream and ripe strawberries in tart shells made with plain pastry, so you can use the filling—even if you don't want to tackle the ethereal Basic Puff Pastry.

Set a large tray of assorted French pastries on the table when you have a coffee, tea or dessert party. It will add plenty of talk, sprinkled with pretty adjectives, to the occasion. Your guests will be flattered to have a chance to help themselves to the flaky, fragile and crisp pastries that once were enjoyed almost exclusively by European royalty.

NAPOLEONS

Elegant—the pride of French menus

½ recipe Basic Puff Pastry (Chapter 2)
Glaze
Nuts
1 recipe Pastry Cream

• Roll chilled pastry on lightly floured surface in 6″ × 15″ rectangle ¼″ thick.

• With sharp knife cut in half, lengthwise. Slant knife slightly as you cut so that one surface of each strip will be broader than the other. (This is important because if they are straight, the tops will be smaller when they puff up.)

• Rinse chilled baking sheet with cold water. Place pastry strips on it with broader surface up. Prick with fork. Chill 30 minutes.

• Bake in hot oven (425°F.) 15 minutes. Turn strips with spatula. Reduce heat to 350° and bake 15 minutes, or until puffed and a rich golden color. Cool.

• Split cool strips to make 3 layers each. Choose the two most attractive for tops. Place them on a rack over tray. Spoon glaze over; let dry at room temperature. Repeat with second coat of glaze. Top with slivered or chopped nuts. Or, if you prefer, decorate with pastry tube, allowing glaze to dry at least 1 hour before decorating. (See Chocolate Stripes.)

• Spread Pastry Cream on two unglazed pastry layers and stack them. Top with a glazed and decorated strip. Repeat this procedure with remaining two strips and top with other decorated strip. Chill at least 30 minutes. Cut each stacked pastry strip in 6 slices. Makes 12.

GLAZE: Combine 1 c. sifted confectioners sugar, ¼ tsp. vanilla, ⅛ tsp. salt and 1½ to 2 tblsp. water.

Note: Bake pastry ahead and freeze, if you wish. Combine with Pastry Cream the day you serve Napoleons. Refrigerate until serving time.

VARIATION

JOSEPHINES: When the two baked strips are split to make 3 layers each, spread top one with thin confectioners sugar frosting and sprinkle with chopped nuts. Stack remaining two layers together with Pastry Cream and add tops. Frosting substitutes for glaze.

CHOCOLATE STRIPES: French chefs omit nuts and pipe 5 lengthwise chocolate stripes on glazed tops of Napoleons for a finishing touch. If you want to try this decorative trim, melt 1 square unsweetened chocolate and mix with 2 tsp. butter. Use the small, straight pastry tube (for writing) to make stripes. Pull a wood toothpick crosswise through Chocolate Stripes at ½" intervals, alternating the direction each time. This gives the classic "wavy" effect on Napoleons.

PASTRY CREAM

Rich, delicious filling for many tarts

3 egg yolks, beaten
½ c. sugar
⅛ tsp. salt
2 tblsp. flour
2 tsp. cornstarch
1 c. light cream
1 tsp. vanilla
¼ c. heavy cream

• Combine egg yolks, sugar, salt, flour and cornstarch in top of double boiler. Gradually stir in light cream.

• Cook over boiling water, stirring constantly, until mixture thickens so it will pile slightly when dropped from spoon. Remove from heat and stir in vanilla. Place waxed paper or saran or other plastic wrap directly on top of mixture. Cool.

• When cold, beat heavy cream until stiff. Fold into custard. Makes 1¾ cups.

BUTTERFLIES

Pastry has many buttery, delicate, crisp layers—immeasurably thin

½   recipe Basic Puff Pastry
        (Chapter 2)
Sugar

• Roll chilled pastry on board lightly sprinkled with sugar (granulated), to make rectangle ¼″ thick. Fold in half. Sprinkle with more sugar and roll again into rectangle ⅛″ thick.
• Trim pastry edges straight with sharp knife. Do not use a sawing motion; make a straight, clean, swift cut. Cut pastry into quarters.
• Sprinkle the quarters lightly with cold water, then with sugar. Stack; then cut into 3″ × ½″ strips. Pick up each strip and give it one twist. Place on chilled baking sheet and press lightly. Chill 30 minutes.
• Bake in hot oven (425°F.) 12 minutes. Reduce heat to 275°F. and bake 10 to 15 minutes, or until golden. Remove immediately from baking sheet. Makes 18 to 20.

PALM LEAVES

A famous French pastry farm cooks can make—guaranteed to impress

½   recipe Basic Puff Pastry
        (Chapter 2)
Sugar

• Roll pastry on surface, sprinkled lightly with sugar, to a rectangle ½″ thick. Sprinkle with sugar. Turn over

and roll into a rectangle three times as long as it is wide and ⅜″ thick. Sprinkle ¼ c. sugar over pastry.
• Fold ends of dough so that they meet in the middle; flatten slightly. Fold folded edges again to meet in the middle and flatten slightly.
• Now fold together lengthwise as you would in closing a book. Press together slightly and refrigerate at least 30 minutes. Then cut in 3 equal portions.
• Chill 2 baking sheets. Remove one from refrigerator and rinse with cold water. Place each pastry roll on its side and slice crosswise in ⅜″ slices. Arrange 12 slices on baking sheet. Chill 30 minutes. Repeat process using other baking sheet and remainder of pastry.
• Bake one sheet at a time. Place in a very hot oven (450°F.) 5 minutes. Reduce temperature to 350°. Quickly turn pastry over, spreading leaf ends apart slightly with spatula. Continue baking until golden and crisp, 15 to 20 minutes. Cool on wire rack. Makes about 24.

CREAM TWISTS

These pastries are the famed French cornets—elegant cream-filled "horns"

½   recipe Basic Puff Pastry
        (Chapter 2)
1   egg white, slightly beaten
Granulated sugar
Whipped cream, sweetened
Walnuts
Shaved chocolate   *more*

• Make twist molds by wrapping strips of aluminum foil around 12 round wood clothespins to cover each completely.

• Roll pastry to 18″ × 12″ rectangle, ¼″ thick. Cut lengthwise into 12 (1″) strips.

• Wrap each strip, overlapping slightly, around a foil-covered clothespin. Do not stretch pastry. Place on baking sheet lined with brown paper.

• Brush with beaten egg white and sprinkle lightly with sugar. Chill 30 minutes.

• Bake in hot oven (425°F.) 10 minutes. Reduce temperature to 350° and continue baking 20 minutes, or until pastry puffs and is golden. While hot, carefully push foil-covered clothespins out with handle of wooden spoon. Return "horns" to oven to dry out inside, 3 to 5 minutes. Cool completely before filling.

• Fill with whipped cream, using pastry bag and a Number 5 tip, ending with a swirl. Or fill with spoon, gently shaking the cream into the pastry "horn." Sprinkle with chopped walnuts and chocolate shavings.

Note: To freeze Cream Twists, refrigerate unbaked pastry-covered clothespins 30 minutes; wrap individually in foil, leaving clothespins in, and freeze. On the day you serve Cream Twists, unwrap and arrange on baking sheet lined with brown paper. Press gently against paper. Brush pastry with beaten egg white and sprinkle lightly with sugar. Bake in very hot oven (450°F.) 5 to 6 minutes; reduce temperature to 350° and bake until pastry puffs and is golden, 5 to 8 minutes. Carefully push out clothespins. Return "horns" to oven to dry out inside, 3 to 5 minutes. Cool on rack before filling.

Sandwich or Shortcake Tarts

Thrifty women often make these little pastries from scraps of leftover pie crust, but many a hostess bakes a supply of the pastry circles especially for shortcakes or pastry sandwiches. That's because they are so easy to fix —there's no shaping other than cutting with a cookie cutter.

A supply of baked pie crust rounds in the freezer is insurance you'll never want for refreshments when you have company. You can combine them with fruit or filling in the twinkling of an eye. You will be limited only by what you have in your freezer, refrigerator and cupboard—and your imagination.

STRAWBERRY ICE CREAM SANDWICHES

Hostess tip: Just right for the party that's coming up—make them ahead

Pastry for 2-crust pie
2 qts. vanilla ice cream
1 qt. strawberries
Sugar

• Divide pastry in halves and roll each half to ⅛″ thickness. Cut in circles with 3″ cookie cutter, preferably cutter with scalloped edge.

• Place on ungreased baking sheet and prick several times with four-tined fork. Bake in very hot oven (450°F.) until lightly browned, 5 to 7 minutes.

• Remove to rack. Cool. Wrap and freeze, if desired. Makes 22 circles.

• Place pan or tray in freezer to chill. Open carton of ice cream. Cut off ½″ lengthwise slice of ice cream. Put remaining ice cream in freezer while you work with slice. Cut ice cream with 3″ cookie cutter with scalloped edge.

• Place a circle of ice cream between two pastry rounds. Put immediately in freezer on chilled pan. Put scraps of ice cream left after cutting circles into chilled bowl and set in freezer.

• Continue in this manner until all the sandwiches are made. Keep in freezer until serving time. Serve topped with strawberries sweetened to taste with sugar. Makes 10 to 11 sandwiches. If you wish to make the sandwiches ahead, freeze them, then cover with airtight wrap and return to freezer.

Note: You will have approximately 3 to 4 c. ice cream scraps left over. Press into bowl, cover with foil or plastic wrap and place in freezer. Use in any way desired.

VARIATIONS

• Use sliced fresh peaches or ripe raspberries instead of strawberries for topping. Substitute other flavors of ice cream for vanilla. Try peach ice cream with raspberry topping.

OPEN-FACE PASTRY TARTS: Spread pastry rounds with softened cream cheese, then with sliced fresh peaches or strawberries, whole raspberries or blueberries. Top with whipped cream. Or top with filling for Vanilla Cream or Chocolate Cream Pie (Chapter 4), or with vanilla or chocolate pudding made from packaged mix, garnishing with whipped cream and a little of the fruit.

LEFTOVER PASTRY TREATS

• Sprinkle rolled pastry with mixture of sugar and cinnamon. Cut in fancy shapes and bake in very hot oven (450°F.) a few minutes, or until lightly browned.

JELLY TARTS: Roll out leftover pastry ⅛″ thick. Cut in circles with 3″ cookie cutter. Remove centers from half of the pastry rounds with small cutter (about size of a thimble). Prick pastry generously and bake on a baking sheet in a very hot oven (450°F.) a few minutes, or until lightly browned. Remove from oven, cool. Top the plain pastry rounds with those with "windows" in the center. Fill with colorful jelly or fruit preserves.

Fix some for the boys with peanut butter spread on the pastry rounds before adding the circles with center cutouts. Garnish them with jelly.

FAST-FIX PIES

All of you have busy seasons when time for baking is short. That's when the quick and easy pie recipes in this chapter will come in handy. Maybe you'll need them most when apple blossoms cloud the air and spring work comes on with a bang, upsetting your cooking schedule and making quick meals a necessity. Or it may be during summer's gardening and food-preserving days or autumn's harvest when you scarcely can get enough time for cooking. Regardless of the season, you'll find the pies made from recipes in this chapter easy to fix and even easier to eat.

You'll notice that some of the recipes call for convenient packaged and canned foods. They do not always make as elegant and delectable pies as some of the more time-consuming "from scratch" recipes in this Cookbook. But we're willing to guarantee that these pies are most acceptable in looks and in taste. If you're serving them to company, you'll be proud of them.

Notice our special Soufflé Pie recipes. They are made by the method FARM JOURNAL home economists best like to use with packaged pie fillings. These are extra-pretty and extra-good pies—Butterscotch Pecan Soufflé Pie, for instance. And as we've mentioned elsewhere in this book, packaged and homemade pie crust mixes are a real help when the cook is in a hurry. So is pastry made with instant-type flour in the electric mixer.

While our fast-fix pies are for busy women who are experienced, excellent pie bakers, they also are for brides and young cooks learning their way around the kitchen. Try Bride's Peach Pie and see if the Praline Topping doesn't make it distinctive and luscious. Make Sunday-Best Banana Pie—we bet you'll agree that the homemaker who invented the recipe has been clever in decorating the pie for the holiday seasons. Don't miss the quintet of quick red cherry pies. And if the weather is hot and company is coming, make no-bake Party Chocolate Pie. No one will guess how little work it is. We promise you compliments on all the pies in this chapter.

Something New—Soufflé Pies

If you're looking for something new and tasty in fast-fix desserts, try our Soufflé Pies. Folding part of the pie filling, made from packaged pudding and pie mix, into the beaten egg whites instead of topping the pie with meringue, distributes flavor throughout the filling. And it's almost no extra work.

You get some charming color contrasts in the layered fillings, too. To see for yourself, start with Butterscotch Pecan Soufflé Pie—you'll like the pie you make. We also predict you'll use the recipe for Butterscotch Pie often, because it has a surprise taste (it's the best way we've discovered in our Test Kitchens for salvaging that half cup of canned pumpkin often left over after baking a pumpkin custard pie).

BUTTERSCOTCH PECAN SOUFFLÉ PIE

Your guests will never guess how easy this pie is to fix—it tastes so good

Baked 8" pie shell
1   (4 oz.) pkg. butterscotch pudding and pie filling mix
2   c. milk
2   eggs, separated
½   c. chopped pecans, toasted
¼   tsp. salt
¼   tsp. cream of tartar
2   tblsp. sugar

• Combine pudding mix, ¼ c. milk and egg yolks in saucepan. Blend thoroughly. Add remaining milk and cook as directed on package. Remove ½ c. hot filling; cool 10 minutes, stirring several times.

• Stir remaining filling until smooth. Add pecans and pour into pie shell.

• Add salt and cream of tartar to egg whites; beat until frothy. Add sugar gradually, beating until stiff peaks form. Stir the ½ c. hot filling until smooth. Fold into egg white meringue in two parts. Pile on hot filling in pie shell; spread evenly out to edges. Bake in slow oven (325°F.) 20 to 22 minutes, until delicately browned. Cool several hours before serving.

BLACK BOTTOM SOUFFLÉ PIE

Not half the work most black bottom pies are—attractive and tasty

Baked 8" pie shell
1   (3¼ oz.) pkg. vanilla pudding and pie filling mix
2   c. milk
2   eggs, separated
1   (6 oz.) pkg. semisweet chocolate pieces
¼   tsp. salt
¼   tsp. cream of tartar
2   tblsp. sugar

• Combine pie filling, ¼ c. milk and egg yolks in saucepan. Blend thoroughly. Add remaining milk and cook as directed on package. Remove ½ c. hot filling; cool 10 minutes, stirring several times.

• Add chocolate pieces to remaining hot filling; stir until melted and smooth. Pour into pie shell.

• Add salt and cream of tartar to egg whites; beat until frothy. Add sugar gradually, beating until stiff peaks form. Stir the ½ c. hot filling until smooth. Fold into egg white meringue in two parts. Pile on hot filling in pie shell; spread evenly out to edges. Bake in slow oven (325°F.) 20 to 22 minutes, until delicately browned. Cool several hours before serving.

LEMON GINGER SOUFFLÉ PIE

Brand-new taste experience—lemon and ginger flavors blend in filling

Baked 8" pie shell
 1 (3⅝ oz.) pkg. lemon pie filling
 ¾ c. sugar
2 ½ c. water
 2 eggs, separated
 ¼ tsp. ginger
 ¼ tsp. salt

• Prepare pie filling as directed on package, using ½ c. sugar, water and egg yolks. Remove 1 c. of the hot filling, stir ginger into it and allow to cool 10 minutes.

• Cool remaining filling 5 minutes, stirring several times. Pour into pie shell.

• Add salt to egg whites; beat until frothy. Add remaining ¼ c. sugar gradually, beating until stiff peaks form.

• Stir the 1 c. of warm filling until smooth. Fold into egg white meringue in two parts. Pile on hot filling in pie shell; spread evenly out to edges.

• Bake in hot oven (400°F.) 10 to 12 minutes, until delicately browned. Cool several hours before serving.

BUTTERSCOTCH PIE

Flavor secret is pumpkin—it mellows the butterscotch-coconut filling

Unbaked 8" pie shell
 1 (4 oz.) pkg. butterscotch pudding and pie filling mix
 1 tsp. cinnamon
 ¼ tsp. nutmeg
 ¼ tsp. salt
 ½ c. cooked or canned pumpkin
 2 c. milk
 2 eggs, slightly beaten
 1 c. flaked coconut

• Combine pie filling mix, spices and salt. Add pumpkin and stir until dry ingredients are moistened. Blend in milk gradually. Stir in eggs, blending well. Stir in coconut.

• Pour into pie shell. Bake in very hot oven (450°F.) 10 minutes. Reduce heat to 325° and continue baking 35 to 40 minutes, or until mixture doesn't adhere to knife when tested halfway between center and outer edge of pie. Cool to serve.

CHERRY CREAM PIE

Don't hesitate to serve this fast-fix pie to guests—they'll brag about it

Baked 9" pie shell
 1 (1 lb.) can pitted tart red cherries (water pack)   *more*

1   envelope unflavored gelatin
¼   c. cold water
1   (3 ¼ oz.) pkg. vanilla pudding
     and pie filling mix
2 ½ c. milk
¼   c. sugar
Few drops of red food color
1   (2 oz.) pkg. dessert topping mix
½   tsp. vanilla

• Drain cherries, saving juice.
• Soften gelatin in water.
• Prepare pie filling as directed on package, using 2 c. milk and 2 tblsp. sugar. Remove 1 c. of hot filling; add gelatin to it and stir until dissolved. Add remaining 2 tblsp. sugar and stir in cherry juice slowly. Add food color to tint mixture delicate pink. Cover and chill in refrigerator until partially set (about 1½ hours).
• Stir remaining hot filling until smooth. Add cherries and pour into pie shell. Cover and cool.
• Prepare dessert topping as directed on package, using ½ c. milk and vanilla. Beat partially set gelatin mixture until smooth. Fold into whipped topping. Pile lightly on cherry filling, spreading evenly to edges. Chill several hours before serving.

CHOCOLATE MOCHA PIE

Two different chocolate layers, distinctive with rich mocha taste

Baked 8″ pie shell
1   (4 oz.) pkg. chocolate pudding
     and pie filling mix
2 ½ c. milk
2   tsp. instant coffee powder
2   tblsp. sugar

1   (2 oz.) pkg. dessert topping mix
½   tsp. vanilla

• Prepare pie filling as directed on package, using 2 c. milk. Remove 1 c. of hot filling. Add instant coffee and sugar; stir to dissolve and blend. Chill thoroughly.
• Cool remaining filling 5 minutes, stirring several times. Pour into pie shell. Cool.
• Prepare dessert topping as directed on package, using remaining ½ c. milk and vanilla. Beat chilled cup of filling until smooth. Fold into topping. Pile lightly on cooled filling in pie shell, spreading evenly to edges. Chill several hours before serving.

BLUSHING APPLE PIE

Excellent way to use canned applesauce—pie filling is blush-red

8″   Graham Cracker Crumb Crust
     (Chapter 2)
2 ½ c. thick applesauce
¼   c. red cinnamon candies (red
     hots)
Whipped cream

• Combine applesauce and red hots in saucepan. Heat just enough to dissolve candy. Cool thoroughly. Pour into cool crumb crust.
• Chill at least 1 hour. Garnish with whipped cream at serving time.

Note: For an attractive pie, save out ⅓ c. crumb mixture when making crust and sprinkle it over top of pie.

BRIDE'S PEACH PIE

Praline Topping adds a gourmet touch

Baked 8" pie shell
1 (1 lb. 13 oz.) can sliced peaches
1 tblsp. cornstarch
Few drops almond extract
Praline Topping (Chapter 9)

• Drain peaches. Measure ¾ c. syrup. Add gradually to cornstarch in saucepan, stirring to blend.
• Cook, stirring constantly, until thick and clear. Add almond extract and drained peaches. Cool and pour into pie shell. Top with Praline Topping (Chapter 9).

Jiffy Holiday Pie

The Oregon homemaker who originated the recipe for this banana pie, likes to feature the dessert in her Sunday-best meals—often on holidays. For Halloween, she tints the whipped cream yellow and makes a pumpkin face on it with orange segments. For the Christmas season, she tints the topping a pale green and adds a wreath of tiny candies of many colors. She says she makes the pie in a few minutes, but that no one guesses she hasn't labored much longer over it. She chills the pie at least two hours before serving, often several hours.

SUNDAY-BEST BANANA PIE

Tasty example of a pie created in the home kitchen of an artist-cook

8" Graham Cracker Crumb Crust

1 (3¼ oz.) pkg. vanilla pudding and pie filling mix
2 c. milk
2 bananas
1 c. heavy cream
½ tsp. vanilla
¼ c. sugar
3 tblsp. finely chopped walnuts

• Put pudding mix and milk in saucepan; cook as directed on package. Cool 5 minutes, stirring once or twice.
• Slice 1 banana and spread over bottom of crust. Pour on pudding mixture. Chill about 3 hours.
• To serve, slice remaining banana over top of pie. Whip cream; add vanilla and sugar. Spread over pie and sprinkle with walnuts.

HURRY-UP MINCEMEAT PIE

Applesauce blends with mincemeat, lemon juice points up fruity flavors

Pastry for 2-crust pie
1 (1 lb. 12 oz.) jar prepared mincemeat (3 c.)
1 c. applesauce
¼ c. lemon juice

• Combine mincemeat, applesauce and lemon juice. Spread in pastry-lined 9" pie pan. Adjust top crust; flute edges and cut vents.
• Bake in hot oven (400°F.) about 40 minutes, or until pie is golden brown.

QUICK CHERRY PIE

You can make this cherry pie "quick as a cat can blink his eye"

Baked 9" pie shell
1 (15 oz.) can sweetened con-
      densed milk (1⅓ c.)
¼ c. lemon juice
1 (1 lb. 4 oz.) can tart cherries
      (1½ c. drained)
¼ tsp. almond extract
Coconut

• Blend the condensed milk with lemon juice. The mixture will thicken slightly.
• Stir in drained cherries and almond extract; pour mixture into baked pie shell. Sprinkle coconut over top. Chill until ready to serve.

CREAM CHERRY PIE

So easy to fix—so color-gay

Baked 9" pie shell
1 (3 oz.) pkg. cream cheese
¼ c. sugar
½ tsp. vanilla
1 c. heavy cream, whipped
1 (1 lb. 5 oz.) can prepared
      cherry pie filling

• Beat together cream cheese, sugar and vanilla until light and fluffy. Fold in whipped cream. Spread evenly in pie shell.
• Spoon pie filling over top. Chill thoroughly before serving.

Note: Substitute other canned fruit pie fillings for the cherry.

CHERRY-CHEESE PIE

No one will guess this beautiful pie is a fast-fix one you made ahead

Pastry for 1-crust pie
1 (1 lb. 6 oz.) can cherry pie
      filling
2 (3 oz.) pkgs. cream cheese,
      room temperature
¼ c. sugar
2 eggs
½ tsp. vanilla
1 c. dairy sour cream

• Line 8" pie pan with pastry and flute edges. Spread half of cherry pie filling over bottom of pastry. Bake in hot oven (425°F.) 15 minutes, or until pastry is browned.
• Meanwhile, soften cream cheese in electric mixer. Blend in sugar gradually; beat in eggs and vanilla. Pour this mixture over hot cherry filling in pie shell. Reduce oven temperature to 350°F. and continue baking 20 minutes.
• Cool pie and place in refrigerator. Before serving, spoon sour cream around rim of pie, and spoon remaining half of cherry pie filling in center.

FROZEN STRAWBERRY PIE

Good insurance that your dessert ready in freezer will please guests

2 (9") Graham Cracker Crumb
      Crusts (Chapter 2)
1 (10 oz.) pkg. frozen strawber-
      ries, thawed
1 c. sugar
2 egg whites
1 tblsp. lemon juice
1 c. heavy cream

• Put berries, sugar, egg whites and lemon juice in mixer bowl; beat 15 minutes at high speed.
• Whip cream and fold into strawberry mixture. Pile high in 9″ foil pie pans lined with crumb crusts. Freeze; remove from freezer and place in plastic bags and seal. Serve without defrosting. Makes 2 pies or 10 servings.

VARIATION

FROZEN PEACH PIE: Substitute 1 (12 oz.) pkg. frozen peaches, thawed, for strawberries and follow directions for Frozen Strawberry Pie, adding ¼ tsp. almond extract to the whipped cream.

PARTY CHOCOLATE PIE

A no-bake pie, cool to make in summer—filling is rich and velvety

9″ Graham Cracker Crumb Crust (Chapter 2)
1 c. butter or margarine
1 ½ c. sugar
3 squares unsweetened chocolate, melted and cooled
¼ tsp. peppermint extract
2 tsp. vanilla
4 eggs

• Cream butter in electric mixer, adding sugar gradually. Add chocolate, peppermint extract and vanilla, mixing well.
• Add eggs, one at a time, beating with electric beater, 5 minutes after adding each egg.
• Pour mixture into crumb pie shell. Chill at least 2 hours. Makes 10 to 12 servings.

CHOCOLATE-PINEAPPLE PIE

Frosty cold—exciting flavor blend

1 pt. chocolate ice cream
1 (8 oz.) can crushed pineapple, drained
1 pt. pineapple sherbet
Shaved semisweet chocolate

• Spread slightly softened chocolate ice cream on sides and bottom of 9″ pie pan, hollowing out in center. Freeze.
• Remove from freezer and spread on pineapple. Freeze.
• Top with pineapple sherbet and shaved chocolate. Freeze.
• Cut in wedges to serve. Makes 6 to 8 servings.

FUDGE NUT CREAM PIE

Creamy and rich with double chocolate flavor of homemade fudge

Baked 9″ pie shell
2 (4 oz.) pkgs. chocolate pudding and pie filling mix
3 c. milk
1 (6 oz.) pkg. semisweet chocolate pieces
2 tblsp. butter or margarine
1 tsp. vanilla
½ c. chopped walnuts
½ c. heavy cream, whipped

• Combine pudding mix, milk and chocolate pieces in saucepan. Cook, stirring constantly, over medium heat until chocolate melts and pudding comes to a boil. Remove from heat and blend in butter and vanilla.
more

• Cool 5 minutes, stirring occasionally. Pour into cool pie shell. Sprinkle chopped nuts over pie, but not quite to edges. Chill. Serve garnished with whipped cream, spooned in ring around edge of pie. Serves 6 to 8.

CHOCOLATE PEANUT PIE

You can omit peanuts, but they add flavor and texture to this party pie

Baked 8″ pie shell
1   (4 oz.) pkg. chocolate pudding and pie filling mix
2   tblsp. brown sugar, firmly packed
½   square unsweetened chocolate
2   c. milk
2   eggs, separated
2   tblsp. butter or margarine
⅓   c. chopped salted peanuts
Meringue (2 egg whites)

• Combine pudding mix, brown sugar, chocolate and ¼ c. milk in saucepan. Add egg yolks and blend well. Then add remaining 1¾ c. milk. Cook over medium heat, stirring constantly, until mixture comes to a boil.
• Remove from heat and stir in butter. Cool at least 5 minutes, stirring two or three times.
• Scatter peanuts in cool pie shell. Pour on chocolate mixture and spread evenly. Top with meringue (see Perfect Meringue for Topping Pies, Chapter 9) and bake in moderate oven (350°F.) until delicately browned, (12 minutes). Cool away from drafts.

VARIATION

• Omit salted peanuts and use Peanut Pie Shell (see Chapter 2) instead of plain pastry pie shell.

CALIFORNIA BROWNIE PIE

A make-ahead pie you can refrigerate 2 or 3 days—also a good freezer

3   egg whites
⅛   tsp. salt
¾   c. sugar
¾   c. fine chocolate wafer crumbs
½   c. chopped walnuts
½   tsp. vanilla
Sweetened whipped cream
Shaved unsweetened chocolate

• Beat egg whites and salt until soft peaks form. Gradually add sugar; beat until very stiff.
• Fold in cookie crumbs, nuts and vanilla. Spread evenly in lightly buttered 9″ pie pan.
• Bake in slow oven (325°F.) about 35 minutes. Cool thoroughly.
• Spread with 1 c. heavy cream, whipped and sweetened with 2 tblsp. sugar; garnish with shaved chocolate. Chill 3 to 4 hours.

Note: For speed, use a potato peeler to shave chocolate.

MALLOW BANANA PIE: Slice bananas in baked 9″ pie shell, top with prepared packaged vanilla pie filling, cover with miniature marshmallows and brown lightly under broiler.

When Company's Coming

The generous woman, who shares this recipe, says she often bakes the pie after friends telephone they'll be stopping by. She serves it fresh out of the oven with tea or coffee. Her guests almost always compliment her on how attractive the pie is and someone usually asks: "May I have the recipe?"

AFTERNOON PARTY PIE

Cookielike crust holds colorful jam— you can fix this one in a jiffy

½ c. butter or margarine
½ c. sugar
1 egg
1 c. sifted flour
⅛ tsp. salt
¼ c. chopped almonds or pecans
1 c. red raspberry jam or preserves
½ c. flaked coconut

• Combine butter, sugar and egg and thoroughly mix. Add flour, salt and nuts. Press mixture into a 9" pie pan. Spread with jam.
• Bake in hot oven (400°F.) until lightly browned, about 15 minutes. Cool on cakerack. (Pie is on the thin side.) Serve sprinkled with coconut. Makes 6 servings.

VARIATION

• Substitute apricot jam or preserves for the raspberry.

WINTER STRAWBERRY-CHEESE PIE

Vary this company dessert with different kinds of fruit preserves

Baked 9" pie shell
1 (8 oz.) pkg. cream cheese
½ c. sugar
3 eggs, beaten
½ c. milk
1 tsp. vanilla
1 (12 oz.) glass strawberry preserves
Whipped cream

• Combine cream cheese, softened at room temperature, and sugar; mix to blend thoroughly.
• Gradually stir in eggs, milk and vanilla. Pour into pie shell.
• Bake in moderate oven (350°F.) 25 minutes. Cool. Top with strawberry preserves and whipped cream or dairy sour cream. Makes 6 to 8 servings.

SUNDAE PIE

Keep one in the freezer for quick use

Baked 9" pie shell
1 qt. vanilla ice cream
Chocolate sauce
Chopped nuts

• Spread slightly softened ice cream in cool pie shell. Wrap in aluminum foil and freeze.
• To serve, cut in wedges and pass a

pitcher of chocolate sauce and small dish of chopped nuts for serving on pie.

Note: Vary the dessert by using different kinds of ice cream and sauces.

ANGEL COCONUT PIE

Looks like a party! A hostess sweet that's a real treat—so easy to fix

1   c. crushed graham crackers
½   c. grated or flaked coconut
½   c. chopped nuts (optional)

5   egg whites
1   c. sugar
Whipped cream
9   maraschino cherries

• Combine graham crackers, coconut and nuts. Mix thoroughly.
• Beat egg whites until stiff. Fold in sugar. Fold in cracker, coconut and nut mixture.
• Spread in well-greased 9″ pie pan. Bake in moderate oven (350°F.) 30 minutes.
• To serve, cut in wedges. Top each with whipped cream and a maraschino cherry. Makes 9 servings.

Pie for the Busy Hostess

If you ever return home late on the day you're having company for dinner, here's just the pie for you to have ready in the refrigerator. Everyone will think it's a cheese pie rather than the easy, make-ahead with a packaged mix the basis of the filling. This is a regal beauty with colorful fruit preserves or sliced, fresh fruit on top of the snowy white filling. Add the decorative trim at the last minute. The best part of the dessert is its wonderful taste.

SNOW CREAM PIE

Favorite with the cook, because it's easy; with guests, because it's good

Graham Cracker Crumb Crust (Chapter 2)
1   (3¾ oz.) pkg. instant vanilla pudding
1   c. dairy sour cream

1   c. milk
½   c. strawberry preserves

• Combine pudding mix with liquids (sour cream and milk) as directed on package. Mixture will be quite liquid.
• Pour into 8″ crumb crust. Chill until set, at least 1 hour, or longer.
• To serve, spoon strawberry preserves over top. Or use other fruit preserves or sweetened sliced fruit, like strawberries or peaches. Makes 6 servings.

Note: Use a baked crumb crust.

SPUR-OF-THE-MOMENT HOSTESS IDEA: When company comes on short notice, one farm woman makes peach pie in a few minutes like this: Drain canned peaches thoroughly. Put ¾ c. syrup drained from fruit in saucepan with 1 tblsp. cornstarch. Cook over low heat until mixture thickens and is clear. Add a drop or two of almond extract,

3 drops of red food color and ½ tsp. grated lemon peel. You have a pink, peach glaze.
• Take a baked pie shell from the freezer. Arrange drained peach halves in it. Spoon glaze over fruit. Garnish pie with whipped cream and serve it with pride. Softened vanilla ice cream may be used instead of whipped cream, if it's easier.

Timesaving Pies

Recipes for the following eight pies are from our TIMESAVING COOKBOOK. They are so quick and easy and such good pies that we felt we must include them in our Fast-Fix Pies chapter.

HAWAIIAN PINEAPPLE PIE

Combine pineapple and coconut in a pie for exotic, tropical flavors

1 pkg. refrigerator coconut cookie dough
1 (3 oz.) pkg. vanilla pudding and pie filling mix
⅛ tsp. salt
½ c. water
1 (20 oz.) can crushed pineapple, drained
1 tblsp. butter or margarine
½ c. heavy cream, whipped
⅓ c. flaked or shredded coconut

• Slice cookie dough in ¼" slices. Arrange slices in 9" pie pan, first lining bottom of pan, then sides. (Let side slices rest on bottom ones to make higher sides.) Bake in moderate oven (375°F.) until lightly browned, 9 to 12 minutes.

• Meanwhile combine pudding mix and salt in saucepan. Blend in water. Add pineapple and cook over medium heat, stirring constantly, until mixture comes to a full boil. Stir in butter.
• Pour hot filling into pie shell. Cool. Spread whipped cream over top. Sprinkle with coconut.

CRANBERRY-MINCEMEAT PIE

Keep the relish on hand for this pie

Unbaked 9" pie shell
3 c. prepared mincemeat
1 c. Cranberry Relish

• Combine mincemeat and Cranberry Relish; pour into pie shell.
• Bake in hot oven (400°F.) 35 minutes.

CRANBERRY RELISH: Put pulp and peel of 4 seeded oranges (medium), 2 lbs. cranberries and 4 cored unpeeled apples (medium) through food grinder. Add 4 c. sugar and mix well. Cover and refrigerate. Or pour into glass jars, leaving ½" head space, seal and freeze. Makes 4 pints.

FROZEN PUMPKIN PIE

Freeze this to serve on short notice

Baked 9" pie shell
1   qt. vanilla ice cream, slightly softened
1   c. canned pumpkin, or cooked, sieved pumpkin
⅓   c. sugar
½   tsp. salt
1   tsp. cinnamon
½   tsp. ginger
½   tsp. ground cloves
¼   c. chopped walnuts

• Beat together ice cream, pumpkin, sugar, salt and spices with electric beater until well blended.
• Pour into pie shell. Sprinkle with nuts. Freeze until firm. If pie is kept longer, store in a plastic bag. Serve frozen. Makes 6 servings.

DANISH RASPBERRY PIE

Filling makes extra-good dessert, too

Baked 8" pie shell
1   c. cold water
1   pkg. Danish-dessert mix, currant-raspberry flavor
1   (10 oz.) pkg. frozen raspberries
1   c. heavy cream, whipped

• Add water to Danish-dessert mix. Bring to boil and boil 1 minute, stirring constantly. Add raspberries; cool.
• Pour into cooled pie shell; refrigerate several hours. Garnish with whipped cream.

BROWNIE PIE

Chocolate lovers laud this pie

Unbaked 9" pie shell
1   (1 lb.) pkg. brownie mix
¼   c. chocolate syrup
¼   c. chopped nuts
Whipped cream

• Prepare brownie mix as directed on package for fudgy brownies. Spread mixture evenly in pie shell. Pour chocolate syrup evenly over top. Sprinkle with nuts.
• Bake in moderate oven (350°F.) 40 to 45 minutes. Serve warm, topped with whipped cream. Makes 10 servings.

NORTH POLE CHERRY PIE

It says: Merry Christmas to all!

Baked 9" pie shell or crumb crust
1   qt. vanilla ice cream
1   (1 lb. 6 oz.) can cherry pie filling

• Spread slightly softened ice cream in pie shell and freeze. (You may tint ice cream delicate green.)
• An hour before serving, spread filling over top. Return to freezer. Serve quickly.

FROZEN MINCEMEAT PIE

Fix it ahead for holiday meals

Baked 9" pie shell
1   qt. vanilla ice cream, slightly softened
1 ½   c. prepared mincemeat

¼ c. chopped nuts
Maraschino cherries, well drained

• Beat together ice cream and mince-meat. Spread into pie shell. Sprinkle with nuts and maraschino cherries, cut in halves.
• Freeze until solid, about 4 hours. If kept longer, place in plastic bag. Serve frozen.

APRICOT PIE À LA MODE

Canned apricots go glamorous in pie

Unbaked 9" pie shell
1   (1 lb. 13 oz.) can apricot halves, drained

1   tblsp. lemon juice
½   c. flour
¾   c. sugar
¼   tsp. cinnamon
¼   tsp. nutmeg
¼   c. butter or margarine
1   pt. vanilla ice cream

• Spread apricots in pie shell; sprinkle with lemon juice.
• Combine flour, sugar and spices. Mix with butter until crumbly. Sprinkle over apricots.
• Bake in hot oven (400°F.) 40 minutes. Serve warm or cold, topped with scoops of ice cream.

PIE TOPPINGS

Toppings are to pie what frostings are to cake—sweet flavor boosters. Spread slightly warm apple pie with Caramel or Molasses Topping, and see what a remarkable difference that homey country-kitchen taste makes. It gives traditional apple pie an exciting new taste.

Try one of the bake-on toppings—there's Spiced Crust Topping, for instance, that turns gold in the oven and leaves the pie crisp on top. Or spoon a glistening glaze over an open-face fruit pie for a finishing touch (see the glacé pies in Chapter 3). Ladle a sweet sauce like Vanilla Cream, reminiscent in flavor of homemade ice cream on apple pie—or Fluffy Orange Sauce. Spoon Amber Caramel Sauce over Pumpkin Pie.

Don't be surprised, when you stop in a neighbor's kitchen for a friendly visit, to find your hostess with one eye on the oven while a topping broils on a pie—Broiled Marshmallow Topping, so delicious on Chocolate Cream Pie. Peanut Butter Cream Topping broiled on banana pie is equally good.

Our grandmothers depended on handsome meringues, swirled whipped cream and scoops of rich, homemade ice cream to top their pies. Grandfathers also had ideas—they frequently poured thick cream over their wedges of fruit pies. It's only recently that the trend to exciting, new pie toppings has picked up momentum.

Besides this chapter of toppings, you'll find recipes for others throughout this Cookbook along with the pies they enhance—Apple-Raisin Pie spread with Orange Frosting, Peach Cream Pie with Lemon Crumb Topping and Concord Grape Pie with a butter-brown sugar streusel containing rolled oats, for examples. We list locations for these toppings at the end of this chapter to help you find them in a hurry.

While some toppings are on the fancy side, most are simple and homespun, like creamy cottage cheese touched with honey and a dash of ginger —delicious on blueberry, peach and our own Peach-Blueberry combination (Chapter 3). We believe you'll not be able to resist the creative toppings for cream pies worked out in our Test Kitchens—they're that unusual.

Gold-Tipped Meringues

Meringues decorate more 1-crust pies than all other toppings put together. And they glorify more lemon pies than any other kind. That's partly because lemon meringue pies long have been farm favorites. But there are other reasons. Meringues are easy to make, too, and they glamorize pies that are lighter endings for hearty meals than 2-crust specials. Then, the practical cook makes meringues with the egg whites left over from fillings that call for yolks.

To be successful with meringue toppings all you need do is *follow the directions* in our recipes. Do pay special attention to dissolving the sugar in the egg whites and to spreading the meringue over the top of the filling so that it touches the edge of the crust around the pie. To keep the topping high and handsome, the way it comes from the oven, protect it from drafts. Home economists sometimes make a screen of stiff paper to stand up around the pie to divert wandering breezes. Let pie cool on rack at least 1 hour.

You can tint meringue before spreading it on pie, if you wish. We like delicate pink meringue on our Pink Party Pie (Chapter 5). And you can put meringue in your pastry tube and press a fluffy collar around the edge of a pie and a design in the center. One farm homemaker says she sometimes makes a meringue lattice on fruit pies with colorful fillings. Here are her directions: Pipe four strips across pie one way (touching ends to crusts), four the other way, slantwise,

so openings will be diamond-shaped. Broil 8″ to 10″ from heat until delicately browned, 2 to 3 minutes.

PERFECT MERINGUE FOR TOPPING PIES

FOR 8″ PIE

2   egg whites
¼   tsp. cream of tartar
⅛   tsp. salt
¼   tsp. vanilla
¼   c. sugar

FOR 9″ PIE

3   egg whites
¼   tsp. cream of tartar
¼   tsp. salt
½   tsp. vanilla
6   tblsp. sugar

FOR 10″ PIE

4   egg whites
¼   tsp. cream of tartar
¼   tsp. salt
½   tsp. vanilla
½   c. sugar

• Have egg whites at room temperature to obtain greatest volume. Place them in a medium bowl with cream of tartar, salt and vanilla.
• Beat with electric or hand beater, at medium speed, until entire mixture is frothy. Do not beat until eggs stiffen.
• Add sugar, a little at a time, beating well after each addition. Do not under-

beat. Beat until sugar dissolves to help prevent beading (those brown syrup drops on top). To test, rub some of the meringue between your fingers to see if it's still grainy. (The grains are undissolved sugar.) Continue to beat until stiff, pointed peaks form when you lift beater slowly.

• Place spoonfuls of meringue around edge of pie filling, spreading it so it touches inner edge of crust to seal all around. This prevents shrinkage. Pile remainder of meringue in center of pie and spread to meet meringue around edge. If the filling is not covered completely, the oven heat may cause it to weep. (Stirring the cooked filling may cause it to weep; water will collect under the meringue.) Lift up meringue over pie in points with back of teaspoon.

• Bake in moderate oven (350°F.) 12 to 15 minutes, or until meringue peaks are golden brown. Too long baking may cause weeping. Cool gradually away from drafts.

COUNTRY-STYLE MERINGUE: With egg whites plentiful in farm kitchens, many country pie bakers like to use 5 egg whites and 10 tblsp. sugar to make a high cover on their 9″ and 10″ pies.

Note: You can substitute 1 tsp. lemon juice for cream of tartar when making meringues for lemon, lime and orange pies. The acid in the juice gives the same result—a wonderful meringue!

Pretty Dress-Ups for Cream Pies

The best way to give pale (but delicious!) cream pies color appeal and extra flavor is to add sweet toppings. This chapter contains several suggestions for fascinating toppings for vanilla-flavored and other cream pies. The directions were developed in our Countryside Kitchens, where taste testers gave them enthusiastic approval and praise.

VANILLA CREAM PIE TOPPINGS

MERINGUE: Combine 3 egg whites, ¼ tsp. salt and ¼ tsp. cream of tartar in small mixing bowl. Beat at high speed until frothy. Gradually add 6 tblsp. sugar, beating at high speed until stiff glossy peaks form and sugar is dissolved. Pile on lukewarm filling, covering evenly out to edges and seal to crust. Bake in slow oven (300°F.) about 20 minutes, or until lightly browned. Cool away from drafts.

JAM MERINGUE: Add ¼ tsp. salt to 3 egg whites. Beat at high speed until frothy. Stir ¼ c. fruit jam until smooth; then add gradually, beating at high speed until stiff glossy peaks are formed. Add a few drops of food color for a delicate color. Spread meringue over lukewarm filling. Bake in slow oven (300°F.) 20 minutes, or until lightly browned.

COCONUT MACAROON TOPPING: Combine 2 slightly beaten egg whites and ⅓ c. sugar. Stir in 1 (3½ oz.) can flaked coconut. Spoon in little mounds all over top of cream filling. Then spread gently to cover completely. Broil 8″ to 10″ from heat, 3 to 4 minutes, or until delicately browned. This browns quickly, so watch carefully.

CONFETTI TOPPING: Combine 1 c. miniature marshmallows, 1 (8½ oz.) can crushed pineapple, well drained (½ c.) and ¼ c. chopped maraschino cherries. Cover cream filling evenly with this mixture. Broil 8″ to 10″ from heat until marshmallows are puffed and soft, but not brown (1 to 2 minutes). Remove from broiler, spread out marshmallows with spatula. Return to broiler until delicate brown (1 to 2 minutes).

Note: You may substitute ½ c. well-drained fruit cocktail for pineapple and cherries in Confetti Topping.

Fluffy Whipped Cream Toppings

No farm woman needs to be reminded how attractive puffs of whipped cream are on pies. But you may have forgotten how your grandmother swirled it on pies and garnished it with homemade jellies or strawberry and other fruit preserves. We borrowed a trick from her for our Snow Cream Pie (Chapter 8)—try it, just in case you've forgotten how pretty and tasty berry preserves are on pie. And we've used jellies, melted, for glazing some of our best 1-crust fruit and berry pies and tarts.

Sweeten whipped cream slightly for topping pies. Add 2 to 4 tblsp. sifted confectioners sugar to 1 c. heavy cream in deep bowl. Chill, then whip until stiff. Makes about 2 cups.

Note: Dairy sour cream frequently substitutes for whipped cream in topping pies. It's one of today's success stories in the food world. The light cream, pasteurized, has a tangy taste and a custardlike consistency, due to the starter or culture added to sour it.

Look up Cherry-Cheese Pie (Chapter 8) and you'll see how fancy sour cream makes this quick-fix pie.

MAPLE CREAM: Whip 1 c. heavy cream. Pour ¼ c. maple syrup in a fine stream over it, carefully folding it in. Cover the top of pumpkin or squash pie with the cream, swirling it attractively.

CREAM LATTICE: Put whipped cream in pastry tube. Press it out on top of a 1-crust pie, making a lattice, or three circles. Or make a collar of whipped cream around edge of pie.

ALMOND CREAM: Chill 1 c. heavy cream, 2 to 4 tblsp. sifted confectioners sugar and ¼ tsp. almond extract in deep bowl. Beat until stiff. Makes about 2 cups. A tasty dress-up for cherry and peach pies!

FLUFFY CARAMEL SAUCE: Add 6 tblsp. brown sugar, firmly packed, and ½ tsp. vanilla to 1 c. heavy cream.

Refrigerate 30 minutes. Whip until stiff. Wonderful on peach, apple and pumpkin pies!

COCOA WHIPPED CREAM: Chill 1½ c. heavy cream, ½ c. sugar and ⅓ c. cocoa in deep bowl. Beat until stiff. Excellent on Vanilla and Banana Cream Pies when serving a crowd (makes enough for 4 pies).

GINGER WHIPPED CREAM: Add 1 tblsp. shaved candied ginger or ½ tsp. powdered ginger to 1 c. heavy cream, whipped.

COFFEE CREAM TOPPING: Chill ¾ c. heavy cream, 2 tblsp. sifted confectioners sugar and 2 tsp. instant coffee powder in bowl. Beat until stiff and fluffy. Marvelous on pumpkin pie and good on any fruit pie.

HONEYED CREAM: Whip 1 c. heavy cream until stiff. Gently stir in about 1 tblsp. strained honey. Extra-good on pumpkin pie.

FLUFFY ORANGE SAUCE

Turns homey cobblers into company fare—especially good on apple cobbler

½ c. sugar
⅛ tsp. salt
½ c. thawed frozen orange juice
    concentrate
2 egg yolks, slightly beaten
1 c. heavy cream, whipped

• Combine sugar, salt and orange juice in saucepan. Cook over low heat, stirring until sugar dissolves.
• Gradually beat a little of the orange mixture into egg yolks. Combine with remainder of hot orange mixture. Cook, stirring constantly, until slightly thickened, about 8 to 10 minutes. Cool.
• About an hour before mealtime, fold in whipped cream. Chill. Makes about 2⅔ cups.

Cheese Makes Pie Extra-Good

Our grandmothers frequently topped fruit pies with spoonfuls of creamy cottage cheese, sprinkled lightly with cinnamon. And men have liked so much to eat Cheddar cheese slices with apple and other fruit pies that the dessert team has gained universal popularity. No clever cook wants to abandon these firmly established customs, but many women also like to find new ways of combining cheese with pie. We give you a few good examples. Try them and then invent a few combinations of your own.

CHEESE CRUST TOPPING

New way to add cheese to apple pie

1 egg white
1 tblsp. grated Parmesan cheese

• Beat egg white until stiff peaks are formed. Fold in cheese.
• Spread over unbaked top crust of apple pie. Bake as directed for regular 2-crust apple pie. Serve warm.

HONEYED CHEESE: Mix 1 tblsp. honey into ½ c. cottage cheese. Add a dash of ginger, if desired. Serve on Peach-Blueberry Pie or on peach and blueberry pies.

ORANGE CHEESE: Soften 1 (3 oz.) pkg. cream cheese with 1 tblsp. orange juice. Spoon on peach or apple pie wedges.

DIFFERENT CHEESE TOPPING: Crumble a little Roquefort or blue cheese on top of apple pie. Return to oven just long enough to heat. A nice change from Cheddar cheese!

FRUIT VELVET TOPPING

Glamorizes vanilla cream pies

2 tblsp. water
3 tblsp. fruit flavor gelatin (strawberry, raspberry or cherry)
1 (3 oz.) pkg. cream cheese
2 tblsp. sugar

⅛ tsp. salt
1 (2 or 2¼ oz.) pkg. dessert topping mix

• Add water to gelatin; dissolve over hot water.
• Have cream cheese at room temperature; stir smooth in small bowl. Add sugar and salt. Add dissolved gelatin gradually, stirring to blend evenly with cheese.
• Prepare dessert topping mix according to package directions. Fold cheese mixture into whipped topping.
• Spread on top of cooled vanilla cream filling in 8″ or 9″ pie shell.
• Refrigerate several hours before serving. For smooth cutting, use warm knife.

VARIATION

• Use ½ c. fruit jam instead of gelatin and water.

Broiled Toppings de Luxe

Some of the most fascinating toppings are broiled after they're spread on ready-to-serve pies. You have to mind what you're doing for a few minutes to see that the topping doesn't brown unevenly or too much. But you'll find it's worth the careful watching for 2 or 3 minutes.

BROILED MARSHMALLOW TOPPING

Excellent on Chocolate Cream Pie

16 marshmallows (¼ lb.)
1   tblsp. milk

¼ tsp. salt
2 egg whites
¼ c. sugar

• Melt marshmallows in milk over hot water; stir until smooth. Let stand over hot water until ready to use.
• Add salt to egg whites; beat until frothy. Add sugar gradually, beating until stiff peaks are formed. Fold in marshmallow mixture. Spread gently over hot cream filling.
• Broil 8″ to 10″ from heat until delicately browned, 2 to 3 minutes. Watch closely, turning to brown evenly.
• Chill thoroughly before serving.

PEANUT BUTTER CREAM TOPPING

Use to top banana pie—a tasty team!

8 marshmallows
1 tblsp. milk
2 tblsp. creamy peanut butter
⅛ tsp. salt
1 egg white
2 tblsp. sugar

• Melt marshmallows in milk over hot water. Add peanut butter; stir until smooth. Let stand over hot water until ready to use.

• Add salt to egg white; beat until frothy. Add sugar gradually, beating until stiff peaks are formed. Fold in marshmallow mixture. Spread gently over hot filling.
• Broil 8″ to 10″ from heat until golden brown, 2 to 3 minutes. Watch closely, turning to brown evenly.
• Chill thoroughly before serving.

Note: Substitute for the meringue in recipe for Banana Meringue Pie (Chapter 4).

Baked-On Pie Toppings

Here are tops for pies that are almost no bother; yet they add distinction, both in flavor and texture. You spread them on the top crust just before you put the pie in the oven to bake. Be sure to notice the different suggestions for types of cookies to use on various kinds of pies in the Cookie Crust Topping recipe.

pie. Mark pieces for cutting while pie is still hot from oven.

Note: Use Butterscotch Nut Cookies on mincemeat; Oatmeal Raisin Cookies on apple; and Sugar Cookies, sprinkled with sugar and cinnamon, on cherry filling.

COOKIE CRUST TOPPING

Clever trick for busy pie bakers

Unbaked pie shell filled with canned
      mincemeat, cherry or apple
      pie filling
¼ roll commercial refrigerator
      cookie dough (14 slices)

• Slice refrigerator cookie dough in ⅛″ slices; cut slices in quarters. Arrange to cover top of filling in pie shell.
• Bake as directed for regular 2-crust

SPICED CRUST TOPPING

It will make your apple pie a favorite at church suppers and bake sales

1 tsp. cinnamon
¼ tsp. nutmeg
⅛ tsp. cloves
1 egg white

• Add spices to egg white and beat until stiff peaks are formed.
• Spread over unbaked top crust of apple pie. Bake as directed for regular 2-crust apple pie. Serve warm.

Wonderful Nutty Tops

Nuts add crunchy texture and rich flavors—both in and on pies. Almost any chiffon pie is enhanced by a sprinkling of chopped nuts at serving time —black walnuts do wonders for chocolate pies. This section deals with nut toppings; the nut pies are in Chapter 4.

CARAMELIZED ALMONDS: Place ¼ c. blanched almonds and 2 tblsp. sugar in skillet. Cook, stirring constantly, until golden brown. Pour on greased baking sheet at once. Cool and break apart. Sprinkle over chiffon pies at serving time.

PEANUT CRUNCH CREAM: Chill ½ c. heavy cream, 1 tblsp. sugar and ½ tsp. vanilla in deep bowl. Beat until stiff. Fold in ¼ c. finely crushed peanut brittle. Excellent on pumpkin pie.

PRALINE TOPPING

Wonderful on all kinds of peach pies

3 tblsp. butter
¼ c. brown sugar
⅓ c. coarsely broken walnuts
1 c. corn flakes

• Melt butter, add sugar and boil 2 minutes.
• Add walnuts and corn flakes. Toss lightly to coat all evenly.
• Cool; crumble over fruit filling in baked pie shell. Chill before serving. Makes enough for 1 (8″ or 9″) pie.

BLACK WALNUT-BROWN SUGAR TOPPING: Combine 3 tblsp. melted butter, ½ c. brown sugar and ¼ c. chopped black walnuts. Sprinkle over top of warm apple or peach pie.

Last-Minute Toppings

You spread these toppings on slightly warm 2-crust pies when you serve them. They are simple to make, but rewarding in taste. Here are a few we predict you'll adopt.

CARAMEL TOPPING

New, marvelous-tasting apple pie trim

⅓ c. sugar
⅓ c. water
2 tblsp. butter
1 tblsp. hot water

• Combine sugar and ⅓ c. water in small heavy saucepan. Boil, without stirring, until golden color—10 to 12 minutes.

• Remove from heat; stir in butter immediately. Then stir in 1 tblsp. hot water. Stir until smooth. Pour into bowl and cool until of spreading consistency.

• Spread over crust of slightly warm apple pie when ready to serve.

BUTTER BALLS: Combine 1½ c. sifted confectioners sugar with ½ c. butter, ¼ tsp. vanilla and ⅛ tsp. nutmeg. Thoroughly mix and chill. Spoon on warm 2-crust apple or peach pie servings or shape in balls and arrange on pie. Add color and flavor by scattering on drained and finely chopped maraschino cherries. A sprinkling of chopped walnuts adds delightful texture and flavor.

SOUR CREAM TOPPING: Combine 1 c. dairy sour cream, 2 tblsp. confectioners sugar and 1 tsp. grated orange peel. Mix and chill. Serve with warm peach pie.

MOLASSES TOPPING

Have the 2-crust apple pie warm, the topping very cold—and enjoy it!

¼   c. butter or margarine
1   c. confectioners sugar
⅛   tsp. nutmeg
1 ½ tblsp. light molasses

• Cream butter and sugar until blended and fluffy. Add nutmeg and molasses and beat to mix thoroughly.
• Chill or freeze. Spoon on individual servings of warm apple pie. Makes ¾ cup.

Pie à la Mode

With ice cream in the freezer, it's no trick to add topknots of it to individual servings. For a special treat, use homemade ice cream.

Here are four much praised recipes from our FREEZING & CANNING COOKBOOK. Use them to dress up your pies. Recommended storage time is up to 1 month.

Don't get in a rut and use only vanilla ice cream. At least dress it up for taste surprises. Swirl a little prepared mincemeat through it and serve on apple pie. Stir crushed fresh or just-thawed frozen strawberries or red raspberries through the softened ice cream and serve on peach pie.

Top apple pie with one of the nut ice creams—coconut, burnt almond, butter pecan or pistachio—or with coffee ice cream. Spoon peach ice cream on blueberry pie, strawberry ice cream on peach pie. Let your imagination be your guide and your family the judge of which combinations hit the jackpot.

COCONUT HONEY ICE CREAM

Makes warm peach pie irresistible

1 ½ c. honey
4   eggs, slightly beaten
3   c. heavy cream
2   tsp. vanilla
½   tsp. lemon extract
½   tsp. salt
3   c. milk
1   (3 ½ oz.) can flaked coconut
2   (8 ½ oz.) cans crushed pineapple

• Add honey to eggs; mix well. Add cream, flavorings, salt and milk; stir until well blended. Chill.   *more*

• Pour into freezer can; put dasher and cover in place. Pack chopped ice and coarse salt around can, 4 parts ice to 1 part salt. Turn dasher.

• When partly frozen, add coconut and pineapple; continue freezing until crank turns hard. Remove dasher. Pack in same ice mixture until serving time. Or spoon into freezer containers; seal, label, date and store in freezer. Makes 1 gallon.

VARIATION

• To intensify coconut flavor, add 2 tsp. coconut extract with lemon extract and vanilla.

MARIELLA'S ICE CREAM

Perfect garnish for fruit pies

1	qt. milk, scalded
4	eggs, beaten
2½	c. sugar
2⅓	to 3 c. heavy cream
1	qt. cold milk
2	tblsp. vanilla
¼	tsp. salt
3	drops lemon extract

• Stir hot milk slowly into eggs and sugar; cook slowly over direct heat until thickened, stirring constantly; cool.

• Add remaining ingredients to cooled egg mixture; stir until smooth. Pour into freezer can; put dasher and cover in place. Pack chopped ice and coarse salt around can, using 4 parts ice to 1 part coarse salt; turn dasher until crank turns hard (about 30 minutes with electric freezer). To store,

spoon lightly into airtight freezer containers (do not pack). Seal, label and date. Freeze. Makes about 1 gallon.

VARIATIONS

CHOCOLATE: Stir 1 (5½ oz.) can chocolate syrup into vanilla mixture.

STRAWBERRY: Mix 3 (10 oz.) pkgs. frozen strawberries, thawed, and ½ c. sugar; stir into vanilla mixture; add red food color for pink ice cream.

Note: You can make 4 batches consecutively. By time the custard for the fourth one is cooked, the first is cool enough to put in freezer can. When that gallon is frozen, the second batch is ready for freezing. This assembly line method makes economical use of ice. A 50 lb. bag of cracked ice is enough to freeze 4 gallons. You save time by using the same bowls and pans for each batch. A good selection to make is 2 gallons of vanilla, 1 of chocolate and 1 strawberry.

QUICK VANILLA ICE CREAM

Soften slightly before spooning on pie

1	tblsp. unflavored gelatin
½	c. cold water
7	c. light cream
1½	c. sugar
1	c. evaporated milk
1	tblsp. vanilla

• Sprinkle gelatin over water to soften.

• Scald 2 c. cream; add gelatin and stir to dissolve. Add sugar; stir to dissolve. Add remaining cream, evaporated milk and vanilla; add slowly to gelatin mixture, stirring.

• Pour into 1 gallon freezer container. Pack with 4 parts ice to 1 part coarse salt; freeze. Makes about 3 quarts.

• Pack in rigid containers with tight lids. Label and date. Store in bottom or coldest part of freezer.

VANILLA CUSTARD ICE CREAM

Its homemade taste enhances pies

2	c. sugar
⅛	tsp. salt
¼	c. cornstarch
1	qt. milk
4	eggs, separated
2	tsp. vanilla
1	(13 oz.) can evaporated milk
1	pt. light cream
½	c. milk (about)

• Thoroughly mix sugar, salt and cornstarch; stir into 1 qt. milk, heated just to boiling point. Remove from heat.

• Beat yolks; gradually add 1 c. of the hot milk mixture, beating constantly. Stir egg yolk mixture into remaining hot milk and bring to a boil. Remove from heat; add vanilla, evaporated milk and cream to hot custard. Cool.

• Fold in egg whites, beaten to stiff but not dry peaks. Pour into 1 gallon freezer container. Add remaining milk to fill can ¾ full.

• Pack with 4 parts ice to 1 part coarse salt; freeze. Makes 1 gallon.

• Package in rigid containers with tight lids. Label and date. Store in coldest part of freezer.

Note: Substitute 2 (13 oz.) cans evaporated milk for light cream, if you wish.

Ice Cream Topping—Farm-Style

The Iowa farm woman who contributes this king-size recipe for Ice Cream Topping says she makes it because her family and other people, especially the men who help occasionally with the work, like it so much on pies, cakes, frozen and fresh fruits and many other desserts. With a supply in the freezer, she can make her pie doubly delicious on short notice. And she always has the important ingredients on hand to whip up 6 quarts—milk, eggs and cream. The topping will keep satisfactorily in the freezer up to a month—if it gets a chance!

The mixture is not as fluffy and light as ice cream made in a crank-type freezer. If you put the topping in the refrigerator or on the counter to soften slightly before serving, it is easier to spoon out and is creamier. The flavors have a chance to mellow, too. Storing the cartons in the freezer away from the freezing surface will keep their contents nearer serving consistency. This holds for all ice cream.

It is not a good idea to freeze Ice Cream Topping or other foods in refrigerator trays unless reserved especially for this purpose. Washing trays used both for food and ice cubes prevents easy removal of ice cubes.

ICE CREAM TOPPING

Serve on slightly warm fruit and berry pies for superb desserts

2   envelopes unflavored gelatin
7½ c. milk
12 eggs, separated
3   c. sugar
½   tsp. salt
3   tblsp. vanilla
6   c. heavy cream

• Soften gelatin in ½ c. milk.
• Combine remaining 7 c. milk, slightly beaten egg yolks, sugar and salt. Add softened gelatin. Cook in heavy pan over low heat, stirring constantly, until mixture thickens slightly. Cool.
• Add vanilla and fold in stiffly beaten egg whites. Pour into 13" × 9" pan.

Cover with foil and place in freezer.
• When frozen, remove from freezer and cut mixture in 6 even blocks. Place 1 block in chilled mixer bowl and return remaining blocks to freezer or refrigerator. When the custard mixture in bowl is barely thawed, beat it until smooth and fluffy.
• Meanwhile, whip 1 c. cream until almost stiff. Fold it into custard mixture and spoon into a quart carton. Return to freezer.
• Repeat with remaining 5 blocks of frozen custard mixture, making 1 qt. Ice Cream Topping at a time.
• To serve, spoon on pieces of pie or other desserts. Makes 6 quarts.

CINNAMON ICE CREAM TOPPING: Blend ¼ tsp. cinnamon into 1 c. slightly softened vanilla ice cream. Spoon on warm apple pie wedges.

Saucy Tops for Pies

Sauces you pass in a pitcher or ladle over pie at serving time provide new taste experiences. The simplest one of all is a pitcher of cream. Just set it on the table and notice how many people will pour it over their pie wedges.

• Combine sugar, syrup and water in small saucepan and bring to a boil. Cook, uncovered, 5 minutes.
• Remove from heat; stir in vanilla. Serve warm or cold. Makes about 1⅓ cups.

AMBER CARAMEL SAUCE

Sweetness to drizzle over whipped cream spread on spicy pumpkin pies

1   c. brown sugar, firmly packed
½   c. light corn syrup
½   c. water
1   tsp. vanilla

VANILLA CREAM SAUCE

Tastes like good homemade vanilla ice cream—spoon over 2-crust fruit pies

1   egg
3   tblsp. sugar
⅛   tsp. salt
¼   c. butter or margarine, melted

½ tsp. vanilla
¾ c. heavy cream

• Beat egg with sugar and salt until fluffy and thick. Beat in butter, a small amount at a time, and stir in vanilla.
• Beat cream until stiff; fold into egg-sugar mixture until all streaks disappear. Chill thoroughly. Makes 2¼ cups.

STRAWBERRY HARD SAUCE

A treasure from a plantation kitchen in Mississippi's fertile Delta region

¼ c. butter or margarine
1 ½ c. confectioners sugar

2 tblsp. crushed fresh strawberries

• Cream butter until fluffy. Beat in sugar, a little at a time, until blended. Then add strawberries and beat until mixture is smooth. Cover and chill. Spoon on individual pie servings. Makes about 1 cup.

VARIATION

VANILLA HARD SAUCE: Omit strawberries in recipe for Strawberry Hard Sauce and add 1 tsp. vanilla. Cover and chill. Sprinkle lightly with mace or nutmeg when serving on apple pie or dumplings. Makes about 1 cup.

More Wonderful Toppings to Try

Here is a list of toppings included with pie recipes elsewhere in this book. You can find them in the chapters indicated, or check the Index.

Chapter 2: Potato Snowcaps
(Frozen)

Chapter 3: Spicy Pecan
Cinnamon Nut
Brown Sugar Streusel
Cinnamon Jelly Glaze
Brown Sugar Syrup
Marshmallow Sauce
Oat Streusel
Lemon Crumb
Spicy
Orange Frosting
Toasted Oat
Crumbly

Chapter 4: Caramelized Pecan
Caramel Sauce
Pecan Meringue

Chapter 5: Chocolate
Chocolate Frosting
Apple Snow

Chapter 6: Blueberry Sauce
Spiced Honey Cream
Orange Biscuit Topping
Cinnamon Syrup

Chapter 7: Sugar Glaze
Cherry Sauce
Orange Cream Dress-Up
Apricot Glaze

Main-Dish Pies

MEAT AND CHICKEN PIES

When fall's first brisk days arrive and harvested vegetables overflow their storage baskets, it's a country custom to get out a rolling pin and fix a meal-in-a-pie. Brimful of fork-tender meat, succulent vegetables and savory gravy, capped with flaky pastry or puffed-up, golden biscuits, meat pies are so satisfying. And they make the cook's work easier, for few accompaniments are needed. Salad or crisp relishes, ice cream or sherbet and a beverage round out the menu.

Notice the variety in our meat pies—especially those made with beef and pork. Our readers, of course, sent us more favorite recipes using ground beef than any other type. They're truly American farm specials. But there are others—Midwestern Casserole Beef Pie with Butter Crumb Biscuits, to name an extra-good one. We believe you'll want to treat your family to it some day soon.

You'll detect intriguing foreign flavors in many pies. That's natural, for Europeans are as fond of these main dishes as we are of steak and potatoes. Exciting recipes for Quebec Pork Pie, Cornish Pasty, English Steak and Kidney Pie and Italian Beef Pie appear in this chapter, among others.

Chicken Pie, Grandmother's wonderful Sunday-dinner standby, has undergone many changes. Crusty, brown Popover Chicken Pie is an example of the new. Double-Crust Chicken Pie represents the traditional—part of its crust bakes in the pie, making dumplings. This old-fashioned Southern chicken dish never will go out of style. And sometime when you're entertaining, or want to surprise the family, try our Individual Chicken-Ham Pies with Rice Crust—delicious!

Be sure to read about the unusual crusts you can make from basic biscuits (Chapter 2). You'll be convinced that while the filling is important, it's often the crust that makes a pie distinctive.

Beef Pies—Hearty and Heartening

Provide a real treat on dark, rainy and cold evenings, when the family seeks the warmth and bright lights of the kitchen at suppertime. Take a brown-topped meat pie from the oven. Let everyone see the rich juices bubbling in the crust's peepholes and savor the aroma. Watch the way everyone hustles around to get ready for supper. No one will forget these home scenes and scents. Psychologists say that pleasing food fragrances are much remembered childhood experiences.

Among the top-ranking meat pies that come to farm tables are the beef and vegetable stews under pastry, biscuits, corn bread or other crusts. You can add your own touches to the fillings or crusts—whatever your family likes. Is it celery, caraway or dill seed, or dill weed? Let the flavors your husband, children and friends appreciate be your guide in converting a homey meat pie into a gourmet dish. Spring a surprise change in flavor occasionally to observe its reception. One country homemaker's stunt is to roll the biscuit dough covering stews in melted butter and fine bread crumbs for golden results. Here is an adapted version of her dish.

1 ½ tsp. salt
⅛ tsp. pepper
¼ c. shortening
2 medium onions, separated in rings
½ c. water
1 can condensed cream of chicken soup
2 c. cubed raw potatoes
Butter Crumb Biscuits
1 can condensed cream of mushroom soup
½ c. dairy sour cream

• Cut steak in 1″ cubes. Dredge with mixture of flour, paprika, ½ tsp. salt and pepper. Place in skillet and brown well in hot shortening. Top with onion rings. Add water and chicken soup. Cover and simmer 45 minutes.
• Add potatoes and remaining 1 tsp. salt. Continue cooking 15 minutes, stirring occasionally.
• Pour hot mixture into 1½ qt. casserole. Top with Butter Crumb Biscuits and bake in hot oven (400°F.) 20 to 25 minutes, or until biscuits are golden.
• Serve with sauce made by heating 1 can mushroom soup and ½ c. dairy sour cream. Makes 6 to 8 servings.

CASSEROLE BEEF PIE

Crumb biscuits atop beef give pie new look and taste—extra-good

2 lbs. round steak
⅓ c. flour
1 tsp. paprika

BUTTER CRUMB BISCUITS

2 c. sifted flour
4 tsp. baking powder
½ tsp. salt
¼ tsp. poultry seasoning
½ tsp. celery seed

½ tsp. onion flakes
¼ c. salad oil
1 c. milk
¼ c. melted butter
1 c. fine bread crumbs

• Sift together into bowl, flour, baking powder, salt and poultry seasoning. Add celery seed and onion flakes; stir in oil and milk. Drop by tablespoonfuls into melted butter, then roll in bread crumbs.
• Place on top hot meat mixture in casserole and bake as directed in Casserole Beef Pie.

STEAK AND ONION PIE

The tantalizing aroma of this pie baking builds eager appetites

Filling:
1 c. sliced onions
½ c. shortening
1 lb. round steak, cut in small pieces
¼ c. flour
½ tsp. paprika
⅛ tsp. ginger
⅛ tsp. allspice
2 tsp. salt
⅛ tsp. pepper
2 ½ c. boiling water
2 c. diced raw potatoes

Egg Crust:
1 c. sifted flour
½ tsp. salt
⅓ c. shortening
1 egg, slightly beaten

Filling: Fry onions slowly in melted shortening, until yellow; remove from fat.

• Roll meat in mixture of flour, spices and seasonings. (Or shake all together in paper bag.) Brown in hot fat.
• Add water; cover and simmer until meat is tender, about 45 minutes.
• Add potatoes and cook 10 minutes longer. Pour into 8″ greased casserole. Place cooked onions on top and cover with Egg Crust.
Egg Crust: Mix flour and salt. Add half of shortening and cut in until as fine as meal. Add remaining shortening and cut in until particles are size of large peas.
• Add egg, mixing thoroughly into a dough. Roll out slightly larger than top of casserole. Make dime-size openings for steam to escape and fit dough over top of casserole; fold under pastry edge and flute.
• Bake in very hot oven (450°F.) 30 minutes. Makes 4 to 6 servings.

STEAK AND KIDNEY PIE

Serve this favorite of English meat-potato-gravy men straight from oven

Pastry for 1-crust pie
1 beef kidney
2 lbs. round steak, cubed
2 tblsp. fat
2 c. chopped onions (2 large onions)
2 tsp. salt
¼ tsp. pepper
½ tsp. dried thyme
1 bay leaf
2 tsp. Worcestershire sauce
2 c. water
4 c. diced raw potatoes (4 medium size)
6 tblsp. flour *more*

• Cover beef kidney with lightly salted water, cover and refrigerate overnight. Drain; cut out tubes and white membrane with scissors. Dice meat.

• Brown kidney and steak in hot fat. Add onions, seasonings and 1½ c. water. Simmer until meat is almost tender, about 1 hour.

• Add potatoes and continue simmering until potatoes are tender, about ½ hour.

• Blend together flour and remaining ½ c. water; stir into meat mixture. Continue cooking and stirring until mixture thickens. Pour into 3 qt. casserole.

• Roll out pastry slightly larger than top of casserole. Place over meat mixture and trim to overhang 1″. Fold under and flute against inside edge of casserole. Cut several steam vents in center.

• Bake in hot oven (425°F.) until lightly browned, about 30 minutes. Makes 8 servings.

Note: You can use the milder-flavored veal or lamb kidney instead of beef kidney, if available. You need not soak it overnight in salted water.

DINNER BEEF PIE

Beef and vegetables in tomato gravy make this plump pie wonderful eating

Pastry for 2-crust pie
2   tblsp. shortening
1 ½ c. chopped celery
1 ½ c. chopped onions
1 ½ c. chopped green pepper
3   c. beef cubes (1″)
1   can condensed tomato soup
2   tblsp. prepared mustard
¼   c. tomato ketchup
¾   tsp. salt

• Heat shortening in skillet, add celery, onions and green pepper; sauté until soft. Stir in beef cubes; cover and simmer 20 minutes. Add soup, mustard, ketchup and salt; heat thoroughly.

• Place meat mixture in pastry-lined 9″ pie pan; adjust top crust, flute edges and cut vents.

• Bake in hot oven (425°F.) 40 to 50 minutes. Makes 6 servings.

Note: Green pepper may be omitted; if so, use 2¼ c. each of celery and onion.

Country Pies Filled with Ground Beef

With ground beef almost always on hand in farm home freezers, it's not surprising that much experimentation with it goes on in country kitchens. It is often the main ingredient in savory meat pies. Two country-kitchen tricks that please—fluffs of mashed potatoes topping the pie in lieu of crust; expertly seasoned ground beef pie shells shaped in a pie pan to hold a variety of tempting fillings.

CHEESEBURGER PIE

If your family likes cheeseburgers in buns, watch them go for this pie

Cheese Pastry for 2-crust pie (Chapter 2)
1   lb. ground beef chuck
½   c. chopped celery
¼   c. chopped onion
2   tblsp. chopped green pepper
1   tsp. salt
¼   tsp. pepper
1   (8 oz.) can tomato sauce
1   tsp. Worcestershire sauce

• Brown beef in skillet, stirring frequently. Add celery, onion, green pepper, salt, pepper, tomato and Worcestershire sauces. Cover and simmer 15 minutes.
• Roll out pastry to 8½″ square by placing 8″ pan on pastry and cutting around it with knife, leaving ½″ margins.
• Place hot meat mixture in 8″ square pan and top with square of pastry, turning under edges.
• Cut remaining pastry into strips and arrange them lattice-style on pastry square, turning under edges.
• Bake in hot oven (400°F.) 30 minutes. Makes 4 servings.

VARIATION

• Use plain pastry for a 1-crust pie instead of Cheese Pastry. Place over top of pie. When baked, sprinkle on ½ c. grated Cheddar cheese and return to oven just long enough to melt cheese.

UPSIDE-DOWN MEAT PIE

Bake this meat loaf under a tent of cheese pastry when you want a change

Pastry for 1-crust pie
1   lb. ground beef chuck
2   tblsp. instant minced onion
1   tsp. salt
1   tsp. prepared mustard
⅛   tsp. pepper
½   c. dry bread crumbs
1   egg, beaten
⅓   c. milk
½   c. ketchup
Parsley

• Combine beef, onion, salt, mustard, pepper, bread crumbs, egg, milk and ⅓ c. ketchup. Place mixture in greased 8″ round cake pan. Pat meat out to within ½″ of sides of pan.
• Roll pastry out to a scant 10″ circle. Place it over meat, tucking it down around meat and pressing it against bottom of pan. Prick pastry all over with a four-tined fork.
• Bake in hot oven (425°F.) until crust is golden, about 40 minutes. Remove from oven and let stand a few minutes. Run spatula under outer edge of pie. Invert serving plate over top of pie pan. Invert both and lift off pie pan.
• Dot top of meat with remaining ketchup and sprinkle with coarsely snipped (with scissors) parsley. If parsley is not available, add color by scattering shreds of yellow cheese over ketchup-dotted meat pie. Makes 6 servings.

SUCCOTASH-BEEF PIE

Southwesterners will step up flavor by adding a little chili powder to filling

Filling:
1 ½ lbs. ground beef
1   c. chopped onion (1 large)
1   c. chopped celery
3   tblsp. flour
1   (1 lb.) can tomatoes
1 ½ tsp. salt
¼   tsp. pepper
1   tsp. Worcestershire sauce
1   c. grated sharp process cheese
2   (10 oz.) pkgs. frozen succotash

Topping:
1   c. cornmeal, yellow or white
¼   c. flour
1   tblsp. sugar
2   tsp. baking powder
½   tsp. salt
1   egg
½   c. milk
¼   c. butter or margarine, melted

Filling: Cook beef, onion and celery in heavy skillet until beef is browned. Stir in flour. Add tomatoes and cook, stirring, until mixture is thickened and bubbling. Stir in seasonings. Cover and simmer until celery is tender, about 15 minutes; stir frequently. Stir in cheese.
• Combine meat mixture and succotash, cooked by package directions, in 3 qt. casserole. Place in moderate oven (375°F.) while you make topping.

Topping: Combine cornmeal, flour, sugar, baking powder and salt. Blend together egg and milk. Stir into corn-meal mixture. Stir in butter. Spread over meat mixture in casserole.
• Bake until topping is golden, about 30 minutes. Makes 8 servings.

EMPANADAS

Serve with bowls of steaming soup and a fruit or vegetable salad

Pastry for 2 (2-crust) pies
1   tblsp. butter
⅓   c. chopped onion
½   c. peeled chopped tomatoes
¼   c. chopped green pepper
½   lb. lean ground beef chuck
¾   tsp. salt
⅛   tsp. pepper
Few drops Tabasco sauce
1   hard-cooked egg, chopped
1 ½ tblsp. seedless raisins
¼   c. chopped green olives

• Melt butter in skillet; add onion, tomatoes and green pepper and cook over low heat until onion is soft. Stir in beef and cook until no pink remains. Remove from heat and stir in remaining ingredients. Cool.
• Roll out pastry. Cut in 4″ rounds. Place 1 tblsp. filling in center of each round. Brush edges with water and fold over dough, pressing edges together firmly. Cut steam vent in top of each.
• Bake in hot oven (425°F.) until lightly browned, about 15 minutes. Makes about 2½ dozen.

Note: These small meat pies are as popular in South America as hot dogs in the U.S.A. They make different and good snacks.

RANCHERS' BEEF TURNOVERS

*You're lucky if you have leftovers, for
these make tasty cold sandwiches*

1	lb. ground lean beef
½	c. chopped onion
¼	c. chopped green pepper
2 ¼	c. biscuit mix
1	tsp. salt
¼	tsp. pepper
⅓	c. ketchup
3	tblsp. butter or margarine
⅔	c. milk
1	(10 ½ oz.) can beef-mushroom gravy (optional)

• Cook beef, onion and green pepper
in skillet until beef is browned. Pour
off excess fat.

• Add ¼ c. prepared biscuit mix, salt,
pepper and ketchup. Cook, stirring
frequently, several minutes.

• Cut butter into remaining 2 c. biscuit mix, until mixture is crumbly.
Blend in milk. Turn out on board
dusted with a little biscuit mix and
knead 8 to 10 times.

• Divide dough in half. Roll each half
into a 10″ square. Divide each into 4
squares. Top each square with about
⅓ c. beef filling. Fold over corner to
corner to make triangles. Seal edges
and cut steam vents in top.

• Bake on greased baking sheet in hot
oven (400°F.) until browned as desired, about 15 minutes. Serve topped
with hot beef-mushroom gravy. Makes
8 turnovers.

Pasty—Family-Size and Individual

Pasty, a meat - and - potato pie
adopted from Cornwall, England, is
popular in this country, especially in
neighborhoods where people of Cornish ancestry live—Mineral Point, Wisconsin, Michigan's Upper Peninsula,
Montana's mining areas and other
places.

For family use, the pasty usually is
large enough to serve everyone at the
table. For lunch boxes and picnic
hampers, individual turnovers are the
rule. They're served cold and are
picked up and eaten from the fingers
when toted; hot in home meals. It was
the custom of miners' wives in Mineral Point to stand in their doorways
at mealtime and shake a white cloth
to call the men home to eat. This part

of the town, now being restored, is
still called Shake-Rag-under-the-Hill.
When the men ate at the lead mines,
their wives wrapped freshly baked pasties in their shawls and carried them
to their husbands.

The most unusual feature of the
true pasty is that no steam vents are
cut in the pastry that holds the savory
meat-and-vegetable filling. For inexperienced cooks this often creates the
problem of sealing the pastry so that
the steam and juices do not escape.
It's an exciting moment when the pasty
is cut at the table and a little of the
fragrant steam spouts out.

Many American cooks depart from
the traditional and cut two slits on top
of individual pasties before baking

them. A Wisconsin custom with family-size pasties is to cut three-cornered openings about 2″ apart. After the pasty has baked half an hour, and once again during the baking, a little cream is poured into the "windows" to insure a juicy filling.

The "a" in pasty is pronounced as in "dash," although some Americans pronounce it as in "pastry." If they do this in the Cornish neighborhoods of Wisconsin and Michigan, they'll be politely corrected.

We give you two recipes for pasty, the family-size and individual.

AMERICAN PIE-PAN PASTY

The original pasty was a big turnover and wasn't baked in a pie pan

Pastry for 2-crust pie
1   lb. ground lean beef chuck
1 ¾ c. diced raw potatoes
¼   c. finely chopped celery
1   tsp. dried onion flakes
1   tsp. salt
¼   tsp. pepper
½   c. grated Cheddar cheese
Paprika

• Combine meat, potatoes, celery, onion, salt and pepper. Place in pastry-lined 9″ pie pan. Sprinkle with grated cheese.
• Adjust top crust; seal. (Do not cut steam vents in it.) Sprinkle lightly with paprika.
• Bake in moderate oven (375°F.) until top is lightly browned, about 1 hour. Serve hot. Makes 6 servings.

CORNISH PASTIES

The traditional recipe for individual pasties—often packed in lunch boxes

Pastry for 1 (10″) 2-crust pie
2   c. thinly sliced raw potatoes
½   c. thinly sliced onion
½   lb. round steak, thinly sliced and cut in ½″ pieces
1 ½ tsp. salt
⅛   tsp. pepper
2   tblsp. butter or margarine

• Divide pastry in three equal parts. Roll one third to make 8″ × 15″ rectangle. Trim edges and cut to make 2 (7″) squares. Place on baking sheet. Repeat with other two thirds of pastry.
• Arrange layer of potatoes on half of each pastry square, top with layer of onion and then with meat. Sprinkle with salt and pepper and dot with butter.
• Moisten pastry edges with cold water and fold over to make triangles; press edges together to make tight seal. (A tight seal retains steam and makes juicy pasties.)
• Bake in moderate oven (375°F.) 1 hour or until meat is tender. Serve hot with chili sauce, ketchup or pickle relish, or serve cold for sandwiches. Makes 6 pasties.

CHILI CON CARNE PIE

Both corn bread and cornmeal mush make good toppings—take your pick

½   c. chopped onion
1   clove garlic, minced
1 ½ lbs. ground beef
1   (8 oz.) can tomato sauce

1   (1 lb.) can tomatoes (2 c.)
1   (20 oz.) can kidney beans, drained (or Mexican-style chili beans)
1   tblsp. chili powder (or less)
1   tsp. salt
¼   c. grated Parmesan cheese
Corn Bread Topping or Mush Topping

• Sauté onion, garlic and beef. Stir in remaining ingredients, except cheese and Topping; simmer 10 minutes.
• Bake as directed with either Topping. Makes 6 servings.

CORN BREAD TOPPING

¾   c. enriched cornmeal
¼   c. sifted flour
½   tsp. salt
1 ½   tsp. baking powder
1   egg
½   c. milk
¼   c. soft shortening
1   tblsp. chopped parsley

• Sift together dry ingredients. Add egg, milk and shortening. Beat with rotary beater until smooth, about 1 minute. Do not overbeat. Stir in parsley. Place hot filling in shallow 2 qt. baking dish; sprinkle with cheese. Spoon Topping around edge of dish. Bake in hot oven (425°F.) 15 to 18 minutes.

MUSH TOPPING

3   c. water
1   c. enriched cornmeal
1   c. cold water
1   tsp. salt
½   tsp. garlic salt
¼   c. finely chopped onion

• Boil 3 c. water. Mix remaining ingredients; stir into boiling water. Cook until thickened, stirring often. Cover; continue cooking over low heat, 10 minutes for yellow cornmeal, 5 minutes for white cornmeal.
• Line greased 9″ × 9″ × 2″ baking dish with two thirds of mush. Add hot filling; sprinkle with cheese. Top with remaining mush.
• Bake in moderate oven (375°F.), about 30 minutes.

HAMBURGER CORN-PONE PIE

Have for supper with creamed peas, coleslaw and strawberry sundae

1   lb. ground beef
⅓   c. chopped onion
1   tblsp. shortening
¾   tsp. salt
1   to 2 tsp. chili powder
1   tsp. Worcestershire sauce
1   c. canned tomatoes
1   (15 ½ oz.) can kidney beans
Corn-Pone Topping

• Brown beef and onion in shortening, stirring. Drain off excess fat. Add seasonings and tomatoes; cover and simmer over low heat 15 minutes. Add kidney beans and heat to boiling.
• Turn into 10″ pie pan and pour over Corn-Pone Topping to cover meat mixture. Bake in hot oven (425°F.) 15 to 20 minutes. Makes 6 servings.

CORN-PONE TOPPING: Sift together ½ c. flour, ¾ tsp. salt and 2 tsp. baking powder; stir in ½ c. cornmeal. Mix thoroughly. Add 1 egg, ¼ c. salad oil and ½ c. milk or enough milk to make a pour batter.

BEEF-ONION PIE

Biscuits, beef and sour cream make this a fancy main-dish pie for company

Biscuit Pie Shell
2 tblsp. butter or margarine
1 c. sliced onion (1 medium-
    large)
1 lb. ground beef
1 tsp. salt
⅛ tsp. pepper
1 tblsp. flour
1 c. dairy sour cream
1 egg, slightly beaten
Paprika

• Melt butter, add onion and cook gently 5 minutes. Add beef and stir with fork until meat loses red color. Remove from heat, drain off excess fat and blend in salt, pepper and flour. Cool slightly.
• Spread meat mixture in Biscuit Pie Shell. Bake in hot oven (400°F.) 5 minutes.
• Meanwhile, combine sour cream and egg.
• Remove pie from oven; reduce heat to 350°F. Spread cream-egg mixture over meat filling. Sprinkle with paprika. Return to oven and bake 30 minutes. Makes 5 to 6 servings.

BISCUIT PIE SHELL: Stir ⅓ c. light cream into 1 c. biscuit mix with fork. Roll out soft dough to fit 9″ pie pan.

BLACK-EYE PEAS AND CHILI PIE

Good, easy Texas-style pie with corn-bread crust—serve with sliced tomatoes

1 (15 oz.) can black-eye peas
    (1 ¾ c.)
1 (15 ½ oz.) can chili con carne
½ c. cornmeal
½ c. flour
1 tblsp. sugar
¼ tsp. salt
2 tsp. baking powder
½ c. milk
1 egg
2 tblsp. soft shortening

• Drain peas, reserving liquid. Combine peas with ¼ c. of the reserved liquid and chili con carne in saucepan. Heat.
• Stir together cornmeal, flour, sugar, salt and baking powder. Add milk, egg and shortening. Beat with rotary beater until smooth, about 1 minute. Do not overbeat.
• Place hot chili mixture in a 1½ qt. greased casserole. Spoon cornmeal mixture over top. Bake in hot oven (400°F.) until lightly browned, about 25 minutes. Makes 4 to 6 servings.

Revival of Shepherd's Pie

Many Monday dinners once featured wonderful Shepherd's Pie made with leftover mashed potatoes, roast beef and gravy from Sunday's feast. They first were made with cooked lamb—hence their name. And to this day, many country cooks champion lamb as the perfect ingredient for the classic pie.

"I stopped making Shepherd's Pies several years ago because I never had enough gravy left to fix them," a farm woman said. But she quickly added,

"Imagine how thrilled I was to discover packaged gravy mixes one day while browsing in a supermarket! Since then, the old-fashioned pies have staged a comeback at our house. However I rarely make one the day after we've had roast. Instead, I freeze the leftover meat, potatoes and gravy (each separately) and make the pie several days later. I've found packaged instant potatoes a help in stretching those left over. In fact, I always keep them in the cupboard."

No doubt nostalgia for the excellent Shepherd's Pies our mothers used to make had something to do with it, but the extra-good taste also helps account for today's renewed interest in the meat-and-potato pie. The following recipe will prompt you to revive this dish you may have forgotten.

UPDATED SHEPHERD'S PIE

Leftover beef in this potato topped pie is a hearty dish with husband appeal

1 ½	c. chopped celery
½	c. chopped onion
½	c. water
4	c. cubed cooked beef pot roast
2	c. leftover gravy
½	c. chopped parsley
1	tsp. salt
3	eggs, separated
3	c. seasoned mashed potatoes
¼	tsp. salt
2	tblsp. grated Parmesan cheese
¼	tsp. paprika
1	c. hot gravy

• Put celery, onion and water in covered saucepan; cook until barely tender. Do not drain. Combine with beef, 2 c. gravy, parsley and 1 tsp. salt in greased 2½ qt. casserole. (If you don't have enough gravy, extend it with gravy mix.)

• Set oven regulator to hot (400°F.). Place casserole in oven to heat while you prepare potatoes.

• Beat egg yolks. Add to mashed potatoes and beat again. (Use instant potatoes, if you wish.)

• Combine egg whites and ¼ tsp. salt. Beat until stiff peaks form. Fold into potatoes and spread over hot meat in casserole. Sprinkle with cheese and paprika.

• Bake until lightly browned, about 25 minutes. Serve with extra gravy. Makes 8 servings.

Note: Follow label directions on 1 (¾ oz.) pkg. gravy mix to make extra gravy.

HAMBURGER-POTATO PIE

Supper's ready! Meat and vegetables topped with potatoes in a hot dish

½	c. chopped onion
1	tblsp. shortening
1	lb. ground beef
½	tsp. salt
⅛	tsp. pepper
1	(1 lb.) can green beans (2 c.)
1	can condensed tomato soup
6	frozen potato Snowcaps (Chapter 2)

Melted butter

• Cook onion in hot shortening until golden; add meat and seasonings;

brown. Add drained beans and soup; heat; pour into 1½ qt. casserole.
· Top with frozen potato Snowcaps; brush with melted butter. Bake in moderate oven (375°F.) 30 minutes, or until Snowcaps are delicately browned. Makes 6 servings.

4-H PIZZABURGERS

Teen-agers like this farm version of pizza that resembles hamburgers

    2   lbs. ground beef
    1   lb. minced ham luncheon meat, ground
    3   (6 oz.) cans tomato paste
    1   tblsp. instant onion
    1½ tsp. orégano
    ½   tsp. sage
    1½ tsp. salt
    ¼   tsp. pepper
    3   c. grated Mozzarella cheese (12 oz.)
    ¼   c. dried parsley
    14 hamburger buns

· Brown beef in skillet; drain off fat. Add luncheon meat, tomato paste, onion, orégano, sage, salt, pepper and 1 c. grated cheese; mix thoroughly. Cool and refrigerate until needed.
· Split hamburger buns. Place ¼ c. meat mixture on bun half. Spread to cover bun. Sprinkle with 1 tblsp. remaining grated cheese and about ½ tsp. dried parsley. Repeat with remaining bun halves.
· Place on baking sheets and bake in very hot oven (450°F.) about 10 minutes, or until cheese is bubbly. Makes 25 to 28 sandwiches.

VEGETABLE BEEF PIE

Cheese potato puffs brown atop a pie long on flavor, short on fixing time

    1   medium onion, chopped
    1   lb. ground beef
    1   tsp. salt
    ¼   tsp. pepper
    1   tblsp. Worcestershire sauce
    ¼   tsp. chili powder
    1   (1 lb.) can green beans, drained
    1   can condensed tomato soup
    6   tblsp. warm milk
    1   egg, beaten
    2   c. mashed potatoes
    ¼   c. sharp grated cheese

· Brown onion and beef; drain fat. In greased 2 qt. casserole, combine beef mixture with next six ingredients.
· Beat milk and egg into potatoes; spoon in ¼ c. mounds over bean mixture, top with cheese.
· Bake in moderate oven (350°F.) 30 minutes or until heated through. Makes 8 servings.

JIFFY MEAT-POTATO PIE

Welcome variety for meat-and-potato families—easy to fix on busy days

    1   lb. ground beef
    1   tsp. salt
    ¼   tsp. pepper
    ½   c. finely chopped onion
    ½   c. soft bread crumbs
    ½   c. milk
    1   egg, beaten
    1   envelope instant mashed potatoes
    ¾   c. shredded sharp process cheese

• Combine beef, salt, pepper, onion, bread crumbs, milk and egg. Mix thoroughly and press in bottom and on sides of 9″ pie pan to line. Bake in moderate oven (350°F.) 35 minutes. Drain off excess fat.

• Prepare potatoes as directed on package. (You can cook and mash potatoes if you prefer.) Spread over meat. Sprinkle with cheese. Return to oven and bake until cheese melts, about 10 minutes. Cut in wedges to serve. Makes 4 servings.

BONELESS STEAK PIE

This farm kitchen special makes a meal along with salad and ice cream

2	lbs. round steak, cut in 1″ cubes
2	tblsp. hot fat
1	c. chopped onion
2	tsp. salt
½	tsp. pepper
1	tblsp. Worcestershire sauce
2	tblsp. chopped parsley
1 ½	c. boiling water
1 ½	c. sliced carrots
½	c. sliced celery
2	tblsp. flour
¼	c. water
4	c. seasoned mashed potatoes
½	c. process cheese spread

• Brown steak cubes in fat. Add onion and cook until soft. Add salt and pepper, Worcestershire sauce, parsley and boiling water. Cover and simmer slowly 30 minutes.

• Add carrots and celery; continue simmering 45 minutes.

• Blend together flour and ¼ c. cold water. Stir into meat mixture and continue stirring until mixture returns to a boil.

• Pour into greased 2½ qt. casserole. Combine hot, seasoned mashed potatoes (may be made from packaged instant mashed potatoes) and cheese spread, stirring until cheese is blended in. Drop by spoonfuls on hot meat around edge of casserole.

• Bake in moderate oven (350°F.) 30 minutes. Makes 6 servings.

BEEF PIE SUPREME

A favorite of meat-and-potato men— from our COUNTRY COOKBOOK

1 ½	lbs. beef for stew (boneless shoulder or chuck)
¼	c. flour
1	tsp. salt
⅛	tsp. pepper
3	tblsp. shortening
1	c. water
1	c. canned tomatoes
2	tsp. Worcestershire sauce
6	carrots
12	small onions
3	c. mashed potatoes
⅓	c. process cheese spread
Melted butter or margarine	

• Cut meat into 1½″ cubes.

• Mix flour, salt and pepper; roll meat in mixture to coat all sides.

• Brown meat well in hot shortening; add water, tomatoes and Worcestershire sauce.

• Peel carrots; cut in 1″ crosswise slices. Peel onions; add to meat.

• Cover tightly. Simmer 2 hours. Stir occasionally to avoid sticking.

more

• Pour into greased 2 qt. casserole.
• With mixer, blend together mashed potatoes and cheese spread. Drop by spoonfuls around rim of casserole.

Brush with melted butter. Bake until bubbly hot in moderate oven (375°F.), about 30 minutes. Makes 6 to 8 servings.

Beef Makes the Crust

Pie shells made with ground beef have an enthusiastic following in many farm homes. If you use fairly lean meat, you'll reduce shrinkage during the baking. In Italian Hamburger Pie you have a blend of meat, tomatoes, cheese and seasonings that explains the name and wonderful taste of the pie. Use this main dish when you're in a hurry. Oven time is only half an hour. You will want to double this recipe for some meals. Or use the larger recipe for Italian Beef Pie in this chapter.

• Drain tomatoes, reserving juice. Measure ½ c. juice, adding water if necessary.
• Combine ground beef, salt, pepper, bread crumbs, onion, garlic and tomato juice. Press into a 9″ pie pan, lining pan.
• Bake in moderate oven (375°F.) 15 minutes. Drain off fat.
• Cut up tomatoes and place in beef pie crust. Sprinkle with parsley, orégano and cheese. Return to oven and bake 15 minutes. Cut in wedges. Makes 4 servings.

ITALIAN HAMBURGER PIE

Something different, colorful and tasty to do with ever popular ground beef

1   (1 lb.) can tomatoes
1   lb. ground beef chuck
1   tsp. salt
¼   tsp. pepper
½   c. soft bread crumbs
⅓   c. finely chopped onion
1   clove garlic, minced
½   tsp. dried parsley
¼   tsp. orégano
½   c. shredded Mozzarella cheese

ITALIAN BEEF PIE

Use Italian-style canned tomatoes instead of regular, if available

2   tsp. salt
2   cloves garlic
2   lbs. ground lean beef chuck
⅓   c. fine dry bread crumbs
¼   tsp. pepper
1   medium onion, chopped (about ¾ c.)
2   (1 lb.) cans tomatoes

1   tsp. seasoning salt
¼   tsp. orégano
¼   tsp. basil
½   c. grated Mozzarella or Parmesan cheese

• Put salt in mixing bowl; add cut cloves garlic and rub to crush. Remove garlic. Add beef, bread crumbs, pepper and onion.
• Drain tomatoes. Measure ¾ c. tomato juice, adding water if necessary. Mix into meat mixture. Pat meat mixture into bottom and on sides of a 10″ pie pan.
• Bake in moderate oven (375°F.) 30 minutes, placing a piece of foil slightly larger than pan on oven rack below pan to catch possible drippings.
• Remove from oven; drain off fat. Arrange drained tomatoes in meat pie shell. Top with seasoning salt, orégano, basil and cheese.
• Return to oven and bake 20 minutes longer. Cool a minute or two, drain off drippings and cut in wedges. Makes 8 servings.

MEAT LOAF PIES

Pastry-wrapped bundles of barbecued meat loaves are supper-party specials

Pastry for 10″ 2-crust pie
1   lb. ground beef chuck
½   lb. ground lean pork
½   lb. liver sausage
2   tblsp. finely chopped onion
2   tblsp. finely chopped green pepper
1   clove garlic, chopped
1 ½ tsp. salt
½   tsp. paprika
¼   tsp. pepper

⅓   c. bread crumbs
Barbecue Sauce

• Combine beef, pork, liver sausage, onion, green pepper, garlic, salt, paprika, pepper and bread crumbs, mixing thoroughly. Shape mixture into 8 square loaves. Place in greased baking pan. Top each meat loaf with 1 tblsp. Barbecue Sauce.
• Bake in moderate oven (350°F.) 15 minutes. Spoon remaining sauce over loaves and continue baking 20 minutes. Remove from baking pan and cool until lukewarm (or bake in advance, cool and refrigerate).
• Divide pastry in half. Roll each half into 12″ square. Cut in fourths. Place each meat loaf diagonally on a square of pastry so that corners of pastry may be brought up over sides of meat loaves. Seal pastry well. Prick each pastry-wrapped meat loaf two or three times.
• Bake in hot oven (425°F.) 20 minutes. Serve hot or cold. Makes 8 servings.

BARBECUE SAUCE: Combine ½ c. ketchup, ¼ c. vinegar, 2 tsp. Worcestershire sauce, ½ clove garlic, finely chopped, 1 tblsp. grated onion, 1 tsp. prepared mustard and 1 tsp. salt. Stir to mix thoroughly.

GOOD IDEA: If you have leftover beef and vegetable stew, reheat it, turn into casserole and top with biscuits (Chapter 2). Bake in very hot oven (450°F.) 20 to 25 minutes, or until biscuits are done.
• You can add a surprise to this guaranteed-to-please pie by using some of the variations for biscuits listed in Chapter 2.

North-of-the-Border Pork Pie

You don't have to visit Canada or our own adjacent north country to enjoy *tourtière,* the famous holiday pork pie. We have two recipes, both from New England farm kitchens.

The true *tourtière* always contains ground lean pork and mashed potatoes in a delicately spiced filling, but there are many variations. We give you the traditional type, which originated in the Province of Quebec. Usually, the cooks there like to double the amount of spices, using ¼ tsp. cloves and ½ tsp. cinnamon in a 9″ pie. While French-speaking people call it *tourtière,* you'll find it's a real treat in our language as Quebec Pork Pie.

The second version—our Good-Neighbor Pork Pie—is an updated recipe from Vermont, with salt, pepper, garlic and vegetables doing the seasoning. While our Canadian neighbors often serve the pie on New Year's Day and during the winter holiday season, it is hearty and tasty for serving throughout the cold months.

One Vermont homemaker who sent us her best-liked pork pie recipe wrote: "My pie-eating men like *tourtière* because it contains two of their favorite foods, meat and potatoes, baked in an envelope of something they're fond of—flaky pastry."

QUEBEC PORK PIE

You can freeze this pie before baking, or freeze just the filling to use later

Pastry for 2-crust pie
1   lb. ground lean pork
½   lb. ground lean beef
3   tblsp. chopped onion
½   tsp. salt
⅛   tsp. pepper
1   c. water
⅛   tsp. cloves
¼   tsp. cinnamon
1½ c. mashed potatoes (2 medium large)

• Combine pork, beef, onion, salt, pepper and water. Cook slowly for 45 minutes. Add cloves and cinnamon; cook 15 minutes longer.
• Add potatoes to meat mixture while hot. Let cool thoroughly, or about 1 hour, so flavors will blend. Turn mixture into pastry-lined 9″ pie pan. Adjust top crust, cut vents and flute edges.
• Bake in hot oven (400°F.) 45 minutes.

GOOD-NEIGHBOR PORK PIE

Brimful of budget meats and savory gravy, capped with golden pastry lid

Pastry for 2-crust pie
6   slices bacon
1   lb. ground lean pork
½   lb. ground veal
1   c. chopped onion
1   clove garlic, minced
¼   c. finely chopped celery
½   tsp. salt
⅛   tsp. pepper
1   beef bouillon cube
¾   c. boiling water
3   tblsp. instant potato flakes

• Chop bacon and cook over medium heat until almost crisp. Add meats, onion, garlic and celery; cook, stirring occasionally, until lightly browned. Drain off excess fat.

• Add seasonings and bouillon cube dissolved in hot water. Cover and simmer 20 minutes.

• Sprinkle 1 tblsp. instant potato flakes over pastry-lined 9″ pie pan. Stir remaining potato flakes into meat mixture. Pour into pie pan, mounding a little in center. Adjust top crust, cut vents and flute edges.

• Bake in hot oven (425°F.) 25 to 30 minutes. Makes 6 servings.

PORK CRANBERRY PIE

Cranberries give the tender, savory pork a delightfully different taste

2 ¼ lbs. lean pork
¼ c. flour
1 tsp. ground sage
¾ tsp. salt
2 slices bacon, chopped
1 c. ground cranberries
⅓ c. sugar
1 c. hot water
Biscuit Crust

• Cut pork in 2″ cubes. Combine flour, sage and salt and toss pork in flour mixture to coat thoroughly. Pan-fry bacon and pork, browning on all sides. Drain off excess fat. Place hot meats in a 1½ qt. casserole.

• Combine cranberries and sugar. Scatter over meat. Add hot water. Cover and bake in hot oven (400°F.) while making Biscuit Crust. Place bis-cuit dough on top of meat and continue baking 20 minutes or until crust is as brown as desired. Makes 6 servings.

BISCUIT CRUST: Sift together 1 c. flour, 1½ tsp. baking powder and ½ tsp. salt. Cut in ¼ c. butter or margarine until mixture resembles coarse crumbs. Stir in ⅓ c. milk all at one time. Stir just to moisten. Knead lightly 8 or 10 times. Pat out or roll out the same size as casserole. Cut round of dough in 6 wedges and arrange on top of pork mixture.

SAUSAGE-EGG SUPPER PIE

A good Ohio cook's interpretation of pizza to fix for the family or teens

Unbaked 9″ pie shell
½ lb. bulk pork sausage
¾ c. chopped onion
½ tsp. orégano
¼ tsp. salt
¼ tsp. pepper
4 eggs
½ c. milk
1 c. shredded sharp Cheddar cheese
⅔ c. canned pizza sauce

• Cook sausage and onion together in skillet, breaking up sausage with fork, until sausage is browned and onion is tender. Drain off excess fat. Add orégano, salt and pepper.

• Beat eggs and milk together. Stir in sausage and cheese. Turn into pie shell and bake in very hot oven (450°F.) 15 minutes. Reduce heat to moderate oven (350°F.) and continue baking until filling is set, 10 to 15 minutes.

more

• Remove from oven and spread top of pie with pizza sauce. Return to oven a minute or two to heat sauce. Makes 6 servings.

SAUSAGE-CORN CUPS

Individual tarts with sausage crust baked in and served from a casserole

1 ½ lbs. bulk pork sausage
2   c. prepared stuffing mix
1   (12 oz.) can whole kernel corn, drained
1   can condensed cream of chicken soup
½   c. milk

• Divide sausage into 6 portions; form into cups about 3″ in diameter. Broil about 5 minutes, or until browned. Pierce bottom of sausage cups with fork to let fat drain.
• Combine stuffing mix and corn. (You can make your own bread dressing or stuffing, seasoning it as you like.) Place one third of mixture in shallow baking dish. Top with sausage cups; fill cups with remaining corn mixture. (You can do this ahead, refrigerate and bake later.)
• Combine soup and milk; stir until smooth. Pour over sausage cups. Bake in slow oven (300°F.) for 30 minutes. Makes 6 servings.

BACON-AND-EGG BREAKFAST PIE

Serve with chilled tomato slices and plenty of steaming hot coffee

Pastry for 2-crust pie
12 slices bacon, cooked

6   eggs
¼   tsp. salt
⅛   tsp. pepper
2   tblsp. chopped parsley
1   tblsp. chopped chives or green onion tops
1   can condensed cream of mushroom soup
3   tblsp. milk

• Place half the bacon strips in bottom of pastry-lined 9″ pie pan.
• Carefully break each egg, keeping yolk whole, into cup. Slip, one at a time, on top of bacon. Sprinkle with salt, pepper, parsley and chives or onion tops. Top with remaining bacon slices. Spoon ½ c. mushroom soup, in small dots, over top.
• Cover with top crust, flute edges and cut steam vents.
• Bake in hot oven (425°F.) 30 minutes, or until lightly browned. Cut in wedges and serve hot with mushroom sauce made by heating remaining mushroom soup combined with milk. Makes 6 servings.

Ham-'n'-Eggs Pie

Here's a pie for which you'll have ingredients on hand. You may want to double the recipe if you have more than five people at your dinner table. It's a wonderful pie for a company supper because it's brimful of country-good foods like ham, eggs and milk.

DEEP-DISH HAM PIE

Home-style meat pie—you can dress it up with cheese pastry lattice top

Cheese Pastry for 1-crust pie
    (Chapter 2)
¼ c. butter or margarine
¼ c. flour
½ tsp. salt
¼ tsp. dry mustard
⅛ tsp. pepper
1 tsp. instant minced onion
2 c. milk
2 hard-cooked eggs, chopped
2½ c. diced cooked ham
1 (8½ oz.) can peas, drained

• Melt butter; blend in flour, salt, mustard and pepper. Add onion and milk; cook over medium heat, stirring constantly, until mixture is thick and smooth. Add eggs, ham and peas.
• Pour hot mixture into 2 qt. casserole. Roll pastry dough slightly larger than top of casserole. Place over warm ham mixture and fold edges under. Flute against inside of casserole. Make steam vents.
• Bake in hot oven (425°F.) until top is browned, about 20 minutes. Makes 4 to 5 servings.

CHEESE-HAM PIES

Pies can be readied for baking in a hurry when you return home late

Cheese Pastry for 2-crust pie
    (Chapter 2)
2 c. diced carrots
2 c. cubed potatoes
3 c. cubed cooked ham
2 tblsp. ham drippings

1 (4 oz.) can sliced mushrooms, drained
2 tblsp. flour
1¼ c. milk
1 tsp. celery seed
¼ tsp. paprika

• Cook carrots and potatoes in salted water until just tender; drain. Arrange in 2 greased 9″ square pans. Divide ham between the 2 pans.
• Heat ham drippings and mushrooms in skillet. Stir in flour until mixture is smooth; add milk and cook until thick and smooth, stirring constantly. Add celery seed and paprika.
• Pour sauce over vegetables and ham in both pans.
• Cover each with pastry, cut vents and flute against pans' edges. Refrigerate until time to bake.
• Bake in hot oven (400°F.) 30 minutes. Makes 12 servings.

CRISSCROSS HAM TAMALE PIE

Widely praised FARM JOURNAL *recipe from our* COUNTRY COOKBOOK

1 (1 lb.) slice ready-to-eat ham or 2½ c. cubed baked ham
3 tblsp. salad oil
¾ c. chopped onion
1 clove garlic, minced
1½ tsp. chili powder
2 tblsp. flour
1 green pepper
2 c. tomato juice
1 (4 oz.) can mushroom stems and pieces
2 c. cooked lima beans (fresh, frozen or canned)
1 (14 oz.) pkg. corn muffin mix
½ c. milk
1 egg, beaten   *more*

• Cut ham into 1″ cubes.

• Heat oil in large skillet. Add onion and garlic. Cook 5 minutes. Add the cubed ham. Sprinkle with chili powder and flour. Continue to cook over moderate heat 10 minutes. Stir occasionally.

• Wash pepper. Remove core. Cut into eighths; add to ham along with tomato juice, mushrooms with liquid and lima beans. Bring to boil; reduce heat, cook 2 or 3 minutes, stirring constantly.

• Pour hot mixture into greased 2 qt. casserole. (A shallow one allows more space for topping.) Place in moderate oven (375°F.) while mixing corn muffin topping.

• Blend corn muffin mix with milk and egg. Spoon over hot ham mixture in a wide crisscross pattern.

• Bake 25 minutes, or until topping is golden brown.

• If meat-and-vegetable mixture is made ahead and chilled in refrigerator, heat it in oven until bubbly hot before adding topping. Makes 6 to 8 servings.

TRIPLE MEAT PIE

Company meat pie with 2 crusts—one of ham, the other pastry

Pastry for 2-crust pie
½ lb. ground lean pork
½ lb. ground veal
1   small onion, chopped (½ c.)
¼ c. chopped parsley
¾ tsp. salt
¼ tsp. pepper
2   tsp. Worcestershire sauce
2   egg yolks, beaten
2   egg whites, stiffly beaten
8   slices baked or boiled ham
     (6 oz.)
Cream (optional)

• Combine pork, veal, onion, parsley, salt, pepper, Worcestershire sauce and egg yolks. Fold in egg whites.
• Arrange half slices of ham so they line pastry-lined 9″ pie pan. Spoon pork mixture over them, mounding it slightly.
• Adjust top crust. Brush with cream for shiny top. Cut vents and flute edges.
• Bake in moderate oven (375°F.) 1 hour. Serve either hot or cold. Makes 6 servings.

Country Chicken Pies

Did you ever, as a child, sit wide-eyed and eager while your grandfather dipped a spoon into the superb chicken pie your grandmother brought steaming hot to the table? It's an unforgettable experience—first, the expectancy and then the fulfillment when you tasted. You'll find modernized old-time recipes for exceptional pies in this chapter along with the new.

Some of our chicken pies contain vegetables. While frozen vegetables often are specified because they're usually available in farm homes and are so handy, you can use cooked fresh or canned vegetables if you prefer.

Cooked turkey may be substituted for chicken in any of these pies—and with equally good results. In some farm kitchens there are larger quantities of the ready-to-use turkey than chicken in the freezer. Pies are a good way to use some of the poultry meat.

Try all these chicken pie recipes to determine which one you and your family and friends like most. Don't overlook the miniature chicken liver pies or tarts, a new type of hot sandwich. We predict that you'll never discover a more appetizing use for those chicken livers.

CHICKEN-POTATO PIE

Chicken and pimiento combine tastily in this hearty main dish

1   frozen Pimiento-Potato Pie Shell (Chapter 2)
4   tblsp. melted butter or margarine
2   tblsp. flour
1   c. chicken broth
Salt and pepper
1   (4 oz.) can sliced mushrooms, drained
½   c. diced celery
1   c. diced cooked chicken

• Remove wrap from frozen Pimiento-Potato Pie Shell. Place in casserole in which it was originally shaped. Drizzle with 2 tblsp. of the melted butter. Cover and bake in hot oven (400°F.) 30 minutes. Uncover and bake 30 minutes.
• Meanwhile, combine the remaining 2 tblsp. melted butter and flour in heavy saucepan. Slowly add broth; stir constantly until sauce is smooth and thick. Season with salt and pepper. Add remaining ingredients; heat. Spoon hot mixture into baked nest for serving. Makes 6 servings.

POPOVER CHICKEN PIE

"Puffed-up" chicken pie is different, new, taste-rewarding and easy to fix

1 ¾   c. flour
2   tsp. salt
¼   tsp. pepper
1   tsp. paprika
8   good-sized pieces fryer chickens (at least 4 lbs.)
⅓   c. vegetable shortening or salad oil
1 ½   tsp. baking powder
4   eggs, slightly beaten
1 ½   c. milk
3   tblsp. melted butter
1   tsp. celery seed

• Combine ¼ c. flour, 1 tsp. salt, pepper and paprika; mix well.
• Use legs and thighs of chicken. Breasts also may be used, but cut them in half. Roll chicken in flour mixture and brown on all sides in shortening. Remove chicken from skillet and drain on paper towels.
• To make batter, sift together remaining 1½ c. flour, baking powder and remaining 1 tsp. salt.
• Blend eggs, milk and butter. Combine flour and egg mixture, beating with rotary beater just enough to make smooth batter. Do not beat more than necessary.
• Pour batter into an 8″ × 12″ × 2″ pan. Arrange browned chicken pieces on top. Sprinkle with celery seed.
• Bake in moderate oven (350°F.) 1

hour, or until puffed and browned. Serve at once. Makes 6 servings.

Note: If you want to serve gravy with the pie, thicken and season chicken broth, if you have it, or heat a can of condensed cream of chicken soup, adding milk for the desired consistency, or use gravy mix. (You can cook the bony chicken pieces in water to make the broth.) If you prefer, bake the chicken pie in a 9" deep pie pan, but you may be able to use only 6 chicken pieces.

CHICKEN AND OYSTER PIE

A Missouri farm woman's delicious way to extend oysters

Pastry for 1-crust pie
3   c. diced cooked chicken
1   c. oysters
6   tblsp. flour
2 ½ c. chicken broth
½   c. finely minced celery
1   tsp. instant onion flakes
1   (10 oz.) pkg. frozen peas and carrots
1   tsp. salt
⅛   tsp. pepper
Paprika

• Place alternate layers of chicken and oysters in bottom of greased 2 qt. casserole.
• Blend together flour and ½ c. chicken broth (or cold water). Add to remaining 2 c. chicken broth. Add celery, onion, salt, pepper and peas and carrots. Cook over medium heat, stirring constantly, until mixture comes to a boil. Simmer 5 minutes. Pour over chicken and oysters.
• Roll pastry slightly larger than top of casserole; place over casserole and trim so it overhangs casserole 1". Fold edge of pastry under and flute against inside edge of casserole. Cut steam vents. Sprinkle with paprika.
• Bake in hot oven (425°F.) until pastry is lightly browned, about 30 minutes. Makes 6 servings.

Chicken Pie Southern-Style

You don't have to live in the South to enjoy Double-Crust Chicken Pie, an old plantation masterpiece . . . make it in your own kitchen. A Georgia farm woman won honors with this recipe in a cooking contest. Serve this pie at your next company or community meal—it's easy to tote. Some Southern homemakers like to double the recipe and bake the pie in a dishpan or roaster!

You may want to follow an old Georgia custom and use your favorite buttermilk biscuits instead of the biscuit mix. Molded cranberry salad and butter beans go well with this.

DOUBLE-CRUST CHICKEN PIE

Two crisp, buttery-brown crusts cover tender chickens, dumplings and gravy

2   (2 ½ lb.) broilers
2   tsp. salt
1 ¼ c. butter or margarine

4 c. biscuit mix
1 ⅓ c. milk
½ tsp. pepper
2 c. boiling water

• Cut chicken into serving pieces; sprinkle with salt; set aside 30 minutes.
• Cut ½ c. butter into biscuit mix. Add milk all at once; stir with fork to soften dough. Beat 12 strokes. Divide into four equal parts.
• Roll out one portion of dough to ¼" thickness (knead each part gently 10 times just before rolling). Cut into 1" × 2" strips; lay strips over bottom of buttered 4 qt. baking dish. Top with half the chicken pieces.
• Place ¼ c. butter in lumps between and on pieces of chicken; sprinkle with ¼ tsp. pepper.
• Roll second dough portion and cut as before; lay pastry strips over chicken until covered.
• Place rest of chicken on this pastry, making sure chicken pieces touch edge of baking dish; add ¼ c. butter in lumps and sprinkle with ¼ tsp. pepper.
• Roll third dough portion large enough to cover chicken; seal it to inside of dish. Cut small hole in center of pastry; pour in enough boiling water to barely float the crust (about 2 c.).
• Bake in very hot oven (450°F.) about 15 minutes, or until brown. Remove from oven; spread with 2 tblsp. softened butter.
• Roll remaining dough large enough to cover first crust; place over top, again sealing to side of dish.
• Return to oven 10 minutes, or until second crust is lightly browned. Remove chicken pie from oven; spread with remaining butter.

• Reduce oven to slow (325°F.); bake 45 minutes or until chicken is tender (add more boiling water as before, if needed). Makes 6 to 8 servings.

CHICKEN SPOONBREAD PIE

Pie wears high, puffy, brown topping

Filling:
5 tblsp. chicken fat
¼ c. chopped celery
2 tblsp. chopped onion
5 tblsp. flour
2 ½ c. chicken broth
1 tsp. salt
¼ tsp. monosodium glutamate
⅛ tsp. pepper
1 tsp. dried parsley
2 ½ c. cubed cooked chicken

Spoonbread:
2 c. boiling water
1 c. white cornmeal
2 tblsp. soft butter
1 c. milk
1 tsp. salt
3 tsp. baking powder
4 eggs, well beaten

Filling: Melt chicken fat in bottom of saucepan. (Extend with butter if necessary to make 5 tblsp., or use all butter.) Add celery and onion and cook until soft, but do not brown. Stir in flour. Add chicken broth and cook, stirring constantly, until mixture boils and is thickened. Add salt, monosodium glutamate, pepper and parsley. Stir in chicken and heat.
• Pour into 3 qt. casserole and place in hot oven (400°F.) and let heat while you make Spoonbread.
Spoonbread: Pour boiling water over

cornmeal. Beat in butter, milk, salt, baking powder and eggs. Pour on top of bubbling hot chicken in casserole. • Bake in hot oven (400°F.) 40 to 45 minutes or until top is browned. Serve at once. Makes 8 servings.

BRUNSWICK CHICKEN PIE

Deep-dish chicken pie inspired by the Deep South's Brunswick Stew

Pastry for 2 (2-crust) pies
1   (4 to 5 lb.) chicken, cut up
2   tsp. salt
2   c. drained whole-kernel corn
2   c. chopped onion
6   c. thick canned tomatoes
4   c. lima beans, fresh or frozen
½   lb. bacon, finely diced
¼   tsp. pepper
¼   tsp. dried thyme
¼   c. soft butter
3   tblsp. flour

• Combine chicken with all ingredients except pastry, butter and flour. Simmer 1 hour. Remove chicken to cool.
• Meanwhile blend butter and flour. Add a little of the stew liquid. Blend; return to stew and cook, stirring constantly, until stew thickens. Cool quickly.
• Remove chicken from bones; cut meat into large pieces and add to cooled stew.
• Line two 2 qt. casseroles with half of pastry. Fill with cooled stew. Top with remaining pastry; seal edges and cut vents in top.
• Cover rim of crust with foil; place in hot oven (425°F.) and bake 15 minutes; reduce heat to 350° and bake

45 minutes. Remove foil and continue baking 15 minutes. Makes 10 to 12 servings.

Note: Unbaked pie freezes well. To bake, place unthawed pie in cold oven. Set oven at hot (425°F.) and bake 30 minutes; reduce heat to 350° and bake about 1½ hours.

LATTICE CHICKEN PIE

Count on this 2-crust pie to make friends and to disappear quickly

1   (3 lb.) broiler-fryer, cut up
3   c. water
3   celery tops
1   tsp. salt
5   peppercorns
Chicken Gravy
1   (10 oz.) pkg. frozen peas, cooked and drained
3   tblsp. chopped pimiento (optional)
2   c. sifted flour
1   tsp. salt
⅓   c. shortening
⅔   c. milk

• Simmer chicken with water, celery tops, 1 tsp. salt and peppercorns until tender, about 1 hour. Remove from broth; cool slightly. Strain broth and make gravy (recipe follows).
• Slip skin from chicken and remove from bones while still warm. Cut into bite-size pieces and combine with peas, pimiento and 2 c. Chicken Gravy.
• Sift flour and 1 tsp. salt in bowl, cut in shortening to make crumbly mixture and stir in milk with fork to make dough that just holds together.

• Turn dough onto lightly floured surface and knead three times; roll two thirds dough in a rectangle about 12″ × 16″. Fit it into a baking dish 10″ × 6″ × 2″. Spoon chicken mixture into pastry-lined dish.

• Roll remaining third of pastry into a rectangle about 14″ × 7″ and cut in 9 long strips from ¾″ to 1″ wide. Lay 5 strips lengthwise over chicken. Cut the remaining 4 strips in half and weave them across long strips to make a lattice. Trim overhang to 1″, turn under and flute against edge of baking dish.

• Bake in hot oven (400°F.) 20 minutes; reduce heat to 350° and bake about 30 minutes longer, or until crust is browned. Serve with remaining Chicken Gravy, heated. Makes 5 to 6 servings.

CHICKEN GRAVY: Melt 6 tblsp. butter or margarine over low heat; stir in 6 tblsp. flour, 1 tsp. salt, ⅛ tsp. pepper, 1 tsp. minced onion and ⅛ tsp. dried marjoram leaves. Cook, stirring constantly, until mixture bubbles. Add 3 c. strained chicken broth gradually, stirring constantly, and 1 tsp. lemon juice. Cook until mixture thickens and boils a minute. Stir in 1 c. light cream. Makes about 4½ c.

HIS AND HER CHICKEN PIE

This pie flatters people by giving them their choice of dark or light meat

Filling:
2 (2½ lb.) frying chickens
5 c. water
½ tsp. salt
1 small onion, sliced
1 carrot, sliced
1 celery stalk, diced
½ tsp. monosodium glutamate
1 c. sliced celery
1 (10 oz.) pkg. frozen mixed vegetables
5 tblsp. flour
½ c. light cream
2½ c. chicken broth
1 tsp. salt
⅛ tsp. pepper

Biscuit Crust:
2 c. sifted flour
4 tsp. baking powder
2 tsp. sugar
1 tsp. salt
½ tsp. cream of tartar
½ c. shortening
⅔ c. milk
Olives, pitted ripe and pimiento-stuffed

Filling: Combine chicken pieces, water, ½ tsp. salt, onion, carrot, diced celery and monosodium glutamate in kettle. Cover and simmer until tender (about 1 hour). Drain and reserve broth. Cool chicken in broth; remove meat from bones, separating dark and light meat.

• Cook sliced celery in salted water until just tender. Add mixed vegetables and cook as directed on package. Drain.

• Blend together flour and cream. Combine in saucepan with broth. Add 1 tsp. salt and pepper and cook over medium heat, stirring constantly, until mixture comes to a boil. Stir in celery and mixed vegetables.

• Place ⅓ of broth mixture in bottom of 2 qt. casserole. Fill one side of casserole with dark meat, the other with light meat. Place toothpick in dark meat side to identify. Pour remaining broth over chicken.

• Place in very hot oven (450°F.) until mixture is bubbly hot. Top with biscuits (recipe follows), cut with doughnut cutter and return to oven. Bake until biscuits are golden, 10 to 12 minutes.

• Remove from oven. Place pitted black olives (ripe) in doughnut holes on side of dark meat, removing toothpick. Place stuffed green olives in holes in biscuits on side holding light meat. Serve at once. Makes 6 to 7 servings.

Biscuit Crust: Sift together flour, baking powder, sugar, salt and cream of tartar. Cut in shortening until mixture resembles coarse crumbs. Add milk all at one time and stir until dough follows fork around bowl. Dough should be soft and easy to handle.

• Turn dough onto lightly floured surface and knead by folding over and pressing with palm of hand 8 to 10 times. Pat or roll to about ½″ thickness and cut with doughnut cutter. Arrange on top of chicken pie as directed.

Note: You can use 2 c. cooked light and 2 c. cooked dark meat to make this pie if you have cooked chicken in the freezer. If you do not have chicken broth, commercially canned broth may be used. Frozen peas may be used instead of mixed vegetables.

MAINE CHICKEN PIE

Chicken and gravy under crisp, flaky pastry—a COUNTRY COOKBOOK *favorite*

Pastry for 2-crust pie
1   (5 lb.) whole stewing chicken

1 ½ qts. water
2   tsp. salt
1   small onion
1   carrot
1   stalk celery
¾   tsp. monosodium glutamate
½   c. sifted flour
½   tsp. onion salt
½   tsp. celery salt
Pepper
3 ½ c. chicken broth
2   or 3 drops yellow food color

• Place chicken in large kettle and add next six ingredients, using ½ tsp. monosodium glutamate and 1 tsp. salt. Simmer, covered, until tender, 3 to 3½ hours. Save broth.

• Remove bird to rack. Strip meat from bones, removing in large pieces. Refrigerate when cool.

• Combine flour, onion salt, celery salt, pepper, 1 tsp. salt and ¼ tsp. monosodium glutamate with ½ c. chicken broth. Mix until smooth.

• Heat 3 c. chicken broth to boiling. Add flour mixture, beating with a wire whip to prevent lumping.

• Cook over medium heat, stirring constantly until mixture is smooth and thickened. Add food color.

• Add chicken and blend well.

• Line 9″ deep-dish pie pan with pastry. Fill with chicken mixture. Adjust top crust, cut vents and flute edges.

• Bake in hot oven (400°F.) 45 minutes, or until browned. Makes 6 to 8 servings.

Note: If you want to freeze this pie, cool, wrap, label and place in freezer. Cool filling before pouring in crust to freeze like unbaked pie. Freeze broth for gravy separately.

INDIVIDUAL CHICKEN-HAM PIES

What a marvelous combination! Rice, chicken and ham expertly seasoned

Rice Crust
3   tblsp. butter
¼   c. flour
2   c. chicken broth
2   tblsp. chopped parsley
2   tsp. salt
¼   tsp. pepper
3   c. diced cooked chicken
1   c. diced cooked ham
⅔   c. grated Cheddar cheese

• Melt butter; add flour and blend. Add chicken broth and cook over medium heat, stirring constantly, until mixture comes to a boil and is thickened. Add parsley, salt, pepper, chicken and ham.
• Pour into rice-lined tart pans. Sprinkle the reserved cup of rice mixture over tops of pies. Sprinkle with cheese.
• Bake in moderate oven (350°F.) 20 minutes. Serve in tart pans.

RICE CRUST: Combine 5 c. cooked rice, 2 beaten eggs, ½ c. melted butter, 1 tsp. salt and ⅛ tsp. pepper. Mix thoroughly. Reserve 1 c. mixture. Pat remaining rice mixture over bottom and on sides of 6 greased (6") tart pans.

VARIATION

ALL-CHICKEN PIES: Omit ham and use 4 c. diced cooked chicken in recipe for Individual Chicken-Ham Pies.

CHICKEN LIVER TARTS

Unusual hot sandwiches to serve with salad or as snack with tomato juice

Pastry for 2 (2-crust) pies
1   lb. chicken livers
3   tblsp. flour
¼   c. chopped onion
¼   c. butter or margarine
2   tsp. Worcestershire sauce
½   tsp. salt
⅛   tsp. pepper
Melted butter
2   tblsp. Parmesan cheese
Paprika

• Dust chicken livers with flour. Cook with onions in ¼ c. butter. Add Worcestershire sauce, salt and pepper. Remove from heat and chop and mash livers until of spreading consistency.
• Divide pastry in fourths and roll each, one at a time, ⅛" thick. Cut in 3" rounds.
• Place half of rounds on baking sheet and top each with 1 tblsp. chicken-liver mixture. Top with other half of pastry rounds and press edges together with tines of fork to seal. Prick tops with fork.
• Brush with melted butter and sprinkle with cheese and paprika. Bake in hot oven (425°F.) 10 to 12 minutes, or until lightly browned. Makes 20 tarts.

Note: Tarts may be made in advance and frozen unbaked. Bake frozen tarts in hot oven (425°F.) 12 to 15 minutes, or until lightly browned. Make smaller tarts to serve as an appetizer.

English Hare Pie

When children have 4-H rabbit projects, their mothers look for recipes to use some of the meat the youngsters produce. Here's a dish adapted by food specialists, U. S. Department of Agriculture. It's an Americanized version with onion and green peppers added—a blend of flavors much enjoyed in many homes.

RABBIT PIE

As English as the Thames—this hare pie has been adapted in this country

Pastry
¼   c. butter or margarine
¼   c. chopped onion
½   c. chopped green pepper
¼   c. sifted flour
4   chicken bouillon cubes
2   c. hot water
Salt
Pepper
3   c. cut-up cooked rabbit meat

• Heat butter in large skillet; add onion and green pepper and cook over low heat about 5 minutes.

• Blend in flour and cook until mixture bubbles. Pour in bouillon, made by dissolving cubes in hot water, stirring constantly. (Use broth in which rabbit was cooked if available, for all or part of bouillon.) Cook until thick and smooth, stirring frequently. Add salt and pepper to taste.

• Add meat to sauce and heat thoroughly. Pour into a 1½ qt. casserole.

PASTRY: Roll out pastry made with 1 c. sifted flour, ½ tsp. salt, ⅓ c. lard and about 2 tblsp. cold water, slightly larger than top of baking dish. Cut slits for steam to escape. Adjust on top of hot rabbit mixture and trim to overhang 1″. Fold under and flute against inside of casserole.

• Bake in hot oven (425°F.) 15 to 20 minutes, or until crust browns and sauce bubbles in vents. Makes 5 to 6 servings.

CHEESE, FISH, SEA FOOD AND VEGETABLE PIES

We're predicting you'll really enjoy drop-in company for lunch when there's a hearty main-course pie practically ready to put in the oven. You can build such appetizing menus around these hot dishes.

Protein foods predominate in these pies—cheese, fish, sea food and eggs. They're good meatless-Friday specials—our Double Corn and Egg Pie, for instance. While the pies are perfect for lunch, they'll serve your whole family well for supper or dinner. Some of them, like Potato and Egg Pie, are hearty breakfast dishes that will start the day right.

If you're having big bowls of steaming beef-vegetable soup, glamorize the meal with our Individual Cheese Tarts or pies. For go-withs, have fruit salad, cookies and a beverage. Take the cookies from the freezer— also the tarts ready for reheating.

Some of the pies in this chapter are ideal for serving when you invite women friends to lunch. Farmhouse Asparagus-Chicken Pie, for instance, is delicious with the green spears arranged in a pastry shell like the spokes of a wheel. And if you're entertaining shrimp fans, do feature this sea food in Shrimp-Cheese Pie or Gulf-Style Shrimp Pie. Don't count the men out —the countryside is filled with farmers who are fond of shrimp. Men also praise our onion pies. One country homemaker says she makes a point of serving piping-hot Herbed Onion and Cheese Pie with sizzling steaks when she's splurging a little for guests. And if your family has little interest in the shiny, purple eggplant from the garden, bake an Eggplant Pie and watch its happy acceptance.

Country cooks show no favoritism in crusts; they use both pastry and biscuit types. Check the ingredients in our recipes—you'll observe most of them are in your cupboard, refrigerator and freezer. So decide on one of the pies in this chapter when you're wondering what to fix for supper.

Win Them to Vegetables with Pies

Farm mothers say that one of the most successful ways of persuading men and children to like vegetables, other than their ever favorite potatoes, is to serve them in pies. Anything held in tender, flaky, golden pastry, or topped by it, has a head start on getting a welcome at farm tables. Once the vegetable is approved in a pie, it also will fare better in other dishes. So pies, country cooks find, are useful in winning friends for garden vegetables.

ONION CHEESE-POTATO PIE

Pretty, tasty economy dish that's especially good with ham or pork

1 frozen Cheese-Potato Pie Shell (Chapter 2)
2 tblsp. melted butter
1 beef bouillon cube
½ c. boiling water
2 c. chopped onions
¼ c. butter or margarine
3 tblsp. flour
1 c. milk
Salt and pepper

• Remove wrap from frozen Cheese-Potato Pie Shell. Place in casserole in which it originally was shaped. Drizzle with melted butter. Cover and bake in hot oven (400°F.) 30 minutes. Uncover and bake 30 minutes.
• Meanwhile, dissolve bouillon cube in boiling water. Add onions; cover and simmer until tender. Drain.
• Melt ¼ c. butter in heavy saucepan. Add flour to make smooth paste. Add milk slowly, stirring constantly until smooth and thickened.
• Season with salt and pepper. Add drained onions. Spoon into baked Cheese-Potato Pie Shell for serving. Makes 6 servings.

CORN-CHEESE PIE

Serve this hearty, hot pie with cold cuts and tomato-lettuce salad

Unbaked 9″ pie shell
1 c. light cream
½ tsp. salt
1 egg, beaten
1 green pepper, chopped (¾ c.)
⅓ c. chopped onion
1 (1 lb.) can cream style corn
½ c. fine bread crumbs
2 tblsp. butter or margarine
⅓ c. grated process American cheese

• Blend cream, salt and egg. Stir in green pepper, onion and corn. Turn into pie shell.
• Scatter bread crumbs over top; dot with butter and sprinkle with cheese.
• Bake in moderate oven (375°F.) until filling is set, about 40 to 45 minutes. Let stand 10 minutes before cutting. Makes 6 servings.

DOUBLE CORN AND EGG PIE

A Friday special—serve with a mixed fruit salad and a green vegetable

Pastry for 2-crust pie
1 (1 lb.) can cream style corn
1 (12 oz.) can Mexicorn
2 tblsp. grated onion
½ tsp. salt
⅛ tsp. pepper
4 hard-cooked eggs, sliced
4 oz. process American cheese, thinly sliced

• Combine corns, onion, salt and pepper, mixing well.
• Arrange sliced eggs in pastry-lined 10″ pie pan to make even layer. Top with corn mixture, then with cheese slices.
• Adjust top crust; flute edges and cut steam vents.
• Bake in hot oven (425°F.) 30 minutes. Let stand 5 minutes before cutting. Makes 8 servings.

HERBED ONION AND CHEESE PIE

Superb with grilled steaks and good with barbecued ribs and other meats

7 tblsp. butter or margarine
2 c. cheese-flavored cracker crumbs
3 large onions, thinly sliced (about 3 c.)
2 eggs, slightly beaten
1 c. milk
1 tsp. salt
¼ tsp. black pepper
⅛ tsp. dried marjoram
⅛ tsp. dried thyme
½ c. shredded sharp Cheddar cheese

• Melt 4 tblsp. butter and toss with 1½ c. cracker crumbs. Press into bottom and on sides of 9″ pie pan to make pie shell. Bake in moderate oven (350°F.) 5 minutes. Cool.
• Melt 2 tblsp. butter in skillet. Add onions, separated into rings. Cover and cook over low heat until onions are soft, 10 to 15 minutes. Stir occasionally. Turn into pie shell.
• Beat eggs with milk, salt, pepper, marjoram and thyme. Add cheese. Melt remaining 1 tblsp. butter in skillet in which onions cooked. Add egg mixture and cook over very low heat, stirring constantly, just until cheese melts. Carefully pour sauce over onions. Top with remaining ½ c. cracker crumbs.
• Bake in very hot oven (450°F.) 15 minutes. Reduce heat to 350°F. and continue baking until filling is set, 10 to 15 minutes. Cut in wedges and serve hot. Makes 8 servings.

ONION PIE

A FARM JOURNAL 5-star success—recipe from COUNTRY COOKBOOK

Caraway Pastry:
1 ½ c. sifted flour
¾ tsp. salt
1 ½ tsp. caraway seeds
½ c. shortening
2 to 3 tblsp. water

Filling:
3 c. thinly sliced peeled onions
3 tblsp. melted butter or margarine
½ c. milk
1 ½ c. dairy sour cream   *more*

1   tsp. salt
2   eggs, well beaten
3   tblsp. flour
Bacon slices

Pastry: Combine flour, salt and cara-way seeds. Add shortening; cut into flour until mixture resembles little peas and coarse cornmeal.
• Gradually add water, tossing with fork until mixture forms a ball that follows fork around bowl.
• Turn onto a lightly floured surface; roll to 11½″ circle of ⅛″ thickness. Fit into a 10″ pie pan; flute edge; prick entire surface with 4-tined fork.
• Bake in hot oven (425°F.) 10 min-utes, or until lightly browned.
Filling: Sauté onions in butter until lightly browned. Spoon into pie shell.
• Add milk, 1¼ c. sour cream and salt to eggs.
• Blend flour with remaining ¼ c. sour cream. Combine with egg mix-ture; pour over onions.
• Bake in slow oven (325°F.) 30 min-utes, or until firm in center. Garnish with crisp bacon. Serve as a main dish. Makes 8 servings.

SPINACH PIE

See if they won't eat spinach fixed this way—a prizewinning luncheon dish

Unbaked 9″ pie shell
10   bacon slices (about ½ lb.)
¾   c. chopped onion (1 medium)
1   (10 oz.) pkg. frozen chopped spinach
4   eggs, slightly beaten
1   c. milk
1   tsp. seasoned salt

• Cut 6 slices bacon in small pieces and pan-fry until crisp. Remove, drain. Cook onion in bacon fat until golden brown. Drain.
• Cook spinach as directed on pack-age. Drain thoroughly.
• Blend eggs, milk and seasoned salt. Add spinach, onion and cooked bacon. Turn into pie shell. Bake in moderate oven (375°F.) until filling is set, 40 to 45 minutes.
• Meanwhile, cut remaining slices of bacon in small pieces and pan-fry until crisp and brown. Drain and sprinkle on top of pie just before serving. Makes 6 servings.

Asparagus and Chicken-Pie Team

Country women long have served asparagus with chicken in special-occasion meals. But we found one farm woman who teams chicken and the green spears in an elegant main-dish pie that her guests praise.

With her Farmhouse Asparagus Pie, she often serves a generous mixed fruit salad in lettuce cups with hot tea or coffee. This 3-piece meal satisfies and it's no trick for the hostess-cook to have everything ready in advance.

By using a 10″ pie pan, you get eight good servings. You can use a 9″ × 9″ × 2″ pan and pastry for a 2-crust pie, but it's more difficult to fit the pastry into the square pan.

FARMHOUSE ASPARAGUS PIE

Company lunch special—so attractive

Unbaked 10" pie shell
20 fresh asparagus spears or 1
    (10 oz.) pkg. frozen aspara-
    gus spears, cooked
1½ c. chopped cooked chicken
 4 slices bacon
 ½ c. shredded natural Swiss cheese
 4 eggs
 1 tblsp. flour
 ½ tsp. salt
 2 c. light cream

2 tblsp. grated Parmesan cheese
Paprika

• Arrange cooked asparagus in bottom of pie shell, spoke-fashion. Top with chicken. Cook, drain and crumble bacon. Scatter it and Swiss cheese over asparagus and chicken.
• Beat together eggs, flour, salt and cream; pour over asparagus. Sprinkle with Parmesan cheese and paprika.
• Bake in moderate oven (375°F.) 45 to 50 minutes or until pie filling is set. Let stand 10 minutes before cutting. Makes 8 servings.

Royal Purple Eggplant Pie

Shiny, purple eggplants that you see in your markets or grow in the garden make excellent hearty pies. Select a vegetable that's firm and heavy for its size. Make sure it's a uniform dark color, free of blemishes (when eggplant ages, it sometimes shrivels and develops a bitter taste).

You need not peel the vegetable for our recipe. Just wash and cut it in cubes. The seasonings suggest dishes popular along Mediterranean shores or in our states bordering the Gulf of Mexico. It's a pie that cuts nicely and adds to the prestige of a vegetable too often neglected in farm kitchens.

EGGPLANT PIE

People who like Italian pizza especially enjoy this—teens, for instance!

Unbaked 9" pie shell
 2 c. cubed unpeeled eggplant

 ¼ c. butter or margarine
 ¾ lb. ground beef chuck
 ½ c. finely chopped onion
 1 clove minced garlic
 1 tblsp. chopped parsley
 ¼ c. chopped celery tops
 1 tsp. salt
 ¼ tsp. orégano
 ⅛ tsp. pepper
 1 (8 oz.) can tomato sauce
 ½ c. shredded Mozzarella cheese

• Place eggplant, washed and cut in ½" cubes, in melted butter in heavy skillet. Cover and cook over medium heat 5 minutes. Remove eggplant.
• Place ground beef, onion and garlic in skillet and cook, stirring, until meat is browned. Add parsley, celery tops, seasonings and tomato sauce. Cook over medium heat 5 minutes, stirring

constantly. Stir in eggplant. Partially cool.
• Turn into pie shell. Bake in moderate oven (375°F.) 45 minutes, until pie is golden brown. Sprinkle cheese over top and return to oven a few minutes until cheese melts. Let stand 5 minutes. Makes 6 servings.

liquid into bowl. Stir in clams, milk, eggs, crackers, bacon and seasonings. Turn into pie shell. Dot with butter. Adjust top crust; flute edges and cut vents.
• Bake in very hot oven (450°F.) 15 minutes. Reduce heat to moderate (350°F.) and bake 30 minutes longer or until golden. Makes 6 servings.

A Down-East Pie Special—Try It

You don't have to live near the ocean to enjoy sea food. Here's a Clam Pie you can fix in the heart of the Rocky Mountains or on the Kansas plains. Do try it. While it's a treat at all times, it's especially refreshing on a cool, rainy evening.

CLAM PIE

New England pie special that will make friends in all parts of the country

Pastry for 2-crust pie
2   slices bacon
2   (8 oz.) cans minced clams
¾   c. milk
2   eggs, well beaten
½   c. coarsely broken oyster
      crackers
1   tsp. onion salt
¼   tsp. pepper
2   tblsp. butter or margarine

• Line 9″ pie pan with half of pastry.
• Pan-fry bacon until crisp. Drain and crumble.
• Drain clams. Measure ¾ c. clam

Eggs and Oysters in Pies

Instead of fretting because fresh oysters in landlocked grocery stores frequently are scarce or rather costly, clever cooks contrive to extend the flavor in interesting ways. They often borrow ideas from famous dishes like the Hangtown Fry of California's gold-rush days, in which oysters and eggs share honors.

Hangtown Supper Pies contain the number of eggs required to stretch a pint of fresh oysters to feed six hungry people. The cook, who revived this ranch version, relies on an old country habit of serving the favorite combination of foods in pastry. This time, it's in flaky tart shells so that everyone has his own share. The pastry takes the role of bread in the meal.

These main-dish individual pies are company fare—perfect for the guest who stops in on a snowy winter or rainy spring evening. You can dress up the little pies with garnishes of lemon slices and show off some of your best homemade pickles as accompaniments. Someway the table talk flourishes when these pies are set before family and friends.

HANGTOWN SUPPER PIES

Example of what imaginative country cooks do with a bounty of fresh eggs

6   baked 6" tart shells (pastry for
        2-crust pie)
6   slices bacon
1   pt. oysters, drained
½   c. flour
10 eggs
1   tblsp. water
¾   tsp. salt
1 ½ c. fine cracker or bread crumbs
¼   c. milk or cream
⅛   tsp. pepper
¼   c. chopped green pepper
¼   c. chopped chives
2   tblsp. butter

• If tart shells are cold, set them on a baking sheet and warm in moderate oven (350°F.) while preparing other ingredients.
• Fry bacon until almost crisp; roll each slice around a fork to make a curl; drain on paper toweling.
• Roll oysters in flour. Beat 1 egg with water; dip oysters in egg mixture mixed with ½ tsp. salt; roll in crumbs. Pan-fry in bacon fat until golden brown on both sides. Drain and keep warm.
• Beat remaining 9 eggs with milk, add remaining ¼ tsp. salt and pepper. Add green pepper and chives. Melt butter in same skillet used for cooking bacon and oysters. Add egg mixture and scramble just until eggs are set.
• Place eggs in bottom of warmed tart shells; top with warm oysters, then with bacon curls. Garnish with lemon slices and pickles, if desired. Makes 6 servings.

SHRIMP-CHEESE PIE

This is a company lunch tempter but don't bypass the family

Unbaked 9" pie shell
1   (6 oz.) pkg. natural Swiss cheese
        slices
1   lb. cleaned and cooked shrimp
2   eggs
2   tblsp. flour
1   c. light cream
½   tsp. dried parsley
½   tsp. onion salt
½   tsp. salt
Paprika

• Place half of cheese slices in bottom of pie shell, top with shrimp, then with remaining cheese.
• Blend together eggs, flour, cream, parsley and salts. Pour over cheese. Dust with paprika.
• Bake in hot oven (400°F.) 40 to 45 minutes. Let stand 5 minutes before cutting. Makes 6 servings.

GULF-STYLE SHRIMP PIE

Makes a little shrimp go a long way

½   lb. bacon, diced
⅓   c. milk
1   tblsp. salad oil
1 ½ c. prepared biscuit mix
1   c. cleaned and cooked shrimp
2   tblsp. chopped green onions
1   clove garlic, minced
2   peeled tomatoes, thinly sliced
½   tsp. crumbled dried sweet basil
¼   tsp. salt
⅛   tsp. pepper
1   (6 oz.) pkg. sliced Mozzarella
        cheese   *more*

• Cook bacon until crisp; drain.
• Stir milk and salad oil into biscuit mix. Mix with a fork. Turn dough on lightly floured surface and roll to fit 9″ pie pan. Crimp edges with fork tines.
• Sprinkle bacon, shrimp, onions and garlic in pie shell. Cover with a single layer of tomatoes. Sprinkle with basil, salt and pepper. Cover with cheese, breaking slices apart to cover tomatoes completely.
• Bake in hot oven (400°F.) 20 to 25 minutes. Serve hot, cut in wedges. Makes 6 servings.

SHRIMP SALAD TARTS

Fruited shrimp salad in pastry shells makes an ideal guest luncheon dish

Cheese Tart Shells:
2   c. sifted flour
1   tsp. salt
½   c. salad oil
1   c. grated Cheddar cheese
3   tblsp. cold water

Filling:
¼   c. mayonnaise
¼   c. dairy sour cream
4   tsp. lemon juice
1   tsp. salt
⅛   tsp. dry mustard
2   c. chopped cooked shrimp
1   c. chopped celery
¼   c. finely chopped green onions
1   c. seedless green grapes, cut in halves
1   medium unpeeled apple, chopped
½   c. chopped pecans

Cheese Tart Shells: Combine flour and salt. Cut in salad oil with pastry blender. Stir in cheese. Add water and toss with fork. Form into smooth ball. Divide in half and roll out each half between waxed paper.
• Cut circles to fit over backs of muffin-cup pans. (A 4½″ circle fits over medium muffin-cup pan.)
• Place each circle over back of cup. Pinch several pleats in pastry so it fits against cup. Bake in hot oven (425°F.) until lightly browned, about 12 minutes. Carefully remove from pans and cool. Makes 15 shells.
Filling: Mix together mayonnaise, sour cream, lemon juice, salt and dry mustard. Combine with remaining ingredients. Serve in Cheese Tart Shells. Makes 5 cups.

CONFETTI-CRUSTED CRAB PIE

This luncheon main dish is ever so tasty with crab and corn chips

Corn Chip Crust:
2   c. finely crushed corn chips
2   tblsp. butter, melted
1   tsp. paprika

Filling:
½   c. chopped green pepper
½   c. finely chopped onion
¼   c. butter or margarine, melted
3   tblsp. flour
1   tsp. salt
¼   tsp. pepper
½   c. milk
1   c. dairy sour cream
½   c. sliced pimiento-stuffed olives
2   (6 oz.) pkgs. frozen crab meat, thawed and flaked

Crust: Combine corn chips, butter and paprika. Reserve ⅓ c. mixture. Press remainder on bottom and side of 9″ pie pan. Bake in moderate oven (375°F.) 10 minutes. Cool.

Filling: Cook green pepper and onion in butter until soft. Blend in flour, salt and pepper. Add milk and sour cream and cook over very low heat, stirring constantly, until thickened.

• Stir in olives and crab meat. Spoon mixture into cool crust. Sprinkle with reserved crust mixture.

• Bake in moderate oven (350°F.) 15 minutes. Serve hot. Makes 6 servings.

Something Special for Supper

Cheese pie rises to the occasion in grand style when served as the main supper or luncheon dish. In spring, serve with tender, new peas seasoned with light cream. Round out your meal with garden lettuce salad—perhaps the oak-leaf variety—if you don't have the makings for the country special, pale-green and white dandelion leaves! Be sure to cook a little snipped green onion with the peas or dried or fresh chopped parsley for extra seasoning.

Start the meal with glasses of tomato juice; end it with old-fashioned tapioca pudding, vanilla-flavored, made with quick-cooking tapioca or a packaged pudding mix. Spoon pretty, pink rhubarb sauce or sugared strawberries, refrigerated until frosty, over the pudding. And if you have sugar cookies, pass them for a bonus. You'll be as happy over your menu as when you discover the season's first violets!

In autumn or winter, serve this cheese pie with buttered succotash and crisp coleslaw, brightened with cut-up red and green peppers or pimientos. Set off the homespun feast with big raisin-stuffed, baked apples and pass your sugar-sprinkled, dark molasses cookies. Have both coffee and milk to drink.

Cheese pie also makes good summer fare. Serve corn on the cob and sliced ripe tomatoes with it then; for dessert, sugared peaches topped with scoops of vanilla ice cream or red raspberry sherbet.

Such menus are the proper setting for French Cheese Pie, a welcome change from the faithful, but overworked, toasted-cheese sandwiches.

FRENCH CHEESE PIE

The French call it Quiche Lorraine—we call it good by any name

Unbaked 9″ pie shell
 6   slices bacon
 ¾   c. chopped onion (1 medium)
1 ¼ c. grated Swiss cheese
 ¼   c. grated Parmesan cheese
 3   eggs, beaten
1 ½ c. light cream
 ½   tsp. salt
 ¼   tsp. pepper

• Cook bacon until crisp. Remove from skillet and crumble; drain off fat. Return 1 tblsp. fat to skillet; add onion and cook gently until tender, but not browned.

• Place bacon, onion and cheeses in pie shell. Blend together eggs, cream, salt and pepper. Pour over mixture in pie shell.

• Bake in moderate oven (375°F.) until mixture is firm and lightly browned, about 45 minutes. Makes 6 servings.

Miniature Cheese Pies

Our miniatures of the famous French Quiche Lorraine are tasty and the hostess can make them ahead and refrigerate or freeze for quick reheating. Our recipe has strictly American accents that make this type of hot sandwich most acceptable. If you wish, you can make the pies smaller than specified in the recipe. Then they become appetizers to serve as snacks.

INDIVIDUAL CHEESE PIES

Take the place of hot sandwiches—excellent with salad or for snacks

6   slices bacon
½   c. chopped onion
1 ½ c. grated aged Swiss cheese (6 oz.)
2   tsp. flour
1   (4 oz.) can mushroom pieces, drained
2   eggs
1   c. light cream or milk
¾   tsp. salt
Pat-in-Pan Tart Shells

• Cook bacon until crisp, remove from skillet, drain and crumble.
• Cook onion in bacon drippings until tender. Remove and drain.
• Combine bacon, cheese, flour and mushrooms. Beat eggs and beat in light cream and salt; add onion.

• Divide cheese-bacon mixture in 12 Pat-in-Pan Tart Shells. Spoon egg mixture over.
• Bake in hot oven (425°F.) 7 minutes. Reduce heat to 300° and bake until egg mixture is set, 10 to 15 minutes. Cool at least 10 minutes before removing from muffin-pan cups. Serve warm. Or refrigerate if you wish to keep the tarts several hours. Reheat in slow oven (300°F.) until heated through, 10 to 15 minutes. You also can freeze the tarts for reheating when needed.

PAT-IN-PAN TART SHELLS

½   c. soft butter or margarine
1   egg yolk
1 ½ c. sifted flour
½   tsp. salt
2   tblsp. milk

• Cream butter in medium bowl with wooden spoon or electric mixer. Beat in egg yolk. Beat in flour and salt, then milk at low speed.
• Shape dough in ball, wrap in waxed paper. Chill 1 hour in refrigerator or 20 minutes in freezer.
• Divide dough in 12 equal balls. Pat into 2½″ muffin-pan cups to make tart shells. Chill in refrigerator 15 minutes before filling and baking as directed in Individual Cheese Pies.

EVERYDAY CHEESE PIE

Tomato adds color—delicious with scalloped corn and tossed green salad

Unbaked 9" pie shell
4   oz. Cheddar cheese, grated
6   slices cooked bacon, drained and crumbled
1   tblsp. grated onion
1   tomato
3   eggs, beaten
1 ¼ c. milk
½   tsp. salt
¼   tsp. pepper
¼   c. chopped parsley

• Sprinkle cheese over bottom of pie shell. Top with bacon and onion. Cut tomato in 6 wedges and arrange over cheese and bacon, spacing so each serving will have a tomato wedge on top.
• Blend together eggs, milk, salt, pepper and parsley. Pour over cheese.
• Bake in moderate oven (350°F.) until set, 50 to 60 minutes. Let stand 10 minutes before cutting. Makes 6 servings.

Breakfast Pie That Pleases

You may have to stretch your imagination to call this dish a pie. But the country cook who sent us the recipe does. She points out that it's double fast to put together when time is short. The potatoes substitute for regular pie crust so that when the wedges are cut it really looks like pie. Her husband says: "It tastes as good as pie!"

Use either your homemade French fries from the freezer, or those you buy at the supermarket to have handy when you need to get a quick, hearty meal.

POTATO AND EGG PIE

Sleight-of-hand pie—bacon, potatoes and eggs cook quickly in skillet

6   slices bacon, chopped
⅓   c. chopped green onions
1   (1 lb.) pkg. frozen French-fried potatoes
2   tsp. salt
8   eggs
⅓   c. light cream or top milk
¼   tsp. pepper

• Cook bacon in 10" skillet until golden. Add onions and continue cooking until onions are limp and bacon is browned. Remove bacon and onions; drain on paper toweling. Keep warm in low oven.
• Pour bacon drippings from skillet; return 3 tblsp. drippings to skillet. Add frozen French fries, sprinkle with 1 tsp. salt; brown, stirring constantly.
• Beat together eggs, cream, remaining 1 tsp. salt and pepper. Pour over potatoes. Cover pan and cook over low heat about 8 minutes. If top is not set then, lift up edges of mixture and

tilt the skillet to let liquid run under. Place under broiler until top is completely set.
• Top with bacon and onions. To serve, cut in wedges. Makes 6 servings.

TUNA SALAD PIE

Excellent selection for women's group luncheon if weather is warm

Baked 9″ pie shell
 2 envelopes unflavored gelatin
 1 c. water
 1 can condensed cream of celery soup
 ½ tsp. salt
 ½ tsp. dry mustard
 ¼ c. lemon juice
 1 tsp. grated onion
 1 c. salad dressing
 2 (6½ to 7 oz.) cans tuna
 1 c. chopped celery
 1 avocado
 1 tblsp. lemon juice

• Sprinkle gelatin on water in saucepan. Place over medium heat, stirring constantly, until gelatin is dissolved, about 3 minutes. Remove from heat.
• Add soup, salt, mustard, ¼ c. lemon juice, onion and salad dressing. Beat with rotary beater until smooth. Chill, stirring occasionally, until mixture mounds when dropped from spoon. Add tuna and celery.
• Peel avocado and dice half of it. Wrap remaining half well in plastic wrap and refrigerate. Chop first avocado half and stir into salad mixture. Spoon into cool pie shell. Chill until firm.
• To serve, cut remaining avocado half into 8 slices, sprinkle with 1 tblsp. lemon juice and arrange on top of pie.

Cut pie in 8 wedges, each trimmed with an avocado slice. Makes 8 servings.

VARIATION

• Add ½ c. chopped cucumber to salad with celery for a cool, refreshing note.

TUNA AU GRATIN PIE

Instead of tuna in the usual casserole, fix a cheese-tuna pie surprise

Unbaked 9″ pie shell
 ¼ c. milk
 1 can condensed cream of mushroom soup
 2 tblsp. flour
 ⅓ c. chopped onion
 2 (6½ oz.) cans tuna
 1 (10 oz.) pkg. frozen peas (2 c.)
 4 oz. pimiento cheese, sliced
 1 c. crushed corn chips

• Combine milk, soup, flour and onion in saucepan. Cook, stirring constantly, until mixture comes to a boil.
• Add tuna and peas; cook over low heat, stirring occasionally, until peas can be separated.
• Pour into pie shell. Top with slices of cheese. Sprinkle with corn chips.
• Bake in hot oven (425°F.) 30 minutes. Makes 6 servings.

TUNA PIZZA

Mildly seasoned pizza—a Friday farmhouse special that children ask for

 1 pkg. hot roll mix
 ¼ c. olive or salad oil
 1 clove garlic, crushed
 2 (6½ to 7 oz.) cans tuna
 ½ c. pitted ripe olives, sliced

2   (8 oz.) cans tomato sauce
1   tsp. dried orégano
¼   tsp. dried basil
¼   tsp. salt
⅛   tsp. pepper
1   (6 oz.) pkg. sliced Mozzarella
     cheese

• Prepare roll mix as directed on package. Divide in half. Roll to fit or press into 2 (12″) greased pizza pans or into 2 (12″) rounds on greased baking sheets.

• Combine olive oil and garlic; brush oil over dough. Drain tuna, reserving oil. Arrange tuna chunks evenly over dough circles. Place olive slices in spaces between tuna.

• Combine oil from tuna and any remaining olive oil, tomato sauce and seasonings. Spread over tuna.

• Top with cheese slices, broken into small pieces. Bake in hot oven (425°F.) 20 minutes or until nicely browned around edges. Makes 2 (12″) pizzas.

Friday Pie

Cans of salmon are at home on farm cupboard shelves . . . insurance for many inviting dishes that can be fixed in a hurry. Salmon pie, for instance. The recipe for our pie comes direct from a Wisconsin kitchen. The crust is biscuitlike and flaky; when baked to a golden brown, it complements the red-fleshed fish.

With this main dish serve buttered corn, broccoli, green beans or peas, depending on what you have in the freezer. A plate of relishes and a sunny compote of canned peaches and apricots complete the meal. How about milk or hot cocoa for a refreshing beverage?

SALMON PIE

Run pie in the oven and relax—your quick meal is under control

1   (1 lb.) can salmon
1   tblsp. grated onion
¼   lb. process sharp cheese, thinly
     sliced
1   can condensed cream of celery
     soup
1   c. flour
1½   tsp. baking powder
½   tsp. salt
3   tblsp. shortening
1   egg
½   c. milk

• Drain salmon, reserving liquid. Flake with fork, removing bones and skin. Place in bottom of 9″ pie pan.

• Top with onion, 2 tblsp. salmon liquid and cheese. Spread ⅓ can celery soup over cheese.

• To make crust, sift together flour, baking powder and salt. Cut in shortening until mixture resembles coarse crumbs. Combine egg and ¼ c. milk. Add to dry ingredients and mix only until all the flour is moistened.

• Place on lightly floured board and knead 8 or 10 times. Roll out slightly larger than top of pie pan. Place over salmon mixture and flute edges against edge of pan. Cut a 1″ square out of center of dough for steam vent.

• Bake pie in moderate oven (375°F.) until lightly browned, 25 to 30 minutes. Cut in wedges. Serve topped with sauce made by heating remaining ⅔ can celery soup and ¼ c. milk. Makes 6 servings.

SALMON POTPIE

Supper in a casserole. Extend menu with coleslaw, canned fruit, cookies

```
3    tblsp. chopped onion
4    tblsp. butter or margarine
¼    c. flour
2    c. milk
½    tsp. salt
⅛    tsp. pepper
1    (1 lb.) can red salmon, broken
     into chunks
1    c. diced cooked carrots
1    c. frozen peas
½    c. grated cheese
Biscuits for topping (1 c. biscuit mix)
```

• Sauté onion in melted butter until tender. Add flour and blend. Slowly add milk, stirring constantly. Cook until thickened. Season with salt and pepper. (Or make the sauce of 1 can cream of chicken soup, adding ½ soup can of milk and the sautéed onion.)

• Add salmon chunks, carrots, uncooked peas, and grated cheese. Pour into casserole. Top with rolled biscuit dough, made by package directions, and cut in pielike wedges. (Or use leftover pastry, cut in circles, instead of biscuit dough.)

• Bake in hot oven (425°F.) 20 min-

utes, until biscuits are brown and mixture is bubbly. Makes 4 to 6 servings.

SALMON CUSTARD PIE

Dill adds a tasty flavor note—serve with green or cabbage salad

```
Unbaked 9″ pie shell
¼    c. chopped green onion
2    tblsp. butter
1    (1 lb.) can salmon
1    tsp. dried dill weed
½    tsp. salt
¼    tsp. pepper
1    c. light cream, scalded
4    eggs, slightly beaten
```

• Bake pie shell in moderate oven (375°F.) 5 minutes.

• Cook onion in butter until soft. Drain salmon, reserving ¼ c. salmon liquid. Remove bones from salmon.

• Place salmon, dill, salt, pepper and salmon liquid in bowl. Mash with fork until well mixed. Add green onion, cream and eggs. Mix well.

• Pour into pie shell and bake in moderate oven (375°F.) until mixture is set, 35 to 40 minutes. Makes 6 servings.

DEEP-DISH FISH PIE

Delicious example of how country cooks team fish with mashed potatoes

```
¼    c. chopped onion
¼    c. sliced carrots
½    c. chopped celery
¼    c. chopped parsley
2    tsp. salt
½    tsp. whole peppercorns
```

2   c. boiling water
1½ lbs. frozen perch fillets, thawed
½   lb. cleaned frozen shrimp
3   tblsp. butter or margarine
3   tblsp. flour
4   c. fluffy seasoned mashed po-
      tatoes
1   c. grated Cheddar cheese

• Combine onion, carrots, celery, parsley, salt, peppercorns and boiling water in saucepan. Bring to a boil and boil 5 minutes.
• Add fillets, cover and simmer gently until tender and flaky, 7 to 10 minutes. Remove fish and place in a greased 9" square pan.
• Add shrimp to fish stock. Cook until water comes to a rolling boil, about 5 minutes. Shrimp will be pink. Remove shrimp and scatter over fish fillets.
• Melt butter in separate saucepan; add flour and blend. Strain fish stock and stir 1½ c. of it into flour mixture. Cook, stirring constantly, until mixture comes to a boil. Pour over fish.
• Combine potatoes with ½ c. cheese. Spread over fish. Bake in moderate oven (350°F.) 30 minutes. Sprinkle remaining cheese over potatoes and return to oven for several minutes until cheese melts. Makes 6 to 8 servings.

ENGLISH FISH PIE

Especially tasty way to serve fish

Pastry for 1-crust pie
2   lbs. fish fillets
3   tblsp. butter
2   tsp. salt
¼   tsp. pepper

2   tblsp. flour
1   c. liquid from cooked fish (add
      milk to make 1 c.)
3   tblsp. fine cracker crumbs
3   hard-cooked eggs, sliced
2   tomatoes, peeled and sliced
2   tblsp. chopped parsley

• Place fish on rack in shallow pan. Brush with 1 tblsp. melted butter; sprinkle with ½ tsp. salt and pepper. Bake in hot oven (400°F.) 15 minutes, until flaky but firm. Save liquid.
• Melt 2 tblsp. butter in saucepan; add flour and ½ tsp. salt. Stir over low heat. Remove from heat; stir in liquid from fish; cook 5 minutes.
• Sprinkle 9" buttered pie pan with 1 tblsp. crumbs. Arrange half of fish over crumbs; top with half the egg and tomato slices. Sprinkle with 1 tblsp. parsley, ½ tsp. salt and 1 tblsp. crumbs. Cover with half of sauce.
• Repeat above for second layer.
• Top with pastry; flute edges and cut vents. Bake in hot oven (400°F.) 35 minutes. Makes 6 servings.

PIZZA

A favorite FARM JOURNAL *version taken from* TIMESAVING COOKBOOK

1   pkg. active dry yeast
1   tsp. sugar
1   c. warm water
3   c. flour
½   tsp. salt
2   tblsp. salad oil
1   lb. Mozzarella, Muenster, proc-
      ess Swiss or American cheese
                                    more

Pizza Sauce
1   (3¾ oz.) can sardines, drained
½   c. Parmesan cheese (about)
Dried orégano

⅛   tsp. pepper
½   tsp. orégano
1   tblsp. salad oil
Dash red pepper (optional)

• Dissolve yeast and sugar in warm (not hot) water. Beat in half the flour; add salt, oil and remaining flour. Mix well; knead until smooth, adding more flour if needed. Place in lightly oiled bowl; turn dough to oil top. Cover; let rise in warm place (85° to 90°F.) until doubled.
• Divide dough in half; roll each half into circle about 13″ in diameter. Place on oiled pizza pan; fold edge under and build up rim slightly. (Or bake on oiled baking sheet in two 8″ × 12″ rectangles, building up dough edges.) Brush with oil.
• Divide remaining ingredients in half. Shred half the Mozzarella cheese and slice the other half.
• On each circle of dough, sprinkle half the shredded Mozzarella; cover with half the sauce. Top with half the sliced Mozzarella and sardines. Sprinkle with half the Parmesan cheese and orégano. (These ingredients make 3 pizzas instead of 2, if you bake them in an electric skillet—see Quick Pizza for directions for baking in skillet.)
• Bake in very hot oven (450°F.) 20 to 25 minutes (until crusty on bottom). Cut each circle into 6 or 8 wedges. Serve hot.

PIZZA SAUCE

1   clove garlic
1   tsp. salt
1   (6 oz.) can tomato juice
1   (8 oz.) can tomato sauce
½   tsp. sugar

• Put garlic through garlic press or mash to a pulp with salt. Combine with remaining ingredients. Do not cook. Makes 1 cup, enough for 2 (12″) pizzas.

PIZZA TOPPINGS: In place of sardines, use chopped or whole anchovies . . . Italian sausage or salami or cold cuts, cut in strips . . . or ground beef (½ lb. to each pizza), seasoned lightly and sautéed in butter. Circle top of any pizza before baking with slices of fresh or canned mushrooms. . . . Sprinkle with chopped chives or parsley, or garnish with chopped stuffed green olives or strips of ripe ones. . . . Decorate top with pattern of raw onion or green pepper rings dipped in salad oil.

VARIATION

QUICK PIZZA: Prepare 1 (15½ oz.) pkg. assembled ready-to-bake pizza mix (contains yeast, flour mixture, sauce and cheese) as directed on package. (Or use hot-roll mix, following directions for pizza on package.) Roll out dough and fit into an oiled, unheated 11″ or 12″ electric skillet; slightly build up dough edge. Add sauce, cheese and chosen topping. Cover; set dial at 300° to 320°F. (low to medium) and bake with vent closed until dough is set, about 30 minutes. Dough browns on bottom of pizza. Slide out with spatula; cut in squares. Serve hot. Makes 4 to 6 servings.

BISCUIT PIZZA

As easy as 1-2-3 to put together and bake for the teen-age crowd

Crust:
- 2 c. flour
- 1 tblsp. baking powder
- 1 tsp. salt
- ⅔ c. milk
- ⅓ c. salad or cooking oil

Filling:
- 1 (6 oz.) can tomato paste
- ¼ c. water
- 1 tsp. dried orégano
- ½ tsp. salt
- ⅛ tsp. pepper
- 1 (8 oz.) pkg. Mozzarella cheese slices, cut in strips

Crust: Sift together flour, baking powder and salt; add milk and oil. Stir with fork until mixture forms a ball. Turn onto lightly floured board and knead 8 to 10 times.

• Roll dough between sheets of waxed paper to fit a 14″ pizza pan or 2 (10″) pie pans.

Filling: Combine tomato paste, water and seasonings. Spread over dough. Place strips of cheese on top.

• Bake in hot oven (425°F.) 15 to 20 minutes. Makes 12 servings.

Cookies

Choice Homemade Cookies from Countryside America

Golden brown cookies, warm and fragrant from the oven—could anything taste better? And what arouses greater enthusiasm—watch the children head for the cookie jar when they return home from school. Notice how your husband lingers in the kitchen if the spicy aroma of cookies, spread on cooling racks, greets him. Doesn't he take seconds—and sometimes thirds?

Don't you yourself recall your mother's wonderful date bars or whatever was her specialty? Maybe your own son, as a serviceman, appreciated your boxes of cookies . . . "love from home." Eating homemade cookies is happiness that builds memories to treasure.

This cookbook contains superior recipes representing all types of cookies; among them are sure to be some you associate with your childhood. We include the best cookies published in FARM JOURNAL through the past twenty years—many of them from country kitchens. But we also feature original Test Kitchen recipes that never before appeared in print.

First in this book you will find recipes for the Big Six traditional cookies—bar, drop, rolled, refrigerator, molded and pressed cookies. The way you handle the dough determines the family to which a cookie belongs—whether you bake it in a pan and cut the cookies with a knife; whether you shape it into rolls and refrigerate them to bake later; roll the dough out thin and use a cutter to form shapes; drop it from a spoon right onto the baking sheet; shape it into balls with your hands; or squirt it from a cookie press.

Newest among the traditionals are the refrigerator cookies, known as icebox cookies before electric refrigerators became commonplace. These are special for women who want to bake thin, crisp cookies without bothering with rolling pin and cookie cutters. It's so much easier, they insist, just to slice dough and bake it.

When Europeans came to America from overseas to establish homes in a new world, the women brought along their treasured cookie recipes, sometimes written down, sometimes memorized. We include some of these old-time specialties, adapting them to the ingredients and appliances and tools we have and to flavors we like. Some of these first colonists made room in their crowded baggage for sandbakelser molds and hand-carved springerle boards or rolling pins. Those who could not bring either the board or rolling pin to use for making these picture cookies improvised by pressing butter molds or glass dishes with cut designs on the rolled cookie dough. You will find in this book up-to-date recipes for Sandbakelser and Springerle and other cookies that originated in many lands. Italy, for example, produced Florentines—rich, melt-in-the-mouth, chocolate-covered cookies flavored with candied orange peel and almonds.

Americans made their own cookie discoveries. Chocolate chip cookies are the classic example. Developed by a Massachusetts home economist who cut up chocolate and added it to her cookie dough when she found her raisin box empty, the cookies caught on at once and skyrocketed to popularity across the country. This book offers you a variety of recipes for this kind of cookie. Try our Cape Cod Chocolate Chip Cookies (molded), Soft Chocolate Chippers (drop) and Chocolate Chip Bars to see which kind you and your family like best.

Cry Baby Cookies, molasses-flavored drop cookies that contain such good things as coconut, nuts, raisins, rate tops with navy men. The first recipes for these cookies are believed to have evolved in kitchens of Maryland's Eastern Shore. Bake them when you want a big batch of cookies to please men. The recipe makes about 9½ dozen cookies, but you can freeze part of the dough to bake later if you like.

Jumbo Sugar Cookies are another all-American treat. The sugar-cinnamon top scents the kitchen delightfully while they bake. One of our home economists who tested this recipe baked a batch and took them to a P.T.A. food sale. They sold fast at 10¢ each! These big cookies are first cousins of Snickerdoodles, an early American, but you handle the dough differently and the ingredients vary somewhat. You'll find recipes for both in our book.

Meringue cookies, or kisses, have been special-occasion treats for generations, the favorite way to use leftover egg whites that accumulated in kitchens where lots of baking was done. You'll be surprised how many appetizing ways this cookbook gives for flavoring meringue cookies and making them distinctive.

Many of our native cookies, once enjoyed, disappeared along

with the special need for them. Boom Cookies are an example. They were giant size—about 5″ in diameter—molasses/coffee-flavored cookies, which hungry lumberjacks joyfully ate at the Boom in Minnesota, a sorting station when logs were floated down the St. Croix River. Gone is the cook shack, the circumstance and the cookies, but our Soft Molasses Cookies in smaller sizes have the same taste provided by molasses, spices and instant coffee powder. It is one recipe of many in this cookbook for molasses cookies.

Christmas and cookies go together, although every season has its cookies. Certainly women bake more cookies for the holidays than at any other time. One reason is the visiting that goes on around the countryside during Yuletide. The traditional refreshments for open houses consist of Christmas cookies with coffee, wine or a fruit drink. In the Bethlehem, Pennsylvania, area, this visiting is called "putzing." It's when a family welcomes neighbors and friends who come to see their crèche under the Christmas tree. The "putz" is the crèche and the name comes from *putzen,* which to Germans means to decorate.

There are many reasons for Christmas cookies other than sharing the treats with visiting friends. They make ideal gifts from the home kitchen to neighbors, shut-ins, business associates and other friends. There also are gift boxes to mail, children home from school eager to feast on Mother's cookies. Cookies are an important part, too, of refreshments served at parties given by clubs and other organizations. And in many homes, Christmas cookies help decorate the gala tree.

Cookies such as White Christmas and brown Spiced Christmas Cookies and Pepper Nuts—the kind grandmothers of Swiss and German descent used to keep in their apron pockets to reward grandchildren for good behavior—still are baked at Christmastime (see Index for the recipes). We give suggestions for decorating these and many other cookies, though all are good plain also. It's the opinion of women who contributed their choice recipes, that the trims justify what they cost in time and effort.

You'll observe recipes in this book that call for frostings, white and tinted to top or coat the cookies and sometimes to put them together in pairs for sandwiches. This dress-up helps both their appearance and disappearance!

You'll find many recipes that call for fillings. In fact, all of the traditional cookie types lend themselves to fillings. One of the favorite types is the bar cookies in which the filling bakes between two layers of dough, sometimes in a jelly roll pan. Some women lament that cookies go so fast, even though they want them to appeal and please. Mothers sometimes have to hide cookies to save them for serving at some special occasion. One mother stores some of her cookies in empty rolled oat boxes because the children never think of looking there for cookies.

To make cookie baking pleasant and memorable, enlist the help of the family, especially with Christmas cookies. You may prefer to bake the cookies and let the children help decorate them—gingerbread boys and animals for Christmas, for instance. Or dream up your own ways to stimulate their interest. We give recipes for making farmyard cookie animals (see Cocoa Cookie Barn), a cookie family, as well as recipe, patterns and directions for making a Christmas gingerbread church. This makes a great Christmas centerpiece and the children will love to help.

In fact, we have included a special section for junior cooks with cookie recipes in their language and with extra how-to detail.

Important as traditional cookies are in our collection, we include many other newer types. Cookie confections have many loyal boosters. These are the easy-to-make cookies that children like to fix for their friends, and also to eat. But homemakers as well like to make cookies that are little work and taste really good. Some of them are no-bake cookies, and several of them require brief *cooking* in a saucepan!

Cookie confections are close kin to candies. You often make them with ready-to-eat cereals or with rolled oats, crackers or vanilla wafers substituting for flour. Many ingredient goodies contribute to their popularity—raisins, marshmallows, chocolate pieces, coconut, nuts.

One of our new cookie triumphs is what we call the pie-bar dessert cookie. It's a cross between a bar cookie and a piece of pie. These luscious cookies that taste like pie salve the calorie-counter's conscience.

Since many women today must stretch time, this book offers quick ways to speedily glamorize packaged store cookies you can keep in your cupboard. The recipes show you how to add homemade touches to cookies you buy.

Today's appliances have speeded up and simplified cookie making. The electric mixer can be used to mix all or part of the dough (see "How to Bake Good Cookies Every Time"). It especially excels for quickly and easily creaming the fat and sugar until light and fluffy, and for thoroughly blending in the eggs and flavoring. The freezer enables women to keep baked cookies or the dough for baking cookies on hand for months.

Most of the recipes in this cookbook are for use in homes located in areas with an altitude under 5,000 feet. But because families living in the mountain states also like homemade cookies, we include the Colorado Basic Cookie Mix for high altitude baking. The basic mix can be used for a wide variety of excellent cookies.

We also give you the recipes for two other popular basic mixes (for altitudes under 5,000 feet): Cookie Starter and Eight-in-One Sugar Cookies. And you'll find many excellent basic recipes with several variations.

For your convenience, we have selected and listed for you cookies appropriate for mailing; to serve at women's luncheon and tea parties; to sell at bazaars; to pack in lunchboxes; to offer at coffee parties; for children to bake; we also list cookies of foreign origin and Christmas specialties.

No one knows where cookies originated, but their name comes from the Dutch word *koekje,* which gets a mention in this old, anonymous American jingle:

> "The British call it biscuit
> And it's *koekje* to the Dutch
> But no matter what you call it
> All cookies please us much."

How to Bake Good Cookies Every Time

You will bake wonderful cookies with the recipes in this cookbook *if* you follow them carefully. To assure you the greatest satisfaction with your results, we pass on some of the points we watch in our Test Kitchens.

COOKIE INGREDIENTS

Flour — Use all-purpose flour in our recipes unless otherwise specified. If a recipe calls for sifted flour, spoon it lightly into measuring cup and level off with straight edge of knife or spatula. Some busy women skip the sifting (we don't recommend) and instead stir the flour in the canister or other container to incorporate air. If you then spoon it lightly into measuring cup and level it off, you sometimes get approximately the same amount as in sifting, but *often you get a little more*. Avoid tapping the cup filled with flour; this packs it.

Fats — The fats called for in this book are butter, regular margarine (in sticks), lard, shortening (it comes in 1- to 3-lb. cans) and salad oil (vegetable). Soft, tub-type margarines are whipped and so contain air and less fat than regular margarine. Use the fat the recipe calls for with one exception: You can substitute shortening for half of the butter listed. For instance, instead of using 1 c. butter, you can use ½ c. each of butter and of shortening.

Many women prefer to use butter in refrigerator cookies because it gets very hard when chilled; the dough slices neatly and evenly. Regular margarine also gives satisfactory results if you freeze the dough or chill it until very cold before slicing.

Pack solid fats firmly in measuring cup and level off. Bring them to room temperature before you start to combine and mix ingredients.

Sugar — Use granulated white sugar (cane or beet) unless otherwise specified. When a recipe calls for brown sugar, use light brown unless dark is designated. Superfine sugar is very fine granulated sugar.

300

Confectioners sugar (called powdered sugar in many areas) should be free of lumps before measuring. Some recipes call for sifted confectioners sugar.

Molasses — Use light molasses unless recipe calls for the dark. You can use either type, but the dark has deeper color and stronger flavor. The light comes from the first boiling of sugar cane, the dark from the second boiling.

Eggs — Recipes in this cookbook were tested with medium to large eggs. If you have small eggs, break two of them into a ¼-cup measure. A medium egg measures about ¼ cup. You can measure the correct amount for the recipe you are using. Since eggs are often the only liquid in cookies, the size used affects the results.

Milk and Cream — When your recipe calls for sweetened condensed milk, read the label on the can to make sure that's what you have. Evaporated milk and sweetened condensed milk both come in cans; they *cannot* be used interchangeably. Recipes calling for buttermilk were tested with commercial cultured type. You can substitute evaporated milk for fresh milk if you mix it with an equal amount of water. A few recipes list packaged instant dry milk powder as an ingredient.

In case you do not have sour milk, measure 1 tsp. vinegar or fresh lemon juice into a ¼-cup measure. Fill with milk and let stand several minutes; then stir and use. (For 1 c. sour milk, use 1 tblsp. vinegar or fresh lemon juice in a 1-cup measure.)

Cream in the recipes is either heavy or whipping (30 to 35% butterfat), coffee or light (18 to 20% butterfat), dairy half-and-half (10 to 12% butterfat) or dairy sour (commercial with 20% butterfat). Do not substitute one kind for another. Our recipes use commercial dairy sour cream.

Chocolate — Recipes in this book may call for one of four kinds of chocolate: unsweetened, semisweet, sweet cooking and no-melt unsweetened chocolate in envelopes. Use the designated type. You can substitute unsweetened chocolate squares for no-melt chocolate when recipe directs it may be done. Melt the squares in a heavy bowl set in a pan of hot, not boiling water, or put the chocolate in the top of a double boiler over hot water. You also can melt it in a small pan over very low heat, stirring constantly, but do watch closely, for chocolate scorches easily. Cool melted chocolate before adding it to other ingredients. Many recipes use chocolate pieces: semisweet, semisweet mint-flavored chocolate and milk chocolate—all have different flavors. Women quite commonly refer to these chocolate pieces as chocolate chips.

If you do not have unsweetened chocolate when ready to bake cookies, you can use 3 tblsp. unsweetened cocoa and 1 tblsp. butter for 1 square unsweetened chocolate. When a recipe calls for cocoa, use the unsweetened.

Peanut Butter — Unless a recipe designates crunchy peanut butter, we used smooth peanut butter in testing.

Rolled Oats — Use either the quick-cooking or regular kind as specified.

Raisins — Seedless raisins, from grapes without seeds, are designated in most recipes, although a few call for seeded raisins, from grapes with seeds that are removed, as the first choice.

Food Color — There are two kinds, liquid and paste. You can use the type you prefer. We found in our testing that the paste gives especially vivid colors, but use it sparingly. Liquid food colors are more widely available. Add them drop by drop until you get the shade you desire. It is easy to mix these colors. For instance, 3 drops of red and 2 of yellow food color make orange.

Decorating Sugars and Candies — Packaged coarse sugar in glistening white and many colors is widely available. Among the other favored cookie decorations are silver, gold and colored dragées, tiny candies of one or many colors and chocolate shot (jimmies).

Nuts — Store nuts in refrigerator or freezer if they are to be kept several days or weeks before use. To chop nuts, spread on wooden board. Hold top of sharp knife close to surface of board with one hand, then move knife handle up and down, and around in a semicircle with other hand so blade contacts uncut nuts. Nut choppers do a good job, too, and so does the electric blender. Chop nuts very fine if recipe calls for grated nuts, or put them through food chopper or chop in blender. When a recipe lists ½ c. nuts (or other measurement), we usually used pecans or walnuts.

UTENSILS AND TOOLS

The tools and utensils you use can simplify cookie baking and contribute to good results. It is especially important to use the pan sizes designated in recipes. Here are the utensils and tools that were especially helpful to home economists perfecting these cookie recipes in our Test Kitchens:

Graduated measuring cups
Measuring cups for liquid
Mixing bowls
Electric mixer (portable or stationary)
Wooden spoon
Small spatula for spreading frosting
Measuring spoons
Double boiler
Rolling pin
Stockinet cover for rolling pin
Pastry cloth
Cookie cutters
Baking sheets—two or more, at least 2" shorter and narrower than the oven. Shiny baking sheets are best for delicate browning. If you have only one baking sheet, use an inverted baking pan for a second one. Or cut heavy-duty aluminum foil to fit your baking sheet. Arrange cookie dough on it while one batch bakes. When the cookies are done, remove them and transfer the foil with the cookies for baking to the hot baking sheet. Put in the oven at once.
Baking pans of standard sizes—8 and 9" square, 13 x 9 x 2" and 15½ x 10½ x 1" jelly roll pan
Broad spatula for removing cookies from baking sheets
Wire cooling racks
Timer
Cookie press

MIXING COOKIES THE RIGHT WAY

Every recipe in this cookbook gives precise directions for mixing the dough, but here are a few general pointers:
Bring ingredients to room temperature before you combine and mix them. This is especially important with solid fats.
Use the electric mixer at medium speed for creaming fats (beating them until light), for creaming together fats and sugar and to blend in eggs and flavorings. You can beat these foods until light and fluffy by hand with a wooden spoon, but we used the electric mixer extensively in testing the recipes. Either add the dry ingredients with the electric mixer at low speed, or mix them in with a wooden spoon.
If the cookie dough seems too soft, chill it an hour or longer. As it becomes firm enough to handle easily, work with a small amount at a

time, leaving the remainder in the refrigerator until you are ready for it. If the dough still seems too soft after chilling, bake a test cookie. If it spreads too much, work 1 to 2 tblsp. flour into the dough.

Here are some of the reasons why your cookie dough is sometimes a trifle too soft: skimpy flour measurement; flour stored in humid place; too generous fat measurement; melted or very soft fat instead of fat at room temperature; large eggs instead of medium size; mixing dough in a very warm kitchen.

When the dough seems too dry, bake a test cookie. If it is dry and crumbly, work 1 to 2 tblsp. soft butter or cream into dough with your hands.

Here are some of the reasons why cookie dough sometimes is a trifle too dry: flour stored in place with low humidity; too generous flour measurement; skimpy fat measurement; soft tub-type margarine instead of regular kind; skimpy liquid measurement; cold fat, such as butter taken directly from refrigerator; small eggs instead of medium size.

Flour has remarkable ability to absorb moisture from the air and to release moisture when stored in a dry place. There is a slight variation in the amount of moisture, due to atmospheric conditions, it can take up in a recipe.

COOKIE BAKING POINTERS

Be sure to heat oven to the correct temperature before putting cookies in to bake. When you bake one batch at a time, place baking sheet on rack in center of oven. If baking two batches at the same time, divide the oven into thirds with racks. Use cool baking sheets for all bakings; cookies spread too much on warm sheets.

Notice whether the recipe calls for a greased baking sheet. If it does, rub the surface lightly with unsalted fat, such as shortening. Some doughs are rich enough that cookies will not stick to ungreased baking sheets and pans. (Ungreased sheets or pans are easier to wash.)

Check cookies for doneness at end of the shortest baking time given in the recipe. When only one baking time is given, test 2 minutes before it ends. Try to avoid overbaking—it makes cookies dry. (Tests for doneness for the different cookie types are given with the recipes.) *Use a timer.*

Remove cookies from baking sheet with wide spatula at once, unless recipe specifies otherwise. When left on baking sheet even a few minutes, they continue to cook. Some recipes direct leaving cookies on baking sheet briefly before removing them. These cookies are fragile and easily broken when hot.

Spread cookies in a single layer on cooling racks. When cooling bar cookies in pan, set it on rack. You cut most bar cookies when cool or at least partly cool. Use a sharp knife.

When a frosting appears with a recipe, it makes enough to frost that amount of cookies unless noted otherwise. So when using the frosting for another cookie, use your judgment about whether it will be enough, too much, or whether you'll have to double the recipe.

HOW TO STORE COOKIES

Once your cookies are baked and thoroughly cooled, store them correctly and in a cool place if possible. This helps them to retain appetizing freshness. Here's the way to do it:

Crisp Cookies — Store in container with loose-fitting lid. If they soften despite your care, spread them on a baking sheet before serving and heat them 3 to 5 minutes in a slow oven (300°).

Soft Cookies — Store them in a container with a tight-fitting lid. If they seem to dry out, add a piece of apple, orange or bread, but replace fruit or bread frequently. You can freshen soft cookies. Before serving, put them in a casserole, cover and heat 8 to 10 minutes in a slow oven (300°).

Bar Cookies — It often is convenient to store them in the pan in which they baked. Lay a piece of plastic wrap over top of cookies; then cover pan with its lid or with foil.

HOW TO FREEZE COOKIES AND COOKIE DOUGH

You can freeze either baked cookies or cookie dough for 9 months to a year. Space in the freezer may determine whether you freeze them baked or unbaked in dough form. Frozen dough frequently takes up less space than baked cookies. Since frosted cookies freeze less satisfactorily than unfrosted, most women prefer to add the frosting shortly before serving them. This gives them a fresh taste. Here's the way to freeze cookies and cookie dough:

Baked Cookies — Layer thoroughly cooled cookies in a rigid container, such as a sturdy box, lined with plastic wrap or aluminum foil. Separate the layers and top with plastic wrap, which clings to them and keeps out the air, or with aluminum foil in which you can seal cookies. Seal foil lining and top covering. Close box, label and freeze. Let cookies thaw unwrapped in package 10 to 15 minutes before serving. *Cookie Dough* — Put dough for *drop* cookies in frozen food containers and cover tightly. Or wrap in plastic wrap sealed with freezer tape, or in aluminum foil. Place the wrapped dough, when frozen, in a plastic bag. When ready to bake, thaw dough just enough so that you can drop it from a spoon.

Pack and freeze *molded* cookie dough like drop cookie dough. When ready to bake, thaw dough just enough so that you can shape it.

Arrange cutout dough for *rolled* cookies in layers in a sturdy box lined with plastic wrap or aluminum foil. Separate layers with plastic wrap or with foil you can seal as for drop cookies. Cover tightly, seal and label. Or spread cookie cutouts on a baking sheet and freeze; then package in the same way. The frozen cutouts are rigid and easier to pack. Put frozen cutouts on baking sheet and bake; no need to thaw.

Shape *refrigerator* cookie dough in rolls of the desired size, wrap tightly in plastic wrap and seal ends with tape, or wrap in aluminum foil. When ready to bake remove from freezer, let thaw just enough so that you can slice the rolls with a sharp knife. You can thaw them in refrigerator for 1 hour and slice.

Freeze dough for *bar* cookies in the pan in which you will bake it. Cover dough with plastic wrap, then with pan lid or foil.

How to Pack Cookies for Mailing

Once you've baked and cooled good cookies, you may get the desire to share some of them with members of your family who are away from home or with friends who live too far away for you to take your prizes to them. You can mail them successfully. No homemade gift travels more extensively than cookies. And no food tastes better to the recipient. If you want your cookies to reach their destination in tiptop condition, follow these rules, which we have tested:

Choose the right cookie for mailing (see Index for suggestions). Soft drop, bar and fruit cookies travel well, while thin, crisp cookies (refrigerator and rolled types) are likely to crumble.

Select a strong packing box; a pasteboard box is not strong enough. Line the box with plastic wrap or aluminum foil.

Have plenty of filler on hand to use between layers of wrapped cookies. You can use shredded or crushed tissue paper, waxed paper or aluminum foil. Popped corn sometimes is used, but occasionally it molds, especially in overseas shipments.

Wrap each cookie separately, or two cookies, back to back, in plastic wrap; fasten with tape.

Place a layer of filler on bottom of box for a cushion. Arrange wrapped cookies close together in neat rows to fill box with some of the filler between each layer. If sending more than one kind of cookie, put the heaviest ones in the bottom of the box.

Spread layer of filler on top. Then lay folded paper napkins or towels on top. Enclose your gift card. Close the box. It should be so full that you have to exert light pressure to close it. Tape box shut. (It's a good idea to write on top the name and address of the person to whom you are mailing the cookies.)

Wrap box with heavy wrapping paper and tie securely. Stick on the clearly addressed label.

Mark the box "FRAGILE—HANDLE WITH CARE," and "PERISHABLE." If you are sending the package overseas, send it by air parcel post if you can.

Bar Cookies

Brownies, rich, moist and fudge-like, top the list of bar cookies. But there are many wonderful-tasting competitors, for the bar cookie family is large. All the cookies you make by spreading dough in a pan and cutting it, after baking, into bars, squares, diamonds and other shapes are generally called "bar cookies."

When women across country send us their favorite cookie recipes, the brownie contributions come in great numbers. Some of them appear on the following pages. They may sound alike but each is different. Try them and find out which you, your family and friends like best—Candy-Top Brownies that make you think they're baked fudge, less sweet California Chocolate Brownies so luscious when topped with whipped cream peaks and frozen, Brownies for a Crowd baked in a jelly roll pan, handsome Two-Tone Brownies and other varieties.

Compare them with the other bars you make from recipes in this section—elegant Cheesecake Squares that melt in the mouth; gently spiced Chocolate/Orange Bars; English Tea Squares with strawberry jam filling. The homemaker who shares the recipe for the Tea Squares says: "They're simply divine, especially when faintly warm."

Bar cookies are so versatile because you can custom-cut them. The size depends mainly on whom you are cutting them for. So consider the sizes indicated in our recipes as suggestions.

Naturally, you want smaller, daintier cookies to serve at a women's party than to pack in a lunchbox or tote to the field to refresh men at work.

Some of our bar cookies can be served for dessert—Frosted Carrot Bars, for instance (cut them somewhat larger than usual). They taste so good that no one will dream the humble vegetable is an ingredient.

Bar cookies make good snacks for people of all ages. Plantation Peanut Cookies or Chocolate Chip Bars will generate special enthusiasm among teen-agers.

Bars are the easiest cookies to bake. You skip rolling, cutting, dropping or shaping the dough and there's only one batch to put in and take from the oven.

Do cut the bars when the cookie is slightly warm or completely cooled unless the recipe designates otherwise. If cut when hot, some bars crumble. Here are other pointers:

Avoid overmixing the dough — makes cookie tops hard. Overmixing the dough will result in a tough textured cookie.

Spread the dough evenly in the pan so all the bars will have the same thickness and texture (some areas in the pan may overbake if spread thinly).

Use the pan size the recipe indicates. If larger, the dough will be thin and unless you reduce the baking time, the cookie will be dry and tough; if smaller, the dough will be thick and may require a longer baking time.

Bake cookies only until they are done. Overbaked cookies are hard and dry; if underdone, doughy. Use the time given in the recipe as a guide for doneness, but also apply the standard tests. Cookies are done if when pressed lightly with a finger, they retain a slight imprint; a toothpick inserted in the center of cake-like bars comes out clean.

BROWNIES FOR A CROWD

Save time—bake cookies in one big pan; they're moist and keep well

½ c. regular margarine	¼ tsp. salt
1 c. sugar	½ c. chopped walnuts
4 eggs	6 tblsp. regular margarine
1 tsp. vanilla	6 tblsp. milk
1 (1 lb.) can chocolate syrup	1 c. sugar
(1½ c.)	½ c. semisweet chocolate pieces
1 c. plus 1 tblsp. sifted flour	1 tsp. vanilla
½ tsp. baking powder	

Beat ½ c. margarine with 1 c. sugar until light and fluffy. Beat in eggs, two at a time, and 1 tsp. vanilla. Mix well. Stir in chocolate syrup.

Sift together flour, baking powder and salt. Stir into chocolate mixture. Add nuts. Pour into well-greased 15½ x 10½ x 1″ jelly roll pan and spread evenly.

Bake in moderate oven (350°) 22 to 25 minutes, or until slight imprint remains when touched lightly with finger. Remove pan to rack, and let cookies cool.

Meanwhile, combine 6 tblsp. margarine, milk and 1 c. sugar in saucepan; stir to mix. Bring to a boil and boil 30 seconds. Add chocolate pieces; stir until mixture thickens slightly and cools. Stir in 1 tsp. vanilla. Spread over cooled cookies, then cut in 2½ x 1" bars. Makes 5 dozen.

CANDY-TOP BROWNIES

These candy-like cookies win compliments; they're good travelers

2 c. sugar	½ c. chopped walnuts
2 eggs	1 egg, beaten
4 squares unsweetened chocolate	2 tblsp. light cream
½ c. butter or regular margarine	2 tblsp. butter or regular
½ c. flour	margarine
2 tsp. vanilla	

Combine 1 c. sugar and 2 eggs; beat.

Melt 2 squares chocolate with ½ c. butter; add to egg mixture. Blend in flour, 1 tsp. vanilla and nuts. Spread in greased 8" square pan.

Bake in moderate oven (350°) 25 to 35 minutes; cool on rack.

Combine remaining 1 c. sugar, beaten egg, cream, 2 squares chocolate, 2 tblsp. butter and 1 tsp. vanilla. Bring to a boil, stirring constantly. Remove from heat and stir until of spreading consistency. Spread over cooled brownies. Cut in 2" squares. Makes 16.

CALIFORNIA CHOCOLATE BROWNIES

These are less sweet than most brownies so you may want to frost them or sprinkle on confectioners sugar . . . they're good keepers

½ c. shortening	¾ c. sifted cake flour
1 c. light corn syrup	¼ tsp. baking powder
2 squares unsweetened chocolate, melted	¼ tsp. salt
	¾ c. chopped nuts
2 eggs, well beaten	Vanilla Cream Icing (see Index)
½ tsp. vanilla	

Cream shortening until fluffy. Gradually beat in corn syrup until thoroughly mixed and light and fluffy. Stir in melted chocolate. Add eggs and vanilla.

Sift together cake flour, baking powder and salt. Add ¼ c. at a time to creamed mixture. Fold in nuts. Pour into well-greased 8″ square pan.

Bake in moderate oven (350°) 30 to 35 minutes, or until slight imprint remains when touched lightly with finger. Set pan on rack to cool completely. Then frost with Vanilla Cream Icing, if desired. Cut in 2″ squares. Makes 16.

Variations

Brownies Made with Cocoa: Omit unsweetened chocolate. Sift 6 tblsp. cocoa with flour. Add 2 tblsp. additional shortening.

Snow Peaked Brownies: When brownies in pan are cool, cut in squares. Do not frost. Remove brownies, one at a time, to baking sheet covered with waxed paper. Beat ½ c. heavy cream until it peaks when beater is removed. Beat in 2 tblsp. sugar and ½ tsp. vanilla. Top each brownie with a teaspoonful of whipped cream, forming a peak. Freeze. When frozen, place in plastic bag and return to freezer. Will keep in good condition up to 3 months.

COTTAGE CHEESE BROWNIES

Two chocolate layers with luscious cheese filling between

3 squares unsweetened chocolate	½ tsp. lemon juice
½ c. butter	½ c. unsifted flour
1¼ c. sugar	½ tsp. baking powder
1½ tsp. vanilla	¼ tsp. salt
1 tblsp. cornstarch	½ c. chopped walnuts
¾ c. creamed cottage cheese	½ tsp. almond extract
3 eggs	

Melt chocolate and 6 tblsp. butter over hot water.

Cream remaining 2 tblsp. butter, ¼ c. sugar and ½ tsp. vanilla. Add cornstarch, cottage cheese, 1 egg and lemon juice; beat until smooth. Set aside.

Beat remaining 2 eggs until thick. With a spoon, gradually stir in remaining 1 c. sugar. Beat with spoon until thoroughly mixed. Stir in chocolate mixture.

Mix and sift together flour, baking powder and salt. Stir into chocolate mixture. Mix in nuts, remaining 1 tsp. vanilla and almond extract. Spoon half of batter into bottom of greased 9″ square pan. Spread evenly.

Cover with cottage cheese mixture. Carefully spoon remaining batter over top. With a spoon, zigzag through batter. Bake in moderate oven (350°) 35 minutes. Cool in pan set on rack 10 minutes, or cool completely. Cut in 2¼″ squares. Makes 16.

HALLOWEEN THREE-DECKER BROWNIES

These orange-and-black treats are brownies in gala, holiday dress

First Deck:

2 squares unsweetened chocolate	½ tsp. vanilla
½ c. butter	½ c. sifted flour
1 c. sugar	½ c. chopped pecans
2 eggs, beaten	

Second Deck:

1 c. confectioners sugar	3 or 4 drops orange food color
2 tblsp. soft butter	(or use mixture of yellow and
2 tsp. milk	red to make orange)
½ tsp. vanilla	

Third Deck:

¼ square unsweetened chocolate   1½ tsp. butter

To make first deck, combine chocolate and butter; melt over hot water. Beat in sugar, eggs and vanilla. Stir in flour and nuts. Bake in greased 8″ square pan in slow oven (325°) 30 to 35 minutes. Cool in pan on rack.

To make second layer, combine confectioners sugar, butter, milk and vanilla to make a smooth mixture. Tint orange with food color. Spread over brownies in pan. Chill 10 minutes.

To make third deck, combine chocolate and butter; melt over hot water. Drizzle from small spoon over top of brownies. Cool in pan on rack, and cut in 2″ squares. Makes 16.

MOCHA BROWNIES

The chocolate/coffee team is tops—do try the frosted brownies

2 squares unsweetened chocolate	¾ c. sifted flour
⅓ c. butter or regular	½ tsp. baking powder
margarine	¼ tsp. salt
2 eggs	2 tblsp. instant coffee powder
1 c. sugar	½ to ¾ c. chopped walnuts
1 tsp. vanilla	(optional)

Melt chocolate and butter together over very low heat, stirring constantly. Set aside to cool.

Beat eggs until light; gradually add sugar and beat until light and fluffy. Add vanilla. Combine with chocolate mixture and mix well.

Sift together flour, baking powder, salt and coffee powder; stir into chocolate mixture and mix well. Fold in nuts. Pour into greased 8″ square pan.

Bake in moderate oven (350°) 30 minutes, or until a slight imprint remains when fingertips touch center top. Cool in pan set on rack, then cut in 2″ squares. Makes 16.

Variation

Frosted Mocha Brownies: Bake brownies as directed. After brownies in pan are cool, but before cutting them, spread with this frosting: Melt 1 square unsweetened chocolate with 1 tblsp. butter or margarine over hot water (or over very low heat, stirring constantly). Blend in 1½ tblsp. very hot and strong liquid coffee and about 1 c. sifted confectioners sugar, enough to make a frosting that spreads smoothly and easily.

ORANGE BROWNIES

The new twist in these brownies is the delicate fresh orange taste

2 squares unsweetened chocolate	½ tsp. grated orange peel
½ c. butter	½ c. sifted flour
2 eggs	⅛ tsp. salt
1 c. sugar	1 c. chopped walnuts
1 tsp. vanilla	

Melt chocolate and butter. Beat eggs; beat in sugar gradually. Beat in butter and chocolate, vanilla and orange peel.

Stir in flour, salt and nuts. Pour into greased 8″ square pan.

Bake in moderate oven (350°) 20 to 25 minutes. Do not over-bake. Cut in 2″ squares. Cool on racks. Makes 16.

Variation

Double Chocolate Brownies: Stir in ½ c. semisweet chocolate pieces along with the nuts.

PINEAPPLE/CHOCOLATE BARS

Pineapple and chocolate unite tastily in these two-tone specials

¾ c. shortening
½ c. sugar
3 eggs
1 tsp. vanilla
½ tsp. ground cinnamon
½ tsp. salt
1 tsp. baking powder

1 c. sifted flour
¼ c. chopped nuts
2 squares semisweet chocolate, melted
1 (8½ oz.) can crushed pine-apple, well drained (⅔ c.)

Combine shortening, sugar, eggs and vanilla; beat until mixture is creamy.

Sift together cinnamon, salt, baking powder and flour. Add to shortening mixture. Stir in nuts.

Divide batter in half. To one half add melted chocolate; spread in greased 9″ square pan. To second half add pineapple; spread over chocolate mixture in pan.

Bake in moderate oven (350°) 35 minutes. Cool in pan on rack. When cool, cut in 3 x 1″ bars. Makes 27.

TWO-TONE BROWNIES

Color contrast of the dark and light layer provides a happy change

⅓ c. shortening
1 c. sugar
2 eggs
½ c. sifted flour
½ tsp. baking powder

½ tsp. salt
1 tsp. vanilla
1 c. chopped nuts
1½ squares unsweetened chocolate, melted

Cream shortening and sugar until light and fluffy; beat in eggs.

Sift dry ingredients together and add to creamed mixture. Mix thoroughly. Stir in vanilla and nuts.

Divide dough in half. To one half, add chocolate and spread in greased 8″ square pan. Spread remaining half of dough on top.

Bake in moderate oven (375°) about 20 minutes, or until a toothpick inserted in center comes out clean. Cool in pan set on rack 10 minutes, or cool completely, then cut in 2″ squares. Makes 16.

BUTTERSCOTCH BROWNIES

Quick-and-easy cookie squares have glossy, caramel-colored tops

1 (6 oz.) pkg. butterscotch pieces   1 c. sifted flour
¼ c. shortening   1 tsp. baking powder
1 c. brown sugar, firmly packed   ½ tsp. salt
2 eggs   ½ c. coarsely chopped walnuts
½ tsp. vanilla

Melt butterscotch pieces and shortening in double boiler over hot water. Remove from heat and stir in brown sugar; cool 5 minutes.

Stir eggs and vanilla into butterscotch mixture to blend thoroughly.

Sift together flour, baking powder and salt. Blend into batter. Stir in nuts. Spread in greased 13 x 9 x 2″ pan and bake in moderate oven (350°) about 25 minutes. Set pan on rack. While still warm, cut in 2″ (about) squares (cookies are especially good warm from the oven). Makes about 2 dozen.

PEANUT BUTTER BROWNIES

Delightful treat for those in your family who like a chewy cookie

6 eggs   1 tblsp. vanilla
3 c. sugar   4 c. unsifted flour
1½ c. brown sugar, firmly packed   1½ tblsp. baking powder
1 c. peanut butter   1½ tsp. salt
½ c. shortening   ½ c. chopped peanuts

Combine eggs, sugars, peanut butter, shortening and vanilla; blend thoroughly.

Add dry ingredients; mix only until dough is smooth. Spread evenly in two lightly greased 15½ x 10½ x 1″ jelly roll pans (or three 13 x 9 x 2″ pans). Sprinkle with peanuts.

Bake in moderate oven (350°) 25 minutes. Cut in 3 x 1″ bars and cool in pans on racks. Makes about 8 dozen.

ALMOND BRITTLE BARS

These cookies remind you of almond brittle—they're really that good

1 c. butter or regular margarine	1 c. sugar
2 tsp. instant coffee powder	2 c. sifted flour
1 tsp. salt	1 (6 oz.) pkg. semisweet chocolate pieces
¾ tsp. almond extract	½ c. finely chopped almonds

Beat together butter, coffee powder, salt and almond extract. Gradually beat in sugar; beat until light and fluffy.

Stir in flour and chocolate pieces. Press batter into ungreased 15½ x 10½ x 1″ jelly roll pan. Sprinkle almonds over top.

Bake in moderate oven (375°) 23 to 25 minutes, or until golden brown. Set pan on rack; cut in 2½ x 1½″ bars while warm. When cool, remove from pan. Makes 40.

NOTE: If you want to break the cookies in irregular pieces, cool baked cookie dough in pan on rack, then break it in pieces with your fingers. Cookies are crisp.

CHOCOLATE CHIP BARS

Keep your cookie jar filled with these for a good hostess reputation

1 c. butter or regular margarine	2 c. sifted flour
1 c. light brown sugar, firmly packed	1 (6 oz.) pkg. semisweet chocolate pieces
1 tsp. vanilla	1 c. chopped pecans or walnuts
⅛ tsp. salt	

Beat butter with sugar until mixture is light and fluffy. Beat in vanilla.

Blend salt with flour and stir into beaten mixture, mixing well. Fold in chocolate pieces and nuts. Press into ungreased 15½ x 10½ x 1″ jelly roll pan.

Bake in moderate oven (350°) 20 minutes. While warm, cut in 2½ x 1½″ bars. Cool in pan on rack. Makes 3 dozen.

CHOCOLATE FUDGE COOKIES

There's a citrus tang in these rich bars fast-made with a cake mix

2 eggs
½ tsp. baking soda
½ c. melted butter
1 tblsp. grated orange peel
1 (about 19 oz.) pkg. devil's food
  cake mix

½ c. sifted flour
1 (6 oz.) pkg. semisweet
  chocolate pieces
⅔ c. chopped walnuts
Confectioners sugar

In a mixing bowl, beat eggs with baking soda. Beat in butter. Add orange peel, cake mix and flour. Stir until all ingredients are moistened (mixture will be stiff). Stir in chocolate pieces and nuts.

Turn batter into greased 15½ x 10½ x 1" jelly roll pan; spread dough evenly over bottom of pan using fork tines. Bake in moderate oven (350°) 12 to 13 minutes, or until toothpick inserted in center comes out clean. (Cookies will not appear to be done.) Place pan on rack to cool. While still warm, cut in 1½" squares; sift confectioners sugar generously over top. Makes about 5½ dozen.

CHOCOLATE MERINGUE BARS

This cookie has everything—eye and appetite appeal and fine flavor

¾ c. shortening
½ c. sugar
½ c. brown sugar, firmly packed
3 eggs, separated
1 tsp. vanilla
1 tsp. baking powder
¼ tsp. baking soda

¼ tsp. salt
2 c. sifted flour
1 (6 oz.) pkg. semisweet
  chocolate pieces
½ c. flaked coconut
½ c. chopped nuts
1 c. brown sugar, firmly packed

Beat together shortening, white sugar and ½ c. brown sugar until light and fluffy. Beat in egg yolks and vanilla to mix well.

Sift together baking powder, baking soda, salt and flour. Add to creamed mixture. Pat into greased 13 x 9 x 2" pan. Sprinkle top with chocolate pieces, coconut and nuts.

Beat egg whites until frothy; gradually add 1 c. brown sugar, beating constantly. Beat until stiff. Spread over cookie dough in pan.

Bake in moderate oven (375°) 25 to 30 minutes. Set pan on rack to cool, then cut in 3 x 1" bars. Makes about 3 dozen.

CHOCOLATE MOLASSES COOKIES

You mix these in a saucepan. Molasses gives the new flavor

½ c. butter or regular margarine
¼ c. molasses
¾ c. brown sugar, firmly packed
1 egg
1 c. sifted flour

½ tsp. salt
½ tsp. baking soda
1 (6 oz.) pkg. semisweet
 chocolate pieces

Heat butter and molasses. Add brown sugar; stir over low heat until sugar is melted. Cool.

Beat egg until light. Add to cooled molasses mixture.

Sift together flour, salt and baking soda. Add with chocolate pieces to molasses mixture. Mix well. Spread in greased 13 x 9 x 2″ pan.

Bake in moderate oven (350°) 20 minutes. Set pan on rack to cool. When cool, cut in 3 x 1″ bars. Makes 39.

CHOCOLATE/ORANGE BARS

Delicately spiced, orange-flavored bars with chocolate-nut topping

1 c. butter or regular margarine
1 c. light brown sugar, firmly
 packed
1 egg yolk
1 tblsp. grated orange peel
2½ c. sifted flour

⅛ tsp. salt
½ tsp. ground allspice
2 (6 oz.) pkgs. milk chocolate
 pieces
⅓ c. chopped walnuts

Beat butter, brown sugar and egg yolk until well blended. Beat in orange peel.

Sift together flour, salt and allspice. Stir into beaten mixture. Mix well. Spread batter in greased 13 x 9 x 2″ pan.

Bake in moderate oven (375°) 15 to 20 minutes, until browned. Remove from oven and top at once with milk chocolate pieces, spreading with spatula as they melt. Sprinkle with nuts. Cool in pan set on rack, then cut in 3 x 1″ bars. Makes 39.

CHOCOLATE/WALNUT COOKIES

Black walnuts lend flavor to these country-kitchen chocolate cookies

1 c. sugar	1 tsp. baking powder
2 eggs, well beaten	¼ tsp. salt
2 squares unsweetened chocolate	1 c. finely chopped black walnuts
½ c. butter or regular margarine	1 tsp. vanilla
1 c. sifted flour	Sifted confectioners sugar

Gradually add sugar to eggs. Melt chocolate with butter; stir into eggs.

Sift together flour, baking powder and salt. Add to first mixture with nuts and vanilla.

Bake in greased 15½ x 10½ x 1" jelly roll pan in moderate oven (350°) 12 to 15 minutes. Cool slightly in pan; dust with confectioners sugar. Cool completely in pan on rack; cut in diamonds, triangles or 1¾" bars. Makes about 7 dozen.

COCOA BARS

A cake-like bar with economical nut and cereal topping—good

2½ c. shortening	1 tblsp. vanilla
2½ c. sugar	2 tsp. salt
1 c. light corn syrup	2½ c. unsifted flour
8 eggs	1 c. chopped walnuts
1⅓ c. cocoa	1 c. oven-toasted rice cereal

Cream shortening and sugar until fluffy. Beat in corn syrup; beat in eggs, one at a time. Blend in cocoa. Add vanilla, salt and flour and blend.

Spread dough into two lightly greased 15½ x 10½ x 1" jelly roll pans (or three 13 x 9 x 2" pans). Combine nuts and cereal; sprinkle over dough.

Bake in moderate oven (350°) about 30 minutes. Cool in pans on racks, then cut in 3 x 1" bars. Makes about 8 dozen.

NOTE: Cereal topping may absorb moisture during storage. To restore crispness, open container of cookies 2 hours before serving.

FUDGE NUT BARS

Luscious fudge nut filling bakes between two layers of cookie mixture

1 c. butter or regular margarine
2 c. light brown sugar, firmly packed
2 eggs
2 tsp. vanilla
2½ c. sifted flour
1 tsp. baking soda
1 tsp. salt
3 c. quick-cooking rolled oats

1 (12 oz.) pkg. semisweet chocolate pieces
1 c. sweetened condensed milk, (not evaporated)
2 tblsp. butter or regular margarine
½ tsp. salt
1 c. chopped nuts
2 tsp. vanilla

Cream together 1 c. butter and sugar. Mix in eggs and 2 tsp. vanilla. Sift together flour, soda and 1 tsp. salt; stir in rolled oats. Add dry ingredients to creamed mixture. Set aside while you make filling.

In a saucepan over boiling water, mix together chocolate pieces, sweetened condensed milk, 2 tblsp. butter and ½ tsp. salt. Stir until chocolate pieces are melted and mixture is smooth. Remove from heat, and stir in nuts and 2 tsp. vanilla.

Spread about two-thirds of cookie dough in bottom of a greased 15½ x 10½ x 1" jelly roll pan. Cover with fudge filling. Dot with remainder of cookie dough and swirl it over fudge filling.

Bake in moderate oven (350°) 25 to 30 minutes, or until lightly browned. Cut in small (2 x 1") bars. Cool in pan on racks. Makes about 6 dozen.

HOSTESS BAR COOKIES

Tempting layered cookies with chocolate tops resemble candy bars

¾ c. butter
¾ c. sifted confectioners sugar
1 tsp. vanilla
1 tblsp. light or heavy cream
2 c. sifted flour
1 (6 oz.) pkg. butterscotch pieces
2 tblsp. light or heavy cream

¼ c. confectioners sugar
1 c. chopped pecans
½ c. semisweet chocolate pieces
2 tblsp. light or heavy cream
¼ c. confectioners sugar
1 tsp. vanilla

Combine butter, ¾ c. confectioners sugar, 1 tsp. vanilla, 1 tblsp. cream and flour in bowl; mix well to form dough. Pat into ungreased

13 x 9 x 2″ pan. Bake in slow oven (325°) 25 minutes. Set pan on rack to cool.

Meanwhile, melt butterscotch pieces in small saucepan over low heat, stirring constantly until smooth. Remove from heat; add 2 tblsp. cream and ¼ c. confectioners sugar and beat until smooth. Fold in pecans. Spread over baked cookie in pan.

Melt chocolate pieces over low heat, stirring constantly. Remove from heat; stir in 2 tblsp. cream, ¼ c. confectioners sugar and 1 tsp. vanilla. Spread on top of filling on cookies. Cut in 3 x 1½″ bars. Makes about 2 dozen.

INDIAN BARS

They're extra-moist chocolate brownies, and that means wonderful

1 c. butter or regular margarine	1½ c. sifted flour
2 squares unsweetened chocolate	1 tsp. baking powder
2 c. sugar	2 tsp. vanilla
4 eggs, slightly beaten	1 c. chopped pecans

Melt butter and chocolate over low heat. Add sugar and eggs, mix thoroughly.

Sift flour with baking powder; stir into creamed mixture. Mix in vanilla and nuts.

Bake in a greased 13 x 9 x 2″ pan in moderate oven (350°) 35 to 40 minutes. Cool completely in pan set on rack. Cut in 3 x 1½″ bars. Makes about 2 dozen.

NOTE: You can cut the recipe in half to make 12 cookie bars. Use an 8″ square pan for baking the cookie mixture.

MARBLEIZED SQUARES

Light brown and dark chocolate variegate attractive, crinkled tops

½ c. butter or regular margarine	1 c. sifted flour
6 tblsp. sugar	½ tsp. salt
6 tblsp. brown sugar, firmly packed	½ tsp. baking soda
	½ c. broken walnuts
1 egg	1 (6 oz.) pkg. semisweet
½ tsp. vanilla	chocolate pieces

Beat butter until light; add white and brown sugars and beat until light and fluffy. Beat in egg and vanilla to mix thoroughly.

Sift together flour, salt and baking soda, and add to first mixture. Stir in nuts. Spread in greased 13 x 9 x 2″ pan. Sprinkle chocolate pieces evenly over top.

Place in moderate oven (350°) 1 minute. Remove from oven and run a knife through dough to marbleize it. Return to oven and bake 12 to 14 minutes. Set pan on rack. When cool, cut in 2″ (about) squares. Makes 2 dozen.

OATMEAL/CHOCOLATE BARS

Thick chewy bars that carry well to picnics and other gatherings

1½ c. brown sugar, firmly packed	1 tsp. salt
¾ c. sugar	1½ tsp. ground cinnamon
1 c. shortening	¾ c. milk
3 eggs	4 c. quick-cooking rolled oats
1 tsp. vanilla	1 (12 oz.) pkg. semisweet
2¼ c. sifted flour	chocolate pieces
1 tsp. baking soda	

Cream sugars with shortening until light and fluffy. Beat in eggs and vanilla.

Sift together flour, soda, salt and cinnamon. Add to creamed mixture along with milk. Stir in oats and chocolate pieces.

Spread batter in greased 15½ x 10½ x 1″ jelly roll pan. Bake in moderate oven (350°) about 30 minutes. While warm, cut in 2 x 1″ bars, but cool completely in pan on rack. Makes about 6 dozen.

SEA FOAM COOKIES

They get their name from meringue top; excellent flavor combination

½ c. shortening	1 tsp. baking soda
½ c. sugar	½ tsp. salt
½ c. brown sugar, firmly packed	3 tblsp. milk
2 eggs, separated	1 (6 oz.) pkg. semisweet
1 tsp. vanilla	chocolate pieces
2 c. sifted flour	1 c. brown sugar, firmly packed
2 tsp. baking powder	¾ c. chopped salted peanuts

Cream shortening with sugar and ½ c. brown sugar until light and fluffy. Beat in egg yolks and vanilla.

Sift together flour, baking powder, soda and salt; stir into creamed mixture alternately with milk. (The dough will be stiff.) Press dough into greased 13 x 9 x 2" pan. Sprinkle evenly with chocolate pieces.

Beat egg whites until soft peaks form; gradually add remaining 1 c. brown sugar and beat, until very stiff and glossy. Spread over dough in pan. Scatter peanuts evenly over top.

Bake in slow oven (325°) 30 to 35 minutes. Cool in pan set on rack, then cut in 3 x 1" bars. Makes 39.

SPICY CHOCOLATE BARS

Chocolate, always good, is even better in this richly spiced cookie

1½ c. shortening	2 tsp. salt
1½ c. sugar	4 tsp. ground cinnamon
1½ c. brown sugar, firmly packed	1 tsp. ground cloves
4 eggs	1 tsp. ground nutmeg
2 tsp. vanilla	2 c. semisweet chocolate pieces
4 c. unsifted flour	(12 oz. pkg.)
2 tsp. baking soda	

Cream shortening and sugars until fluffy. Beat in eggs, one at a time. Add vanilla.

Blend in dry ingredients; add chocolate pieces. Spread evenly in two ungreased 15½ x 10½ x 1" jelly roll pans. Bake in moderate oven (375°) 20 minutes. Cut in 3 x 1" bars; cool in pans on racks. Makes about 8 dozen.

NOTE: Instead of adding chocolate pieces to the batter, you can sprinkle them over top of dough before baking. Cookies may also be baked in three 13 x 9 x 2" pans instead of the two jelly roll pans.

TOFFEE COOKIE SQUARES

Rich cookies that taste like toffee. Bake them for Christmas presents

½ c. butter or regular margarine	½ tsp. salt
½ c. shortening	2 c. sifted flour
1 c. brown sugar, firmly packed	1 (6 oz.) pkg. semisweet
1 egg yolk, unbeaten	chocolate pieces
1 tsp. vanilla	½ c. chopped nuts

Cream together butter, shortening, brown sugar and egg yolk. Stir in vanilla, salt and flour.

Pat mixture into lightly greased 15½ x 10½ x 1" jelly roll pan. Bake in slow oven (325°) 15 to 20 minutes.

Melt chocolate pieces; spread over warm baked mixture. Sprinkle with chopped nuts; cut in 2" squares while warm. Cool in pan on rack. Makes 3 dozen.

COCONUT/MOLASSES WUNDERBARS

A molasses/coconut candy, chocolate-coated, inspired this duplicate of the flavor combination in cookies—they're mighty good eating

½ c. butter or regular margarine
¾ c. brown sugar, firmly packed
¼ c. dark molasses
2 eggs
1 tsp. vanilla

1 c. sifted flour
¼ tsp. salt
1 c. flaked coconut
4 (¾ oz.) milk chocolate candy bars

Cream butter and brown sugar until light and fluffy. Beat in molasses, eggs and vanilla to mix well.

Mix flour and salt thoroughly; gradually stir into creamed mixture. Stir in coconut.

Spread in greased 9" square pan. Bake in moderate oven (350°) about 25 minutes, or until lightly browned. Remove from oven and set pan on rack. Immediately place chocolate candy, broken in pieces, over the top. When chocolate melts, spread it evenly over top.

Cool completely in pan, then cut in 1½" squares. Makes 3 dozen.

FILLED OATMEAL BARS

It's the taste of chocolate-coated raisins that makes these so good

1 (15 oz.) can sweetened condensed milk (not evaporated)
2 squares unsweetened chocolate
2 c. seedless raisins
1 c. butter or regular margarine

1⅓ c. brown sugar, firmly packed
1½ tsp. vanilla
2 c. sifted flour
¾ tsp. salt
½ tsp. baking soda
2½ c. quick-cooking rolled oats

Combine sweetened condensed milk and chocolate; heat over boiling water until chocolate melts, stirring occasionally. Remove from heat; stir in raisins. Set aside to cool slightly.

Beat butter until light; beat in brown sugar and vanilla until fluffy.

Sift together flour, salt and baking soda; add rolled oats. Mix with creamed mixture until crumbly.

Press half of dough evenly into ungreased 13 x 9 x 2″ pan. Cover with chocolate mixture. Sprinkle with remaining half of dough; press down slightly.

Bake in moderate oven (375°) about 25 minutes, or until golden brown. Set pan on rack to cool. Cut, while slightly warm, in 2 x 1″ bars. Makes about 4 dozen.

SPICY APPLE BARS

Cut cookies larger and serve warm with vanilla ice cream on top for a compliment-winning dessert

½ c. shortening	1 tsp. ground cinnamon
1 c. sugar	½ tsp. ground nutmeg
2 eggs	¼ tsp. ground cloves
1 c. sifted flour	1 c. quick-cooking rolled oats
1 tsp. baking powder	1½ c. diced peeled apples
½ tsp. baking soda	½ c. coarsely chopped walnuts
½ tsp. salt	Sifted confectioners sugar
1 tblsp. cocoa	

Cream together shortening and sugar until light and fluffy; beat in eggs, one at a time.

Sift together flour, baking powder, baking soda, salt, cocoa and spices; add to creamed mixture. Stir in rolled oats, apples and nuts. Spread in greased 13 x 9 x 2″ pan.

Bake in moderate oven (375°) about 25 minutes. Cool slightly in pan on rack; cut in 2 x 1½″ bars. Sprinkle with confectioners sugar. Makes about 2½ dozen.

APPLESAUCE FUDGIES

The applesauce keeps the cookies moist longer than most brownies

2 squares unsweetened chocolate	1 c. sifted flour
½ c. butter	½ tsp. baking powder
½ c. sweetened applesauce	¼ tsp. baking soda
2 eggs, beaten	¼ tsp. salt
1 c. brown sugar, firmly packed	½ c. chopped walnuts
1 tsp. vanilla	

Melt chocolate and butter together.

Mix applesauce, eggs, sugar and vanilla. Sift dry ingredients into applesauce mixture. Stir until blended; add chocolate and stir well.

Pour into greased 9″ square pan. Sprinkle with walnuts. Bake in moderate oven (350°) 30 minutes. Cut in 2¼″ squares and cool in pan on racks. Makes 16.

APRICOT BARS

Color-bright bits of apricot and fruity topping make these luscious

1 c. dried apricots	1 tsp. baking powder
1 c. boiling water	¾ tsp. salt
½ c. butter or regular margarine	2 tsp. orange juice
2 c. brown sugar, firmly packed	2 tsp. lemon juice
2 eggs	1 tsp. grated orange peel
1 tsp. vanilla	2 tsp. soft butter
1 tsp. grated orange peel	1 c. sifted confectioners sugar
1¾ c. sifted flour	½ c. chopped walnuts

Put apricots in small bowl; pour on boiling water. Let stand 5 minutes. Then drain and cut in small bits with kitchen scissors.

Cream together ½ c. butter and brown sugar until light and fluffy; beat in eggs, vanilla and 1 tsp. orange peel.

Sift together flour, baking powder and salt; blend into creamed mixture. Stir in apricots.

Spread in greased 15½ x 10½ x 1″ jelly roll pan and bake in moderate oven (350°) about 20 minutes. Let cool in pan set on rack 10 minutes.

Meanwhile, blend orange and lemon juices, 1 tsp. orange peel, 2 tsp. butter and confectioners sugar, beating until smooth. Spread on cookies that have cooled 10 minutes in pan. Sprinkle with walnuts, pressing them in lightly so they will adhere to cookies. Complete cooling, then cut in 2¼ x 1¼″ bars. Makes about 56.

LUSCIOUS APRICOT BARS

Tang of apricots makes these special

⅔ c. dried apricots	½ tsp. baking powder
½ c. butter	¼ tsp. salt
¼ c. sugar	½ tsp. vanilla
1⅓ c. sifted flour	½ c. chopped almonds
1 c. brown sugar, firmly packed	Confectioners sugar (optional)
2 eggs, well beaten	

Rinse apricots; cover with water and simmer 10 minutes. Drain, cool and chop.

Combine butter, white sugar and 1 c. flour; mix until crumbly. Pack into greased 9″ square pan. Bake in moderate oven (375°) 20 minutes.

Gradually beat brown sugar into eggs. Sift together remaining flour, baking powder and salt. Add to egg mixture; mix well. Add vanilla, ¼ c. almonds and apricots. Spread on baked layer. Sprinkle with remaining nuts.

Bake in moderate oven (350°) about 20 minutes. Cool in pan on rack. Cut in 1½″ squares. If you wish, sprinkle lightly with confectioners sugar. Makes 2½ dozen.

CRAN/APRICOT SCOTCHIES

Red filling has luscious tang, contrasts beautifully with snowy coating

1 c. apricot pulp (cooked dried apricots put through food mill), or drained and strained canned apricots	2 tsp. butter
	1½ c. brown sugar, firmly packed
	¾ c. butter or regular margarine
	2 eggs
½ c. cooked or canned whole cranberry sauce	1 c. flaked coconut
	3¾ c. sifted flour
½ c. sugar	2 tsp. cream of tartar
1 tblsp. flour	1 tsp. baking soda
1 tblsp. lemon juice	1 tsp. salt
2 tblsp. orange juice	Confectioners sugar (for coating)

Combine apricot pulp, cranberry sauce, sugar mixed with 1 tblsp. flour, lemon and orange juices and 2 tsp. butter in saucepan. Bring to a boil, stirring constantly. Reduce heat and simmer, stirring constantly, 5 minutes. Set filling aside to cool before using.

Cream together brown sugar and ¾ c. butter until light and fluffy. Beat in eggs. Add coconut; stir to mix.

Sift together flour, cream of tartar, baking soda and salt; stir into creamed mixture. Pat half of mixture into greased 13 x 9 x 2" pan.

Spoon cooled filling evenly over dough in pan. Sprinkle remaining half of dough over top (it will be crumbly, but will spread and cover during baking).

Bake in moderate oven (350°) 30 minutes. Cool in pan on rack. Cut in 3 x 1" bars and roll in confectioners sugar. Makes about 3 dozen.

NOTE: The filling is rather soft when cookies come from oven, but it firms when cooled completely. If you want to serve cookies before thorough cooling, use 1½ tblsp. flour instead of 1 tblsp. to thicken filling.

CHERRY/WALNUT BARS

Pink-frosted cookies with shortbread base, rich candy-like topping

2¼ c. sifted flour	½ tsp. vanilla
½ c. sugar	1 (2 oz.) jar maraschino cherries
1 c. butter	½ c. chopped walnuts
2 eggs	1 tblsp. softened butter
1 c. brown sugar, firmly packed	1 c. confectioners sugar
½ tsp. salt	½ c. flaked coconut (optional)
½ tsp. baking powder	

Mix flour, sugar and 1 c. butter until crumbly. Press into ungreased 13 x 9 x 2" pan. Bake in moderate oven (350°) 20 minutes, or until crust is lightly browned.

Blend together eggs, brown sugar, salt, baking powder and vanilla.

Drain and chop cherries, reserving liquid. Stir chopped cherries and walnuts into blended mixture. Spread on top of baked crust. Return to oven and bake 25 minutes. Remove from oven; cool in pan on rack.

Combine softened butter and confectioners sugar with enough reserved cherry liquid to spread. Spread on cookies; sprinkle with coconut, if you wish. When icing has set, cut in 2 x 1" bars. Makes 48.

MARSHMALLOW/CHERRY BARS

Tall, dainty-pink marshmallow topping with dots of red cherries

¾ c. butter or regular margarine
⅓ c. brown sugar, firmly packed
1½ c. sifted flour
2 envelopes unflavored gelatin
½ c. cold water
2 c. sugar

½ c. cherry juice and water
1 (8 oz.) jar maraschino cherries,
 drained and chopped
½ c. chopped almonds
3 drops red food color
½ tsp. almond extract

Combine butter, brown sugar and flour; mix well and press into ungreased 13 x 9 x 2″ pan. Bake in slow oven (325°) 30 minutes. Set aside to cool.

Soften gelatin in ½ c. water.

Combine white sugar and juice drained from cherries (with enough water added to make ½ c.). Bring to a boil over medium heat and boil 2 minutes. Remove from heat and stir in softened gelatin. Beat with electric mixer at medium speed until very stiff, about 20 minutes (mixture climbs beaters as it thickens).

Fold in cherries and almonds. Add food color and almond extract. Spread on top of baked crust in pan. Let stand at room temperature until topping sets. Cut in 2 x 1″ bars. Cover pan with lid or foil and leave in a cool place until time to serve. Makes about 48.

HERMITS—SEA-VOYAGE COOKIES

You don't have to tax your imagination to appreciate how marvelous New England Hermits tasted to men at sea. Canisters, lovingly filled and tucked into chests, went on clipper ships from Massachusetts to many faraway places. Eyes brightened when the cookies appeared, for they brought remembrances of home. Good travelers and keepers.

These hearty American cookies, spiced and fruited, never went out of style. Good today served with hot coffee. Our recipe comes from Cape Cod.

NEW ENGLAND HERMITS

Roll cookies in confectioners sugar for a homey, quick dress-up

½ c. butter	1 tsp. ground cinnamon
½ c. sugar	½ tsp. ground cloves
2 eggs	¼ tsp. ground nutmeg
½ c. molasses	⅛ tsp. ground allspice
2 c. sifted flour	3 tblsp. chopped citron
½ tsp. salt	½ c. chopped raisins
¾ tsp. baking soda	½ c. currants
¾ tsp. cream of tartar	¼ c. chopped walnuts

Cream butter with sugar until light and fluffy. Beat in eggs and molasses.

Sift together flour, salt, baking soda, cream of tartar and spices; stir into creamed mixture. Stir in citron, raisins, currants and nuts.

Spread batter evenly in greased 13 x 9 x 2″ pan. Bake in moderate oven (350°) about 20 minutes, or until done. (Touch lightly with fingertip. If no imprint remains, cookies are done.)

Set pan on rack to cool, cutting in 3 x 1″ bars while slightly warm. Cool completely before removing from pan. Makes 39.

TEATIME CURRANT COOKIES

Remember how Grandma's currant teacakes tasted? Moist, tender!

1 c. dried currants	1¾ c. sifted flour
1 c. water	¼ tsp. salt
½ c. salad oil	1 tsp. baking soda
1 egg	½ c. chopped pecans
1 c. sugar	1 c. sifted confectioners sugar

Place currants and water in 1-qt. saucepan; bring to a boil. Remove from heat, add salad oil and let cool.

Beat egg slightly; gradually add sugar, beating until thoroughly mixed. Beat in thoroughly cooled currant mixture.

Sift flour, salt and baking soda together and add to currant mixture. Stir in nuts.

Spread in greased 13 x 9 x 2″ pan; bake in moderate oven (375°) 20 minutes (test for doneness with a wooden toothpick). Remove from oven and set pan on rack to cool 10 minutes. Cut in 2¼ x 1″

bars (about) and roll in confectioners sugar. Cool completely on racks. Makes 4 dozen.

CHINESE CHEWS

Distinctive, marvelous in taste and good keepers if you hide them

1 c. sugar	1 c. chopped pitted dates
¾ c. sifted flour	1 c. chopped nuts
1 tsp. baking powder	2 eggs, beaten
¼ tsp. salt	Confectioners sugar

Sift sugar, flour, baking powder and salt into bowl. Stir in dates and nuts.

Add eggs; mix thoroughly. Spread in greased 15½ x 10½ x 1″ jelly roll pan. Bake in moderate oven (375°) about 20 minutes.

Cut in 2 x 1″ bars while warm; sprinkle lightly with confectioners sugar. Cool in pan set on rack. Makes about 6 dozen.

DATE-FILLED OAT COOKIES

Lemon peel and spices give tantalizing fragrance, distinctive taste

1 c. chopped dates	¾ tsp. ground cinnamon
½ c. sugar	½ c. light brown sugar, firmly
¼ c. orange juice	packed
½ c. water	1 tsp. grated lemon peel
1 c. sifted flour	½ c. butter or regular margarine
¼ tsp. salt	¼ c. milk
¼ tsp. baking soda	1½ c. quick-cooking rolled oats
¼ tsp. ground nutmeg	

Combine dates, sugar, orange juice and water in small saucepan. Cook, stirring, until thick; set aside to cool. You'll have about 1¾ c. filling.

Sift together flour, salt, baking soda, nutmeg and cinnamon. Add brown sugar and lemon peel, blending well. Blend in butter with pastry blender, as for pie crust. Add milk; stir in rolled oats.

Spread half of dough in greased 8″ square pan. Spread date filling evenly over top.

Roll remaining half of dough between sheets of waxed paper into an 8″ square to fit pan. Fit dough over filling.

Bake in moderate oven (350°) 25 to 30 minutes. Cool in pan set on rack. Cut in bars about 2½ x 1". Makes 2 dozen.

DATE/NUT BARS

These cake-like cookies and coffee make great evening refreshments

1 c. sifted confectioners sugar
1 tblsp. oil
2 eggs, beaten
¼ c. sifted cake flour
¼ tsp. salt

½ tsp. baking powder
¾ c. chopped nuts
1 c. chopped dates
1 tsp. vanilla
Confectioners sugar (for tops)

Add 1 c. confectioners sugar and oil to eggs; blend well.

Add sifted dry ingredients. Stir in nuts, dates and vanilla.

Pour into greased 9" square pan. Bake in slow oven (325°) 25 minutes. Cool slightly in pan on rack. Cut in 3 x 1" bars; sprinkle with confectioners sugar. Makes 27.

DATE SANDWICH BARS

Easy to tote when you're asked to bring cookies. They'll win praise

¼ c. sugar
3 c. cut-up dates
1½ c. water
¾ c. soft butter or regular
  margarine

1 c. brown sugar, firmly packed
1¾ c. sifted flour
½ tsp. baking soda
1 tsp. salt
1½ c. quick-cooking rolled oats

Mix sugar, dates and water, and cook over low heat until mixture thickens. Stir to prevent scorching. Set aside to cool.

Thoroughly mix butter and brown sugar. Beat until fluffy.

Stir flour, baking soda and salt together. Stir into the brown sugar-butter mixture. Add rolled oats and mix well. Divide in half and spread one part into greased 13 x 9 x 2" pan. Flatten and press it down with hands so the mixture will cover the bottom of the pan.

Spread the cooled date mixture on top. Sprinkle evenly with the second half of the rolled oat mixture. Pat it down lightly with hands.

Bake in hot oven (400°) 25 to 30 minutes, or until a delicate brown. Remove from oven; while warm, cut in 2 x 1½" bars. Remove bars at once from pan to racks to finish cooling. Makes about 30.

FRENCH BARS

Delicate as spice cake. Dress up cookies with Orange Butter Frosting

2¼ c. brown sugar, firmly packed
4 eggs, well beaten
1½ c. soured evaporated milk
 (see Note)
1½ tsp. baking soda
2¼ c. unsifted flour
1 tsp. ground cinnamon

½ tsp. salt
1½ c. chopped walnuts
1½ c. cut-up dates
1 c. toasted flaked coconut
Orange Butter Frosting (recipe
 follows)

Add sugar to eggs and beat until thick. Stir in soured evaporated milk.

Blend in dry ingredients. Stir in nuts, dates and coconut. Do not overmix batter.

Spread dough evenly in two lightly greased 15½ x 10½ x 1" jelly roll pans (or three 13 x 9 x 2" pans). Bake in moderate oven (350°) about 20 minutes. Cool in pans on racks. Frost if desired, and cut in 2½ x 1" bars. Makes 80.

N O T E : To sour evaporated milk, pour 1½ tblsp. vinegar into a 2-cup measure. Add evaporated milk until measurement is 1½ c. Stir well and set aside a few minutes before using.
Orange Butter Frosting: Combine 1 lb. confectioners sugar, sifted, with ¼ c. butter, ¼ c. orange juice, ½ tsp. salt and 1 tsp. grated orange peel. Beat until creamy. Spread on cooled bars. (Let frosting set before cutting cookies).

NUT AND FRUIT BARS

It's wonderful how fast these date cookies sell at Christmas bazaars

3 eggs
1 tsp. vanilla
1 c. sugar
1 c. sifted flour
½ tsp. salt
1 tsp. baking powder

1 c. chopped walnuts
1 (8 oz.) pkg. pitted dates
1 (6 oz.) jar maraschino
 cherries, drained
Confectioners sugar

Combine eggs and vanilla. Beat well. Add sugar and flour sifted with salt and baking powder; blend well. Stir in nuts and fruits.

Bake in greased 15½ x 10½ x 1" jelly roll pan in moderate oven

(350°) 30 minutes. Cool in pan on rack. Cut in 2″ squares. Sprinkle with confectioners sugar. Store in airtight box. Makes 3 dozen.

ORANGE/DATE BARS

These are "candy cookies"; roll moist bars in confectioners sugar

½ lb. pitted dates
2 tblsp. flour
1 c. water
¾ c. shortening
1 c. brown sugar, firmly packed
1 tsp. vanilla
2 eggs

1 tsp. baking soda
1¾ c. sifted flour
½ tsp. salt
½ c. chopped nuts (optional)
1 (16 oz.) pkg. candy orange
  slices (gumdrops)

Put dates, 2 tblsp. flour and water in small saucepan. Bring to a boil and cook until mixture is thick. Set aside to cool.

Cream shortening, brown sugar and vanilla until light and fluffy. Beat in eggs.

Sift together baking soda, 1¾ c. flour and salt; add to creamed mixture. Stir in nuts. Spread half of dough in bottom of greased 13 x 9 x 2″ pan.

Cut candy orange slices in lengthwise thirds; cover dough in pan with candy arranged in straight rows crosswise in pan. Spread cooled date mixture on top of orange slices. Carefully top with remaining half of dough.

Bake in moderate oven (350°) 40 minutes. Cool in pan on rack, then cut between orange slices to make bars about 2 x 1″. Makes about 4 dozen.

ORANGE/DATE DAINTIES

Orange/date flavors blend and lift these out of the commonplace

1 c. finely cut dates
1 c. orange juice
2 tsp. grated orange peel
¼ c. regular margarine
½ c. sugar
1 egg

1 c. sifted cake flour
¼ tsp. baking soda
½ tsp. baking powder
⅛ tsp. salt
¼ c. orange juice
¾ c. crushed corn flakes

Combine dates and 1 c. orange juice in heavy pan. Cook over low heat, stirring, until mixture is thick and smooth. Cool slightly; stir in orange peel and set aside.

Beat together margarine and sugar until light and fluffy. Beat in egg to blend well.

Sift together cake flour, baking soda, baking powder and salt. Add alternately with ¼ c. orange juice to beaten mixture, beating after each addition.

Spread batter in lightly greased 15½ x 10½ x 1″ jelly roll pan. Top batter with reserved orange-date mixture, spreading evenly. Sprinkle corn flakes over the top.

Bake in moderate oven (375°) about 25 minutes. Set pan on rack; while still hot, cut in 2″ squares. Makes about 40.

TREASURE BARS

Nuts, coconut, dates or chocolate are the hidden treasure in these

1 c. sifted flour	½ tsp. baking powder
½ c. brown sugar, firmly packed	¼ tsp. salt
½ c. butter	1 c. chopped walnuts
2 eggs	1 c. shredded coconut
1 c. brown sugar, firmly packed	½ c. chopped dates or semisweet
1 tsp. vanilla	chocolate pieces
1 tblsp. flour	

Combine 1 c. flour and ½ c. brown sugar; cut in butter. Press into greased 13 x 9 x 2″ pan. Bake in moderate oven (350°) 12 minutes. Cool on rack 5 minutes.

Meanwhile, beat eggs slightly. Add 1 c. brown sugar gradually, beating until light and fluffy. Blend in vanilla.

Sift together 1 tblsp. flour, baking powder and salt. Stir into egg mixture. Stir in nuts, coconut and dates. Spread over baked crust. Return to oven and bake 25 minutes. Cool in pan on rack, then cut in 2½ x 1½″ bars. Makes about 2½ dozen.

CALIFORNIA LEMON BARS

Hostess favorite—rich cookies, great with beverages and ice cream

1 c. sifted flour	2 tblsp. flour
½ c. butter or regular margarine	1½ c. confectioners sugar
¼ c. confectioners sugar	1 tsp. vanilla
2 eggs, beaten	2 tblsp. melted butter or
1 c. sugar	margarine
½ tsp. baking powder	1 tblsp. milk (about)
2 tblsp. lemon juice	

Blend 1 c. flour, ½ c. butter and ¼ c. confectioners sugar as for pastry. Press into ungreased 8″ square pan. Bake in moderate oven (350°) 20 minutes.

Combine eggs, sugar, baking powder, lemon juice and 2 tblsp. flour. Pour onto baked bottom layer and bake in moderate oven (350°) 25 minutes. Cool slightly in pan.

Combine 1½ c. confectioners sugar, vanilla, 2 tblsp. butter and enough milk to make mixture of spreading consistency. Spread on top of baked cookies in pan. Cool in pan on rack, then cut in 2½ x 1¼″ bars. Makes 1½ dozen.

LEMON MERINGUE BARS

These cookies taste like lemon meringue pie—and that's good!

½ c. butter or regular margarine	2 tsp. finely grated lemon peel
½ c. sifted confectioners sugar	½ c. sugar
2 eggs, separated	½ c. chopped walnuts
1 c. sifted flour	16 walnut halves
¼ tsp. salt	

Cream butter until light and fluffy. Gradually beat in confectioners sugar. Beat in egg yolks to blend.

Combine flour and salt; sift into egg yolk mixture. Stir in lemon peel. Spread evenly in greased 8″ square pan.

Bake in moderate oven (350°) about 10 minutes, until lightly browned. Remove from oven. Set oven regulator to hot (400°).

Beat egg whites until they form stiff moist peaks; gradually beat in ½ c. sugar, blending well. Stir in chopped nuts. Spread meringue evenly over baked layer. Return to hot oven (400°) and bake about

5 to 7 minutes, until lightly browned. Remove from oven and partially cool in pan set on wire rack. Cut in 2″ squares and top each square with a walnut half. Makes 16.

LEMON/COCONUT SQUARES

Delicate texture, fresh lemon flavor make these cookies special

Cookie Dough:
1½ c. sifted flour   ½ c. butter or regular margarine
½ c. brown sugar, firmly packed

Filling:
2 eggs, beaten   2 tblsp. flour
1 c. brown sugar, firmly packed   ½ tsp. baking powder
1½ c. flaked or shredded coconut   ¼ tsp. salt
1 c. chopped nuts   ½ tsp. vanilla

Frosting:
1 c. confectioners sugar   Juice of 1 lemon
1 tblsp. melted butter or regular
   margarine

Mix together ingredients for cookie dough; pat down well in buttered 13 x 9 x 2″ pan. Bake in very slow oven (275°) 10 minutes.

To make filling, combine eggs, sugar, coconut, nuts, flour, baking powder, salt and vanilla. Spread on top of baked mixture. Bake in moderate oven (350°) 20 minutes.

While still warm, spread with frosting made by combining confectioners sugar, melted butter and lemon juice. Cool slightly; cut in 2″ squares. Complete cooling in pan on racks. Makes about 24.

LEMON LOVE NOTES

Snowy confectioners sugar coating contributes to the cookies' charms

½ c. butter   ½ tsp. baking powder
1 c. sifted flour   2 eggs, beaten
¼ c. confectioners sugar   2 tblsp. lemon juice
1 c. sugar   2 tsp. grated lemon peel
2 tblsp. flour

Mix butter, 1 c. flour and confectioners sugar. Press into an ungreased 8″ square pan. Bake in moderate oven (350°) 8 minutes or until golden. Cool in pan on rack.

Combine sugar, 2 tblsp. flour and baking powder. Add eggs, lemon juice and peel. Mix well. Pour evenly over baked, cooled mixture in pan.

Bake in moderate oven (350°) 25 minutes. (Top puffs up in baking, but falls in cooling.) Cool in pan on rack and cut in 2″ squares. Sprinkle with confectioners sugar, if desired. Makes 16.

COFFEE COOKIE BARS

A hearty cookie, moist and tasty—a fine coffee accompaniment

1 c. brown sugar, firmly packed	½ tsp. baking soda
¼ c. shortening	½ tsp. salt
1 egg	½ c. hot, strong coffee
1 tsp. vanilla	½ c. raisins
1½ c. sifted flour	½ c. chopped nuts
½ tsp. ground cinnamon	Caramel Icing (recipe follows)
½ tsp. baking powder	

Cream sugar and shortening until light and fluffy. Beat in egg and vanilla.

Sift together flour, cinnamon, baking powder, baking soda and salt, and add alternately with hot coffee to creamed mixture. Stir in raisins and nuts.

Spread dough in greased 13 x 9 x 2″ pan. Bake in moderate oven (350°) 25 minutes. While hot, spread with Caramel Icing. Set pan on rack to cool, then cut in 2 x 1″ bars. Makes about 4 dozen.

Caramel Icing: Combine 3 tblsp. brown sugar, firmly packed, 3 tblsp. butter and 1 tblsp. dairy half-and-half, light cream or milk in 1-qt. saucepan. Bring to a boil. Remove from heat and gradually add 1 c. sifted confectioners sugar, beating constantly. If icing is not smooth, place over low heat, stirring constantly, until lumps of sugar disappear. Makes enough to ice cookies baked in a 13 x 9 x 2″ pan.

FRUIT BARS

Excellent cookies to mail for gifts—they're good keepers

2 c. seedless raisins	1 c. sugar
1½ c. chopped mixed candied fruit	1 c. brown sugar, firmly packed
1 c. chopped walnuts	2 eggs, beaten
½ c. orange or pineapple juice	4½ c. sifted flour
2 tsp. vanilla	2 tsp. ground cinnamon
1 c. butter or regular margarine	2 tsp. baking powder
	1 tsp. baking soda

Rinse raisins in hot water, drain; dry on towel.

Combine raisins, candied fruit, nuts, juice and vanilla; let stand.

Cream together butter, sugars and eggs. Sift together dry ingredients and add in thirds to creamed mixture; mix until smooth. Add fruit mixture; blend well. Let stand 1½ hours in refrigerator, or overnight.

When ready to bake, spread dough in greased 15½ x 10½ x 1″ jelly roll pan. Bake in hot oven (400°) 15 to 20 minutes, until lightly browned. Cool in pan set on rack. When cool, cut in bars about 3 x 1″. Makes about 4 dozen.

RAISIN-FILLED BARS

Cooked raisin filling produces cookies that are good—like raisin pie

2 c. raisins	1½ c. quick-cooking or regular rolled oats
1⅓ c. water	
3 tblsp. cornstarch	1 c. melted butter or regular margarine
2 tblsp. cold water	
1 c. sugar	1½ c. sifted flour
1 tsp. vanilla	1 tsp. baking soda
1 c. brown sugar, firmly packed	½ tsp. salt
	1 c. chopped nuts

To make filling, cook raisins in 1⅓ c. water until tender. Dissolve cornstarch in 2 tblsp. cold water. Add sugar and cornstarch to raisins; stir until mixture thickens. Remove from heat, add vanilla and set aside to cool.

Add brown sugar and oats to melted butter; mix well.

Sift together flour, soda and salt; add to sugar-butter mixture. Stir in nuts. Pack half of mixture into bottom of greased 9″ square pan. Spread raisin filling evenly on top. Then top with remaining crumb mixture.

Bake in moderate oven (350°) 30 minutes. Set pan on rack to cool 10 minutes, or cool completely, then cut in 3 x 1″ bars. Makes about 27.

FAVORITE HONEY BARS

These chewy cookies are good. Play smart and double the recipe

½ c. shortening	½ tsp. baking powder
½ c. sugar	¼ tsp. salt
½ c. honey	1 c. quick-cooking rolled oats
1 egg, well beaten	1 c. flaked coconut
⅔ c. sifted flour	1 tsp. vanilla
½ tsp. baking soda	½ c. chopped nuts

Cream shortening, sugar and honey until light and fluffy. Add egg and blend.

Sift flour with soda, baking powder and salt; add to creamed mixture. Add oats, coconut, vanilla and nuts.

Spread in greased 15½ x 10½ x 1″ jelly roll pan; bake in moderate oven (350°) 20 to 25 minutes. Cool in pan on rack. When cool, cut in 2½ x 1½″ bars. Makes about 3 dozen.

N O T E : To trim, sprinkle confectioners sugar over tops of bars before serving.

HONEY/ALMOND TRIANGLES

A honey-almond topping bakes right on these rich, tasty cookies

½ c. butter	1¾ c. sifted flour
¼ c. sugar	½ c. sugar
2 tblsp. honey	2 tsp. baking powder
2 tblsp. milk	¼ tsp. salt
1 c. chopped, slivered or sliced almonds	½ c. butter
1 tsp. almond extract	1 egg

In saucepan combine ½ c. butter, ¼ c. sugar, honey, milk, almonds and almond extract. Bring to a full rolling boil, stirring constantly. Set aside to cool slightly.

Sift together flour, ½ c. sugar, baking powder and salt. With pastry blender, cut in ½ c. butter until particles are very fine.

Beat egg with a fork until blended; add to crumb mixture, tossing with a fork to mix. Gather dough and work with hands until mixture holds together. With lightly floured fingertips, press evenly over bottom of lightly greased 15½ x 10½ x 1″ jelly roll pan.

Pour honey-almond topping over dough and spread evenly. Bake in moderate oven (350°) 20 to 25 minutes, or until a deep golden color. Place pan on rack at least 10 minutes, or until cool. Cut in 2½″ squares, then cut each square diagonally to make triangles. Makes 4 dozen.

HONEYED LEMON SLICES

Honey and lemon blend their flavors in these superlative cookie bars

1 c. brown sugar, firmly packed	1 c. honey
2 c. sifted flour	2 tblsp. butter
½ c. butter or regular margarine	¼ c. lemon juice
1 c. cookie coconut	3 eggs, beaten

Blend together brown sugar, flour, ½ c. butter and coconut. Pat two-thirds of mixture into ungreased 9″ square pan.

In small saucepan, cook together honey, 2 tblsp. butter, lemon juice and eggs, stirring constantly, until mixture thickens. Cool and spread over mixture in pan. Sprinkle remainder of brown sugar mixture over top.

Bake in moderate oven (350°) 40 minutes. Cut in 1½″ squares and cool in pan on rack. Makes about 3 dozen.

LEBKUCHEN

Spicy German Christmas cookies with glazed tops—good keepers

¾ c. honey	1 tsp. ground cinnamon
¾ c. sugar	1 tsp. ground allspice
1 large egg	¼ tsp. ground cloves
1 tsp. grated lemon peel	⅓ c. chopped citron
1 tblsp. milk	½ c. chopped blanched almonds
2¾ c. sifted flour	1 c. sifted confectioners sugar
½ tsp. salt	4 tsp. water (about)

In large saucepan heat honey slightly, but do not boil. Remove from heat and stir in sugar. Beat in egg, then add lemon peel and milk.

Sift together flour, salt, cinnamon, allspice and cloves. Stir, a little at a time, into honey mixture. Stir in citron and almonds. Form dough into a ball; wrap in waxed paper and chill several hours or overnight.

Divide dough in half and let stand 15 to 20 minutes to warm slightly to make spreading in pans easier. Spread each half in a greased 13 x 9 x 2" pan (use a metal spoon moistened in water to spread dough).

Bake pans of dough separately in hot oven (400°) about 15 minutes, or until lightly browned. (Or test for doneness by touching lightly with fingertip. If no imprint remains, cookies are done.)

Place pans on cooling racks and brush cookie tops at once with confectioners sugar mixed with enough water to make a smooth icing. While still warm, cut in 3 x 1" bars or diamond shapes; remove from pans to cool on racks. When cool, store cookies in airtight containers. They will keep several weeks. Four or five days before serving, a cut apple or orange placed in canisters mellows and improves flavor of cookies. Makes about 6 dozen.

ENGLISH TEA SQUARES

Jam-filled bars are all-purpose cookies—serve with tea or coffee

¾ c. butter or regular margarine	¼ tsp. ground allspice
1 c. sugar	1 c. chopped almonds or walnuts
1 egg	½ c. strawberry jam
1 tsp. vanilla	3 tblsp. confectioners sugar
2 c. sifted flour	

Beat butter until light; add sugar and beat until light and fluffy. Beat in egg and vanilla to blend well. Stir in flour, allspice and almonds.

Spoon about half of mixture into lightly greased 9" square pan. Carefully spread strawberry jam over top. Top with remaining dough.

Bake in moderate oven (350°) 40 to 45 minutes, or until delicately browned. Remove to cooling rack and sift confectioners sugar over top. When cool, cut in 1½" squares. Makes 3 dozen.

JINGLE JAM BARS

You bake cake-like batter on berry jam and cut it in luscious ribbons

¼ c. butter	¾ c. sifted cake flour
1 c. red raspberry jam	1 tsp. baking powder
4 eggs	1 tsp. salt
¾ c. sugar	Confectioners sugar
1 tsp. vanilla	

Melt butter in 15½ x 10½ x 1" jelly roll pan. Mix jam with butter and spread evenly over bottom of pan.

Beat eggs until thick and lemon colored. Add sugar, 1 tblsp. at a time, beating after each addition. Add vanilla.

Sift together remaining dry ingredients and fold into egg mixture in 2 parts. Spread batter evenly over jam mixture in pan. Bake in hot oven (400°) 15 to 18 minutes. Remove from oven and let stand in pan for 5 minutes.

Then invert pan on sheet of wrapping paper or towel lightly dusted with confectioners sugar. Let stand 2 or 3 minutes. Then lift pan gradually, allowing cake to fall out slowly. Assist carefully with spatula, if necessary.

Cut cake crosswise in two equal pieces. Invert one piece over the other so that jam edges are together. Use paper to assist in turning one piece over the other. Cut in 2½ x 1½" bars. Cool on racks. Makes 20.

N O T E : You can use strawberry, apricot or other jam instead of raspberry.

MARMALADE BARS

If you're looking for a superb go-with for tea or coffee, here it is

1 c. orange marmalade	1½ c. sifted flour
½ c. chopped pecans	1 tsp. baking powder
½ c. flaked coconut	¼ tsp. baking soda
½ c. regular margarine	¼ tsp. salt
1 c. brown sugar, firmly packed	1 c. quick-cooking rolled oats
1 egg	Orange Confectioners Frosting
2 tblsp. orange juice	(recipe follows)

Combine marmalade, pecans and coconut. Set aside.

Beat margarine and brown sugar until light and fluffy. Beat in egg and orange juice to mix well.

Sift together flour, baking powder, soda and salt. Add to beaten mixture. Fold in rolled oats. Spread half of dough into well-greased 13 x 9 x 2" pan. Drop teaspoonfuls of marmalade mixture over dough and spread evenly to cover. Drop remaining half of dough over top. Carefully spread over filling.

Bake in moderate oven (350°) 35 to 38 minutes. While warm, frost with Orange Confectioners Frosting. Cool in pan set on rack, then cut in 3 x 1" bars. Makes 39.

Orange Confectioners Frosting: Combine 2 tblsp. soft margarine, 1½ c. sifted confectioners sugar and 2 to 3 tblsp. orange juice (or enough to make a frosting of spreading consistency). Beat until smooth.

SWEDISH ALMOND SHORTBREAD

A crisp bar, subtly flavored with toasted almonds; sugar-sprinkled

2 c. butter
1 c. sugar
6 c. unsifted flour
1 tblsp. vanilla

½ tsp. salt
1 c. toasted slivered almonds
Sugar (for top)

Cream butter and sugar until fluffy. Work in flour, vanilla and salt. Roll out dough to fit two ungreased 15½ x 10½ x 1" jelly roll pans (or three 13 x 9 x 2" pans).

Sprinkle with almonds and sugar. Cut unbaked dough in 2½ x 1½" bars. Bake in moderate oven (350°) about 15 minutes. Immediately recut bars along same lines. Cool in pans on racks. Makes 80.

BRAZIL NUT BARS

Distinctive holiday cookies with a rich, nutty flavor—try them

2 c. sifted flour
2 tsp. baking powder
¾ tsp. salt
½ tsp. ground cinnamon
½ c. shortening
⅓ c. butter or regular margarine

1 c. light brown sugar, firmly
  packed
2 eggs, beaten
1 tsp. vanilla
1 c. thinly sliced or chopped
  Brazil nuts
1 egg white

Sift together flour, baking powder, salt and cinnamon.

Cream together shortening, butter and brown sugar until light and fluffy. Add eggs and vanilla; beat until light. Add sifted dry ingredients and half of nuts. Spread in greased 15½ x 10½ x 1" jelly roll pan, or two 8" square pans.

Beat egg white slightly. Brush over dough; sprinkle with remaining nuts. Bake in moderate oven (350°) 20 to 30 minutes. Cut in 2 x 1" bars. Cool in pans on racks. Makes about 6 dozen.

BROWN SUGAR CHEWS

No-fat cookies have crisp crust, and chewy, sweet walnut centers

1 egg	¼ tsp. salt
1 c. brown sugar, firmly packed	¼ tsp. baking soda
1 tsp. vanilla	1 c. chopped walnuts
½ c. sifted flour	

Combine egg, brown sugar and vanilla. Mix thoroughly.

Sift together flour, salt and baking soda; stir into brown sugar mixture, then stir in nuts.

Spread in greased 8" square pan. Bake in moderate oven (350°) 15 to 18 minutes. Cool in pan on rack, then cut in 1½" bars. (Chews are soft when warm.) Makes 25.

BROWN SUGAR/NUT BARS

Cut these chewy cookies in small squares—they're rich, satisfying

1 lb. brown sugar	1 tsp. baking powder
1 c. butter	½ tsp. salt
2 eggs	1 c. coarsely chopped walnuts
2 c. sifted flour	

Cook sugar and butter in top of double boiler over hot water until sugar dissolves. Cool.

Add eggs, one at a time, beating thoroughly after each addition. Stir in remaining ingredients. Spread in ungreased 15½ x 10½ x 1" jelly roll pan. Bake in moderate oven (350°) 25 minutes. While hot, cut in 2" squares or desired size. Cool in pan on rack. Makes about 35.

BUTTERSCOTCH STRIPS

Cookies three ways—strips, man-size squares and a four-layer stack

½ c. butter	½ c. chopped nuts
2 c. brown sugar, firmly packed	½ tsp. salt
2 eggs	2 tsp. vanilla
2 c. sifted flour	Confectioners sugar
2 tsp. baking powder	

Melt butter, add to sugar and cool. Blend in eggs. Stir in remaining ingredients.

Spread in lightly greased 13 x 9 x 2" pan. Bake in slow oven (325°) about 30 minutes. While still warm, cut into 24 strips about 3 x 1½". Roll in confectioners sugar. Cool on racks. Makes 2 dozen.

NOTE: These may be cut in 12 (3 x 3") squares for man-size cookies.

Variation

Butterscotch Stack: Mix dough as directed and divide into four equal portions. Roll or pat out each portion into an 8" circle between two pieces of waxed paper (draw an 8" circle on counter top for guide).

Chill circles in refrigerator until top piece of paper can be peeled off easily; transfer circles on waxed paper to lightly greased baking sheets.

Bake in slow oven (325°) about 20 minutes. You may bake two at a time by using both oven shelves; be sure to exchange top and bottom baking sheets after 10 minutes in the oven for even browning.

Remove from baking sheet and cool on rack. When cool, peel off paper. Stack circles, spreading each with filling of whipped cream or scoops of softened ice cream. Freeze. To serve, let stand at room temperature about 15 minutes. Cut into wedges. Makes 10 to 12 servings.

CHEESECAKE BARS

They taste like cheesecake and that means rich and luscious

⅓ c. butter or regular margarine   1 (8 oz.) pkg. cream cheese
⅓ c. brown sugar, firmly packed   1 egg, beaten
1 c. sifted flour   2 tblsp. milk
½ c. chopped walnuts   1 tblsp. lemon juice
¼ c. sugar   ½ tsp. vanilla

Cream butter and brown sugar until light; add flour and chopped walnuts. Cream with spoon until mixture forms crumbs. Set aside 1 c. mixture for topping. Press remaining crumb mixture into ungreased 8″ square pan.

Bake in moderate oven (350°) 12 to 15 minutes. Set pan on rack to cool.

Combine white sugar and cream cheese; beat until smooth. Add egg, milk, lemon juice and vanilla. Beat thoroughly to mix. Spread evenly in pan over baked crumbs. Sprinkle reserved 1 c. crumbs over top.

Bake in moderate oven (350°) 25 to 30 minutes. Set pan on rack to cool. Cut in 2 x 1″ bars and store in refrigerator. (Cookies are perishable and must be kept in refrigerator until eaten.) Makes 32.

FROSTED CARROT BARS

Carrots are the mystery ingredient in these wonderfully moist cookies

4 eggs   3 c. finely grated carrots (9 medium)
2 c. sugar
1½ c. salad oil   1½ c. flaked coconut
2 c. sifted flour   1½ c. chopped walnuts
2 tsp. baking soda   Cream Cheese Frosting (recipe follows)
2 tsp. ground cinnamon
1 tsp. salt

Beat eggs until light; gradually beat in sugar. Alternately add salad oil and flour sifted with soda, cinnamon and salt. Mix well.

Fold in carrots, coconut and walnuts. Spread evenly in two greased 13 x 9 x 2″ pans.

Bake in moderate oven (350°) 25 to 30 minutes. Set pans on racks and cool. Spread with Cream Cheese Frosting, then cut in 3 x 1″

bars. Remove from pans and place in covered container. Store in refrigerator or freezer. Makes 6½ dozen.

Cream Cheese Frosting: Blend 1 (3 oz.) pkg. cream cheese with 1 tblsp. dairy half-and-half or whole milk. Add 2½ c. sifted confectioners sugar, 3 tblsp. dairy half-and-half or whole milk (or enough to make a frosting of spreading consistency), 1 tsp. vanilla and ⅛ tsp. salt. Beat to mix.

PENUCHE DREAM BARS

And we give you a chocolate variation—try both and take your pick

Bottom Layer:

½ c. shortening
½ c. brown sugar, firmly packed
1 c. sifted flour

½ tsp. salt
2 tblsp. milk

Top Layer:

2 eggs
1 c. brown sugar, firmly packed
1 tsp. vanilla
½ tsp. salt
2 tblsp. flour

½ tsp. baking powder
1 (3½ oz.) can flaked coconut
(1⅓ c.)
1 c. chopped pecans

For bottom layer, cream shortening and brown sugar until light and fluffy. Mix together flour and salt; add to creamed mixture. Stir in milk. Pat evenly in greased 9″ square pan.

Bake in slow oven (325°) about 20 minutes, until light brown. Remove from oven.

To make top layer, combine eggs, brown sugar and vanilla; beat until mixture thickens.

Sift together salt, flour and baking powder; add to egg mixture. Mix well; stir in coconut and pecans. Spread evenly over baked bottom layer.

Bake in slow oven (325°) about 20 minutes, until golden brown. Set pan on rack and let cool, then cut in 2¼ x 1″ bars. Makes 3 dozen.

Variation

Chocolate Dream Bars: Make and bake bottom layer as for Penuche Dream Bars, but use ⅓ c. butter or regular margarine instead of ½ c.

shortening. Make top layer, substituting 1 (6 oz.) pkg. semisweet chocolate pieces for the coconut. Spread on baked layer and bake 15 to 20 minutes. Cool in pan on rack. Spread Easy Chocolate Icing on top and cut in 2¼ x 1" bars.

Easy Chocolate Icing: Melt 1 tsp. butter with 1 square unsweetened chocolate over warm, not boiling, water. Remove from heat and stir in 1½ to 2 tblsp. hot water. Add enough sifted confectioners sugar (about 1 c.) to make icing that spreads easily. Beat until smooth. Makes enough to ice from 3 to 4 dozen cookies, depending on size, or a 9" square pan of cookies.

PLANTATION PEANUT COOKIES

Cookies look and taste much like peanut brittle—a teen-age favorite

½ c. butter or shortening	1 c. sifted flour
½ c. brown sugar, firmly packed	¼ tsp. baking soda
1 egg, slightly beaten	½ tsp. ground cinnamon
1 tsp. vanilla	½ c. coarsely chopped salted
½ c. finely chopped salted	peanuts
peanuts	

Cream butter until light; beat in brown sugar until fluffy. Beat in 2 tblsp. beaten egg and vanilla to mix well. Add the ½ c. finely chopped peanuts.

Blend together flour, baking soda and cinnamon; add to creamed mixture. With floured fingers, pat dough on greased baking sheet to make a rectangle 14 x 10". Brush top with remaining egg and sprinkle with coarsely chopped peanuts.

Bake in slow oven (325°) 20 to 22 minutes. Press lightly with finger. If a slight imprint remains, cookies are done. Use care not to overbake. While warm, cut in 3½ x 1½" bars (or break in irregular pieces). Cool in pan on rack. Makes 2 dozen.

PECAN CHEWS

Easy-to-make cookies with a caramel, toasted-nut flavor

¾ c. butter
1½ c. brown sugar, firmly packed
1 egg
1 tsp. vanilla

½ tsp. salt
2 c. sifted flour
1 c. chopped toasted pecans
(see Index)

Cream butter and brown sugar until light and fluffy. Beat in egg, vanilla and salt. Blend in flour and nuts.

Spread dough in lightly greased 15½ x 10½ x 1" jelly roll pan. Bake in moderate oven (375°) about 15 minutes, or until lightly browned. Cool in pan on rack, then cut in 3 x 1" bars. Makes about 4 dozen.

NUT-CRESTED COOKIE SQUARES

Serve these candy-like cookies during the holidays with fruit punch

1 c. butter
1 c. brown sugar, firmly packed
1 tsp. vanilla
1 egg
2 c. sifted flour

⅛ tsp. salt
1 (6 oz.) pkg. semisweet
chocolate pieces
½ c. finely chopped nuts

Cream butter until fluffy; add brown sugar and beat until light. Add vanilla and egg; then add the flour and salt. Blend well.

Spread evenly about ¼" thick on greased baking sheet. Bake in moderate oven (350°) 15 minutes.

Meanwhile melt chocolate pieces.

Remove baking sheet from oven and at once spread melted chocolate over top to frost evenly. Sprinkle with nuts. Cut in 2" squares while still hot. Cool in pan on racks. Makes about 4 dozen.

SOUTHERN PRALINE BARS

Rich butterscotch flavor makes these chewy, frosted bars favorites

½ c. lard
1½ c. brown sugar, firmly packed
2 eggs
1½ c. sifted flour
1 tsp. baking powder

1 tsp. salt
2 tsp. vanilla
¾ c. chopped pecans
Praline Frosting (recipe follows)

Melt lard in 2-qt. saucepan. Add remaining ingredients, except frosting, and mix well. Spread in greased 13 x 9 x 2" pan.

Bake in moderate oven (350°) 25 to 30 minutes. Cool slightly in pan on rack, then spread with Praline Frosting. When cool, cut in 2 x 1½" bars. Makes about 2½ dozen.

Praline Frosting: Melt together in saucepan 2 tblsp. butter, ¼ c. brown sugar, firmly packed, and 2 tblsp. light cream or milk. Stir in about 1 c. sifted confectioners sugar (enough to make a frosting of spreading consistency) and beat until smooth.

Variation

Coconut Praline Bars: Substitute ¾ c. flaked coconut for the pecans and bake as directed.

SWEDISH HEIRLOOM BARS

Dainty tea-party cookies accented with cinnamon—a women's special

1 c. sugar
1 c. shortening
½ tsp. vanilla
1 egg, separated

2 c. sifted flour
½ tsp. salt
1 tblsp. ground cinnamon
1 c. finely chopped nuts

Cream sugar, shortening and vanilla until mixture is light and fluffy. Beat in egg yolk.

Sift together flour, salt and cinnamon; stir into creamed mixture and mix well. Spread dough in greased 15½ x 10½ x 1" jelly roll pan (dough will be spread thin).

Beat egg white until frothy and spread over top of dough. Sprinkle nuts evenly over egg white topping.

Bake in moderate oven (350°) about 20 minutes. Cool in pan on rack 10 minutes, then cut in 2 x 1½" bars. Makes about 50.

SPEEDY COOKIES SUPREME

Quick and easy—youngsters like the pronounced brown sugar flavor

2 c. brown sugar, firmly packed   2 c. sifted flour
2 eggs   1 c. broken nuts
½ c. butter or shortening

Combine 1 c. brown sugar, 1 egg, beaten, butter and flour. Blend thoroughly. Press dough onto greased large baking sheet (about 17 x 14").

Beat the remaining egg and spread over top of dough on baking sheet; sprinkle with ½ c. brown sugar, then with nuts. Scatter remaining ½ c. brown sugar over top.

Bake in moderate oven (350°) about 15 minutes, until light brown. Cool on baking sheet set on rack 10 minutes, then cut in 2" squares, or desired shapes. Makes about 4½ dozen.

TOFFEE STICKS

These take more time to make than many bars, but they are worth it

¾ c. butter or regular margarine   1 (6 oz.) pkg. butterscotch pieces
½ c. brown sugar, firmly packed   ¼ c. light corn syrup
1 egg yolk   1 tblsp. water
1 tsp. vanilla   ¼ tsp. salt
¼ tsp. salt   Toasted slivered almonds
1½ c. sifted flour   (for top)
2 tblsp. shortening

Blend together butter, brown sugar, egg yolk, vanilla and salt. Stir in flour. Spread mixture in greased 13 x 9 x 2" pan.

Bake in moderate oven (350°) 20 minutes, or until nicely browned. Cool slightly in pan on rack.

Combine shortening, butterscotch morsels, corn syrup, water and salt in saucepan. Heat and stir until smooth; spread over top of baked dough. Sprinkle on almonds. Allow topping to set, then cut in 2 x 1" sticks. Makes about 4 dozen.

WALNUT BARS

Chewy nut cookies have crackly tops—they disappear fast

¾ c. sifted flour	2 c. brown sugar, lightly packed
¼ tsp. salt	2 eggs
¼ tsp. baking soda	1 c. coarsely chopped walnuts

Sift together flour, salt and soda. Add sugar and eggs, mix well; then beat quickly until fluffy. Add nuts.

Bake in greased 9″ square pan in moderate oven (350°) 30 minutes. Cool in pan on rack, then cut in 2 x 1″ bars. Makes about 32.

WALNUT/CINNAMON SQUARES

This recipe and variations make eight different kinds of cookies

1 c. butter	2 c. sifted flour
1 c. sugar	1 tsp. ground cinnamon
1 egg, separated	1 c. finely chopped walnuts

In a mixing bowl, cream together butter and sugar. Beat in egg yolk to mix thoroughly.

Sift together flour and cinnamon; stir into creamed mixture and mix thoroughly. Spread dough evenly over bottom of lightly greased 15½ x 10½ x 1″ jelly roll pan.

Beat egg white slightly; brush over top of dough. With fingertips, smooth surface. Sprinkle nuts over dough and press in.

Bake in very slow oven (275°) 1 hour. While still hot, cut in 1½″ squares; cool in pans on racks. Makes about 5½ dozen.

Variations

Austrian Almond Squares: Make dough for Walnut/Cinnamon Squares, but substitute 1 tsp. ground nutmeg for the cinnamon and 1 c. chopped or sliced almonds for the walnuts. Bake as directed.

Orange/Pecan Flats: Make cookies as directed for Walnut/Cinnamon Squares, but add 1 tblsp. grated orange peel along with egg yolk. Omit cinnamon and use chopped pecans instead of walnuts.

Turkish Cardamoms: Make cookies as directed for Walnut/Cinnamon Squares, but substitute 1 tsp. ground cardamom for the cinnamon and 1 c. chopped filberts or hazelnuts for the walnuts.

Macadamia Nut Gingers: Make cookies as directed for Walnut/ Cinnamon Squares, but substitute 1 tsp. ground ginger for the cinnamon and use finely chopped roasted salted macadamia nuts instead of walnuts.

Peanut Salts: Make cookies as directed for Walnut/Cinnamon Squares, except use 1 c. brown sugar, firmly packed, instead of white sugar. Omit cinnamon, and use salted roasted peanuts instead of walnuts.

Brown Sugar Spice Crisps: Make cookies as directed for Walnut/ Cinnamon Squares, substituting 1 c. light brown sugar, firmly packed, for the white sugar. Use 1½ tsp. ground cinnamon instead of 1, and add ¾ tsp. ground nutmeg, ¾ tsp. ground ginger and ¼ tsp. ground cloves along with cinnamon. Omit walnuts, topping only with egg white.

Lemon or Lime Sugar Crisps: Make cookies as directed for Walnut/ Cinnamon Squares, but add 2 tblsp. grated lemon or lime peel along with egg yolk. Omit cinnamon and walnuts.

GOLDEN COCONUT DIAMONDS

You brush icing on these Danish cookies luscious with coconut

1 c. butter	1 c. sifted confectioners sugar
1 c. sugar	(about)
Few drops yellow food color	2 tblsp. light rum, or about 1 tsp.
1 c. flaked coconut	rum flavoring plus 2 tsp. water
2 c. sifted flour	

Cream together butter and sugar until light and fluffy. Beat in food color; stir in coconut. Gradually stir in flour to make a smooth dough.

With lightly floured fingertips, press dough evenly over bottom of greased 15½ x 10½ x 1" jelly roll pan. Bake in slow oven (325°) 25 to 30 minutes, or until lightly browned.

Mix confectioners sugar and rum to make a thin icing. While cookies are hot, drizzle on icing and quickly brush it over cookies to form a glaze. While still warm, cut cookies in 8 lengthwise strips, then diagonally in 1" wide strips to make diamonds. Cool in pan on rack. Makes about 80.

CRUMBLE COOKIES

This three-generation family recipe came from England with the home-maker's grandmother. Easy to make, great with tea or milk

1 c. dark brown sugar, firmly packed	1 c. butter
	2¼ c. sifted flour

Combine all ingredients in large bowl of electric mixer; beat at medium speed to mix thoroughly. Press over bottom of ungreased 13 x 9 x 2″ pan.

Bake in moderate oven (350°) 15 to 17 minutes, or until golden brown. Set pan on rack. Cut in 2″ squares while warm; let cool a few minutes before removing from pan. Makes about 28.

FROSTED MOLASSES CREAMS

Coffee flavors these molasses cookies and the frosting they wear

½ c. shortening	¾ tsp. salt
½ c. sugar	¼ tsp. baking soda
1 egg, beaten	1 tsp. ground cinnamon
½ c. molasses	½ tsp. ground cloves
⅓ c. strong, hot coffee	Creamy Coffee Icing (recipe follows)
1½ c. sifted flour	
1½ tsp. baking powder	

Cream together shortening and sugar; blend in egg, molasses and coffee.

Sift together dry ingredients; add to creamed mixture and blend well. Pour into greased and waxed-paper lined 13 x 9 x 2″ pan.

Bake in moderate oven (350°) 25 minutes. While warm, frost with Creamy Coffee Icing. Cool in pan on rack, then cut in 3 x 1″ bars. Makes about 39.

Creamy Coffee Icing: Cream ¼ c. butter or margarine with 2 c. confectioners sugar. Add about 2 tblsp. cold coffee, enough to make an icing of spreading consistency; mix until smooth.

OATMEAL SHORTBREADS

Try these nutty, not-too-sweet cookies as an accompaniment to cheese

1½ c. sifted flour   ⅔ c. quick-cooking rolled oats
⅔ c. brown sugar, firmly packed   1 c. butter

Combine all ingredients in large mixing bowl. With pastry blender or fingers, cut or rub ingredients together until well blended and crumbly. Press firmly and evenly into greased 15½ x 10½ x 1″ jelly roll pan. (Lightly flour fingertips if necessary to prevent sticking.)

Bake in slow oven (300°) 40 to 45 minutes, or until deep golden. While still hot, cut in 2 x 1½″ bars. Cool in pan on rack. Makes about 4 dozen.

Drop Cookies

Bite into plump, golden drop cookies and you'll often discover happy surprises in our recipes—dates, raisins, currants, cherries, nuts, chocolate pieces, citron, coconut and other treats. These are the substantial family cookies that usually travel successfully and keep well (if you hide them). They fill more cookie jars than any other kind and contribute much to the fame of country kitchens.

Next to bars, drop cookies are the easiest type to make. True, you do have several bakings, but if pressed for time, you can divide the dough and freeze part of it to bake when you have a little leisure or want to serve freshly baked cookies with coffee to business callers or neighbors who stop by.

Many cookies that once were rolled and cut now are represented in the drop cookie family. Try Grandma's Soft Sugar Cookies in this section and see if they don't remind you of the rolled cookies you used to eat at your grandmother's house. They're big and fat, with a glistening sprinkle of sugar and a raisin decoration in the center.

It's a real sacrifice not to give honorable mention to many of our drop cookie recipes. For instance, Hampshire Hermits, in which the flavors of citron and Lemon Glaze blend so harmoniously. And if you like fig cookies, you'll want to try California Fig Cookies. They're *really* good.

The dough for drop cookies is soft enough to drop from a spoon. Use a kitchen spoon rather than a measuring spoon, and take slightly rounded rather than level spoonfuls (unless recipe specifies otherwise). Push dough off the spoon with a rubber spatula or another spoon. Make the drops the same size and peak them up so they will bake evenly and look attractive. Bake them *just until done,* or until a slight imprint remains when you touch a cookie lightly with your finger. Remove from baking sheet unless the recipe directs otherwise. If left on a hot sheet, they continue to bake and may overbake.

You also will find several crisp cookies in this section that start as drops of dough. Sesame Wafers are an excellent example. So are see-through, party lace cookies, flat or rolled (after baking) the Swedish way.

The generous collection of oatmeal cookie recipes includes the favorites of the countryside, be they crisp, chewy or soft. Among them are Rookie Cookies, which, as some women know from experience, greatly please men.

ALMOND JEWELS

Cookies bright as a Mexican fiesta with that Chinese-almond taste

2 c. sifted flour	1 egg
½ tsp. baking powder	¾ tsp. vanilla
¼ tsp. salt	¾ c. chopped almonds
½ c. butter or regular margarine	Gumdrops
¾ c. sifted brown sugar, firmly packed	Almonds (for tops)

Sift together flour, baking powder and salt.

Cream butter; add sugar gradually; cream until light and fluffy. Beat in egg and vanilla; stir in chopped nuts. Add dry ingredients and mix.

Drop teaspoonfuls of dough 1½ to 2″ apart onto lightly greased baking sheet. Decorate tops with pieces of bright gumdrops (not licorice) and insert lengthwise slices of almonds in cookie centers.

Bake in moderate oven (350°) 12 to 15 minutes. Cool cookies on racks. Makes 3½ dozen.

ANISE DROPS

Cookies make their own creamy white topping while they bake

3 eggs	½ tsp. salt
1 c. plus 2 tblsp. sugar	1 tsp. anise extract or 3 tblsp.
1¾ c. sifted flour	anise seeds
½ tsp. baking powder	

Beat eggs with electric mixer at medium speed until fluffy. Gradually add sugar, beating constantly. Continue to beat for 20 minutes.

Reduce speed of mixer to low and add flour sifted with baking powder and salt. Beat in anise extract. Drop dough by teaspoonfuls about ½″ apart onto well-greased baking sheet, swirling dough to make a round cookie. Let stand at least 8 hours to dry, preferably overnight.

Bake in slow oven (325°) about 10 minutes, or until cookies are a creamy golden color, not brown, on bottom. Remove cookies to rack to cool. Makes about 50.

BLACK WALNUT COOKIES

Tastes like sour cream cookies Grandma served with applesauce

½ c. shortening	1 tsp. ground cinnamon
¾ c. sugar	½ tsp. salt
1 egg	¼ tsp. baking soda
½ tsp. vanilla	½ c. dairy sour cream
2 c. sifted flour	½ c. chopped black walnuts
1 tsp. baking powder	

Cream shortening and sugar until light and fluffy. Beat in egg and vanilla.

Sift together dry ingredients. Add to creamed mixture, alternately with sour cream. Stir in walnuts.

Drop by teaspoonfuls about 2″ apart onto greased baking sheet. Press flat with bottom of drinking glass, dipping glass into sugar before pressing each cookie.

Bake in moderate oven (375°) 9 to 12 minutes. Remove cookies and cool on racks. Makes 4½ dozen.

BEST-EVER BUTTERSCOTCH COOKIES

One of the best-tasting cookies ever baked in Countryside Kitchens

1 tblsp. vinegar	1 tsp. baking soda
1 c. evaporated milk (about)	½ tsp. baking powder
½ c. butter or regular margarine	½ tsp. salt
1½ c. brown sugar, firmly packed	⅔ c. chopped walnuts or pecans
2 eggs	Brown Butter Frosting (recipe
1 tsp. vanilla	follows)
2½ c. sifted flour	Walnut or pecan halves

Put vinegar in a 1-cup measure; add evaporated milk and set aside.

Beat butter until light; add brown sugar and beat until mixture is light and fluffy. Beat in eggs and vanilla to blend thoroughly.

Sift together flour, baking soda, baking powder and salt.

Stir evaporated milk and add alternately with dry ingredients to creamed mixture. Stir in chopped nuts. Drop rounded tablespoonfuls of dough about 2½" apart onto lightly greased baking sheet.

Bake in moderate oven (350°) 10 to 12 minutes, or until lightly browned and barely firm to touch. Remove cookies and cool on racks. When cool, spread with Brown Butter Frosting and press a walnut or pecan half in each cookie. Makes about 5 dozen.

Brown Butter Frosting: Melt ½ c. butter in small saucepan and cook over medium heat, stirring constantly, until butter stops bubbling and is nut-brown in color (do not scorch). Combine with 2 c. sifted confectioners sugar and 2 to 4 tblsp. boiling water; beat until smooth and of spreading consistency. Makes enough to frost about 5 dozen cookies.

BUTTERSCOTCH DROPS

These soft, chewy, delicious, easy, economical cookies always please

1 c. shortening	3½ c. sifted flour
2 c. brown sugar, firmly packed	1 tsp. baking soda
2 eggs	1 tsp. salt
½ c. buttermilk or water	

Mix shortening, brown sugar and eggs. Stir in buttermilk.

Sift together flour, soda and salt, and add to first mixture. Chill. Drop by teaspoonfuls about 2" apart onto lightly greased baking sheet. Bake in hot oven (400°) 8 to 10 minutes until set (almost no imprint when touched with finger). Makes 6 dozen.

CASHEW DROPS

Pleasant surprise: biting into a whole-cashew center

½ c. butter or regular margarine	¾ tsp. baking soda
1 c. brown sugar, firmly packed	¼ tsp. salt
1 egg	⅓ c. dairy sour cream
½ tsp. vanilla	1¾ c. whole cashew nuts
2 c. sifted flour	Golden Butter Glaze (recipe
¾ tsp. baking powder	follows)

Cream butter and sugar until light and fluffy. Beat in egg and vanilla to mix thoroughly. Add sifted dry ingredients alternately with sour cream, blending well. Carefully fold in nuts.

Drop by well-rounded teaspoonfuls 2″ apart onto greased baking sheet.

Bake in hot oven (400°) 8 to 10 minutes. Remove cookies and cool on racks. Top with Golden Butter Glaze, if desired. Makes about 4 dozen.

Golden Butter Glaze: Melt ½ c. butter in saucepan over medium heat until it turns *light* golden brown (use care not to overbrown). Remove from heat and add 3 c. sifted confectioners sugar, 1 tsp. vanilla and enough hot water (3 to 4 tblsp.) to make a glaze that will spread smoothly. Beat well. Makes enough to frost or glaze 4 dozen cookies, depending on size.

CORN FLAKE COOKIES

Coconut takes the spotlight in these extra-good, crisp cookies

2 c. sifted flour	1 c. brown sugar, firmly packed
1 tsp. baking soda	2 eggs, well beaten
½ tsp. salt	1 tsp. vanilla
½ tsp. baking powder	2 c. flaked or shredded coconut
1¼ c. shortening	2 c. corn flakes
1 c. sugar	

Sift together flour, soda, salt and baking powder.

Cream shortening; gradually add sugars; beat until light. Add eggs and vanilla.

Combine dry ingredients and creamed mixture; add coconut and corn flakes.

Drop small teaspoonfuls 1½″ apart onto greased baking sheet.

Bake in moderate oven (350°) 8 to 10 minutes, or until delicately browned. Spread on racks to cool. Makes 8 dozen.

CREAM CHEESE DROP COOKIES

Lemon and cheese flavors blend tastily in these drop cookies

¾ c. butter	2 tsp. grated lemon peel
1 (3 oz.) pkg. cream cheese	2 c. sifted cake flour
1 c. sifted confectioners sugar	1 c. chopped pecans
1 tblsp. lemon juice	Sifted confectioners sugar (for
1 tsp. vanilla	rolling)

Cream butter and cream cheese until light and fluffy. Gradually add 1 c. confectioners sugar, beating thoroughly. Stir in lemon juice, vanilla and lemon peel. Add flour and mix well. Stir in nuts.

Drop by scant teaspoonfuls about 2″ apart onto ungreased baking sheet. Bake in slow oven (300°) about 25 minutes, until set but not brown. While hot roll in sifted confectioners sugar. Cool on racks. Makes 4 dozen.

GUESS-AGAIN COOKIES

The slightly salty, crisp bits in these rich cookies are potato chips!

1 c. butter or regular margarine	2 c. sifted flour
½ c. sugar	½ c. crushed potato chips
1 tsp. vanilla	½ c. chopped pecans

Beat butter, sugar and vanilla until light and fluffy. Add flour, potato chips and nuts; mix well.

Drop by scant teaspoonfuls 2″ apart onto ungreased baking sheet. Flatten by pressing with bottom of drinking glass, greased and dipped in sugar (grease and sugar glass as needed).

Bake in moderate oven (350°) 10 to 11 minutes. Remove to racks to cool. Makes about 5 dozen.

MAPLE WAFERS

You can bake these maple cookies even if you live far from sugar bush country. Try frosting on your favorite sugar cookies, too

3 tblsp. butter or regular margarine	1 tsp. cream of tartar
½ c. maple-blended syrup	½ tsp. baking soda
1 egg, beaten	¼ tsp. salt
2 tblsp. milk	¾ c. chopped nuts
1 c. sifted flour	Maple Frosting (recipe follows)

Melt butter. Remove from heat and stir in maple syrup. Add egg and milk and mix well.

Sift together flour, cream of tartar, baking soda and salt. Add to maple syrup mixture; blend well. Fold in nuts. Chill thoroughly (batter thickens).

Drop dough by teaspoonfuls 2″ apart onto lightly greased baking sheet. Bake in hot oven (400°) 8 to 10 minutes. Remove cookies and cool on racks. When cool, spread with Maple Frosting. Makes about 2 dozen.

Maple Frosting: Heat ¼ c. butter until light golden brown. Stir in 1 c. sifted confectioners sugar, ⅛ tsp. salt, ¾ to 1 tsp. maple flavoring and 1 tblsp. hot water, or enough to make frosting that will spread smoothly on wafers.

POTATO CHIP COOKIES

Something different! These chewy cookies will be the talk of your next coffee party when you reveal what's in them

1 c. shortening	1 tsp. vanilla
1 c. sugar	2 c. sifted flour
1 c. brown sugar, firmly packed	1 c. crushed potato chips
2 eggs	

Beat shortening until light; gradually add white and brown sugars, beating constantly. When light and fluffy, add eggs, one at a time, beating after each addition. Add vanilla and beat to blend thoroughly.

Stir in flour, then fold in potato chips. Drop by rounded teaspoonfuls 2″ apart onto lightly greased baking sheet. Flatten with floured fork tines.

Bake in moderate oven (350°) 12 to 15 minutes, or until light golden brown. Spread on racks to cool. Makes about 5 dozen.

SALTED PEANUT COOKIES

Red-skinned and creamy white peanuts dot these brown cookies

1 c. shortening	1 tsp. baking powder
2 c. brown sugar, firmly packed	½ tsp. baking soda
2 eggs	2 c. quick-cooking rolled oats
1 tsp. vanilla	1 c. corn flakes
2 c. sifted flour	1 c. salted peanuts (skins on)

Cream shortening and brown sugar until light and fluffy. Beat in eggs to mix thoroughly. Beat in vanilla.

Sift together flour, baking powder and soda; stir into creamed mixture. Then fold in rolled oats, corn flakes and peanuts. Drop by rounded teaspoonfuls 2″ apart onto greased baking sheet.

Bake in moderate oven (350°) 10 to 12 minutes. Spread on racks to cool. Makes about 7 dozen.

SESAME WAFERS

Dainty, crisp and rich-flavored—taste-testers were enthusiastic

¾ c. melted butter or regular margarine

1½ c. light brown sugar, firmly packed

1 tsp. vanilla

1 egg

1 c. Toasted Sesame Seeds (recipe follows)

1¼ c. sifted flour

¼ tsp. baking powder

¼ tsp. salt

Cream butter and sugar until light and fluffy. Add vanilla and egg; beat to mix thoroughly. Stir in sesame seeds.

Sift together flour, baking powder and salt; stir into creamed mixture. Drop half teaspoonfuls of dough about 2″ apart onto lightly greased baking sheet.

Bake in moderate oven (375°) about 5 to 6 minutes, or until edges brown (bottoms of cookies brown and burn quickly). Remove from oven and transfer cookies at once to racks to cool. Makes about 7 dozen.

Toasted Sesame Seeds: Spread seeds in a shallow pan and heat in a moderate oven (350°) about 20 minutes, until they turn a pale brown; stir occasionally. Remove from oven and cool. (Watch while they are in the oven to prevent scorching.)

SOUR CREAM DROP COOKIES

New version of old-time sour cream cookies uses dairy sour cream

1 c. shortening

2 c. sugar

1 tsp. vanilla

3 eggs

1 c. dairy sour cream

5 c. sifted flour

½ tsp. baking soda

3 tsp. baking powder

1 tsp. salt

1½ c. chopped walnuts

2 tblsp. sugar

1 tsp. ground cinnamon

Beat shortening until light; add 2 c. sugar and beat until fluffy. Beat in vanilla and eggs to mix thoroughly. Beat in sour cream.

Sift together flour, baking soda, baking powder and salt. Add to creamed mixture. Fold in chopped nuts. Chill 1 hour, or until dough is easy to handle.

Drop dough by teaspoonfuls about 2" apart onto lightly greased baking sheet.

Combine 2 tblsp. sugar with cinnamon. Lightly grease bottom of drinking glass (2¼" in diameter) and dip in cinnamon/sugar mixture. Press cookies flat.

Bake in moderate oven (350°) about 12 minutes. Remove to racks to cool. Makes about 6 dozen.

CHOCOLATE BANANA COOKIES

Delicious way to salvage very ripe bananas—tasty, moist cookies

1 c. sugar	2½ c. sifted flour
⅔ c. shortening	2 tsp. baking powder
2 eggs	¼ tsp. salt
1 tsp. vanilla	¼ tsp. baking soda
1 c. mashed bananas (2½ medium)	Chocolate Frosting (recipe follows)
1 (6 oz.) pkg. semisweet chocolate pieces, melted	

Beat together sugar and shortening until mixture is light and fluffy. Beat in eggs and vanilla, mixing well. Add bananas and melted chocolate.

Sift together flour, baking powder, salt and baking soda. Add to beaten mixture. Drop by teaspoonfuls about 2" apart onto lightly greased baking sheet.

Bake in moderate oven (350°) 10 minutes. Remove cookies and cool on racks; then frost with Chocolate Frosting, if desired. Makes about 5 dozen.

Chocolate Frosting: Combine 2 tblsp. soft butter, 2 squares unsweetened chocolate, melted, 3 tblsp. warm water and 2 c. sifted confectioners sugar. Beat until smooth.

CHOCOLATE CHEESE COOKIES

Crisp cookies with a delicate flavor of chocolate and cream cheese

½ c. butter
½ c. shortening
1 (3 oz.) pkg. cream cheese
1½ c. sugar
1 egg
½ tsp. vanilla

2 squares semisweet chocolate,
   melted and cooled slightly
2¼ c. sifted flour
1½ tsp. baking powder
½ tsp. salt
2 tblsp. milk
½ c. chopped nuts (optional)

Beat butter, shortening and cream cheese until light. Gradually add sugar, beating until mixture is light and fluffy. Beat in egg, vanilla and melted chocolate.

Sift together flour, baking powder and salt. Add alternately with milk to chocolate mixture. Stir in nuts.

Drop by teaspoonfuls 2″ apart onto lightly greased baking sheet. Bake in moderate oven (350°) about 15 minutes. Remove cookies and cool on racks. Makes about 4½ dozen.

N O T E : Use unsweetened instead of semisweet chocolate for a more pronounced chocolate flavor.

CHOCOLATE HERMITS

Make dainty, tea-size or man-size cookies according to your needs. Top with a chocolate confectioners sugar frosting (see Index)—*a decorative curl for dainty cookies, a generous covering for others*

1⅓ c. sifted flour
2 tsp. baking powder
½ tsp. salt
1 tsp. ground cinnamon
½ c. shortening
1 c. sugar
1 egg, well beaten

3 squares unsweetened
   chocolate, melted
1 tsp. vanilla
⅓ c. milk
1 c. chopped raisins
1 c. chopped nuts

Sift together flour, baking powder, salt and cinnamon.

Cream shortening; add sugar gradually; cream until fluffy.

Add egg to creamed mixture with chocolate; blend well. Add vanilla and milk. Stir in dry ingredients, raisins and nuts. Mix well; chill 30 minutes.

Drop by teaspoonfuls about 2″ apart onto greased baking sheet. Bake in moderate oven (350°) 15 minutes. Remove cookies and cool on racks. Makes 2 dozen.

CHOCOLATE MARSHMALLOW CAKELETS

Cookies resemble little cakes, ideal for cold weather because chocolate topping sometimes gets sticky when it's hot and humid

½ c. shortening
1 c. brown sugar, firmly packed
1 egg
1¾ c. sifted flour
½ tsp. baking soda
½ tsp. salt
½ c. cocoa
½ c. milk

½ c. chopped walnuts
18 regular marshmallows (about), cut in halves
1 (6 oz.) pkg. semisweet chocolate pieces
2 tblsp. butter
½ tsp. ground cinnamon

Beat shortening until light; add brown sugar and beat until fluffy. Beat in egg to blend.

Sift together flour, baking soda, salt and cocoa. Beat flour mixture alternately with milk into creamed mixture. Stir in walnuts.

Drop rounded teaspoonfuls of dough 2″ apart onto lightly greased baking sheet. Bake in moderate oven (350°) 12 to 15 minutes. Remove from oven and top with marshmallow halves. Set pan on rack until cookies are cool enough to handle.

Melt chocolate pieces with butter; stir in cinnamon. Holding cookies in hand, use a small spatula and swirl their tops with chocolate mixture to cover marshmallows. Cool cookies on racks. Makes about 3 dozen.

CHOCO-MARSHMALLOW COOKIES

Fat marshmallows atop chocolate cookies go fancy with frosting

1¾ c. sifted cake flour
½ tsp. salt
½ tsp. baking soda
½ c. cocoa
½ c. shortening
1 c. sugar
1 egg

1 tsp. vanilla
¼ c. milk
18 regular marshmallows, cut in halves
Cocoa Frosting (recipe follows)
36 pecan halves (½ c.)

Sift together flour, salt, soda and cocoa.

Cream shortening and sugar; add egg, vanilla and milk, beating well. Add dry ingredients and mix. Drop by teaspoonfuls about 2" apart onto greased baking sheet.

Bake in moderate oven (350°) 8 minutes (don't overbake). Remove from oven and press a marshmallow half, cut side down, on top of each cookie. Bake 2 minutes longer. Remove cookies and cool on racks. Top with Cocoa Frosting, then with a pecan half. Makes 3 dozen.

Cocoa Frosting: Combine 2 c. sifted confectioners sugar, 5 tblsp. cocoa and ⅛ tsp. salt. Add 3 tblsp. soft butter or margarine and 4 to 5 tblsp. light cream. Blend until smooth.

CHOCOLATE POTATO COOKIES

A homey pioneer favorite made with buttermilk—moist, good keepers

½ c. shortening	1½ c. sifted flour
1 c. brown sugar, firmly packed	½ tsp. salt
1 egg	½ tsp. baking soda
1 tsp. vanilla	¾ c. buttermilk
2 squares unsweetened	½ c. chopped walnuts or pecans
chocolate, melted	½ recipe for Chocolate Frosting
½ c. unseasoned mashed	(see Index)
potatoes (room temperature)	

Cream together shortening and brown sugar until light and fluffy. Beat in egg and vanilla to mix well. Add chocolate and mashed potatoes and beat until smooth.

Sift together flour, salt and baking soda; add alternately with buttermilk to creamed mixture. Stir until smooth, then add nuts. Drop by rounded teaspoonfuls 2" apart onto greased baking sheet.

Bake in hot oven (400°) about 10 minutes, or until cookies, when touched with finger, spring back (do not overbake). Let remain on baking sheet a minute or two before removing to racks for cooling. While *still warm,* spread on Chocolate Frosting. Makes 4½ dozen.

CHOCOLATE SANDWICH TREASURES

Favorite of a Pennsylvania woman—keeps well, sells fast at bazaars

1 c. milk	4 c. sifted flour
5 tblsp. flour	2 tsp. baking soda
1 c. confectioners sugar	½ tsp. baking powder
1 c. shortening	½ tsp. salt
¼ tsp. salt	1 c. buttermilk
½ c. shortening	¾ c. boiling water
2 c. sugar	½ c. cocoa
2 eggs	2 drops red or green food color
1 tsp. vanilla	(optional)

To make filling, combine ½ c. milk with 5 tblsp. flour and mix to a smooth paste. Add remaining ½ c. milk. Cook over medium heat, stirring, until mixture thickens. Set aside to cool.

In large mixer bowl, beat at medium speed confectioners sugar, 1 c. shortening and ¼ tsp. salt until light and fluffy. Add cooked mixture and continue beating until fluffy. Set aside while you bake cookies. (You'll have 2½ cups.)

To make cookie dough, beat ½ c. shortening until light; gradually add white sugar and beat until mixture is light and fluffy. Beat in eggs and vanilla to mix well.

Sift together 4 c. flour, baking soda, baking powder and ½ tsp. salt. Alternately add with buttermilk to creamed mixture.

Pour boiling water over cocoa and stir to mix. Cool and add to dough, mixing well.

Drop by teaspoonfuls (not heaping) 1″ apart onto lightly greased baking sheet. Bake in moderate oven (350°) 8 minutes. Remove from pan and cool on racks.

When cookies are cool, put together in pairs with filling spread between. You'll use 2 c. to fill cookies. Tint remaining ½ c. filling a delicate pink or green with 2 drops red or green food color, or leave filling untinted. Drop a little on top of each cookie sandwich. A nut or flaked coconut may be placed on top for decoration. Makes 5 dozen filled cookies.

NOTE: When the Pennsylvania homemaker who contributed this recipe wants to give the cookies a special appeal for guests, she divides the filling in quarters and places each part in a small bowl. She leaves one part creamy white, tints the other three delicately with food color—pink, green and yellow-orange. Then she decorates the tops of the sandwiches with a bit of the filling, adding nuts or flaked coconut for a trim.

FLORENTINES DIRECT FROM ITALY

Many American tourists in Europe resolve, once they get home, to duplicate the Florentines they ate in Italy. These cookies are almost a confection—half candy, half cookie. They are rich, sweet and excellent with coffee for evening refreshments. It's the combination of flavors—candied orange peel, chocolate and cream—plus the crisp texture that makes the cookies so rewarding.

Their name comes from the city of Florence, according to most food historians, back in the 15th or 16th century.

Our taste tests revealed that many people on this side of the Atlantic Ocean prefer a little less candied orange peel than Europeans like. Our recipe calls for ¾ cup finely chopped peel, but there's no law against using 1 to 1½ cups of it.

FLORENTINES

Lacy cookies for special occasions, painted with melted chocolate

¾ c. heavy cream
¼ c. sugar
¼ c. sifted flour
½ c. very finely chopped slivered blanched almonds

¾ c. very finely chopped candied orange peel (4 oz. pkg.)
2 (4 oz.) bars sweet cooking chocolate

Stir cream and sugar together to blend well. Stir in flour, almonds and orange peel. Drop by scant teaspoonfuls about 1¼″ apart onto heavily greased and floured baking sheet. *Flatten cookies with spatula;* they will be about ½ to ¾″ apart after flattening.

Bake in moderate oven (350°) about 10 to 12 minutes, until cookies brown lightly around edges. (Centers of cookies will be bubbling when you remove them from oven.) Let stand 2 or 3 minutes or until they become firmer. Place on wire rack or waxed paper to cool.

Meanwhile, melt chocolate over hot, not boiling, water. When cookies are cool, turn upside down and brush with melted chocolate. Let dry several hours or overnight at room temperature to give chocolate time to set. (In hot, humid weather, use chocolate confection coating, melted, instead of sweet cooking chocolate.) Store in covered container in refrigerator or freezer. Makes about 4 dozen.

FROSTED DROP BROWNIES

Frost some cookies white, some with chocolate to provide interest

½ c. butter or regular margarine
¾ c. sugar
1 egg
2 squares unsweetened chocolate, melted
1¾ c. sifted flour
½ tsp. baking soda

½ tsp. salt
½ c. milk
1 tsp. vanilla
½ c. chopped nuts
Shiny White Icing or Chocolate Icing
36 walnut or pecan halves

Cream butter and sugar until fluffy. Add egg and beat well. Stir in melted chocolate.

Sift together flour, baking soda and salt. Add alternately with the milk to the chocolate mixture. Stir in vanilla and nuts.

Drop by teaspoonfuls 2″ apart onto ungreased baking sheet; bake in hot oven (400°) 8 to 10 minutes. Remove cookies and cool on racks. Drop 1 tsp. Shiny White or Chocolate Icing onto center of each cookie and swirl with a fork. Top with walnut or pecan halves. Makes 3 dozen cookies.

Shiny White Icing: Add enough cream or milk to 2 c. sifted confectioners sugar to make icing of spreading consistency. Add ½ tsp. vanilla. (Tint part of the icing a delicate pink with a few drops red food color. Flavor with peppermint extract, if you like.)

Chocolate Icing: Add 1 square unsweetened chocolate, melted, to 1 c. sifted confectioners sugar; beat in enough cream or milk to make icing of spreading consistency. Add ½ tsp. vanilla.

MALTED CHOCOLATE DROPS

Just the cookie chocolate lovers adore—try the frosted variation

⅔ c. butter or regular margarine	¼ tsp. salt
¾ c. sugar	¼ c. cocoa
2 eggs	1 c. chocolate-flavored instant
1 tsp. vanilla	malted milk powder
2 c. sifted flour	¼ c. water
2 tsp. baking powder	1 c. chopped walnuts

Beat butter and sugar together until light and fluffy. Beat in eggs and vanilla to mix well.

Sift together flour, baking powder, salt, cocoa and malted milk powder. Add alternately with water to creamed mixture. Fold in nuts. Chill several hours.

Drop teaspoonfuls of dough 2″ apart onto greased baking sheet. Bake in moderate oven (350°) about 12 minutes. Remove cookies and cool on racks. Makes about 4 dozen.

Variation

Frosted Malted Chocolate Drops: When cookies are cool frost with Chocolate Malt Frosting.

Chocolate Malt Frosting: Melt 1 square unsweetened chocolate and 1 tblsp. butter over very low heat (or over hot water), stirring constantly. Mix in 1 tblsp. warm water, 2 tblsp. chocolate-flavored instant malted milk powder, 2 tblsp. light cream or dairy half-and-half and 1 c. sifted confectioners sugar, or enough to make a frosting of spreading consistency.

PENNSYLVANIA DUTCH COOKIE-PIES

A teen-age enthusiasm. Filling is good with other cookies, too

1½ c. sugar	½ tsp. cream of tartar
¼ c. shortening	½ tsp. baking soda
½ c. cocoa	1 tsp. salt
1 egg	¾ c. buttermilk
1 tsp. vanilla	Fluffy Refrigerator Filling
2 c. sifted flour	(recipe follows)

Cream together sugar and shortening until light and fluffy. Beat in cocoa and egg. Add vanilla.

Sift together flour, cream of tartar, baking soda and salt; add alternately with buttermilk to creamed mixture. Mix well.

Drop by teaspoonfuls about 2" apart onto greased baking sheet. Bake in moderate oven (375°) 10 to 12 minutes. Remove cookies to racks and cool.

Spread flat sides (bottoms) of cooled cookies with Fluffy Refrigerator Filling and put together in pairs. (If you like, you can sprinkle filling with flaked coconut before putting together.) Makes 26 cookie-pies.

Fluffy Refrigerator Filling: Place 2½ tblsp. flour in 1-qt. saucepan. Measure ½ c. milk. Add a little milk to flour and stir to make a smooth paste. Add remaining milk; cook and stir until mixture thickens. Cool.

In a small mixing bowl, cream together ½ c. butter or shortening, ½ c. sugar, ⅛ tsp. salt and 1 tsp. vanilla until light and fluffy. Slowly add thickened flour-milk mixture, beating constantly, until filling is light and fluffy. Makes about 1¾ cups.

NOTE: You will have ⅓ to ⅔ c. filling left over after using for Pennsylvania Dutch Cookie-Pies. The woman who shares this recipe says it's a planned leftover. She stores the filling in a covered jar in the refrigerator and uses it to spread on other cookies or cupcakes she bakes. The filling in the refrigerator remains soft and fluffy. She often doubles the recipe to make more filling to refrigerate.

PINEAPPLE/CHOCOLATE CHIP COOKIES

Big recipe for family—good keepers, have mild pineapple flavor

½ c. butter	4 c. sifted flour
½ c. shortening	½ tsp. baking soda
1 c. brown sugar, firmly packed	½ tsp. salt
1 c. white sugar	1 c. chopped walnuts
2 eggs	1 (6 oz.) pkg. semisweet
1 tsp. vanilla	chocolate pieces
1 c. crushed pineapple with juice	

Cream together butter, shortening and sugars until light and fluffy. Beat in eggs, one at a time, and vanilla. Stir in pineapple.

Sift together flour, baking soda and salt; divide in half. Add first half to creamed mixture. When well blended, add second half. Stir in nuts and chocolate pieces.

Drop batter by teaspoonfuls 2" apart onto greased baking sheet. Bake in hot oven (400°) 15 minutes. Remove cookies to racks and cool. Makes about 7 dozen.

SOFT CHOCOLATE CHIPPERS

Children like to come home to these chocolate-dotted goodies

½ c. shortening
1 c. brown sugar, firmly packed
1 egg
1 tsp. vanilla
1¾ c. sifted flour

½ tsp. baking soda
½ tsp. salt
¼ c. buttermilk
1 (6 oz.) pkg. semisweet chocolate pieces

Beat shortening until light; add brown sugar and beat until light and fluffy. Beat in egg and vanilla to blend well.

Sift together flour, baking soda and salt. Add alternately with buttermilk to creamed mixture. Beat until smooth. Add chocolate pieces and mix well.

Drop about 2" apart onto greased baking sheet. Flatten with a spoon. Bake in moderate oven (375°) 8 to 10 minutes, until lightly browned. Remove to cooling racks. Makes about 3 dozen.

SOUR CREAM CHOCOLATE COOKIES

These quick-to-make cookies have the good taste sour cream imparts

½ c. butter
1 c. brown sugar, firmly packed
1 egg
2 squares unsweetened chocolate, melted
1½ c. sifted flour
¼ tsp. baking powder

¼ tsp. salt
¼ tsp. baking soda
½ c. dairy sour cream
1 c. chopped walnuts
1 tsp. vanilla
Cocoa Frosting (recipe follows)

Cream together butter and brown sugar. Add egg and blend well. Beat in chocolate.

Sift together flour, baking powder, salt and soda; add to creamed mixture alternately with sour cream. Stir in nuts and vanilla.

Drop by teaspoonfuls about 2" apart onto greased baking sheet. Bake in moderate oven (375°) 8 minutes. Remove cookies and cool on racks, then frost with Cocoa Frosting. Makes 5 dozen.

Cocoa Frosting: Heat 3 tblsp. milk. Add 1½ c. sifted confectioners sugar, 3 tblsp. butter and 3 tblsp. cocoa. Blend together until of spreading consistency.

TWO-TONE JUMBLES

Try these 2-in-1 cookies—plain and chocolate sour cream treats

¼ c. shortening	2¾ c. sifted flour
¼ c. butter	½ tsp. baking soda
1 c. brown sugar, firmly packed	1 tsp. salt
½ c. sugar	1 c. dairy sour cream
1 tsp. vanilla	1 square unsweetened chocolate,
2 eggs	melted
1 c. chopped walnuts or pecans	

Beat together shortening, butter, brown and white sugars and vanilla until light and fluffy. Beat in eggs to mix well. Stir in ½ c. walnuts.

Sift together flour, baking soda and salt. Add alternately to creamed mixture with sour cream. Divide dough in half. Add chocolate to one half.

Drop chocolate dough from teaspoon 2″ apart onto lightly greased baking sheet. Drop equal size spoonfuls of plain dough next to and touching chocolate mounds (they will bake together as one). Sprinkle with remaining ½ c. nuts, pressing them in lightly.

Bake in moderate oven (375°) about 12 minutes, until almost no imprint remains after touching center of cookie with finger and until lightly browned. Remove cookies to racks to cool. Makes about 3½ dozen.

TWO-WAY COOKIES

As easy to bake chocolate/orange and coconut cookies as one kind

4 c. sifted flour	3 eggs
1 tsp. salt	1 tsp. vanilla
1 tsp. baking soda	½ tsp. orange extract
1 c. regular margarine	1 (6 oz.) pkg. semisweet
1 c. sugar	chocolate pieces
1¼ c. light brown sugar, firmly packed	1 (3½ oz.) can flaked coconut

Sift together flour, salt and baking soda.

Cream margarine until fluffy; gradually add sugars. Add eggs, one at a time, beating thoroughly after each addition. Add vanilla; blend. Add sifted dry ingredients. Mix well. Divide batter in half.

Add orange extract and chocolate pieces to one half dough and coconut to other half. Drop by rounded teaspoonfuls about 2" apart onto greased baking sheet.

Bake in a moderate oven (350°) 12 to 15 minutes. Remove cookies and cool on racks. Makes about 6 dozen.

CARAMEL APPLE COOKIES

You can frost the cookies before freezing or just before serving

½ c. shortening	1 tsp. ground cloves
1⅓ c. brown sugar, firmly packed	½ tsp. ground nutmeg
	1 c. grated peeled apples
1 egg	1 c. light raisins
2¼ c. sifted flour	½ c. apple juice
1 tsp. baking soda	1 c. chopped walnuts
½ tsp. salt	Caramel Icing (recipe follows)
1 tsp. ground cinnamon	

Cream shortening, sugar and egg until light and fluffy. Sift together dry ingredients and add to creamed mixture. When well blended, stir in remaining ingredients, except icing.

Drop by level tablespoonfuls 3" apart onto greased baking sheet. Bake in moderate oven (350°) about 12 minutes, or until lightly browned.

Remove cookies and cool on racks. When cool, spread with Caramel Icing. Makes about 4 dozen.

Caramel Icing: Combine ¼ c. butter and ¼ c. brown sugar, firmly packed, in saucepan; cook until sugar dissolves, about 3 minutes. Add 1½ c. sifted confectioners sugar, ¼ tsp. salt and 2½ tblsp. dairy half-and-half or light cream; beat until smooth. (If frosting becomes too thick when spreading on cookies, thin it by adding a little more cream.)

GLAZED APPLE COOKIES

These big, spicy cookies travel and keep well, taste wonderful

½ c. shortening

1⅓ c. brown sugar, firmly
 packed

1 egg

2 c. sifted flour

1 tsp. baking soda

½ tsp. salt

1 tsp. ground cinnamon

½ tsp. ground cloves

¼ tsp. ground nutmeg

1 c. coarsely chopped nuts

1 c. finely chopped peeled apple
 (2 medium)

1 c. raisins

¼ c. milk

1½ c. sifted confectioners sugar

1 tblsp. butter

⅛ tsp. vanilla

2½ tblsp. light cream or dairy
 half-and-half (about)

Beat together shortening and brown sugar until light and fluffy. Beat in egg to blend thoroughly.

Sift together flour, baking soda, salt, cinnamon, cloves and nutmeg. Stir half the dry ingredients into creamed mixture. Stir in nuts, apple and raisins; then stir in remaining half of dry ingredients and milk. Mix well.

Drop from tablespoon 1½″ apart onto lightly greased baking sheet. Bake in hot oven (400°) 10 to 12 minutes. Remove cookies to racks and while still warm, spread with glaze.

To make glaze, combine confectioners sugar, butter, vanilla and enough cream to make glaze of spreading consistency. Beat until smooth. Spread on warm cookies. Makes about 3 dozen.

BANANA DROP COOKIES

Cake-like banana cookies are coated with cinnamon-sugar and bran

1 c. whole bran cereal

6 tblsp. sugar

½ tsp. ground cinnamon

1 c. sugar

½ c. shortening

¼ c. butter

2 eggs

1½ tsp. vanilla

1 c. mashed bananas (3 medium)

2½ c. sifted flour

3 tsp. baking powder

1 tsp. salt

Place bran cereal on sheet of waxed paper; roll fine with rolling pin. Add 6 tblsp. sugar and cinnamon; mix well. Set aside.

Beat 1 c. sugar, shortening and butter until light and fluffy. Beat in eggs and vanilla to mix thoroughly. Stir in bananas.

Sift together flour, baking powder and salt. Stir into banana mixture. Drop by teaspoonfuls into bran mixture and tumble until they are well coated. Place 2″ apart on greased baking sheet.

Bake in hot oven (400°) about 10 minutes. Remove cookies and cool on racks. Makes 4½ dozen.

CITRUS/NUT DROPS

Cookies flavored with orange and lemon, wear red cherry hats

½ c. shortening
¼ c. sugar
1 egg yolk
½ tsp. vanilla
2 tblsp. evaporated milk
1 tsp. grated orange peel

1 tsp. grated lemon peel
1¼ c. sifted flour
1 egg white, slightly beaten
¾ c. finely chopped nuts
Candied cherry halves (for tops)

Cream together shortening and sugar until light and fluffy. Beat in egg yolk, vanilla, evaporated milk and orange and lemon peels. Mix in flour.

Dip tablespoonfuls of dough in egg white. Lift out with fork, and dip one side in nuts. Place nut side up 2″ apart on greased baking sheet; press a cherry half into each.

Bake in slow oven (325°) 20 minutes. Remove cookies and cool on racks. Makes about 2 dozen.

CHRISTMAS DROP COOKIES

Gay with holiday colors, but festive for parties at all seasons

1 lb. dates, chopped
½ c. chopped walnuts
½ c. chopped maraschino
  cherries
1 c. sugar

1 tsp. vanilla
3 egg whites, stiffly beaten
1 c. sifted flour
Maraschino cherry pieces (for tops)

Combine dates, nuts and cherries. Mix in sugar and vanilla. Add egg whites to fruit mixture alternately with flour. (If mixture is dry, add a little cherry juice.)

Drop by teaspoonfuls about 2″ apart onto greased baking sheet. Top with pieces of cherries.

Bake in moderate oven (350°) about 20 minutes, until lightly browned. Remove cookies and cool on racks. Store in tightly covered container. (They keep indefinitely, and are better with aging.) Makes 4 dozen.

CRY BABY COOKIES

They're favorites of men. That's why we give you a giant-size recipe

1 c. plus 2 tblsp. shortening	1 tsp. salt
1 c. plus 2 tblsp. sugar	1½ tsp. baking soda
1 c. light molasses	2 c. shredded coconut
2 eggs, well beaten	2 c. chopped walnuts
4¾ c. sifted cake flour	1½ c. raisins
1 tblsp. baking powder	1 c. milk

Cream shortening; beat in sugar, molasses and eggs.

Sift together flour, baking powder, salt and soda; combine with coconut, walnuts and raisins. Add alternately with milk to creamed mixture.

Drop tablespoonfuls 2" apart onto greased baking sheet. Bake in moderate oven (375°) 10 minutes. Remove cookies and cool on racks. Makes about 9½ dozen.

DATE/NUT DROPS

Chewy cookies rich flavored with nuts, dates and brown sugar—good

2 c. chopped dates	1 tsp. vanilla
½ c. sugar	4 c. sifted flour
½ c. water	1 tsp. baking soda
1 c. butter or regular margarine	1 tsp. salt
1 c. sugar	1 tsp. ground cinnamon
1 c. brown sugar, firmly packed	1½ c. chopped nuts
3 eggs	

Combine dates, ½ c. sugar and water in saucepan. Cook, stirring occasionally, until mixture is the consistency of very thick jam. Cool.

Cream butter; add sugars gradually, beating until light and fluffy. Beat in eggs and vanilla.

Sift together dry ingredients. Add to creamed mixture, blending thoroughly. Stir in nuts and date mixture.

Drop by rounded teaspoonfuls about 2" apart onto greased baking sheet. Bake in a moderate oven (375°) 12 to 15 minutes. Remove cookies and cool on racks. Makes 12 dozen.

OREGON DATE SURPRISES

Walnut-stuffed dates are the unusual ingredient in these cookies

36 pitted dates (8 oz.)	1¼ c. sifted flour
½ c. large walnut pieces (36)	½ tsp. baking soda
¼ c. butter or regular margarine	1 tsp. baking powder
¾ c. brown sugar, firmly packed	¼ tsp. salt
1 egg	½ c. dairy sour cream
1 tsp. vanilla	Vanilla Cream Icing (see Index)

Stuff each date with a walnut piece. Set aside.

Beat together butter and brown sugar until light and fluffy. Beat in egg and vanilla to blend well.

Sift together flour, baking soda, baking powder and salt. Add to creamed mixture alternately with sour cream. Add stuffed dates and stir until they are well coated with batter.

Drop from teaspoon about 2″ apart onto lightly greased baking sheet, allowing 1 date to each cookie. Bake in moderate oven (375°) about 10 minutes. Remove cookies and cool on racks. If you like, frost with Vanilla Cream Icing. Makes 3 dozen.

N O T E : If you shell walnuts, first soak them overnight in salt water. Then the nut meats will come out whole.

RAGGED ROBINS

These dainty cookies are ideal for serving with ice cream, puddings

2 eggs	1 c. chopped dates
½ c. sugar	2 c. corn flakes
1 tsp. vanilla	¼ c. confectioners sugar
1 c. chopped walnuts	

Beat eggs until lemon-colored; gradually beat in sugar and vanilla to blend thoroughly. Stir in walnuts and dates. Fold in corn flakes.

Drop by teaspoonfuls 2″ apart onto lightly greased baking sheet. Bake in moderate oven (350°) 12 to 15 minutes. Cool 1 or 2 minutes on baking sheet, then remove to cooling rack. While still warm, roll in confectioners sugar. When cool, store cookies in loosely covered container. Makes about 3½ dozen.

CALIFORNIA FIG COOKIES

A recipe from the state that grows figs—and knows how to use them

1 c. chopped golden or black figs (½ lb.)	1 tsp. vanilla
	2 c. sifted flour
⅓ c. water	2 tsp. baking powder
1 c. butter or regular margarine	½ tsp. salt
½ c. sugar	Walnut or pecan halves
½ c. brown sugar, firmly packed	(optional)
1 egg	

Cook figs with water, stirring frequently, until thickened, about 5 minutes. Set aside to cool.

Beat butter with both sugars until light and fluffy; beat in egg and vanilla to blend well.

Sift together flour, baking powder and salt. Mix into creamed mixture. Then stir in cooled figs.

Drop by teaspoonfuls about 2" apart onto lightly greased baking sheet. Press a walnut half on top of each cookie. Bake in moderate oven (375°) 10 to 12 minutes, until lightly browned. Remove cookies and cool on racks. Makes 4 dozen.

FAMILY COOKIES

These soft cookies contain healthful vegetable and fruit ingredients

1 c. regular margarine	4½ c. sifted flour
2 c. sugar	½ tsp. salt
3 eggs	1 tsp. baking soda
1 c. cut-up carrots, ground	¼ tsp. ground allspice
1 large apple, ground	¼ tsp. ground cloves
1 large orange, ground	½ tsp. ground nutmeg
1 c. dates, ground	1 tsp. ground cinnamon
1 c. raisins, ground	1 c. chopped walnuts

Beat margarine until light; gradually add sugar and beat until light and fluffy. Beat in eggs until well blended. Fold in carrots and fruits.

Sift together flour, salt, baking soda and spices. Add to first mixture. Fold in nuts.

Drop by teaspoonfuls 2" apart onto lightly greased baking sheet and bake in moderate oven (350°) 10 to 12 minutes. Remove cookies and cool on racks. Store in airtight container. Makes about 7½ dozen.

HOLIDAY FRUITCAKE COOKIES

Glamor cookies with gay green and red topknots—a yuletide treat

4 c. sifted flour	1 c. chopped pecans
1 tsp. baking soda	1 c. candied cherries, cut in
1 tsp. salt	quarters
1 c. shortening	2 c. cut-up dates
2 c. brown sugar, firmly packed	1 c. candied fruits and peels
2 eggs, beaten	Red or green candied cherries
⅔ c. buttermilk	(for tops)

Sift together flour, soda and salt.

Cream shortening; add brown sugar and eggs; beat until light and fluffy. Add buttermilk and sifted dry ingredients, then fold in nuts, cherries, dates and candied fruits. Chill dough.

Drop dough by teaspoonfuls about 2" apart onto lightly greased baking sheet. Top each cookie with green or red cherry half.

Bake in moderate oven (375°) 8 to 10 minutes. Remove cookies and cool on racks. Makes 8 dozen.

FRUITED DROP COOKIES

There are many ways to introduce healthful fruit, wheat germ and rolled oats in meals, but when it comes to pleasant eating, none surpasses Fruited Drop Cookies. The recipe comes from a Tennessee woman who invented it; she says the cookies are husband-inspired. Because her husband is a great cookie fan, she decided to make them contribute to his nutrition. Result: Fruited Drop Cookies. Once you make them, you'll know why the hearty, good-for-you cookies are so popular in her family.

FRUITED DROP COOKIES

Serve these with glasses of milk or with hot coffee for a treat

½ c. finely cut dried apricots	1 tblsp. lemon juice
½ c. chopped dried prunes	1½ c. quick-cooking rolled oats
½ c. seedless raisins	2 tblsp. wheat germ
¾ c. water	2 c. sifted flour
½ c. regular margarine	1 tsp. baking soda
½ c. sugar	½ tsp. baking powder
½ c. brown sugar, firmly packed	½ tsp. salt
1 egg	⅓ c. chopped nuts

Combine apricots, prunes and raisins with water in saucepan. Heat and simmer about 5 minutes, stirring frequently. (Mixture is thick; watch carefully.) Set aside to cool.

Beat margarine until light; gradually add white and brown sugars, beating until light and fluffy. Beat in egg and lemon juice to blend well. Add fruit, rolled oats and wheat germ and mix well.

Sift together flour, baking soda, baking powder and salt. Fold into fruit mixture along with nuts. Chill.

Drop dough by teaspoonfuls 1″ apart onto lightly greased baking sheet. Bake in moderate oven (375°) 12 to 15 minutes. Remove cookies and cool on racks. Store in tightly covered container. Makes about 4½ dozen.

FRUITY GUMDROP COOKIES

Apples, gumdrops and raisins—no wonder the cookies are so tasty

2 c. sifted flour	1 egg, beaten
½ tsp. salt	¾ c. thick applesauce
2 tsp. baking powder	1 c. gumdrops, cut in small pieces
½ tsp. ground cinnamon	(no black candies)
½ c. shortening	1 c. raisins
½ c. sugar	

Sift together flour, salt, baking powder and cinnamon.

Cream shortening and sugar; add egg and applesauce; mix well.

Add flour mixture; stir until well blended; stir in gumdrops (no black candies) and raisins.

Drop by teaspoonfuls about 2″ apart onto lightly greased baking sheet. Bake in hot oven (400°) 10 to 15 minutes, until lightly browned. Transfer to cooling rack. Makes 4 dozen.

NOTE : You can use drained, crushed pineapple or canned peaches, drained and mashed, instead of applesauce. Rolled oats may be substituted for the gumdrops.

HAMPSHIRE HERMITS

Tangy Lemon Glaze is perfect on these citron-flavored cookies

⅔ c. butter or regular margarine
1 c. light brown sugar, firmly
   packed
2 eggs
2 tblsp. dairy sour cream
   or buttermilk
1¾ c. sifted flour
1¾ tsp. ground cinnamon

¼ tsp. ground ginger
¼ tsp. cloves
¼ tsp. baking soda
⅛ tsp. salt
1 c. chopped nuts
½ c. chopped raisins or currants
½ c. finely chopped citron
Lemon Glaze (recipe follows)

Beat butter until light. Gradually add brown sugar and beat after each addition until light and fluffy. Beat in eggs, one at a time, beating to mix thoroughly. Stir in sour cream.

Sift together flour, spices, baking soda and salt. Add to creamed mixture and beat until batter is smooth. Gradually add nuts, raisins and citron.

Drop batter from tablespoon 2″ apart onto greased baking sheet. Bake in moderate oven (350°) about 12 to 15 minutes, until cookies are golden brown. Remove cookies to racks and while warm, brush with Lemon Glaze. Makes about 3 dozen.

Lemon Glaze: Add 2 tblsp. lemon juice to 1 c. sifted confectioners sugar. Stir until smooth; brush over warm cookies (glaze is thin and tart).

LEMON DROP COOKIES

Crushed candy sweetens, adds lemony flavor to dotted cookies

½ c. boiling water (about)	¼ c. shortening
¼ c. dried currants	½ c. chopped candied cherries
2 c. sifted flour	1 egg, beaten
3 tsp. baking powder	½ tsp. vanilla
1 tsp. salt	⅓ c. milk
1 c. finely crushed candy lemon drops	

Pour boiling water over currants to cover; let stand 5 minutes. Drain and spread currants on paper toweling.

Sift together flour, baking powder and salt. Crush about ¼ c. lemon drops at a time between two sheets of aluminum foil; measure and stir each fourth at once into flour mixture before they stick together. Mix flour mixture and crushed lemon candy well. Blend in shortening with pastry blender until crumbly. Add cherries and currants.

Combine egg, vanilla and milk, and stir into flour mixture with fork. Stir until dough clings together in a ball.

Drop by teaspoonfuls about 1" apart onto greased baking sheet. Bake in moderate oven (350°) about 15 minutes. Transfer cookies to rack to cool. Makes about 3½ dozen.

MULTI-FRUITED DROPS

Crisp cookies—grated citrus peel enhances other fruit flavors

1 c. butter or regular margarine	½ tsp. baking soda
1 c. sugar	1½ c. quick-cooking rolled oats
1 c. brown sugar, firmly packed	1 tblsp. grated orange peel
2 eggs	1 tblsp. grated lemon peel
1 tsp. vanilla	1 c. chopped dates
2 c. sifted flour	1 c. seedless raisins
½ tsp. salt	1 c. chopped nuts
1 tsp. baking powder	1 c. flaked coconut

Cream together butter and sugars until light and fluffy. Beat in eggs and vanilla to mix thoroughly.

Sift together flour, salt, baking powder and soda. Mix into creamed mixture. Add remaining ingredients and mix well.

Drop from teaspoon about 2" apart onto greased baking sheet. Bake in moderate oven (375°) 12 minutes. Remove to racks to cool. Makes about 8 dozen cookies.

OLD-FASHIONED HERMITS

Seeded raisins make country-kitchen treats tasty—good travelers

1 c. shortening	1 tsp. salt
2 c. brown sugar, firmly packed	1 tsp. ground nutmeg
2 eggs	1 tsp. ground cinnamon
½ c. cold coffee	1½ c. chopped nuts
3½ c. sifted flour	2½ c. seeded raisins or currants
1 tsp. baking soda	

Thoroughly mix together shortening, sugar and eggs. Stir in cold coffee.

Sift together dry ingredients and stir into shortening mixture. Stir in nuts and raisins. Chill at least 1 hour.

Drop rounded teaspoonfuls of dough 2" apart onto lightly greased baking sheet. Bake in moderate oven (375°) 8 to 10 minutes. Test for doneness by touching lightly with fingertip. If almost no imprint remains, cookies are done. Use care not to overbake. Remove to racks to cool. Makes about 7½ dozen.

ORANGE COOKIES

For parties spread Orange Icing over tops of cake-like treats

⅔ c. shortening	½ tsp. salt
1 c. sugar	½ tsp. baking soda
2 eggs, slightly beaten	½ c. orange juice
1 tblsp. grated orange peel	½ c. chopped nuts
2¼ c. sifted flour	

Cream together shortening and sugar.

Combine eggs, creamed mixture and orange peel.

Sift together flour, salt and baking soda.

Add to creamed mixture alternately with orange juice; mix until well blended. Add nuts.

Drop by tablespoonfuls about 2″ apart onto greased baking sheet. Bake in moderate oven (375°) 10 minutes, or until golden brown. Remove cookies and cool on rack. Makes 3 dozen.

Orange Icing: Blend together 2½ tblsp. butter or regular margarine and 1½ c. sifted confectioners sugar. Stir in 1½ tblsp. orange juice and 2 tsp. grated orange peel. Blend until smooth.

ORANGE/CARROT COOKIES

Cheerful as Kansas sunflowers and kind to the budget—attractive, too

1 c. shortening	2 c. sifted flour
¾ c. sugar	2 tsp. baking powder
1 c. mashed cooked carrots	½ tsp. salt
1 egg	Golden Glow Topping (recipe
1 tsp. vanilla	follows)

Cream shortening and sugar until fluffy. Add carrots, egg and vanilla; mix well.

Sift together flour, baking powder and salt; add to carrot mixture; mix well. Drop batter by teaspoonfuls about 2″ apart onto greased baking sheet.

Bake in moderate oven (350°) about 20 minutes. Place cookies on racks to cool. While warm, spread with Golden Glow Topping. Makes 5 dozen.

Golden Glow Topping: Combine juice of ½ orange; grated peel of 1 orange, 1 tblsp. butter or regular margarine and 1 c. sifted confectioners sugar. Blend until smooth.

ORANGE/COCONUT CRISPS   *very good*

Friends will make a point to stop by for these crisp 3″ cookies

2 eggs	2½ c. sifted flour
⅔ c. salad oil	2 tsp. baking powder
1 c. sugar	½ tsp. salt
¼ c. thawed frozen orange juice	1 c. cookie coconut
concentrate	

Beat eggs with fork until well blended. Stir in oil. Blend in sugar until mixture thickens. Stir in orange juice concentrate.

Sift together flour, baking powder and salt; add with coconut to egg mixture. Stir until well blended.

Drop by teaspoonfuls about 2″ apart on ungreased baking sheet. Stamp each cookie flat with bottom of drinking glass dipped in sugar. (Lightly oil glass, then dip in sugar. Continue dipping in sugar for each cookie.)

Bake in hot oven (400°) 8 to 10 minutes. Remove immediately from baking sheet to cooling rack. Makes 3 dozen.

NOTE: Balls of cookie dough, rolled in sugar, may be packaged and frozen for future use. To bake: remove as many balls as desired from package, place on baking sheet and let stand about 30 minutes at room temperature. Bake as directed.

ORANGE-GLAZED PRUNE COOKIES

Brown cookies with yellow topknots hold prune and orange flavors

2 c. brown sugar, firmly packed	1 tsp. ground cinnamon
1 c. butter or shortening	½ tsp. salt
2 eggs, beaten	2 c. chopped cooked prunes
½ c. milk	1 c. chopped walnuts
3½ c. sifted flour	1 tsp. vanilla
1 tsp. baking powder	Orange Glaze (recipe follows)
1 tsp. baking soda	

Cream together sugar and butter; stir in eggs and milk.

Sift together flour, baking powder, soda, cinnamon and salt; stir into creamed mixture. Add prunes, nuts and vanilla.

Drop by teaspoonfuls onto greased baking sheet. Bake in moderate oven (350°) 15 to 20 minutes, until lightly browned. Remove cookies and cool on racks.

Spread tops of cooled cookies with a thin layer of Orange Glaze. Makes 8½ dozen.

Orange Glaze: Combine 3 c. confectioners sugar, grated peel of 1 orange and ¼ c. orange juice. Blend thoroughly until smooth.

PRUNE COOKIES

Spiced drop cookies topped with prune hats—try these soon

2 c. sugar	½ tsp. ground allspice
1 c. shortening	1 tsp. ground cinnamon
3 eggs	¼ tsp. ground nutmeg
1 c. finely cut cooked prunes	¼ tsp. ground cloves
3 c. sifted flour	¾ c. chopped walnuts
1 tsp. baking soda	Cooked prunes, pitted (for tops)
½ tsp. salt	

Combine sugar, shortening, eggs and prunes; beat until well blended.

Sift together dry ingredients; add in thirds to beaten mixture. Stir in walnuts.

Drop dough from teaspoon about 2″ apart onto ungreased baking sheet. Top each with a quarter of a cooked prune, skin side up.

Bake in moderate oven (375°) 12 to 14 minutes. Remove cookies and cool on racks. Makes about 5 dozen.

N O T E : If batter seems too stiff, add a small amount of prune juice.

GOLDEN PINEAPPLE COOKIES

You paint cookie tops with pineapple juice-confectioners sugar icing

½ c. shortening	2 c. sifted flour
1 c. brown sugar, firmly packed	1½ tsp. baking powder
1 egg	¼ tsp. baking soda
1 tsp. vanilla	⅛ tsp. salt
1 (8½ oz.) can crushed pineapple	1 c. sifted confectioners sugar

Cream shortening with brown sugar until light and fluffy. Add egg and vanilla and beat well to mix thoroughly.

Drain pineapple, reserving juice. Add pineapple to creamed mixture. Sift together flour, baking powder, baking soda and salt; stir into creamed mixture.

Drop by teaspoonfuls 1½ to 2″ apart onto greased baking sheet. Bake in slow oven (325°) about 15 minutes, until golden. Remove from baking sheet and cool on racks.

Stir 4 tsp. reserved pineapple juice into confectioners sugar. Beat until smooth. Brush on cookies. Makes about 4 dozen.

PUMPKIN COOKIES

Children eat these soft cookies without making crumbs

½ c. shortening	4 tsp. baking powder
1¼ c. brown sugar, firmly packed	½ tsp. salt
2 eggs	½ tsp. ground cinnamon
1 tsp. vanilla	½ tsp. ground nutmeg
1½ c. mashed cooked or canned	1 c. raisins
pumpkin	1 c. chopped nuts
2½ c. sifted flour	

Cream together shortening and brown sugar. Add eggs; beat thoroughly. Mix in vanilla and pumpkin.

Sift together dry ingredients. Blend into creamed mixture. Stir in raisins and nuts.

Drop dough by heaping teaspoonfuls about 2" apart onto greased baking sheet. Bake in a moderate oven (375°) about 15 minutes, until lightly browned. Remove cookies and cool on racks. Makes 5 dozen.

PUMPKIN/PINEAPPLE COOKIES

Taste like your best pumpkin pie with faint pineapple undertone

½ c. butter or regular margarine	1 c. quick-cooking rolled oats
1 c. brown sugar, firmly packed	2 c. sifted flour
½ c. sugar	½ tsp. baking powder
1 egg	½ tsp. baking soda
1 c. canned pumpkin	½ tsp. salt
½ c. drained crushed pineapple	2 tsp. ground cinnamon
1 c. coarsely cut-up pecans	¼ c. milk

Cream butter and sugars until light and fluffy. Beat in egg, then beat in pumpkin and pineapple. Stir in nuts and oats.

Sift together dry ingredients and add alternately with milk to creamed mixture.

Drop by teaspoonfuls about 2" apart onto greased baking sheet.

Bake in moderate oven (350°) 8 to 10 minutes. Place cookies on racks to cool. Makes 6 dozen.

GRANDMA'S RAISIN COOKIES

To keep cookies until mealtime, hide them from your family

1½ c. seedless raisins	2 tsp. baking powder
1½ c. water	1 tsp. baking soda
1½ c. shortening	½ tsp. salt
2 c. sugar	1 c. chopped walnuts
2 eggs	Caramel Frosting (recipe
1 tsp. vanilla	follows)
4 c. sifted flour (about)	

Cover raisins with water and cook gently about 20 minutes. Drain, saving 1 c. liquid. Cool.

Beat shortening and sugar until light and fluffy. Beat in eggs and vanilla to mix thoroughly.

Sift together flour, baking powder, baking soda and salt. Stir into creamed mixture alternately with reserved 1 c. raisin liquid. Stir in raisins and nuts.

Drop dough from tablespoon 2″ apart onto greased baking sheet. Spread out with bowl of spoon. Bake in moderate oven (375°) 10 to 12 minutes. Place cookies on racks and while still warm, spread tops with Caramel Frosting. Makes 5½ dozen.

Caramel Frosting: Combine in saucepan 1½ c. brown sugar, firmly packed, ¾ c. evaporated milk and ¼ c. regular margarine. Cook until sugar dissolves and margarine is melted. Remove from heat and cool slightly. Add 1 tsp. vanilla and enough sifted confectioners sugar (about 3 c.) to make a frosting of spreading consistency. If frosting gets too thick, add a few drops of milk.

RANCH HOUSE RAISIN COOKIES

You cook the raisins before you stir them into the cookie mixture

½ c. raisins
1 c. water
1 c. brown sugar, firmly packed
½ c. shortening
1 egg
½ tsp. vanilla

1¾ c. sifted flour
½ tsp. salt
½ tsp. baking powder
½ tsp. baking soda
½ c. chopped nuts

Bring raisins to a boil with water. Cool thoroughly.

Cream sugar and shortening until fluffy. Add egg and vanilla. Beat to mix.

Sift together flour, salt, baking powder and soda. Alternately add to creamed mixture with cooled raisins (there should be ½ c. liquid with raisins; if not, add water to make ½ c.). Stir in nuts.

Drop dough by teaspoonfuls at least 2" apart onto greased baking sheets.

Bake in moderate oven (350°) 10 to 12 minutes. Remove cookies and cool on racks. Makes 4 dozen.

RAISIN/CARROT COOKIES

Good family-style cookies that keep well if given a chance

1 c. sifted flour
¼ c. nonfat dry milk powder
¼ tsp. baking soda
1 tsp. baking powder
¼ tsp. ground nutmeg
¼ tsp. ground cinnamon
½ tsp. salt
⅓ c. shortening
⅓ c. brown sugar, firmly packed

½ c. molasses
1 egg, beaten
1 c. shredded carrots (or sweet potato)
1 tsp. grated lemon peel
½ c. ground or finely chopped raisins
1¾ c. quick-cooking rolled oats

Sift together flour, dry milk powder, soda, baking powder, nutmeg, cinnamon and salt.

Cream together shortening, sugar and molasses; add egg, then dry ingredients; stir until well blended.

Add carrots, lemon peel, raisins and oats; mix well. (If dough is too stiff, add a few drops of milk.) Chill.

Drop by teaspoonfuls about 2" apart onto lightly greased baking sheet. Bake in hot oven (375°) 10 to 12 minutes, until lightly browned. Remove cookies and cool on racks. Makes 5 dozen.

RAISIN/KETCHUP COOKIES

Ketchup gives cookies a rose-beige color and faint spicy taste—fresh Lemon Glaze contributes pleasing piquant flavor contrast

1 c. regular margarine	½ tsp. baking soda
½ c. sugar	⅛ tsp. salt
½ c. light brown sugar, firmly packed	¼ c. tomato ketchup
	¾ c. raisins
2 eggs	½ c. chopped nuts
1 tsp. vanilla	Lemon Glaze (recipe follows)
2¾ c. sifted flour	

Beat margarine until light. Gradually add white and brown sugars, beating constantly. Beat until light and fluffy. Beat in eggs and vanilla to blend well.

Sift together flour, baking soda and salt. Stir into creamed mixture alternately with ketchup. Fold in raisins and nuts. Drop heaping teaspoonfuls of dough 2" apart onto lightly greased baking sheet.

Bake in moderate oven (375°) 10 to 12 minutes, or until edges are browned and almost no imprint remains when touched lightly with fingertip. Remove cookies to cooling racks. Brush on Lemon Glaze while cookies are hot. Makes about 4 dozen.

Lemon Glaze: Combine 1½ c. sifted confectioners sugar with 2 tblsp. strained lemon juice; stir until smooth. If mixture is not thin enough to make a transparent glaze on cookies, add more lemon juice, 2 or 3 drops at a time until of right consistency. Makes ½ cup.

PECAN LACE ROLL-UPS

For women's luncheons tie bright ribbons around the crisp roll-ups

2 eggs	¼ c. melted butter or regular margarine
⅔ c. brown sugar, firmly packed	
1 tsp. vanilla	¼ c. sifted flour
	⅔ c. finely chopped pecans

Beat eggs until they thicken. Add brown sugar, 1 tblsp. at a time, beating constantly. Beat in vanilla to blend well. Slowly add slightly cooled butter. Fold in flour and pecans.

Place a tablespoonful of batter on well-greased baking sheet, spreading it to make a circle 4″ in diameter. Repeat process, having no more than 4 cookie circles 2″ apart on baking sheet at a time.

Bake in moderate oven (375°) 5 to 6 minutes, or until browned. Remove from oven and let cool about 30 seconds, then slip wide spatula under cookie to loosen it. Place the handle of a wooden spoon on one end of cookie and quickly roll up loosely to make a fat cylinder. Place on rack to cool. Repeat with other baked cookies. Then bake and roll the remainder of the batter in the same way (no more than 4 cookies at a time). Makes 15.

SWEDISH LACE COOKIES

The thin, crisp, brown lace-like cookie saddles or roll-ups always get attention. They're much easier to make than you may think

½ c. butter or regular margarine   1 tsp. baking powder
1½ c. regular rolled oats   1 tblsp. flour
1 egg   Dash of salt
⅔ c. sugar

Melt butter and pour over rolled oats.

Beat egg until light; then beat in sugar. Stir together baking powder, flour and salt to blend. Add to egg mixture, then add rolled oats.

Drop tablespoonfuls of batter 3″ apart onto greased and lightly floured baking sheet. Bake in moderate oven (375°) about 8 to 10 minutes, until golden brown.

Place on cooling rack; let stand about 1 minute (cookies should still be hot and pliable). Lift cookies off quickly with wide spatula and place over broomstick, wrapped with aluminum foil, propped across two coffee or shortening cans or pans. Gently press cookies to make them the shape of a saddle. Work fast. If cookies get too cold, they break in shaping. You can return the baking sheet to the oven for a minute if they cool too fast. Makes about 20 cookies.

Variation

Lace Roll-Ups: While cookies are warm, roll up around handle of a wooden spoon to make fat cylinders. These cookies are easier to store than the saddle shapes.

WALNUT LACE COOKIES

These see-through cookies are thin, fragile, crisp and delicious

⅓ c. sifted flour	1 c. brown sugar, firmly packed
½ tsp. baking powder	1 egg, slightly beaten
⅛ tsp. salt	1 c. chopped walnuts
¼ c. butter or regular margarine	

Sift together flour, baking powder and salt.

Blend butter, brown sugar and sifted dry ingredients with pastry blender as for pie crust. Add egg and mix thoroughly. Stir in walnuts.

Drop thin batter by half teaspoonfuls about 2″ apart onto heavily greased baking sheet. (Cookies spread during baking.) Bake in moderate oven (375°) 5 to 6 minutes. Remove from baking sheet at once and cool on racks. Makes about 5½ dozen.

GINGER NUGGETS

Team these cookies with glasses of milk for after-school snacks

3 c. sifted flour	¼ tsp. ground cloves
1 c. nonfat dry milk powder	1 c. shortening
1½ tsp. salt	1½ c. molasses
2 tsp. baking soda	¼ c. sugar
1 tsp. ground cinnamon	1 egg
½ tsp. ground ginger	

Sift together flour, dry milk powder, salt, soda and spices.

Cream together shortening, molasses and sugar.

Add egg, mix well. Add dry ingredients, and mix well. Chill.

Drop from teaspoon about 2″ apart onto greased baking sheet.

Bake in moderate oven (375°) 10 to 15 minutes, until done. Remove cookies and cool on racks. Makes about 8 dozen.

MOLASSES/WHOLE WHEAT COOKIES

Raisins and whole wheat flour make these molasses cookies special

½ c. nonfat dry milk powder
½ tsp. baking soda
2 tsp. baking powder
½ tsp. salt
⅓ c. shortening
¾ c. molasses

1 tsp. vanilla
2 eggs, beaten
1 c. plus 2 tblsp. whole wheat
   flour
½ c. raisins

Sift together dry milk powder, soda, baking powder and salt.

Cream together shortening, molasses, and vanilla; add eggs, blend well.

Add sifted ingredients and whole wheat flour; stir until thoroughly mixed. Add raisins (whole, chopped or ground).

Drop by teaspoonfuls about 2″ apart onto lightly greased baking sheet. Bake in moderate oven (350°) 10 to 12 minutes, until lightly browned. Remove cookies and cool on racks. Makes 4 dozen.

PEANUT/MOLASSES COOKIES

Cookies fruited with prunes are a pleasing texture and flavor surprise

1 c. sifted flour
½ tsp. salt
1 tsp. baking powder
¼ tsp. baking soda
¼ c. shortening
¼ c. brown sugar, firmly packed

½ c. molasses
½ c. crunchy peanut butter
½ tsp. vanilla
1 egg
2 tblsp. milk
1 c. chopped, uncooked prunes

Sift together flour, salt, baking powder and soda.

Cream together shortening, sugar, molasses, peanut butter and vanilla. Add egg and milk; mix well. Add dry ingredients; stir until well blended. Add chopped prunes.

Drop by teaspoonfuls onto lightly greased baking sheet. Bake in moderate oven (375°) 10 to 15 minutes, or until done.

Transfer cookies to cooling rack. Store in tightly covered container. Makes 5 dozen.

SOFT MOLASSES COOKIES

Family-style, generous cookies like Grandma used to make—updated

1 c. butter or regular margarine	1 tsp. instant coffee powder
1 c. sugar	2 tsp. ground cinnamon
1 large egg	1 tsp. ground ginger
1 c. light molasses	½ tsp. ground cloves
4¾ c. sifted flour	¾ c. milk
3 tsp. baking soda	Raisins or walnut halves
½ tsp. salt	

Beat butter until light; gradually add sugar and beat until fluffy. Beat in egg to blend thoroughly; then beat in molasses.

Sift together flour, baking soda, salt, coffee powder and spices. Add to first mixture alternately with milk. Beat about 30 seconds.

Drop dough by heaping teaspoonfuls about 2" apart onto lightly greased baking sheet, using care to keep cookies round. Press a raisin in center of each cookie.

Bake in moderate oven (375°) about 12 to 15 minutes, or until done. Place cookies on racks to cool. Makes about 5½ dozen.

SOFT MOLASSES DROPS

Ideal for mailing overseas and wonderful eating at home and abroad

¾ c. butter	2 tblsp. molasses
1½ c. brown sugar, firmly packed	1 tsp. baking soda
3 eggs	3 c. sifted flour
1 tsp. vanilla	1 c. raisins

Cream together butter and sugar until light and fluffy. Beat in eggs and vanilla to mix well.

Combine molasses and baking soda. Add to creamed mixture. Gradually stir in flour. Add raisins.

Drop by teaspoonfuls 2" apart onto greased baking sheet. Bake in moderate oven (350°) 8 minutes, or until brown. Cool cookies on racks. Makes about 6 dozen.

SLAPJACKS

The Pennsylvania Dutch created these molasses/coconut cookies

¾ c. butter or regular margarine
3 c. brown sugar, not firmly
   packed
1 c. light or dark molasses
1½ tsp. baking soda

3 c. sifted flour
¼ tsp. salt
½ c. cookie coconut
½ c. chopped walnuts

Cream butter and brown sugar until light and fluffy. Blend in molasses.

Sift together baking soda, flour and salt; add to creamed mixture, beating to mix thoroughly. Add coconut and nuts. Chill thoroughly for several hours, or overnight.

Drop dough by teaspoonfuls 2″ apart onto greased baking sheet. Bake in moderate oven (350°) 12 to 14 minutes. Cool 2 or 3 minutes on baking sheet before removing to cooling rack. Makes about 7 dozen.

COCONUT/NUTMEG COOKIES

Serve these with lemon sherbet for a wonderful flavor combination

1 (1 lb. 3 oz.) pkg. yellow or
   white cake mix
1 c. flaked coconut
½ c. butter or regular margarine

1 tsp. ground nutmeg
1 egg
2 tblsp. cold water

Combine all ingredients and mix until well blended.

Drop teaspoonfuls of mixture onto lightly greased baking sheet. Bake in moderate oven (350°) 12 to 15 minutes, until lightly browned. Transfer cookies to cooling rack. Makes 3½ dozen.

HONEYED GINGERSNAPS

Sugar sparkles on top of brown cookies—crisp outside, chewy within

⅔ c. sugar
¼ c. butter or regular margarine
1 tsp. ground ginger
½ tsp. ground cinnamon
½ tsp. baking soda
½ tsp. salt

½ tsp. vanilla
1 egg
½ c. honey
1½ c. sifted flour
Sugar for topping (about ¼ c.)

Combine ⅔ c. sugar, butter, ginger, cinnamon, baking soda, salt and vanilla in large mixing bowl. Cream until light and fluffy. Add egg and beat until very fluffy. Blend in honey. Add flour, a little at a time, and blend well.

Drop by teaspoonfuls 2½" apart onto lightly greased baking sheet. Sprinkle with sugar.

Bake in moderate oven (350°) 10 to 15 minutes, until lightly browned. Remove at once from baking sheet to racks to cool thoroughly. Makes about 4 dozen.

SWEDISH SPICE SPECIALS

Cardamom and orange peel contribute delightful, distinctive flavor

2 c. sifted flour
½ c. sugar
½ tsp. baking soda
½ c. light corn syrup
½ c. regular margarine or butter

1 tsp. ground cardamom
¼ tsp. ground ginger
¼ tsp. ground cloves
2 tsp. finely grated orange peel
1 egg

Sift flour with sugar and soda.

Combine corn syrup, margarine, spices and orange peel in saucepan; heat just until mixture boils and margarine melts. Remove from heat and cool.

Beat egg in large bowl. Slowly pour the cooled syrup into the egg. Stir in flour-sugar mixture all at once; blend well.

Drop by teaspoonfuls 2" apart onto greased baking sheet. Bake in moderate oven (350°) 10 to 12 minutes, until lightly browned. Transfer cookies to racks to cool. Makes about 3 dozen.

Very good

CIRCLE RANCH OAT COOKIES

Nicely spiced, big soft cookies—store airtight to retain freshness

1 c. shortening	1 tsp. baking soda
1½ c. brown sugar, firmly packed	¾ tsp. salt
	1 tsp. ground cinnamon
2 eggs	½ tsp. ground nutmeg
½ c. buttermilk	3 c. quick-cooking rolled oats
1¾ c. sifted flour	½ c. chopped walnuts
1 tsp. baking powder	¾ c. dried currants or raisins

Beat shortening until light; add brown sugar and beat until fluffy. Beat in eggs to mix well. Stir in buttermilk.

Sift together flour, baking powder, baking soda, salt, cinnamon and nutmeg; stir into beaten mixture. Stir in rolled oats, nuts and currants.

Drop dough by tablespoonfuls 2″ apart onto lightly greased baking sheet. Bake in hot oven (400°) about 8 minutes. Cool slightly on baking sheet; then remove to racks to complete cooling. Makes about 5 dozen.

NOTE: You can use sweet milk instead of buttermilk, but decrease baking soda to ¼ tsp. and increase baking powder to 2 tsp.

FRESH-FROM-THE-OVEN COOKIES

The contributor of the recipe for Oatmeal/Coconut Crisps and its variations keeps the dough in a tight container in her refrigerator for several days—sometimes a few weeks. It's a great recipe; she finds it easier to bake a few cookies at a time. And, in addition, she can always serve cookies with that wonderful fresh-from-the-oven aroma and taste.

OATMEAL/COCONUT CRISPS

Taste-testers voted these the best oatmeal cookies they've sampled

2 c. butter or regular margarine	3 c. sifted flour
2 c. brown sugar, firmly packed	2 tsp. salt
2 c. sugar	2 tsp. baking soda
2 tsp. vanilla	6 c. quick-cooking rolled oats
4 eggs	1½ c. flaked coconut

Cream together butter and brown and white sugars until fluffy. Stir in vanilla; then add eggs, one at a time, beating after each addition.

Sift together flour, salt and baking soda. Add to creamed mixture. Stir in rolled oats and coconut. Drop by teaspoonfuls about 2" apart onto well-greased baking sheet.

Bake in moderate oven (350°) 10 to 15 minutes. Cool cookies on racks. Makes 14 dozen.

NOTE: You can omit the 1½ c. coconut and divide dough into thirds. Add ⅓ c. flaked coconut to one part, ⅓ c. raisins to second part and ⅓ c. chopped walnuts to the third part.

Variations

Oatmeal/Raisin Cookies: Use 1½ c. raisins instead of the coconut.
Oatmeal/Nut Cookies: Use 1½ c. chopped walnuts instead of the coconut.
Oatmeal/Butter Crisps: Omit the flaked coconut.

OATMEAL CHIPPERS

Nuggets of chocolate lift these cookies above the commonplace

½ c. butter or regular margarine	1 tsp. salt
½ c. shortening	1 tsp. ground cinnamon
1 c. sugar	1 tsp. ground nutmeg
1 c. brown sugar, firmly packed	2 c. quick-cooking rolled oats
2 eggs	1 (6 oz.) pkg. semisweet
1 tsp. vanilla	chocolate pieces
2 c. sifted flour	1 c. chopped walnuts
1 tsp. baking soda	

Cream together butter and shortening. Add sugars gradually, beating until light and fluffy. Beat in eggs and vanilla.

Blend in sifted dry ingredients, mixing thoroughly. Stir in oats, chocolate pieces and nuts.

Drop by rounded teaspoonfuls about 2″ apart onto greased baking sheet. Bake in moderate oven (375°) 9 to 12 minutes. Remove cookies and cool on racks. Makes 8 dozen.

OATMEAL DROP COOKIES

Coffee party treats—apricot or other fruit jam adds a color note

½ c. butter or regular margarine	2½ c. sifted flour
½ c. shortening	1 tsp. baking soda
1 c. brown sugar, firmly packed	1 tsp. salt
¾ c. sugar	1 tsp. ground cinnamon
2 eggs	2 c. quick-cooking rolled oats
½ c. water	½ c. apricot jam
1 tsp. vanilla	

Cream together butter and shortening. Gradually beat in sugars until mixture is light and fluffy. Add eggs, water and vanilla. Beat well.

Sift together flour, soda, salt and cinnamon. Blend into creamed mixture. Stir in oats.

Drop rounded teaspoonfuls about 3″ apart onto ungreased baking sheet. Make an indentation in each with tip of spoon. Fill with apricot jam (about ½ tsp.). Top with 1 tsp. dough.

Bake in hot oven (400°) 10 to 12 minutes. Remove cookies and cool on rack. Makes 4 dozen.

JEWELED OATMEAL DROPS

Gumdrops add chewy texture, color and flavor to these crisp cookies

1 c. shortening	½ tsp. baking soda
1 c. brown sugar, firmly packed	1 tsp. baking powder
1 c. sugar	¾ tsp. salt
2 eggs	2 c. quick-cooking rolled oats
1 tsp. vanilla	1 c. cut-up assorted gumdrops
2 c. sifted flour	(no black candies)

Beat shortening until light. Add sugars and beat until fluffy. Beat in eggs and vanilla to mix thoroughly.

Sift together flour, baking soda, baking powder and salt; add to beaten mixture. Mix well.

Stir in rolled oats and gumdrops. Drop by teaspoonfuls about 2″ apart onto lightly greased baking sheet.

Bake in moderate oven (375°) about 10 to 12 minutes. Remove from baking sheet to rack and let cool. Makes 5½ dozen.

N O T E : Cut gumdrops with scissors moistened in cold water.

Variation

Orange Jeweled Oatmeal Drops: Substitute 18 candy orange slices, cut in small pieces, for the assorted gumdrops.

ORANGE/OATMEAL SCOTCHIES

An orange-coconut blend flavors these crisp brown oatmeal cookies

¾ c. shortening	1½ c. quick-cooking rolled oats
1½ c. brown sugar, firmly packed	½ c. flaked coconut
	2 c. sifted flour
2 eggs	2 tsp. baking powder
1 tblsp. grated orange peel	½ tsp. baking soda
6 tblsp. orange juice	½ tsp. salt

Cream shortening and sugar until light and fluffy. Beat in eggs to mix thoroughly. Then beat in orange peel and juice. Stir in rolled oats and coconut.

Sift together remaining dry ingredients; stir into first mixture.

Drop by teaspoonfuls 2″ apart onto lightly greased baking sheet.

Bake in hot oven (400°) 8 to 10 minutes. Remove cookies and cool on racks. Makes about 5½ dozen.

OVERNIGHT MACAROONS

Easy-to-make, delicious, inexpensive—cookies look like brown lace

4 c. quick-cooking rolled oats	2 eggs, beaten
2 c. brown sugar, firmly packed	1 tsp. salt
1 c. salad oil	1 tsp. almond extract

Combine rolled oats, brown sugar and salad oil in large mixing bowl; mix well. Cover and let stand overnight.

In the morning, blend eggs, salt and almond extract into oat mixture. Let stand 5 minutes.

Drop batter from teaspoon 2″ apart onto lightly greased baking sheet. Bake in slow oven (325°) 15 minutes. Remove cookies and cool on racks. Makes 4 dozen.

SCOTCH MOLASSES COOKIES

Thin, crisp oatmeal cookies have attractive lacy edges. Good!

¾ c. sifted flour	½ tsp. ground cloves
½ c. sugar	2½ c. quick-cooking rolled oats
2 tsp. baking powder	1 c. raisins
½ tsp. salt	⅔ c. melted shortening
2 tsp. baking soda	1 egg, beaten
1 tsp. ground cinnamon	¾ c. molasses
½ tsp. ground nutmeg	1 tblsp. milk

Sift together dry ingredients.

Combine oats and raisins; sift flour mixture over top.

Combine remaining ingredients in bowl. Pour over dry ingredients; mix well. Drop by teaspoonfuls 2 to 3″ apart onto greased baking sheet.

Bake in moderate oven (350°) 8 to 12 minutes. Spread on racks to cool. Makes 3 dozen.

PUMPKIN/OATMEAL DROPS

Not too sweet; mild, spicy and good keepers if you hide them

¾ c. butter or regular margarine
1½ c. sugar
2 eggs
1 c. canned pumpkin
1 tsp. vanilla
1½ c. sifted flour
2 tsp. baking powder
½ tsp. baking soda

½ tsp. salt
1 tsp. ground cinnamon
½ tsp. ground nutmeg
⅛ tsp. ground cloves
1½ c. quick-cooking rolled oats
½ c. shredded coconut
½ c. chopped nuts

Cream together butter and sugar. Beat in eggs; add pumpkin and vanilla.

Sift together flour, baking powder, soda, salt and spices. Stir into creamed mixture. Add oats, coconut and nuts.

Drop by teaspoonfuls 2″ apart onto greased baking sheet. Bake in moderate oven (375°) about 12 minutes. Remove cookies and cool on racks. Makes 6 dozen.

ROOKIE COOKIES

For hearty cookies that are extra-chewy use regular rolled oats

2 eggs
2 c. brown sugar, firmly packed
1 c. melted butter or regular
    margarine
2 c. sifted flour
1 tsp. baking powder
½ tsp. baking soda

½ tsp. salt
4 c. regular rolled oats
1 c. chopped nuts
1 c. shredded coconut
½ c. raisins
½ c. water (about)

Beat eggs; blend in sugar and butter.

Sift together flour, baking powder, soda and salt. Stir into egg mixture. Stir in remaining ingredients, adding enough water to moisten well. Mix thoroughly.

Drop by teaspoonfuls about 2″ apart onto greased baking sheet. Bake in moderate oven (350°) about 15 minutes. Remove cookies and cool on racks. Makes 6 dozen.

N O T E : For less chewy cookies use 3½ c. quick-cooking rolled oats instead of the regular.

WHEAT/OAT CRISPS

It's a wonder that anything so "good for you" can taste so good

¾ c. shortening	1 tsp. salt
1 c. brown sugar, firmly packed	½ tsp. baking soda
½ c. white sugar	3 c. quick-cooking rolled oats
1 egg	2 tblsp. wheat germ
¼ c. water	½ c. flaked coconut
1 tsp. vanilla	½ c. chopped nuts
1 c. stone ground whole wheat flour	¼ c. semisweet chocolate pieces (optional)

Beat shortening with sugars until light and fluffy. Beat in egg, water and vanilla until creamy.

Stir together flour, salt and baking soda to mix. Stir into creamed mixture and blend well. Add rolled oats, wheat germ, coconut and nuts. Drop by teaspoonfuls 2" apart onto lightly greased baking sheet. Top each cookie with a chocolate piece.

Bake in moderate oven (350°) 12 to 15 minutes. Transfer cookies to racks to cool. Makes 5 dozen.

GRANDMA'S SOFT SUGAR COOKIES

Grandma centered seeded raisins in her memorable man-size cookies

1 c. sugar	3½ c. sifted flour
1 c. brown sugar, firmly packed	2 tsp. baking powder
½ c. butter	1 tsp. cream of tartar
½ c. shortening	¾ tsp. salt
2 eggs	¾ tsp. baking soda
1 tsp. vanilla	1 c. buttermilk
½ tsp. lemon extract	⅓ c. sugar (for tops)
1 tsp. ground nutmeg	Seeded raisins (or seedless)

Beat together white and brown sugars, butter and shortening until light and fluffy. Beat in eggs, vanilla and lemon extract to mix well.

Sift together nutmeg, flour, baking powder, cream of tartar, salt and soda. Add alternately with buttermilk to creamed mixture.

Drop tablespoonfuls of dough 2½" apart onto greased baking sheet. With the back of the spoon's bowl, spread round and round with the outer edge of the cookies a little thicker than the centers. Sprinkle generously with sugar and place a fat seeded raisin in the center of each cookie.

Bake in hot oven (400°) about 10 minutes. For softer cookies, bake in hot oven (425°) about 8 minutes, or until no indentation remains when you touch the center of the cookie with your fingertip. Remove cookies and cool on racks. Makes 4 dozen.

POWDERED SUGAR COOKIES

Rich, dainty cookies that can be either molded or dropped

⅓ c. shortening	1 tsp. baking soda
½ c. butter	1 tsp. cream of tartar
1½ c. confectioners sugar	¼ tsp. salt
1 egg	1 c. chopped pecans
1 tsp. vanilla	¾ c. confectioners sugar (for
¼ tsp. almond extract	coating)
2½ c. sifted flour	

Beat shortening and butter until light; gradually add 1½ c. confectioners sugar, beating constantly. Beat in egg, vanilla and almond extract to mix well.

Sift together flour, baking soda, cream of tartar and salt. Add to creamed mixture. Stir in nuts.

Drop by teaspoonfuls 1″ apart onto ungreased baking sheet. (Or shape in 1″ balls.) Bake in hot oven (400°) 8 to 10 minutes. Remove to cooling racks, and while still warm, roll in confectioners sugar. When cool, roll in confectioners sugar again for snowy white coating. Makes about 6 dozen.

Rolled Cookies

When lights and decorations go up along main streets across the country, rolling pins and cookie cutters of many shapes soon come to light in the kitchen. Then, more than at any other season, rolled cookies have top popularity. By the time Christmas arrives, cookie stars, hearts, crescents, jaunty gingerbread boys and animals dangle from the branches of twinkling Christmas trees.

We tell you how to glamorize cookies by sprinkling them before baking with coarse white or colored decorating sugar, tiny colored candies, chocolate shot (jimmies), chopped nuts, silver and gold dragées and other simple trims. You can also spread baked cookies with frosting or a glaze, or put them together in pairs with frosting or filling. (Be sure to try our Raisin-Filled Cookies with a choice of three other fillings.)

If you want a picture-pretty tray or plate of cookies to set—as for a buffet supper—bake our beautiful Wild Rose Cookies, dainty Cheese/Jam Cookie Tarts and Frosted Diamond Cookies (a Pennsylvania Dutch specialty containing caraway seeds).

Among our rolled cookies are also some imported recipes from faraway places, all adapted to American tastes—Finnish Stars, Orange Wreaths from Mexico and Chinese Almond Cookies.

Do bake our traditionals. We recommend the Frosted Ginger Creams, an unforgettable molasses cookie. And don't miss the big recipe for Gingerbread Christmas Cookies, ideal for cutting into different shapes for yuletide. We also include Hard-Cooked Egg Cookies, a delightful yellow rolled cookie.

Some women bake rolled cookies the year around, time being their only limitation. But beginners and women inexperienced in rolling dough are sometimes loath to try them. It's really simple to roll cookie dough if you use good recipes and follow the rules. Number one is to chill the dough if it seems soft. When it gets firm, take only the amount you can work with at a time from the refrigerator.

Roll it on a pastry cloth with a stockinet-covered rolling pin. Rub a little flour into the cloth and stockinet with your hands to discourage the dough from sticking. Repeat if necessary, but be stingy with flour —adding too much makes cookies tough.

Roll from the center of the mound of dough as you do for pie crust. When you cut dough with the cookie cutter, start at the edges and work to the center. Dip the cutter in flour and shake off the excess. Repeat as often as necessary to prevent dough from sticking. Cut with pressure and keep scraps to a minimum by cutting cookies close together. For the last baking, gather the scraps, shape into a mound, roll and cut. These cookies will be less tender than those rolled only once.

If you do not have cookie cutters in assorted shapes, why not start a collection, adding one or two a year? Many women say this is a rewarding hobby. If you (or another family member) have artistic leanings you also can draw and cut patterns from cardboard. Grease the patterns well before laying them on the rolled dough; cut around them with a pointed knife.

Lift cutouts to the baking sheet on a wide spatula to avoid stretching them out of shape. Bake cookies only until delicately browned unless recipe specifies otherwise.

ALMOND QUARTER-MOONS

Recipe for the dainty crescents is from an almond grower's wife

2¾ c. sifted flour	1½ c. sugar
1½ tsp. baking powder	½ tsp. almond extract
¼ tsp. salt	2 eggs, beaten
¾ c. butter or regular margarine	½ c. ground unblanched almonds

Sift together flour, baking powder and salt.

Cream butter and sugar until light and fluffy. Add almond extract and eggs; beat well. Add sifted dry ingredients and almonds and mix well. Chill.

Roll dough about ⅛" thick. Cut with crescent-shaped cutter. Place about 2" apart on ungreased baking sheet. Bake in moderate oven (350°) 8 to 10 minutes. Remove cookies and cool on racks. Makes about 10 dozen.

SPECIAL-OCCASION JELLY COOKIES

Jelly in country kitchens is more than a spread for hot biscuits, toast or jelly roll. It's also a favored ingredient in many dishes, including cookies like these Almond/Jelly Cookies.

Jelly touches these crisp, rich cookies with bright color and supplies that luscious fruity flavor. They're at their best served the same day you bake them, although you can freeze them successfully to bring out on short notice when you want to give your guests a true country-kitchen treat. The combination of almond/jelly flavors makes these cookie sandwiches exceptional.

When we first made them, we used currant jelly, as suggested by the North Dakota woman who contributed this recipe. You can substitute any kind you especially like or have in your cupboard. We found both apricot and peach jams also made delightful fillings.

ALMOND/JELLY COOKIES

Grated almonds speckle cookie sandwiches filled with tart-sweet jelly

1 c. butter	⅛ tsp. salt
1 c. plus 2 tblsp. sugar	1 c. grated unblanched almonds
¼ tsp. vanilla	(about ¾ c. before grating)
1½ c. sifted flour	½ c. currant jelly

Beat butter until light; add sugar and vanilla and beat until fluffy. Add flour and salt, blended together, and then the almonds.

Cover bowl tightly and chill overnight or several hours.

Roll dough very thin with waxed paper placed over dough to make rolling easier. Cut with 2½″ round cutter.

Place cookies 1″ apart on lightly greased baking sheet and bake in slow oven (300°) 8 to 10 minutes, until they start to brown around edges. Remove cookies to cooling rack. While still warm, spread half of cookies with currant jelly and top with other half of cookies. Complete cooling on racks. Makes 3 dozen.

N O T E : You can crush almonds fine with a rolling pin if a hand-turned grater is not available.

APPLESAUCE ROLL-UP COOKIES

Slice and bake one roll; freeze the other roll for baking later

1¾ c. applesauce (16½ oz. can)   1 c. shortening
¾ c. cut-up dates   3 eggs
½ c. sugar   4 c. sifted flour
1 tblsp. grated orange peel   ¼ tsp. salt
1 c. chopped nuts   ½ tsp. baking soda
2 c. brown sugar, firmly packed

To make filling, combine applesauce, dates and white sugar. Cook over low heat, stirring until thick, about 12 minutes. Remove from heat; stir in orange peel and nuts. Set aside to cool (you'll have 3 c. filling).

Beat brown sugar with shortening until light and fluffy. Beat in eggs to mix well.

Sift together flour, salt and baking soda. Add to creamed mixture, and mix thoroughly. Divide in half. Roll each half about ¼" thick on waxed paper to make a 15 x 12" rectangle.

Spread 1½ c. filling over each half of dough. Roll up like jelly roll (each roll will be about 16" long). Wrap tightly in waxed paper and refrigerate overnight, or at least several hours.

With a sharp knife, cut dough in ¼" slices; place 1½ to 2" apart on lightly greased baking sheet. Bake in moderate oven (350°) about 12 minutes, until lightly browned. Transfer cookies to racks to cool. Store cookies in container with loose-fitting lid. Makes about 10 dozen.

N O T E : If cookies lose crispness on standing, spread on baking sheet and heat in slow oven (300°) about 5 minutes. If you like, sift confectioners sugar mixed with cinnamon over slightly warm cookies. Use the proportion of 1 tsp. ground cinnamon to ½ c. confectioners sugar. Especially good with coffee.

BROWN-EYED SUSANS

These yellow and brown cookies bring beauty to any tea table

1 c. butter or regular margarine	3¼ c. sifted flour
1 c. sugar	1 tblsp. baking powder
1 egg	1 tsp. salt
½ tsp. almond extract	⅓ c. semisweet chocolate
¼ tsp. yellow food color	pieces (64)

Cream butter and sugar together until light and fluffy. Beat in egg, almond extract and food color.

Sift together flour, baking powder and salt. Gradually blend into creamed mixture.

Turn dough onto lightly floured surface; knead gently to form a ball. Wrap in plastic wrap or waxed paper and chill several hours, or until dough can be handled easily.

Divide dough in fourths. Roll one fourth at a time to make a 12 x 6″ rectangle. Cut each rectangle into strips ¾″ wide and 6″ long. On long side of strip cut slits ½″ apart and three-fourths of the way through to opposite side. Roll each strip like a jelly roll. (Dough has tendency to break when rolled; hold roll together with fingers and pinch slightly on bottom when placing on baking sheet. This spreads the blossoms.) Place about 1″ apart on ungreased baking sheet. Turn cut ends down a little to form flower petals. Center a chocolate piece, flat side up, in each flower.

Bake in moderate oven (375°) 8 to 10 minutes, until browned. Remove from oven; cool slightly on baking sheet set on rack. Remove from baking sheet and cool completely on racks. Makes about 64.

Variation

Festival Squares: Divide dough for Brown-Eyed Susans in half. Make flower cookies with one half, Festival Squares with the other half: Roll dough into two 12 x 6″ rectangles. Cut in 2″ squares with knife; then cut two ½″ slits in each side of squares. Bake and cool like Brown-Eyed Susans. Then drop Vanilla Cream Icing in irregular amounts from teaspoon onto centers of cookies. For the most charming cookies, divide icing into four parts. Leave one white and tint the others with food color in pastel shades of pink, green and yellow. Makes 3 dozen.

Vanilla Cream Icing: Stir together 2 c. sifted confectioners sugar, ¼ tsp. salt and 1 tsp. vanilla; add enough milk or water (about 2 tblsp.) to make an icing that spreads easily. Beat well. Spread on cookies with pastry brush, or drop from spoon, as directed in recipe.

BUTTER CRISPIES

Freeze some of these to bring out for company—they're good keepers

1 c. butter	⅛ tsp. salt
1 c. sugar	¾ tsp. ground nutmeg
1 egg	1 tsp. baking soda
3½ c. sifted flour	½ c. buttermilk

Cream butter until light and fluffy. Gradually beat in sugar and egg.

Combine flour, salt, nutmeg and baking soda. Sift into creamed mixture alternately with buttermilk. Chill at least an hour or until firm.

Roll out a small part of dough at a time, keeping remaining dough in refrigerator until ready to roll. Roll very thin. Cut with 2½" round or fancy cookie cutters. Place ¼ to ½" apart on ungreased baking sheet.

Bake in moderate oven (350°) 8 to 10 minutes, until lightly browned. Remove from baking sheet to wire racks to cool. Makes 5½ dozen.

CHEESE/JAM COOKIE TARTS

Brown rims of cookie dough frame fruit jams of festive colors

1 c. butter	½ c. jam (grape, apricot, peach
1 (8 oz.) pkg. cream cheese	or berry)
2 c. sifted flour	

Beat together butter and cream cheese until light and fluffy. Blend in flour. Chill overnight.

Roll dough about ⅛" thick and cut with 2" round cutter. Spread tops with jam; arrange ½" apart on ungreased baking sheet. (Cookies shrink during baking.)

Bake in moderate oven (350°) 10 to 12 minutes. Remove cookies and cool on racks. Makes about 6 dozen.

NOTE: Store cookies in container with loose lid in a cool place, or package and freeze them. To use if frozen, thaw in wrapper at room temperature about 15 minutes. To restore crispness to stored cookies, spread them on baking sheets and heat in slow oven (300°) about 5 minutes.

CHINESE ALMOND COOKIES

An Iowa country woman, member of a gourmet club, serves these with tea for dessert after an oriental-type meal.

The inspiration to make Chinese Almond Cookies followed a trip to California and an afternoon spent browsing around San Francisco's Chinatown. Back home in her farm kitchen, she set out to duplicate the cookies she saw in an oriental bakery and tasted in a Chinese dinner. Luckily, she used lard for shortening; this gave her product that characteristic texture that all authentic Chinese almond cookies have. By baking them in a slow oven, she achieved the right color—no browning except a delicate shading around the edges. Her cookies, with almonds centered on top, capture the delightful flavor that makes this type of cookie the top oriental favorite of Americans.

CHINESE ALMOND COOKIES

Go Chinese with these creamy white cookies, a top oriental favorite

1 c. lard, butter or regular
    margarine
1 c. sugar
1 egg
¾ tsp. almond extract
2¾ c. sifted flour

½ tsp. baking soda
½ tsp. salt
24 whole almonds (about), split
    lengthwise in halves
    (about ¼ c.)

Beat together lard and sugar until light and fluffy. Beat in egg and almond extract to blend well.

Sift together flour, baking soda and salt; add to creamed mixture. Shape dough with hands to form a ball.

Roll dough a scant ¼" thick and cut with 2" round cutter. Place 2" apart on ungreased baking sheet. Put an almond half in the center of each cookie.

Bake in slow oven (325°) 15 to 20 minutes, or until cookies brown very lightly around edges. Carefully remove cookies with broad spatula to cooling rack. (They are fragile when hot.) When cool, store in covered container in a cool place, or freeze. Makes about 3½ dozen.

CLOTHESPIN COOKIES

These fascinating cookies will be the talk of your coffee party

3¼ c. sifted flour	1¼ c. warm water
1 tsp. salt	2 egg yolks
2 tblsp. sugar	Chocolate/Marshmallow Filling
2 c. shortening	(recipe follows)

Blend together flour, salt, sugar and ½ c. shortening as for pie crust. Stir in warm water. Then add egg yolks and mix well. Cover bowl and chill 1 hour.

Remove dough from refrigerator and roll in rectangle ¼" thick. Spread with ½ c. shortening. Fold one half of dough (greased top) over on other half; refrigerate another hour. Repeat this process two more times, each time spreading ½ c. shortening on dough.

Roll a fourth of dough at a time, leaving remaining dough in refrigerator until ready to work with it. Cut in strips 1" wide, 4" long. Wind each strip loosely around a clean wooden clothespin. Lay in ungreased 15½ x 10½ x 1" jelly roll pan.

Bake in hot oven (425°) 10 to 12 minutes. Place clothespins with cookies on cooling racks. In 2 or 3 minutes, gently twist pins and slip off cookies. (They are crisp and break easily so work carefully.) When cool, fill with Chocolate/Marshmallow Filling.

To fill, cut a small hole in corner of small plastic bag. Partly fill with Chocolate/Marshmallow Filling, leaving remaining filling in refrigerator until needed. Squeeze out filling, first into one end of cookie and then in other end to fill completely. Store filled cookies in refrigerator until serving time. Makes 9 dozen.

NOTE: Cookies may be refrigerated a few days and then filled. Or freeze cookies and fill them when needed.

CHOCOLATE/MARSHMALLOW FILLING

This luscious filling and the crisp cookies are great teammates

¼ c. flour
1 c. milk
½ c. butter
½ c. sugar
½ c. confectioners sugar

½ c. marshmallow creme
1 tsp. vanilla
2 to 4 squares unsweetened
    chocolate, melted and cooled

Mix flour with a little milk to make a smooth paste; add remaining milk and cook, stirring constantly, until mixture thickens. Set aside to cool.

Cream together butter and sugars until light and fluffy, using electric mixer on high speed. Add thickened flour-milk mixture and beat well. Then beat in the marshmallow creme and vanilla. Stir in chocolate. Cover and chill before using. Makes 2 cups.

N O T E : You can use 2 to 4 squares unsweetened or semisweet chocolate in the filling. What you use and how much is a matter of personal preference.

COCOA/MOLASSES COOKIES

Long-time favorites in Dutch neighborhoods in Hudson River Valley

1 c. butter
½ c. sugar
1 c. light molasses
1 egg
1 tsp. vanilla

3 c. sifted flour
1 tsp. salt
½ c. cocoa
Vanilla Glaze (see Index)

Cream butter and sugar until light and fluffy. Beat in molasses, egg and vanilla to mix well.

Sift together flour, salt and cocoa; stir into creamed mixture. Chill dough.

Roll dough rather thick, about ¼", and cut into 4 x 2½" rectangles. (Use an empty luncheon meat can for a cutter, or a 4 x 2½" rectangular cutter or a knife. Cookies cut with the empty can or cutter have rounded corners.) Place ½" apart on lightly greased baking sheet.

Bake in moderate oven (350°) about 10 minutes. Remove cookies and cool on racks, then spread with Vanilla Glaze. Makes 3 dozen.

CORNMEAL COOKIES

The unusual ingredient in these crisp, raisin treats is cornmeal

1½ c. sifted flour	¾ c. sugar
½ tsp. baking powder	1 egg
½ tsp. salt	½ tsp. lemon extract
½ c. cornmeal	¼ c. milk
½ tsp. ground nutmeg	½ c. chopped raisins
½ c. shortening	5 tblsp. sugar (for topping)

Sift together flour, baking powder, salt, cornmeal and nutmeg.

Beat together shortening and ¾ c. sugar until light and fluffy. Beat in egg and lemon extract. Alternately add milk and sifted dry ingredients. Beat until smooth. Stir in raisins.

Roll dough out on lightly floured board to ¼" thickness; cut with 2½" round cutter. Place 1" apart on greased baking sheet; sprinkle with sugar. Bake in moderate oven (375°) 12 to 15 minutes. Remove cookies and cool on racks. Makes 29 cookies.

DATE PINWHEELS

Two-tone pinwheels add charm to a tray or plate of one-color cookies

1⅓ c. chopped dates	1⅓ c. brown sugar, firmly packed
½ c. sugar	2 eggs
½ c. water	2⅔ c. sifted flour
½ c. chopped nuts	½ tsp. salt
⅔ c. shortening	½ tsp. baking soda

Combine dates, sugar, water and nuts in saucepan; cook until thick. Set aside to cool.

Cream shortening; beat in brown sugar. Beat in eggs to mix thoroughly.

Sift together dry ingredients; add to creamed mixture and blend well. Chill thoroughly.

Divide dough in half; roll each half in a rectangle ¼" thick. Spread each with date filling and roll up like a jelly roll. Wrap in waxed paper and chill overnight.

Cut dough in ⅛" slices and place 1½" apart on greased baking sheet. Bake in moderate oven (375°) 8 minutes, or until lightly browned. Remove cookies and cool on racks. Makes about 5 dozen.

PINK AND WHITE FROSTED DIAMONDS

Pennsylvania Dutch women of Moravian faith invented these cookies and named them Moravian seed cookies. Your fondness for them will depend on how much you enjoy the flavor of caraway.

Tradition requires that you cut the pastry-like dough in diamond shapes, frost them in white and sprinkle on coarse pink sugar.

Diamonds are easy to cut with a knife, although you can use a cookie cutter if you have one. Just roll the dough in a rectangle and cut 2″ diagonal strips one way, and then the other. And you have no scraps of dough to reroll and bake.

FROSTED DIAMOND COOKIES

Guaranteed to please caraway fans—also to dress up the cookie tray

½ c. butter	1 tsp. caraway seeds
½ c. sugar	White Mountain Frosting
2 eggs	(recipe follows)
1 tsp. vanilla	¼ c. coarse pink decorating
3 c. sifted flour	sugar (about)
⅛ tsp. salt	

Beat butter until light; gradually add sugar and beat until mixture is fluffy. Beat in eggs and vanilla to blend thoroughly.

Sift together flour and salt; add to creamed mixture. Stir in caraway seeds.

Roll dough thin, not more than ⅛″, and cut in 2″ diamonds with sharp knife or cookie cutter. Place ½″ apart on lightly greased baking sheet.

Bake in slow oven (325°) 10 to 12 minutes. Remove cookies and cool on racks. Then spread with White Mountain Frosting and sprinkle with pink sugar. Makes about 6½ dozen.

White Mountain Frosting: Combine 1 c. sugar, ⅛ tsp. cream of tartar and ¼ c. water in small saucepan. Place over heat and stir until sugar dissolves. Continue cooking syrup to soft ball stage (236°).

Meanwhile, add ⅛ tsp. salt to 1 egg white and beat until stiff. Pour hot syrup in a fine stream into egg white, beating constantly until frosting is of spreading consistency.

DOUBLE CREAM COOKIES

Tea party tidbits—tiny, rich cookies put together with frosting

1 c. soft butter	2 c. sifted flour
⅓ c. heavy cream	Creamy Frosting (recipe follows)

Mix together butter, cream and flour; chill thoroughly. Roll ⅛" thick and cut in 1½" rounds. Place on waxed paper heavily sprinkled with sugar and turn to coat circles.

Place about 2" apart on ungreased baking sheet; prick tops with fork in three or four places. Bake in moderate oven (375°) about 8 minutes, until puffy, but not browned. Place cookies on racks to cool. Put together in pairs with Creamy Frosting. Makes about 5 dozen double cookies.

Creamy Frosting: Blend together ¼ c. butter, ¾ c. sifted confectioners sugar, 1 egg yolk and 1 tsp. vanilla or ¼ tsp. almond extract. Beat until smooth.

FIG BARS

The moist fig filling in these butter cookies is not overly sweet

1 c. butter	1 tsp. baking powder
2 c. brown sugar, firmly packed	1½ c. ground figs
3 eggs	1 c. water
1 tsp. vanilla	¾ c. sugar
1 tblsp. lemon juice	3 tblsp. flour
4 c. sifted flour	¼ c. chopped walnuts
1 tsp. salt	2 tblsp. orange juice
1 tsp. baking soda	

To make dough, cream butter and brown sugar. Add eggs, vanilla and lemon juice; beat. Stir together 4 c. flour, salt, baking soda and baking powder; blend into creamed mixture. Chill.

Meanwhile, prepare fig filling. Boil figs in water 5 minutes. Blend sugar and 3 tblsp. flour; stir into figs. Cook over low heat, stirring frequently, until thick. Stir in nuts and orange juice. Cool.

Divide chilled dough in half. Roll each half in a rectangle 18 x 12 x ⅛" on well-floured pastry cloth. Cut into four 3" wide strips. Put cooled filling down center of strips. Using a spatula, fold dough over filling. Cut strips in half; transfer strips, seam side down, to ungreased baking sheet, about 2″ apart. Bake in moderate oven (375°) about 15 minutes. Transfer bars to racks to cool. Cut in 2″ bars. Makes about 5 dozen.

FIG/ORANGE-FILLED SQUARES

Fork tines make decorative edge on two sides of plump turnovers

2 c. finely chopped dried figs	1 egg
½ c. white sugar	2 tblsp. milk
1 c. orange juice	1 tsp. vanilla
Dash of salt	3 c. sifted flour
½ c. sugar	½ tsp. salt
½ c. brown sugar, firmly packed	½ tsp. baking soda
1 c. shortening	

To make filling, combine figs, ½ c. white sugar, orange juice and dash of salt in small saucepan. Cook, stirring occasionally, until thick. Set aside to cool. You will have 2 cups.

Cream together ½ c. white sugar, brown sugar and shortening until light and fluffy. Add egg, milk and vanilla; beat well.

Sift together flour, ½ tsp. salt and baking soda; stir into creamed mixture. Chill dough at least 1 hour.

Divide dough into quarters. Roll one quarter at a time on lightly floured board to make a 12 x 8″ rectangle. Cut crosswise into 6 strips, each 2″ wide. Spread fig filling over half of strips; then top with remaining strips. Press lengthwise edges with floured tines of fork to seal. Cut in 2″ lengths. Repeat with remaining portions of dough.

Place 2″ apart on ungreased baking sheet and bake in moderate oven (350°) about 10 minutes. Transfer cookies to rack to cool. Makes about 4 dozen.

FINNISH STAR COOKIES

These decorative cookies are rich like pastry—with date filling

1 c. sugar	1 c. butter
1 c. finely cut dates (½ lb.)	½ c. water
1 c. water	1 tblsp. light cream or milk
1½ c. sifted flour	2 tblsp. sugar (for tops)

To make filling, combine 1 c. sugar, dates and 1 c. water in saucepan. Bring to a boil over medium heat; reduce heat to low and continue cooking and stirring until filling thickens. Set aside to cool.

Blend flour with ½ c. butter with pastry blender as for pie crust. Slowly add ½ c. water; mix well and chill thoroughly.

Roll dough ⅛" thick. Spread about a third of remaining ½ c. butter over half of dough. Fold buttered half over other half of dough and roll to ⅛" thickness. Repeat spreading with butter and rolling two more times.

Cut dough in 2½" squares. Cut 1" slash in each corner of squares and place about 1 tsp. cooled date filling on center of each square. Fold one point of each slashed corner to center to make pinwheel, and pinch edges to seal. Brush with cream and sprinkle with sugar.

Arrange about 2" apart on ungreased baking sheet and bake in hot oven (400°) about 10 minutes. Transfer cookies to racks to cool. Makes about 5 dozen.

FORTUNE COOKIES, AMERICAN STYLE

Bake fortune cookies for the next social gathering at your house; they're fun for people of all ages. The homemade version tastes better than the Chinese, but differs in shape—flatter, with a small center peak.

The recipe for Mom's Fortune Cookies comes from an Illinois woman who has been baking them off and on for more than 10 years. Stored in a covered container and put in a cold place or the freezer, they keep for several months. It's convenient to keep them on hand to bring out on short notice.

The Illinois mother always writes messages to insert in a few cookies she saves especially for her children. That explains the name of the recipe. Her motherly notes run from "I love you" and "It's your turn to feed the cat" to "You're an exceptional child—exceptionally untidy and sweet."

Adult messages are predictions, such as "You'll meet a stranger this week who will bring you happiness" and "If your birthday is between May 1 and August 25, this is your year for exciting travel."

Here's the recipe for the cookies. You'll enjoy using your imagination when you write the fortunes to enclose in them.

MOM'S FORTUNE COOKIES

These cookies liven up parties; make them ahead to have on hand

1 c. sugar	⅓ c. milk
⅔ c. shortening	3 c. sifted flour
2 eggs	3 tsp. baking powder
1 tsp. vanilla	½ tsp. salt

Cream sugar and shortening until light and fluffy. Beat in eggs, vanilla and milk to mix thoroughly.

Sift together flour, baking powder and salt. Stir gradually into creamed mixture. Chill well.

Roll dough ⅛″ thick and cut with 2″ round cutter. Place about 1″ apart on ungreased baking sheet.

Type or write your own messages on little slips of paper; fold small and place like tent in center of each cookie on baking sheet. Place another cut-out cookie on top and press edges together to seal.

Bake in hot oven (400°) 10 to 12 minutes. Remove cookies and cool on racks. Makes about 5½ dozen.

FRUIT BLOSSOM COOKIES

Charming as an old-fashioned flower garden in full bloom

⅔ c. shortening	1½ tsp. baking powder
¾ c. sugar	¼ tsp. salt
1 egg	2 tblsp. milk
½ tsp. vanilla	Citrus/Raisin (or other) Filling
2 c. sifted flour	(recipe follows)

Cream together shortening and sugar. Add egg; beat until light and fluffy. Add vanilla.

Sift together dry ingredients. Add to creamed mixture along with milk. Divide dough in half. Chill 1 hour.

Roll out half of dough; keep the rest chilled. Roll 1/16 to ⅛″ thick. Cut with 2″ scalloped cookie cutter. Place about ½ tsp. Citrus/Raisin Filling in centers of half the cookies. Place 1½″ apart on greased baking sheet. Cut out centers of remaining half of cookies with 1″ round cutter; place on filled bottoms and press edges with fork to seal. Repeat this process with remaining half of dough.

Bake in moderate oven (350°) 10 to 12 minutes. Transfer cookies to racks to cool. Makes about 2 dozen.

CITRUS/RAISIN FILLING

Do try the fruity variations—they add color and taste contrasts

¼ c. chopped seedless raisins	4 tsp. water
½ tsp. grated orange peel	2 tblsp. sugar
1 tblsp. orange juice	½ tsp. flour
½ tsp. lemon juice	⅛ tsp. salt

Combine all ingredients in heavy saucepan. Bring to a boil, stirring constantly. Cook over medium heat about 5 minutes, stirring occasionally. Cool. Makes about ¼ cup.

Variations

Fig Filling: Substitute chopped dried figs for the raisins.
Apricot Filling: Substitute finely chopped, soft, dried apricots for raisins and add 1½ tsp. orange juice, ¼ tsp. lemon juice, 3 tblsp. water and 1 tsp. flour.
Pineapple Filling: Combine in saucepan ¾ tsp. cornstarch and ¼ c. crushed pineapple, undrained. Cook until clear, stirring constantly. Cool.
Cherry Filling: Mash ¼ c. cherry pie filling. Add a few drops almond extract, if desired.

GINGER COOKIES FOR A CROWD

A big recipe to make when you wish to put cookies in the freezer

5½ c. sifted flour	1 c. shortening
1 tblsp. baking soda	1 c. sugar
2 tsp. baking powder	1 egg, beaten
1 tsp. salt	½ tsp. vanilla
¾ tsp. ground ginger	1 c. dark molasses
1 tsp. ground cinnamon	½ c. strong coffee

Sift together flour, soda, baking powder, salt, ginger and cinnamon.
Cream shortening; add sugar gradually; beat until light; add egg and vanilla.

Add molasses and coffee, then sifted dry ingredients; mix well; chill.

Roll out on lightly floured board ¼" thick; cut with round 2" cutter.

Place about 2" apart on greased baking sheet. Bake in hot oven (400°) 8 to 10 minutes. Spread on racks to cool. Makes 12 dozen.

GINGERBREAD CHRISTMAS COOKIES

Few goodies you make in your kitchen say Merry Christmas more eloquently than gingerbread cookies. You may consider them old-fashioned, but they're as up to date as the carols you sing or the Santa Claus to whom children write such adorable letters. These spicy molasses cookies are especially inviting on Christmas trees, and lend themselves to decorating.

Aside from tradition and tastiness, gingerbread cookies have many qualities that recommend them. You can bake them ahead. They keep satisfactorily for weeks either in the freezer or a cool place. You can cut them in many fancy shapes, such as animals, stars, bells, Christmas trees or whatever forms you wish, including plain and scalloped rounds. And you can decorate them with raisins, currants, candies and white or tinted icing. The dark brown cookie makes an excellent background to show off the trimmings.

Our Gingerbread Christmas Cookies recipe makes cookies that do not break easily. For this reason alone they are a fine choice for Christmas trees. You can hang them on your big tree or a smaller one decorated entirely with cookies. The cookie tree can be a small evergreen. Or cut a flat triangular Christmas tree from a piece of soft-board. Cover it with green felt and pin the cookies to the felt, using red and green ribbons you pull through holes made in the cookies before baking.

There are two ways to make the holes in the cookies: 1) Insert 1½" length of drinking straw into each unbaked cookie in the place you want the hole. Remove the straws before cookies are cool. Pull green and red ribbons through the holes and tie in bows or loops. 2) For each cookie, loop a 5 to 6" length of string on baking sheet. Press unbaked cookie on a string, leaving at least 1" overlap to hold cookie securely.

If you have such a hospitality cookie tree, you will need a reserve supply of cookies to replace those your visitors enjoy taking off and eating. Our recipe for Gingerbread Christmas Cookies makes about 12 dozen 2½″ round cookies. It's easy to cut the recipe in half if you want to bake a smaller batch.

GINGERBREAD CHRISTMAS COOKIES

Cookies are sturdy, crisp and hard—taste like gingerbread. The little pigs with pink icing curls for tails make a hit with a crowd

½ c. shortening	1 tsp. ground allspice
1 c. brown sugar, firmly packed	1½ c. dark molasses
2 tsp. baking soda	⅔ c. water
2 tsp. salt	6½ c. sifted flour (about)
1 tsp. ground cinnamon	Ornamental Icing (optional,
1 tsp. ground ginger	see Index)
1 tsp. ground cloves	

Cream shortening, sugar, baking soda, salt and spices together until light and fluffy. Beat in molasses. Stir in water.

Gradually stir in enough flour to make a stiff dough (about 6½ c.). Shape dough in ball with hands, wrap in plastic wrap or waxed paper and refrigerate several hours or overnight.

Roll out dough, a small amount at a time, ⅛ to ¼″ thick. Cut with desired cutter; slip a broad spatula under cookie and transfer it to lightly greased baking sheet. Arrange cutouts a short distance apart on baking sheet (they spread very little).

Bake in moderate oven (350°) 10 to 12 minutes, or until cookies are lightly browned. Remove from baking sheet to racks and cool. Decorate with Ornamental Icing, if you wish. Makes about 12 dozen.

Gingerbread Boys: Cut rolled dough for Gingerbread Christmas Cookies with 6″ gingerbread boy cutter. Place them about ½″ apart on lightly greased baking sheet. Place heads of cutout boys on loops of string or insert drinking straws, as described. For each cookie, dip 3 raisins in slightly beaten egg white and press firmly, an equal distance apart, into cookie to represent shirt buttons (you'll need about 12 dozen raisins). For red buttons press in cinnamon candies (red hots) instead of raisins. Carefully move the legs and arms of the boys in different positions to provide animation and variety. Bake cookies, remove drinking straws, if used, and cool on racks. Decorate after cooling, or after freezing or storing. Use Ornamental Icing put through a decorating tube or small plastic bag with small hole cut in one corner. Use to draw faces on gingerbread boys, changing the features to give them a variety of expressions. The recipe for Gingerbread Christmas Cookies makes about 4 dozen 6" Gingerbread Boys.

Gingerbread Pigs: Cut the recipe for Gingerbread Christmas Cookies in half. Roll dough as directed, and cut with pig-shaped cookie cutter. Bake, cool and decorate with Ornamental Icing. You can outline each pig cookie with a thin white line of icing and make icing circles or dots for eyes. Tint a little icing pink with red food color and use it to make a curl on each pig cookie to represent its tail. Makes 64.

N O T E : Children delight in animal cookies. Among their favorites are rooster, hen, rabbit, reindeer and horse cookies.

OLD-FASHIONED GINGER CREAMS

Almost everyone cherishes memories of cookies especially enjoyed in childhood. Frosted Ginger Creams are more than a dream. A California homemaker-home economist developed her own recipe for Frosted Ginger Creams, the cookies she ate when a child on visits to an aunt.

She had never acquired the recipe—not written down. But when she had a home of her own, she baked ginger/molasses cookies until she duplicated the favorites of her childhood.

When we tested her recipe, every member of our taste panel gave the cookies an A-1 rating. Bake a batch soon. Your friends and family will rejoice in these old-fashioned treats.

FROSTED GINGER CREAMS

These white-iced ginger cookies are soft, flavorful—and keep well

1 c. shortening	½ tsp. baking powder
1 c. brown sugar, firmly packed	1 tsp. salt
2 eggs	2 tblsp. butter or regular
1 c. dark molasses	margarine
2 tblsp. vinegar	2 c. sifted confectioners sugar
5 c. sifted flour (about)	1 tsp. vanilla
1 tblsp. ground ginger	3 tblsp. milk or cream
1 tblsp. baking soda	

Cream together shortening and brown sugar until light; beat in eggs, one at a time, beating well to blend. Add molasses and vinegar.

Sift together 4 c. flour, ginger, soda, baking powder and salt; stir into batter. Add additional flour to make a soft dough easy to roll.

Roll dough on lightly floured surface; cut in 2 or 3″ circles. Place about 1″ apart on lightly greased baking sheet.

Bake in moderate oven (375°) 10 to 15 minutes. Remove cookies and cool on wire racks.

Meanwhile, blend butter and confectioners sugar together, add vanilla and milk and beat until smooth. Spread over tops of cooled cookies, leaving a ¼″ rim of brown cookie around the white frosting. Store in airtight containers. Makes 5½ dozen.

GRAPEFRUIT SUGAR COOKIES

These dainty cookies make talk at tea parties—guests ask why they're so good. Candied peel is the secret

1 c. butter	½ tsp. salt
1¼ c. sugar	¾ c. finely chopped Candied
2 eggs	Grapefruit Peel (recipe
3 c. sifted flour	follows)
2½ tsp. baking powder	

Cream butter and sugar; add eggs and beat until fluffy.

Sift together dry ingredients; mix in grapefruit peel. Add to creamed mixture. Divide dough in half; place in covered container and chill in refrigerator several hours.

Roll dough about ¼″ thick on floured board; cut with floured cutter.

Place 1 to 1½″ apart on greased baking sheet and bake in moderate oven (375°) 8 to 10 minutes. Remove cookies and cool on racks. Makes about 5 dozen.

CANDIED GRAPEFRUIT PEEL

Keep this handy—it makes icings and cookies special

Select and wash thick-skinned grapefruit. Cut into quarters and remove pulp. Put peel in saucepan; cover with cold water. Weight down peel with a plate. Let stand several hours or overnight. Drain.

With scissors, cut peel into strips about ¼″ wide.

Cover peel with cold water and slowly bring to a simmer (180°) in a saucepan. Remove from heat, cover pan and let stand about 1 hour; drain. Repeat process until peel no longer tastes bitter (about 3 times).

Cover again with water and boil until yellow peel is tender, about 15 minutes. Drain well in colander. Press out water. Pack peel firmly into measuring cup to measure.

Return peel to saucepan. For each cup of peel, add 1 cup of sugar. Place over medium heat; stir until sugar has dissolved (peel forms its own liquid).

Cook peel over medium heat, stirring frequently, until sugar syrup is concentrated; reduce heat to low (syrup should boil gently). Continue cooking until the grapefruit peel is semitransparent and most of the sugar syrup has boiled away.

Drain in colander. Separate pieces of peel on baking sheets and allow to stand until they feel fairly dry. Sprinkle with enough sugar to give a crystalline look.

Store in tightly covered cans, or in plastic bags in the freezer.

HARD-COOKED EGG COOKIES

Cinnamon and nuts splash the tops of the rich, tasty, yellow cookies

1 c. butter or regular margarine	3 c. sifted flour
1 c. sugar	1 egg, slightly beaten
1 egg	1 tsp. sugar
5 sieved hard-cooked egg yolks (about 1 c.)	2 tsp. ground cinnamon
	½ c. chopped nuts
1 tblsp. finely grated lemon peel	

Beat butter, 1 c. sugar and 1 egg to blend thoroughly. Add hard-cooked egg yolks and lemon peel. Stir in flour.

Roll dough about ¼" thick on lightly floured surface; cut with 2" round cutter. Place ½" apart on ungreased baking sheet. Brush tops of cookies with slightly beaten egg.

Combine 1 tsp. sugar and cinnamon; sprinkle with nuts over cookies.

Bake in slow oven (325°) 20 to 25 minutes, or until delicately browned. Remove cookies and cool on racks. Store in container with loose-fitting lid to retain crispness. Makes about 52.

Variation

Molded Hard-Cooked Egg Cookies: Instead of rolling dough, shape in 1″ balls. Place 2″ apart on ungreased baking sheet. Flatten by pressing with lightly greased bottom of juice glass. Brush tops with slightly beaten egg, sprinkle with sugar-cinnamon mixture and nuts, and bake like cutout cookies. Makes about 68.

HONEY WAFERS

Honey, spices and bran make these crisp, dainty cookies delicious

½ c. butter
½ c. honey
2 c. sifted flour
1 tsp. baking soda

½ tsp. ground cinnamon
¼ tsp. ground cloves
¼ tsp. ground allspice
¼ c. crushed bran flakes

Cream together butter and honey.

Sift together flour, baking soda, cinnamon, cloves and allspice. Mix with bran flakes.

Combine dry ingredients with honey and butter. Chill 1 hour, or until firm enough to roll easily.

Roll ⅛″ thick on lightly floured board. Cut with floured cookie cutter. Place about 2″ apart on greased baking sheet; bake in moderate oven (350°) 8 to 10 minutes. Remove cookies and cool on racks. Makes 3 dozen.

EASTER LAMB COOKIES

Stand lambs in green cellophane grass on a tray for a centerpiece

1 c. regular margarine
⅔ c. sugar
1 egg
1 tsp. vanilla
2½ c. sifted flour

½ tsp. baking powder
1 egg, separated
1 c. cookie coconut
¼ tsp. water
2 drops red or blue food color

Beat together margarine and sugar until light and fluffy. Beat in 1 egg and vanilla to blend thoroughly.

Sift together flour and baking powder. Add to creamed mixture. Divide dough in half; wrap each half in waxed paper and chill.

On lightly floured surface, roll half of dough very thin, less than ⅛″ if possible. Cut with lamb cookie cutter or pattern.

Beat white from separated egg until foamy. Brush onto unbaked cookies. Sprinkle with half of cookie coconut. Place 1″ apart on greased baking sheet.

Bake in moderate oven (350°) 7 to 10 minutes. Place cookies on racks to cool.

Meanwhile, roll second half of dough; cut in same way, but decorate before baking with egg yolk paint: Beat yolk from separated egg with water; add food color. Paint on unbaked cookies; sprinkle with coconut and bake as for first half of cookies. Makes about 76 (38 from each half of dough).

LEMON/ALMOND RICHES

Almond daisies with red centers top these Christmas beauties

1 c. butter or regular margarine
1 c. sugar
1 egg, separated
1 tblsp. finely grated lemon peel
¼ tsp. salt
2 c. sifted flour
½ c. finely chopped blanched almonds

1 tsp. water
2 tblsp. sugar (for tops)
2 c. whole blanched almonds (about ¾ lb.)
1 (4 oz.) pkg. candied cherries, cut in halves

Beat butter and 1 c. sugar together until light and fluffy. Beat in egg yolk and lemon peel.

Blend together salt and flour and stir into beaten mixture. Stir in chopped almonds. Shape dough in ball, flatten on lightly floured surface and roll ¼" thick. Cut with 2" round cutter.

Slightly beat egg white diluted with water; brush over tops of cookies. Sprinkle lightly with sugar. Press whole almonds around edge of cookies like daisy petals, 5 petals to a cookie. Place a cherry half, rounded side up, in center of each cookie.

Place cookies 1½" apart on lightly greased baking sheet. Bake in slow oven (325°) 15 to 17 minutes, or until cookies brown around edges. Remove cookies and cool on racks. Makes 3½ dozen.

Variation

Lemon-Flavored Riches: Omit almond daisy trim, placing a half candied cherry in center of each cookie before baking.

MINCEMEAT/CHEESE COOKIES

Perfect non-sweet addition to cookie tray—taste like mincemeat pie!

1 c. butter or regular margarine	1 (9 oz.) pkg. prepared
2 c. grated Cheddar cheese	mincemeat
(½ lb.)	½ c. water
2 c. sifted flour	

Cream butter until light; add cheese (at room temperature) and cream until well blended. Stir in flour; mix well and chill.

Meanwhile, cook mincemeat and water until slightly thickened. Set aside to cool.

Roll dough ⅛" thick on lightly floured surface; cut in 2" circles. Put half of circles about 1" apart on lightly greased baking sheet. Place 1 tsp. cooled mincemeat mixture in center of each cookie on baking sheet. Top each with another circle of dough; press edges with fork to seal. Prick cookie tops in several places with tines of kitchen fork.

Bake in moderate oven (350°) 15 minutes, or until lightly browned. Remove cookies to racks to cool. Makes 3½ dozen.

MINCEMEAT-FILLED OATSIES

Substantial and luscious—men especially like this oatmeal cookie

1 c. sifted flour	¾ c. sugar
1 tsp. baking soda	5 c. quick-cooking rolled oats
¼ tsp. salt	1 c. prepared mincemeat
1 tsp. vinegar	1 tsp. lemon juice
½ c. milk	¼ c. water
½ c. butter or regular margarine	6 tblsp. sugar

Sift together flour, baking soda and salt.

Combine vinegar and milk; stir to mix and set aside.

Beat butter until light; gradually beat in ¾ c. sugar. Beat until fluffy.

Add half of flour mixture, the milk and then remaining flour mixture. Mix thoroughly and fold in rolled oats. Chill 4 hours or longer.

Meanwhile, combine mincemeat, lemon juice, water and 6 tblsp. sugar in saucepan. Bring to a boil, stirring constantly. Set aside to cool.

Roll dough, one-third at a time, leaving remaining dough in refrigerator until ready to work with it. Roll dough thin, about ⅛". Cut with 2½" round cutter.

Spread 1 tsp. cooled mincemeat mixture on half the cookies. Top with remaining cookies. Place 1" apart on ungreased baking sheet.

Bake in moderate oven (350°) 10 to 13 minutes. Remove cookies and cool on racks. Makes 3½ dozen.

Variation

Date-Filled Oatsies: Substitute 1 c. chopped dates for mincemeat in filling.

COUNTRY MOLASSES COOKIES

Make these cutouts as varied as the shape of your cookie cutters

1 c. sugar	1 tsp. baking soda
1 c. shortening	½ tsp. baking powder
1 c. light molasses	1 tsp. ground ginger
1 tblsp. vinegar	1 tsp. ground cinnamon
6 c. sifted flour	2 eggs, beaten
½ tsp. salt	

Combine sugar, shortening, molasses and vinegar in saucepan; bring to boil and cook 2 minutes. Cool.

Sift together flour, salt, soda, baking powder and spices.

Add eggs to cooled molasses mixture. Add dry ingredients and mix well. Chill.

Roll out dough on lightly floured board, about ⅛ to ¼" thick. Cut with cookie cutters of desired shapes; place 1" apart on greased baking sheet.

Bake in moderate oven (375°) 8 to 10 minutes, or until done. Transfer cookies to racks to cool. Makes about 12 dozen.

CRISP MOLASSES COOKIES

Fancy—spread cookies with white frosting, sprinkle with pink sugar

3 c. sifted flour
1 tsp. salt
1 tsp. baking soda
2 tsp. ground cinnamon
2 tsp. ground ginger
⅓ c. sugar

¾ c. shortening
1⅓ c. molasses
Nuts, colored decorating sugar or
  grated orange peel (for
  decorations)

Sift together dry ingredients; cut in shortening.

Heat molasses; add to flour mixture. Chill until stiff enough to roll (3 hours or overnight). Roll very thin, about $\frac{1}{16}''$, on lightly floured board. Cut with cookie cutter (leaves, butterflies, gingerbread men or other shapes). Decorate with nuts, colored sugar or orange peel.

Place about 2″ apart on lightly greased baking sheets. Bake in hot oven (400°) 7 to 8 minutes, or until lightly browned. Spread on racks to cool. Makes 6 dozen.

NOTE: To make drop cookies, do not chill dough. After mixing, drop from teaspoon about 2″ apart onto lightly greased baking sheet. Flatten with bottom of glass; bake as for rolled cookies.

MOLASSES WAGON WHEELS

Children adore these big cookies—with "spokes" of white icing

½ c. shortening
1 c. sugar
1 c. dark molasses
½ c. water
4 c. sifted flour
1 tsp. baking soda
1½ tsp. salt
1½ tsp. ground ginger
½ tsp. ground cloves

¼ tsp. ground nutmeg
¼ tsp. ground allspice
¼ c. sugar (for tops)
66 raisins (about ⅓ c.)
1 c. sifted confectioners sugar
¼ tsp. salt
½ tsp. vanilla
1 tblsp. light cream or dairy half-
  and-half

Cream shortening and 1 c. sugar until light and fluffy. Beat in molasses and water to mix thoroughly.

Sift together flour, soda, 1½ tsp. salt and spices; stir into creamed mixture. Chill several hours or overnight.

Roll dough ¼" thick. Press into 3" circles with large glass, or cut with 3" round cutter. Sprinkle tops with sugar. Place ¼ to ½" apart on greased baking sheet. Press 3 large raisins in center of each dough circle.

Bake in moderate oven (350°) about 12 minutes, until almost no imprint remains when touched lightly with finger. Remove from oven, but leave on baking sheet a few minutes before transferring to cooling racks.

Meanwhile, blend confectioners sugar, ¼ tsp. salt, vanilla and cream together until smooth. When cookies are cool, make spokes of wheel with icing put through small plastic bag, with small hole in one corner, and outline raisin center to simulate wheel's hub. Makes about 22.

NEW MOONS

Dainty crisp crescents shine with glaze—a special-occasion cookie

1 c. butter or regular margarine	1½ c. grated (not ground)
1¼ c. sugar	blanched almonds (½ lb.)
2 tsp. grated lemon peel	1 tsp. vanilla
¼ tsp. salt	2 c. sifted confectioners sugar
1⅓ c. sifted flour	2½ tblsp. boiling water
	1 tsp. vanilla

Cream butter and sugar until light and fluffy. Add lemon peel, salt, flour, almonds and 1 tsp. vanilla; mix thoroughly. Chill dough.

Roll dough ⅛" thick and cut with crescent cutter. Place about ½" apart on ungreased baking sheet. Bake in moderate oven (375°) 8 to 10 minutes.

Meanwhile, combine confectioners sugar, boiling water and 1 tsp. vanilla. Spread over tops of warm cookies. If glaze gets too thick to spread thinly on cookies, add a few drops of hot water. Place cookies on racks to complete cooling. Makes 10 dozen.

NORWEGIAN HEIRLOOM COOKIES

Cut in squares or diamonds—the granulated sugar coating sparkles

1 c. butter	2 c. sifted flour
½ c. sugar	1 c. finely chopped nuts
2 tsp. vanilla	¼ c. sugar (for coating)

Cream butter and ½ c. sugar until light and fluffy. Add vanilla and mix well. Stir in flour and nuts. Chill until firm enough to roll.

Roll dough ¼" thick and cut with knife in 2" squares or diamonds. Place ½" apart on ungreased baking sheet.

Bake in moderate oven (375°) 8 to 10 minutes. While warm roll in sugar. Cool on racks. Makes 5 dozen.

NOTE : Put nuts through nut chopper twice or chop very fine with a knife.

NUT BUTTER COOKIES

Rich cookies—you may want to double recipe for special occasions

1 c. sifted flour	¼ c. apricot or red raspberry
⅓ c. sugar	jam (about)
⅔ c. finely chopped pecans	Viennese Chocolate Frosting
½ c. butter	(recipe follows)
	Pecan halves (about 18)

Sift together flour and sugar; add chopped pecans and mix well. Blend in butter with fork or pastry blender until dough holds together. (Dough will be crumbly.) Chill until easy to handle.

Roll dough on lightly floured surface to ⅛" thickness. Cut in 2" circles and place ½" apart on ungreased baking sheet. Bake in moderate oven (375°) 7 to 10 minutes. Remove from oven and let stand 1 to 2 minutes before removing from baking sheet. Cool completely on racks.

Make sandwich cookies by spreading half the cookies with a thin layer of jam and topping with other half of cookies. Spread Viennese Chocolate Frosting on top of sandwiches and place a pecan half on top of each frosted sandwich. Makes about 1½ dozen.

Viennese Chocolate Frosting: Cream together 2 tblsp. butter and ⅓ c. confectioners sugar until light and creamy. Blend in 1 square unsweetened chocolate, melted and cooled.

CALL THEM DISHPAN OR OATMEAL/MOLASSES COOKIES

Big, chewy Oatmeal/Molasses Cookies, made from a recipe that appeared in Farm Journal, are enjoying great popularity in country kitchens. A farm woman in New York State likes to bake the 6 dozen cookies from our recipe in installments because it's easier to find time to get one baking sheet in the oven than several. (Also, her family thinks no cookie can surpass one just out of the oven.) She calls them Dishpan Cookies because the Illinois woman who contributed the recipe to Farm Journal said her grandmother mixed the dough in a dishpan.

Here's the way she makes the cookies in installments: "I shape the dough in rolls 3″ in diameter, wrap them tightly in foil or plastic wrap and store them in the refrigerator or freezer—the freezer if I'm not going to bake them for a week or longer. When I want to bake cookies, I slice the dough ¼″ thick and bake it as the recipe directs."

OATMEAL/MOLASSES COOKIES

A big recipe for big cookies—put some in freezer to have handy

8½ c. sifted flour	2 c. light molasses
1 tblsp. salt	4 eggs, beaten
2 tblsp. baking soda	¼ c. hot water
8 c. quick-cooking rolled oats	3 c. seedless raisins
2½ c. sugar	2 c. ground black walnuts or
1 tblsp. ground ginger	English walnuts
2 c. melted shortening	Sugar (for tops)

Reserve ½ c. flour. Sift together 8 c. flour, salt and baking soda.

In a very large bowl or dishpan, mix rolled oats, sugar and ginger. Stir in shortening, molasses, eggs, hot water, sifted dry ingredients, raisins and nuts. Work dough with hands until well mixed. Add the reserved ½ c. flour if needed to make dough workable.

Roll dough to ¼″ thickness; cut with 3½″ round cutter. Place 2 to 3″ apart on lightly greased baking sheet. Brush with water and sprinkle with sugar.

Bake in moderate oven (375°) 8 to 10 minutes. Remove cookies to racks to cool. Makes 6 dozen.

OPEN-HOUSE COOKIES

When it's Christmas time in the Bethlehem, Pennsylvania, area, families visit from one neighbor's home to another to view one another's putz, or Nativity Scene. It's an old Pennsylvania Dutch custom, on these occasions, for the hostess to pass traditional cookies.

Many of them are in camel, donkey, star and other fascinating shapes. From women in this community come recipes for three of the favorites, Spiced Christmas Cookies (often called Brown Christmas Cookies), White Christmas Cookies and Pepper Nuts (Pfeffernuesse).

All three recipes make dozens of cookies. And all keep well so you can bake them ahead. Store them in airtight containers or package and freeze. The secret to success in making these treats is to chill the dough overnight before working with it. And do roll Spiced and White Christmas cookies very thin.

SPICED CHRISTMAS COOKIES

Crisp, brown and molasses-flavored cookies to decorate if you wish

1 c. butter	5 c. sifted flour
1½ c. brown sugar, firmly packed	1 tblsp. ground cinnamon
2 c. molasses	1½ tsp. ground ginger
2 tblsp. light cream or dairy half-and-half	½ tsp. ground cloves

Cream butter; gradually add sugar, beating until light and fluffy. Beat in molasses; blend in cream.

Sift together dry ingredients; stir into creamed mixture. Store in covered bowl in refrigerator overnight.

Roll dough thin, using floured pastry cloth on board and rolling pin. Cut in animal shapes.

Place 1 to 1½" apart on greased baking sheet. Bake in moderate oven (350°) 10 to 12 minutes. Remove cookies and cool on racks. Makes 19 dozen.

WHITE CHRISTMAS COOKIES

Sugar, spice and everything nice—cookies are crisp and straw-colored

1 c. butter	4 c. sifted flour
2 c. sugar	⅛ tsp. ground nutmeg
4 eggs, beaten	⅛ tsp. ground cinnamon

Cream butter; gradually add sugar and beat until light and fluffy. Beat in eggs.

Sift together dry ingredients; stir into creamed mixture (dough should be stiff). Store in covered bowl in refrigerator overnight.

Roll dough very thin, using floured pastry cloth on board and rolling pin. Cut in star shapes. Place 1 to 1½" apart on greased baking sheet.

Bake in moderate oven (350°) 10 to 12 minutes, or until crisp and straw-colored. Remove cookies and cool on racks. Makes 16 dozen.

PEPPER NUTS

Store these spicy, hard cookies in airtight containers. You can add a slice of apple to mellow them

3 eggs, beaten	2 tblsp. ground cinnamon
3½ c. brown sugar, firmly packed	1 tblsp. ground cloves
	Ornamental Icing (see Index)
4 c. sifted flour	Red cinnamon candy (optional)
1 tsp. baking powder	

Combine eggs and sugar; beat well.

Sift together dry ingredients; add gradually to egg-sugar mixture (dough will be very stiff).

Divide dough. Roll with hands on lightly floured board into rolls the thickness of your middle finger. Cut in ½" slices. Place 1 to 1½" apart on greased baking sheet.

Bake in slow oven (300°) 30 minutes. Remove cookies and cool on racks.

Shortly before serving you can top each pepper nut with a dab of Ornamental Icing and a red cinnamon candy (red hots), if you like. Makes 27 dozen.

ORANGE WREATHS

Recipe is from Mexico where cookies accompany hot chocolate

½ c. butter or regular margarine	2 c. sifted flour
¼ c. sugar	2 tsp. baking powder
2 tsp. grated orange peel	1 egg white, beaten until foamy
3 egg yolks, well beaten	

Cream butter, sugar and orange peel together until light and fluffy. Beat in egg yolks and mix well.

Mix and sift together flour and baking powder; add a little at a time to the creamed mixture. Beat after each addition until dough is moderately stiff.

Roll dough on lightly floured surface to ½" thickness. Cut with 2½" doughnut cutter. Place about 2" apart on lightly greased baking sheet. Brush tops of cookies with egg white.

Bake in moderate oven (375°) about 20 minutes, or until golden brown. Remove from baking sheet and cool on racks. Makes about 1 dozen.

N O T E : Gather scraps of dough and centers of rings together in a ball; roll, cut and bake.

PARTY WHIRLS

Pretty pink, brown and cream-colored cookie pinwheels—delicious

1 c. butter	½ tsp. salt
1 c. sugar	½ tsp. ground cinnamon
2 eggs	3 drops red food color
½ tsp. vanilla	½ square semisweet chocolate,
3 c. sifted flour	melted

Beat together butter and sugar until light and fluffy. Beat in eggs and vanilla to blend well.

Sift together flour, salt and cinnamon; add to creamed mixture. Divide dough in thirds. Tint one-third pink with red food color (stir in food color with a spoon); color the second part brown with melted chocolate, and leave the last third untinted.

Roll each third of dough separately on lightly floured waxed paper into a 13 x 10" rectangle. Cover baking sheet with waxed paper; hold over untinted dough, invert and remove waxed paper from top of dough on baking sheet. Flip pink rectangle of dough over onto untinted dough and remove waxed paper from it. If edges are not quite even, straighten them by gently rolling with a rolling pin. Then turn chocolate dough onto pink dough and remove waxed paper from it. Straighten edges if necessary. Chill until firm.

Remove dough from refrigerator and roll up tightly as for jelly roll, using waxed paper under dough to help shape the log. Wrap tightly in waxed paper and chill. If you do not want to bake the cookies within three days, cut the long log in half, wrap each log in aluminum foil and store in freezer until ready to bake.

To bake, cut dough in ⅛ to ¼" slices with sharp knife. Place ½" apart on ungreased baking sheet and bake in hot oven (400°) about 8 minutes. Remove cookies to cooling racks. Makes about 7 dozen.

AMERICAN SAND TARTS

Crisp cookies, thin as paper, have true buttery flavor, nut trim

1 c. butter	1 egg white, slightly beaten
2¼ c. sugar	Almonds or peanuts
2 eggs	Ground cinnamon
4 c. sifted flour	

Cream butter and sugar until light and fluffy. Beat in eggs, mixing well. Stir in flour. Chill dough thoroughly.

Roll dough very thin and cut with 2½" round cutter. Brush centers of rounds with egg white and put ½ almond or peanut in center of each cookie. Brush again with egg white and sprinkle nuts with a trace of cinnamon.

Place cookies about ½" apart on ungreased baking sheet. Bake in hot oven (400°) about 5 minutes. Remove cookies to cooling racks. Makes about 12 dozen.

SCOTCH SHORTBREAD COOKIES

Buttery-rich, extra-good cookies—tint the dough if you like

1 c. butter
¾ c. confectioners sugar
2 c. sifted flour

Cream butter until light. Add sugar (sift if not smooth) and beat until light and fluffy. Add flour and mix to make a soft dough.

Pat or roll on floured surface to ⅓ to ½" thickness. Cut with 2½" cookie cutter or knife. (You can gently flute edges with fingers as for pie crust. Or decorate by pricking cookies with fork.)

Bake on ungreased baking sheet in slow oven (325°) about 20 minutes, until cookies are very delicately browned. Remove cookies and cool on racks. Makes 28 to 30.

STAR COOKIES

Sugar cookies cut in yuletide star shape. Icing will glamorize them

3 c. sifted flour	1¼ c. sugar
2 tsp. baking powder	1 tsp. vanilla
½ tsp. salt	1 egg
½ c. shortening	1 tblsp. milk
½ c. butter or regular margarine	

Sift together flour, baking powder and salt.

Cream shortening and butter with sugar until light and fluffy. Add vanilla, egg and milk; beat thoroughly. Add dry ingredients and mix well. Chill dough 1 hour for easy handling.

Divide dough in fourths; roll out each portion ⅛" thick. Cut with 2½" star-shaped cookie cutter. Place 1½ to 2" apart on greased baking sheet.

Bake in moderate oven (375°) 8 to 10 minutes. Remove cookies and cool on racks. Makes 7 dozen.

SPRINGERLE—THE PICTURE COOKIE

Springerle is a time-tested, German Christmas cookie with many fans on this side of the Atlantic Ocean. It's one of the first cookies to bake for the yuletide since it needs to mellow from 5 to 8 weeks. Often it's baked and waiting for Christmas even before Thanksgiving.

Traditionally, you sprinkle anise seeds over the surface on which you let the cookie dough stand overnight. You can use oil of anise instead of the seeds if you prefer. Our recipe gives directions for both flavorings.

These are picture cookies. You stamp the designs on the rolled cookie dough either with a board or rolling pin in which designs of birds and flowers are carved. You will find both the boards and rolling pins in housewares departments, especially in late autumn; occasionally you can find interesting old ones in antique shops.

In our tests we discovered it is somewhat easier to use the design board instead of a roller. Certainly this is true for inexperienced springerle bakers. It is important to press the board down firmly on the rolled dough so it leaves a clear print of the design. Lift the board off the dough with steady hands to avoid blurred pictures. If you use the rolling pin, roll it with a little pressure across the sheet of dough *only once.*

Adding too much flour produces a hard cookie. If the dough sticks to board or pin, use care in flouring it. We found chilling the dough 1 hour before rolling helps. Be sure not to roll the dough too thin, for if you do, it's almost impossible to get good imprints.

Making these cookies is a two-day operation because after rolling the dough you let it stand overnight (at least 10 hours) at room temperature before baking. Store the baked cookies in a container with a tight lid and set them in a cool place.

One more pointer: The cookies should not be brown—just a hint of yellow around the edges.

SPRINGERLE

Give these cookies time to mellow—they're well worth waiting for

4 eggs	¼ tsp. salt
2 c. sugar	2 tblsp. melted butter
4 c. sifted cake flour	1 tblsp. anise seeds
1 tsp. baking powder	

Using electric mixer at low speed, beat eggs in large bowl. Gradually add sugar, then beat at medium speed about 10 minutes. (You can use a hand rotary beater, but if you do, increase beating time to 30 minutes.)

Sift together flour, baking powder and salt; blend into egg mixture alternately with butter, mixing well. Cover dough with waxed paper or foil and chill 1 hour.

Dust surface lightly with flour and pat out or roll half of the dough at a time to almost, but not quite, ½" thickness.

Lightly flour springerle board and press it firmly down on dough. Lift board up carefully so as not to mar lines of the design. If board sticks to dough, lightly flour it and the top of the dough. Then brush off flour after removing board. (If you use springerle rolling pin, roll the dough to a flat sheet ½" thick. Then roll over it with springerle rolling pin just once to press in designs.)

Lightly grease baking sheet and sprinkle evenly with anise seeds.

Lift dough carefully to baking sheet, cover loosely with waxed paper and let stand overnight.

When ready to bake, cut dough to cookie size along lines made by springerle board (or rolling pin). Separate on baking sheet by ½" space.

Bake in moderate oven (350°) 5 minutes, then reduce heat to slow (300°) and continue baking about 10 minutes longer. Remove cookies and cool on racks. Makes about 3½ dozen.

NOTE: You can use 6 drops anise oil instead of the anise seeds. Add it to the beaten eggs. Superfine granulated sugar gives the best results in this recipe, but you can use regular granulated sugar.

RAISIN-FILLED COOKIES

Dark fruit filling shows through window in tender, light brown cookies

½ c. shortening	2½ c. sifted flour
1 c. sugar	¼ tsp. baking soda
2 eggs	½ tsp. salt
1 tsp. vanilla	Raisin Filling (recipe follows)

Mix together shortening, sugar and eggs. Stir in vanilla and mix thoroughly.

Sift together flour, soda and salt. Blend into sugar/egg mixture. Chill thoroughly.

Roll dough thin, about $\frac{1}{16}$", and cut with 2½" round cutter. (Or use any desired shape cutter.) Place half of cookies 1" apart on lightly greased baking sheet. Spread a generous teaspoonful of cooled Raisin Filling on each. Cut centers out of other half of cookies, using a small heart, star or other shaped cutter. Place over cookies on baking sheet. Press edges together with floured fork tines or fingers.

Bake in hot oven (400°) 8 to 10 minutes, or until cookies are lightly browned. Spread on racks to cool. Makes about 3½ dozen.

Raisin Filling: In a small saucepan, combine 2 c. ground or finely cut raisins, ¾ c. sugar and ¾ c. water; cook slowly, stirring constantly, until mixture thickens. Remove from heat; stir in ½ c. chopped walnuts (optional) and 1 tsp. finely grated lemon or orange peel. Cool before using.

Variations

Prune-Filled Cookies: Cook 2⅔ c. prunes; drain and mash (you should have 2 c.). Substitute for raisins in Raisin Filling.

Date-Filled Cookies: Substitute 2 c. finely cut-up or ground dates for raisins in Raisin Filling.

Raisin Turnovers: Cut cookie dough in 3″ instead of 2½″ rounds. Place 1 tsp. Raisin Filling on each cookie. Fold over and press edges to seal. Bake like Raisin-Filled Cookies. Makes about 6 dozen.

N O T E : You can use prune or date filling instead of Raisin Filling to make turnovers.

GRIDDLE COOKIES—BACK IN STYLE

Grandmother used to bake cookies on the griddle to avoid heating the oven in midsummer. Children stopping in her kitchen, hopeful of a handout, remembered how good the warm cookies were with glasses of cold lemonade or bowls of ice cream. No childhood eating experience could be more memorable. So it's good news that the cookies again are coming off griddles to please people of all ages.

Give freezers the thanks. Today's cooks roll and cut the dough and stack the circles with foil between like hamburger patties. As they are wrapped in packages and frozen, it's easy to bring the desired number out. Bake them in your electric skillet—at the table, if that's convenient.

RAISIN GRIDDLE COOKIES

Keep packages of dough in your freezer to bake on short notice

3½ c. sifted flour	1 tsp. ground nutmeg
1 c. sugar	1 c. shortening
1½ tsp. baking powder	1 egg
1 tsp. salt	½ c. milk
½ tsp. baking soda	1¼ c. raisins

Sift dry ingredients together into bowl. Cut in shortening until mixture is mealy.

Beat egg, add milk and blend. Add egg mixture and raisins to flour mixture. Stir until all the ingredients are moistened and dough holds together.

Roll on lightly floured board to ¼″ thickness. Cut with 2″ round cookie cutter.

Heat griddle until a few drops of water dance on it. (Do not overheat griddle.) Oil griddle lightly and place cookies on it. As the bottoms brown, the tops become puffy. Then turn and brown on other side. Serve warm. Makes about 4 dozen.

Variation

Lemon Griddle Cookies: Make dough for Raisin Griddle Cookies, but omit raisins and add 1 tsp. grated lemon peel. Bake as directed.

LEMON SUGAR COOKIES

A time-tested recipe that makes bar, rolled and drop cookies

½ c. butter or regular margarine	1½ tsp. baking powder
1 c. sugar	2 c. sifted flour
1 egg	¼ c. milk
½ tsp. vanilla	1 egg white, slightly beaten
2 tsp. grated lemon peel	(optional)
¼ tsp. salt	Sugar (optional)

Cream butter and sugar thoroughly. Add egg, vanilla and lemon peel. Beat until mixture is light and fluffy.

Sift dry ingredients. Stir into creamed mixture together with milk. Divide dough in half. Chill 1 hour.

Roll out half of dough on floured board, keeping the other half chilled until ready to use. Roll ¼" thick.

Cut into bars and place about 2" apart on greased baking sheet.

If desired, brush with slightly beaten egg white and sprinkle with sugar. Repeat with remaining dough.

Bake in moderate oven (350°) 12 to 15 minutes. Remove cookies and cool on racks. Makes 2 dozen.

Variations

Chocolate Chip Cookies: Add ½ c. semisweet chocolate pieces to dough.

Grease and flour two 9" square baking pans. Spread half the dough in each. Bake in moderate oven (350°) 25 minutes, or until light brown.

While still warm cut into 3" squares. Cool in pan on racks. Makes 1½ dozen.

Nut/Sugar Cookies: Mix ½ c. finely chopped nuts into dough. Roll dough and bake as directed.

Coconut Cookies: Add ½ c. shredded coconut. Make drop cookies and place 2″ apart on greased baking sheet.

Raisin Cookies: Add ½ c. seedless raisins. Make drop cookies and place 2″ apart on greased baking sheet.

Spiced Sugar Cookies: Add ¼ tsp. ground nutmeg and ½ tsp. ground cinnamon to dough, omitting lemon peel. Roll dough. Bake as directed.

SUGAR COOKIES

Sugar-topped, old-fashioned cookies—men say: "Make them bigger"

1 c. shortening	3 c. sifted flour
1 c. sugar	1 tsp. salt
1 c. dairy sour cream	1 tsp. baking powder
3 egg yolks, beaten	½ tsp. baking soda
1 tsp. vanilla	Sugar (for tops)

Cream shortening and sugar thoroughly; add sour cream, egg yolks and vanilla.

Sift together dry ingredients; add to creamed mixture, blending well; chill.

Shape into balls, working with small portions at a time, keeping remaining dough chilled.

Roll out ⅛″ thick on lightly floured surface. Cut with floured 2½″ cutter (sprinkle cutouts with sugar).

Place about 2″ apart on greased baking sheet. Bake in moderate oven (375°) about 15 minutes. Transfer cookies to racks to cool. Makes 6 dozen.

THUMBPRINT COOKIES

Rich and tender rather than sweet—beautiful on tray or plate

¾ c. butter or regular margarine	½ tsp. salt
1 (3 oz.) pkg. cream cheese	¼ tsp. baking powder
2 c. sifted flour	⅓ c. jam or jelly
2 tblsp. sugar	

Cream together butter and cream cheese until light and fluffy.

Sift together flour, sugar, salt and baking powder. Stir into creamed mixture, blending thoroughly.

Roll out on lightly floured surface into a square about ½" thick. Cut into 1½" squares.

Place about 1" apart on ungreased baking sheet. With your thumb make an indentation in center of each cookie. Fill with ½ tsp. jam or jelly.

Bake in a moderate oven (350°) 20 to 25 minutes. Remove cookies and cool on racks. Makes 2½ dozen.

N O T E : For fancy cookies, use jellies or jams of different kinds and colors.

WEDDING RING COOKIES

Gold and silver cookies—ideal for bridal showers, anniversaries

1 c. butter	1 tblsp. water
1¾ c. sifted flour	1 egg white, lightly beaten
1½ tsp. grated lemon peel (optional)	½ c. coarsely chopped blanched almonds
1 tblsp. light cream or dairy half-and-half	⅓ c. yellow sugar
	Silver dragées

Blend butter and flour with pastry blender until mixture is crumbly. Add lemon peel, cream and water; mix with hands to form a stiff dough. Shape in ball and refrigerate to chill thoroughly.

Divide dough in half; keep one half in refrigerator while working with other half. Roll dough on lightly floured surface to ¼" thickness. Cut out rings with doughnut cutter. Brush one side of rings with egg white; dip this side of cookies in almonds. Press almonds lightly so they will adhere. Sprinkle with yellow sugar. Repeat with remaining half of dough.

To make double rings, cut one ring and link it through another ring on lightly greased baking sheet. Decorate one of the rings with silver dragées.

Bake 6 double rings at a time in hot oven (425°) about 8 minutes, or until cookies brown around edges. Remove from oven and let cookies cool on baking sheet a few minutes. Transfer with metal spatula to cooling racks. Makes 18 to 19 double rings.

N O T E : You can bake some of the decorated rings singly for guests who like smaller servings than the double rings.

WILD ROSE COOKIES

These cookies are buttery rich, like shortbread, and party pretty

1 c. butter or regular margarine	2¼ c. sifted flour
½ c. very fine granulated sugar (super fine)	Pink decorating sugar
	Yellow decorating sugar, or tiny yellow candies
¼ tsp. vanilla	

Cream butter with sugar until light and fluffy; beat in vanilla.

Divide flour in thirds. Stir first third into creamed mixture and blend well. Repeat with second third and then with last third. Knead gently until smooth, about 5 minutes. Shape in ball, wrap in clear plastic wrap or waxed paper and chill several hours, or overnight.

Divide dough in fourths. Pat one portion at a time ¼" thick on lightly floured surface. Cut with 2½" round scalloped cutter. Place dough cutouts ½ to 1" apart on ungreased baking sheet. Sprinkle liberally with pink sugar, leaving ¾" circle in center uncovered.

Cut a circle of stiff paper about the same size of cookies and cut out a ¾" circle in center. Lay on cookie and carefully spoon yellow sugar into hole in paper; lift off paper. Or, if you can find small yellow candies, use them for cookie centers.

Bake in slow oven (325°) 12 to 15 minutes, until firm, but do not brown. Transfer cookies to racks and cool. Makes 5 dozen.

N O T E : You can bake the cookies after adding pink sugar, cool them and add dots of frosting, tinted yellow, to make the centers. Use ½ recipe for Ornamental Icing. For dainty teatime cookies, use a 1" round, scalloped cookie cutter.

ORNAMENTAL ICING

Write and draw on cookies with this icing to give them a festive look

1½ to 2 c. confectioners sugar
1 to 2 tblsp. slightly beaten egg white (about)

Combine confectioners sugar with enough egg white to make an icing you can put through decorating tube or small plastic bag with small hole cut in one corner, but which will have enough consistency to hold its shape on cookies. A second batch of icing can easily be made if needed.

CHRISTMAS COOKIE CENTERPIECES

You can bake rolled cookies and put them together to make charming yuletide centerpieces. It takes time to bake the cookies, to build with them and to add decorations, but when you see the way the children and guests of all ages admire your creation, you'll know the minutes were well spent.

The trick is to divide the work. Bake the cookies ahead and freeze them or store them in a cold place. It helps to have them on hand when you are ready to start assembling the scenes.

We give you recipes, patterns and directions for two cookie centerpieces. Take your pick of a country barnyard scene, made with chocolate-flavored cookies, or a Christmas church built with sugar cookies. Snow (frosting) trims both of them.

SUGAR-SYRUP CEMENT

This sweet syrup holds cookies in place when building with them

For Barn: Melt ½ c. sugar in a heavy shallow skillet (at least 12" across); use lowest heat to melt sugar. For silo, melt another ½ c. sugar.

For Church: Melt 2 c. sugar.

Stir constantly while sugar melts, so that it won't burn. Keep syrup on medium heat while you use it. Be sure to use a wide skillet, so you can dip edges of long cookies into the syrup easily, as you put pieces together.

Work slowly when putting barn or church together. Make sure pieces are "glued" firmly before adding another.

General Directions: Enlarge patterns as indicated (each square equals 1 square inch) and cut from cardboard. Use them to cut cookie pieces.

Dust cardboard patterns with flour and cut around them with a sharp knife.

Bake cookie pieces one day; assemble and decorate cookie scene the next (or store baked cookies in freezer).

Check baked cookies against patterns; trim edges with a sharp knife while cookies are still warm.

GINGER COOKIE CHURCH

Put cookie pieces together with "cement"; arrange trees and fence, build gumdrop bushes and blanket with icing—use photo as guide

1 c. shortening	1 c. dark corn syrup
1 c. brown sugar, firmly packed	2 eggs, beaten
1 tblsp. grated lemon peel	5½ to 6 c. sifted flour
1 tblsp. ground cinnamon	1 tsp. salt
1 tblsp. ground ginger	1¼ tsp. baking soda

Cream shortening; add brown sugar, lemon peel and spices; blend.

Bring syrup to a boil; pour into creamed mixture; stir until well blended.

Add eggs and blend.

Sift 3 c. flour with salt and baking soda; add to mixture. Stir in 2½ c. flour, a little at a time.

Turn out on lightly floured surface and knead about 10 minutes, using remaining ½ c. flour if necessary.

Chill 1 hour.

Separate dough into several sections. (It is slightly stiffer than ordinary dough. This prevents crumbling.) Roll out each section to ¼" thickness. Transfer to greased baking sheet; smooth out dough with rolling pin. Dust patterns for church pieces with flour; place over dough and cut out with sharp knife. Mark "logs" on doors and sides of church with a two-tined fork or a knife.

Bake in moderate oven (375°) 12 to 15 minutes for large pieces, 5 to 7 for smaller pieces. Remove cookies and cool on racks.

Snow Icing: Place 1 lb. confectioners sugar in mixing bowl. Beat 3 egg whites slightly with a fork; add to confectioners sugar and beat with electric mixer on low speed for 1 minute. Add 1 tblsp. white vinegar; beat 2 minutes more at high speed, or until stiff and glossy —as for stiff meringue. Use as directed to decorate cookie church.

To Assemble Church: Cover heavy cardboard 20 x 18" with cotton. Wet your thumb and push a path through the cotton, leading to the church door.

Diagrams show how church and steeple go together. First, fasten colored cellophane or tissue paper over windows of church with flour paste.

Cut fence pieces and weave together (see photo)

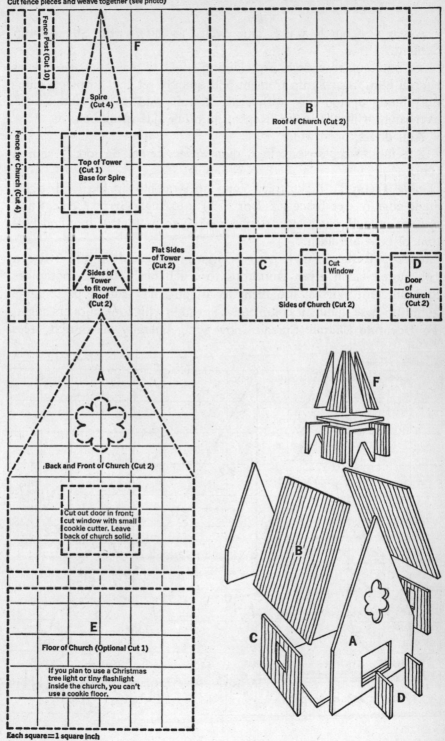

Fence Post (Cut 10)

Fence for Church (Cut 4)

Spire (Cut 4)

F

B
Roof of Church (Cut 2)

Top of Tower (Cut 1)
Base for Spire

Flat Sides of Tower (Cut 2)

Sides of Tower to fit over Roof (Cut 2)

C

Cut Window

D
Door of Church (Cut 2)

Sides of Church (Cut 2)

A

Back and Front of Church (Cut 2)

Cut out door in front; cut window with small cookie cutter. Leave back of church solid.

E

Floor of Church (Optional Cut 1)

If you plan to use a Christmas tree light or tiny flashlight inside the church, you can't use a cookie floor.

Each square = 1 square inch

Assemble church walls; glue walls to floor with Sugar-Syrup Cement.

To put roof on church, dip slanting edges of walls on one side of church into Sugar-Syrup Cement and quickly set roof in place, carefully lining up top edge with peak of walls and leaving about a 1″ overhang on 3 other sides. Repeat on other side of church.

Add doors, open wide.

Assemble steeple, spire first, then tower; center on top of church roof.

Cookie Trees: To make trees stand up straight, dip the long, right-angle edge of tree brace (X-2 or Y-2) into Sugar-Syrup Cement and press it at right angle against tree cookie, so bottom of tree and bottom of base are flush.

Gumdrop Bushes: You'll need 1 large green gumdrop and 3 dozen (or more) small green gumdrops for each bush. Break toothpicks into different lengths; use them to attach small gumdrops to large gumdrop base, hiding it completely. Sprinkle with confectioners sugar.

To Decorate Church: Spread Snow Icing liberally on church, trees

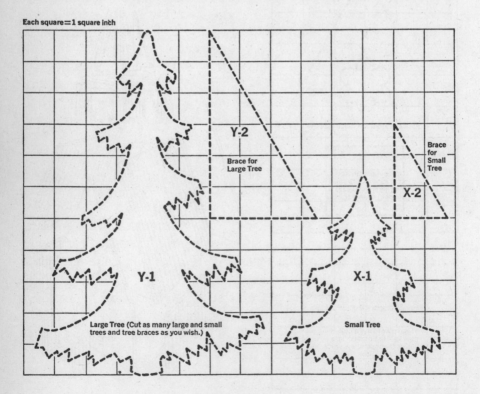

Each square = 1 square inch

Y-2
Brace for Large Tree

Brace for Small Tree

X-2

Y-1

X-1

Large Tree (Cut as many large and small trees and tree braces as you wish.)

Small Tree

and fence after they've been put together (see photo). Icicles will form naturally if you apply icing from the top.

Sprinkle with confectioners sugar while icing is still moist, for a look of new-fallen snow. Shake sugar through a fine sieve.

COCOA COOKIE BARN

A good "building dough" especially flavored for chocolate lovers

1⅓ c. shortening	1 tsp. baking soda
2 c. sugar	1 tsp. salt
2 eggs	½ c. cocoa
4⅔ c. flour	½ c. milk
2 tsp. baking powder	

Cream shortening and sugar until light and fluffy; add eggs and beat well.

Sift together dry ingredients; add alternately with milk to creamed mixture, mixing well. Chill dough.

Roll out small amount of dough at a time ⅛" thick on lightly floured pastry cloth. Cut desired shapes (see patterns).

Bake on greased baking sheets in slow oven (325°) 10 to 15 minutes. Remove cookies and cool on racks.

White Decorating Frosting: Combine 2 egg whites, 1½ c. sugar, ⅓ c. water, 2 tsp. light corn syrup and ⅛ tsp. salt in top of double boiler; beat 1 minute. Cook over boiling water, beating constantly, until mixture stands in stiff peaks. Remove from heat; transfer to mixing bowl; beat until smooth. Use at once.

Red Decorating Frosting: Beat together 4 c. confectioners sugar, ⅛ tsp. salt, 2½ tsp. red food color, 6 drops yellow food color and 4½ to 5 tblsp. milk until of stiff spreading consistency.

To Assemble Barn Scene: Cover heavy cardboard 30 x 20" with foil. Set decorated barn and silo at one end. Frost board with another batch of White Decorating Frosting, leaving unfrosted area for pond; swirl frosting for drifts. Don't worry if the roof isn't quite straight— just cover the defects with frosting.

Make pretzel fence. Set decorated animals and trees in frosting snow (prop with toothpicks till frosting dries).

Silo: Cut 30 circles from dough with 2" cookie cutter. Bake, cool and glue in a stack with Sugar-Syrup Cement.

Animals and Trees: Use any cookie cutters you have, or make your

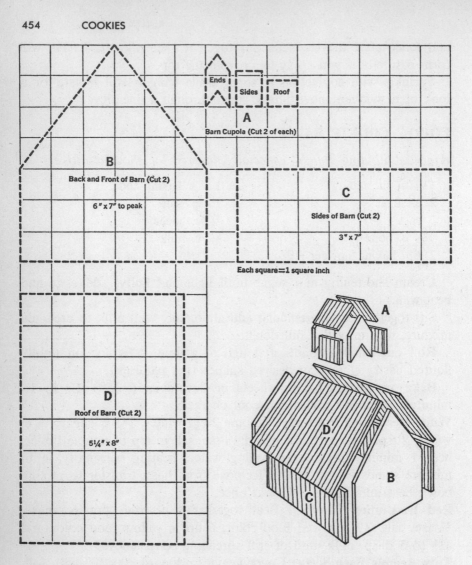

Ends

Sides Roof

A

Barn Cupola (Cut 2 of each)

B

Back and Front of Barn (Cut 2)

6 " x 7" to peak

C

Sides of Barn (Cut 2)

3" x 7"

Each square=1 square inch

D

Roof of Barn (Cut 2)

5¼" x 8"

A

D

B

C

own patterns by tracing from magazines or cards. Give animals character by drawing features (wings, ears, eyes) in dough with toothpick before baking.

To Decorate Barn: Use Red Decorating Frosting for sides of barn and silo. Apply with small-blade spatula to make ridges (see photo).

Use 1 batch of White Decorating Frosting for roof of barn, cupola, to make peak of silo and (with decorating tube) for features on animals, trees, barn windows and doors.

COOKIE FAMILY IN A CHRISTMAS HOUSE

Cookie dolls all dressed up for the holidays—a whole family of them in a cozy Christmas House—are an ideal gift for children. They will tote this present around until they finally can no longer resist eating them.

Children will sense the love you put into the homemade gift. Most of them will keep the pretty house and store their personal treasures in it.

We give you the recipe and patterns for making the Cookie Family and directions for the Christmas House.

COOKIE FAMILY

It's easiest to bake cookies one day and decorate them the next

⅔ c. shortening

1½ c. sugar

2 eggs

1 tsp. vanilla

1 tblsp. milk

3¼ c. sifted flour

2½ tsp. baking powder

½ tsp. salt

Decorating Frosting

Mix shortening, sugar and eggs. Stir in vanilla and milk.

Sift together flour, baking powder and salt. Blend into creamed mixture. Chill.

Roll out dough ⅛" thick on floured board or pastry cloth. Dust cardboard patterns with flour. Lay patterns on dough and cut out designs with point of paring knife. Use spatula to move to lightly greased baking sheet. Do not stretch dough.

Before baking Cookie Girl, insert a short piece of paper drinking straw in dough through which to tie hair bow.

Bake in hot oven (400°) 5 to 7 minutes, until lightly browned. Transfer cookies to racks to cool. Cool before frosting. Makes 7 cookie families.

Decorating Frosting:

⅓ c. butter or regular margarine

3 c. sifted confectioners sugar

1½ tblsp. water (about)

Cream butter and sugar thoroughly. Add enough water to make frosting of spreading consistency.

PATTERNS FOR THE COOKIE FAMILY
(*Each square = ½ inch*)

Divide frosting into 7 small dishes and add food color as follows:
White: ⅓ c. for Father's and Boy's shirts, and for dress trimmings.
Brown: Add 2 tsp. cocoa to ¼ c. frosting. For eyes, hair for Father, Mother's and Boy's shoes.
Pink: Add red to ¼ c. frosting. For Mother's dress.
Red: Add red plus small amount of yellow to 2 tblsp. frosting. For Girl's dress, all mouths.
Green: Add green to 2 tblsp. frosting. For Boy's trousers.
Yellow: Add yellow to 1 tblsp. frosting. For Girl's hair.
Orange: Add yellow plus small amount of red to 2 tblsp. frosting. For Dog.

Let one color frosting dry well before using second on the same cookie.

Spread frosting with narrow spatula. Use paint brush for facial features.

When frosted cookies are completely dry, add white trim on dresses, using decorating tube.

Use narrow red ribbons to tie cookies onto sheet of white cardboard that fits into hosiery-type box.

CHRISTMAS HOUSE

Decorate a hosiery-type box about ¾" to 1" thick to look like a house for the cookie family. Sketch a design to fit box lid (suggestions follow). A red house looks especially festive. To make it, cover lid and bottom of box separately with red wrapping paper. On the lid, paste a roof cut from gray paper; draw shingles on roof. Add a scalloped cornice along roof edge, cut from white paper. Cut a window from yellow paper; cut a Christmas tree from green paper and decorate it with colored signal dots (from stationery store). Paste tree on window and window on house. Add white shutters and white window frame. Cut a white door and paste it in place. Cut dark green bushes and gold lanterns to paste on each side of door. Finally, decorate door with wreath cut from an old Christmas card.

To mount cookies, cut a piece of stiff cardboard to fit inside box. Arrange cookies and mark where holes for ribbon should be made: on both sides of man's neck, both sides of woman's waist, through hair-ribbon hole in girl's head and on opposite side, on both sides of boy's neck and on both sides of dog's neck. Make holes with ice pick or sharp knife. Tie cookies in place with ¼" red ribbon.

Refrigerator Cookies

Making refrigerator cookies is a two-act performance. Act one: mix, shape and freeze or refrigerate the dough; act two: slice and bake. The action may take place days, weeks or months apart. It's this division of work that elevates refrigerator cookies to first place among summer homemade cookies.

Even if it's hot and humid, you can slice off just enough cookies to meet your immediate needs and bake them quickly without heating the kitchen too much. Country women like to bake the cookies right after breakfast before the sun turns on full heat. Of course the cookies are favorites at all seasons, but summer is their heyday.

You need only a few rules for successful refrigerator cookies. One is to shape the dough in smooth, firm rolls with your hands. Make them the diameter you want your cookies; they spread little in baking. Wrap them tightly in waxed paper, twisting both ends to seal. If you freeze the dough, overwrap with foil. Or wrap them with foil or plastic wrap, taping edges. Most cookie doughs will keep well 3 to 5 days in the refrigerator, 6 months in the freezer.

Use a knife with a long, sharp blade to slice the dough from ⅛ to ¼″ in thickness. The thinner the slices, the crisper the cookies will be. Be sure they are cut to the same thickness so they will bake in the same number of minutes. Bake them until they are lightly browned unless recipe directs otherwise. If you add nuts to the dough, chop them very fine or they will make it difficult to slice cookies neatly.

Refrigerator cookies need no decoration. But for special occasions you can sprinkle waxed paper with decorating sugar or with tiny multicolored candies, finely chopped nuts, chocolate shot (jimmies) or finely crushed stick candy. Turn the roll of cookie dough round and round on the waxed paper to coat it with the decoration. Then wrap and chill or freeze. When baked, the cookies have fancy rims.

You can also tint light-colored dough with food color or press a nut or drop a dab of jelly on cookie slices just before you bake them.

Or top ready-to-bake cookies with peaks of meringue, tinted if you like. Our Meringue-Topped Cookies are tasty beauties, especially when you flavor the meringue with peppermint, tint it pink and sprinkle with pink sugar—or coconut or chocolate shot.

Filled refrigerator cookies are so easy to fix. When the slices of dough are on the baking sheet, drop a bit of filling on each one and lay another cookie on top. Try our fruity Mincemeat/Lemon Filling. You can also put *baked* refrigerator cookies together with filling to make sandwiches—to prove that two cookies taste better than one!

For cookies that are on the salty rather than the sweet side, make Old Salts. They're a great snack or appetizer. Our Molasses Almond Cookies are unusual, too—the topping bakes right with the cookies. Our recipe suggests that you shape both the rolls of dough and topping in rolls 1″ in diameter. This produces small cookies which are ideal for tea and other parties. You may prefer to double the recipe and make 2″ rolls.

You'll find recipes for many kinds of refrigerator cookies that are wonderful with ice cream, sherbet, iced or hot tea and coffee, lemonade and other fruit drinks. They also are perfect partners for party punch.

ALMOND REFRIGERATOR COOKIES

A simplified, American version of Chinese cookies—crisp, lacy, rich

1 c. butter or regular margarine	½ tsp. almond extract
2 c. sifted flour	1 egg yolk
¾ tsp. salt	1 tblsp. water
¾ c. sugar	½ c. blanched almonds, cut in
½ tsp. vanilla	halves (see Index)

Cut butter into flour with pastry blender as for pie crust. Work in salt, sugar, vanilla and almond extract with hands. Shape in two long rolls 1 to 1½″ in diameter. Wrap tightly in plastic wrap or waxed paper and refrigerate 1 hour, or until firm.

Cut rolls in ¼″ slices and place 1″ apart on lightly greased baking sheet. Brush top of each cookie sparingly with egg yolk mixed with water. Press an almond half in center of each.

Bake in hot oven (400°) 8 to 10 minutes, or until lightly browned. Cool slightly on baking sheet before removing to cooling rack. (If

you do not cool them a little on baking sheet, they will crumble.)
Makes about 6½ dozen.

RICH ANISE COOKIES

Keep several rolls in the refrigerator—excellent with ice cream

1 c. butter or regular margarine	½ tsp. vanilla
1 (3 oz.) pkg. cream cheese	2½ c. sifted flour
1 c. sugar	½ tsp. salt
1 egg yolk	2 tsp. anise seeds, crushed

Cream butter, cream cheese and sugar together until light. Add egg
yolk and vanilla and beat until light and fluffy.

Combine flour, salt and anise seeds. Blend into creamed mixture
until smooth. Shape in two rolls about 2″ in diameter on lightly
floured waxed paper. Wrap rolls tightly in waxed paper and chill at
least 2 hours or overnight.

Cut dough in thin slices, about ⅛″ thick; place about 2″ apart on
ungreased baking sheet. Bake in moderate oven (350°) 10 to 12
minutes, or until cookie edges are browned. Remove cookies and
cool on racks. Makes about 6 dozen.

Variation

Rich Nutmeg Cookies: Omit anise seeds from Rich Anise Cookies
and add 1 tsp. ground nutmeg with the flour.

BUTTERSCOTCH REFRIGERATOR COOKIES

Keep a few cans of dough in freezer to bake on short notice

3½ c. sifted flour	2 c. brown sugar, firmly packed
1 tsp. salt	2 eggs, well beaten
1 tsp. ground cinnamon	2 tblsp. warm water
1 tsp. baking soda	1 tsp. vanilla
½ c. shortening	1 c. chopped nuts
½ c. butter	

Sift together flour, salt, cinnamon and soda.

Cream shortening and butter; gradually add sugar; beat until light.
Add eggs, water and vanilla; mix well.

Combine dry ingredients and creamed mixture; blend well. Add
nuts.

Shape dough into roll 2″ in diameter. Wrap tightly in waxed paper and chill thoroughly—overnight for best results. When ready to bake, cut in ⅛″ slices.

Bake 1½″ apart on ungreased baking sheet in hot oven (400°) 10 to 12 minutes. Spread on racks to cool. Makes 6 dozen.

BLACK WALNUT COOKIES

Descendant of Pennsylvania Dutch slapjacks—cookies taste great

6 c. sifted flour	2¼ c. brown sugar, firmly packed
1 tsp. salt	½ c. sugar
½ tsp. baking soda	2 eggs, beaten
1 tsp. cream of tartar	2 tsp. vanilla
1¾ c. butter or regular margarine	1½ c. black walnuts
	1½ c. flaked or shredded coconut

Sift together flour, salt, soda and cream of tartar.

Cream butter; add brown and white sugars gradually and beat until fluffy. Add eggs and vanilla; mix well.

Grind nuts and coconut together in food chopper using medium blade, or use blender. Add to creamed mixture. Add sifted dry ingredients and blend well. Chill.

Shape dough in four rolls about 2″ in diameter. Wrap tightly in waxed paper and chill thoroughly.

Cut rolls in ⅛″ slices; place about 1″ apart on ungreased baking sheet. Bake in moderate oven (350°) 10 to 12 minutes. Remove cookies and cool on racks. Makes 8 to 9 dozen.

BLUSHING REFRIGERATOR COOKIES

The pink glow of cookies contrasts charmingly with their gay red tops

1 c. butter	5 drops red food color
½ c. sugar	2¾ c. sifted flour
½ c. brown sugar, firmly packed	½ tsp. baking soda
2 eggs	½ tsp. salt
1 tsp. vanilla	Red decorating sugar (for tops)

Combine butter, sugars, eggs and vanilla; beat until very light. Add food color.

Sift together flour, baking soda and salt. Stir into first mixture. Mix with hands until dough is smooth. Shape in two rolls, each 2″

in diameter and about 9½" long. Wrap tightly in waxed paper, twisting ends. Chill in refrigerator overnight or a couple of days, or freeze.

When ready to bake, cut dough in thin slices, about ⅛" thick, with a sharp knife. Arrange ½" apart on ungreased baking sheet. Sprinkle tops with red sugar.

Bake in hot oven (400°) 6 to 8 minutes. Remove from baking sheet and cool on racks. Makes 8 dozen.

Variations

Chocolate Wafers: Make like Blushing Refrigerator Cookies, only omit food color and red decorating sugar, and add 2 squares unsweetened chocolate, melted and cooled, to butter. Sprinkle tops of wafers before baking with finely chopped nuts or green decorating sugar, or decorate them, when cool, with Ornamental Icing (see Index).

Filled Refrigerator Cookies: Make half of recipe for Blushing Refrigerator Cookies, but omit food color and red decorating sugar. Place half of the cookies on baking sheet; top each with ½ tsp. Mincemeat/Lemon Filling, then top with another cookie and bake as directed. Makes 2 dozen.

Mincemeat/Lemon Filling: Stir together ¼ c. prepared mincemeat, 2 tblsp. chopped walnuts and 2 tsp. grated lemon peel.

CHOCOLATE COOKIE SANDWICHES

Fill with pastel pink and green frosting for a festive party tray

½ c. shortening
½ c. sugar
1 egg
3 tblsp. milk
2 squares unsweetened
  chocolate, melted and cooled

1¾ c. sifted flour
1 tsp. salt
½ tsp. baking powder
Peppermint Frosting (recipe
  follows)

Cream shortening and sugar until fluffy; beat in egg, milk and chocolate.

Sift together flour, salt and baking powder. Stir into creamed mixture. Shape dough in two smooth rolls about 2" in diameter, 6" long. Wrap each in waxed paper and chill several hours until firm, or overnight.

Slice rolls thin, about ⅛", with sharp knife. Place 1½" apart on lightly greased baking sheet. Bake in moderate oven (375°) 7 to 10 minutes (watch carefully). Remove cookies and cool on racks. Spread half the cookies with Peppermint Frosting. Top with remaining cookies. Makes 2½ dozen.

Peppermint Frosting: Combine 2 c. sifted confectioners sugar, 1½ tblsp. butter and 2½ tblsp. dairy half-and-half or light cream. Beat until smooth. Add 3 to 4 drops peppermint extract. Divide in half; to one part add 3 drops red food color, to the other, 2 drops green food color.

CHOCOLATE FILLED COOKIES

Partially melted chocolate candy wafers form the luscious filling

1 c. butter	2½ c. sifted flour
1 c. sugar	¼ tsp. cream of tartar
1 egg	40 thin round chocolate candy
1 tsp. vanilla	wafers

Cream butter and sugar until light and fluffy. Add egg and vanilla. Beat well.

Sift flour and cream of tartar; add to creamed mixture and beat until blended. Chill until dough is firm enough to handle. Then shape dough in two rolls, each about 10" long. Wrap tightly in waxed paper or plastic wrap and chill overnight.

Cut one roll of dough in ⅛" slices. Place 20 rounds 1 to 1½" apart on ungreased baking sheet. Place a chocolate wafer on each. Top with 20 more rounds of dough. Press dough circles together, completely covering chocolate wafers. Repeat with other roll of dough.

Bake in moderate oven (375°) about 10 minutes, or until cookies are delicately browned. Transfer cookies to racks to cool. Makes 40.

NOTE: Work with half of dough at a time, keeping the remaining dough in refrigerator.

CHOCOLATE MINT WAFERS

Chocolate/mint flavors complement each other in these thin cookies

¼ c. heavy cream	⅛ tsp. peppermint extract
1 tblsp. vinegar	2 c. sifted flour
½ c. shortening	¾ c. cocoa
1 c. sugar	½ tsp. baking soda
1 egg	¼ tsp. salt

Combine heavy cream and vinegar in measuring cup; set aside.

Cream together shortening and sugar; stir in egg and peppermint extract.

Sift together remaining dry ingredients; add alternately with heavy cream to creamed mixture. Mix thoroughly. Divide dough in half and shape into two rolls. Wrap tightly in waxed paper and chill several hours in refrigerator.

Cut dough in ⅛″ slices with sharp knife; place 1½″ apart on ungreased baking sheet. Bake in moderate oven (350°) 15 minutes. Remove cookies and cool on racks. Makes 3 dozen.

EASY DATE FILL-UPS

For crisper cookies refrigerate filling and add just before serving

½ c. butter	1 tsp. vanilla
½ c. lard	2½ c. sifted flour
½ c. dairy sour cream	2 c. quick-cooking rolled oats
¾ c. brown sugar, firmly packed	1¼ c. halved dates (8 oz.)
2 tsp. baking soda	½ c. sugar
1 tsp. salt	¼ c. water

Blend together butter, lard, dairy sour cream, brown sugar, baking soda, salt and vanilla. Add flour and oats and mix well.

Divide dough in half. Shape each part in a roll 2″ in diameter. Wrap in foil or waxed paper and refrigerate overnight, or at least 8 hours. (For faster chilling place in freezer.)

To bake, cut dough in ⅛″ slices; place about 1″ apart on ungreased baking sheet. Bake in moderate oven (350°) 8 to 12 minutes, or until light golden brown. Remove cookies and cool on racks.

To make filling, combine dates, white sugar and water in saucepan. Cook over medium heat until thick and smooth, stirring constantly. Cool until lukewarm.

At serving time, spread half of cooled cookies on bottom sides with date filling; top with remaining cookies. Makes about 4 dozen.

Variation

Austrian Cookie Rounds: Omit the date filling. Melt together in custard cup, set in hot water, ½ c. semisweet chocolate pieces and 1 tblsp. shortening. Spread on half of cookies while still slightly warm to coat them with a glaze. Let harden. Before serving, spread a thin layer of currant or other red jelly on the unglazed cookies and top with a glazed cookie, glazed side up.

FINNISH SHORTBREAD COOKIES

Rich cookies, a treat from Finnish kitchens—we give you variations

2 c. butter	⅛ tsp. salt
1 c. sugar	Chopped almonds
4 c. sifted flour	Sugar (for tops)

Cream butter and 1 c. sugar thoroughly. Add flour and salt. Shape in long, slender rolls 1" in diameter. Wrap rolls tightly in waxed paper and chill thoroughly.

Cut dough in ½" slices; place ½ to 1" apart on ungreased baking sheet. Press each circle down with your thumb. Sprinkle with almonds, then with sugar.

Bake in hot oven (400°) 7 to 10 minutes. (Cookies should not brown.) Remove cookies and cool on racks. Makes about 14 dozen.

NOTE: You can take the dough from the refrigerator and bake cookies whenever convenient. It's a good idea to chill the dough at least 24 hours.

Variations

Easter Shortbreads: Prepare dough for Finnish Shortbread Cookies; chill thoroughly (do not form in rolls). Divide chilled dough in thirds, and work with one part at a time. Roll dough ⅛" thick on lightly floured surface. Cut first third of dough with Easter bunny cookie cutter; arrange ½" apart on ungreased baking sheet. Do not sprinkle with almonds. Bake in hot oven (400°) 8 minutes. Remove cookies and cool on racks. Repeat with second third of dough, but cut with chicken cookie cutter. Then roll and cut last portion of dough with an Easter cross cookie cutter. (All cutters are from 2 to 2½" at longest or widest place.)

When all cookies are cool, frost tops with Tinted Frosting. Use pink dragées for bunny eyes, green dragées for chicken eyes and three silver dragées to decorate each cross (one dragée centered in each extension of the cross). Spread frosted cookies out in tight container with waxed paper between layers if they are to be held a few hours or a couple of days before serving. Set in a cold place. Cookies are especially handsome served on a purple or black lacquer or a silver tray. Makes 5 dozen.

Tinted Frosting: Beat together until smooth 2 c. sifted confectioners sugar, 1 tsp. vanilla and 3 to 4 tblsp. milk, enough to make a frosting of spreading consistency. Divide in thirds. To one part, add 1 drop of red food color to make a delicate pink frosting for the bunnies; to the second part, add 2 drops yellow food color to make frosting for chickens; and to the last third, add 1 drop green food color to make a pale green frosting for the crosses.

FRESH LEMON COCONUT COOKIES

Lemon peel provides a fresh citrus taste that's wonderful with coconut

¼ c. butter	¾ c. shredded coconut
¼ c. shortening	1¾ c. sifted flour
1 c. sugar	½ tsp. salt
1 egg	2 tsp. baking powder
2 tsp. grated lemon peel	

Cream together butter, shortening and sugar. Add egg and beat until light and fluffy. Add lemon peel and coconut; stir to blend.

Sift together dry ingredients; stir into creamed mixture. Divide dough in half and shape into rolls. Wrap tightly in waxed paper and store in refrigerator at least several hours.

Cut dough in thin slices with sharp knife; place 1½" apart on ungreased baking sheet. Bake in hot oven (400°) 10 minutes. Remove cookies and cool on racks. Makes about 4 dozen.

LEMON THINS

Just right to escort ice cream, sherbet, light puddings and fruits

1 c. butter or regular margarine	½ tsp. baking powder
½ c. sugar	⅛ tsp. salt
1 egg, beaten	1 tblsp. lemon juice
2 c. sifted flour	½ tsp. grated lemon peel

Cream together butter and sugar; add egg; mix well.

Sift together flour, baking powder and salt; combine with sugar mixture. Add lemon juice and peel.

Form into rolls 1½ to 2″ in diameter; wrap tightly in waxed paper and chill.

Slice very thin. Bake 1½″ apart on ungreased baking sheet in moderate oven (375°) 8 to 10 minutes. Remove cookies and cool on racks. Makes 5 to 6 dozen.

MERINGUE-TOPPED COOKIES

Beauties—pink, peppermint-flavored meringue with pink sugar trim

1 c. butter or regular margarine	½ tsp. cream of tartar
1½ c. sugar	¼ tsp. almond extract
3 eggs, separated	Colored decorating sugar,
2 tsp. grated orange peel	decorating candies or flaked
3 c. sifted flour	coconut (optional)
¼ tsp. salt	

Beat butter until light. Add ¾ c. sugar and beat until light and fluffy. Beat in egg yolks and orange peel to blend well.

Stir together flour and salt; add to creamed mixture. Shape in two rolls 1½″ in diameter. Wrap tightly in waxed paper, twisting ends, and refrigerate overnight.

Cut dough in ¼″ slices. Place about 1″ apart on ungreased baking sheet.

Beat egg whites with cream of tartar until foamy. Gradually add remaining ¾ c. sugar and beat until stiff, but not dry. Fold in almond extract. Drop by teaspoonfuls onto cookie slices. Sprinkle top of meringue with colored sugar, decorating candies or flaked coconut.

Bake in moderate oven (350°) 10 to 12 minutes, or just until delicately browned. Remove cookies to cooling rack. Makes about 5 dozen.

NOTE: For fascinating holiday cookies, tint meringue with food color; omit almond extract and flavor with other extracts. Use peppermint extract for pink or green meringues, lemon extract for yellow meringues and orange extract for orange-colored meringues (mixture of red and yellow food color makes orange). Sprinkle tops of meringues with colored sugar to match color of meringue, or with decorating candies, silver or other colored dragées, flaked coconut or chocolate shot (jimmies). A tray of these handsome, buttery rich cookies provides decorative and delicious hospitality for a party or open house.

MINCEMEAT REFRIGERATOR COOKIES

Mincemeat is the seasoning in this big recipe—makes 9 dozen

¾ c. butter	3 c. sifted flour
1 c. sugar	½ tsp. baking soda
1 egg	½ tsp. salt
½ tsp. vanilla	1 tsp. ground cinnamon
1 tsp. finely grated lemon peel	½ c. chopped walnuts
¾ c. prepared mincemeat	

Cream together butter and sugar until light and fluffy. Beat in egg, vanilla and lemon peel. Stir in mincemeat.

Sift together flour, baking soda, salt and cinnamon; gradually add to creamed mixture, mixing well. Stir in nuts.

Divide dough in half. Place each part on a lightly floured sheet of waxed paper and form in a roll 1½" in diameter, about 12" long. (Sprinkling waxed paper with a little flour helps you to shape smooth rolls.) Wrap rolls in waxed paper and refrigerate several hours, overnight or 2 or 3 days.

With sharp knife, cut dough in ⅛" slices; place 1½" apart on ungreased baking sheet. Bake in moderate oven (375°) about 10 minutes. Remove cookies to cooling racks at once. Makes 9 dozen.

MOCHA NUT COOKIES

Chocolate and coffee combine in these distinctive cookies

½ c. shortening
1 c. sugar
1 egg
2 squares unsweetened chocolate, melted

½ c. chopped walnuts or pecans
1 c. sifted flour
¼ tsp. salt
1 tsp. baking powder
2 tsp. instant coffee powder

Cream together shortening and sugar. Add egg and beat until light and fluffy. Stir in chocolate and nuts.

Sift together dry ingredients and add to creamed mixture; blend thoroughly. Divide dough in half and shape into rolls. Wrap tightly in waxed paper; chill in refrigerator at least several hours.

Cut dough in ⅛″ slices; place 1½″ apart on ungreased baking sheet. Bake in moderate oven (375°) 15 minutes. Remove cookies and cool on racks. Makes about 6 dozen.

MOLASSES/ALMOND COOKIES

Little coffee-flavored molasses cookies with a baked-on topping

½ c. shortening
3 tblsp. light molasses
1 tsp. instant coffee powder
½ tsp. vanilla
1½ c. sifted flour

¼ tsp. salt
¼ tsp. baking soda
½ c. butter
½ c. confectioners sugar
½ c. chopped almonds

Beat shortening until light. Gradually beat in molasses. Stir in coffee powder and vanilla.

Sift together flour, salt and baking soda. Add to molasses mixture. Form dough into a roll 1″ in diameter, about 13″ long. Wrap tightly in waxed paper, twisting ends, and chill in refrigerator 2 hours or overnight.

Combine butter, confectioners sugar and almonds. Shape in roll 1″ in diameter; wrap tightly in waxed paper, twisting ends. Chill 2 hours or overnight.

To bake, cut each roll in ¼″ slices; place dough slices about 1″ apart on ungreased baking sheet and top with almond slices. Bake in moderate oven (350°) 10 to 12 minutes. Remove cookies and cool on racks. Makes about 4 dozen.

OATMEAL/MAPLE COOKIES

Whole wheat flour and maple flavoring give the cookies distinction

1 c. soft butter	1 c. quick-cooking rolled oats
1 c. brown sugar, firmly packed	¼ c. chocolate shot (jimmies)
1 tsp. maple flavoring	¼ c. finely chopped walnuts
1½ c. whole wheat flour	

Cream butter, brown sugar and flavoring together until fluffy. Stir in flour and oats; mix until blended.

Divide dough in half. Shape each half into a roll 1½" in diameter. Roll one roll in chocolate shot and the other in nuts. Wrap tightly in waxed paper; chill several hours or overnight.

Cut ¼" slices and place 1½" apart on ungreased baking sheet. Bake in moderate oven (350°) 12 to 15 minutes. Cool on baking sheet until firm before removing to cooling rack. Makes 6 dozen.

OLD SALTS

Perfect snack—hide or they'll disappear. Salted tops, sweet inside

1 c. shortening	¼ tsp. salt
1 c. sugar	½ tsp. baking powder
1 egg	½ tsp. baking soda
1 tsp. vanilla	3 c. quick-cooking rolled oats
1¼ c. sifted flour	Salt (for tops)

Cream shortening and sugar until light and fluffy. Beat in egg and vanilla to mix thoroughly.

Sift together flour, ¼ tsp. salt, baking powder and soda; add to creamed mixture. Stir in rolled oats.

Divide dough in quarters and place each part on sheet of lightly floured waxed paper. Shape in roll 1" in diameter and about 12" long. Wrap in waxed paper and chill several hours or overnight. (It's easier to shape soft dough on waxed paper lightly floured.)

Cut in ¼" slices (dough will be crumbly and cannot be cut thinner). Sprinkle tops lightly with salt. Place about 1" apart on greased baking sheet.

Bake in moderate oven (375°) 10 to 12 minutes. Let stand a couple of minutes before removing from baking sheet to rack for cooling. Makes about 12 dozen.

SIX-IN-ONE REFRIGERATOR COOKIES

You make 18 dozen cookies of six flavors from one batch of dough

2 c. butter
1 c. sugar
1 c. light brown sugar, firmly packed
2 eggs, beaten
1 tsp. vanilla
4 c. flour
1 tsp. baking soda
½ tsp. salt

½ c. shredded coconut
½ c. finely chopped pecans
½ tsp. ground nutmeg
1 tsp. ground cinnamon
1 square unsweetened chocolate, melted
¼ c. finely chopped candied cherries

Cream butter. Gradually add sugars; cream until light and fluffy. Add eggs and vanilla; mix well.

Sift together flour, soda and salt; gradually add to creamed mixture, beating well after each addition.

Divide dough in six parts. Add coconut to one part; pecans to second; nutmeg and cinnamon to third; melted chocolate to fourth; and candied cherries to fifth. Leave the last portion plain. Chill 30 minutes, or longer.

Shape dough into six rolls about 1¾" in diameter. Wrap tightly in plastic wrap or waxed paper and refrigerate overnight, or freeze.

When ready to use, slice with sharp knife in ⅛" slices. (If frozen, thaw just enough to slice.) Place on lightly greased baking sheet.

Bake in moderate oven (375°) 10 to 12 minutes, until lightly browned. Remove cookies and cool on racks. Makes 18 dozen.

Molded Cookies

Christmas Cane Cookies tied with red ribbons . . . two-color cookie snails, or Swirls . . . Chocolate Bonbon Cookies with shiny pink Peppermint Glaze . . . Mexican Fiesta Balls dotted with cherries and fragrant with coffee—these will give you an idea of charming cookies you can make with recipes in this section.

Our molded cookies come in many sizes and shapes. Among the tasty tidbits are Spanish Wedding Cakes made from lemon-flavored cookie dough wrapped around almonds. Frosted Yule Logs resemble short, fat pencils coated with nuts. And Honeyed Yo-Yos are big, plump cookies sweetened and flavored with honey and brown sugar. Put together in pairs with apricot or other jam between, they really look like yo-yos. Men especially think they're right, both in size and taste.

This cookbook contains several superior recipes for sugar cookies. But our Molded Sugar Cookies take second place to none of them. They won several blue ribbons at fairs for the woman who shares the recipe with you. If you like sugar cookies that are golden and crisp on the outside and soft within, this recipe is for you.

Molded cookies especially delight women who like to create beautiful food and who like to shape dough with their hands. The technique can give you the same sort of satisfaction an artist experiences from molding clay.

Though fascinating, these cookies are not difficult to make, nor unduly time consuming. But do plan to spend enough time to achieve artistic results.

Rules are few—it's imaginative work and defies many cut-and-dried regulations. The dough has to be right. If it's too soft, chill it until you can easily handle it.

Balls of dough are the beginning of many molded cookies. Some of them retain their spherical shape during the baking, while others, such as Snickerdoodles, flatten. Some cookies are flattened before you put them in the oven. Use the bottom of a glass tumbler, greased lightly every time you press it on the dough. Some recipes recommend that you dip the glass lightly in flour or in sugar. And you flatten some cookies with the floured tines of a fork, pressed crosswise and then lengthwise to make a design.

Gather cheer, if you're new at this baking art, by reminding yourself that the more cookies you mold, the faster you'll do it well. Mothers report that some children excel in shaping cookie dough. Give them an opportunity to participate.

ALMOND BUTTERBALLS

Right for teas, parties, receptions—a hostess favorite

1 c. butter or regular margarine	2 c. sifted flour
¼ c. confectioners sugar	1 c. chopped almonds
1 tsp. vanilla	Confectioners sugar (for coating)
⅛ tsp. almond extract	

Cream butter and ¼ c. confectioners sugar until light and fluffy; add flavorings.

Stir in flour and almonds; blend well.

Form dough into tiny balls; place about 1" apart on ungreased baking sheet. Bake in moderate oven (350°) about 20 minutes.

Roll cookies in confectioners sugar while warm. Cool on racks. Makes about 6 dozen.

BLACK WALNUT CRESCENTS

Serve these with applesauce for a great winter supper dessert

½ c. butter	2 tsp. vanilla
½ c. shortening	2 c. sifted flour
⅓ c. sugar	½ c. chopped black walnuts
2 tsp. water	Confectioners sugar (for dipping)

Cream butter and shortening until light; add sugar, cream until light and fluffy. Beat in water, vanilla, flour and nuts. Chill 4 hours, or overnight.

Shape dough in rolls about 15" long and ½" in diameter; then cut in 3" lengths. Shape in crescents.

Place about ½" apart on ungreased baking sheet, and bake in slow oven (325°) 12 to 15 minutes. Do not let cookies brown. Cool slightly on baking sheet, then remove from baking sheet and dip in confectioners sugar. Place on racks to cool. Makes about 44.

N O T E : Black walnuts have a pronounced flavor. If you wish to decrease it, put 2 tblsp. chopped black walnuts in a ½ c. measure and fill with chopped walnuts, English-type.

CHRISTMAS CANE COOKIES

There's a hint of peppermint in these entwined red and creamy white butter cookie strips, shaped like canes for the yuletide

1 c. butter or regular margarine	½ tsp. salt
1 c. sifted confectioners sugar	½ tsp. red food color
1 egg	¼ c. crushed red and white
1½ tsp. vanilla	peppermint candy
½ tsp. almond extract	¼ c. sugar
2½ c. sifted flour	

Beat butter and confectioners sugar until mixture is light and fluffy. Beat in egg, vanilla and almond extract to blend well.

Mix flour and salt and stir into creamed mixture. Divide in half. Blend food color into one half. Work with ¼ plain dough and ¼ tinted dough. Keep remainder of dough in refrigerator until you are ready to use it.

Take 1 tsp. plain dough and roll with hands into a strip 4" long. Then roll 1 tsp. tinted dough into a strip the same length. Lay the two strips side by side and twist together, holding both ends of strips, to make a red and white striped rope. Place the rope on ungreased baking sheet and curve one end to make the cane's handle. Repeat, making one cane at a time so the dough will not dry out and be difficult to twist and shape. Place canes about 1" apart on baking sheet (12 will fit on one baking sheet). Then repeat with remaining portions of dough.

Bake in moderate oven (375°) about 10 minutes. Remove from baking sheet at once. Combine candy and white sugar; sprinkle on hot cookies. Cool on racks. Makes about 4 dozen.

EASY CANE COOKIES

Cookies are dappled with red flakes of peppermint candy—tie the canes with Christmas ribbons for a festive look

1 c. butter or regular margarine	2½ c. sifted flour
1 c. confectioners sugar	½ tsp. salt
1 egg	½ c. crushed red and white
1 tsp. vanilla	peppermint candy
¼ tsp. peppermint extract	2 tblsp. sugar

Beat together butter and confectioners sugar until light and fluffy. Beat in egg, vanilla and peppermint extract to blend well.

Combine flour and salt and stir into creamed mixture. Wrap dough in waxed paper and chill at least 1 hour.

When ready to shape, mix crushed candy with white sugar. Roll 1 level measuring tablespoonful of dough on surface sprinkled with small amount of crushed candy mixture to make a 6" rope. Place on greased baking sheet. Curve one end down to form handle of cane. Repeat until all the crushed candy mixture and dough have been used.

Bake in moderate oven (375°) about 12 minutes, until lightly browned. Remove at once from baking sheet and cool on racks. Makes about 3½ dozen.

NOTE: You can use stick candy of different colors and different extracts instead of the peppermint candy.

CHOCOLATE BONBON COOKIES

Tiny cookies with a shiny red peppermint glaze—for holiday parties

2 c. sifted flour	1 square unsweetened chocolate,
½ tsp. baking powder	melted
½ tsp. salt	1 tsp. vanilla
½ c. butter or regular margarine	Peppermint Glaze (recipe
½ c. sugar	follows)
1 egg	Silver dragées, nuts or canned
	frostings (for decorations)

Sift together flour, baking powder and salt.

Cream butter and sugar together until light and fluffy. Beat in egg, melted chocolate and vanilla. Stir in flour mixture, a third at a time, blending well. The dough will be stiff.

Roll rounded teaspoonfuls of dough, one at a time, into balls between hands. Place balls about 2" apart on lightly greased baking sheet.

Bake in moderate oven (350°) about 12 minutes, until firm. Remove from baking sheet to wire racks. Repeat until all dough is baked. Cool thoroughly.

To glaze cookies, arrange at least 1" apart on racks over waxed paper. Spoon Peppermint Glaze over to cover cookies completely (scrape glaze that drips onto waxed paper back into bowl). Spoon a second coating of glaze over the cookies; let cool. Trim with silver dragées, nuts or frostings from pressurized cans. Makes about 31.

NOTE: For Christmas holidays, use green frosting to make holly leaves, dots of red frosting for holly berries.

PEPPERMINT GLAZE

Perfect for chocolate cookies; tint glaze pink or green if you wish

3 c. sifted confectioners sugar   ¼ tsp. red food color (optional)
2 to 3 tblsp. water   ¼ tsp. peppermint extract

Combine all ingredients and beat until smooth. The glaze should be thin enough to pour from a spoon. If it gets too thick while working with it, add a few drops of water and beat until smooth. Makes about 1 cup.

Variation

Vanilla Glaze: Omit peppermint extract and red food color; add ½ tsp. vanilla and make glaze as directed.

CAPE COD CHOCOLATE CHIP COOKIES

A great 20th century cookie that rates among the all-time champions

1 c. butter or regular margarine	1 tsp. baking soda
¾ c. brown sugar, firmly packed	1 tsp. salt
¾ c. sugar	1 (6 oz.) pkg. semisweet
2 eggs	chocolate pieces
1 tsp. vanilla	½ c. chopped walnuts
2¼ c. sifted flour	

Cream butter until fluffy; gradually add sugars and beat until light and fluffy. Beat in eggs and vanilla, mixing well.

Sift together flour, baking powder and salt; add to creamed mixture and blend. Stir in chocolate pieces and nuts. Chill dough several hours or overnight.

Roll dough by teaspoonfuls between palms of hands and place 2″ apart on greased baking sheet. Flatten balls with fingertips to make flat rounds. Bake in moderate oven (350°) 10 to 12 minutes, or until light golden brown. Cool a few minutes on baking sheets before removing to racks to cool. Makes about 6½ dozen.

HOSTESS CINNAMON BALLS

Cookie balls wear cinnamon-walnut-sugar coating—they're special

½ c. butter or regular margarine	1 tsp. baking powder
1 c. sugar	¼ tsp. salt
1 egg, unbeaten	½ c. finely chopped nuts
1 tsp. vanilla	1 tblsp. ground cinnamon
1¼ c. sifted flour	1 tblsp. sugar

Cream butter and 1 c. sugar. Add egg and vanilla; beat well for 2 minutes with electric mixer at medium speed.

Sift together flour, baking powder and salt; add to creamed mixture; chill.

Mix nuts, cinnamon and 1 tblsp. sugar.

Mold dough into walnut-size balls; roll each in nut mixture.

Place balls 2½″ apart on greased baking sheet. Bake in moderate oven (350°) 12 to 15 minutes. Remove cookies and cool on racks. Makes about 20.

CHOCOLATE CRACKLES

Use confectioners sugar to put designs on these soft chocolate party
cookie balls. The tops crackle in baking—a hostess favorite

2 eggs
1 c. sugar
1 tsp. vanilla
3 squares unsweetened chocolate, grated
2 c. finely grated (chopped very fine) pecans (7½ oz.)

¼ c. finely ground dry bread crumbs
2 tblsp. flour
¾ tsp. ground cinnamon
⅛ tsp. salt
¼ c. confectioners sugar (for coating)

Beat eggs with sugar and vanilla to blend well. With spoon, mix in chocolate, pecans, bread crumbs, flour, cinnamon and salt. Chill dough until easy to handle.

Shape part of dough at a time in 1" balls, leaving remaining dough in refrigerator until ready to work with it. Roll balls in confectioners sugar and arrange 1" apart on greased baking sheet.

Bake in slow oven (325°) 12 to 15 minutes (they will be soft and crackled on top). Remove cookies and cool on racks. Store in tightly covered container. Makes about 3½ dozen.

EASY CHOCOLATE CRACKLES

These cookies made with cake mix have a moist, fudge-like center

1 (1 lb. 2½ oz.) pkg. devil's food cake mix
2 eggs, slightly beaten

1 tblsp. water
½ c. shortening
Confectioners sugar (for coating)

Combine cake mix, eggs, water and shortening. Mix with a spoon until well blended.

Shape dough into balls the size of walnuts. Roll in confectioners sugar.

Place 1½" apart on greased baking sheet. Bake in moderate oven (375°) 8 to 10 minutes. Remove cookies and cool on racks. Makes 4 dozen.

CHOCOLATE MACAROONS

If you like chocolate and chewy cookies, these will please you

½ c. shortening	2 c. sugar
4 squares unsweetened chocolate	4 eggs
2 c. sifted flour	2 tsp. vanilla
2 tsp. baking powder	Confectioners sugar (for coating)
½ tsp. salt	

Melt together shortening and chocolate.

Sift together flour, baking powder and salt.

Add sugar to chocolate, stirring until smooth. Add eggs singly, beating well after each; add vanilla.

Add flour mixture; blend thoroughly.

Chill dough 2 to 3 hours.

Dip out rounded teaspoons of dough; form into small balls. Roll each in confectioners sugar. Place about 2" apart on lightly greased baking sheet.

Bake in moderate oven (375°) about 10 minutes. (Do not overbake. Cookies should be soft when taken from oven.) Remove cookies and cool on rack. Makes 5 to 6 dozen.

COCONUT CRISPIES

Crisp cookies with crinkled tops—perfect with ice cream

½ c. regular margarine	1 c. sifted flour
½ c. sugar	½ tsp. baking soda
½ c. brown sugar, firmly packed	½ tsp. salt
1 egg	½ c. crushed corn flakes
½ tsp. vanilla	½ c. flaked coconut

Beat together margarine and white and brown sugars until light and fluffy. Beat in egg and vanilla to blend well.

Sift together flour, baking soda and salt. Stir into creamed mixture. Fold in corn flakes and coconut. Chill until dough can easily be shaped in balls.

Shape dough by teaspoonfuls in little balls; place 2" apart on lightly greased baking sheet. Bake in moderate oven (350°) about 10 minutes, or until cookies are lightly browned. Remove at once from baking sheet to racks to cool. Store these thin crisp cookies in container with loose-fitting lid. Makes 50.

NOTE : You'll need 2 c. corn flakes to make about ½ c. crushed.

VIENNESE CRESCENTS

Use almonds in crescents for the Vienna version; or use pecans, shape in balls and you have Mexican Wedding Cakes

1 c. butter
¾ c. sugar
1½ tsp. vanilla

2½ c. sifted flour
1 c. ground almonds (or pecans)
Confectioners sugar (for coating)

Cream butter until light; gradually add sugar and beat until light and fluffy. Beat in vanilla.

Gradually blend in flour and nuts. Chill dough thoroughly so it will handle easily.

Form teaspoonfuls of dough into crescents; place ¾" apart on ungreased baking sheet. Bake in moderate oven (350°) 12 to 15 minutes, or until lightly browned. Cool slightly; remove from baking sheet and, while warm, roll in confectioners sugar. Cool on racks. Makes about 7½ dozen.

CRISSCROSS COOKIES

A winner because it has that wonderful lemon/brown sugar taste

4 c. sifted flour
1½ tsp. baking soda
2 tsp. cream of tartar
1 tsp. salt
1⅓ c. shortening

2½ c. brown sugar, firmly packed
1½ tsp. vanilla
1 tsp. lemon extract
3 eggs, beaten

Sift together flour, soda, cream of tartar and salt.

Cream shortening; add brown sugar gradually. Add vanilla, lemon extract and eggs; beat until light and fluffy. Add sifted dry ingredients and mix until smooth. Chill several hours.

Roll level tablespoons of dough into balls the size of a small walnut. Place about 1" apart on greased baking sheet. Press lightly with tines of fork, making a crisscross pattern.

Bake in moderate oven (375°) 8 to 10 minutes. Remove cookies and cool on racks. Makes 8 dozen.

HEIRLOOM DANISH COOKIES

A rich version of sugar cookies; dress them up for the holidays

½ c. shortening
½ c. regular margarine
1 c. sugar
1 egg
1 tsp. vanilla

2 c. sifted flour
½ tsp. baking soda
½ tsp. cream of tartar
2 to 3 tblsp. sugar (for tops)

Cream together shortening, margarine, 1 c. sugar, egg and vanilla until light and fluffy.

Sift together flour, baking soda and cream of tartar. Gradually stir into creamed mixture to make a smooth dough. Chill thoroughly.

Roll dough in ¾″ balls; place 1½″ apart on ungreased baking sheet and flatten with fork. Sprinkle with sugar.

Bake in slow oven (325°) 12 to 15 minutes. Remove cookies to racks to cool. Makes about 6 dozen.

N O T E : You can tint cookie dough and sprinkle with colored sugar to match. A few red and green cookies are pretty in a Christmas gift package.

DOUBLE TREAT COOKIES

Cookies full of children's favorites—better make a triple batch

2 c. sifted flour
2 tsp. baking soda
½ tsp. salt
1 c. shortening
1 c. sugar
1 c. brown sugar, firmly packed

2 eggs
1 tsp. vanilla
1 c. peanut butter
1 c. chopped salted peanuts
1 (6 oz.) pkg. semisweet
chocolate pieces

Sift together flour, baking soda and salt.

Beat together shortening, white and brown sugars, eggs and vanilla until fluffy. Blend in peanut butter. Add sifted dry ingredients. Stir in peanuts and chocolate pieces.

Shape batter into small balls and place about 2″ apart on ungreased baking sheet. Flatten with a drinking glass dipped in sugar. Bake in moderate oven (350°) 8 minutes, or until brown. Transfer cookies to racks to cool. Makes 7 dozen.

GREEK EASTER COOKIES

Excellent with coffee! These cookies are rich, but not very sweet

½ c. butter	7 c. sifted flour
1 c. sugar	3½ tsp. baking powder
½ c. salad oil	1 tsp. salt
½ c. melted shortening	1 egg yolk
⅔ c. milk	2 tblsp. milk
2 eggs	2½ tblsp. sesame seeds
1 tsp. vanilla	

Cream butter until light and fluffy; gradually beat in sugar, salad oil, melted shortening and milk. Beat in 2 eggs and vanilla.

Sift together flour, baking powder and salt, and gradually add to creamed mixture to make a soft dough.

Shape in 1½″ balls and work each ball under fingers on lightly floured surface to make a rope 7 to 8″ in length. Twist each strip of dough and shape in double twist, making 2 loops like a figure 8 with ends overlapping slightly. Place about ½″ apart on ungreased baking sheet.

Combine egg yolk and milk; brush on cookies. Sprinkle with sesame seeds.

Bake in moderate oven (350°) about 20 minutes, or until golden. Cool slightly on baking sheet on rack; then remove from baking sheet and cool completely on racks. Makes about 5 dozen.

FOUR-FROM-ONE ANGEL COOKIES

This cookie cookbook contains many favorite recipes from Farm Journal readers, among them these Angel Cookies. An upstate New York woman says: "They are our best-liked cookies. It's a big recipe that makes about nine dozen so I make four different kinds.

"I divide the dough in quarters and bake the first portion plain. I roll the balls of dough from the second portion in flaked or cookie coconut. To the third, I add ½ c. semisweet chocolate pieces, to the fourth, ½ c. chopped salted peanuts."

You may think of other ways to introduce variety and interest to the cookie plate or tray.

ANGEL COOKIES

Keep a supply in your freezer ready to serve with coffee or tea

1 c. butter or regular margarine	4½ c. sifted flour
1 c. lard	2 tsp. baking soda
1 c. sugar	2 tsp. cream of tartar
1 c. brown sugar, firmly packed	2 tsp. salt
2 eggs	1 c. chopped nuts
2 tsp. vanilla	White sugar (for dipping)

Cream together butter, lard and white and brown sugars. Beat in eggs, one at a time, to mix thoroughly. Add vanilla.

Sift together flour, baking soda, cream of tartar and salt. Add to creamed mixture. Stir in nuts. Chill dough until it is easy to handle.

Shape dough in balls the size of walnuts; dip tops in sugar. Arrange about 2″ apart on lightly greased baking sheet. Sprinkle several drops of water on each cookie.

Bake in moderate oven (350°) 15 minutes. Remove cookies and cool on racks. Makes 9 dozen.

N O T E : You can divide the ingredients in half to bake 4½ dozen cookies.

GINGER BLOSSOM COOKIES

Nuts make cream-colored centers for brown cookies—attractive

¾ c. shortening	1 tsp. ground cinnamon
1 c. brown sugar, firmly packed	½ tsp. ground cloves
¼ c. light molasses	2 tsp. baking soda
1 egg, beaten	¼ tsp. salt
2¼ c. sifted flour	25 blanched almonds
1 tsp. ground ginger	

Cream shortening and sugar; add molasses and egg; blend well. Sift dry ingredients; add to creamed mixture; mix well.

Roll into balls about 1½″ in diameter; place 2½″ apart on greased baking sheet. Flatten slightly; press almond in center of each.

Bake in moderate oven (350°) 12 to 15 minutes. Remove cookies and cool on racks. Makes 25.

CRACKLE-TOP GINGER COOKIES

To make cookie tops glisten, sprinkle with sugar before baking

1 c. shortening	2 tsp. baking soda
2 c. brown sugar, firmly packed	2 tsp. ground ginger
1 egg, well beaten	1 tsp. vanilla
1 c. molasses	1 tsp. lemon extract
4 c. sifted flour	Sugar (for tops)
½ tsp. salt	

Cream shortening; gradually add brown sugar. Blend in egg and molasses; beat until light and fluffy.

Sift together dry ingredients; gradually blend into creamed mixture. (Dough should be soft but not sticky, or tops won't crackle.)

Add vanilla and lemon extract. Chill about 4 hours, or until dough can be handled with light dusting of flour on hands and board.

Shape dough into balls about 1½″ in diameter. Place 3″ apart on greased baking sheet. (Do not flatten.)

Bake in moderate oven (350°) 12 to 15 minutes, or until brown. Sprinkle with sugar, then remove from baking sheet with pancake turner. Spread on racks to cool. Makes about 30.

HONEY/NUT COOKIES

Good keepers if you hide them—rich and crisp but not too sweet

1 c. butter or regular margarine	1 tsp. ground cinnamon
¼ c. honey	1 c. chopped walnuts
2 c. sifted flour	Confectioners sugar (for tops)

Cream butter until light; add honey and beat to mix thoroughly. Sift flour and cinnamon together; beat into creamed mixture. Stir in nuts.

Shape in 1½″ balls; place about 2″ apart on lightly, greased baking sheet. Flatten with bottom of drinking glass dipped in flour. Bake in slow oven (325°) 15 minutes, or until lightly browned. Cool on baking sheet a few minutes; place on racks and while still warm, dust with confectioners sugar. Makes about 5 dozen.

HONEYED YO-YOS

Put flat sides together with jam—big sandwiches resemble yo-yos

1 c. shortening	3½ c. sifted flour
1 c. brown sugar, firmly packed	2 tsp. baking soda
3 eggs	¼ tsp. salt
⅓ c. honey	¾ c. apricot jam
1 tsp. vanilla	

Cream together shortening and brown sugar until light and fluffy. Beat in eggs. Add honey and vanilla and beat to mix thoroughly.

Sift together flour, baking soda and salt. Add to creamed mixture. Chill overnight, or several hours until firm.

Shape dough in balls the size of large walnuts. Place 2″ apart on ungreased baking sheet. Bake in moderate oven (350°) 10 to 12 minutes, until almost no imprint remains when you press cookie lightly with finger. Transfer cookies to racks and cool.

Put flat bottom sides of cookies together in pairs with apricot jam (or other fruit jam) between. Makes about 2½ dozen.

JELLY DIAGONALS

Use jelly, jam or preserves of another color for half the batch for contrast—try apricot and grape preserves for interesting effect

¾ c. butter	½ tsp. baking powder
⅔ c. sugar	½ tsp. ground nutmeg
1 egg	¼ tsp. salt
2 tsp. vanilla	¼ c. apricot jam or preserves,
2 c. sifted flour	or currant jelly

Cream butter until light; add sugar and beat until fluffy. Beat in egg and vanilla to mix thoroughly.

Sift together flour, baking powder, nutmeg and salt. Stir into creamed mixture; mix thoroughly.

Divide dough in quarters. Form each part into a roll about 12″ long, ¾″ in diameter. Place two rolls at a time 4″ apart on ungreased baking sheet; have the rolls at least 2″ from edges of baking sheet. Make a depression about ⅓″ deep lengthwise down the center of each roll. You can do this with a knife handle. Fill the cavity with jam, preserves or jelly (you'll need about 1 tblsp. for each roll).

Bake in moderate oven (350°) 15 to 20 minutes, until lightly browned around edges. While warm, cut in diagonal slices, about 10 to a roll. Cool cookies on racks. Makes 40.

BRAZILIAN LACE-EDGED COOKIES

Lacy edges give these cookies a gay look—nice for entertaining

¼ c. soft butter or regular margarine
1½ c. brown sugar, firmly packed
2 tblsp. water

1 c. sifted flour
1 tsp. ground cinnamon
1 c. chopped Brazil nuts

Cream butter; add sugar gradually and cream until light and fluffy. Blend in water.

Sift flour and cinnamon; add nuts. Combine mixtures.

Shape dough in small balls, about 1". Place 2" apart on greased baking sheet.

Bake in slow oven (325°) about 15 minutes.

Remove from oven; let stand about 30 seconds before lifting from baking sheet with wide spatula. (If cookies get too crisp to come off smoothly, return to oven and heat about a minute to resoften.) Remove cookies and cool on racks. Makes about 5 dozen.

LEMON ANGEL COOKIES

Lemon-filled meringue tops these lovely hostess specials

⅔ c. shortening
1 c. brown sugar, firmly packed
2 eggs
1 tsp. vanilla
2 c. sifted flour

1 tsp. salt
1 tsp. baking soda
3 egg whites
¾ c. sugar
Lemon Filling (recipe follows)

Beat shortening with brown sugar until light and fluffy. Beat in the 2 eggs, one at a time, and vanilla to mix well.

Sift together flour, salt and baking soda and add to creamed mixture. Chill dough 1 hour.

Beat egg whites until foamy; add sugar gradually and beat until stiff peaks form. Set aside.

Shape chilled dough into balls, using 1 tsp. dough for each ball.

Place 2" apart on ungreased baking sheet. Flatten to ⅛" thickness with bottom of 2" juice glass.

Top each cookie with 1 tsp. meringue. With the spoon, make a hollow in center of meringue on cookie. Bake in slow oven (325°) 10 to 12 minutes, or until cookies are cream-colored. Cool cookies on racks, then fill depressions in meringue on top of cookies with lukewarm Lemon Filling. Store cookies in refrigerator until time to serve them. Makes 4 dozen.

NOTE: You can fill these cookies with other fillings, jelly or jam or whipped cream just before serving.

LEMON FILLING

Filling on meringue-topped cookies will have a dull, yellow look

1 c. sugar	3 egg yolks
2 tblsp. cornstarch	¼ c. lemon juice
¼ tsp. salt	1 tsp. grated lemon peel
¼ c. water	1 tblsp. butter

Combine ½ c. sugar, cornstarch and salt in small saucepan, mixing well. Stir in water. Cook over low heat, stirring constantly, until mixture thickens (it will not be clear).

Beat together egg yolks and ½ c. sugar. Blend a little of the hot mixture into egg yolks, then add to mixture in saucepan. Cook over low heat, stirring constantly, about 2 minutes, or until mixture thickens; remove from heat.

Stir in lemon juice, lemon peel and butter. Cool until lukewarm.

LEMON SNOWBALLS

A great hostess favorite—pure white cookies accented with lemon

½ c. shortening or butter	¼ tsp. cream of tartar
⅔ c. sugar	3 tblsp. lemon juice
2 tsp. grated lemon peel	1 tblsp. water
1 egg	½ c. chopped nuts
1¾ c. sifted flour	Confectioners sugar (for coating)
½ tsp. baking soda	

Cream together shortening, sugar and lemon peel until light and fluffy. Add egg; beat until smooth.

Sift together flour, baking soda and cream of tartar. Add to creamed mixture alternately with lemon juice and water.

Stir in nuts. Chill dough.

With floured hands, form dough into small balls and place 1" apart on ungreased baking sheet. Bake in moderate oven (350°) 8 to 10 minutes. Remove from sheet and roll immediately in confectioners sugar. Cool on racks. Makes 3½ dozen.

Variation

Orange Snowballs: Omit lemon peel and lemon juice. Substitute grated orange peel and orange juice. Use pecans for nuts.

MEXICAN FIESTA BALLS

Chocolate, coffee and maraschino flavors blend in these gala cookies

1 c. butter	½ tsp. salt
½ c. sugar	1 c. finely chopped nuts
2 tsp. vanilla	½ c. chopped drained maraschino
2 c. sifted flour	cherries
¼ c. cocoa	1 c. confectioners sugar (for
1 tblsp. instant coffee powder	coating)

Beat butter until light; gradually add sugar. Beat until light and fluffy. Add vanilla and beat to blend well.

Sift together flour, cocoa, coffee powder and salt; gradually add to creamed mixture. Blend in nuts and cherries; chill until easy to handle.

Shape dough into balls 1" in diameter and place 1" apart on ungreased baking sheet. Bake in slow oven (325°) 20 minutes. Remove cookies to cooling racks and, while warm, roll in confectioners sugar. Makes 5 dozen.

MEXICAN SEED COOKIES

Anise and sesame seeds give these thin sugar cookies a new taste

1 tblsp. whole anise seeds	1 egg
2 tblsp. boiling water	2 c. sifted flour
⅔ c. sugar	1 egg, lightly beaten
¾ c. butter or regular margarine	⅓ c. toasted sesame seeds (see
⅛ tsp. baking soda	Index)

Combine anise seeds and boiling water and let stand.

Beat together sugar and butter until fluffy. Beat in soda and 1 egg. Drain anise seeds and add to mixture.

Stir in flour, a little at a time, and mix well. Wrap dough in waxed paper and chill overnight.

When ready to bake, roll dough into ½" balls. Place about 3" apart on ungreased baking sheets. Flatten to 1/16" thickness with the bottom of a glass. Brush tops with lightly beaten egg. Sprinkle each with toasted sesame seeds.

Bake in hot oven (400°) 7 to 8 minutes, or until lightly browned. Remove cookies and cool on racks. Makes 6 dozen.

MEXICAN THUMBPRINTS

The custard filling bakes in these rich and luscious party cookies

1 egg yolk	½ c. sugar
1 tblsp. sugar	2 egg yolks
1 tblsp. flour	1 tsp. vanilla
¼ tsp. vanilla	2¼ c. sifted flour
Dash of salt	1 tsp. baking powder
½ c. heavy cream	⅛ tsp. salt
1 c. butter	

To make filling, blend 1 egg yolk with 1 tblsp. sugar, 1 tblsp. flour, ¼ tsp. vanilla and dash of salt in top of double boiler. Add the cream gradually and blend well. Cook over water, stirring constantly, until custard is thick and smooth. Cover surface of custard with waxed paper or plastic wrap. Chill thoroughly.

To make cookies, beat butter until light; gradually add ½ c. sugar and beat until fluffy. Beat in 2 egg yolks and 1 tsp. vanilla to blend well.

Sift together 2¼ c. flour, baking powder and ⅛ tsp. salt. Mix into egg yolk mixture to blend thoroughly. Chill dough until easy to handle, at least 1 hour.

Shape heaping teaspoonfuls of dough into balls; place 1″ apart on ungreased baking sheet. With thumb, press medium-size indentations in each dough ball. Put ¼ tsp. filling in each.

Bake in moderate oven (350°) 13 to 15 minutes, or until light brown. Remove cookies and cool on racks. Makes 4½ dozen.

MOLASSES BUTTERBALLS

Easy to make and really delicious—brown cookies in white dress

1 c. butter or regular margarine	2 c. finely chopped walnuts
¼ c. molasses	Confectioners sugar (for
2 c. sifted flour	coating)
½ tsp. salt	

Cream butter; add molasses.
Sift flour and salt; stir in nuts.

Add flour mixture to creamed mixture; blend well. Shape dough into small balls, about 1″ in diameter.

Place about 1″ apart on ungreased baking sheet. Bake in moderate oven (350°) 25 minutes, or until lightly browned. Roll in confectioners sugar while warm. Cool cookies on racks. Makes about 4 dozen.

SPICY MOLASSES BALLS

Brown sugar adds to the tastiness of these spicy, country specials

¾ c. shortening	2 tsp. baking soda
1 c. brown sugar, firmly packed	1 tsp. ground cinnamon
1 egg	1 tsp. ground ginger
¼ c. molasses	½ tsp. ground cloves
2½ c. sifted flour	Sugar (for dipping)
¼ tsp. salt	

Cream shortening and brown sugar; blend in egg and molasses.
Sift together remaining ingredients, except sugar; stir into creamed

mixture; mix well. Shape into ¾" balls; dip tops in sugar. Place 2" apart on greased baking sheet.

Bake in moderate oven (350°) 12 to 15 minutes. Remove cookies and cool on racks. Makes about 4 dozen.

PARTY PINKS

Crisp cookies with pink tops bring glamor to festive entertaining

¾ c. butter or regular margarine	1½ c. sifted flour
1½ c. sifted confectioners sugar	¼ tsp. salt
1 tsp. vanilla	1 egg white, slightly beaten
3 drops red food color (about)	1 c. finely chopped pecans
1 egg yolk	

Cream butter, sugar and vanilla until light and fluffy. Add food color to make a delicate pink. Take out ¼ c. mixture and refrigerate.

To remainder of creamed mixture add egg yolk, flour and salt; mix thoroughly. Shape in balls about 1" in diameter. Dip in egg white, then in nuts.

Place 1½" apart on ungreased baking sheet. Bake in moderate oven (350°) 10 minutes. Remove from oven and quickly make indentation in each cookie by pressing with back of ¼ tsp. measuring spoon (round bowl). Return to oven and bake about 7 minutes longer.

Transfer from baking sheet to racks. When cool, place ¼ tsp. reserved pink creamed mixture in the center of each cookie. Makes 3 dozen.

PEANUT/APPLE COOKIES

Apple gives these cookies their moistness, peanut butter, the flavor

½ c. shortening	½ c. grated peeled apple
½ c. smooth peanut butter	1½ c. sifted flour
½ c. sugar	½ tsp. baking soda
½ c. brown sugar, firmly packed	½ tsp. salt
1 egg	½ tsp. ground cinnamon
½ tsp. vanilla	

Cream together shortening, peanut butter and sugars until light and fluffy. Beat in egg, vanilla and apple to mix well.

Sift together remaining dry ingredients; stir into creamed mixture to blend well. Chill several hours.

Work with a fourth of dough at a time, leaving remaining dough in refrigerator until ready to use. Shape in 1″ balls and place 1½″ apart on greased baking sheet. Flatten balls with a fork moistened in cold water.

Bake in moderate oven (350°) 12 to 15 minutes. Remove cookies and cool on racks. Makes about 5 dozen.

PEANUT BLOSSOM COOKIES

Chocolate stars make pretty centers and make cookies look festive

1 c. shortening	2 tsp. baking soda
1 c. sugar	1 tsp. salt
1 c. brown sugar, firmly packed	2 tblsp. milk
2 eggs	½ c. sugar (for dipping)
1 c. peanut butter	Chocolate candy stars for
3½ c. sifted flour	centers (about 1 lb.)

Cream shortening, 1 c. white sugar and brown sugar together until light and fluffy. Beat in eggs and peanut butter.

Sift together flour, baking soda and salt and stir into creamed mixture. Add milk and mix.

Shape in 1 to 1½″ balls with hands; dip in ½ c. sugar and arrange 2 to 3″ apart on lightly greased baking sheet. Bake in moderate oven (350°) 7 minutes. Remove from oven and quickly press a small chocolate candy star in center of each cookie. (Candy will fall off cookie when cooled unless it is pressed in before cookie is completely baked.) Return to oven and bake 5 to 7 minutes longer.

Remove from baking sheet to racks and cool. Makes about 10 dozen.

PEANUT DROPS

These cookies have crisp, ragged tops with flashes of red cherries

¼ c. butter or regular margarine	¼ c. butter
½ c. peanut butter	⅓ c. sugar
½ c. brown sugar, firmly packed	1 egg
½ c. sugar	½ c. chopped salted peanuts
1 egg	3 c. corn flakes
1¼ c. sifted flour	¼ c. chopped drained
¼ tsp. baking soda	maraschino cherries
¼ tsp. salt	

To make cookie dough, beat ¼ c. butter and peanut butter together;

gradually add brown sugar and ½ c. white sugar and beat until light and fluffy. Beat in 1 egg to mix thoroughly.

Sift together flour, baking soda and salt. Add to first mixture; mix well.

Make topping by creaming together ¼ c. butter and ⅓ c. white sugar. Add remaining ingredients and beat well.

Shape cookie dough into 1" balls; place 2" apart on lightly greased baking sheet and flatten with a fork. Top each cookie with about 2 tblsp. topping.

Bake in moderate oven (375°) 12 to 15 minutes. Transfer cookies to racks to cool. Makes 34.

PECAN BONBONS AND LOGS

For variety bake part of dough in logs—bonbons are very pretty

2 c. sifted flour	2 tsp. vanilla
¼ c. sugar	2½ c. finely chopped pecans
½ tsp. salt	Confectioners sugar (for coating)
1 c. butter or regular margarine	

Sift flour, sugar and salt into mixing bowl. Blend in butter and vanilla with pastry blender. Add 2 c. nuts.

Shape half the dough into ½" balls. Roll in remaining nuts. Place about 1½" apart on greased baking sheet and bake in moderate oven (350°) 15 to 20 minutes. Cool cookies on racks.

Roll remaining dough into logs; bake. While warm, roll in confectioners sugar. Makes 4 dozen.

PECAN COOKIES

Jewel-like centers make these a pretty addition to the party tray

2 c. ground pecans	⅓ c. strawberry preserves
⅔ c. sugar	18 candied or maraschino
½ tsp. salt	cherries, cut in halves
2 egg whites	

Combine pecans and sugar. Add salt and egg whites and mix until mixture is completely moistened.

Form into small balls (mixture will be moist). Place about 2" apart on ungreased baking sheet. Press a small hole in center of each ball with your fingertip. Fill with strawberry preserves. Top with cherry halves, cut side down.

Bake in moderate oven (350°) about 15 minutes. Remove from baking sheet at once to prevent sticking. Cool on racks. Makes 3 dozen.

PECAN DROPS

The brown beauties with red-cherry trim are perfect for Christmas

1 c. butter or regular margarine	2 c. sifted flour
½ tsp. salt	1 c. finely chopped pecans
½ c. sifted confectioners sugar	Candied cherries, cut in sixths
1 tblsp. vanilla	

Blend together butter, salt, sugar and vanilla. Add flour and pecans; mix well; chill.

Shape into small balls; place about 2″ apart on lightly greased baking sheet. Press small hole in center of each ball with fingertip; insert piece of cherry in each. Bake in moderate oven (350°) about 15 minutes. Remove cookies and cool on racks. Makes 5 dozen.

PECAN FINGER COOKIES

Pecan halves in cookie jackets—a tasty addition to the teatime tray

1 c. butter	¼ tsp. salt
½ c. sugar	1 c. pecan halves
2 tsp. vanilla	¼ c. confectioners sugar (for
2 c. sifted flour	coating)

Beat butter until light; add sugar and vanilla and beat until mixture is fluffy.

Blend together flour and salt; stir into creamed mixture and mix well. With the fingers, shape rounded teaspoonfuls of dough around each pecan half. If dough is soft, chill before using. Cut pecan halves in two if necessary.

Place about 1″ apart on lightly greased baking sheet; bake in moderate oven (350°) 15 to 18 minutes, or until a light brown. While cookies are still warm, roll in confectioners sugar. Cool on racks. Makes about 4½ dozen.

Variation

Coconut/Pecan Finger Cookies: Before baking cookies, dip them in

1 egg white beaten lightly with 1 tblsp. water and roll in ¾ c. flaked coconut.

PECAN PUFFS

Pecan cookie balls are snowy white with confectioners sugar coating

½ c. butter	2 c. sifted flour
½ c. regular margarine	1 c. finely chopped pecans
6 tblsp. confectioners sugar	¾ c. confectioners sugar (for
6 tblsp. water	coating)
2 tsp. vanilla	

Place butter, margarine, 6 tblsp. confectioners sugar, water, vanilla, flour and nuts in bowl. Mix with electric mixer at medium speed. Chill dough briefly, about 1 hour.

Pinch off pieces of dough about the size of walnuts. Roll between hands to form balls. Place 1½" apart on ungreased baking sheet. Bake in moderate oven (350°) 18 to 20 minutes. While warm, roll in confectioners sugar. Cool on racks. For a heavier coating, roll again in confectioners sugar when cool. Makes 4 dozen.

PEPPARKAKOR

Black pepper gives "bite" to these Swedish gingersnaps

1 c. sugar	1 tblsp. ground ginger
1 c. butter or lard	½ tsp. black pepper
1 c. light molasses	3½ c. sifted flour
1 tsp. baking soda	Sugar (for dipping)
1 tsp. salt	

Cream sugar and butter until light and fluffy. Beat in molasses.

Sift together baking soda, salt, ginger, pepper and flour; add to creamed mixture and beat to mix well. Chill dough until easy to handle.

Shape dough with hands into balls the size of large marbles. Dip in sugar before baking. Place 1½" apart on lightly greased baking sheet.

Bake in moderate oven (350°) 12 to 15 minutes, or until lightly browned. Cool on baking sheet 1 minute, then transfer to rack to cool completely. Makes about 7 dozen.

PRETZEL COOKIES

Pretzel shape adds charm to a tray of assorted cookies—rich-tasting

⅔ c. butter
½ c. sugar
½ tsp. vanilla
3 eggs

⅛ tsp. salt
3 c. sifted flour
½ c. sugar (for dipping)
½ c. finely chopped walnuts

Cream butter with ½ c. sugar until light and fluffy. Beat in vanilla and 2 eggs to mix thoroughly. Combine salt and flour; add to creamed mixture. Knead dough until smooth. Set aside for 1 hour or longer.

Take up small portions of dough (the size of large walnuts) and roll under hands on pastry cloth or board into 7" lengths with the diameter of a pencil. Form in pretzel shapes. Brush with remaining egg, slightly beaten, then dip tops in remaining ½ c. sugar and nuts.

Place about 1" apart on ungreased baking sheet; bake in slow oven (325°) about 25 minutes, or until cookies are a very light brown. Remove cookies and cool on racks. Makes about 40.

RIBBON COOKIES

Colorful cookies for your party—serve them with steaming hot coffee

1 c. butter or regular margarine
1½ c. sugar
1 egg
1 tsp. vanilla
2½ c. sifted flour
1½ tsp. baking powder
½ tsp. salt

¼ c. chopped candied red cherries
¼ c. chopped candied green cherries
⅓ c. semisweet chocolate pieces, melted over hot, not boiling, water
¼ c. chopped pecans

Cream butter and sugar until light and fluffy. Add egg and vanilla; beat.

Sift together flour, baking powder and salt; blend half into butter-sugar mixture; stir in remaining flour mixture until blended.

Divide dough in three parts. Add red cherries to one, green cherries to second and chocolate and pecans to the third part.

Line bottom and sides of 9 x 5 x 3" loaf pan with foil. Pat red cherry dough into bottom of pan; pat chocolate dough over this; pat green cherry dough over top. Press each layer down firmly. Cover and refrigerate for several hours.

Turn out of pan. Cut in half lengthwise. Slice each bar in ⅛″ thick slices. Place 1½″ apart on ungreased baking sheet. Bake in hot oven (400°) 10 to 12 minutes. Remove cookies and cool on racks. Makes 8 dozen.

SANDBAKELSER

In Sweden these fragile sand tarts are served upside down on blue plates—or fill upright tarts with whipped cream at serving time

⅓ c. blanched almonds	1 egg white
½ c. butter	1 tsp. vanilla
½ c. sugar	1¼ c. sifted flour

Put almonds through fine blade of food chopper twice. Set aside.

Mix together well butter, sugar, unbeaten egg white and vanilla. Stir in flour and almonds. Cover and chill 2 hours or longer.

With lightly floured fingers, press dough over bottom and sides of sandbakelser molds (they're like tiny fluted tart pans). Press dough as thin as possible, or about ⅛″ thick. Set on ungreased baking sheet.

Bake in moderate oven (350°) about 12 minutes, or until very delicately browned. Cool 3 minutes or until molds are cool enough to handle. Tap molds lightly on table to loosen cookies. Cool on racks. Makes 2½ to 3 dozen, depending on size of molds and thinness of cookies.

SAND BALLS

Honey enhances flavor; roll twice in sugar for snowy white coating

1 c. butter	¼ tsp. salt
½ c. confectioners sugar	1 tsp. vanilla
2 tblsp. honey	¾ c. chopped walnuts
2¼ c. sifted flour	Confectioners sugar (for coating)

Cream butter, confectioners sugar and honey together thoroughly. Add flour, salt, vanilla and nuts. Mix with hands, if necessary, to blend well.

Form into balls 1″ in diameter and chill thoroughly.

To bake, place cookie balls 2½″ apart on greased baking sheet. Bake in moderate oven (375°) 14 to 17 minutes. While still warm, roll in confectioners sugar. Cool cookies on racks. Then roll in confectioners sugar again. Makes 4 dozen.

SNICKERDOODLES

Generations of boys and girls have returned home from school happy to find the kitchen fragrant with cinnamon-sugar and the cookie jar filled with freshly baked Snickerdoodles. These cookies are just as popular today as they were long ago. The Pennsylvania Dutch proudly claim them as their invention, but the cookies were not strangers in New England homes, for most of the very old regional cookbooks with age-yellowed pages include the recipe, as do later editions. Good recipes always have journeyed from one section of the country to another because women like to share their favorites. Evidence of this is the thousands of recipes they sent to FARM JOURNAL for possible use in this cookbook.

Recipes undergo changes with the years. Originally, Snickerdoodles often were either rolled or drop cookies, sprinkled with sugar and cinnamon. Many women today prefer to shape the dough in small, even-sized balls and to roll them in a cinnamon-sugar mixture, the true Cape Cod way. The molded cookies come from the oven in almost perfect rounds. Our recipe is for this kind.

SNICKERDOODLES

The crisp cookies with crinkly sugar-cinnamon tops always please

½ c. butter or regular margarine	2 tsp. cream of tartar
½ c. lard	1 tsp. baking soda
1½ c. sugar	¼ tsp. salt
2 eggs	2 tblsp. sugar
1 tsp. vanilla	1 tsp. ground cinnamon
2⅔ c. sifted flour	

Beat butter and lard until light; add 1½ c. sugar and beat until fluffy. Beat in eggs and vanilla.

Sift together flour, cream of tartar, baking soda and salt; add to beaten mixture.

Combine 2 tblsp. sugar and cinnamon.

Shape dough in small balls, about 1″, and roll in sugar-cinnamon mixture. Place 2″ apart on ungreased baking sheet. Bake in hot oven (400°) 8 to 10 minutes. (Cookies flatten during baking.) Remove cookies and cool on racks. Makes about 6 dozen.

SWIRLS

These decorative, two-color cookies will provide party conversation

1 c. butter or regular margarine	½ tsp. vanilla
½ c. sifted confectioners sugar	¼ tsp. almond extract
2¼ c. sifted flour	3 drops red food color
¼ tsp. salt	12 drops yellow food color

Beat butter until light; add confectioners sugar and beat until fluffy.

Sift together flour and salt and blend well into creamed mixture. Divide dough in half. Leave one half plain and blend vanilla into it with electric mixer on low speed. To remaining half add almond extract and food colors to produce an orange-colored dough. Chill thoroughly.

Take 1 teaspoonful plain dough and shape into a pencil-like roll 6" long. Repeat with tinted dough. (If dough gets warm while working with it and sticks to surface, lightly flour surface.) Lay the two rolls side by side on ungreased baking sheet and coil them. Repeat with remaining dough, leaving 1" between coils.

Bake in hot oven (400°) about 8 minutes, or until cookies are set but not browned. Remove cookies and cool on racks. Makes 3 dozen.

CRACKLED SUGAR COOKIES

An old-fashioned cookie: subtle lemon flavor, pretty, crinkled top

1 c. shortening (part butter)	¼ c. sugar
1½ c. sugar	1 tsp. grated orange peel
6 egg yolks, or 3 eggs, beaten	½ tsp. grated lemon peel
1 tsp. vanilla	2 tblsp. finely chopped black
½ tsp. lemon extract	walnuts
½ tsp. orange extract	½ tsp. ground nutmeg
2½ c. flour	1 tblsp. brown sugar
1 tsp. baking soda	2 tblsp. sugar
1 tsp. cream of tartar	¼ c. chocolate shot (jimmies)

Cream shortening and 1½ c. sugar until fluffy. Add yolks and flavorings; beat.

Combine flour, baking soda and cream of tartar; add to creamed mixture. Shape in 1" balls. Divide balls in thirds.

Combine ¼ c. sugar with orange and lemon peels; roll one-third of balls in mixture.

Roll second third of balls in mixture of nuts, nutmeg, brown sugar and 2 tblsp. sugar.

Roll remaining balls in chocolate decorations (jimmies).

Place cookie balls about 2″ apart on ungreased baking sheet. Bake in moderate oven (350°) 12 to 15 minutes. Remove cookies and cool on racks. Makes about 5 dozen.

JUMBO SUGAR COOKIES

Extra-crisp, big, thin cookies with crinkled tops sell fast at bazaars

2 c. sugar	1 tsp. baking soda
1 c. shortening	1 tsp. salt
2 eggs	1 tsp. ground cinnamon
2 c. sifted flour	(for tops)
2 tsp. cream of tartar	2 tblsp. sugar (for tops)

Beat together 2 c. sugar and shortening until light and fluffy. Beat in eggs to mix thoroughly.

Sift together flour, cream of tartar, baking soda and salt. Stir into creamed mixture. On lightly floured waxed paper, form dough into four rolls, each about 12″ long and 1 to 1¼″ in diameter. Cut in 1″ slices. Dip tops of cookies in mixture of cinnamon and 2 tblsp. sugar. Place 3″ apart, cinnamon-sugar sides up, on greased baking sheet.

Bake in moderate oven (375°) about 12 minutes. Let stand on baking sheet 1 minute before removing to cooling racks. Makes 4 dozen.

MOLDED SUGAR COOKIES

Have won blue ribbons in baking contests—crisp crust, soft interior

2½ c. sifted flour	1 c. butter
2 tsp. cream of tartar	1 tsp. vanilla
1 tsp. baking soda	1 c. sugar
½ tsp. salt	2 eggs, beaten

Sift together flour, cream of tartar, baking soda and salt.

Cream butter, vanilla and sugar until light and fluffy. Add eggs and beat well. Add sifted dry ingredients, a fourth at a time, stirring to mix thoroughly. Chill 1 hour.

Shape dough in 1" balls and place 2½" apart on greased baking sheet. Flatten by pressing with bottom of drinking glass coated with sugar. (Dip bottom of glass in sugar before flattening each cookie.)

Bake in moderate oven (375°) 8 minutes, or until golden. Remove cookies to racks to cool. Makes about 5½ dozen.

DOUBLE VANILLA BARS

These cookies, twice flavored with vanilla, win praise and disappear fast. Keep Vanilla Sugar on hand for a gourmet touch in baking

5 egg yolks	3¾ c. sifted flour
1 c. plus 2 tblsp. sugar	⅛ tsp. salt
2 tsp vanilla	Vanilla Sugar (recipe follows)
1 c. butter	

Beat egg yolks until light. Gradually beat in sugar, beating after each addition. Then beat 3 minutes longer. Beat in vanilla.

With pastry blender, cut butter into flour mixed with salt until particles are fine. Add to egg mixture and blend. Then knead with hands until dough is smooth. Chill 1 hour.

Pinch off dough, about 1 tblsp. at a time; flour hands and roll into strips about 2" long and ½" thick. Place 1" apart on ungreased baking sheet.

Bake in moderate oven (350°) 12 to 15 minutes, or until golden brown. Cool about 3 minutes before removing from baking sheet to racks. Carefully dip each cookie while warm into Vanilla Sugar to coat completely. Cool, then dip again in Vanilla Sugar. (If you wish, you can use sifted confectioners sugar instead of the Vanilla Sugar.) Makes about 5½ dozen.

Vanilla Sugar: Sift 1 (1 lb.) pkg. confectioners sugar into a container with a tight-fitting lid. Split a vanilla bean (available at many spice and flavoring counters) lengthwise; cut up and add to container of sugar. Cover and let stand 3 days or longer before using. Sugar will keep for months if tightly covered. You will need about half of it to coat these cookies.

SPANISH WEDDING CAKES

You wrap these cookies with lemon flavor around almonds

1 c. butter
¼ c. sifted confectioners sugar
1 tblsp. grated lemon peel
1 tblsp. water
2½ c. sifted flour

¼ tsp. salt
½ c. whole blanched almonds (about)
¾ c. confectioners sugar (for coating)

Cream butter until light and fluffy. Stir in ¼ c. confectioners sugar, lemon peel and water.

Mix flour with salt; beat into butter mixture. Knead with hands until dough is light.

Pinch off 1 heaping teaspoonful of dough at a time; press it flat and then press it around a whole almond to cover completely. Shape like a little loaf. Place about 1" apart on lightly greased baking sheet.

Bake in moderate oven (350°) about 15 minutes, or until cookies start to brown around bottom. Take care not to overbake. Remove from baking sheets and cool 2 or 3 minutes on racks, then roll in confectioners sugar. Cool completely and then roll again in confectioners sugar. Store in airtight container. Makes about 4 dozen.

FROSTED YULE LOGS

Shape of yule logs adds interest to Christmas cookie tray or box

1 c. butter or regular margarine
¾ c. sugar
1 egg
1 tsp. vanilla
3 c. sifted flour

½ tsp. ground nutmeg
¼ c. sugar
1 c. finely chopped pecans
1 egg white

Beat butter until light; add ¾ c. sugar and beat until light and fluffy. Beat in egg and vanilla to blend well.

Sift together flour and nutmeg; stir into creamed mixture. Shape dough into fat pencil-shaped rolls, each about 2" long, to represent yule logs.

Combine remaining ¼ c. sugar and pecans. Beat egg white slightly. Dip yule logs into egg white and then roll in nut mixture. Place 1" apart on lightly greased baking sheet.

Bake in moderate oven (375°) about 10 minutes, until browned. Remove cookies and cool on racks. Makes 6 dozen.

Pressed Cookies

Give a cookie press to a woman who likes to bake and turn her loose in her kitchen. Sweet things happen—like tender-crisp, buttery-rich cookies in many designs. Spritz, the highly revered Swedish pressed cookies, are the kind most frequently made, but different forms or shapes, flavors and decorations result in great variety. It seems incredible that so many delicacies can come from the same dough until you start using a press.

Among the designs in spritz that attract attention are the letter cookies. You'll find two recipes for them in this section, Lindsborg Letter Spritz, from a Swedish-American community in Kansas, and Lemon Cookie Letters.

You'll want to try our Royal Crowns, a splendid pressed cookie in which hard-cooked egg yolks are an ingredient.

As the term "pressed" suggests, you put the dough through a cookie press with one of a variety of plates inserted to produce cookies of the shape desired. Women who bake this kind of cookie consider it easy and quick.

The beauty of pressed cookies is partly in their design or shape. They all taste wonderful. Serve them undecorated or fancied up as you wish. You can top them, before baking, with bits of candied fruits, raisins, currants or chopped nuts. Or you can add decorations after baking, arranging them in designs and securing them to the cookie with drops of corn syrup or egg white. Use coarse colored sugar, multicolored tiny candies, dragées or tiny red cinnamon candies for the trims. And if you're in the mood, tint the dough with food color before you put it in the press.

The dough for pressed cookies needs to be right. Butter is the first choice of fats, but you can use regular margarine or shortening. Be sure to have the fat at room temperature before you start to mix the dough. Beat it with the electric mixer at medium speed until soft, or beat it with a spoon. Gradually add the sugar, beating all the time, and continue beating until the mixture is light and fluffy, but do not overbeat.

When the dough is ready, test it by pressing a small amount through the press. It should be pliable and soft, but not crumbly. Unless the dough is soft or the recipe directs that you chill it, work with it at room temperature. Dough that's too cold crumbles. When the dough seems too soft, add 1 to 2 tblsp. flour; if too stiff, add 1 egg yolk.

Put about one-fourth of the dough in the press at a time. Hold the press so it rests on the baking sheet unless you are using a star or bar plate. Press dough onto a cool baking sheet; if it is warm, the fat in the dough melts and the cookies will not adhere to the sheet when you lift off the press. Do not remove press until the dough forms a well-defined design. You may need to wait a few seconds to give it time to cling to the baking sheet. You will not need to exert pressure on the press or the handle if the dough is right.

Pressed cookies are rich. Bake them on an ungreased baking sheet until they are set. You bake some pressed cookies until lightly browned around the edges, while others are not browned at all.

ORANGE/CHEESE COOKIES

Rows of ridges on cookies make them look like little washboards

1 c. butter or regular margarine	1 tblsp. orange juice
1 (3 oz.) pkg. cream cheese	2½ c. sifted flour
1 c. sugar	1 tsp. baking powder
1 egg	Dash of salt
1 tblsp. grated orange peel	

Combine butter and cream cheese; beat until light. Gradually add sugar, beating until mixture is fluffy. Beat in egg, orange peel and juice to blend thoroughly.

Sift together flour, baking powder and salt. Add to creamed mixture, blending well.

Put plate with narrow slit in cookie press. Put a fourth of dough into press at a time and press rows of strips of dough about 1″ apart onto ungreased baking sheet. With knife, mark strips in 2″ lengths.

Bake in moderate oven (375°) 8 to 10 minutes, until very delicately browned. Immediately cut strips into pieces on knife marks. Remove cookies and cool on racks. Makes about 12½ dozen.

NOTE: Sprinkle some of the cookies before baking with chocolate shot (jimmies) for a tasty, interesting touch.

PEANUT BUTTER PRESSED COOKIES

Glamorize peanut butter cookies by shaping them with cookie press

¾ c. butter or regular margarine   ½ tsp. vanilla or almond extract
3 tblsp. peanut butter   1¾ c. sifted flour
½ c. sugar   ¼ tsp. salt
1 egg yolk

Beat together butter and peanut butter until light. Gradually beat in sugar, beating until light and fluffy. Beat in egg yolk and vanilla to blend thoroughly.

Sift together flour and salt. Add to creamed mixture; mix to a smooth dough.

Fit desired plate into cookie press. Put one-fourth of the dough in cookie press at a time. Force cookies 1" apart onto ungreased baking sheet. Bake in moderate oven (375°) 8 to 10 minutes, or until delicately brown. Remove cookies and cool on racks. Makes about 3 dozen.

ROYAL CROWNS

A tasty, unusual, regal addition to the holiday cookie collection

4 hard-cooked egg yolks   ½ tsp. almond extract
½ tsp. salt   2½ c. sifted flour
1 c. butter or regular margarine   Red or green candied cherries
⅔ c. sugar

Force egg yolks through a coarse sieve with back of spoon. Add salt and mix.

Cream together butter and sugar until light and fluffy. Add almond extract and egg yolks. Add flour and mix well.

Place dough in cookie press. Force dough through crown design 1 to 2" apart onto lightly greased baking sheet. Decorate with bits of candied cherries.

Bake in moderate oven (375°) 7 to 10 minutes. Remove cookies and cool on racks. Makes 6 dozen.

SPRITZ

Change shape of these tender cookies with different press plates

1 c. butter
⅔ c. confectioners sugar
1 egg
1 egg yolk

1 tsp. almond extract, vanilla or
  ¼ c. grated almonds
2½ c. sifted flour

Combine butter, sugar, egg, egg yolk and almond extract. Work in flour.

Use a fourth of the dough at a time; force it through cookie press 1″ apart onto ungreased baking sheet in desired shapes. Bake in hot oven (400°) 7 to 10 minutes, or until set but not browned. Remove cookies and cool on racks. Makes 4 to 6 dozen, depending on size.

CHOCOLATE SPRITZ

The potent chocolate flavor of these crisp cookies delights many. They add charming contrast to a tray of light-colored spritz

1 c. butter or regular margarine
⅔ c. sugar
1½ squares unsweetened
  chocolate, melted
3 egg yolks

1 tsp. vanilla, or ¾ tsp. almond
  extract
⅛ tsp. salt
2½ c. sifted flour

Cream butter with sugar until light and fluffy. Beat in chocolate, egg yolks and vanilla. Stir salt into flour to mix thoroughly. Work into creamed mixture, a little at a time.

Divide dough into fourths and put each part through cookie press ½ to 1″ apart on ungreased baking sheet. (Use whatever shaped disk in press you like.)

Bake in hot oven (400°) 7 to 10 minutes, until cookies are set, but do not brown. Remove at once to racks to cool. Makes about 7 dozen.

NOTE: See recipe in Index for Date/Nut Kisses if you want to use leftover egg whites in a delicious treat.

SPRITZ CHOCOLATE SANDWICHES

Pretty-as-a-picture, special-occasion spritz taste simply great—slender cookies with chocolate filling and chocolate-nut ends

1 c. butter or regular margarine	½ tsp. salt
1¼ c. sifted confectioners sugar	Buttery Chocolate Frosting
1 egg	(recipe follows)
1 tsp. vanilla	1 c. chopped walnuts
2½ c. sifted flour	

Beat butter until light; gradually add sugar, beating after each addition. Beat until light and fluffy. Beat in egg and vanilla to blend well.

Sift together flour and salt. Gradually add to creamed mixture, mixing well.

Put star plate in cookie press. Place a fourth of dough in press at a time. Press out to make 2½" strips about 1" apart on ungreased baking sheet.

Bake in hot oven (400°) 6 to 8 minutes, or until very delicately browned. Place cookies at once on cooling rack. When cool, put cookies together in pairs with Buttery Chocolate Frosting between. Dip ends of sandwiches in the frosting and then in chopped nuts. Makes 69 sandwiches.

Buttery Chocolate Frosting: Beat 3 tblsp. butter until light and fluffy. Add 1½ squares unsweetened chocolate, melted. Beat in ¾ tsp. vanilla, ⅛ tsp. salt, 3½ c. sifted confectioners sugar and enough dairy half-and-half or light cream (about 6 tblsp.) to make frosting of spreading consistency.

PINEAPPLE SPRITZ

Decorate them with silver or colored dragées for special occasions

1½ c. butter or regular margarine	4½ c. sifted flour
	1 tsp. baking powder
1 c. sugar	Dash of salt
1 egg	Silver and colored dragées
2 tblsp. thawed frozen pineapple juice concentrate	(optional)

Beat together butter and sugar until light and fluffy. Beat in egg and pineapple juice concentrate to blend thoroughly.

Sift together flour, baking powder and salt. Add to creamed mixture, blending well. (Dough will be stiff.)

Put rosette or other plate into cookie press. Put a fourth of dough in press at a time. Press out dough designs about 1″ apart onto ungreased baking sheet. Decorate with silver and colored dragées.

Bake in moderate oven (375°) 8 to 10 minutes, until firm but not brown. Remove at once from baking sheet to cooling racks. Makes 9 dozen.

SCANDINAVIAN SPRITZ

Crisp, buttery-tasting, fragile—serve with fruit punch or coffee

2¼ c. sifted flour
½ tsp. baking powder
¼ tsp. salt
1 c. butter or regular margarine

¾ c. sugar
3 egg yolks, beaten
1 tsp. almond extract, or ¼ c. grated almonds

Sift together flour, baking powder and salt.

Cream butter; add sugar gradually and beat until light. Add egg yolks and almond extract. Add dry ingredients; work with hands if dough seems crumbly.

Using a fourth of dough at a time, force it through cookie press 1 to 2″ apart onto ungreased baking sheet in desired shapes. Bake in hot oven (400°) 7 to 10 minutes, until set but not brown. Remove cookies and cool on racks. Makes about 6 dozen.

LEMON COOKIE LETTERS

Cookie initials will honor a guest, a school team or any occasion

1 c. butter or regular margarine
½ c. sugar
½ c. brown sugar, firmly packed
1 tsp. grated lemon peel
1 tblsp. lemon juice

1 egg
2½ c. sifted flour
¼ tsp. baking soda
⅛ tsp. salt

Beat butter until light; beat in sugars until light and fluffy. Beat in lemon peel and juice and egg to blend thoroughly.

Sift together flour, baking soda and salt. Add to creamed mixture, blending well.

Fill press with a fourth of dough at a time. Press letters about 1″ apart on ungreased baking sheet. Bake in moderate oven (375°)

10 to 12 minutes, until light brown on edges. Remove from baking sheet to cooling racks. Makes about 8½ dozen.

LINDSBORG LETTER SPRITZ

A Kansas version of Swedish spritz—they always start conversation

1 c. butter or regular margarine	2 c. sifted flour
¾ c. sugar	1 tsp. baking powder
1 egg yolk	⅛ tsp. salt
¾ tsp. almond extract or vanilla	

Cream butter with sugar until light and fluffy. Beat in egg yolk and almond extract. Beat until very fluffy.

Sift together flour, baking powder and salt; gradually add to creamed mixture, beating with mixer on low speed. Beat just enough to blend. Shape dough in ball, wrap in waxed paper and chill several hours or overnight.

Let dough warm slightly before using (very cold dough does not easily leave press). Using cookie press with star-shaped disk, press out dough in long, straight strips on cold, ungreased baking sheet.

Cut each strip in 4" pieces and shape in letters such as S, R, A, B, Y, U and O (or shape as desired). You will need to add pieces of dough to form some letters. Place ½ to 1" apart on ungreased baking sheet.

Bake in moderate oven (350°) 8 to 10 minutes, or until edges of cookies are a golden brown. Remove cookies to wire racks and cool. Makes about 6 dozen.

NOTE: To store, pack in containers in layers with waxed paper between. Freeze or keep in a cool place.

Meringue Cookies

The old-fashioned name for these small, airy clouds of flavorful sweetness we call meringue cookies is "kisses." By whatever name, they're delicious. Serve them with red-ripe strawberries or juicy sliced peaches and cream or ice cream. Or garnish ice cream sundaes with our little puffs, Miniature Meringues. And if wondering what dessert to take to the picnic, consider non-gooey meringues as the companion to fruit to eat from the hand—grapes, sweet cherries or pears.

Meringues are versatile—you can use your ingenuity to add charm and flavor to them. For a Valentine luncheon or party, bake our Jeweled Meringues, dotted with tiny red cinnamon candies, in heart shape. Add chopped dates and nuts to meringue cookies and you have our Date/Nut Kisses, which enhance any assortment of holiday or special-occasion cookies.

Tint meringue in pastel shades with food colors before baking for color-schemed effects at showers and receptions. Sprinkle coarse red sugar over meringue rosettes and you'll have our Holiday Party Kisses. They look like lovely red and white roses on the cookie tray at open houses and inspire word bouquets to the hostess.

Meringues are easy to make. Beat the egg whites with the electric mixer at medium speed until foamy. Continue to beat while you gradually add the sugar. Then beat until mixture is stiff and glossy. Drop it from a teaspoon to form peaks or put it through a pastry tube with the rosette or one of the other tips. Space the meringues about 1" apart on greased baking sheets or on brown paper spread on baking sheets. Bake until set; then remove from baking sheet and cool on racks in a place free of drafts. Notice the time for baking listed in the recipe you are using. Some meringue cookies come from the oven white, while others take on a delicate beige around the edges.

Thrifty women to this day think meringue cookies are the best way to use leftover egg whites.

COCONUT KISSES

If you like macaroons you'll enjoy these chewy, moist cookies

¼ tsp. salt	½ tsp. vanilla or almond extract
½ c. egg whites (4 medium)	2½ c. shredded coconut
1¾ c. sugar	

Add salt to egg whites and beat until foamy. Gradually beat in sugar. Continue beating until mixture stands in stiff peaks and is glossy. Fold in vanilla and coconut.

Drop by heaping teaspoonfuls 2″ apart onto greased baking sheet. Bake in slow oven (325°) 20 minutes, or until delicately browned and set. Remove from baking sheet and cool on racks. Makes about 3 dozen.

Variations

Walnut Kisses: Substitute finely chopped walnuts for the coconut in recipe for Coconut Kisses.

Chocolate/Coconut Kisses: Follow directions for making Coconut Kisses, but stir in 1 square unsweetened chocolate, melted and cooled until lukewarm, before folding in coconut.

CORN FLAKE KISSES

An inexpensive sweet to serve with apples or grapes for dessert

¼ tsp. salt	1 tsp. grated orange peel or
2 egg whites	vanilla
1 c. sugar	3 c. corn flakes

Add salt to egg whites and beat until foamy. Gradually beat in sugar. Continue beating until mixture stands in peaks and is glossy. Fold in orange peel and corn flakes.

Drop by teaspoonfuls 2″ apart onto greased baking sheet. Bake in moderate oven (350°) 15 to 18 minutes, or until set and delicately browned. Remove from baking sheet and cool on racks. Makes about 3 dozen.

DATE/NUT KISSES

You can depend on these easy-to-make party treats to please

3 egg whites
1 c. sugar
¼ tsp. salt

1 tsp. vanilla
¾ c. chopped walnuts
¾ c. chopped dates

Put egg whites, sugar, salt and vanilla in top of double boiler; stir to blend. Place over boiling water and beat with rotary beater until mixture stands in peaks. (To prevent meringues from being lumpy, scrape bottom and sides of pan occasionally with rubber scraper.) Stir in nuts and dates at once.

Drop heaping teaspoonfuls of mixture about 2" apart onto lightly greased baking sheets (let one sheet wait while you bake the other).

Bake in slow oven (300°) 12 to 15 minutes, or until very lightly browned. Remove from baking sheet immediately and cool on racks. Makes about 40.

N O T E : Date/Nut Kisses offer an ideal way to use the 3 leftover egg whites when you make Chocolate Spritz (see Index).

HOLIDAY PARTY KISSES

Red and green rosettes—the small meringues are perfect for Christmas

3 egg whites
⅛ tsp. salt
⅛ tsp. cream of tartar

¾ c. sugar
Red and green decorating sugar

Beat egg whites with electric mixer at medium speed until froth starts to appear. Add salt and cream of tartar. Continue beating for 5 minutes, or until soft peaks form. Gradually add half the white sugar, beating constantly; then beat 5 minutes. Add remaining half of white sugar in the same way. After beating for 5 minutes, continue beating until the sugar is completely dissolved.

Remove beater and place the meringue mixture in a pastry tube with rosette end. Press it out to make rosettes 1" apart on brown paper spread over a baking sheet. (Or drop mixture from teaspoon.) Sprinkle half the meringues with red sugar, the other half with green sugar.

Bake in very slow oven (250°) 1 hour, or until meringues are firm, but not browned. (When done, meringues should lift off paper easily.) Remove from paper and cool on racks. Makes 26.

NOTE: When making meringues or kisses, or anything that uses only egg whites, slip the leftover yolks into a wire sieve immersed in a pan of simmering water. Simmer for 5 minutes. Remove and dry, then press the yolks through the sieve. Use to garnish salads, cooked buttered vegetables, creamed vegetables, soups and other dishes. One wonderful way to salvage egg yolks is to make Hard-Cooked Egg Cookies or Royal Crowns (see Index).

DEBBIE'S PEPPERMINT KISSES

A 12-year-old Hoosier girl bakes these for her mother's parties

4 egg whites	1½ c. brown sugar, firmly
¼ tsp. salt	packed
¼ tsp. cream of tartar	1 (12 oz.) pkg. semisweet
1 tsp. peppermint extract	chocolate pieces

Beat egg whites, salt, cream of tartar and peppermint extract together until soft peaks form.

Add brown sugar gradually, beating all the time. Beat until stiff peaks form.

Set aside 48 chocolate pieces and fold remainder into egg white mixture.

Drop teaspoonfuls 1" apart onto plain paper spread on baking sheet. Top each with a chocolate piece.

Bake in slow oven (300°) 20 to 25 minutes, or until set and slightly brown. Remove from paper while slightly warm, this way: Remove paper from baking sheet, spread a wet towel on the hot baking sheet and place the paper of kisses on top. Let stand only 1 minute. The steam will loosen the kisses and they will slip off easily on a spatula. Makes about 4 dozen.

NOTE: Instead of plain paper, you can line the baking sheet with waxed paper.

PINK KISSES

These lovely pink meringues are chewy like coconut macaroons

1 (3 oz.). pkg. strawberry flavor gelatin	⅔ c. egg whites (about 5 to 7)
1 c. sugar	¾ tsp. almond extract
¼ tsp. salt	1 (3½ oz.) can flaked coconut

Combine gelatin, sugar and salt.

Beat egg whites at high speed on electric mixer, gradually adding gelatin-sugar mixture. Add almond extract and continue beating until glossy and stiff peaks form. Stir in coconut.

Place brown paper on baking sheet. Drop mixture by heaping teaspoonfuls about 1" apart onto paper. Bake in very slow oven (275°) 35 to 40 minutes. Remove from paper and cool on racks. Makes 62.

Variation

Pink Raspberry Kisses: Substitute raspberry flavor gelatin for the strawberry, and bake as directed.

JEWELED MERINGUES FOR ENTERTAINING

These cookies have an easy-do aspect: You put the meringues in the oven in the evening, turn off the heat and forget them until morning when they'll be baked. Place them in a container, cover loosely with waxed paper and set in a cool place.

If you wish, you can freeze them. Wrap each meringue in plastic wrap and place in a plastic bag, or wrap with heavy-duty aluminum foil. They'll stay in good condition up to a month. To use, take meringues from bag or remove foil and let stand at room temperature in their individual wraps for 4 to 6 hours. Then unwrap and serve.

The cinnamon candies do not melt during baking. In addition to contributing flashes of bright color to the snowy-white meringues, and a texture contrast, they provide a taste of cinnamon. They're especially appropriate for the yuletide season and for Valentine parties, when touches of red in food are so inviting. Many hostesses like to serve the meringues with ice cream.

JEWELED MERINGUES

Especially pretty for a Valentine special—if shaped like hearts

2 egg whites	½ tsp. vanilla
⅛ tsp. salt	½ c. red cinnamon candies (red
½ tsp. cream of tartar	hots)
¾ c. sugar	

Beat egg whites until foamy. Add salt and cream of tartar. Beat until stiff peaks form. Add sugar, 1 tblsp. at a time, beating after each addition. Stir in vanilla. Fold in candies.

Drop mixture by teaspoonfuls 1 to 1½" apart onto lightly greased baking sheet. Place in moderate oven (350°); turn off heat. Leave in oven overnight. (Do not open oven door before at least 2 hours have passed.) Meringues do not brown. Remove from baking sheet and cool on racks. Makes 25.

MERINGUES À LA BELLE

Crackers give these crunchy, crisp kisses a faint salty taste

3 egg whites	1 tsp. vanilla
¾ c. sugar	⅔ c. crushed saltine crackers
½ tsp. baking powder	½ c. chopped nuts

Beat egg whites until frothy. Gradually add sugar, beating until meringue stands in soft peaks; scrape bottom and sides of bowl occasionally with rubber spatula. Blend in baking powder and vanilla. Fold in crackers and nuts.

Drop mixture by rounded teaspoonfuls 1" apart onto two lightly greased baking sheets. Bake one sheet at a time in slow oven (300°) about 20 minutes. Remove from baking sheets at once and cool on racks. Makes about 3 dozen.

MINIATURE MERINGUES

Serve these atop or alongside fruit, chocolate or other sundaes

1 large egg white	⅓ c. very fine granulated sugar
Few grains salt	(superfine)
	¼ tsp. vanilla

With electric mixer at medium speed, beat egg white and salt until mixture stands in soft, tilted peaks. Beat in sugar, 1 tblsp. at a time; continue beating until sugar is dissolved. (Rub a little of mixture between thumb and forefinger to determine if grains of sugar are dissolved.) Stir in vanilla.

Drop by rounded teaspoonfuls 1″ apart onto well-greased baking sheet. Bake in very slow oven (250°) 45 minutes, until firm and crisp, but not browned. Remove with metal spatula to wire racks to cool. Store in container with loose-fitting lid, or freeze in tightly covered container. Use to garnish ice cream or as an accompaniment to it. Makes 20 to 24.

BIT O' NUT SWEETS

Meringue cookies that taste like candy. So little work and so good

2 egg whites	½ c. chopped dates
2 c. brown sugar, firmly packed	½ c. chopped candied lemon
2 c. sliced Brazil nuts	peel, or other candied fruit

Beat egg whites until stiff. Beat in brown sugar gradually. Work in nuts, dates and lemon peel. Drop by teaspoonfuls 1″ apart onto greased baking sheet.

Bake in very slow oven (250°) 30 minutes. Remove from baking sheet immediately and cool on racks. Makes about 5 dozen.

Variation

Double Date Sweets: Omit candied lemon peel, and increase amount of chopped dates to 1 c.

Cookie Confections

To make cookie confections is to cook young. They're short on work, long on good eating.

No need to get out your electric mixer to make cookie confections. Nor will you have to heat the oven for some of them. Holiday Fruit Bars, for instance. Full of good things, such as dates, candied cherries, nuts and vanilla wafers, the bars are "No-Bake." Chocolate/Peanut Crunchers also skip the oven.

Another characteristic of many cookie confections is the absence of flour from the ingredient list. Substituting for it often are foods made with flour or from grains, such as graham crackers, whole or in crumbs, vanilla wafers, rolled oats and other cereal representatives from supermarket shelves.

All cookie confections are a cross between cookies and candy; those that contain no food made with flour or cereals are more candy-like. Date/Coconut Balls and Carnival Candy Cookies are two tasty examples. It's this union of cookie and candy qualities that makes them "confections."

Look at the recipe for Basic Graham Cracker Mix and the intriguing cookies in which it appears. You press the mix into a pan, spread or pour on something luscious, bake, cool and cut it into bars. For example, an easy chocolate filling makes Fudgies distinctive; the refreshing lemon tang in Lemon-Filled Bars explains why hostesses like to serve them with fruit salads.

You'll find great variety in our cookie confections. In some—Swedish Almond Creams, for instance—you lay graham crackers over the bottom of the pan, top with filling and bake. You take a couple more steps with Graham Cracker Bars: Top the filling with a layer of graham crackers and spread on frosting. These are make-ahead specials; you refrigerate them overnight before cutting in bars and serving. You get them ready the day before your party.

The adaptability of cookie confections deserves as much credit for their astonishing success as the ease with which you fix them.

They're the answer to so many occasions. For snacking they have few equals and Potpourri Cookies are outstanding in this category. To make them you melt together chocolate pieces, marshmallows and butter and pour the mixture over crisp, oven-toasted rice cereal, salted peanuts and broken pretzel sticks. Your friends will enjoy nibbling on them while watching television with you.

Today's youngsters like quick results and turn to confection-making —easier to make than candy, and the results are foolproof. Join the ranks of up-to-date cooks and build up your repertoire of cookie confections from the recipes that follow.

BASIC GRAHAM CRACKER MIX

This is the starting point for any of the four recipes that follow

2¼ c. graham cracker crumbs
½ c. melted butter
½ c. sugar

Combine all ingredients, and use as directed.

COCONUT CARAMEL BARS

With the basic mix on hand, you can have cookies in 20 minutes

Basic Graham Cracker Mix   ⅓ c. light or heavy cream
28 caramels (½ lb.)   1 c. flaked coconut

Press two-thirds Basic Graham Cracker Mix over bottom of 13 x 9 x 2" pan.

Melt caramels with cream over hot water. Stir in coconut. Spoon here and there over crumbs in pan. Spread carefully to cover crumbs. Sprinkle with remaining third of graham cracker mix; press down firmly.

Bake in moderate oven (375°) 15 minutes. Cool partially in pan set on rack; then cut in 3 x 1" bars, or any desired size. Makes 39.

Variation

Nut Caramel Bars: Substitute 1 c. chopped nuts for coconut in Coconut Caramel Bars.

FUDGIES

The easy-to-make fudge filling makes these chocolate-delicious

Basic Graham Cracker Mix
1 (15 oz.) can sweetened
   condensed milk (not
   evaporated)

1 (6 oz.) pkg. semisweet
   chocolate pieces
½ c. chopped nuts

Press two-thirds Graham Cracker Mix over bottom of 13 x 9 x 2" pan.

Heat sweetened condensed milk in saucepan. Blend in chocolate pieces and stir until mixture thickens. Stir in nuts. Pour evenly over mix in pan. Sprinkle with remaining third of mix. Press down firmly.

Bake in moderate oven (375°) 15 minutes. Cool slightly in pan set on rack; then cut in 2" squares, or desired size. Makes 2 dozen.

LEMON-FILLED BARS

Serve these tangy lemon bars with dessert fruit cups and salads

Basic Graham Cracker Mix
2 eggs, slightly beaten
½ c. water
1 c. sugar

3 tblsp. lemon juice
2 tsp. grated lemon peel
2 tblsp. butter

Press all but 1 c. Graham Cracker Mix over bottom of 13 x 9 x 2" pan.

Combine remaining ingredients, except mix, in saucepan. Cook over low heat, stirring constantly, until very thick and clear. Pour over basic mix in pan. Sprinkle on remaining mix; press down.

Bake in moderate oven (375°) 20 minutes. Partially cool in pan set on rack; then cut in 3 x 1" bars, or desired size. Makes 39.

MATRIMONIAL GRAHAM BARS

You'll like the happy marriage of date and graham cracker flavors

Basic Graham Cracker Mix
1½ c. halved pitted dates

⅔ c. water
¼ c. sugar

Press two-thirds of Basic Graham Cracker Mix over bottom of 13 x 9 x 2" pan.

Cook dates, water and sugar together until thick and smooth, stirring frequently. Spoon here and there over crumbs in pan; spread carefully to cover. Sprinkle remaining third of basic mix over date filling; press down firmly.

Bake in moderate oven (375°) 15 minutes. Partially cool in pan set on rack; then cut in 3 x 1″ bars, or desired size. Makes 39.

CANDY BAR COOKIES

Here's the top favorite new recipe from an experienced cookie baker

½ c. butter or regular margarine
1 c. fine graham cracker crumbs
1 (6 oz.) pkg. semisweet
chocolate pieces
1 (6 oz.) pkg. butterscotch
pieces

1 c. flaked coconut
1 c. broken nuts
1 (15 oz.) can sweetened
condensed milk (not
evaporated)

Melt butter in 13 x 9 x 2″ pan. Sprinkle graham cracker crumbs evenly over bottom of pan. Then sprinkle on chocolate pieces. Next sprinkle on butterscotch pieces, then the coconut. Sprinkle on nuts. Dribble sweetened condensed milk over top.

Bake in moderate oven (375°) about 25 minutes. Set pan on rack and cut in 3 x 1″ bars when partly cooled, but while still warm. Remove from pan when cool. Makes 39 bars.

CHOCOLATE/COCONUT BARS

Many popular cookies contain graham crackers—here's a good one

2 c. crushed graham crackers
¼ c. sugar
½ c. melted butter or regular
margarine

1 (15 oz.) can sweetened condensed milk (not evaporated)
2 c. flaked coconut
1 (6 oz.) pkg. semisweet
chocolate pieces

Combine graham crackers, sugar and butter. Mix well and pat into ungreased 13 x 9 x 2″ pan. Bake in moderate oven (350°) 15 minutes.

Combine sweetened milk and coconut. Spread on baked layer. Return to oven and bake 15 minutes longer.

Melt chocolate pieces and spread over baked layers. Cool in pan set on rack, then cut in 2½ x 1¼″ bars. Makes about 3 dozen.

DATE MALLOW CHEWS

Three sure-fire goodies in these bars: dates, nuts and marshmallows

½ c. butter
1 (10½ oz.) pkg. miniature
marshmallows
1¼ c. cut-up dates
2 c. graham cracker crumbs

½ c. chopped nuts
1 square semisweet chocolate
2 tblsp. milk
1 tblsp. butter
1 c. confectioners sugar

Melt ½ c. butter in 3-qt. saucepan. Add marshmallows and cook over low heat until melted, stirring constantly. Stir in dates, graham cracker crumbs and nuts. Press into buttered 9" square pan.

Combine chocolate, milk and 1 tblsp. butter in small saucepan over low heat; stir constantly until chocolate and butter are melted. Stir in confectioners sugar. Spread over mixture in pan. Let stand in pan until set, then cut in 1½" squares. Makes 3 dozen.

DATE/MARSHMALLOW BALLS

Skip-the-oven cookies, sweet and rich—a real confection treat

1½ c. chopped dates
1¼ c. chopped nuts
2 c. miniature marshmallows

3½ c. graham cracker crumbs
1 (6½ oz.) pkg. fluffy white
frosting mix

Combine dates, 1 c. nuts, marshmallows and 2½ c. graham cracker crumbs. Mix thoroughly.

Prepare frosting mix as directed on package. Add to the date mixture and mix until completely moistened.

Combine remaining ¼ c. nuts and 1 c. graham cracker crumbs in small bowl.

Form date mixture into 1½" balls. Roll in graham cracker crumbs and nuts. Store in covered container at least 12 hours to mellow. Makes 3 dozen.

FRUITCAKE SQUARES

This holiday bar cookie was rated "yummy" by taste-testers

6 tblsp. butter or regular margarine
1½ c. graham cracker crumbs
1 c. shredded coconut
2 c. cut-up mixed candied fruit
1 c. dates

Flour
1 c. coarsely chopped walnuts or pecans
1 (15 oz.) can sweetened condensed milk (not evaporated)

Melt butter in 15½ x 10½ x 1" jelly roll pan. Sprinkle on crumbs; tap sides of pan to distribute crumbs evenly. Sprinkle on coconut. Distribute candied fruit as evenly as possible over coconut.

Cut dates into a small amount of flour so they won't stick together. Distribute dates over candied fruit. Sprinkle on nuts. Press mixture lightly with hands to level it in pan. Pour sweetened condensed milk evenly over top.

Bake in moderate oven (350°) 25 to 30 minutes. Cool completely in pan on rack before cutting in 1½" squares. Remove from pan. Makes 70.

GRAHAM CRACKER BARS

Simple start with graham crackers ends up with elegant cookies

30 graham crackers
1 c. brown sugar, firmly packed
½ c. butter or regular margarine
½ c. milk
1 c. flaked coconut

1 c. graham cracker crumbs
2 c. confectioners sugar
5 tblsp. melted butter
3 tblsp. dairy half-and-half
½ tsp. vanilla

Line bottom of greased 13 x 9 x 2" pan with 15 graham crackers.

In saucepan, combine brown sugar, ½ c. butter, milk, coconut and graham cracker crumbs. Bring to a boil and cook, stirring constantly, until thick, about 10 minutes. (Mixture burns easily.) Spread evenly on top of whole graham crackers in pan. Top with remaining 15 graham crackers to cover.

Beat together confectioners sugar, melted butter, dairy half-and-half and vanilla until mixture is smooth. Spread on top of graham crackers in pan.

Cover with waxed paper and let stand in refrigerator overnight before cutting in 3 x 1" bars. Makes 39.

JIFFY CANDY COOKIES

Children like to make these cookies that taste like candy bars

18 graham crackers, broken into small pieces
1 (15 oz.) can sweetened condensed milk (not evaporated)
1 (6 oz.) pkg. semisweet chocolate pieces
½ c. chopped pecans
½ c. flaked coconut

Combine all ingredients. Pour into greased 8" square pan. Bake in moderate oven (350°) 35 minutes.

While warm, cut in 1½" squares and place on cooling rack. Makes about 25.

NOTE: These cookies will firm when cool.

MAGIC COOKIE BARS

Cut bars to fit appetites—these cookies are almost like candy

½ c. regular margarine, melted
1½ c. graham cracker crumbs
1 c. chopped nuts
1 (6 oz.) pkg. semisweet chocolate pieces
1 (6 oz.) pkg. butterscotch pieces
1½ c. flaked coconut
1 (15 oz.) can sweetened condensed milk (not evaporated)

Cover bottom of 13 x 9 x 2" pan with melted margarine. Sprinkle evenly with graham cracker crumbs.

Sprinkle nuts, then chocolate pieces, butterscotch morsels and coconut over crumbs. Pour sweetened condensed milk over coconut.

Bake in moderate oven (350°) 25 to 30 minutes, until lightly browned. Cool in pan set on rack 15 minutes, then cut in 3 x 1½" bars. Lift from pan with spatula and complete cooling on rack. Makes 2 dozen.

PRALINE COOKIES

"Child pleasers" . . . these candy-like cookies are made in minutes

24 graham crackers
1 c. light brown sugar, firmly packed
½ c. butter or regular margarine
1 c. chopped pecans

Line the bottom of a greased 15½ x 10½ x 1" jelly roll pan with graham crackers.

Place brown sugar and butter in small saucepan; bring to a rolling boil over medium heat and cook 1½ minutes. Remove from heat. When mixture has stopped bubbling, stir in nuts. Spoon it on and spread over graham crackers.

Bake in moderate oven (350°) 10 minutes. Cool in pan on rack, then cut in 2 x 1" bars. Makes about 48.

SEVEN-LAYER BARS

Just layer ingredients in pan—easy and delicious

¼ c. butter or regular margarine
1 c. graham cracker crumbs
1 c. shredded coconut
1 (6 oz.) pkg. semisweet
   chocolate pieces

1 (6 oz.) pkg. butterscotch
   pieces
1 (15 oz.) can sweetened condensed milk (not evaporated)
1 c. chopped nuts

Melt butter in 13 x 9 x 2" pan. Sprinkle crumbs evenly over butter; tap sides of pan to distribute crumbs evenly. Sprinkle on coconut, chocolate and butterscotch pieces.

Pour sweetened condensed milk (not evaporated) evenly over top. Sprinkle on nuts and press lightly into pan.

Bake in moderate oven (350°) 30 minutes. Cool in pan on rack, then cut in 2 x 1" bars. Makes about 40.

SWEDISH ALMOND CREAMS

Creamy almond candy on crisp graham crackers—wonderful taste

15 graham crackers
¼ c. light or heavy cream
¾ c. sugar
¼ c. light corn syrup

½ c. butter
¾ c. sliced almonds
¼ tsp. almond extract

Arrange graham crackers to cover bottom of heavily buttered 13 x 9 x 2" pan.

Combine cream, sugar, corn syrup and butter in small saucepan; boil 3 minutes. Stir in almond slices and extract. Pour over crackers in pan.

Bake in moderate oven (375°) 10 minutes, or until lightly browned. Partially cool on rack, then cut in 3 x 1" bars. Makes 39.

THREE-LAYER CHOCOLATE SQUARES

The cookies to make when your oven is busy—they taste wonderful

½ c. butter or regular margarine
¼ c. cocoa
½ c. sifted confectioners sugar
1 egg, slightly beaten
2 tsp. vanilla
3 c. graham cracker crumbs
½ c. chopped pecans
¼ c. butter or regular margarine

1 tsp. cornstarch
2 tsp. sugar
3 tblsp. light cream or evaporated milk
1 tsp. vanilla
2 c. sifted confectioners sugar
1 (9¾ oz.) sweet chocolate candy bar

Melt ½ c. butter. Add the following ingredients, one at a time, stirring after each addition: cocoa, ½ c. confectioners sugar, egg, 2 tsp. vanilla, cracker crumbs and pecans. Stir until mixture is well blended, then press it into lightly greased 13 x 9 x 2" pan.

Melt ¼ c. butter. Combine cornstarch and 2 tsp. sugar; add to butter and blend thoroughly. Add cream; cook, stirring constantly, until thick and smooth. Cool; add 1 tsp. vanilla and 2 c. confectioners sugar. Blend well and spread over first layer. (Drop by teaspoonfuls and spread carefully—this is a stiff mixture.)

Melt chocolate bar over hot water; spread it over the cream filling. Cool in pan on rack, and cut in 1" squares before chocolate sets completely. Makes about 9 dozen.

HALLOWEEN TREATS

Let your youngsters make these cookies for trick or treat visitors

2 c. sugar
⅔ c. milk
6 tblsp. peanut butter

1 tsp. vanilla
1¼ c. crumbled soda crackers (40 squares)

Heat together sugar and milk in 2-qt. saucepan; boil 3 minutes. Remove from heat; add peanut butter. Then add vanilla and crackers. Mix well. Cool, then form into 1" balls. Makes 34.

COCONUT/CORN FLAKE CRISPIES

Chocolate topknots help to make party cookies out of the cereal base

3 egg whites	2 c. crushed corn flakes
¼ tsp. salt	1⅓ c. flaked coconut
1 c. sugar	½ c. chopped pecans
1 tsp. vanilla	

Beat egg whites until frothy; add salt and gradually beat in sugar. Continue beating until very stiff and glossy. Stir in vanilla, corn flakes, coconut and pecans.

Drop heaping teaspoonfuls of dough 2″ apart onto ungreased brown wrapping paper covering baking sheet.

Bake in slow oven (325°) 15 to 18 minutes, until set and delicately browned. Remove from oven and lift off paper holding cookies; lay wet towel on hot baking sheet. Place paper of cookies on towel; let stand 1 minute (steam will loosen cookies). Lift cookies with spatula to cooling rack. Makes 40.

Variations

Chocolate/Coconut Crispies: Make like Coconut/Corn Flake Crispies, but stir 2 squares unsweetened chocolate, melted and slightly cooled, into batter. Bake as directed.

Chocolate-Topped Crispies: Melt together over hot water 1 (6 oz.) pkg. milk chocolate pieces, 2 tblsp. shortening and 2 tblsp. shaved paraffin. Hold the baked cookies, one at a time, in the hand and dip tops in mixture.

PEANUT CHEWS

Peanut butter fans will like these crunchy cookies—fine for snacks

9 c. corn flakes	¼ c. butter or regular margarine
1½ c. sugar	¾ c. water
¼ tsp. salt	2 tsp. vanilla
¾ c. light corn syrup	½ c. crunchy peanut butter

Place corn flakes in a bowl.

Combine sugar, salt, corn syrup, butter and water in saucepan. Bring to a boil and reduce heat. Continue to cook to the hard ball stage (250°), using care not to overcook.

Remove from heat and stir in vanilla and peanut butter. Pour mixture over corn flakes.

Toss with a fork to cover corn flakes with syrup completely. Work quickly.

Drop in clusters onto waxed paper. Makes about 40.

PEANUT BUTTER DROPS

A quick confection; nutritious too—children like these

1 c. sugar
1 c. light corn syrup
½ c. peanut butter

4 c. ready-to-eat high protein cereal
1 c. thin pretzel sticks, broken in 1" lengths

Mix sugar and syrup in large saucepan. Bring to a boil over medium heat; cook about 30 seconds. Remove from heat and add peanut butter. Stir until smooth. Stir in cereal and pretzel sticks.

Drop by tablespoonfuls onto waxed paper. Makes about 4½ dozen.

DATE/COCONUT BALLS

Snowy coconut decorates these baked-in-a-skillet date cookies

2 tblsp. butter
1 c. sugar
2 eggs, beaten
1 c. chopped dates

½ c. chopped nuts
2 c. oven-toasted rice cereal
1 c. flaked coconut

Put butter in heavy skillet with sugar, eggs and dates. Cook over medium-low heat, stirring constantly, until mixture leaves sides of skillet. (Mixture burns easily.)

Remove from heat; add nuts and cereal. Shape in 1" balls with hands; roll in coconut. Store in tightly covered container (cookies are good keepers). Makes 38.

COCONUT CRISPS

Cookie bars, luscious with dates, nuts and snowy coconut topknots

6 c. oven-toasted rice cereal
1 c. chopped walnuts
¾ c. butter or regular margarine
1¼ c. sugar
2 tblsp. milk

¼ tsp. salt
1 c. chopped dates
1 tblsp. vanilla
2 tblsp. lemon juice
1 (3½ oz.) can flaked coconut

Combine cereal and walnuts in greased 13 x 9 x 2" pan.

Combine butter, sugar, milk, salt and dates in saucepan. Cook to the soft ball stage (240°); stir occasionally. Remove from heat and add vanilla and lemon juice.

Pour hot syrup over cereal/nut mixture; stir lightly to coat cereal. Spread mixture evenly in pan. Sprinkle coconut over top and press mixture firmly into pan. Let set 4 hours or longer.

When firm, cut in 3 x 1¼" bars. Makes 2½ dozen.

POTPOURRI COOKIES

Perfect snack to munch on while watching television or visiting

1 (6 oz.) pkg. semisweet
  chocolate pieces
½ c. butter or regular margarine
1 (10 oz.) pkg. marshmallows
4 c. oven-toasted rice cereal

2 c. salted Spanish peanuts
2 c. raisins
2 c. broken pretzel sticks (about
  ½" lengths)

Melt chocolate pieces, butter and marshmallows in top of double boiler over simmering water. Stir to blend.

Combine rice cereal, peanuts, raisins and broken pretzel sticks in a greased large bowl. Pour melted chocolate mixture over and stir to coat all pieces. With two teaspoons form into clusters; drop onto greased baking sheets. Cool until set. Makes 5 dozen.

PUFFED-UP RICE FINGERS

Candied fruits add color and flavor to these crunchy cereal bars

5 c. puffed rice
¼ c. diced mixed candied fruit
½ c. coarsely chopped nuts
½ c. sugar
¾ c. dark corn syrup

⅓ c. water
½ tsp. salt
1 tblsp. butter or regular margarine

Spread puffed rice in shallow pan and heat in moderate oven (350°) about 10 minutes. Then turn into a greased large bowl. Stir in fruit and nuts.

In medium-size saucepan stir together sugar, corn syrup, water and salt. Cook over medium heat to soft ball stage (236° on candy thermometer). Stir in butter.

Stir hot syrup mixture into puffed rice until evenly coated. Using greased hands, pack mixture firmly into greased 13 x 9 x 2" pan. Cut in 3 x 1" bars. Makes 39.

CHOCOLATE OATSIES

Shortcut to hospitality—make these fast-fix, candy-good cookies

2 c. sugar
½ c. milk
¼ c. butter or regular margarine
⅓ c. cocoa

3 c. quick-cooking rolled oats
½ c. flaked or shredded coconut
½ c. peanut butter
1 tsp. vanilla

Combine sugar, milk, butter and cocoa in saucepan. Boil 1 minute. Remove from heat.

Mix in rest of ingredients.

Drop by teaspoonfuls onto waxed paper. Makes 30.

FARMHOUSE CHOCOLATE CRUNCH

These chewy cookies containing black walnuts are cousins of candy

⅔ c. butter or regular margarine
½ c. light corn syrup
1 tsp. salt
3 tsp. vanilla
1 c. brown sugar, firmly packed

4 c. quick-cooking rolled oats
2 (6 oz.) pkgs. semisweet chocolate pieces
½ c. chopped black walnuts

Melt butter in a large saucepan. Add syrup, salt, vanilla, brown sugar and rolled oats; mix well. Press into a well-greased 15½ x 10½ x 1" jelly roll pan.

Bake in hot oven (425°) 12 minutes. During the last 2 minutes of baking, sprinkle on chocolate pieces. When they melt, remove pan from oven and spread chocolate evenly to cover top. Sprinkle with chopped nuts. Cut in 1½" squares while still warm. Cool in pan on rack. Recut when cool. Makes about 70.

PEANUT CANDY-BAR COOKIES

Chewy, toffee-like bars topped with tasty peanut-chocolate

2 c. quick-cooking rolled oats	1 tsp. vanilla
1 c. graham cracker crumbs	½ c. salted peanuts
¾ c. brown sugar, firmly packed	1 (6 oz.) pkg. semisweet
½ c. melted butter	chocolate pieces
½ c. dark corn syrup	½ c. peanut butter
¼ tsp. baking soda	

Combine all ingredients, except chocolate pieces and peanut butter. Spread or press into greased 13 x 9 x 2" pan. Bake in moderate oven (375°) 15 to 20 minutes, or until light golden brown.

Meanwhile, melt together chocolate pieces and peanut butter over hot water. Spread over baked cookie while warm. Cool slightly in pan set on rack, then cut in 3 x 1" bars. Makes 39.

CEREAL SLICES

These crunchy confection cookies really rate high with youngsters

½ c. butter	4 c. assorted bite-size shredded
1 (10½ oz.) pkg. miniature	cereal biscuits (wheat, rice
marshmallows	and corn)
2 c. salted peanuts	

Melt butter in 3-qt. saucepan. Add marshmallows and cook over low heat, stirring constantly, until melted. Stir in nuts and cereals (oat puffs are good included in this combination).

Divide mixture in half on sheets of foil or waxed paper. Shape each half in a 15" long roll, using fork and side of foil or waxed paper to aid in the shaping. Wrap rolls tightly and refrigerate until firm. To serve, cut in ½" slices. Makes 5 dozen.

CHOCOLATE/PEANUT CRUNCHERS

Chocolate-marshmallow mix covers salted peanuts and crisp cereals

¼ c. butter
1 (6 oz.) pkg. semisweet
   chocolate pieces
1 (10½ oz.) pkg. miniature
   marshmallows

1½ c. salted peanuts
2 c. assorted bite-size shredded
   cereal biscuits (wheat, corn
   and rice)

Melt butter in 3-qt. saucepan over low heat. Add chocolate pieces and marshmallows; cook and stir constantly until melted, smooth and syrupy. Stir in peanuts and cereal (oat puffs are good included in assortment).

Spread in buttered 9″ square pan, using 2 forks to spread evenly. When firm, cut in 1½″ squares. Makes 3 dozen.

SPICY CRUNCH

If you want a snack guests rave about, here's the recipe to use

3 c. puffed oat cereal
2 c. shredded rice, bite-size
   biscuits
2 c. shredded corn, bite-size
   biscuits
2 c. shredded wheat, bite-size
   biscuits
1 c. raisins

1 c. pecan halves
½ c. butter or regular margarine
1⅓ c. brown sugar, firmly
   packed
¼ c. light corn syrup
2 tsp. ground cinnamon
½ tsp. salt

Butter a large bowl and toss cereals, raisins and pecans in it to mix.

Combine butter, brown sugar, corn syrup, cinnamon and salt in a heavy skillet. Stir constantly over medium heat until boiling. Boil 3 minutes.

Pour the hot syrup over cereal mixture in the bowl; stir to coat thoroughly.

Spread on two buttered baking sheets. Cool. When firm, break into pieces. Makes about 2½ quarts.

APRICOT/COCONUT BALLS

The refreshing tart-sweet flavor of apricots pleases everyone

1 c. apricot preserves
2 tblsp. butter
2½ c. vanilla wafer crumbs

2 c. flaked coconut
¼ c. currants (optional)
½ tsp. rum flavoring (optional)

Combine apricot preserves and butter in saucepan. Bring to a boil. Stir in vanilla wafer crumbs, ½ c. coconut, currants and rum flavoring.

Place remaining 1½ c. coconut in shallow dish. Drop teaspoonfuls of apricot mixture into coconut and roll to coat thoroughly. Shape into balls. Place on waxed paper. Makes 3½ dozen.

HOLIDAY FRUIT BARS

Ideal no-bake fruit cookies for Christmas celebrations and gifts

½ c. butter
1 (10½ oz.) pkg. miniature
  marshmallows
¾ c. chopped nuts

1 c. candied cherries, cut in
  halves
1 c. dates, cut in halves
1½ c. vanilla wafer crumbs

Melt butter in 3-qt. saucepan. Add marshmallows; cook over low heat, stirring constantly, until melted. Add remaining ingredients; mix thoroughly.

Spread mixture in buttered 9" square pan, using fork to spread evenly. When ready to serve, cut in 1½" squares. Makes 3 dozen.

Variation

Cereal Christmas Fruit Bars: Substitute 1½ c. oven-toasted rice cereal for vanilla wafer crumbs.

ALMOND BARS

These skip-the-oven cookies are so easy to make and so good to eat

¾ c. blanched almonds
¼ c. candied cherries
¼ c. toasted flaked or shredded
  coconut
1 tblsp. butter or regular
  margarine

1½ tblsp. honey
¼ tsp. almond extract
1 (4 oz.) pkg. sweet cooking
  chocolate

Grind almonds and cherries together. Add coconut.

Cream butter, honey and almond extract together; add ground mixture; mix well. Shape into large rectangle on waxed paper.

Melt chocolate; spread over top; chill until firm. Cut in 2½ x 2" bars. Makes 18 to 20.

ALMOND BONBONS

This new almond Christmas special adds distinction to the cookie tray

3 c. finely chopped blanched almonds (1 lb.)

3 egg whites, stiffly beaten

1 tblsp. heavy cream

1 tsp. almond extract

2 c. sifted confectioners sugar

1 tsp. water

1 tblsp. lemon-flavored iced tea mix

Chocolate pieces or nuts (for centers)

Sugar or tiny multicolored decorating candies

Combine almonds, stiffly beaten egg whites, heavy cream, almond extract, confectioners sugar, water and tea mix. Stir until ingredients are well blended.

Butter hands lightly (mixture is somewhat sticky) and form in 1" balls around chocolate pieces or nuts (one in each ball). Roll half of balls in sugar, the other half in colored candies. Makes about 5 dozen.

CARNIVAL CANDY COOKIES

Colored marshmallows give a festive look to these chocolate drops

1 (6 oz.) pkg. semisweet chocolate pieces

¼ c. peanut butter

2 tblsp. light corn syrup

2 tblsp. shortening

1 c. salted peanuts

1 c. colored miniature marshmallows

Melt together in saucepan over low heat chocolate pieces, peanut butter, corn syrup and shortening. Stir until smooth. Cool slightly, then stir in peanuts and marshmallows; avoid overstirring.

Drop by teaspoonfuls onto waxed paper. Let set until firm. Makes about 2 dozen.

Variation

Peanut/Cereal Candy Cookies: Use ½ c. salted peanuts and ½ c. oat puffs (cereal circles) in Carnival Candy Cookies instead of 1 c. salted peanuts.

CASSEROLE COOKIES

A Missouri school teacher contributed this recipe. She says she makes the confection cookies every yuletide season. The teachers take turns providing candy daily for their lounge the week before the holiday vacation. Casserole Cookies disappear quickly, which is adequate proof of their popularity.

You bake the cookie mixture in a casserole. A crust forms on top, but it disappears when you stir the hot cookies with a spoon. When mixture cools, you shape the cookies in 1″ balls and roll them in granulated sugar. The white sugar granules glisten on the dark cookie balls.

CASSEROLE COOKIES

A cookie-candy hybrid, baked in a casserole—inviting and rewarding

2 eggs	1 c. flaked coconut
1 c. sugar	1 tsp. vanilla
1 c. chopped walnuts	¼ tsp. almond extract
1 c. chopped dates	¼ c. sugar (for coating)

Beat eggs well; gradually add 1 c. sugar, beating until mixture is light and fluffy. Stir in nuts, dates, coconut, vanilla and almond extract. Turn into ungreased 2-qt. casserole.

Bake in moderate oven (350°) 30 minutes. Remove from oven and while still hot, stir well with wooden spoon. Let cool, then form into 1″ balls. Roll in ¼ c. sugar. Makes about 34.

COCONUT/DATE MARBLES

These attractive cookie marbles taste like date bars—party fare

1 egg	1 c. finely cut dates (8 oz.)
½ c. sugar	1 (7 oz.) pkg. cookie coconut
1 tsp. vanilla	½ c. finely chopped pecans
⅛ tsp. salt	4 drops red food color

Beat egg until foamy; gradually beat in sugar, vanilla and salt. Beat until fluffy. Stir in dates, ¾ c. coconut and pecans. Spread in greased 9" square pan.

Bake in slow oven (300°) about 30 minutes, or until golden. (Test by pressing lightly with fingertip. If cookie springs back, it is done.)

Set pan on rack to cool. Cut in 1½ x 1" bars. Roll each bar in hands to make a 1" ball. Tint half of the remaining coconut pink with red food color. Roll half the cookie balls in pink coconut, the other half in white. Makes about 4 dozen.

CHOCOLATE/PEANUT CLUSTERS

They'll remind you of candy, but you bake them like cookies—good

⅙ c. sifted flour	2 squares unsweetened
⅔ c. sugar	chocolate, melted
½ tsp. salt	2 tsp. light corn syrup
⅓ c. shortening	1 tsp. vanilla
1 egg	2½ c. unsalted peanuts

Sift flour, sugar and salt into bowl. Add shortening, egg, chocolate, corn syrup and vanilla; mix well. Add nuts.

Drop teaspoonfuls of dough 1" apart, onto greased baking sheet. Bake in moderate oven (350°) 8 minutes.

Cool cookies before removing to wire rack—they're very tender when hot! Makes 3 dozen.

Variations

Chocolate/Raisin Clusters: Use only 1½ c. peanuts and add 1 c. raisins.

Chocolate/Date Clusters: Use 1½ c. chopped walnuts instead of peanuts and 1 c. chopped dates.

DATE/NUT MACAROONS

They're moist, chewy, tasty and so easy to make. Try them soon

⅔ c. sweetened condensed milk (not evaporated)	1 c. chopped nuts
	1 c. chopped, pitted dates
1 c. flaked or shredded coconut	1 tsp. vanilla

Mix together all ingredients. Shape into balls and place about 1" apart on greased baking sheet.

Bake in moderate oven (350°) 10 to 12 minutes, until golden brown. Remove cookies and cool on racks. Makes about 2 dozen.

ROCKY ROAD FUDGE BARS

They're dual purpose—serve these treats as cookies or candy

½ c. light corn syrup
½ c. sugar
1 (6 oz.) pkg. semisweet
  chocolate pieces

¼ c. peanut butter
½ c. chopped nuts
2 c. miniature marshmallows

Combine corn syrup and sugar in saucepan; bring to a boil and boil 2 minutes. Stir in chocolate pieces and peanut butter; cool slightly. Add nuts and marshmallows, stirring just enough to distribute.

Spread evenly in buttered 9" square pan. To serve, cut in 1½" squares. Makes 3 dozen.

Variations

Rocky Road Fudge Slices: If desired, shape Rocky Road Fudge Bars mixture into two 10" rolls. (Mixture is somewhat soft and is a little difficult to handle, but slices are very attractive.) Wrap rolls tightly in aluminum foil or waxed paper and refrigerate until firm. To serve, cut in ¼ to ½" slices.

Cereal Rocky Road Fudge Slices: Make like Rocky Road Fudge Slices, but substitute 2 c. oat puffs (cereal circles) for the marshmallows.

SOUTHERN CANDY-COOKIES

Luscious butterscotch mix coats raisins, nuts and marshmallows

½ c. light corn syrup
½ c. brown sugar, firmly packed
½ c. peanut butter
1 (6 oz.) pkg. butterscotch
  pieces

2 c. light raisins (seeded)
½ c. chopped pecans
2 c. miniature marshmallows

Bring to a boil corn syrup and brown sugar; boil 2 minutes. Remove from heat; blend in peanut butter and butterscotch pieces. Stir in raisins, pecans and marshmallows, using care not to overmix.

Drop by rounded teaspoonfuls onto waxed paper. To hasten setting, place in refrigerator. Makes about 3½ dozen.

COCONUT MARZIPANS

Fruit flavor gelatin contributes color and zip to these cookies

1 (3 oz.) pkg. fruit flavor
  gelatin
2⅓ c. flaked or cookie
  coconut (7 to 8 oz. pkg.)
½ c. sweetened condensed milk
  (not evaporated)

¼ c. heavy or light cream
¼ c. sugar
¼ c. butter
1 c. confectioners sugar

Set aside 1 tblsp. gelatin to use in glaze. Combine coconut, sweetened condensed milk and remaining gelatin (strawberry, cherry, lemon, lime or orange). Mix thoroughly.

Form mixture into cookies in shape of berries or fruit to correspond to flavor of gelatin; let stand a few minutes.

Meanwhile, make glaze: Combine cream, sugar, butter and reserved gelatin in small saucepan. Boil 2 minutes; stir in confectioners sugar. Drop shaped cookies, one at a time, into glaze to coat. Lift out of glaze with fork, allowing excess to drip off. Place on waxed paper. (If necessary, thin glaze with a little milk while coating cookies.) Makes about 2½ dozen.

Pie-Bar Dessert Cookies

Our pie-bar dessert cookies, inspired by popular pies, prove there is something new under the sun—something mighty good to eat. The idea for this cross between cookies and pies came about through concern about calories.

Many Americans in this diet-conscious age try to skip dessert yet long for at least a few bites of delicious sweetness to top off the meal or to enjoy with coffee at evening social affairs. Our food editors in their travels around the country asked: "What is your favorite dessert? What would you choose if you were not counting calories?" Men promptly replied: Pies. And a surprising number of women gave the same answer.

With this in mind when we were working on this cookie book, some creative Test Kitchen work evolved our recipes for small cookies that taste like pies. We call them pie-bar dessert cookies. Taste-testers rated them as tasty as the pies from which they descend. We knew from that moment we had the right rich, satisfying miniature desserts.

The cookies, with the exception of Pumpkin Pie Squares, are finger food. It's easier to eat the spicy, pumpkin cookies with a fork. But there's nothing wrong about serving any of these pie-bar cookies on a small plate with a fork and coffee alongside.

Neither is there any reason why you can't cut these cookies a little larger, although if much bigger, you defeat the major reason for them —cookies small enough to please weight-watchers and permit them to have dessert without feeling guilty.

Which pie-bars taste best? Is it Sour Cream/Raisin, Golden Lemon, Brownie or Chess? Or are Pecan and French Apple Pie-Bars even better? Try all 15 of these exciting cookies and the variations before you decide.

CRAN/APPLE PIE-BARS

Sugar glistens on lattice top over cranberry-orange filling

2 c. sifted flour
½ tsp. salt
⅔ c. shortening
2 tblsp. butter or regular margarine
5 to 6 tblsp. water

1 (10 oz.) pkg. frozen cranberry-orange relish, thawed
1 c. finely chopped apple
⅓ c. sugar
Sugar (for top)

To make crust, combine flour and salt; cut in shortening and butter until particles are the size of small peas. Add water gradually, while stirring with a fork, until mixture is moist enough to hold together. Reserve ⅓ of dough to use for topping.

Roll remaining ⅔ of dough on floured surface to make a 14 x 9" rectangle. Place on ungreased baking sheet.

To make filling, combine cranberry-orange relish, apple and ⅓ c. sugar. Spread over pastry, leaving a ½" margin on all sides.

Roll out remaining ⅓ of dough. Cut in strips about ½" wide, half of them 14" long, the other half 9" long. Crisscross over filling to make a lattice top; fold lower crust up over. Sprinkle with sugar.

Bake in hot oven (400°) 30 to 35 minutes, or until pastry is golden brown. Cool in pan on rack. Cut in 2 x 1½" bars. Makes about 3½ dozen.

NOTE: Cookies lose some of their crispness after standing 24 hours. To serve them the second or third day after baking, heat them in a very slow oven (250°) about 10 minutes to restore crispness.

FRENCH APPLE PIE-BARS

Cookies never were better! That's the verdict of men taste-testers

2 c. sifted flour
1 tsp. salt
¾ c. shortening
4 to 5 tblsp. water
4 c. thinly sliced peeled apples

½ c. sugar
½ c. brown sugar, firmly packed
¼ c. flour
¼ tsp. ground cinnamon

To make crust, combine 2 c. flour with salt; cut in shortening until particles are size of small peas. Set aside 1 c. mixture. To the remainder, add water gradually, while stirring with a fork, just until dough is moist enough to hold together. Form into a square. Roll on floured board to a 14 x 10" rectangle. Fit into ungreased 13 x 9 x 2" pan.

Combine apples with white sugar. Place in pastry-lined pan.

Combine reserved crumb mixture with brown sugar, ¼ c. flour and cinnamon; sprinkle over apples.

Bake in hot oven (400°) 35 to 40 minutes, or until apples are tender and top is golden brown. Cool in pan on rack. Cut in 2" (about) squares. Makes 2 dozen.

BROWNIE PIE-BARS

A rich cream cheese crust holds the cake-like chocolate-nut filling

⅓ c. shortening	2 eggs
1 (3 oz.) pkg. cream cheese	⅓ c. flour
1¼ c. sifted flour	½ c. chopped nuts
½ tsp. salt	½ tsp. baking powder
4 to 5 tblsp. water	½ tsp. salt
½ c. butter or regular margarine	½ tsp. vanilla
2 squares unsweetened	¼ c. sifted confectioners sugar
chocolate	(for coating)
1 c. sugar	

To make crust, soften shortening with cream cheese (at room temperature). Add 1¼ c. flour and ½ tsp. salt. Mix just until particles are the size of small peas. Add water gradually, while stirring with a fork, until dough is moist enough to hold together.

Form dough into a square. Roll out on lightly floured surface to 14 x 10" rectangle. Fit into ungreased 13 x 9 x 2" pan.

To make filling, melt butter with chocolate in saucepan over very low heat. Stir in remaining ingredients, except confectioners sugar; beat to mix well. Pour into pastry-lined pan.

Bake in moderate oven (350°) 40 to 45 minutes. Cool in pan on rack; sprinkle with confectioners sugar. Cut in 2" (about) squares. Makes 2 dozen.

Variation

Frosted Brownie Pie-Bars: Omit sprinkling with confectioners sugar, and spread with this frosting: Melt together 1 (1 oz.) envelope no-melt unsweetened chocolate, or 1 square unsweetened chocolate, 2 tblsp. butter and 1 tblsp. milk. Stir in 1 c. confectioners sugar. Beat until smooth, adding a few drops of milk if necessary to make frosting of spreading consistency. Spread over cooled Brownie Pie-Bars.

DANISH CARAMEL PIE-BARS

We also give a speedy Americanized version of "caramelettes"

1½ c. sifted flour	1 egg
⅓ c. sugar	1 c. sugar
¼ tsp. salt	¾ c. light cream
½ c. butter	¾ c. sliced almonds

Combine flour, ⅓ c. sugar, salt and butter until mixture is crumbly. Blend in egg. Press mixture with fingers into bottom and ½" up sides of ungreased 9" square pan.

Melt 1 c. sugar in heavy skillet over medium-low heat, stirring constantly, until it turns a light caramel color. Add cream very slowly, stirring constantly. When mixture is smooth, remove from heat and stir in almonds. Pour into crust-lined pan.

Bake in moderate oven (350°) 30 to 35 minutes, or until edges are golden brown. Cool in pan on rack. Cut in 1½" squares. Makes 3 dozen.

Variations

American Caramel Pie-Bars: Make like Danish Caramel Pie-Bars, substituting this speedy filling for the one in which you melt the sugar: Combine ⅔ c. caramel sundae sauce, ¼ c. light cream, 1 tblsp. melted butter and ¾ c. sliced almonds. Pour into crust-lined pan and bake as directed.

Danish Caramel Tarts: Press crust for Danish Caramel Pie-Bars into 18 ungreased 2½" muffin-pan cups to cover bottom and ½" up sides. (Or use small tart pans.) Place rounded tablespoonfuls caramel filling in each muffin-pan cup. Bake in moderate oven (350°) about 25 minutes. Cool; loosen carefully and remove from pans. Makes 1½ dozen.

CHEESE PIE-BAR COOKIES

Between crisp undercrust and crumb top there's a velvety, lemon-flavored filling reminiscent of the best cheese cakes and pies

1¾ c. sifted flour	½ c. dairy sour cream
⅓ c. sugar	2 eggs
¼ tsp. salt	1 tsp. grated lemon peel
⅔ c. butter	⅓ c. sugar
1 (3 oz.) pkg. cream cheese	

Combine flour, ⅓ c. sugar and salt; using electric mixer on low speed, cut in butter until particles are fine like cornmeal. Set aside ⅓ of mixture for topping. Press remaining ⅔ of mixture into bottom of ungreased 9" square pan. Bake in moderate oven (350°) 15 minutes.

To make filling, soften cream cheese by beating with sour cream. Blend in eggs, lemon peel and ⅓ c. sugar. Pour over crust in pan. Sprinkle with reserved crust mixture.

Bake in moderate oven (350°) 30 to 35 minutes, or until filling is set. Cool in pan on rack. Cut in 1½" squares and store in refrigerator until serving time. Makes 3 dozen.

CHESS PIE BARS

For dessert cut larger squares; top with whipped cream or ice cream

1½ c. sifted flour	½ c. melted butter
¼ c. brown sugar, firmly packed	2 tblsp. milk
½ c. butter or regular margarine	1 tblsp. flour
1 c. brown sugar, firmly packed	2 eggs
½ c. sugar	½ c. chopped nuts

Combine 1½ c. flour and ¼ c. brown sugar; cut in butter, using mixer on low speed, until particles are fine. Press mixture into bottom of ungreased 13 x 9 x 2" pan. Bake in moderate oven (375°) 10 minutes.

Meanwhile, combine remaining ingredients in mixing bowl; beat well. Pour over crust in pan; bake in moderate oven (375°) 20 to 25 minutes, or until golden brown. Cool in pan on rack; then cut in 2" squares. Makes about 2 dozen.

FRENCH CHOCOLATE PIE-SQUARES

Chocolate creams is a good name for these specials

1⅔ c. graham cracker crumbs	2 (1 oz.) envelopes no-melt
¼ c. sugar	unsweetened chocolate or 2
⅓ c. melted butter	squares unsweetened chocolate,
½ c. butter	melted
1 c. confectioners sugar	2 eggs
	1 tsp. vanilla

Combine graham cracker crumbs, sugar and melted butter. Set aside ⅓ of mixture for topping. Press remaining mixture into bottom of ungreased 9″ square pan.

Bake in moderate oven (375°) 8 minutes. (Omit baking, if you wish.)

To make filling, cream ½ c. butter with confectioners sugar until very light and fluffy. Blend in chocolate. Add eggs and vanilla; beat well. Spread over crust in pan. Sprinkle with reserved crust mixture. Refrigerate.

To serve, cut in 1½″ squares. Makes 3 dozen.

NOTE: Keep cookies in refrigerator. The filling softens at room temperature.

GLAZED JAM PIE-BARS

A cake-like filling bakes in a crust; spread jam and frosting on top

1⅓ c. sifted flour	⅔ c. sugar
½ tsp. salt	2 eggs
¼ c. shortening	½ tsp. baking powder
¼ c. butter	½ tsp. salt
3 to 4 tblsp. water	1 tsp. vanilla
½ c. fruit or berry jam, or	1 c. sifted flour
preserves	Rum Frosting (recipe follows)
½ c. butter	

Mix 1⅓ c. flour and ½ tsp. salt. Using electric mixer at low speed, cut in shortening and ¼ c. butter until particles are fine. Add water gradually, while stirring with fork, until dough is moist enough to hold together.

Roll out dough on floured surface to a 14 x 10″ rectangle. Fit into ungreased 13 x 9 x 2″ pan. Spread jam over bottom.

To make filling, cream ½ c. butter and sugar until light and fluffy. Add eggs, baking powder, ½ tsp. salt and vanilla. Beat well. Blend in 1 c. flour. Spread carefully over jam-topped dough in pan.

Bake in moderate oven (375°) 30 to 35 minutes, or until golden brown. While warm spread with Rum Frosting. Cool in pan on rack, then cut in 2″ (about) squares. (These cookies are good keepers.) Makes 2 dozen.

Rum Frosting: Blend together until smooth 2 tblsp. soft butter or regular margarine, 1 c. confectioners sugar, 1 tblsp. milk and ½ tsp. rum flavoring.

LEMON FLUFF PIE-BARS

Filling separates to form a creamy layer on bottom, spongy fluff on top, like lemon sponge pie. Cookies are light and refreshing

⅓ c. butter	¼ c. flour
¼ c. confectioners sugar	2 eggs, separated
1 c. sifted flour	1 tblsp. grated lemon peel
¼ c. butter or regular margarine	¼ c. lemon juice
1 c. sugar	1 c. milk

To make crust, soften ⅓ c. butter with confectioners sugar; blend in 1 c. flour. Press mixture into bottom of ungreased 9″ square pan. Bake in moderate oven (350°) 12 minutes.

To make filling, cream together ¼ c. butter, sugar and ¼ c. flour. Beat in egg yolks, lemon peel and juice. Blend in milk.

Beat egg whites until they stand in peaks (stiff, but not dry). Fold into filling mixture and pour into baked crust.

Bake in moderate oven (350°) 35 to 40 minutes, or until deep golden brown. Cool in pan on rack and cut in 2 x 1″ bars. Makes 3 dozen.

GOLDEN LEMON PIE-BARS

Crisp crust holds tart-sweet filling—a treat for lemon pie fans

1⅓ c. sifted flour	1 c. sugar
½ tsp. salt	2 tblsp. flour
½ c. shortening	2 eggs
2 to 3 tblsp. water	1 tblsp. grated lemon peel
⅓ c. butter	¼ c. lemon juice

To make crust, mix 1⅓ c. flour with salt; cut in shortening to form particles the size of small peas. Set aside ⅓ c. mixture for topping. To the remainder add water gradually, while stirring with a fork, until dough is moist enough to hold together.

Roll dough out on floured surface to make a 10″ square. Fit into ungreased 9″ square pan.

To make filling, cream butter with sugar. Blend in 2 tblsp. flour, eggs, lemon peel and juice. Pour into pastry-lined pan. Sprinkle top with reserved ⅓ c. crust mixture.

Bake in hot oven (400°) 30 to 35 minutes, or until golden. Cool in pan on rack. Cut in 1½″ squares. Makes 3 dozen.

MINCEMEAT PIE-BARS

For a holiday dessert cut in 3- or 4-inch bars, top with ice cream

2½ c. sifted flour	5 to 6 tblsp. water
1 tsp. salt	2 c. prepared mincemeat
1 c. shortening	2 tblsp. sugar (for tops)

Combine flour and salt; cut in shortening until particles are the size of small peas. Gradually add water, while stirring with a fork, until dough is moist enough to hold together.

Divide dough in half. Roll one part on floured surface to make a 14 x 9″ rectangle. Place on ungreased baking sheet. Spread mincemeat to within ½″ of edges.

Roll remaining half of dough to 14 x 9″ rectangle. Place on top of mincemeat; seal edges with a fork. Prick top generously with fork. Sprinkle with sugar.

Bake in hot oven (400°) 25 to 30 minutes, or until golden brown. Serve warm or cold, cut in 2″ (about) squares. Makes 28.

PECAN PIE-BARS

To serve these luscious cookies for dessert, top with whipped cream

½ c. butter	2 tblsp. flour
1¼ c. sifted flour	3 eggs
¼ c. sugar	1 tsp. vanilla
½ c. brown sugar, firmly packed	¼ tsp. salt
1 c. light or dark corn syrup	½ to 1 c. chopped pecans

To make crust, cut butter with 1¼ c. flour and sugar until particles are fine like cornmeal. Press into bottom of ungreased 9" square pan. Bake in moderate oven (350°) 15 minutes.

Combine remaining ingredients in mixing bowl, beating until well blended. Pour over partially baked crust in pan.

Bake in moderate oven (350°) 30 to 35 minutes, or until golden brown and knife inserted in center comes out clean. Cool in pan on rack. Cut in 1½" squares. Makes 3 dozen.

Variation

Chocolate Pecan Pie-Bars: Make like Pecan Pie-Bars, but in filling use light corn syrup and add 2 (1 oz.) envelopes no-melt unsweetened chocolate, or 2 squares unsweetened chocolate, melted. Bake 35 minutes after pouring filling into crust.

PUMPKIN PIE SQUARES

Serve these pumpkin squares with coffee for a perfect dessert after a big meal or for evening refreshments that will be talked about

1 c. sifted flour	¾ c. sugar
½ c. quick-cooking rolled oats	½ tsp. salt
½ c. brown sugar, firmly packed	1 tsp. ground cinnamon
½ c. butter or regular margarine	½ tsp. ground ginger
1 (1 lb.) can pumpkin (2 c.)	¼ tsp. ground cloves
1 (13½ oz.) can evaporated milk	½ c. chopped pecans
	½ c. brown sugar, firmly packed
2 eggs	2 tblsp. butter

Combine flour, rolled oats, ½ c. brown sugar and ½ c. butter in mixing bowl. Mix until crumbly, using electric mixer on low speed. Press into ungreased 13 x 9 x 2" pan. Bake in moderate oven (350°) 15 minutes.

Combine pumpkin, evaporated milk, eggs, white sugar, salt and spices in mixing bowl; beat well. Pour into baked crust. Bake in moderate oven (350°) 20 minutes.

Combine pecans, ½ c. brown sugar and 2 tblsp. butter; sprinkle over pumpkin filling. Return to oven and bake 15 to 20 minutes, or until filling is set. Cool in pan on rack and cut in 2" (about) squares. Makes 2 dozen.

DANISH RAISIN PIE-BAR COOKIES

Cookies have luscious soft filling—serve with a fork, if you like

1 c. butter or regular margarine	2 c. sifted flour
1½ c. sugar	½ tsp. salt
3 eggs	1 (1 lb. 6 oz.) can raisin pie
1 tsp. vanilla	filling (2 c.)

Beat butter with sugar until light and fluffy. Beat in eggs and vanilla to mix well.

Sift together flour and salt; add a little at a time to creamed mixture, beating after each addition. Divide dough in half. Spread one half in greased 15½ x 10½ x 1" jelly roll pan. Carefully spread raisin pie filling evenly over dough.

Drop remaining half of dough over filling with spoon or cake decorator to form a lattice (lattice spreads in the baking). Bake in moderate oven (350°) 28 to 30 minutes, or until golden. Set pan on rack to cool, then cut in 2½ x 1" bars. Cookies are best served the same day they are baked, or frozen. Makes 5 dozen.

RAISIN CREAM PIE-BARS

Tasty cookies are rich like raisin cream pie, so cut into small bars

½ c. butter	2 c. ground raisins
1¼ c. sifted flour	½ c. sugar
½ c. quick-cooking rolled oats	1 c. light cream
½ c. brown sugar, firmly packed	¼ tsp. salt
¼ tsp. salt	1 tblsp. lemon juice

To make crust, combine butter, flour, rolled oats, brown sugar and ¼ tsp. salt; mix until crumbly. Press 2 c. mixture into bottom of ungreased 9" square pan. Set aside remainder of crumb mixture for topping.

To make filling, combine raisins, sugar, cream and ¼ tsp. salt. Cook, stirring, until thick. Remove from heat and stir in lemon juice. Spread over crust in pan. Top with reserved crumb mixture.

Bake in moderate oven (375°) 35 to 40 minutes, or until golden brown. Cool in pan on rack. Cut in 1½" squares. Makes 3 dozen.

SOUR CREAM/RAISIN PIE-BARS

Praises skyrocket for these cookies inspired by sour cream raisin pie

1½ c. sifted flour	¾ c. sugar
½ tsp. salt	1 tblsp. flour
⅓ c. shortening	1 tsp. ground cinnamon
¼ c. butter or regular margarine	¼ tsp. ground nutmeg
2 to 3 tblsp. water	⅛ tsp. ground cloves
1 c. dairy sour cream	½ c. seedless raisins
2 eggs	¼ c. brown sugar, firmly packed

Mix 1½ c. flour with salt; cut in shortening and butter until particles are the size of small peas. Set aside ⅔ c. mixture for topping.

To remaining mixture, gradually add water, while stirring with a fork, until dough is just moist enough to hold together. Roll out on floured surface to make a 10" square; fit into ungreased 9" square pan.

Combine dairy sour cream, eggs, sugar, 1 tblsp. flour, spices and raisins; beat well to blend. Pour into pastry-lined pan.

Blend brown sugar into reserved crumb mixture; sprinkle over filling. Bake in moderate oven (375°) 30 to 35 minutes, or until light golden brown. Cool in pan on rack. Cut in 1½" squares. Makes 3 dozen.

NOTE: The filling has a custard base. Store cookies in refrigerator if not used soon after baking and cooling.

Ready-Made Cookies

When you're too busy to bake cookies and the supply in the freezer has vanished, depend on packaged cookies from the supermarket to serve when company comes. Just transform the basic cookies with your own special touches and they will have both a homemade taste and also appearance.

Take Marshmallow Gingersnaps. All you do to glamorize the crisp, spicy cookies is to lay marshmallow halves on them and broil about 5 minutes. Then you spread on a speedy orange confectioners sugar frosting. They're yummy and easy to fix.

Flat oatmeal cookies respond kindly to dress-ups. For our Date Betweens, put the cookies together in pairs with a quickly cooked date filling for pleasing sandwiches.

Another type of store cookie you can personalize speedily is short-bread. For Fudge Shortbread Squares you arrange the square short-bread cookies in a pan, spoon on a fast-fix chocolate frosting and chill in the refrigerator until set. Then you cut them into 2" bars.

You can accomplish so much with vanilla wafers plus imagination in so few minutes. Try Chocolate-Coated Wafers for an adventure in rapid cooking. After a few tries at "dress-ups," you'll be ready to branch out on your own in personalizing the cookies you buy.

Keep a few packages in the cupboard to fix up in a jiffy when you need something delicious to serve with tea, coffee, a fruit drink or ice cream. If friends telephone to say they're coming over, you can have a plate of pretty cookies ready for thoughtful hospitality by the time they arrive. They'll be impressed.

MARSHMALLOW GINGERSNAPS

Gingersnaps taste great topped with marshmallows, orange icing

15 regular marshmallows, halved   1 tsp. grated orange peel
30 gingersnaps   1 tblsp. butter
1 c. confectioners sugar   1 to 2 tblsp. orange juice

Place a marshmallow half, cut side down, on each gingersnap. Arrange on ungreased baking sheet and put in very slow oven (200°) 5 minutes. Remove from oven and press marshmallows down slightly.

Combine confectioners sugar, orange peel and butter, and add orange juice until of spreading consistency. Beat until smooth. Spread over marshmallow-topped gingersnaps. Makes 2½ dozen.

ORANGE/COCONUT TOPPERS

Orange/coconut top complements the spicy flavor of gingersnaps

2 tblsp. butter   2 tsp. grated orange peel
½ c. sugar   1 tblsp. orange juice
½ c. flaked coconut   4 dozen gingersnaps

Melt butter in small saucepan; stir in sugar, coconut, orange peel and juice. Spread a scant teaspoonful on each gingersnap, almost to edges.

Arrange on ungreased baking sheet and bake in very hot oven (450°) 5 minutes, or until topping is bubbly. Remove cookies and cool on racks. Makes 4 dozen.

DATE BETWEENS

Orange/date filling between oatmeal cookies makes a real treat

½ c. cut-up dates   2 tblsp. sugar
⅓ c. orange juice or water   40 small flat oatmeal cookies
1 tsp. grated orange peel
   (optional)

Combine dates, orange juice, orange peel and sugar in small saucepan. Cook over medium heat, stirring constantly, until thick.

Put cookies together in pairs with about 1 tsp. date filling between. Makes 20.

Variation

Date-Filled Specials: Substitute small flat butter cookies or vanilla wafers for the oatmeal cookies.

OATMEAL TOSCAS

Bake these cookies with Swedish almond topping only 5 minutes

¼ c. sugar	½ c. sliced almonds
1 tsp. flour	⅛ tsp. almond extract
2 tblsp. light cream or milk	2 dozen flat oatmeal cookies
2 tblsp. butter	

In a small saucepan combine sugar and flour; stir to mix. Add cream and butter. Bring to a full boil, stirring constantly. Remove from heat and stir in almond slices and almond extract. Place a teaspoonful on center of each oatmeal cookie. Place cookies on ungreased baking sheet.

Bake in very hot oven (450°) 5 minutes, or until topping is bubbly. Cool cookies on racks. Makes 2 dozen.

FUDGE SHORTBREAD SQUARES

Quick and easy fudge on shortbread cookies makes them festive

16 shortbread square cookies	1 (6 oz.) pkg. semisweet
½ c. sweetened condensed milk	chocolate pieces
(not evaporated)	½ c. chopped nuts
	½ tsp. vanilla

Arrange cookies in bottom of lightly greased 8″ square pan.

Cook condensed milk and chocolate pieces over low heat, stirring occasionally, until thick, smooth and shiny. Stir in nuts and vanilla. Spoon over cookies in pan; carefully spread to cover. (You can sprinkle 2 shortbread cookies, crumbled, over top if you wish.) Refrigerate until set.

Cut in 2″ squares to serve. Makes 16.

PEANUT/DATE SHORTIES

Date/peanut filling on shortbread cookies, topped with chocolate

½ c. peanut butter
2 tblsp. butter
1 c. cut-up dates
1 c. confectioners sugar
36 shortbread cookies

½ c. semisweet chocolate pieces
2 tblsp. butter
2 tblsp. milk
½ c. confectioners sugar

Combine peanut butter, 2 tblsp. butter, dates and 1 c. confectioners sugar; add a few drops of milk if necessary to mix. Place 1 teaspoonful of mixture on each cookie.

Melt chocolate pieces and 2 tblsp. butter in milk by heating over hot water. Stir in ½ c. confectioners sugar and beat until smooth and shiny. (Add more milk if necessary.)

Dip tops of cookies in chocolate frosting. Spread on racks until chocolate hardens. Makes 3 dozen.

AUSTRIAN TORTELETTES

Jelly spread between cookies and frosting is a tasty surprise

¼ c. red jelly or jam (about)
36 shortbread square cookies
(10 oz. pkg.)
¼ c. sliced filberts

½ c. sugar
2 tblsp. milk
2 tblsp. butter
½ c. semisweet chocolate pieces

Spread about ½ tsp. jelly over top of each cookie. Sprinkle with filberts.

Combine sugar, milk and butter in small saucepan. Bring to a boil; boil 1 minute. Remove from heat and stir in chocolate pieces. Continue to stir until smooth and of spreading consistency. If mixture is not smooth and shiny, thin with a few drops of milk. Spread on tops of cookies. Additional sliced filberts may be scattered over tops of cookies before chocolate hardens. Makes 3 dozen.

Variation

Peanut Prizes: Omit jelly and filberts. Top each cookie with 1 tsp. peanut butter, then spread on chocolate mixture.

CARAMEL SUNDAE COOKIES

These quick-fix cookies will become favorites at your house

14 caramels (¼ lb.)
2 tblsp. light cream or dairy
    half-and-half
2 tblsp. butter
½ c. confectioners sugar
¼ c. chopped nuts

⅛ tsp. peppermint extract
    (optional)
4 dozen vanilla wafers
½ c. milk chocolate pieces
1 tblsp. shortening

Melt together over hot water caramels, cream and butter. Stir in confectioners sugar, nuts and peppermint extract. Place a scant teaspoonful on top each vanilla wafer.

Melt chocolate pieces and shortening over hot water. Stir to mix and spoon a small amount on top of caramel-topped wafers. Makes 4 dozen.

N O T E : Double the recipe for caramel mixture and chocolate topping for 1 (10 to 12 oz.) pkg. vanilla wafers.

Variations

Chocolate/Caramel Sundae Cookies: Substitute small chocolate cookies for the vanilla wafers.
Shortbread/Caramel Sundae Cookies: Substitute shortbread cookies for the vanilla wafers.
Butter Cookie/Caramel Sundae: Substitute small butter cookies for the vanilla wafers.

CHERRY/CHOCOLATE CREAMS

Maraschino cherries nestle in creamy fondant under the glaze

1 egg white
2 tblsp. maraschino cherry
    juice
4 c. confectioners sugar
4½ dozen vanilla wafers

27 maraschino cherries, halved
    and well drained
1 (6 oz.) pkg. milk chocolate
    pieces
¼ c. maraschino cherry juice
2 tblsp. shortening

Beat together egg white, 2 tblsp. maraschino cherry juice and confectioners sugar. (Add a few drops of milk if too thick.) Place a teaspoonful of this fondant on top each vanilla wafer; press a cherry half, cut side down, on top.

To make glaze, melt together milk chocolate pieces, ¼ c. maraschino cherry juice and shortening in small saucepan. Stir until smooth. Place ½ tsp. glaze on top each cherry half on cookie, allowing it to run down on fondant topping. Makes 4½ dozen.

CHOCOLATE-COATED WAFERS

Fix vanilla wafers this way when you're having discerning guests

1 (6 oz.) pkg. mint or semisweet chocolate pieces	4 dozen vanilla wafers
2 tblsp. shortening	Cookie coconut or chopped nuts (optional)
2 tblsp. shaved paraffin	

Melt together chocolate pieces, shortening and paraffin over hot water. Stir to blend.

Dip vanilla wafers, one at a time, in chocolate mixture to coat. Lift out with 2 forks, allowing excess chocolate to drip off. Let harden on racks. If desired, decorate tops of wafers before topping hardens with cookie coconut, or with chopped nuts. Makes 4 dozen.

Variation

Butterscotch Favorites: Substitute butterscotch pieces for the chocolate pieces.

CHOCOLATE RUM BALLS

Cookies prettied up like this look and taste like chocolate candy

2 tblsp. butter	4 dozen vanilla wafers
1 c. confectioners sugar	½ c. milk chocolate pieces
1 to 2 tblsp. milk	1 tblsp. shortening
½ to 1 tsp. rum extract	1 tblsp. shaved paraffin

Melt butter in small saucepan over medium heat to a delicate brown. Blend in confectioners sugar. Gradually add milk until of spreading consistency. Stir in rum extract.

Spread mixture generously on bottom sides of half of vanilla wafers. Top with remaining half of cookies, bottom side down.

Melt milk chocolate pieces with shortening and paraffin over hot water; stir to blend. Drop cookie sandwiches into chocolate. Coat on both sides and lift out with 2 forks, letting excess chocolate drop off. Cool on racks. Makes 2 dozen.

MINT STUFFIES

Plain vanilla wafers, dressed up, become pretty party fare

3 tblsp. butter

2 c. confectioners sugar

2 tblsp. crème de menthe, or
½ tsp. peppermint extract and
a few drops green food color

1 to 2 tblsp. milk

4 dozen vanilla wafers

½ c. semisweet mint chocolate
pieces

1 tblsp. shortening

Combine butter, confectioners sugar, crème de menthe and enough milk to make frosting of spreading consistency. Put 1 scant teaspoonful of mixture on each vanilla wafer.

Melt mint chocolate pieces and shortening over hot water. Spoon over frosted vanilla wafers. Let cookies cool before serving. Makes 4 dozen.

PARTY-GOERS

Picture-pretty cookies. Gelatin both tints and flavors coconut

1 (3 oz.) pkg. strawberry flavor
gelatin

⅔ c. sweetened condensed milk
(not evaporated)

2⅓ c. flaked coconut (7 oz.)

2 tblsp. butter

3 tblsp. milk

3 tblsp. sugar

1 c. confectioners sugar

3 dozen vanilla wafers

Reserve 1 tblsp. gelatin for frosting; combine remaining gelatin and sweetened condensed milk. Stir in coconut. Refrigerate 1 to 2 hours.

To make frosting, combine reserved 1 tblsp. gelatin, butter, milk and white sugar; boil 2 minutes. Stir in confectioners sugar.

Shape chilled coconut mixture into ¾" balls; press one ball firmly down on each vanilla wafer. Spread frosting over topping and cookie. It may be necessary to thin frosting with a few drops of water while spreading on cookies. Makes 3 dozen.

NOTE: You can substitute gelatin of other flavors and colors, such as raspberry, cherry, lime, orange and lemon, for the strawberry flavor gelatin.

BOYS' SPECIAL

You can make one snack cookie sandwich using the ingredients given here—or you can make them by the dozen on short notice

1 tsp. peanut butter

2 flat unfilled cookies (large butter cookies, chocolate chip, etc.)

4 or 5 miniature marshmallows

6 to 8 semisweet chocolate pieces

Spread a thin layer of peanut butter on bottom side of a flat cookie. Top with marshmallows and chocolate pieces.

Broil until marshmallows are puffy and chocolate pieces appear melted. Top with another cookie, bottom side down. Makes 1 cookie sandwich.

CHILDREN'S SPECIAL

Their favorites combined—marshmallows, chocolate, peanut butter

½ c. peanut butter

24 chocolate chip or chocolate cookies

12 marshmallows, halved

1 square semisweet chocolate

1 tblsp. butter

1 tblsp. milk

1 c. confectioners sugar

Spread 1 tsp. peanut butter in center of each cookie top. Place a marshmallow half, cut side down, on peanut butter centers.

In small saucepan, melt chocolate and butter with milk over low heat, stirring constantly. Stir in confectioners sugar. Beat until smooth, adding a few drops of milk if necessary for spreading consistency. Spread over marshmallow-topped cookies. Makes 2 dozen.

CHOCOLATE/COCONUT RIBBONS

Ribbons of chocolate decorate coconut bar cookies—really delicious

1 (6 oz.) pkg. semisweet chocolate pieces

½ c. peanut butter

32 coconut bar cookies

Melt together over low heat, stirring constantly, chocolate pieces and peanut butter. Let stand until cool, but not set.

Arrange 4 coconut bars, in a single row with ends touching, on sheet of foil or waxed paper. Spread generously with the chocolate/peanut mixture.

Top with second layer of cookies, using half cookies at each end. Again spread with chocolate/peanut mixture. Repeat with third layer of cookies. Top with frosting, then a fourth layer of cookies.

Repeat procedure, using remaining 16 cookies. Wrap in foil or waxed paper and refrigerate several hours.

To serve, cut in ½″ slices with a sharp knife. Cookies slice easier the day they are made because chocolate hardens more if left longer. If not used, place sliced cookies on plate and slip into a plastic bag. Makes 32.

FROSTED FIG BARS

Glamorize tiny fig-filled cookies this easy way for your tea party

30 fig-filled bar cookies	1½ tblsp. orange juice
(1 lb.)	1 tsp. grated orange peel
2½ tblsp. butter	½ c. cookie coconut
1½ c. sifted confectioners sugar	

Cut cookie bars lengthwise in halves.

Combine butter, confectioners sugar, orange juice and orange peel. Beat until smooth.

Place coconut in shallow dish.

Hold a half cookie in one hand; spread top with frosting, using a small spatula. Dip cookie top in coconut. Place on waxed paper. Makes 5 dozen.

Variation

Snowy Topped Fig Bars: Follow recipe for Frosted Fig Bars, but omit orange juice and peel and in their place use 1½ tblsp. light cream or milk and ½ tsp. vanilla. (Add enough cream or milk to make frosting of spreading consistency.)

LAZY DAISY SUGAR COOKIES

Good family dessert: these cookies with broiled tops, and ice cream

2 tblsp. melted butter
½ c. brown sugar, firmly packed
1 tblsp. light cream or milk

½ c. cookie coconut or finely chopped nuts
12 large sugar cookies

Combine butter, sugar, cream and coconut. Spread a scant tablespoonful on each cookie.

Place cookies on ungreased baking sheet and broil until topping is bubbly. Remove cookies to rack to cool. Makes 1 dozen.

Cookies to Make from a Mix

A country cookie custom worthy of a wider adoption than it enjoys today is the use of a homemade cookie mix. Once you make it and have it on hand, it's no trick to bake a hurry-up batch of cookies. We give you recipes for a mix adapted to kitchens located in high country and two mixes for use in locations under 5,000 feet elevation.

BAKING COOKIES IN HIGH ALTITUDES

One of the easiest, quickest and most successful ways to bake good cookies if you live in a high altitude area is to use a reliable home-made mix. You can buy mixes in packages in mountainous regions that are adapted to high elevations, but it is an economy to make your own. Home economists at the Colorado State University Agricultural Experiment Station have developed a basic mix that is responsible for many of the best cookies that come from home ovens in high country. The recipe for it and for a variety of superior cookies made from it were evolved in the altitude laboratory where the various conditions due to different altitudes are simulated.*

Home economists at the Agricultural Experiment Station and women throughout the Western mountain region have told Farm Journal food editors about the pointers to heed in making the mix. They say it is important to follow the directions with precision because at high altitudes recipes are more sensitive to slight changes than in lower places. Here are some of their suggestions: Measure accurately. Use the ingredients specified; substitutions will disappoint you. Be sure to use hydrogenated shortening, which is available in practically all food markets. It's a good idea to have all the ingredients at room temperature before you start combining them. (You will

* From *Cookie Recipes from a Basic Mix for High Altitudes* by Dr. Ferne Bowman and Dr. Edna Page, Colorado State University.

notice that baking powder is the variable ingredient in the following recipe. The amount for your altitude is given in a table that follows the recipe.)

COLORADO BASIC COOKIE MIX

9 c. sifted flour	1 tblsp. salt
3 c. instant nonfat dry milk powder	4 c. hydrogenated shortening
Baking powder (see table below)	4 c. sugar

Combine flour, dry milk powder, baking powder and salt. Sift together twice.

Soften shortening in 6-qt. (or larger) bowl with electric mixer at medium speed, or with large wooden spoon. Gradually add sugar, beating constantly, until mixture is light and fluffy.

Gradually add dry ingredients, blending them into mixture with electric mixer at low speed, or cut them in with pastry blender as for pie crust. Mixture will resemble coarse cornmeal.

Store in large covered container at room temperature. Mix will keep for several weeks. To use, stir with fork before measuring, then lightly spoon mix into measuring cup and level with straight edge of knife or spatula—do not pack it. Makes about 19 cups.

Amount of Baking Powder to Use

At 5,000 feet—3 tblsp.

At 7,500 feet—2 tblsp. plus ¾ tsp.

At 10,000 feet—1 tblsp. plus 1½ tsp.

If the altitude at which you live is not exactly 5,000, 7,500 or 10,-000 feet, use the one nearest to your altitude. For example, if your elevation is 6,000 feet, use the baking powder indicated for 5,000 feet.

FAVORITE COOKIES FROM THE BASIC MIX

Here are recipes for some of the best liked cookies made with the Colorado Basic Cookie Mix. Women in high country say they prefer to make comparatively small- or medium-size batches because the cookies are so quick to mix and bake. They like to serve them fresh and fragrant from the oven.

BROWNIES 1

6 squares semisweet chocolate	¼ c. water
2 c. Colorado Basic Cookie Mix	2 tsp. vanilla
2 eggs	½ c. chopped walnuts

Melt chocolate over hot water.

Combine all ingredients and blend thoroughly. Spread in greased and floured 9″ square pan and bake in moderate oven (350°) 25 to 30 minutes. Set pan on rack; when slightly cool, cut in 2 x 1½″ bars. Makes about 2 dozen.

BROWNIES 2

2 squares unsweetened chocolate	¼ c. water
2 c. Colorado Basic Cookie Mix	2 tsp. vanilla
2 eggs	½ c. chopped walnuts
½ c. brown sugar, firmly packed	

Melt chocolate over hot water.

Blend all ingredients thoroughly. Spread in greased and floured 9″ square pan and bake in moderate oven (350°) 25 to 30 minutes. Set pan on rack; when slightly cool, cut in 2 x 1½″ bars. Makes about 2 dozen.

CHEWY DATE/NUT BARS

3 c. Colorado Basic Cookie Mix	1 tsp. vanilla
2 tblsp. water	1 c. chopped dates
2 eggs	1 c. coarsely chopped walnuts
¼ c. brown sugar, firmly packed	

Blend all ingredients thoroughly. Spread in greased 13 x 9 x 2″ pan.

Bake in moderate oven (350°) 35 to 40 minutes. Cool in pan on rack, then cut in 2 x 1″ bars. Makes about 4 dozen.

CRISPY BARS

2 c. Colorado Basic Cookie Mix

¼ c. brown sugar, firmly packed

2 eggs

¼ tsp. salt

¾ c. brown sugar, firmly packed

1 tsp. vanilla

1 c. shredded or flaked coconut

1 c. oven-toasted rice cereal

1 c. broken walnuts

Combine cookie mix and ¼ c. brown sugar. Press into greased 9" square pan.

Beat eggs until frothy; add salt. Gradually add ¾ c. brown sugar, beating until thick. Add vanilla, coconut, cereal and nuts. Mix thoroughly. Spread over layer in pan.

Bake in slow oven (325°) 25 to 30 minutes. Cool in pan on rack, then cut in 2 x 1½" bars. Makes about 2 dozen.

DATE LAYER BARS

3 c. Colorado Basic Cookie Mix

1¾ c. quick-cooking rolled oats

1 lb. chopped dates

1 tblsp. lemon juice

1½ c. water

¼ c. brown sugar, firmly packed

2 tblsp. water

Combine cookie mix and rolled oats. Press 2½ c. of mixture into greased 13 x 9 x 2" pan.

Combine dates, lemon juice and 1½ c. water; cook over low heat until mixture is the consistency of thin jam. Spread over crumb layer in pan.

Blend brown sugar and 2 tblsp. water into remaining crumb mixture. Sprinkle over date mixture in pan and press down lightly.

Bake in moderate oven (350°) 30 to 35 minutes. Cool in pan on rack, then cut in 2 x 1" bars. Makes about 4 dozen.

PECAN BARS

2¼ c. Colorado Basic Cookie Mix

2 tblsp. water

3 eggs

1 c. brown sugar, firmly packed

½ tsp. vanilla

1 c. chopped pecans

Blend 2 c. cookie mix, water and 1 egg thoroughly. Spread in greased 13 x 9 x 2" pan. Bake in moderate oven (375°) 8 to 10 minutes.

To make topping, beat 2 eggs until foamy. Add brown sugar, ¼ c. cookie mix and vanilla. Blend thoroughly. Stir in nuts. Spread over baked layer.

Return to moderate oven (350°) and bake 20 to 25 minutes. Cool in pan on rack, then cut in 2 x 1″ bars. Makes about 4 dozen.

CHERRY DROPS

3 c. Colorado Basic Cookie Mix
2 eggs

½ c. coarsely chopped drained maraschino cherries
½ c. chopped pecans

Blend cookie mix and eggs. Add cherries and nuts. Drop by teaspoonfuls about 2″ apart onto ungreased baking sheet.

Bake in moderate oven (375°) 10 to 12 minutes. Remove cookies and cool on rack. Makes 3½ to 4 dozen.

CHOCOLATE DROPS

2 c. Colorado Basic Cookie Mix
3 tblsp. cocoa
1 egg

2 tblsp. water
1 tsp. vanilla
½ c. chopped walnuts

Blend all ingredients thoroughly. Drop by teaspoonfuls about 2″ apart onto ungreased baking sheet.

Bake in moderate oven (375°) 10 to 14 minutes. Remove cookies and cool on racks. Makes 3 dozen.

CHOCOLATE CHIP COOKIES

4 c. Colorado Basic Cookie Mix
1 egg
2 tblsp. water
1½ tsp. vanilla

¼ c. brown sugar, firmly packed
1 (6 oz.) pkg. semisweet chocolate pieces
1 c. chopped walnuts

Blend all ingredients thoroughly. Drop by teaspoonfuls about 2″ apart onto ungreased baking sheet.

Bake in moderate oven (375°) 10 to 13 minutes. Remove cookies and cool on racks. Makes 5 dozen.

CRISP CHOCOLATE DROPS

4 squares semisweet chocolate   1 tsp. vanilla
2 c. Colorado Basic Cookie Mix   ½ c. chopped nuts
2 tblsp. water

Melt chocolate over hot water.

Blend all ingredients thoroughly. Drop by teaspoonfuls about 2" apart onto ungreased baking sheet.

Bake in moderate oven (375°) 10 to 12 minutes. Remove cookies and cool on racks. Makes 3 to 3½ dozen.

COCONUT COOKIES SUPREME

2 c. Colorado Basic Cookie Mix   1 tsp. vanilla
1 egg   ½ c. shredded coconut
2 tblsp. water   ½ c. chopped walnuts

Blend all ingredients thoroughly. Drop by teaspoonfuls about 2" apart onto lightly greased baking sheet.

Bake in moderate oven (375°) 12 to 15 minutes. Remove cookies and cool on racks. Makes 3 dozen.

LEMON DROPS

2 c. Colorado Basic Cookie Mix   1 tblsp. lemon juice
1 egg   1½ tsp. grated lemon peel

Blend all ingredients thoroughly. Drop by teaspoonfuls about 2" apart onto ungreased baking sheet.

Bake in moderate oven (375°) 10 to 12 minutes. Remove cookies and cool on racks. Makes 2½ dozen.

MINCEMEAT COOKIES

2 c. Colorado Basic Cookie Mix   ½ tsp. vanilla
½ c. prepared mincemeat   1 tblsp. water
1 egg   ½ c. chopped walnuts

Blend all ingredients thoroughly. Drop by teaspoonfuls about 2" apart onto ungreased baking sheet.

Bake in moderate oven (375°) 10 to 12 minutes. Remove cookies and cool on racks. Makes 3 to 4 dozen.

OATMEAL COOKIES

1 c. raisins	½ tsp. ground allspice
2 c. Colorado Basic Cookie Mix	1 egg
1 c. quick-cooking rolled oats	1½ tsp. vanilla
2 tblsp. brown sugar	½ c. chopped walnuts
½ tsp. ground cinnamon	

Cover raisins with water and simmer 5 minutes. Drain, reserving ½ c. raisin water.

Blend raisins and reserved ½ c. raisin water with remaining ingredients thoroughly. Drop by teaspoonfuls about 2" apart onto ungreased baking sheet.

Bake in moderate oven (375°) 13 to 15 minutes. Remove cookies and cool on racks. Makes 3½ to 4 dozen.

CINNAMON COOKIES

2½ c. Colorado Basic Cookie Mix	1 tsp. vanilla
½ c. sugar	1½ tsp. ground cinnamon
1 egg	¼ c. finely chopped nuts

Combine cookie mix, sugar, egg and vanilla; blend thoroughly. Combine cinnamon and nuts.

Form dough into small balls, about 1" in diameter; roll in cinnamon-nut mixture. Place 2" apart on ungreased baking sheet.

Bake in moderate oven (375°) 12 to 15 minutes. Remove cookies and cool on racks. Makes 3½ dozen.

MOLASSES COOKIES

4 c. Colorado Basic Cookie Mix	½ tsp. ground ginger
¼ tsp. ground cloves	1 egg
½ tsp. ground cinnamon	¼ c. molasses

Blend all ingredients thoroughly. Refrigerate dough 1 hour.

Form dough into small balls, about 1" in diameter; place 1 to 2" apart on lightly greased baking sheet. Flatten cookies with bottom of glass covered with damp cloth.

Bake in moderate oven (375°) 8 to 10 minutes. Remove cookies and cool on racks. Makes 5 to 6 dozen.

PEANUT BUTTER COOKIES

4 c. Colorado Basic Cookie Mix   1 egg
½ c. brown sugar, firmly packed   1½ tsp. vanilla
1 c. peanut butter   1 tblsp. water

Blend all ingredients thoroughly. Form dough into small balls, about 1″ in diameter, and place 1 to 2″ apart on ungreased baking sheet. Flatten cookies with tines of fork.

Bake in moderate oven (375°) 10 to 12 minutes. Remove cookies and cool on racks. Makes 7 dozen.

THUMBPRINTS

1 (3 oz.) pkg. cream cheese   9 drained maraschino cherries,
2 c. Colorado Basic Cookie Mix   cut in fourths
¾ tsp. vanilla   Jelly or tinted frosting
1 egg white, slightly beaten   (optional)
¾ c. finely chopped nuts

Soften cream cheese. Add cookie mix and vanilla and blend thoroughly. Form dough into small balls, about 1″ in diameter. Dip into egg white, then roll in nuts. Place 1 to 2″ apart on greased baking sheet and press top of each cookie with thumb.

Bake in moderate oven (350°) 5 minutes, or until puffy. Remove from oven and quickly press top of each cookie with thumb to make indentation.

Return to oven and bake about 10 minutes longer. Place cookies on racks to cool. Place a maraschino cherry quarter or a bit of jelly or tinted frosting in center of each cookie. Makes 2½ to 3 dozen.

SUGAR COOKIES

3 c. Colorado Basic Cookie Mix   ½ tsp. almond extract, or
1 egg   ¾ tsp. vanilla
   Sugar

Blend all ingredients thoroughly. Roll dough ⅛ to ¼″ thick and cut with a round cookie cutter the size you like, or have. (Chill the dough 2 to 3 hours or overnight before rolling if it is difficult to handle.) Place 1 to 2″ apart on ungreased baking sheet.

Bake in moderate oven (375°) 8 to 10 minutes. Place cookies on racks to cool. Sprinkle with sugar, or decorate as desired. Makes 3 dozen.

COOKIE STARTER

This mix is versatile. We give you seven good cookies to make with it

2¼ c. sifted flour
¾ tsp. salt
1 c. butter or regular margarine

Sift flour and salt into bowl.
Cut in butter until mixture resembles coarse bread crumbs.
Store in clean jar with tight-fitting lid. Keep in refrigerator or freezer. Makes 3 to 4 cups.

Tips on using mix

Let the crumbs reach room temperature before adding other ingredients. Loosen with a fork if mix is too compact. Your electric mixer can help you make cookie dough from the mix.

To short-cut cookie making, shape dough into roll; wrap and chill thoroughly. Slice and bake cookies as desired. When dough is cold, allow more time for baking. To get a thicker cookie, shape teaspoonfuls of dough with fingers and roll in palms of hands into balls; stamp with flat-bottomed glass and bake.

When you bake and then freeze, wrap cookies in foil or plastic wrap, or store them in freezer containers.

OLD ENGLISH GINGER CONES

If cookies break in rolling, return them to oven for 1 minute

1 c. Cookie Starter
¼ tsp. baking soda
1½ tsp. ground ginger
¼ tsp. ground nutmeg
¼ tsp. ground cinnamon

¼ c. dark brown sugar, firmly packed
1 tblsp. dark molasses
1 tblsp. buttermilk
Sifted confectioners sugar

Combine all ingredients, except confectioners sugar, and mix well. Form dough into ball; chill 2 hours.
Shape in 1" balls. Roll in confectioners sugar, then pat very thin with glass dipped in confectioners sugar. Place 3" apart on greased baking sheet.

Bake in moderate oven (350°) 4 minutes.

Remove cookies while still hot. Twist over wooden spoon handle and sprinkle with sugar. Cool on racks. Makes 1½ dozen.

BLIND DATES

You shape and bake dough around dates—add charm to cookie tray

1 (3 oz.) pkg. cream cheese (room temperature)	2 tblsp. confectioners sugar
	24 pitted dates
1 c. Cookie Starter	Sifted confectioners sugar
½ tsp. vanilla	

Combine first 4 ingredients. Form into four balls.

Chill dough 2 hours.

Work with one ball at a time, and roll ⅛" thick on board dusted with confectioners sugar.

Cut in rounds with 2½" cutter.

Place date in center of each round. (Date may be stuffed with nut, or use ½ date and 1 nut.) Fold edges over and pinch ends to points.

Place 1" apart on lightly greased baking sheet, seam side down. Bake in moderate oven (350°) 10 to 12 minutes.

Sprinkle with confectioners sugar. Remove cookies and cool on racks. Makes 2 dozen.

ICE CREAM WAFERS

Wonderful ice cream accompaniment! Wafers are thin and crisp

1 c. Cookie Starter	⅓ c. sugar
½ tsp. vanilla	½ tsp. baking powder
1 egg yolk	Sifted confectioners sugar

Mix all ingredients, except confectioners sugar.

Chill dough thoroughly.

Sprinkle board and rolling pin with confectioners sugar. Roll small amount of dough ⅛" thick.

Cut with small cookie cutter and place 1" apart on greased baking sheet. Bake in moderate oven (350°) about 6 minutes, until cookies are lightly browned.

Dust with confectioners sugar. Remove cookies and cool on racks, Makes 3 dozen.

Variations

Oriental Almond Cookies: Make up Ice Cream Wafers recipe, substituting ½ tsp. almond extract for the vanilla.

Chill dough until firm enough to handle, about 1 hour.

Shape into balls about 1" in diameter. Flatten with glass dipped in confectioners sugar.

Place cookies 3" apart on lightly greased baking sheet.

Beat egg white with fork. Brush a little on each cookie.

Decorate each cookie with slivered, blanched almonds to make flower.

Bake in moderate oven (350°) about 12 minutes. Remove cookies and cool on racks. Makes 2 dozen.

Orange and Lemon Wafers: Make up Ice Cream Wafers recipe omitting vanilla and adding grated peel of 1 orange and grated peel of ½ lemon.

Roll out and cut cookies into different shapes. Place 1" apart on lightly greased baking sheet. (Or roll into balls, using 1 teaspoon dough for each cookie. Dip fork into confectioners sugar and make waffle design by crisscrossing with fork. Don't mash cookies too flat.)

Bake in moderate oven (350°) 10 minutes. Decorate with strips of orange peel. Remove cookies and cool on racks. Makes 1½ dozen.

Sesame Cookies: Make Ice Cream Wafers recipe, substituting ¼ tsp. baking soda and ½ tsp. cream of tartar for baking powder. Add ½ c. toasted coconut and ¼ c. sesame seeds (if unavailable add another ¼ c. toasted coconut).

Mix ingredients well.

Shape dough into roll. Chill 15 minutes.

Slice ⅛" thick and place 1" apart on greased baking sheet. Bake in moderate oven (350°) 15 minutes, or until lightly browned. Remove cookies and cool on racks. Makes 2½ dozen.

NOTE: In Charleston, South Carolina, they're called Benne Cookies—benne is the colloquial name for sesame seeds.

Victorian Spice Cookies: Make up Ice Cream Wafers recipe using brown sugar instead of white, and ¼ tsp. baking soda instead of baking powder. Add ½ c. chopped walnuts, 1 tsp. cocoa, ⅛ tsp. ground nutmeg, ½ tsp. ground cinnamon and ¼ tsp. ground allspice.

Mix together all ingredients. Form into balls using 1 tsp. dough for each.

Put 1″ apart on greased baking sheet. Make hole in centers of cookies with fingertip. Place ¼ tsp. firm jelly in each hole.

Bake in moderate oven (350°) about 10 minutes, or until cookies are firm. Remove cookies and cool on racks. Makes 2½ dozen.

EIGHT-IN-ONE SUGAR COOKIES

Many women praised this mix when it appeared in Farm Journal

2 c. butter or regular margarine	6½ c. sifted flour
2 c. sugar	1 tblsp. cream of tartar
1 c. brown sugar, firmly packed	2 tsp. baking soda
4 eggs	¼ c. milk

Cream together butter and sugars until smooth and fluffy. Stir in unbeaten eggs, one at a time.

Sift together dry ingredients; add to creamed mixture alternately with milk. Mix thoroughly.

Divide dough in eight 1-cup lots. Wrap each tightly in foil or plastic wrap; freeze. Then place in plastic bag. To use, thaw dough just enough that you can shape or drop it. Place about 2″ apart on greased baking sheet and bake in moderate oven (375°) 10 to 15 minutes. Spread cookies on racks to cool. Mix makes 8 cups dough; each cup makes 2 to 3 dozen cookies, depending on the kind you bake.

N O T E : This dough, tightly wrapped, will keep several days in refrigerator. Freeze as recipe directs for longer storage.

Chocolate Chip Balls: Knead into 1 c. cookie dough, 1 tblsp. cocoa and ⅓ c. semisweet chocolate pieces. Shape into about 24 round balls; flatten slightly with spatula. Bake as directed.

Coconut/Almond Cookies: Knead into 1 c. cookie dough, 1 c. flaked coconut and ¼ tsp. almond extract. Shape into about 24 balls; place on greased baking sheet and press flat with spatula. Top each with a piece of candied cherry. Bake as directed.

Pecan Balls: Knead into 1 c. cookie dough, ½ c. finely chopped pecans and ¼ tsp. vanilla. Shape into 24 round balls. Bake as directed.

Ginger Cookie Balls: Stir into 1 c. cookie dough, 1 tblsp. dark molasses and ¼ to ½ tsp. ground ginger. Shape into about 24 balls (dip fingers occasionally in water so dough doesn't stick to hands). Bake as directed.

Gumdrop Cookie Balls: Mix into 1 c. cookie dough, ½ c. finely cut gumdrops (cut with scissors). Shape into 24 balls; crisscross with a fork. Bake as directed.

Fruit 'n Spice Drop Cookies: Stir into 1 c. cookie dough, ½ c. cooked and drained and chopped dried fruit, 2 tblsp. brown sugar, ¼ tsp. ground cinnamon and ⅛ tsp. ground cloves. Drop by teaspoonfuls 2″ apart onto greased baking sheet. Bake as directed. Makes 30.

Orange Wafers: Stir into 1 c. cookie dough, ¼ tsp. grated orange peel and ¼ c. sugar mixed with 4 tsp. orange juice. Drop by teaspoonfuls 2″ apart on greased baking sheet. Bake as directed. Makes 24 thin cookies.

Banana/Lemon Drops: Stir into 1 c. cookie dough, ¼ c. mashed ripe banana, ½ tsp. grated lemon peel and ¼ tsp. lemon juice. Drop 1 teaspoonful at a time into finely rolled corn flakes. Coat by turning gently with spoon. (Dough is very soft.) Place 2″ apart on greased baking sheet and bake as directed. Watch carefully so cookies do not scorch. Makes 2 dozen.

Cookies Children Will Love to Make

If your daughter has never baked cookies, you'll find easy-to-follow, step-by-step recipes in this section especially for beginning cooks. It's really *her* cookbook within *your* cookbook. They'll answer the questions she would otherwise have to ask you—will give her a feeling of independence and achievement. Let her use these recipes and she'll not have to bother Mother. What's more, she'll make good cookies.

After your youngster (boys like to bake cookies, too) has made these recipes successfully, she is ready to branch out and try other recipes on the preceding pages. We suggest, in a list preceding the Index, some of the easier ones that will appeal to young people.

The recipes in this section were developed in Farm Journal Countryside Test Kitchens especially for beginners in baking. We have taken them from our book for beginning cooks, Let's Start to Cook. These cookie recipes go into much more detail than the others and are easy to read and follow.

BAR COOKIES

These are the cookies that are easiest to bake. You spread the dough in a greased pan and bake it the way you bake cakes. Then you cut the cookie into squares or bars.

Here are some recipes for bar cookies almost everybody loves. So get out your measuring cup, mixing bowl and get going.

Do's for bar cookies

1. Do use the pan size the recipe recommends. If your pan is too large, the dough spreads thinner in the pan and it overbakes; the cookies will be tough and dry. If the pan is too small, the dough spreads too thick in it and the cookies may not bake through.

2. Do mix the dough the way the recipe directs. Overmixing gives bar cookies hard, crusty tops.

3. Do spread the dough evenly in the pan with a spatula or spoon so that all of it will bake in the same number of minutes.

4. Do watch the clock. When the time for baking is almost up, make the fingerprint test: When the cookies are lightly browned and a few minutes before the baking time is up, lightly press the top of the cookie with a fingertip. If your finger makes a slight dent or imprint that remains, the cookie is done. Overbaking makes cookies dry and crumbly.

5. Do cool the cookies in the pan at least 10 minutes before cutting. Cutting the bars while they are hot makes the cookies crumble.

FUDGE BROWNIES

For a surprise, frost these brownies with chocolate and white frostings and arrange like a checkerboard

2 (1-ounce) squares unsweetened chocolate	½ teaspoon salt
	1 cup sugar
⅓ cup soft shortening	2 eggs
¾ cup sifted flour	1 teaspoon vanilla
½ teaspoon baking powder	½ cup chopped or broken nuts

Start heating the oven to 350°. Lightly grease an 8 x 8 x 2-inch pan with unsalted shortening or salad oil.

Put the chocolate and shortening in the top of the double boiler and melt them over hot, not boiling, water. Or melt them in a small saucepan over low heat, watching all the time so chocolate won't burn. Cool until lukewarm.

Sift the flour onto a square of waxed paper or into a bowl and then measure. Sift the measured flour with the baking powder and salt. Set aside.

Beat the sugar and eggs together in a large bowl with a spoon, or with an electric mixer on medium speed, until light. If you use an electric mixer, stop the mixer two or three times and scrape sides of bowl with a rubber spatula.

Beat the cooled chocolate-shortening mixture and vanilla into the egg-sugar mixture. Stir in the flour mixture or beat it in with the electric mixer on low speed. Stir in the nuts and mix well. (If you like, you can divide the nuts in half. Stir ¼ cup into the cookie dough and sprinkle the other ¼ cup on top of dough in pan just before baking.)

Spread evenly in the greased pan with the back of a spoon or a spatula. Bake on the rack in the center of the oven 20 to 25 minutes. The crust on top will have a dull look when the cookie is done.

Remove the pan from the oven and set it on a wire rack to cool about 10 minutes, or until completely cooled, before cutting. Cut into 16 (2-inch) bars.

For a change

Before cutting the baked Brownies into squares or bars, sprinkle the top lightly with powdered sugar.

BROWNIES À LA MODE

Here's a dessert that you won't go wrong on if your friends or family are chocolate fans. (That means most Americans!) Bake the Fudge Brownies dough in a greased 9-inch round layer cake pan. Set the pan on a wire rack to cool. To serve, cut the cookie in pie-shaped pieces and top each triangle with vanilla ice cream. Pass a pitcher of chocolate sauce to pour over it. You can buy the sauce in a jar or can, or make it.

MAGIC PARTY SQUARES

The magic of these cookies is the way you frost them with milk chocolate candy bars. And their wonderful taste!

½ cup regular margarine or butter (¼ pound)	2 tablespoons water
	1 teaspoon vanilla
1 cup brown sugar, firmly packed	3 (1-ounce) milk chocolate
¾ cup sifted flour	candy bars
¾ cup quick-cooking rolled oats	¼ cup chopped nuts
1 egg	

Start heating the oven to 375°.

Put the margarine, brown sugar, flour and rolled oats in a medium bowl and mix well with a pastry blender. Be sure the margarine is evenly distributed. Add the egg, water and vanilla and beat with a spoon to mix thoroughly.

Spread evenly in an ungreased 9 x 9 x 2-inch pan with the back of a spoon or a spatula. Bake on the rack in the center of the oven about 22 to 25 minutes. The crust on top will have a dull look when the cookie is done.

Remove the pan from the oven and top at once with the chocolate candy bars. Let stand about 2 minutes or until the heat softens the candy. Spread the melted chocolate over the top of the cookie to make a frosting. Sprinkle the frosting with chopped nuts. Cool in pan on rack and cut into about 20 bars, or any number you like. (*Double Magic:* You can double this recipe and bake the cookie in a 13 x 9 x 2-inch pan. You'll need to bake it longer, about 35 to 40 minutes in all.)

CANDY BAR COOKIES

The 4-H Club girl who shares this recipe with us says the cookies taste like candy bars. Her friends agree

1 cup brown sugar, firmly packed	1 teaspoon salt
½ cup soft butter	4 cups quick-cooking rolled oats
½ cup light corn syrup	½ cup peanut butter
3 teaspoons vanilla	1 cup semisweet chocolate pieces

Start heating the oven to 350°. Grease a 13 x 9 x 2-inch pan with unsalted shortening or salad oil.

With a spoon or electric mixer on medium speed, mix the brown sugar and butter in a large bowl until light and fluffy. Add the corn syrup, vanilla, salt and rolled oats and beat on low speed to mix ingredients well.

Spread the mixture evenly in the greased pan with the back of a spoon or spatula. Bake on the rack in the center of the oven 15 minutes.

While the mixture bakes, mix the peanut butter and chocolate in a small bowl.

Remove the pan from the oven and at once spread the peanut butter-chocolate mixture evenly over the top to cover until the heat melts the chocolate. Cool in pan on rack, then cut into 27 bars and remove from the pan with a spatula.

RICH BUTTERSCOTCH BARS

If you have a 1-pound box of brown sugar in the cupboard, use it.
Then you don't have to measure or roll out lumps

1 pound brown sugar (2¼ to
  2⅓ cups, firmly packed)
1 cup soft butter
2 eggs
2 cups unsifted flour

1 teaspoon baking powder
½ teaspoon salt
1 cup coarsely chopped or
  broken walnuts

Cook the sugar and butter in the top of the double boiler over hot, not boiling, water until the sugar dissolves. Or cook them in a medium saucepan over low heat. Cool until lukewarm.

Start heating the oven to 350°.

Add the eggs, one at a time, to the butter-sugar mixture and beat thoroughly after adding each egg.

Stir together the flour, baking powder and salt to mix well. Add to the butter-sugar mixture and stir in the nuts.

Spread evenly in an ungreased 15½ x 10½ x 1-inch pan (jelly roll pan). Bake on the rack in the center of the oven 25 minutes or until the cookie is a delicate brown; a slight dent is left when you touch the top lightly with a fingertip.

Remove the pan from the oven and set it on a wire rack. Cut while hot into 40 bars, or as many as you like.

DATE LOGS

Chop and measure at the same time—cut the dates fine with scissors
and let them drop into the measuring cup

¾ cup sifted flour
1 cup sugar
1 teaspoon baking powder
¼ teaspoon salt

1 cup pitted finely cut-up dates
1 cup chopped walnuts
3 eggs, well beaten
Confectioners sugar

Start heating the oven to 325°. Grease a 9 x 9 x 2-inch pan with unsalted shortening or salad oil.

Sift the flour onto a square of waxed paper or into a bowl and then measure. Sift the measured flour with the sugar, baking powder and salt into a medium bowl. Stir the finely cut dates, walnuts and the well-beaten eggs into the flour mixture.

Spread evenly in the greased pan with the back of a spoon or a spatula. Bake on the rack in the center of the oven 35 to 40 minutes or until the cookie is a delicate brown; a slight dent is left when you touch the top lightly with a fingertip.

Remove the pan from the oven and set it on a wire rack until completely cool. Then, cut cookie into 48 strips or logs, or any number you like, and roll them in confectioners sugar.

DROP COOKIES

You don't have to use your imagination to figure out how drop cookies got their name—you drop the soft dough from a spoon onto a baking sheet. They're really push-and-drop cookies because you have to push the dough off the spoon with a teaspoon or a rubber spatula. If you heap the drops of cookie dough up in the center to make little peaks, the cookies will be especially attractive.

To give drop cookies a fancy look in a jiffy, press bits of nuts or candied cherries on the center of each cookie before baking. Or spread the baked and cooled cookies with cake frosting, either a quick-to-fix confectioners sugar frosting or a packaged frosting mix.

CHOCOLATE/NUT DROPS

Use a little showmanship and dress up these cookies—lightly press a nut on each one before baking

½ cup soft butter or regular margarine	½ teaspoon salt
6 tablespoons brown sugar	Few drops hot water
6 tablespoons honey	½ teaspoon vanilla
1 egg	1 (6-ounce) package semisweet chocolate pieces
1¼ cups sifted flour	½ cup chopped walnuts
½ teaspoon baking soda	

Start heating the oven to 375°. Grease a baking sheet with unsalted shortening or salad oil.

Beat the butter, brown sugar and honey together until light and fluffy. Add the unbeaten egg and beat well to mix.

Sift the flour onto a square of waxed paper or into a bowl and then measure. Sift the measured flour with the baking soda and salt.

Stir into the creamed mixture. Add the hot water and beat to mix. Stir in the vanilla, chocolate pieces and nuts.

Drop 2 inches apart from a teaspoon onto a greased baking sheet. Bake on the rack in the center of the oven 10 to 12 minutes or until the cookies are a delicate brown; a slight dent shows when you touch the top lightly with a fingertip.

Remove the pan from the oven and set it on a wire rack to cool slightly. Then remove the cookies from the baking sheet with a wide spatula and spread them on a wire rack to finish cooling. Makes about 36 cookies.

MOLASSES LOLLYPOP COOKIES

Wonderful party favors and Christmas gifts for the young fry. You can get skewers at dime stores and meat counters

½ cup soft butter or regular margarine	1 teaspoon ground ginger
½ cup sugar	½ teaspoon ground cinnamon
1 egg	½ teaspoon ground cloves
½ cup light molasses	½ teaspoon ground nutmeg
2½ cups sifted flour	2 tablespoons water
¼ teaspoon salt	Wooden skewers, about 24, 4½
1 teaspoon baking soda	inches long

Start heating the oven to 375°.

Beat the butter and sugar with an electric mixer on medium speed or with a spoon until light and fluffy. Add the egg and molasses and beat to mix well.

Sift the flour onto a square of waxed paper or into a bowl and then measure. Sift the measured flour with the salt, baking soda and spices. Add half of it to the molasses mixture and beat with the electric mixer on low speed to mix. Add the water and stir until smooth. Then mix in the second half of the flour mixture. Stir until smooth.

Drop rounded tablespoonfuls of the dough 4 inches apart onto an ungreased baking sheet. Insert the pointed end of a wooden skewer (popsicle stick) into each cookie with a twisting motion.

Bake on the rack in the center of the oven 10 to 12 minutes or until the cookies are a delicate brown; a slight dent shows when you touch the cookie lightly with a fingertip.

Remove the pan from the oven and let it stand 1 minute. Then, with a wide spatula, carefully remove the lollypops to a wire rack to cool.

When the cookies are cool, decorate them as you like. One good way is to spread them with confectioners sugar mixed with a little milk until smooth and just thick enough to spread on the cookies. Use candies, raisins, tiny candy red hots, small gumdrops and chocolate pieces to make faces and flaked or shredded coconut for hair. Wonderful for a children's party or gifts to your friends. Makes about 24 large cookies.

ORANGE/COCONUT CRISPS

Use the orange juice as it comes from the can—just thaw

2 eggs	2½ cups sifted flour
⅔ cup salad oil	2 teaspoons baking powder
1 cup sugar	½ teaspoon salt
¼ cup frozen orange juice concentrate, thawed	1 cup packaged cookie coconut

Start heating the oven to 400°.

Beat the eggs with a fork or a wire whisk in a medium bowl. Stir in the salad oil and sugar and beat until the mixture thickens. Stir in the orange juice (do not dilute).

Sift the flour onto a square of waxed paper or into a bowl and then measure. Sift the measured flour with the baking powder and salt. Add with the coconut to the egg mixture. Stir to mix well.

Drop teaspoons of dough about 2 inches apart onto an ungreased baking sheet. Press each cookie flat with the bottom of a drinking glass, oiled lightly with salad oil and dipped in sugar. Dip the glass in the sugar before flattening each cookie. Bake on the rack in the center of the oven 8 to 10 minutes or until the cookies are a delicate brown; a slight dent shows when you touch the top lightly with a fingertip.

Remove the pan from the oven and take the cookies from the baking sheet with a wide spatula. Spread them on a wire rack to cool. Makes about 36.

TWICE-AS-GOOD COOKIES

Melted chocolate makes these chip cookies different

1 (6-ounce) package semisweet chocolate pieces
1 cup sifted flour
½ teaspoon baking soda
½ teaspoon salt
½ cup soft butter or regular margarine

½ cup sugar
1 egg
¼ cup warm water
½ cup chopped or broken walnuts

Melt ½ cup of the chocolate pieces in the top of the double boiler over hot, not boiling, water or in a small saucepan over low heat. Cool until lukewarm.

Sift the flour onto a square of waxed paper or into a bowl and then measure. Sift the measured flour with the baking soda and salt. Set aside.

Beat the butter, sugar and egg in the large bowl of the electric mixer, on medium speed, until the mixture is light and fluffy, or beat with a spoon.

Beat in the melted chocolate and warm water. Then beat in flour mixture on low speed just enough to mix, or mix in with a spoon.

Stir in the walnuts and the rest of the chocolate pieces with a spoon. Chill in the refrigerator at least 30 minutes.

Start heating the oven to 375°. Lightly grease a baking sheet with unsalted shortening or salad oil.

Drop rounded teaspoons of the dough onto the greased baking sheet about 3 inches apart. Bake on the rack in the center of the oven 10 to 12 minutes or until a slight dent shows when you touch the top lightly with a fingertip.

Remove the pan from the oven and take the cookies from the baking sheet with a wide spatula. Spread them on a wire rack to cool. Makes 36.

MOLDED COOKIES

If you have ever enjoyed modeling with clay, you'll love to make molded cookies. You shape the stiff dough with your hands, often into balls. To keep the dough from sticking to your hands, chill it thoroughly in the refrigerator. Then rub your hands lightly with flour or a little confectioners sugar before making the balls. You may have to flour or sugar your hands several times while shaping a batch of cookies.

Often recipes direct that you flatten the balls of dough after they are on the baking sheet. Sometimes you use a fork, sometimes the bottom of a glass, dipped in sugar. Then there are thumbprint cookies—you press a hollow in each cookie with your thumb, which you fill with goodies before or after baking. Some of the cookie balls flatten while they bake; some keep their shape. You'll find all kinds among our recipes.

SNACK TIME PEANUT COOKIES

For a snack that satisfies, serve these cookies with glasses of cold milk, cups of hot cocoa or fruit juice

½ cup soft butter or regular
    margarine
½ cup peanut butter
½ cup sugar
½ cup brown sugar, firmly
    packed

1 egg
1¼ cups unsifted flour
½ teaspoon baking powder
¾ teaspoon baking soda
¼ teaspoon salt

In a medium bowl, beat the butter, peanut butter, white and brown sugars and the egg together until the mixture is light and fluffy.

Stir the flour, baking powder, baking soda and salt together in another medium bowl and then stir it into the peanut butter mixture. Chill the dough 1 hour, or until you can handle it easily.

Start heating the oven to 375°. Lightly grease a baking sheet with unsalted shortening or salad oil.

Shape the chilled dough into balls the size of large walnuts. Arrange them on the greased baking sheet about 3 inches apart. Dip a fork into flour and press it first one way and then the other to flatten each cookie and make a crisscross design.

Bake on the rack in the center of the oven until set, but not hard, or about 10 to 12 minutes. Remove from oven and spread cookies on rack to cool. Makes 36.

THUMBPRINT COOKIES

You make a hollow in the cookie balls with your thumb before baking to fill with treats when the cookies are cool

½ cup sifted confectioners sugar
1 cup soft butter or regular
   margarine
½ teaspoon salt

1 tablespoon vanilla
2 cups sifted flour
1 cup finely chopped or broken pecans

Sift the confectioners sugar and measure. Beat it, the butter, salt and vanilla together until fluffy.

Sift the flour onto a square of waxed paper or into a bowl and then measure. Stir the sifted flour and pecans into the confectioners sugar mixture. Mix well. Chill in the refrigerator at least an hour so dough will shape easily.

When you are ready to bake the cookies, start heating the oven to 350°.

Shape the chilled dough into small balls. Place them 3 inches apart on an ungreased baking sheet. Press a small hole in the center of each ball with your thumb tip.

Bake on the rack in the center of the oven about 15 minutes, or until lightly browned and set. Remove from oven and spread cookies on rack to cool. Makes 60 small cookies.

REFRIGERATOR COOKIES

Among cookies that were invented in American kitchens are the refrigerator cookies. They contain so much shortening that you have to chill them several hours before baking, which is how they got their name. The shortening makes refrigerator cookies especially crisp.

You shape the cookie dough into long rolls, wrap them in waxed paper, plastic wrap or aluminum foil and chill them in the refrigerator several hours or overnight. Then the shortening hardens and they're easy to slice and bake. If carefully wrapped so they won't dry out, you can keep the rolls of dough in the refrigerator 3 to 5 days. Then you can slice off and bake the cookies when you wish. Serve them warm from the oven—they're so good when freshly baked.

Or you can freeze the wrapped rolls of dough in the freezer and bake them any time within 6 months. When you're ready for some cookies, take the wrapped frozen dough from the freezer and leave it in the refrigerator for an hour, or on the kitchen counter 30 minutes. The rolls of dough will be just right for slicing. You will find many excellent refrigerator cookie dough rolls in the supermarket. All you have to do is slice and bake them.

Refrigerator cookies are thin and crisp. Remember that the thinner you slice them, the crisper they will be.

REFRIGERATOR SCOTCHIES

Shape the roll of refrigerator dough as big around as you want your cookies—2½ inches is a good size

1 cup soft butter or regular margarine	2 eggs
½ cup white sugar	1½ teaspoons vanilla
½ cup brown sugar, firmly packed	2¾ cups sifted flour
	½ teaspoon baking soda
	1 teaspoon salt

Beat the butter, white and brown sugars, eggs and vanilla until fluffy and well mixed.

Sift the flour onto a square of waxed paper or into a bowl and then measure. Sift the measured flour with the baking soda and salt. Add about half of it to the shortening-sugar mixture and stir to mix well. Gradually add the rest of the flour mixture, working it into the dough with the hands. Mix thoroughly.

Press and shape the dough into a long smooth roll about 2½ inches in diameter. Wrap it tightly in waxed paper or aluminum foil and chill several hours or overnight.

When you are ready to bake some of the cookies, start heating the oven to 400°.

Remove the dough from the refrigerator, unwrap it and cut off thin (⅛-inch) slices—eight slices from an inch of dough! Use a knife with a thin, sharp blade for slicing so the cookie edges will be neat. Rewrap the unused dough and put it back in the refrigerator. The dough will keep 3 to 5 days.

Place the slices a little distance apart on an ungreased baking sheet and bake on the rack in the center of the oven 6 to 8 minutes, or until cookies are lightly browned.

Remove the pan from the oven, lift the cookies from the baking sheet with a wide spatula and spread them on a wire rack to cool. This recipe will make about 75.

CHOCOLATE REFRIGERATOR COOKIES

Slices of chocolate and nuts—pretty, too, if you add fancy edges

1½ (1-ounce) squares
unsweetened chocolate
½ cup soft butter or regular
margarine
1 cup light brown sugar, firmly
packed
1 egg

½ teaspoon vanilla
2 cups sifted flour
½ teaspoon baking powder
¼ teaspoon baking soda
¼ teaspoon salt
3 tablespoons milk
½ cup finely chopped nuts

Put the chocolate in the top of the double boiler and melt over hot, not boiling, water or melt it in a small saucepan over low heat. Cool until lukewarm.

Beat the butter and brown sugar with the electric mixer on medium speed or with a spoon until light and fluffy. Add the egg, chocolate and vanilla. Beat to mix thoroughly.

Sift the flour onto a sheet of waxed paper and then measure. Sift the flour with the baking powder, baking soda and salt into a medium bowl. Add some of it to the chocolate mixture, then add a little of the milk. Beat on mixer's low speed or with a spoon after each addition. Keep on adding the flour mixture and milk, first one and then the other, until all of these ingredients are used.

Stir in the nuts. They must be chopped very fine so the chilled dough can be sliced easily.

Shape the dough in two smooth rolls with your hands—make them about 2½ inches in diameter. Wrap them tightly in aluminum foil or waxed paper, twisting the ends of the paper so they will stay in place. Chill several hours or overnight.

When ready to bake the cookies, start heating the oven to 400°. Unwrap the rolls of dough and cut each into thin slices with a sharp knife. Place the slices a little distance apart on an ungreased baking sheet.

Bake on the rack in the center of the oven 6 to 10 minutes.

Remove the pan from the oven, lift the cookies from the baking sheet with a wide spatula and spread them on a wire rack to cool. Makes 46 to 48 cookies.

For a change

Fancy Edge Cookies: When you take the roll of dough from the refrigerator, sprinkle a sheet of waxed paper with little candies of many colors (nonpareils), chocolate shot (jimmies) or finely chopped nuts. Unwrap the roll of cookie dough and turn it around in these tiny candies to coat well. Then, slice and bake the cookies.

ROLLED COOKIES

Get out the rolling pin and cookie cutters before you start to make these cookies. They are a little more difficult to make than other cookies because you have to roll the dough, but this isn't hard if you chill the dough first and use the pastry cloth and stockinet-covered rolling pin. (Rub a little flour into the pastry cloth with your hand. It will disappear into the meshes in the cloth. Brush off any loose flour on the pastry cloth. Then roll the stockinet-covered rolling pin around on the pastry cloth.)

You can dress up rolled cookies in many ways. Just cutting them with various cookie cutters of many shapes gives them a different look. And you can sprinkle the unbaked cookie cutouts with sugar —white or colored—tiny candies or chopped nuts. Also you can spread the cooled, baked cookies with confectioners sugar icing—white or tinted with food color.

Bake these cookies only until they're light brown. Baking them longer will give you a tough, dry cookie.

EXTRA-GOOD SUGAR COOKIES

Sprinkle cookies with sugar before baking—they'll glisten

⅔ cup soft shortening	2 cups sifted flour
¾ cup sugar	1½ teaspoons baking powder
1 egg	¼ teaspoon salt
¾ teaspoon vanilla	4 teaspoons milk
¼ teaspoon almond extract	

Beat the shortening and sugar together until light and fluffy. Add the egg and beat to mix well. Add the vanilla and almond extracts. (You can use 1 teaspoon vanilla and omit the almond extract.) Mix thoroughly.

Sift the flour onto a square of waxed paper and then measure. Sift the measured flour with the baking powder and salt. Stir it into the sugar-shortening mixture along with the milk. Divide the dough in half and chill in the refrigerator 1 hour or until the dough is easy to handle.

Start heating the oven to 375°. Grease a baking sheet with unsalted shortening or salad oil.

Roll the dough, half of it at a time, from the center to the edge until it is ⅛ to ¼ inch thick. (The thinner you roll the dough, the crisper the cookies will be.) Cut with a 3- or 4-inch round cookie cutter.

Use a wide spatula to place the cookies ½ inch apart on the greased baking sheet.

Bake on the rack in the center of the oven 8 to 9 minutes, or until the cookies are light brown.

Remove the pan from the oven at once and use a wide spatula to place the cookies on a wire cooling rack. Makes about 24 cookies.

For a change

Polka Dot Cookies: Dot the tops of cooled Extra-Good Sugar Cookies with dabs of chocolate frosting.

Painted Cookies: Stir ¼ teaspoon cold water into 1 egg yolk. Divide the egg yolk among 3 or 4 small custard cups and tint each part a different bright color with food color of red, green, yellow and pink. Stir to mix the food color and egg yolk. When cookies are ready to bake, paint a design on the top of each with the tinted egg yolk. Use a small, clean, pointed brush for each color. If the egg yolk thickens while standing, add a few drops of cold water and stir.

Cookies on Sticks: Arrange popsicle sticks or wooden skewers with pointed ends on a greased baking sheet and place a round of cookie dough on the pointed end of each skewer. Allow at least ½ inch between each cookie. Bake like Extra-Good Sugar Cookies. Remove the pan from the oven and at once place a chocolate-coated candy mint on the center of each cookie. The candy will melt enough to stick to the cookie when it is cool. Use a wide spatula to place the cookies on wire racks to cool.

Funny Face Cookies: While Cookies on Sticks are hot, you can decorate them with chocolate pieces instead of mints to make the features of a funny face. Let Funny Face Cookies cool before handling them so that the decorations will stay on. Or frost the tops of the cooled cookies and decorate them with little candies and nuts.

CHOCOLATE PINKS

Flatter everyone by writing his name on the dark chocolate cookies

2 (1-ounce) squares un-
  sweetened chocolate
¾ cup soft shortening
1 cup sugar
1 egg
¼ cup light corn syrup

2 cups sifted flour
¼ teaspoon salt
1 teaspoon baking soda
1 teaspoon ground cinnamon
Pink Icing

Melt the chocolate in the top of the double boiler over hot, not boiling, water or in a saucepan over low heat. Cool until lukewarm.

Beat together the shortening, sugar and egg until light and fluffy. Stir in the chocolate and corn syrup.

Sift the flour onto a square of waxed paper or into a bowl and then measure. Sift the measured flour with the salt, baking soda and cinnamon into the chocolate mixture. Beat to mix well.

Divide the dough into three parts and chill it in the refrigerator at least 1 hour.

When you are ready to bake the cookies, start heating the oven to 350°.

Place ⅓ of the dough on a lightly floured pastry cloth. Keep the rest of the dough in the refrigerator until you are ready to roll it.

Roll the dough from the center to the edge ⅛ inch thick and cut it with a lightly floured cookie cutter. To avoid stretching the cookie cutouts, use a wide spatula to place them ½ inch apart on an ungreased baking sheet.

Bake on the rack in the center of the oven 10 to 12 minutes.

Remove the pan from the oven and take the cookies from the baking sheet with a wide spatula. Spread them on a wire rack to cool.

Roll, cut and bake the remaining two parts of the dough and the scraps, gathered together, in the same way.

When the cookies are cool, spread their tops with a creamy confectioners sugar icing, tinted pink. Makes about 30 to 36.

PINK ICING

1 cup sifted confectioners sugar
¼ teaspoon salt
½ teaspoon vanilla

1 to 1½ tablespoons light
  cream or water
Red food color

Sift the confectioners sugar onto a square of waxed paper or into a bowl and then measure. Put the measured powdered sugar, salt and vanilla in a small bowl. Add the cream or water and mix well with a spoon or with the electric mixer on low speed to make an icing that you can spread.

Tint the frosting pink with a few drops of red food color.

Spread it on the cookies with a spatula. Or make Pink Icing a little thicker, this way—use only about ¾ tablespoon of cold water or 1 tablespoon cream. Write names on the cookies with a toothpick dipped in the icing. Nice for a party.

GRANDMA'S MOLASSES COOKIES

They taste like molasses cookies Grandma used to make but they're topped with a sweet, shiny Sugar Glaze

4 cups sifted flour	½ cup soft shortening
1 teaspoon baking soda	¾ cup sugar
½ teaspoon baking powder	¾ cup light molasses
1 teaspoon salt	½ cup buttermilk
2 teaspoons ground ginger	Sugar Glaze (recipe follows)

Sift the flour onto a square of waxed paper and then measure. Sift the measured flour with the baking soda, baking powder, salt and ginger into a medium bowl. Set aside.

Beat the shortening in a large bowl with the electric mixer on medium speed or with a spoon until light and fluffy. Gradually add the sugar and beat until very fluffy.

Stir in a little of the flour mixture, then a little molasses and buttermilk. Keep adding the flour and the molasses and milk until you have used all of them. Start and end the mixing by adding some of the flour. Mix well.

Divide the dough into four parts. Cover and chill it at least 4 hours or overnight.

When you are ready to bake the cookies, start heating the oven to 400°. Lightly grease a baking sheet with unsalted shortening or salad oil.

Roll out ¼ of the dough at a time from the center to the edge to ¼-inch thickness if you want fat, soft cookies, or to ⅛-inch thickness if you want thinner, more crisp cookies. Use a floured cutter to make the cutouts. To avoid stretching the cutouts, use a wide spatula to place them about ½ inch apart on the baking sheet.

Bake on the rack in the center of the oven 7 to 10 minutes.

Remove the pan from the oven and take the cookies from the baking sheet with a wide spatula. Spread them on a wire rack to cool. When partly cooled, spread with Sugar Glaze. Makes about 48 cookies.

SUGAR GLAZE

Put 2 cups sifted confectioners sugar and 2 to 3 tablespoons milk in a medium bowl. Stir until smooth. Spread on tops of Grandma's Molasses Cookies while they are slightly warm.

For a change

Gingerbread Boys: Cut the dough for Grandma's Molasses Cookies, rolled ¼ inch thick, with a floured gingerbread-boy cutter. Lift the cutouts with a wide spatula or pancake turner onto a lightly greased baking sheet. Press raisins into the dough for the eyes, nose, a mouth with a smile and shoe and cuff buttons. Use bits snipped from red or green gumdrops with scissors for coat buttons. Bake like Grandma's Molasses Cookies. You can move the legs and arms of the gingerbread boys on the baking sheet, before baking, to make them look as if they're dancing or running.

GIANT RAISIN COOKIES

Man-sized cookies big enough to satisfy the hungriest cookie eaters. There's a hint of orange flavor

½ cup raisins	4 cups sifted flour
1½ cups soft shortening	2 teaspoons salt
1½ cups sugar	1½ teaspoons baking powder
2 large eggs	⅓ cup milk
2 teaspoons vanilla	Sugar (for tops)
1 teaspoon grated orange peel	Raisins (for tops)

Cut the raisins coarsely with scissors.

Beat the shortening and sugar together in a large bowl with the electric mixer on medium speed or with a spoon until fluffy. Add the eggs, vanilla and orange peel. Beat well.

Sift the flour onto a square of waxed paper and then measure. Sift the measured flour with the salt and baking powder. Stir a little of the flour into the shortening-sugar mixture, then stir in a little milk. Mix well. Do this until all the flour and milk are used.

Stir in the cut-up raisins.

Divide the dough into three parts and chill 1 hour or longer in the refrigerator.

Start heating the oven to 375°. Grease a baking sheet with unsalted shortening or salad oil.

Roll one part of the dough at a time from the center to the edge on a lightly floured surface until a little less than ¼ inch thick.

Cut cookies by cutting around an empty 1-pound coffee can or its lid with a small knife. Place them 1 inch apart on greased baking sheets.

Sprinkle the circles of dough with sugar. Cut the raisins in strips with scissors. Press the raisins into the cookies to make initials or names.

Bake on the rack in the center of the oven 10 to 12 minutes, or until a light brown.

Remove the pan from the oven and lift the cookies from the baking sheet with a wide spatula. Place them on a wire rack to cool. Store them in a jar with a loose lid. Makes 35.

COOKIE CONFECTIONS

Here are the easiest of all cookies to make. You don't bake them. So get out a saucepan, stirring spoon and your measuring tools and stir up a batch of cookies in a jiffy. We predict you'll have beginner's luck with them—that means *good* luck.

BUTTERSCOTCH CRUNCHIES

You can make these crunchy cookies with any ready-to-eat cereal flakes. So look in your cupboard and take your pick

2 (6-ounce) packages butterscotch pieces
½ cup peanut butter
6 cups corn flakes

In a large saucepan cook and stir butterscotch pieces and peanut butter over medium heat until the mixture melts. Remove from the heat and stir in the corn flakes with a spoon. Mix well.

Drop teaspoonfuls of the mixture onto a sheet of waxed paper. Let set. Makes 36.

NO-BAKE CHOCOLATE COOKIES

Stir these cookies up in a jiffy when something to nibble is in order. Let your guests help you make them

2 cups sugar	1 teaspoon salt
½ cup milk	3 cups quick-cooking rolled oats
1 stick butter or regular	1 teaspoon vanilla
margarine (¼ pound)	½ cup broken walnuts
3 tablespoons cocoa	1 cup flaked coconut

Put the sugar, milk, butter, cocoa and salt in a large saucepan and bring to a boil. Remove from the heat and stir in the rolled oats, vanilla, nuts and coconut.

Drop from a teaspoon onto waxed paper to make 48.

SAUCEPAN PEANUT COOKIES

Top favorites of schoolboys, fathers and new cooks. No wonder— use whatever cereal flakes you have

1 cup light corn syrup	1½ cups peanut butter
1 cup sugar	4 cups cereal flakes

Mix the corn syrup and sugar in a medium saucepan. Bring the mixture to a full boil. Remove from the heat and stir in the peanut butter and cereal flakes. Mix well.

Drop heaping teaspoonfuls onto a buttered baking sheet. Makes 48.

Cookies for Special Occasions

Once you've baked a variety of cookies from recipes in this cookbook, you'll want to choose the kinds you like but for different occasions. We list suggestions for you to consider to help you select a recipe to meet a special need.

Many cookies are exceptionally versatile and suitable for different occasions. For instance, some of those that originated in faraway places frequently are traditionals on the Christmas cookie tray but are also good travelers in lunchboxes. Children, of course, like just about all cookies, although those in our junior cookie section (see Cookies Children Will Love to Make in Index) and some of the cookie confections are probably most popular with them.

We based our selections primarily on the reactions of our tastetesters—men, women and children—and what women who contributed their favorite recipes to this cookbook told us about them. Many superior recipes in this book do not appear on our lists—these are merely suggested "starters."

(See Index for Recipes)

DAINTY HOSTESS COOKIES

Cheesecake Squares
Cheese Pie-Bar Cookies
Chess Pie-Bars
Chocolate Bonbon Cookies
Chocolate Cookie Sandwiches
French Chocolate Pie Squares
Grapefruit Sugar Cookies
Holiday Party Kisses
Jam/Cheese Cookie Tarts
Jeweled Meringues
Lemon/Coconut Squares

Meringue-Topped Cookies
Mocha Balls
Molasses/Almond Cookies
Nut Butter Cookies
Pumpkin Pie Squares
Ribbon Cookies
Royal Crowns
Spritz Chocolate Sandwiches
Swirls
Walnut Lace Cookies
Wild Rose Cookies

COMPANY AND COFFEE PARTY SPECIALS

Almond Butterballs
Butter Crispies
Chocolate Meringue Bars
Chocolate/Orange Bars
Date-Filled Oat Cookies
English Tea Squares
French Bars
Frosted Carrot Bars

Frosted Ginger Creams
Hampshire Hermits
Hard-Cooked Egg Cookies
Mom's Fortune Cookies
New Moons
Sesame Wafers
Southern Praline Bars

CHRISTMAS COOKIE FAVORITES

Brazil Nut Bars
Christmas Drop Cookies
Citrus/Nut Drops
Easy Cane Cookies
French Bars
Frosted Yule Logs
Fruitcake Squares

Gingerbread Christmas Cookies
Mincemeat/Cheese Cookies
Pretzel Cookies
Rich Anise Cookies
Spiced Christmas Cookies
Star Cookies
White Christmas Cookies

COOKIES FROM FARAWAY PLACES

Chinese Almond Cookies
Danish Raisin Cookies
Finnish Shortbread Cookies
Finnish Star Cookies
Florentines
Golden Coconut Diamonds
Greek Easter Cookies
Lebkuchen
Mexican Fiesta Balls

Orange Wreaths
Pepparkakor
Pepper Nuts
Sandbakelser
Spanish Wedding Cakes
Springerle
Swedish Almond Shortbread
Viennese Crescents

COOKIES FOR LUNCHBOXES

Chocolate Chip Bars
Chocolate Potato Cookies
Cornmeal Cookies
Fruity Gumdrop Cookies
Honeyed Yo-Yos

Indian Bars
Jeweled Oatmeal Drops
Orange/Carrot Cookies
Raisin-Filled Cookies
Rookie Cookies

GOOD SELLERS AT BAZAARS

Candy-Top Brownies
Chocolate Sandwich Treasures
Cocoa Bars
Cry Baby Cookies
Date-Filled Oat Cookies
Jumbo Sugar Cookies

Marshmallow/Cherry Bars
Nut and Fruit Bars
Oatmeal/Molasses Cookies
Snickerdoodles
Spicy Apple Bars
Two-Tone Jumbles

COOKIES THAT MAIL WELL

Applesauce Fudgies
Brownies for a Crowd
California Fig Cookies
Circle Ranch Oat Cookies
Fruit Bars
Glazed Apple Cookies
Grandma's Raisin Cookies

Hampshire Hermits
Multi-Fruited Drops
Oatmeal Chocolate Bars
Oregon Date Surprises
Pumpkin Cookies
Raisin/Ketchup Cookies
Two-Tone Jumbles

CHILDREN'S FAVORITES—TO EAT

Chocolate/Coconut Bars
Chocolate Marshmallow
   Cakelets
Chocolate/Peanut Crunchers
Date 'Mallow Chews

Double Treat Cookies
Grandma's Soft Sugar Cookies
Peanut Candy-Bar Cookies
Potpourri Cookies
Soft Chocolate Chippers

CHILDREN'S FAVORITES—TO MAKE

Butterscotch Crunchies
Candy Bar Cookies
Chocolate/Nut Drops
Chocolate Oatsies
Chocolate/Peanut Clusters
Chocolate/Peanut Crunchers
Chocolate Pinks
Chocolate Refrigerator Cookies
Date Logs
Date/Nut Macaroons
Extra-Good Sugar Cookies
Fudge Brownies
Giant Raisin Cookies
Grandma's Molasses Cookies

Jiffy Candy Cookies
Magic Party Squares
Molasses Lollypop Cookies
No-Bake Chocolate Cookies
Orange/Coconut Crisps
Peanut Butter Drops
Potato Chip Cookies
Refrigerator Scotchies
Rich Butterscotch Bars
Rocky Road Fudge Bars
Saucepan Peanut Cookies
Snack Time Peanut Cookies
Thumbprint Cookies
Twice-as-Good Cookies

Bread

ALL ABOUT BREADS

If you like to settle down to read cookbooks, we invite you to this fascinating story of bread. Plump loaves, shiny-brown rolls and luscious coffee breads will pop out of the pages. You'll sniff in imagination the most enchanting of all fragrances, that of yeast bread leaving the oven. You'll remember the crunch of the knife as it cuts through the golden crust, and you'll almost taste the wheaty goodness of bread slices spread with butter.

You will marvel at the wonderful, faster-to-make breads that have been emerging from test kitchens—and country kitchens—as some of you recall Grandmother's friendly kitchen and the irresistible smell of her beautiful breads. Our new simplified versions retain the old flavors, good looks and aroma.

Food fragrances, psychologists say, linger in memory more strongly than tastes. This may explain why, when we asked many men and women for their most cherished childhood food memories, they mentioned warm homemade bread more times than all other kinds of foods put together. They talked of oven-fresh bread spread with butter and homemade berry jam . . . bowls of steaming vegetable-beef scented soup along with hot corn bread for supper on evenings when rain splashed against windowpanes . . . warm sugary-cinnamon rolls brought over by a neighbor to say: "Merry Christmas to your house from ours." Country hostesses know there's nothing like the aroma of yeast bread to sharpen appetites and build anticipation for the meal that is about ready.

For good measure we include in this cookbook, along with yeast-leavened breads, some of the great quick breads that so successfully dress up meals with so little effort—biscuits, muffins, popovers, pancakes, waffles, nut and fruit breads and gingerbread, for instance. Excellent packaged mixes for these breads line supermarket shelves. You use them, too, but there are occasions when you want to stir up "from scratch" quick breads like those in this book. They, too, are easier than ever to make.

Bread in History

The story of bread is the story of wheat. When a Kansas farmer described the best memory of his childhood home, he said: "I picture level, emerald wheat fields in spring which, at harvest time, ripple gold in the wind. Our fields stretched from back of the barn as far as you could see."

Breadmaking started about 10,000 years ago, so far as we know. The place was the Fertile Crescent, the part of the Middle East that follows an imaginary line drawn from Egypt through Palestine and Syria and south along the Euphrates and Tigris rivers to the Persian Gulf. There wheat first was a grass.

No one knows who made the first loaf of bread during the dawn of civilization, but we believe it was unleavened bread baked by the sun. During the excavation of the location where Ur, an ancient city near the Persian Gulf, once flourished, archaeologists discovered—and lighted—ovens used for bread baking that had been idle 3,900 years. These are thought to be the oldest ovens in the world. The Egyptians usually get credit for inventing the oven and discovering leavening. Bread baking improved greatly with their use. Bakers vied with one another to produce fancy loaves for offerings to pagan gods. You can see drawings of some of these breads in the Pharaohs' tombs in the Valley of the Kings. Bread frequently was money. Egyptians paid the slaves who built their historic pyramids with three loaves of bread and two jugs of beer a day for each worker.

The Greeks refined the milling of flour and also baking methods; the Romans learned from them and carried their skills to what now is Europe. The Romans also improved the cultivation of wheat and developed new varieties.

When the Christian era began, bread continued as the staff of life. Jesus, teaching his followers to pray, said: "Give us this day our daily bread." Early Christians, instead of baking bread for pagan gods, fashioned fancy loaves for feasting on church holidays, such as Christmas and Easter, and to give thanks at the end of the harvest season, much the way we celebrate on Thanksgiving Day. Food traditions live long and die slowly. We have turkey, cranberries and pumpkin pie for our November holiday, while people in Europe still feature their traditional breads on special days. You will find many recipes for Americanized versions of these lovely, delicious breads in this cookbook. When you bake them and serve them on holidays and special occasions, you'll find that old customs reflect a luster on today's breads.

Immigrants to what today is the United States brought their prized bread recipes to their new homes. No wonder our heritage is so rich. We have adopted and taken to our tables the great breads of the world. French bread no longer belongs only to France, or Stollen to Germany.

Original American Breads

During the early colonial years, corn was more plentiful than wheat, so corn bread was more common than wheat bread. Friendly Indians showed colonists how to grow corn and how to prepare it for food. Pioneer women improved on the cooking techniques. When people traveled, they went on foot or horseback, sleeping and eating in the forests. They carried corn bread for sustenance. That's why it was called journeycake. When roads and taverns were built and stagecoaches carried passengers, journeycake somehow became johnnycake, a name many easterners still use for corn breads. The kinds of breads made with cornmeal were—and still are—almost without limit. Every region has its specialties.

From the start southerners showed a preference for white cornmeal, northerners for yellow. Spoon breads, light and tasty, graced Southern tables. And on the frontier, pioneers, when they ran out of starter or yeast, made salt-rising bread. They stirred together water, a little water-ground cornmeal (ground between stones by water power), potatoes and salt; they set the mixture, uncovered, in a warm place, exposing it to the air until bacteria fell into it and formed gas or caused fermentation. Then they removed the potatoes and used the liquid as leavening for the one-time famous bread, made with white flour.

Another native yeast-leavened corn bread is Anadama Batter Bread (see Index). A Massachusetts fisherman, tired of the cornmeal mush his wife, Anna, spooned up for his meals, added molasses and yeast to it and baked the first loaf of this bread while muttering: "Anna-dam'er, Anna-dam'er" (or so the legend goes). This batter bread, toasted, still has a loyal following in New England.

Southern Beaten Biscuits

No discussion of our original breads is complete without a salute to beaten biscuits, perhaps the South's greatest contribution. These light brown, crusty biscuits differ from other kinds in that you serve them cold. Southern hostesses often pull them apart (they divide in half easily) and tuck in thin slices of cooked country ham for superlative sandwiches.

The tiny, thin biscuits start out as a stiff dough. The trick is to beat the dough, placed on a wooden block, with mallet, rolling pin, hammer or some other device until it blisters and becomes smooth. No one today has time to beat the dough 100 strokes for everyday meals (200 strokes for company) so you no longer hear the thump, thump, thump in kitchens.

While most beaten biscuits now are commercially made, a poultryman on

Maryland's Eastern Shore says they come daily from the kitchen in his home and other kitchens in the neighborhood. A machine takes over the work of beating, however. You put the dough through rollers, something like old-fashioned clothes wringers, to blister and smooth it.

The dough, rolled less than a half inch thick, is cut with small cutters, some of which used to have stickers in them to prick biscuit tops. Women now prick each biscuit with a fork. They bake them in a moderate oven until they're a pale gold (see Index for Beaten Biscuits).

Sour Dough

Sour dough breads of the Old West also have their champions today. Occasionally they are older men, many of whom once spent considerable time in cattle and sheep camps, where a crock of sour dough starter was a staple item. The starter, part of which was saved from one baking to the next, usually leavened sour dough biscuits and pancakes and gave them the characteristic tangy flavor.

The starters for some sour dough breads made today have their beginning in milk, according to a California rancher's wife. You pour the milk into a stone crock or glass container (never metal) and let it stand, uncovered, in a warm place (about 80°) 24 hours or until it bubbles or ferments.

If bubbling occurs, add 1 c. flour to the milk and let the mixture stand in a warm place (80°) 2 to 4 days, depending on how long it takes the entire surface of the mixture to bubble and give off a sour aroma. You can't expect to be successful every time you try to make this starter, for it often takes repeated attempts. That is why few women now make it and why ranchers and miners, in pioneer days, rode or walked miles to get a starter from a relative or friend. But once

you get your starter, you save back some of it at each baking, add equal parts of water and flour and leave it, uncovered, at room temperature until it bubbles. Then you cover and store it in the refrigerator. Usually it will keep up to two weeks, but for best results, use it once a week.

You cannot expect to duplicate in a home kitchen San Francisco's famed sour dough French breads, which visitors to the city frequently buy at the airport and carry for gifts to many parts of the country, especially to Hawaii. These marvelous commercial breads are made with hard wheat flour and with special starters, some of them many years old and guarded by bakers like pots of gold. The commercial bakeries also have special humidity-controlled ovens.

We give you in this cookbook FARM JOURNAL's modified and easier method of making sour dough starters and recipes for biscuits and griddlecakes which they leaven. Dehydrated commercial sour dough starter in packages may be found in some health food stores and specialty shops. Once you make your starter with it from directions that come with the dehydrated product, handle it the same way as homemade starters.

Boston Brown Bread

Another historic bread that deserves a mention is steamed Boston Brown Bread, a quick bread especially enjoyed in New England as a companion to a pot of baked beans. The custom of having this team of foods for supper on Saturday nights is a Puritan tradition that time has not erased. We steam our Boston Brown Bread (see Index) in tin fruit cans from the supermarket; these loaves make the right size slices.

Flour for "the Staff of Life"

The basic ingredients for yeast breads are wheat flour, yeast, liquid—usually water or milk—salt, sugar and fat—lard, butter, margarine, salad oil or shortening. More flour is used than any other ingredient. The magic in flour is gluten, a protein. When you mix flour with liquid and manipulate the mixture by beating, stirring and kneading, the gluten develops in long elastic strands that stretch and trap the bubbles of carbon dioxide gas which yeast gives off as it grows. It's these bubbles that cause dough to rise and bread to become light. Gluten thus forms the "framework" of bread, enabling the loaf to hold its shape when baked.

Hard wheats contain more gluten than soft wheats. Some supermarkets carry bags of flour labeled "high protein" and "for breadmaking," but most flour marketed today is all-purpose, a blend of hard and soft wheats. It contains enough gluten for bread-making and not too much for cake-making. As its name implies, it's a flour for all cooking and baking purposes.

Most flours today are enriched to provide good nutrition. The millers add vitamins and minerals to equal the natural supply in whole wheat grains. Because rye and whole wheat flours contain less gluten than all-purpose flour, you combine white flour with them when baking yeast breads.

Flour has the ability to absorb moisture from the air during humid or rainy weather. Then it cannot absorb as much liquid in the mixing bowl as when the air is dry. That's why flour measurements for yeast breads have to be approximate, within a certain range. The general rule, unless the recipe specifies otherwise, is to add flour until you have dough as soft as you can handle.

Yeast Makes Dough Rise

Yeast consists of living plants, which feed upon sugar and flour as they multiply. They give off carbon dioxide gas, which, as we have mentioned, makes dough rise. Women haven't always had it so good with yeast as they do today. Bread bakers in the ancient world used "barm," the thick scum on top of fermenting wine, for leavening. Sometime along history's path, women began to make their own yeast from hops. Unfortunately, the strength of this homemade product varied. In our grandmothers' day, cakes of dry yeast, containing a few slow-growing yeast plants, were used. To give the yeast time to grow, bread bakers set a sponge of water, flour and the crumbled yeast cake, and let it stand overnight in a warm place. By morning the yeast plants had multiplied enough that the ingredients for bread could be mixed. The other type of yeast then available was moist compressed yeast that was perishable.

During World War II, research workers discovered how to remove water from moist yeast. Active dry yeast was the result. Its first purpose was to give our military forces, regardless of where in the world they were stationed, fresh-baked yeast bread. This active dry yeast had remarkable keeping qualities, providing it was stored in airtight packages. Soon this yeast came to kitchen cupboards and was on hand ready for use. All a woman had to do (or has to do today) was look on the label for the expiration date stamped on it (usually about a year after yeast is packaged). Since yeast is a living plant, even though dehydrated, it cannot live forever.

Changes were recently made in this active dry yeast. It now comes in finer particles, which eliminates the necessity of dissolving it in water before you add it with other ingredients to the mixing bowl. Look at the new breadmaking methods in this cookbook—Instant Blend, Short-Cut Mixer, CoolRise and Rapidmix—to see how this improvement in yeast simplifies breadmaking (see Index for each of these methods). Try them to find out how easy they are and what fine bread they make.

Compressed yeast is still available in some communities. As mentioned, this moist yeast is perishable, but you can keep it in the refrigerator up to two weeks. Many country women keep compressed yeast up to six months in their freezers. Once you thaw it, however, use it immediately. One package of active dry yeast works the same as a ⅗ oz. cake of compressed yeast. You follow the recipes in the section "Conventional Method" when you bake with this yeast, crumbling and dissolving it in lukewarm liquid.

Ways to Make Bread

Women have baked satisfying breads for thousands of years, but never did homemade bread taste better than it does today. And never did breadmakers have it so easy. This is due primarily to the application of science and management to this branch of cookery, which simplifies and speeds up the process. The electric mixer whirls away and takes over a major share of the work on mixing the dough. Your oven's automatic heat control provides the right baking temperature. Electric knives slice bread, even when warm, to perfection. And you use very warm tap water right from your hot water faucet for the liquid in some of the methods.

Kneading continues to be important in most methods and gives you the feel of the springy, pliable dough that you can work with as the artist works with clay. And as you knead, trouble and frustrations disappear and thoughts of the something good you are creating replace them. For those of you who do not enjoy or have the time for kneading, this cookbook also gives recipes for the batter breads, where beating substitutes for kneading—also the newer Easy Mixer Method with the beating plus only about 1 minute of kneading.

Rising traditionally follows the kneading or beating, but in the Cool-Rise and Short-Cut Mixer Methods, the dough (covered) has a 20-minute rest on the board before you shape it into loaves. You have to use especially designed recipes whenever you give dough this rest period instead of the traditional first rising . . . we give you several of them. Temperature is important in encouraging dough to rise—85° is about right. The dough needs to be in a place free from drafts, which could cause the temperature to fluctuate.

Recipes You'll Find in This Cookbook

There's a fabulous collection of conventional yeast bread recipes in this cookbook. They are outstanding selections from farm and ranch kitchens across the country. We handpicked them and then tested the recipes to get acquainted with them—to be sure directions were clear, and to know how to describe their virtues to you. You can follow these conventional recipes exactly, or you can alter some of the steps in making the dough the newer and quicker ways, as we explain in another section (see Index for Newer Ways to Bake Bread). Do try the new ways on your own treasured bread recipes, too.

To name the best recipes in this cookbook is impossible. We believe all of them are good. First of all, we nominate for honors the several versions of just plain white, whole wheat and rye breads. Try them all and then you can settle on your favorites. The whole wheat breads have different, interesting flavors; some contain honey, others molasses. And there's one with a surprisingly good, faint lemon taste. There are all kinds of rye breads, those flavored with caraway seeds, grated orange peel or anise seeds. And there's one with the dill-caraway combination of flavors that's a natural for cheese sandwiches.

The bread specialties are a delight. Orange-Nut-Glazed Raisin Bread, flavored with a hint of ginger and orange peel, is distinctive and tasty. We're proud of the Cracked Wheat Bread a Minnesota farm woman bakes for her family and for her church bake sales, where it's a best seller. Finnish Coffee Bread, with its subtle cardamom taste, can't be surpassed. Braid strands of the dough, bake them in loaf pans, spread confectioners sugar frosting on top and you have superior coffee bread. Bake the unbraided dough in loaf pans, omit the frosting and you have a superb plain bread that gets compliments whenever you serve it. Lovely yellow-pink slices of Tomato Bread, framed with golden crust, always bring praises for their delicate, spicy flavor.

Dainty Brioche from our own Test Kitchens is a true treat. Our rolls made with sour cream also are country specials—Holiday Cream Twists, to name one. Potato Puffs, Bran Rolls and Perfect Buns are among other favorites. Hot Cross Buns await the Easter season. What a shame not to mention all of these hot rolls, which truly are miniature loaves of yeast bread, but made with a softer dough and baked faster and oftener at a higher temperature.

We can't leave out our crisp pizza crust. Our teen taste-testers voted this the best they ever had. You can make it ahead and freeze it; bake it when you want to serve pizza. Different fillings are described.

The many coffee breads from faraway places, adapted to the American scene, deserve a spotlight. Every woman can find at least a dozen kinds she'd be happy to feature at a coffee party. Reading recipes for them is something like taking a trip abroad: Grecian Feast Loaf, Austrian Gugelhupf, Norwegian Jule Kage, Glazed Danish Twist, German Stollen and Russian Kulich.

Quick breads—the kind you frequently bake when you say to a caller, "Stay for supper"—make up about a third of the book. We've found easy ways to make traditional kinds. For instance, if you don't want to spend time steaming our Boston Brown Bread to serve at your bean supper, try our Oven-Baked Brown Bread.

Quick breads, like yeast-leavened types, have a history. Many of them are descendants of the coarse hearth breads primitive people made. The "cakes" King Arthur forgot to watch in his peasant hut were among the forerunners of today's highly refined and delicious hot breads.

We hope you'll get as much pleasure and satisfaction in baking, serving and eating breads made by recipes in this cookbook as we enjoyed preparing them for you. And we also hope you'll bake breads frequently for your family—that you won't save them only for guests. Homemade breads deliver big batches of cheer to the dining table. They're a symbol of home. Good luck. And many bakings!

YEAST BREADS

Conventional Method
for Baking Bread

There's more than one way to bake good yeast bread. This section deals with today's Conventional Method. Home economists sometimes call it the straight-dough method because you combine all the ingredients at one time. It's quite different from the sponge method of our grandmothers—after supper on the farm, a frequent remark of women once was: "I must set the sponge." These earlier bread bakers stirred together dry, slow-acting yeast, liquid and some of the flour and put the sponge-like batter in a warm place overnight. Next morning they added the remaining ingredients to the spongy, bubbling mixture to make their dough.

Recently there has been a revolution in breadmaking techniques. Many companies—flour milling companies and yeast manufacturers—have been working on short cuts for breadmaking. Each manufacturer's test kitchens have produced new recipes following their timesaving techniques, and we present them to you in this book.

We also, however, give you an excellent collection of breads made by the Conventional Method—treasures from farm and ranch kitchens all over the country. Even though you switch to newer ways of bread baking, hold onto your best-liked recipes that follow the Conventional Method and add our collection in this section. Progress, after all, is keeping the best of the old and accepting the best of the new.

With a few simple changes in combining the ingredients, you can use these Conventional Method recipes with the Rapidmix and Instant Blend Methods, in which the active dry yeast is not predissolved in water and the electric mixer does a lot of the work.

Whichever method you use, read the pointers on bread baking which follow, especially if you're inexperienced in handling yeast doughs.

Pointers for Baking Perfect Bread

How to Recognize Top Quality. The loaf is plump and it has a tender, golden crust. The crust may be crisp, but if you brush a little soft or melted butter on it while the loaf is warm, it is shiny and soft. Along the sides of the loaf, just below the top crust, there's an even, slight break, often called the shred. The texture is fine-grained. If you feel a slice of the loaf, it is soft, springy and a little moist. The bread tastes good when cold and when warm.

Flour. The kind used in the recipes in this cookbook is all-purpose flour, which is milled from blended soft and hard wheats. In some supermarkets, flours, labeled "high protein" and "for breadmaking" are available and they may be used. They are especially desirable for CoolRise breads, which are described in the section Newer Ways to Bake Bread (see Index).

We recommend sifting the flour before measuring in both quick breads and conventional breads to get uniform results. But we stir, rather than sift, whole wheat and rye flours. Most of the rye flour in national distribution is medium rye. This is what our recipes in this book call for.

Yeast. There are two kinds of yeast in some markets, active dry and compressed. Since active dry yeast is available almost every place, we list it in our recipes. You can substitute a cake of compressed yeast for a package of active dry yeast in breads made by the Conventional Method, but dissove it in lukewarm water

(85°) instead of the warm water (110 to 115°) used for active dry yeast. You can dissolve compressed yeast in lukewarm water, milk, potato water, diluted evaporated milk, reconstituted nonfat dry milk or a combination of these liquids. The trend is away from predissolving active dry yeast in water, as recipes in Newer Ways to Bake Bread indicate.

Yeast is a plant; in its rapid growth it produces carbon dioxide gas, or bubbles, that causes dough to rise. Yeast grows best at a temperature of 80 to 85°. This is the ideal temperature for dough during the rising processes.

Liquids. Water, milk and potato water are the most common liquids. Unpasteurized milk must be scalded and cooled until lukewarm to destroy an enzyme that makes bread gummy. Generally pasteurized milk need not be scalded. Buttermilk does not require scalding. Water produces a bread with crisp crust and wheaty flavor. Bread made with milk has a more velvety grain, creamy white crumb and browner crust than that made with water. Potato water adds a characteristic flavor and moisture to bread; it gives a loaf of a little greater volume, but slightly coarser in texture.

Sugar. It contributes flavor to bread. Sugar also helps yeast to manufacture gas bubbles and the crust to brown beautifully during baking.

Salt. It contributes flavor, and helps control the action of yeast; if you use too much it checks the growth. Measure it accurately because altering the amount may throw the recipe out of balance.

Fat. Use lard, butter, margarine, vegetable shortening or salad oil, as the recipe suggests. It makes for tenderness, improves the keeping quality and flavor and aids in the browning. Fat also lubricates the gluten meshwork so the dough can expand easily.

How Much Flour to Add. Add enough flour at mixing or kneading time to prevent the dough from sticking to your hands—keep it as soft as you can handle it. If you add flour after the dough has risen, it may make dark streaks and coarsen texture.

To Knead. Turn dough out on lightly floured board or other surface (sticks less to a board). Flatten it with the palms of your hands. Then pick up the edge farthest from you and fold it over to the edge nearest you. Curve your hands over the dough and push gently, but firmly, three or four times with the heel of your hands. Turn the dough a quarter of the way around, fold it over on itself again and push. Repeat this folding, turning and pushing until the dough is smooth and elastic. Use a rocking-rolling motion as you knead. The dough, when kneaded enough, not only looks very smooth, but it also no longer has a sticky feel. (If you are kneading dough that contains fruits, like raisins, for instance, and nuts, look at the dough between the bits of fruit and nuts to see if it is smooth.)

To Rise. The correct temperature is necessary and humidity helps. Place dough in lightly greased bowl; turn it over to grease top. Cover with a sheet of waxed paper and a clean towel to prevent dried crust from forming. Let rise in a warm, humid place (80 to 85°) free from drafts. An unheated oven is an ideal place. Set a pan on the lower rack or the bottom of the oven and fill it with hot water. Or place the bowl of dough in an empty cupboard and set pans of warm water around it. Another way to keep yeast dough and batter warm during rising is to fill a large saucepan or bowl about two thirds full of hot water. Place a wire cooling rack over the top and set the bowl of dough on the rack. In very hot weather, it may be desirable to set the bowl of dough in a pan of cool, but not cold, water. Let dough rise until doubled. To test when it is doubled, press with the tips of two fingers lightly and quickly ½″ into the dough. If the dent stays, the dough is doubled.

To Punch Down. Plunge fist into dough to collapse it; fold edges over to center. Turn dough over in bowl. Let rise again until doubled if recipe so directs.

How to Shape an Oblong Loaf. Turn risen dough onto board; divide and let rest as recipe directs. Flatten dough with hands. Then with rolling pin roll it into a rectangle the size recommended in the recipe. Starting at the narrow side farthest from you, roll tightly like a jelly roll, sealing with each turn. Seal the long seam well; then seal ends of loaf by pressing firmly with sides of hands to make a thin, sealed strip. Use care not to tear dough. Fold sealed ends under. Place loaf, seam side down, in a greased loaf pan of the size specified in the recipe. You may lightly brush top of loaf with salad oil or melted butter. Cover and let rise until doubled or until dent made by gently pressing sides of dough with finger does not disappear. Do not let bread rise too much or it may crumble, be coarse-grained and have a yeasty flavor.

Baking Tips. Place loaves on center shelf in a preheated oven unless recipe directs otherwise. If you are baking 2 loaves, leave at least 2" between pans. If you are baking 3 or 4 loaves, stagger them on 2 shelves. When you bake a large loaf, you can keep the top from browning too much by baking it on the shelf placed at the lowest oven level. Or you can cover the bread loosely, if it starts to brown too fast, with aluminum foil during the last 20 minutes of baking.

For loaves with sides browned like the top and bottom crusts, use anodized aluminum (dull finish), ovenproof glass or darkened metal loaf pans. Shiny metal pans reflect the heat away from the bread. When baking bread in glass pans, the oven temperature needs to be 25° lower than for metal. Recipes in this cookbook indicate when glass baking pans are used, and the temperature given in such recipes is correct. When there is no mention of the pan, other than size, it is a metal pan. The standard loaf pan sizes are 9×5×3" and 8½-×4½×2½".

When baking time is up, remove one loaf from pan and tap the bottom or side of the loaf with forefinger. If there is a hollow sound, the bread is done. If there is no such hollow sound, return bread to oven and bake 5 minutes longer, then test again.

To Cool Bread. Remove bread from pans or baking sheet as soon as baked to prevent steam forming and making bread soggy. Place on wire racks. Cool in place free from drafts to prevent cracking of crust.

The Big Three Breads

The big three yeast-leavened, loaf breads, no matter how you bake them, are white, whole wheat and rye. In this cookbook, we give you several recipes for each that produce the kind of homemade breads farm people rate superior (see Index for those not in this section). Then we also give you recipes for specialty breads—raisin, cheese, orange, prune, cracked wheat, herb and potato, to name a few. Try several of them to find out which kinds are the most praised by your family and friends. It's quite an exciting game to play and one that brings a lot of eating pleasure to your table.

BEST-EVER WHITE BREAD

This is a 2-loaf recipe—dough is easy to handle, loaves are plump

2 c. milk
2 tblsp. sugar
2 tsp. salt
1 tblsp. lard or shortening
1 pkg. active dry yeast
¼ c. warm water (110 to 115°)
6 to 6½ c. sifted all-purpose
   flour

• Scald milk. Stir in sugar, salt and lard. Cool to lukewarm.
• Sprinkle yeast on warm water; stir

to dissolve. Add yeast and 3 c. flour to milk mixture. Beat with spoon until batter is smooth and sheets off spoon. Or beat with electric mixer at medium speed until smooth, about 2 minutes, scraping bowl occasionally.

• Add enough remaining flour, a little at a time, first by spoon and then with hands, to make a dough that leaves the sides of the bowl. Turn onto lightly floured board; cover and let rest 10 minutes.

• Knead until smooth and elastic, 8 to 10 minutes. Round up into a ball and put into lightly greased bowl; turn dough over to grease top. Cover and let rise in warm place until doubled, about 1½ hours. Punch down, cover and let rise again until almost doubled, about 45 minutes.

• Turn onto board and shape into ball. Divide in half. Shape into loaves and place in 2 greased 9×5×3″ loaf pans. Cover and let rise until doubled, about 1 hour.

• Bake in hot oven (400°) 35 minutes, or until deep golden brown. Place on wire racks and let cool away from drafts. Makes 2 loaves.

Note: Just double the recipe for Best-Ever White Bread if you want to bake 4 loaves.

Roll Out the Bubbles

When you get ready to shape dough into loaves, roll it with rolling pin. This removes the big bubbles that otherwise would make holes in the bread. Pay special attention to rolling out bubbles in edges of dough.

RICH WHITE BREAD

This bread makes superlative toast

1   c. milk
2   tblsp. sugar
2   tsp. salt
2   tblsp. lard or shortening
2   pkgs. active dry yeast
½   c. warm water (110 to 115°)
2   eggs
5½ to 6 c. sifted all-purpose flour

• Scald milk; stir in sugar, salt and lard. Cool to lukewarm.

• Sprinkle yeast on warm water; stir to dissolve. Add yeast, eggs and 2¾ c. flour to milk mixture. Beat with spoon until batter is smooth and sheets off spoon. Or beat with electric mixer at medium speed until smooth, about 2 minutes, scraping bowl occasionally.

• Add enough remaining flour, a little at a time, first with spoon and then with hands, to make a dough that leaves sides of bowl. Turn onto lightly floured board, cover and let rest 10 minutes.

• Knead until smooth and elastic, 8 to 10 minutes. Round up into ball and place in lightly greased bowl; turn dough over to grease top. Cover and let rise in a warm place until doubled, 1 to 1½ hours.

• Punch down, cover and let rise until almost doubled, about 30 minutes. Turn onto board and shape into ball; divide in half. Shape into loaves and place in 2 greased 9×5×3″ loaf pans. Cover and let rise in warm place until dough reaches top of pan on sides, fills corners and top is rounded above pan.

• Bake in hot oven (400°) 30 to 40

minutes, or until golden brown. Place on wire racks and cool away from drafts. Makes 2 loaves.

ZUCCHINI MARMALADE

Serve as spread on toasted homemade bread—zucchini adds crunch

2 lbs. young zucchini squash
Juice of 2 lemons
1 tsp. grated lemon peel
1 (13½ oz.) can crushed
     pineapple, drained
1 (1¾ oz.) pkg. powdered fruit
     pectin
5 c. sugar
2 tblsp. finely chopped
     crystallized ginger

• Peel squash and cut in thin slices. Measure 6 c. sliced zucchini into a large kettle.
• Add lemon juice, peel and crushed pineapple. Bring to a boil. Lower heat and simmer, uncovered, until squash is tender but holds its shape, about 15 minutes.
• Add fruit pectin. Place over high heat and bring to a boil. Stir in sugar and ginger. Bring to a full rolling boil and boil hard 1 minute, stirring constantly.
• Remove from heat; skim off any foam. Stir and skim 5 minutes to cool slightly and prevent fruit from floating.
• Ladle into hot, sterilized jars; seal with hot paraffin. Makes 5 half pints.

To Slice Warm Bread

Lay the fragrant, hot loaf on its side on bread board. Cut in neat slices with an electric knife.

WHOLE WHEAT BREAD

Homemade bread at its best—this has a rich wheat flavor and is light

1 pkg. active dry yeast
¼ c. warm water (110 to 115°)
½ c. brown sugar
1 tblsp. salt
2½ c. lukewarm water
¼ c. shortening
3½ c. whole wheat flour
4 c. sifted all-purpose flour

• Sprinkle yeast on ¼ c. warm water; stir to dissolve.
• Dissolve brown sugar and salt in lukewarm water. Add with shortening, whole wheat flour (stirred before measuring) and 1 c. all-purpose flour to yeast. Beat thoroughly to mix well.
• Stir in remaining flour to make a dough that leaves the sides of the bowl. Turn out on floured board, cover and let rest for 10 to 15 minutes. Knead until smooth and elastic, about 10 minutes.
• Place in greased bowl; turn dough over to grease top. Cover and let rise in warm place until doubled, about 1½ hours.
• Punch down. Turn onto board and divide in half; round up each half to make a ball. Cover and let rest 10 minutes.
• Shape into loaves and place in 2 greased 9×5×3″ loaf pans. Let rise until dough reaches top of pan on sides and the top of loaf is well rounded above pan, about 1¼ hours.
• Bake in moderate oven (375°) about 45 minutes, covering loosely with sheet of foil the last 20 minutes if necessary, to prevent excessive browning. Makes 2 loaves.

HONEY WHOLE WHEAT BREAD

A group of Nebraska wheat growers voted this their favorite—recipe from our Freezing & Canning Cookbook

2 pkgs. active dry yeast
5 c. warm water (110 to 115°)
6 tblsp. lard or other shortening
¼ c. honey
4 c. whole wheat flour
½ c. instant potatoes (not reconstituted)
½ c. nonfat dry milk
1 tblsp. salt
6½ to 8 c. sifted all-purpose flour

• Sprinkle yeast on ½ c. warm water; stir to dissolve.
• Melt lard in 6-qt. saucepan; remove from heat, add honey and remaining 4½ c. warm water.
• Mix whole wheat flour (stirred before measuring), instant potatoes, dry milk and salt. Add to saucepan; beat until smooth.
• Add yeast and beat to blend. Then with wooden spoon mix in enough all-purpose flour, a little at a time, to make a dough that leaves the sides of the pan. Turn onto lightly floured board and knead until smooth and satiny and small bubbles appear, 8 to 10 minutes.
• Place in lightly greased bowl; turn dough over to grease top. Cover and let rise in warm place until doubled, 1 to 1½ hours. Punch down dough, turn onto board and divide in thirds. Cover and let rest 5 minutes. Shape into 3 loaves and place in greased 9×5×3″ loaf pans. Cover and let rise until doubled, about 1 hour.
• Bake in hot oven (400°) about 50 minutes, or until bread tests done. Remove from pans and cool on wire racks. Makes 3 loaves.

Note: You may use 1 c. mashed potatoes in place of instant potatoes. Combine with the honey-water mixture.

Extra-good Rye Bread

Swedish women make many kinds of rye breads, all of them good. Usually they flavor their loaves with grated orange peel, caraway seeds or anise seeds. Our Swedish Rye Bread Supreme recipe comes from a farmer's wife in McPherson County, Kansas, who lived in Sweden until she was of high school age. You have a choice of flavorings. Try all three and see which one gets the most compliments.

SWEDISH RYE BREAD SUPREME

Take your pick of caraway or anise seeds or orange peel for flavoring

¼ c. brown sugar
¼ c. light molasses
1 tblsp. salt
2 tblsp. shortening
1½ c. boiling water
1 pkg. active dry yeast
¼ c. warm water (110 to 115°)
2½ c. rye flour
2 to 3 tblsp. caraway seeds
3½ to 4 c. sifted all-purpose flour

• Combine brown sugar, molasses, salt and shortening in large bowl; pour on boiling water and stir until sugar is dissolved. Cool to lukewarm.
• Sprinkle yeast on warm water; stir to dissolve.
• Stir rye flour (stir before measuring) into brown sugar-molasses mix-

ture, beating well. Stir in yeast and caraway seeds; beat until smooth.

• Mix in enough of the all-purpose flour, a little at a time, first with spoon and then with hands, to make a smooth soft dough. Turn onto lightly floured board; knead until satiny and elastic, about 10 minutes. Place dough in lightly greased bowl; turn dough over to grease top. Cover and let rise in warm place until dough is doubled, 1½ to 2 hours.

• Punch down; turn dough onto lightly floured board and divide in half. Round up dough to make 2 balls. Cover and let rest 10 minutes. Shape into loaves and place in 2 greased 8½ × 4½ × 2½" loaf pans. Cover and let rise in a warm place until almost doubled, 1½ to 2 hours.

• Bake in moderate oven (375°) 25 to 30 minutes, covering with sheet of aluminum foil the last 15 minutes if loaves are browning too fast. Turn onto wire racks to cool. Brush loaves with melted butter while warm if you like a soft crust. Makes 2 loaves.

VARIATIONS

Orange-Flavored Rye Bread: Omit caraway seeds and use instead 2 tblsp. grated orange peel.

Anise-Flavored Rye Bread: Omit caraway seeds and in their place use 1 tsp. anise seeds.

Round Loaf Rye Bread: Shape the 2 balls of dough by flattening them slightly instead of shaping into oblongs. Place loaves on opposite corners of greased baking sheet instead of in loaf pans. Let rise and bake as as directed for Swedish Rye Bread Supreme.

Dark Rye Bread

Practically every country in Europe has its own version of rye bread. Most of the breads are darker and coarser than the preceding Scandinavian recipe produces. Pumpernickel is a good example. This bread carries the name of the Swiss baker, Pumper Nickel, who first made it to stretch the limited amount of flour during a wheat shortage. You will notice that our recipe calls for cornmeal, mashed potatoes and whole wheat flour, in addition to rye flour. You can add caraway seeds if you like.

PUMPERNICKEL

A dark moist bread full of flavor— excellent for cheese sandwiches

3   c. cold water
¾   c. cornmeal
¼   c. dark molasses
1   tblsp. caraway seeds
2   tblsp. shortening
4   tsp. salt
1   pkg. active dry yeast
¼   c. warm water (110 to 115°)
2   c. mashed potatoes, made
      with packaged instant mix
5   c. rye flour
6½ to 7 c. whole wheat flour

• Combine cold water and cornmeal in saucepan. Bring to a boil and cook until thick, about 2 minutes, stirring constantly. Remove from heat, add molasses, caraway seeds, shortening and salt. Pour into a large mixing bowl.

• Sprinkle yeast over warm water; stir to dissolve. Add cold potatoes and yeast to cornmeal mixture. Gradually add rye flour and then whole wheat flour (stirred before measuring), to form a stiff dough. Knead on well-floured board until no longer sticky, 10 to 15 minutes (be sure not to underknead).

• Place in greased bowl; turn dough over to grease top. Cover and let rise in warm place until doubled, 2 to 2½ hours. Punch down dough. Knead on board sprinkled with whole wheat flour until dough no longer is sticky, adding more flour if necessary. Divide into 4 equal portions. Shape into round or oblong loaves. Place 2 loaves on each of 2 greased baking sheets, sprinkled liberally with cornmeal. Cover and let rise again in warm place 45 minutes (dough will not double in volume)

• Bake in moderate oven (375°) 40 to 45 minutes. Remove from oven and cool on wire racks. Makes 4 loaves.

Note: For a crisp crust, brush top of loaves with cold water just before baking. For a tender crust, brush with melted butter.

Specialty Breads Start with Raisins

Raisin loaves are international bread favorites. Their goodness depends to no small extent on using soft, plump raisins. If you've had your supply in the cupboard some little time and the raisins seem a little dry, pour boiling water over them. Let stand a few minutes and drain well. Or you may place raisins in a sieve and steam over boiling water.

Toasted raisin bread enjoys continuous popularity. Spread liberally with butter and orange or apricot marmalade, it's mighty inviting alongside a cup of hot tea or coffee. One of our good farm cooks tells how she prevents the glaze or frosting from melting in the electric toaster and making an annoying clean-up job. She inserts two or three wooden toothpicks in each slice of bread just under the top crust. The picks hold the sweet topping above the toaster, away from the heat.

ORANGE-NUT-GLAZED RAISIN BREAD

Rich golden loaves, so delicious . . .
The orange glaze contains walnuts

1 c. milk
1½ tsp. salt
½ c. sugar
½ c. soft butter or shortening
2 pkgs. active dry yeast
¼ c. warm water (110 to 115°)
5¼ to 5¾ c. sifted all-purpose
     flour
2 eggs
1 tsp. grated orange peel
1 tsp. ginger
1½ c. raisins
Orange-Nut Glaze

• Scald milk. Pour over salt, sugar and butter in large bowl. Blend and cool to lukewarm.

• Sprinkle yeast on warm water; stir to dissolve. Add to milk mixture with 2½ c. flour. Beat 2 minutes with electric mixer at medium speed, scraping bowl occasionally. Or beat with spoon until smooth, about 100 strokes.

• Beat in eggs, orange peel, ginger,

raisins and ½ c. flour. Then mix in enough remaining flour, a little at a time, first with spoon and then with hands, to make a soft dough that leaves the sides of bowl.
• Turn onto lightly floured board. Knead just until smooth, about 50 strokes. Round up in ball. Place in a lightly greased bowl; turn dough over to grease top. Cover and let rise in warm place until doubled, 1 to 1½ hours.
• Punch down and let rest for 15 minutes. Divide in half. Shape into loaves and place in 2 greased 8½×-4½×2½" or 9×5×3" loaf pans. Make 3 diagonal slashes ¼" deep across top of each loaf.
• Cover and let rise in warm place only until doubled, about 1 hour.
• Bake in moderate oven (375°) 40 to 50 minutes. Cover with sheet of foil after first 20 minutes of baking if loaves are browning too fast. Remove loaves from pans; place on wire racks. Spread Orange-Nut Glaze on tops, then cool. Makes 2 loaves.

Orange-Nut Glaze: Blend 1 c. sifted confectioners sugar, 2 tsp. soft butter and ½ c. finely chopped walnuts; add 2 to 4 tblsp. orange juice to make glaze of spreading consistency.

CINNAMON TWIST BREAD

Lovely to look at—wonderful to eat

1   c. milk
¼   c. shortening
½   c. sugar
2   tsp. salt
2   pkgs. active dry yeast
½   c. warm water (110 to 115°)
6   c. sifted all-purpose flour
2   eggs, slightly beaten

½   c. sugar
1   tblsp. cinnamon
1   tblsp. soft butter

• Scald milk; stir in shortening, ½ c. sugar and salt. Cool to lukewarm.
• Sprinkle yeast on warm water in large bowl; stir to dissolve. Stir in 3 c. flour, eggs and milk mixture. Beat with electric mixer 2 minutes at medium speed, scraping bowl occasionally. Or beat by hand until batter sheets off spoon. Mix in enough remaining flour with hands, a little at a time, to make a soft dough that cleans the sides of bowl. Turn out onto lightly floured board; knead until smooth, about 10 minutes. Place in lightly greased bowl; turn dough over to grease top. Cover and let rise in warm place until doubled, about 1½ hours.
• Punch down; cover and let rise again until almost doubled, about 30 minutes. Turn onto board; divide in half. Round up each half to make a ball. Cover and let rest 10 minutes.
• Roll each half into a 12×7" rectangle. Combine ½ c. sugar and cinnamon; save out 1 tblsp. for topping. Sprinkle dough rectangles evenly with sugar-cinnamon mixture. Sprinkle 1 tsp. cold water over each rectangle. Spread smooth with spatula. Roll as for jelly roll, starting at narrow end. Seal long edge; tuck under ends. Place, sealed edge down, in 2 greased 9×5×3" loaf pans. Cover and let rise until almost doubled, 45 to 60 minutes.
• Brush tops of loaves with soft butter and sprinkle with reserved sugar-cinnamon mixture.
• Bake in moderate oven (375°) 35 to 40 minutes. Cover tops of loaves

with aluminum foil the last 15 minutes of baking, if necessary, to prevent excessive browning. Remove from pans and cool on wire racks. Makes 2 loaves.

WHEAT GERM BREAD

Good for you and extra-good tasting

1 ¾ c. milk
2 tblsp. sugar
1 tblsp. salt
¼ c. shortening
2 pkgs. active dry yeast
½ c. warm water (110 to 115°)
⅓ c. wheat germ
5 to 6 c. sifted all-purpose
   flour
Melted butter or margarine
Sesame seeds

• Scald milk; add sugar, salt and shortening. Stir and cool to lukewarm.
• Sprinkle yeast on warm water; stir to dissolve.
• Combine milk mixture, yeast, wheat germ and 2½ c. flour. Beat with electric mixer at medium speed, scraping bowl occasionally, 2 minutes. Or beat by hand until batter is smooth.
• Mix in enough remaining flour with spoon and hands to make a dough that leaves the sides of bowl. Turn onto board and knead until smooth and elastic, about 10 minutes. Place in lightly greased bowl; turn dough over to grease top. Cover and let rise in warm place until doubled, about 1 hour. Punch down; cover and let rise until doubled, about 30 minutes.
• Turn dough onto board; divide in half. Round up to make 2 balls. Cover and let rest 10 to 15 minutes. Shape into 2 loaves and place in greased 9×5×3" loaf pans. Cover and let rise until almost doubled, 50 to 60 minutes. Brush tops of loaves with butter and sprinkle with sesame seeds.
• Bake in hot oven (425°) 25 to 30 minutes, or until bread tests done. Makes 2 loaves.

OLD-FASHIONED OATMEAL BREAD

Loaves with tempting homemade look and taste go fast at bake sales

2 c. milk
2 c. quick rolled oats, uncooked
¼ c. brown sugar, firmly packed
1 tblsp. salt
2 tblsp. shortening
1 pkg. active dry yeast
½ c. warm water (110 to 115°)
5 c. sifted all-purpose flour
   (about)
1 egg white
1 tblsp. water
Rolled oats

• Scald milk; stir in 2 c. rolled oats, brown sugar, salt and shortening. Remove from heat and cool to lukewarm.
• Sprinkle yeast on warm water; stir to dissolve.
• Add milk mixture and 2 c. flour to yeast. Beat with electric mixer on medium speed, scraping the bowl occasionally, 2 minutes. Or beat with spoon until batter is smooth.
• Add enough remaining flour, a little at a time, first with spoon and then with hands, to make a soft dough that leaves the sides of the bowl. Turn onto floured board; knead until dough is smooth and elastic, 8 to 10 minutes. Place in lightly greased bowl; turn dough over to grease top. Cover and

let rise in warm place until doubled, 1 to 1½ hours. Punch down and let rise again until nearly doubled, about 30 minutes.

• Turn onto board and divide in half. Round up to make 2 balls. Cover and let rest 10 minutes. Shape into loaves and place in greased 9×5×3" loaf pans. Let rise until almost doubled, about 1 hour and 15 minutes. Brush tops of loaves with egg white beaten with water and sprinkle with rolled oats.

• Bake in moderate oven (375°) about 40 minutes. (If bread starts to brown too much, cover loosely with sheet of aluminum foil after baking 15 minutes.) Makes 2 loaves.

Cracked Wheat Bread Sells Fast

A Minnesota farm woman grinds some of their new crop of wheat every year to make a dark bread, flecked with crunchy bits of cracked wheat. Her family and friends are fond of her tasty loaves. She also bakes them for her church's food sales, and customers buy them almost as soon as they arrive.

She wraps each loaf in clear plastic wrap to keep it fresh and to show off its golden beauty. She cuts some loaves in half and wraps them separately so that everyone can see the interesting color and texture of the inside of the loaves. Families of two buy up these half loaves, which look so good that they encourage more people to buy whole loaves.

Once you bake this bread and taste it, you'll not wonder at its popularity.

If you don't have your own wheat to grind, you can buy cracked wheat in packages at health food stores.

CRACKED WHEAT BREAD

Disappears fast at church bake sales

1   c. milk
1 ½ tblsp. shortening
1 ½ tsp. salt
1 ½ tblsp. molasses
1   pkg. active dry yeast
1 ¼ c. warm water (110 to
        115°)
1   c. rye flour
1   c. cracked wheat
4   to 4 ½ c. sifted all-purpose
        flour

• Scald milk; add shortening, salt and molasses. Cool to lukewarm.

• Sprinkle yeast on warm water in large mixing bowl; stir to dissolve. Stir in rye flour, cracked wheat, 1½ c. all-purpose flour and milk mixture. Beat with electric mixer at medium speed for 2 minutes, scraping bowl occasionally.

• Stir in remaining flour, a little at a time, to make a dough that leaves the sides of the bowl. Turn onto lightly floured board and knead until satiny and elastic, about 10 minutes.

• Place in lightly greased bowl; turn dough over to grease top. Cover and let rise in warm place until doubled, 1 to 1½ hours. Punch down, cover and let rise again until doubled, about 45 minutes.

• Turn dough onto board; divide in half. Round up in balls, cover and let rest 10 minutes. Shape into loaves and place in 2 greased 9×5×3" loaf pans. Cover and let rise again until doubled, about 1 hour.

• Bake in moderate oven (375°) 45 minutes, covering with foil last 10 minutes to prevent excessive browning. Turn from pans onto wire racks. Brush tops of warm loaves with melted butter if desired. Makes 2 loaves.

Roadside Potato Bread

Plump, richly browned loaves of potato bread are farm kitchen specialties. Many women treasure their mothers' recipes for them, but almost every home baker now simplifies her recipes by using packaged instant potatoes. This eliminates the work of peeling, cooking and mashing. Frequently milk substitutes for potato water; it gives the bread increased nutritional value and helps ovens to brown the crusts beautifully.

The recipe that follows comes from a Pennsylvania farmer's wife; she calls the loaves Roadside Potato Bread. That's because her mother used to sell them at a roadside market.

"When September nights have a cidery fragrance of orchards and vineyards and the smell of new-mown hay," she says, "I start thinking of the cold weather ahead. I visualize my kitchen filled with the aroma of baking bread. By the time the first frosts swagger across the fields, I have my bread recipe file on the counter top. Roadside Potato Bread will be one of my first bakings. We like it toasted and spread with homemade jelly or jam. It's just the change we need at breakfast to start busy, chilly days in good spirits."

Here is her version of the heirloom recipe.

ROADSIDE POTATO BREAD

Dusting cornmeal inside greased pans gives crust an interesting look

3½ c. milk
6   tblsp. sugar
6   tblsp. lard or butter
2   tsp. salt
¼   c. instant mashed potatoes (not reconstituted)
2   pkgs. active dry yeast
½   c. warm water (110 to 115°)
10 to 11 c. sifted all-purpose flour
3   tblsp. cornmeal

• Scald milk; pour into large bowl and stir in sugar, lard, salt and instant mashed potatoes. Cool to lukewarm.
• Sprinkle yeast on warm water; stir to dissolve.
• Add yeast and 4 c. flour to milk mixture. Beat 2 minutes with electric mixer at medium speed, or until batter is smooth. Or beat by hand. Mix in just enough of remaining flour, a little at a time, first with spoon and then with hands, to make a dough that leaves the sides of bowl.
• Turn onto lightly floured board; cover and let rest 10 to 15 minutes. Knead until smooth, about 10 minutes. Place in greased bowl; turn dough over to grease top. Cover and let rise in warm place until doubled, 1½ to 2 hours. Punch down dough; cover and let rise again until doubled, about 45 minutes.
• Turn onto board and divide in 3 equal parts; round up in balls, cover and let rest 10 minutes.
• Meanwhile, grease 3 (8½ × 4½ × 2½") loaf pans. Sprinkle bottoms and sides of pans with cornmeal (1 tblsp. to each pan).

• Shape dough into loaves; place in pans, cover and let rise until doubled, 50 to 60 minutes.

• Bake in moderate oven (375°) 45 minutes, or until loaves are rich brown and have a hollow sound when tapped with fingers. Remove from pans; cool on wire racks. Makes 3 loaves.

ITALIAN BREAD

Long kneading gives this the characteristics of Italian—and French— loaves

2   pkgs. active dry yeast
2½ c. warm water (110 to 115°)
7¼ to 7¾ c. sifted all-purpose
        flour
1   tblsp. salt
Yellow cornmeal
1   egg white, slightly beaten
1   tblsp. cold water

• Sprinkle yeast on warm water; stir to dissolve.

• Add 2 c. flour and beat thoroughly; stir in salt. Stir in 4½ c. flour (about) a cupful at a time; the dough will be stiff.

• Turn onto a lightly floured board, cover with a clean towel and let rest 10 to 15 minutes. Knead 15 to 25 minutes, until dough is smooth and very elastic, working in ¾ to 1¼ c. more flour. Do not underknead.

• Place in lightly greased bowl; turn dough over to grease top. Cover and let rise in a warm place free from drafts until doubled, about 1½ hours. Punch down, let rise again until doubled, about 1 hour.

• Turn onto lightly floured board, divide in half, cover and let rest 10 minutes.

• Roll each half in a 15×12″ rectangle; the dough will be about ¼″ thick. Starting with the long side, roll up tightly, sealing each turn well with the hands. Roll the ends between hands to taper them and place diagonally, seam side down, on greased baking sheet sprinkled with cornmeal. Cut slits ⅛″ deep and 2″ apart on tops of loaf. Combine egg white and cold water. Brush on tops and sides of loaves. Cover with towel wrung from water, but do not let it touch the bread; prop it with iced tea glasses turned upside down. Let rise in warm place until doubled, 1 to 1½ hours.

• Place a large, shallow pan on the floor or low rack of a moderate oven (375°); fill with boiling water. Bake loaves about 20 minutes, or until light brown. Brush tops and sides again with egg white-water mixture. Bake 20 minutes longer, or until loaves are a golden brown. Cool. Makes 2 loaves.

VARIATIONS

Italian Bread—Round Loaves: Shape each half of dough into a ball instead of into a long loaf. Place on baking sheet, sprinkled with cornmeal, and with sharp knife make 3 or 4 cuts ⅛″ deep on tops of loaves. Brush with egg white-water mixture and let rise and bake like Italian Bread.

French Bread: Much French Bread is made exactly like Italian Bread, but sometimes either 1 tblsp. sugar or 1 tblsp. melted shortening is added.

Summer Flour Storage

If space permits, keep flour in freezer during the extremely hot weather.

PIZZA SANDWICHES

Make these appetizing sandwiches with Italian Bread for a teen treat

• Cut 1 loaf Italian Bread in half lengthwise. Spread with butter. Combine ¾ c. lean ground beef, ½ c. grated Parmesan cheese, ½ tsp. dried orégano leaves, 1 tsp. salt, ⅛ tsp. pepper, 1½ tblsp. minced onion and 1½ (6 oz.) cans tomato paste.

• Spread mixture on cut sides of bread. Place, cut side up, on baking sheet. Top with thin slices of 2 ripe tomatoes. Bake in moderate oven (350°) 20 minutes.

• Remove from oven; top with 8 slices process American cheese. Return to oven until cheese melts, about 5 minutes. Cut to make 8 to 10 servings.

BREAD STICKS

Sticks are jaunty served from a tall glass—serve with Italian dishes

¾ c. milk
1 tblsp. sugar
2 tsp. salt
1 tblsp. soft shortening
1 pkg. active dry yeast
¼ c. warm water (110 to 115°)
3 to 3¼ c. sifted all-purpose
   flour
Bread Stick Topping

• Scald milk. Remove from heat and add sugar, salt and shortening. Blend and cool to lukewarm.

• Sprinkle yeast over warm water; stir to dissolve.

• Add the milk mixture and 1½ c. flour to the yeast. Beat with electric mixer at medium speed until smooth, scraping the bowl occasionally (100

strokes by hand). Add more flour, a little at a time, first with spoon and then with hand, until dough leaves the sides of bowl.

• Turn dough onto lightly floured board. Knead until smooth and elastic, about 8 minutes. Place in lightly greased bowl; turn dough over to grease top. Cover and let rise in warm place until doubled, about 45 minutes.

• Turn dough onto board and roll to a 16×6″ rectangle. From wide side, cut into ½″ strips. Roll each strip under hand to make pencil shape. Dough strips will be 8″ long. Place a little apart on 2 greased baking sheets. Let rise in warm place 15 minutes. Brush sticks with Topping.

• Bake in hot oven (400°) 10 to 15 minutes, or until golden brown. Cool on wire racks. Makes 32 bread sticks.

Bread Stick Topping: Mix 1 egg white with 1 tblsp. water. Brush on bread sticks just before baking; sprinkle with poppy or sesame seeds or coarse salt.

VARIATION

Crunchy Bread Sticks: Place the cooled sticks on 2 ungreased baking sheets. Place in very slow oven (250°), turning occasionally, for 45 to 60 minutes, or until evenly browned. Cool on racks.

Hold That Air

When slashing or scoring the tops of loaves, as for French and some rye breads, use care not to drive out the air and flatten the loaf. Make shallow cuts with a very sharp knife or a safety razor blade.

CHEESE BREAD

A favorite from our Country Cookbook; *excellent for toasting, as a base for creamed foods*

1 ¾ c. milk
¼   c. sugar
2   tsp. salt
2   tblsp. butter
3   c. shredded process cheese
1   pkg. active dry yeast
¼   c. warm water (110 to 115°)
5 ½ c. sifted all-purpose flour

• Scald milk; remove from heat and stir in sugar, salt, butter and 2 c. cheese. Stir constantly until cheese melts. Cool to lukewarm.

• Sprinkle yeast on warm water; stir to dissolve.

• Combine cheese mixture, yeast, 2½ c. flour and remaining 1 c. cheese. Beat with electric mixer at medium speed, scraping the bowl occasionally, 2 minutes. Or beat by hand until batter is smooth.

• Add enough remaining flour, a little at a time, first by spoon and then with hands, to make a dough that leaves the sides of bowl. Turn onto lightly floured board and knead until smooth and elastic, 8 to 10 minutes. Place in lightly greased bowl; turn dough over to grease top. Cover and let rise until doubled, about 1½ hours.

• Turn onto board; punch down and divide into thirds. Round up to make 3 balls, cover and let rest 10 minutes. Shape into loaves and place in 3 greased 9×5×3″ loaf pans. Cover and let rise until almost doubled, about 1 hour.

• Bake in moderate oven (375°) about 40 minutes. (Bread browns easily. If it starts to brown too much, cover loosely with sheet of aluminum foil the last 20 minutes of baking.) Makes 3 loaves.

ONION BREAD

Bread has beef-onion taste; team it with vegetable salad or soup

2   c. water
1   (1 ⅜ oz.) pkg. onion soup
      mix
2   tblsp. sugar
1   tsp. salt
2   tblsp. grated Parmesan cheese
2   tblsp. shortening
1   pkg. active dry yeast
¼   c. warm water (110 to 115°)
5 ½ to 6 c. sifted all-purpose
      flour

• Bring 2 c. water to boiling in saucepan; add soup mix and simmer, covered, 10 minutes. Stir in sugar, salt, cheese and shortening; cool to lukewarm.

• Sprinkle yeast on warm water in large bowl; stir to dissolve. Stir in onion soup mixture and 2½ c. flour. Beat with electric mixer at medium speed, scraping the bowl occasionally, 2 minutes, or by hand until batter sheets from spoon. Mix in remaining flour, a little at a time, first with spoon and then with hands, until dough leaves the sides of bowl. Dough will be moderately stiff. Turn onto lightly floured board.

· Knead until dough is smooth, place in lightly greased bowl and turn dough over to grease top. Cover and let rise in warm place until doubled, about 1½ hours. Punch down, turn onto board and divide in half. Cover and let rest 10 minutes. Shape into loaves and place in 2 greased 9×5×3″ loaf pans. Cover and let rise until doubled, about 1 hour.

· Bake in hot oven (400°) 30 to 40 minutes, or until browned. Makes 2 loaves.

ORANGE BREAD

Favorite from our Freezing & Canning Cookbook; *spread with ground dates and nuts for party sandwiches*

    2   pkgs. active dry yeast
    ½   c. warm water (110 to 115°)
    1½ c. warm orange juice (110 to
        115°)
    5   to 6 c. sifted all-purpose
        flour
    ½   c. sugar
    2   tsp. salt
    ¼   c. soft lard or butter
    ¼   c. grated orange peel

· Sprinkle yeast on warm water in large bowl; stir to dissolve. Add orange juice and 2 c. flour. Beat with electric mixer at medium speed 2 minutes, scraping bowl occasionally, or beat by hand until smooth. Stir in sugar, salt, lard and orange peel. Mix

in enough remaining flour, a little at a time, first with spoon and then with hands, to make a dough that leaves sides of bowl.

· Turn out on lightly floured board and knead until satiny and elastic, 5 to 8 minutes. Place in lightly greased bowl; turn dough over to grease top. Cover and let rise in warm place until doubled, about 1½ hours.

· Punch down. Turn onto board and divide in half. Cover; let rest 5 minutes. Shape into 2 loaves and place in greased 8½ × 4½ × 2½″ loaf pans. Brush tops lightly with butter, cover and let rise until doubled, about 1 hour.

· Bake in moderate oven (375°) about 45 minutes (watch bread—it browns quickly). Cover with foil after baking 30 minutes if loaves start to brown too much. Cool. Makes 2 loaves.

VARIATION

Orange-Cinnamon Swirl: Roll half of dough into rectangle ¼″ thick, 6″ wide, 20″ long. Brush with 1 tblsp. melted butter. Mix 3 tblsp. sugar and 1½ tsp. cinnamon. Sprinkle evenly over dough, reserving 1 tblsp. for top of loaf. Roll like jelly roll, starting at narrow end. Seal ends. Place, seam side down, in a greased 8½ × 4½ × 2½″ loaf pan. Sprinkle with reserved sugar-cinnamon mixture. Cover and let rise until a little more than doubled, about 1¼ hours.

· Bake in moderate oven (375°) about 45 minutes. Cool on wire rack. Makes 1 loaf.

GOLDEN PUMPKIN BREAD

Cheerful yellow color with brown crust—it has faint pumpkin pie taste

1   c. milk
1   c. canned pumpkin
¼   c. shortening
¼   c. sugar
2   tsp. salt
1   tsp. cinnamon
½   tsp. ginger
½   tsp. cardamom
2   pkgs. active dry yeast
½   c. warm water (110 to 115°)
6½   c. sifted all-purpose flour
2   eggs

• Scald milk; stir in pumpkin, shortening, sugar, salt and spices. Cool to lukewarm.

• Sprinkle yeast on warm water; stir to dissolve.

• Add 3 c. flour, milk mixture and eggs to yeast. Beat with electric mixer at medium speed 2 minutes, scraping the bowl occasionally. Or beat by hand until batter is smooth.

• Mix in enough remaining flour, a little at a time, first with spoon and then with hands, to make a dough that leaves the sides of bowl.

• Turn onto lightly floured board. Knead until smooth and elastic, 8 to 10 minutes. Place in lightly greased bowl and turn dough over to grease top. Cover and let rise in warm place until doubled, 1 to 1½ hours. Punch down. Turn onto board, divide in half and round up to make 2 balls. Shape in loaves and place in 2 greased 9×5×3″ loaf pans. Brush tops of loaves with melted butter. Cover and let rise until almost doubled, about 50 minutes.

• Bake in moderate oven (375°) about

35 minutes, or until bread tests done. Makes 2 loaves.

VARIATION

Spiced Pumpkin Raisin Bread: Stir 1½ c. seedless raisins into batter before adding second portion of flour with spoon and hands when making Golden Pumpkin Bread.

PRUNE BREAD

Another popular bread from our Freezing & Canning Cookbook—moist loaves are excellent for toast

2   pkgs. active dry yeast
2   c. warm water (110 to 115°)
½   c. nonfat dry milk (not reconstituted)
½   c. sugar
1½   tsp. salt
1   tsp. cinnamon
8   to 9 c. sifted all-purpose flour
½   c. soft butter or lard
3   eggs, beaten
2   tblsp. grated lemon peel
2   c. cooked, pitted and chopped prunes

• Sprinkle yeast on ½ c. warm water in big bowl; stir to dissolve. Add remaining water, dry milk, sugar, salt, cinnamon and 3 c. flour. Stir until smooth.

• Add 3 c. flour and remaining ingredients. Stir until well blended. Mix in enough remaining flour, a little at a time, first with spoon and then with hands, to make a dough that leaves the sides of bowl. Dough will be soft.

• Turn onto board; knead thoroughly, about 5 minutes. Add more flour, if needed, to prevent dough sticking to board.

• Place in lightly greased bowl; turn dough over to grease top. Cover and let rise in warm place until doubled, about 1½ hours. Punch down, turn onto board and divide dough in thirds. Cover and let rest 5 minutes. Shape into 3 loaves and place in greased 8½ × 4½ × 2½" loaf pans. Brush with melted fat; let rise until doubled, about 1 hour.

Bake in moderate oven (375°) about 50 minutes. Remove from pans and cool on wire racks. Makes 3 loaves.

HUNGARIAN WHITE BREAD

Here's a delicious way to use herbs— they provide a subtle fine flavor

2   pkgs. active dry yeast
2   c. warm water (110 to 115°)
6   to 7 c. sifted all-purpose flour
3   tblsp. sugar
2   tsp. salt
2   tblsp. salad oil
¼   tsp. anise
½   tsp. fennel

• Sprinkle yeast on warm water; stir to dissolve.
• Blend in 3 c. flour, sugar, salt, oil and herbs. Beat with electric mixer on medium speed about 2 minutes, scraping the bowl occasionally, or until batter is smooth. Or beat about 100 strokes with a spoon.
• Add enough remaining flour, a little at a time, first with a spoon and then with hands, to make a dough that leaves the sides of bowl. Turn onto lightly floured board, let rest 10 minutes and knead until dough is smooth and elastic (little bubbles will show beneath surface).
• Place in lightly greased bowl; turn dough over to grease top. Cover with clean towel and let rise in a warm place free from drafts until doubled, 45 minutes to 1 hour.
• Punch down dough, turn over in bowl, cover and let rise 15 minutes more. Turn out onto board, divide in half, and shape into 2 round loaves. Cover and let rest 10 minutes. Cut 3 or 4 slits ⅛" deep on top of each loaf. Place on opposite corners of a greased 15½ × 12" baking sheet, or on 2 baking sheets. Cover and let rise in a warm place until almost doubled, 40 to 50 minutes.
• Bake in hot oven (400°) 30 to 40 minutes, or until well browned. Remove from baking sheet and cool on racks. Makes 2 round loaves.

Note: If you like a soft crust, brush tops and sides of loaves while hot with butter or shortening.

TOMATO BREAD

Pretty pink bread —a meat and cheese sandwich special

2   c. tomato juice
2   tblsp. butter
3   tblsp. sugar
1   tsp. salt
¼   c. tomato ketchup
1   pkg. active dry yeast
¼   c. warm water (110 to 115°)
7   c. sifted all-purpose flour
     (about)

• Heat tomato juice and butter together until butter is melted. Add sugar, salt and ketchup. Let cool to lukewarm.
• Sprinkle yeast on warm water; stir to dissolve.
• Add tomato mixture and 3 c. flour to yeast. Beat with electric mixer at

medium speed, scraping the bowl occasionally, 2 minutes. Or beat by hand until smooth.

• Mix in enough remaining flour, a little at a time, first with spoon and then with hands, to make a soft dough that leaves the sides of bowl. Turn onto lightly floured board and knead until smooth and elastic, 8 to 10 minutes. Place in lightly greased bowl; turn dough over to grease top. Cover and let rise in warm place until doubled, 1 to 1½ hours. Punch down and divide in half. Cover and let rest 10 minutes. Shape into loaves and place in greased 9×5×3″ loaf pans. Cover and let rise until almost doubled, about 1 hour.

• Bake in hot oven (425°) about 25 minutes, or until bread tests done. Makes 2 loaves.

• Mix in remaining flour, a little at a time, until dough leaves the sides of bowl.

• Turn onto lightly floured board and knead until smooth and elastic, 8 to 10 minutes. Place in lightly greased bowl; turn dough over to grease top. Cover and let rise in warm place until doubled, 1 to 1½ hours. Punch down; cover and let rise again until almost doubled, about 45 minutes.

• Turn dough onto board, divide in half and round up to make smooth balls. Cover and let rest 10 to 15 minutes. Shape into loaves and place in 2 greased 9×5×3″ loaf pans. Cover and let rise until doubled, about 1 hour.

• Bake in hot oven (400°) 35 minutes, or until bread tests done. Makes 2 loaves.

HERB BREAD

Perfect companion for chicken

1 ½   c. milk
¼   c. sugar
1   tblsp. salt
2   tsp. celery seeds
1   tsp. ground sage
2   pkgs. active dry yeast
½   c. warm water (110 to 115°)
¼   c. shortening
2   eggs, slightly beaten
7½   c. flour (about)

• Scald milk; stir in sugar, salt, celery seeds and sage. Cool to lukewarm.

• Sprinkle yeast on warm water; stir to dissolve.

• Combine milk mixture, shortening, eggs and 3 c. flour; add yeast. Beat with electric mixer at medium speed, scraping bowl occasionally, 2 minutes. Or beat with spoon until smooth.

Feather-light, Tender Rolls

The country hostess knows what piping hot, homemade rolls do for guest meals. When she passes hot rolls, whatever else she has on the table seems special, too. A Hoosier farmer's wife says: "Because my homemade rolls attract so much favorable attention, I try to get double duty out of them. I like to have them ready to bake so that I can run them in the oven when guests drive into the yard. That heavenly, yeasty aroma of baking bread greets them at the door and is a promise of something wonderful to come. It works like a charm. The anticipation is great, and there's no letdown at mealtime."

Excellent rolls are simple to bake. The important point is to keep the dough soft—as soft as you can handle. You can take a choice of rolls that you knead briefly, those you don't knead at all or refrigerator rolls. We give you recipes for all.

To dramatize your hot rolls, form the dough in different shapes. It may take a litte practice, but we tell you how. Pass a napkin-lined basket or tray of cloverleafs, knots and braids, for instance.

Serve the rolls so hot that the butter spread on melts pronto. If you need to warm them at mealtime, put them in a brown paper bag in a moderate oven (350°) for 15 to 20 minutes. Or if they're frozen, wrap them in aluminum foil and heat in a hot oven (400°) about 20 minutes. One more point to heed—after baking, remove rolls at once from pans or baking sheet. Cool on wire racks if you do not serve right away.

HOW TO SHAPE ROLLS

Cloverleafs: Shape dough in long rolls 1″ in diameter. Cut off 1″ pieces and form each into a small ball. Place 3 balls in each greased muffin-pan cup. Balls should touch bottom of cups and fill them half full. Brush with melted butter or margarine.

Four-Leaf Clovers: Place 2″ ball of dough in each greased muffin-pan cup. With scissors cut surface of each ball in half and then across again to make fourths.

Butterhorns: Roll dough ¼″ thick, brush with melted butter or margarine and cut in 12″ circle. Cut circle in 16 pie-shaped pieces. Starting at wide or curved end, roll up. Place, point end down, on greased baking sheet, 2″ apart.

Crescents: Make like Butterhorns, but curve ends of each roll on baking sheet to make crescent shapes.

Fan-Tans. Roll dough ⅛″ thick into an oblong. Brush with melted butter or margarine. Cut in strips 1½″ wide. Stack 6 strips; cut in 1½″ pieces. Place cut side down, in greased muffin-pan cups.

Pan Rolls. Shape dough in 2″ balls. Dip in melted butter or margarine. Place in greased round layer cake pans, letting balls just touch one another.

Dinner Rolls: Shape dough in 2″ balls. Roll each ball with floured hands until 4″ long. Roll ends between hands to taper. Place on greased baking sheet, 2″ apart.

Parkerhouse Rolls: Roll dough ¼″ thick on lightly floured board; cut in rounds with 2½″ floured biscuit or cookie cutter. Brush with melted butter. Make a crease in each round just off center with back of table knife. Fold larger side of each round over other side, overlapping slightly. Seal end edges. Brush with melted butter; place rolls about 1″ apart on greased baking sheet.

Butterfly Rolls: Roll dough into rectangle about ¼″ thick, 6″ wide. Brush with melted butter or margarine and roll like a jelly roll. Cut in 2″ widths. Make a depression down center of each with a small wooden handle. Place on greased baking sheet.

Easter Bunnies: Shape dough into long ropes ¾ to 1″ in diameter; cut in 10 to 12″ lengths. Tie in loose knots, bringing ends straight up to make ears. Press in raisins for eyes. Brush with 1 egg yolk beaten with 1 tblsp. water. Let rise on greased baking sheet. After baking and while still warm, frost lightly with Confectioners Sugar Frosting (see Index), tinting some of frosting a pale pink for bunnies' ears.

Roll dough into an oblong about 12" long and a scant ½" thick. Cut in strips ½" wide, 6" long, and shape rolls as follows:

Snails: Hold one end of strip on greased baking sheet and twist. Wind strip round and round to make coil. Tuck end under.

Figure 8s: Hold one end of strip in one hand; twist other end, stretching strip slightly until the two ends, when placed together on greased baking sheet, make a Figure 8.

Twists. Make like Figure 8s, but give each circle of Figure 8 an additional twist before placing on greased baking sheet.

Knots: Form loop of strip and ease one end through loop to make a knot. Press ends down on greased baking sheet.

Rosebuds: Form twisted strip into a loop; pull one end up through center of loop (making a knot) and bring other end over the side and under.

Braids: Form several ropes of dough ½" in diameter. Braid 3 ropes into a long braid. Repeat with other ropes. Cut braids into 3½" lengths. Pinch together at both ends; then gently pull to lengthen braids. Lay on greased baking sheets; brush lightly with melted butter.

RICH HOT ROLLS

Light, tender, rich, delicious

¾   c. milk
½   c. shortening
½   c. sugar
1   tsp. salt
2   pkgs. active dry yeast
½   c. warm water (110 to 115°)
4¼ to 4¾ c. sifted all-purpose
        flour
2   eggs

• Scald milk; add shortening, sugar and salt. Cool to lukewarm.
• Sprinkle yeast on warm water; stir to dissolve.
• Add 1½ c. flour to milk mixture; beat well by hand or with electric mixer at low speed 1 minute. Beat in eggs and yeast.
• Gradually stir in enough remaining flour, a little at a time, to make a soft dough that leaves the sides of bowl. Turn onto lightly floured board; knead until smooth, satiny and no longer sticky, 5 to 8 minutes.
• Place in lightly greased bowl; invert to grease top. Cover and let rise in warm place until doubled, 1 to 1½ hours. Punch down and turn onto board. Divide in half and shape as desired (see How to Shape Rolls).
• Brush tops lightly with melted butter; let rise until doubled, 30 to 45 minutes.
• Bake in moderate oven (375°) 12 to 15 minutes, or until golden brown. Makes about 30 rolls, exact number depending on shape and size.

VARIATIONS

Plain Rolls (less rich): Reduce sugar to ¼ c. and shortening to ⅓ c. in recipe for Rich Hot Rolls.

Cinnamon Rolls: Divide risen dough for Rich Hot Rolls in half. Roll each half into a 16×8″ rectangle. Combine 1 c. sugar, ½ c. melted butter and 1 tblsp. cinnamon. Spread half of mixture on each rectangle. If you like, scatter ⅓ c. raisins over each rectangle. Roll lengthwise as for jelly roll; seal edges. Cut in 1″ slices. Place, cut side down, in 2 well-greased 9×9×2″ pans. Cover and let rise until doubled, 30 to 40 minutes. Bake in moderate oven (375°) 20 to 25 minutes. Remove to wire racks. Makes 32 rolls.

Note: Frost rolls with Confectioners Sugar Frosting, if you like.

Butterscotch Rolls: Use one half of risen dough for Rich Hot Rolls. Roll dough into a 16×8″ rectangle. Brush with ¼ c. melted butter. Sprinkle with ⅓ c. brown sugar combined with 1 tsp. cinnamon. Roll lengthwise as for jelly roll; seal edges. Cut in 1″ slices.
• Pour ¼ c. melted butter into a 9×9×2″ pan; grease sides of pan. Stir ½ c. brown sugar and 1 tblsp. light corn syrup into butter in pan; mix well. Heat slowly, stirring constantly, until mixture is syrupy and spreads evenly over bottom. Remove from heat. Sprinkle with ⅓ c. finely chopped pecans.
• Place rolls, cut side down, over syrup mixture. Cover and let rise until doubled, 30 to 45 minutes. Bake in moderate oven (375°) about 20 minutes. Cool 3 minutes in pan; then invert on rack (place waxed paper under rack to catch any drippings). Makes 16 rolls.

EVERYDAY ROLLS

Rolls are not rich—they taste like warm fresh-baked loaf bread

1   c. milk
2   tblsp. sugar
1   tsp. salt
2   tblsp. shortening
1   pkg. active dry yeast
¼   c. warm water (110 to 115°)
3½ c. sifted all-purpose flour
1   egg
Melted butter

• Scald milk; add sugar, salt and shortening. Cool to lukewarm.
• Sprinkle yeast on warm water; stir to dissolve.
• Combine milk mixture and 1 c. flour; beat 1 minute with electric mixer at low speed. Add yeast and egg. Beat again with electric mixer until smooth.
• Stir in remaining flour, a little at a time, beating after each addition, until you have a soft dough. Cover and let rise in warm place until doubled, 1 to 1½ hours. Turn out onto lightly floured board, toss to coat with flour and knead about 15 strokes to force out large bubbles and to smooth dough.
• Shape in 2″ balls and place close together in greased 9″ layer cake pan. Brush tops with melted butter. Cover and let rise until doubled, 30 to 45 minutes.
• Bake in moderate oven (375°) 25 to 30 minutes, or until golden. Turn out onto wire rack. Serve hot. Makes 16 rolls.

For Soft Golden Crusts

Brush yeast bread or rolls right after baking with melted butter.

Crusty Brown Rolls

There are four important rules to heed in baking crusty rolls:
• Use water for the liquid. Milk makes soft crusts.
• Brush rolls with water or Egg Wash during the rising and before baking. We give you directions for each type of roll.
• Bake rolls in a steam-filled oven (see recipe).
• Rub no shortening on the rolls before or after baking.

CRUSTY BROWN ROLLS

Hard, chewy, delicious—so popular we reprinted recipe from Cooking for Company

    2   pkgs. active dry yeast
    1 ¾ c. warm water (110 to 115°)
    4   tsp. sugar
    2   tsp. salt
    2   tblsp. melted shortening
    6 ½ to 7 c. sifted all-purpose flour
    3   egg whites, beaten stiff
    Egg Wash

• Sprinkle yeast on warm water; stir to dissolve. Add sugar, salt, shortening and 2 c. flour; beat well. Add egg whites. Add remaining flour until dough leaves the sides of bowl when you stir it.
• Turn out on lightly floured surface. Knead until dough is smooth and elastic, and tiny blisters show on the surface (about 5 minutes).
• Place in a lightly greased bowl; turn dough over to grease top. Cover with a damp cloth.
• Let rise in a warm place until doubled, about 1 hour. Punch down.

• You may shape the dough at this point. For superior results, let the dough rise again until doubled; then punch it down and shape.
• Follow directions for shaping given with each type roll (see Variations).
• Place rolls on greased baking sheets sprinkled lightly with cornmeal. Brush with Egg Wash or with water. Cover and let rise until doubled, about 20 minutes. Brush again with Egg Wash or water.
• Bake in a hot oven (425°) 20 minutes, or until brown and crusty. Place a large shallow pan of boiling water on the bottom of oven to provide steam while the rolls bake. This makes the rolls crusty. Makes about 3 dozen rolls.

Egg Wash: Beat slightly 1 egg white with 1 tblsp. water. Brush on rolls.

VARIATIONS

French Rolls: Shape raised dough in 3″ balls; flatten under hands to make 4″ circles or 6″ tapered oblongs ¾″ thick. Use a very sharp knife or razor to make shallow cuts about ¼″ deep on top. Place on baking sheet, brush with Egg Wash; sprinkle with poppy or sesame seeds. Let rise until doubled, brush again with Egg Wash and bake.

Onion Rolls: Shape raised dough in 3″ round rolls ½″ thick; make hollow in centers with fingers. Fill with an onion mixture made by soaking 3 tblsp. instant minced onion in 3 tblsp. cold water, then drained and mixed with 1 tblsp. poppy seeds. Brush with Egg Wash; let rise until doubled; brush again with Egg Wash. Bake.

Salty Caraway Crescents: Divide the raised dough into 4 portions. Roll each portion into a very thin 16" square; cut each into 16 (4") squares. Roll each, starting at a corner, diagonally to opposite corner; seal, curve ends and roll gently under the palms of the hands to lengthen slightly. Place on baking sheet. Brush with Egg Wash. Let rise until doubled; brush again with Egg Wash. Sprinkle with coarse salt crystals and caraway seeds. Bake 10 minutes; brush again with Egg Wash; bake 5 minutes more, or until browned.

Note: Table salt may be used, but coarse salt such as that used for pickling and curing meat gives better results. It is available in nearly all food stores.

Italian Bread Sticks: Divide raised dough into 4 portions; roll out each portion to 7×4" rectangle. Cut lengthwise in ½" strips. Roll under hands to make strips 8" long. Place on baking sheet 1" apart. Brush with water; let rise and brush again with water before baking.

POTATO PUFF ROLLS

Try these piping hot, feather-light rolls next time there's company

½ c. mashed potatoes
1 c. milk
¼ c. shortening
¼ c. sugar
1 tsp. salt
1 pkg. active dry yeast
¼ c. warm water (110 to 115°)
4 to 4½ c. sifted all-purpose
    flour
1 egg

• Prepare potatoes from packaged instant mashed potatoes (do not season).

Recipe for 1 serving usually makes ½ c. Or cook potatoes and mash, but do not season.
• Scald milk. Add shortening, sugar, salt and potatoes. Cool to lukewarm.
• Sprinkle yeast on warm water; stir to dissolve. Combine milk mixture, yeast, 2 c. flour and egg. Beat well by hand or with electric mixer at medium speed, scraping the bowl occasionally, to make smooth mixture, about 2 minutes. Stir in enough remaining flour, a little at a time, to make a soft dough that leaves the sides of bowl.
• Turn onto lightly floured board and knead until satiny and elastic, 5 to 10 minutes. Place in lightly greased bowl; turn dough over to grease top. Cover and let rise in warm place until doubled, 1 to 1½ hours. Punch down.
• Turn onto board. Shape into a ball, cover and let rest 10 minutes. Pinch off small pieces of dough and shape in balls to half fill greased muffin-pan cups. Cover and let rise until almost doubled, about 1 hour.
• Bake in hot oven (400°) 10 to 12 minutes. Makes about 34 rolls.

Baking in High Country

Yeast doughs rise faster in high altitudes and many breads are coarse-grained. To bake fine-textured loaves with our recipes, make one of these changes:
• *Let dough rise a shorter time—just until it is barely doubled.*
• *Use less yeast than the recipe specifies.*
• *Punch down the dough two times, instead of once, so the dough will rise three times, instead of two.*

PERFECT BUNS

Buns are uniform in size and shape if you bake them in 4" foil tart pans

½ c. milk
2 tblsp. sugar
1 ½ tsp. salt
¼ c. shortening
1 pkg. active dry yeast
½ c. warm water (110 to 115°)
3 c. sifted all-purpose flour
1 egg, beaten
1 egg (for glaze)
2 tblsp. water
½ tsp. sesame or poppy seeds
       (optional)

• Scald milk; pour into bowl over sugar, salt and shortening. Stir; cool to lukewarm.
• Sprinkle yeast on warm water; stir to dissolve.
• Add yeast, 1½ c. flour and beaten egg to milk mixture. Beat with electric mixer at medium speed until batter is smooth, about 2 minutes; or beat by hand. Mix in remaining flour, a little at a time, with spoon or hands. Cover and let rest 15 minutes.
• Toss dough onto floured board until it no longer is sticky. Divide into 12 equal portions. Shape each portion into a smooth ball. (Dough may be somewhat sticky and difficult to shape into a ball. If so, toss each ball into a little flour on the board.)
• Place each ball in a greased 4" foil tart pan (the disposable kind). Flatten tops of buns by pressing dough down gently with fingertips. Set pans on two baking sheets; cover, let rise in warm place until doubled. (If you do not have tart pans, you can bake the buns on greased baking sheets, but their shape may not be uniform.) If oven is not in use, place buns in oven with pan of boiling water on oven floor.
• Brush with mixture of 1 egg, beaten with 2 tblsp. water. If desired, sprinkle each bun with sesame or poppy seeds.
• Bake in hot oven (400°) 12 minutes, changing position of baking sheets during baking. Cool 5 minutes; turn out on wire racks. Buns may be frozen. Serve warm or cool. Makes 12 buns.

BRAN ROLLS

These tender, light rolls go together fast—there's no kneading or shaping

1 pkg. active dry yeast
½ c. warm water (110 to 115°)
½ c. boiling water
½ c. shortening
⅓ c. sugar
½ c. whole bran
¾ tsp. salt
1 egg
3 c. sifted all-purpose flour

• Sprinkle yeast on warm water; stir to dissolve.
• Pour boiling water over shortening in mixing bowl; stir in sugar, bran and salt. Cool to lukewarm. Beat egg with rotary beater and add to bran mixture. Stir in yeast and mix well.
• Stir in flour, ½ c. at a time. Cover and let rise in warm place until almost doubled, about 2½ hours. Punch down. Drop dough from spoon into greased muffin-pan cups, filling cups half full. Cover and let rise until doubled, about 1 hour.
• Bake in moderate oven (375°) 15 minutes. Makes 2 dozen rolls.

REFRIGERATOR WHOLE WHEAT ROLLS

Serve piping hot with plenty of butter —we guarantee compliments

1 ¾ c. milk
½ c. sugar
1 tblsp. salt
3 tblsp. shortening
2 pkgs. active dry yeast
½ c. warm water (110 to 115°)
4 to 4½ c. whole wheat flour
3 c. sifted all-purpose flour
2 eggs, beaten

• Scald milk; add sugar, salt and shortening. Cool to lukewarm.
• Sprinkle yeast on warm water; stir to dissolve.
• Combine milk mixture, 1 c. whole wheat flour (stirred before measuring) and 1 c. all-purpose flour. Beat well with electric mixer at medium speed, scraping bowl occasionally, 2 minutes. Or beat by hand. Add yeast mixture and eggs and beat well. Stir in enough remaining flours, a little at a time, to make a soft dough that leaves the sides of bowl. Place in greased bowl; turn dough over to grease top. Cover and place in refrigerator (dough will keep in refrigerator about 3 days).
• Remove from refrigerator about 2 hours before you wish to serve rolls. Turn dough onto floured board; knead very lightly a few times. Shape as desired and place in greased pans or on baking sheets. Cover, let rise in warm place until doubled, 1 to 1½ hours.
• Bake in hot oven (400°) 15 to 20 minutes. Brush with melted butter. Makes 4 dozen rolls.

Note: See Index for Rich Refrigerator Dough and recipes made with it.

Coffee Breads and Rolls for All Occasions

You can take a bread tour of Europe without leaving home. Just sit down in a comfortable chair and relax while you read the pages that follow. Travel with me from the north —Norway, Sweden, Denmark and Finland—to Vienna, the waltz capital and a city of fabulous breads; to Greece, Russia, Yugoslavia, Hungary, Czechoslovakia, Germany, France, Italy and England—the Grand Tour!

As you read about the Easter, New Year, Christmas and other festive sweet breads, you won't want to wait for a holiday to treat your family and friends to the world's great classic breads. Bake them the year round —they're good any time. For the holiday seasons most women like to dress them up a little more with frosting, nuts and candied fruit.

Many of these recipes come from farm and ranch kitchens. Most of them started out as heirlooms handed from mother to daughter for several generations. American homemakers adapted the recipes to the ingredients available, to improved new breadmaking techniques and to the modern equipment in their kitchens. Their imagination and skill have resulted in tasty breads made in less time. Notice how a Minnesota farm woman makes a basic mix to speed holiday and special-occasion baking.

Turn the pages and stimulate your appetite with the recipes for our splendid collection of these sweeter, richer breads and rolls, the kind you serve with coffee and tea and even sometimes for dessert. Some are the new versions of breads from faraway places; others are favorite breads originated in U.S. country kitchens. These yeast breads are easier to bake than you may think.

Honeyed Danish Twist

An unusual shape adds interest to a loaf of bread. Glazed Danish Twist is a good example; it resembles a big, fat pretzel. Hunt up the pretzels in your supermarket and take some home with you to use as a guide when you shape the dough.

Our Danish Twist has a rich brown crust that glistens with Honey Glaze, which contributes a delicate sweet flavor and a shiny coating to the golden loaf.

GLAZED DANISH TWIST

A shiny, nut-sprinkled coffee bread shaped like a giant golden pretzel

½   c. milk
¼   c. sugar
1   tsp. salt
2   tblsp. shortening
1   pkg. active dry yeast
¼   c. warm water (110 to 115°)
2¾ c. sifted all-purpose flour
    (about)
1   egg
1   tblsp. softened butter
3   tblsp. sugar
½   tsp. cinnamon
Honey Glaze
Chopped nuts

• Scald milk; pour into large bowl and add ¼ c. sugar, salt and shortening. Cool to lukewarm.
• Sprinkle yeast on warm water; stir to dissolve.
• Add 1 c. flour, egg and yeast to milk mixture; beat with electric mixer at medium speed, scraping the bowl occasionally, for 2 minutes, or until smooth; or beat vigorously with spoon. Stir in remaining flour, a little at a time, until soft dough is easy to handle. (Add more flour if needed.)
• Sprinkle about 2 tblsp. flour on board and turn out dough. Knead about 5 minutes, or until dough is smooth, satiny and elastic.
• Shape dough in smooth ball and place in lightly greased bowl; turn dough over to grease top. Cover with a clean towel and let rise in a warm place free from drafts until doubled, about 2 hours. Punch down dough and shape into a ball. Cover and let rest 5 minutes.
• Flatten dough and roll out to make a narrow strip 6″ wide, ¼″ thick and 23″ long. Spread with softened butter and sprinkle with 3 tblsp. sugar blended with cinnamon.
• Roll up from long side to make a long, slender roll; seal edges by pressing firmly. Leave roll on board and twist by rolling one end away from you, the other toward you. Lift carefully to baking sheet to avoid untwisting; shape like a pretzel, tucking ends of dough under "pretzel" to prevent untwisting. Cover and let rise in a warm place free from drafts until doubled, about 1 hour.
• Bake in moderate oven (350°) 25 to 30 minutes.
• Remove from oven and immediately brush on Honey Glaze;

sprinkle with chopped walnuts or slivered almonds. Then place loaf on wire rack to cool. Makes 1 large loaf.

Honey Glaze: Combine 2 tblsp. sugar, ¼ c. honey and 1 tblsp. butter in small saucepan. Bring to a boil, stirring occasionally. Brush hot mixture over Danish Twist.

Beautiful Viennese Striezel

Every country on the map of Europe boasts of beautiful braided loaves of yeast bread. The Viennese call theirs Striezel. Sometimes the bakers stack the braids three or four stories high; other times they use only two braids, one on top of the other. Our Striezel has two braids topped off with a plump twist of dough.

The secret of keeping the braids from slipping out of place while the dough rises and bakes is to make a depression with the hands lengthwise down the center of the loaf. You lay the braid in this "trench."

Try our recipe, even if you've never attempted to make a braided loaf, and see if you don't find it's easier than you believed it would be. Our Striezel contains raisins, candied cherries and orange peel, but you can omit these flavorful fruits if you prefer a plainer loaf made with the basic sweet dough. You also can leave off the frosting, but spreading it on is no chore (after cooling or freezing the Striezel), and sprinkling on nuts (chopped candied cherries, too, for the holidays) gives the fascinating brown loaf a gala look.

VIENNESE STRIEZEL

This 3-story braided loaf is handsome, and it tastes as good as it looks

½ c. milk
¼ c. sugar
1 tsp. salt
2 tblsp. shortening
1 pkg. active dry yeast
¼ c. warm water (110 to 115°)
2 ¾ to 3 c. sifted all-purpose flour
1 egg
¼ c. raisins
¼ c. chopped candied cherries
2 tblsp. chopped candied orange peel
¼ tsp. nutmeg
Frosting
Chopped nuts

• Scald milk; pour into a large bowl and add sugar, salt and shortening. Cool to lukewarm.
• Sprinkle yeast on warm water; stir to dissolve.
• Add 1 c. flour, egg and yeast to milk mixture; beat with electric mixer at medium speed, scraping the bowl occasionally, for 2 minutes, or until smooth. Or beat vigorously with spoon. Stir in raisins, cherries, orange peel and nutmeg. Stir in enough remaining flour, a little at a time, to make a soft dough, easy to handle.
• Sprinkle about 2 tblsp. flour on board and turn out dough. Knead about 5 minutes or until dough is smooth, satiny and elastic.
• Shape dough into a ball and place in lightly greased bowl; turn dough over to grease top. Cover with clean towel and let rise in a warm place free from drafts until doubled, about 2¼ hours.

• Punch down. Cover and let rest 5 to 10 minutes.
• Divide dough into 9 pieces of equal size. Shape each piece into a ball, ccver and let rest 5 minutes. Roll each ball under the hands to make a strand 15″ long. Place 4 strips on lightly greased baking sheet and braid, starting at the center and braiding to each end. With the sides of the hands make a depression down the center of the braid. (This helps to keep the next braid in place.)
• Braid 3 strands loosely, again braiding from the center to both ends. Lay this braid on top of braid on baking sheet. Make a depression down the center of this braid.
• Twist the 2 remaining strands loosely around each other. Lay the twist in the depression on the second tier of braids. Bring the ends of twist down over ends of loaf; tuck ends of twist under the loaf. Cover with towel and let rise in warm place free from drafts until doubled, about 1½ hours.
• Bake in moderate oven (350°) 35 to 40 minutes. Remove from baking sheet and place on wire rack. When cool, spread with Frosting and sprinkle with chopped nuts. Makes 1 large loaf.

Viennese Striezel Frosting: To ½ c. sifted confectioners sugar add ¼ tsp. vanilla and enough milk or cream (about 2½ tsp.) to make a smooth frosting.

When Freezing Bread

Bake yeast breads to be frozen to a light golden brown. This prevents the separation of the crust from the inside of loaf.

A Farm Woman's Baking Plan

A clever Minnesota farm woman fixes a Sweet Dough Basic Mix for her own style of coffee breads and rolls. It's her solution to the problem of finding time to bake different kinds. She gets the mix ready a day or several days ahead, divides it into 4 portions, which she covers and stores in a cool place. The idea started in a visit with her county Extension home economist.

"It's a real blessing," she says, "to have the mix ready to go, especially at exciting times, such as the holidays, when there's so much I want to do in the kitchen. Because I work with a comparatively small amount of dough at a time, I do all the mixing with a spoon and my hands. I don't get out the mixer, which is such a big help when I bake larger batches of bread."

Taste-testers gave the breads made by her recipes a vote of excellence. Try them and see if you don't rate their judgment as superior.

SWEET DOUGH BASIC MIX

A fix-ahead mix—so handy for making delicious coffee breads and rolls

8 ½ c. sifted all-purpose flour
⅓ c. nonfat dry milk
½ c. sugar
4 tsp. salt
¼ c. lard

• Combine flour, dry milk, sugar and salt; stir to mix thoroughly.
• Cut in lard with pastry blender.

Divide in 4 equal portions. Each portion makes approximately 2 c. plus 2 tblsp. Basic Mix.

TO USE SWEET DOUGH BASIC MIX

1 portion Sweet Dough Basic Mix
1 pkg. active dry yeast
⅔ c. warm water (110 to 115°)
1 egg, beaten

• Place Basic Mix in large bowl; make a hollow in center.
• Sprinkle dry yeast on warm water; stir to dissolve. Add egg and pour into hollow in dry ingredients. Beat with spoon until smooth and satiny. If the dough is too soft to handle, work in a little more flour.
• Turn onto lightly floured board and knead until smooth and satiny, 3 to 5 minutes. Place in lightly greased bowl; turn dough over to grease top. Cover with a clean towel and let rise in a warm place free from drafts until doubled, 1 to 1½ hours.
• Punch down. Let rise again until doubled, 45 minutes to 1 hour. You are ready to make a coffee bread or rolls with this light dough.

NORWEGIAN JULE KAGE

Slices of this Christmas bread display a tempting sprinkling of fruits

1 portion risen dough from Sweet Dough Basic Mix
2 tblsp. currants
¼ c. seedless raisins
¼ c. cut-up candied fruits
¼ tsp. ground cardamom
Egg Yolk Glaze

• Place dough on lightly floured board; roll gently to flatten. Sprinkle currants, raisins, candied fruits and cardamom on half of the dough; fold other half over on the fruits. Knead gently to mix fruits through the dough, about 3 minutes. Shape into a ball, cover and let rest 10 minutes.
• Place dough on a greased baking sheet, cover and let rise in warm place until doubled, about 1 hour and 15 minutes. Brush with Egg Yolk Glaze.
• Bake in moderate oven (350°) 30 minutes. Makes 1 round loaf.

Egg Yolk Glaze: Mix with fork 1 egg yolk and 2 tblsp. cold water.

HOUSKA

This braided Bohemian Christmas bread is a treat to see and to eat

1 portion risen dough from Sweet Dough Basic Mix
1 tsp. grated lemon peel
2 tblsp. cut-up mixed candied fruits
2 tblsp. raisins
2 tblsp. slivered almonds
Confectioners sugar

• Place dough on lightly floured board. Flatten gently with rolling pin. Sprinkle half of dough with lemon peel, candied fruits, raisins and almonds. Fold other half of dough over fruit and nuts and knead gently, 3 to 5 minutes, to distribute fruits and nuts through dough.
• Divide the dough in half. Cut one half in 4 pieces, the other half in 5 pieces. Roll strips under hand to make slender rolls about ½″ thick and 12″ long. Place 4 strips on greased baking sheet and braid, starting at the

center and braiding to each end. Make a depression with sides of hands lengthwise down the center of the braid. Braid 3 strips, from center to each end, and lay on top of braid on baking sheet. Twist remaining 2 strips and lay on top of braids, tucking ends under loaf. Let rise until doubled, about 1 hour and 15 minutes.
· Bake in moderate oven (350°) 25 minutes. Cool on wire rack. Before serving sprinkle with sifted confectioners sugar. Makes 1 loaf.

MINCEMEAT COFFEE BREAD

As American as the Fourth of July and wonderfully good—pretty, too

1   portion risen dough from
        Sweet Dough Basic Mix
1½ c. ready-to-use mincemeat
Lemon-Orange Butter Frosting
Nuts, coarsely chopped
Maraschino cherries, sliced and
        well drained

· Place risen dough on lightly floured board; divide in half. Cover with clean towel and let rest 20 minutes.
· Roll out each half to make a 14×8" rectangle. Place each on a greased baking sheet. Spread ¾ c. mincemeat lengthwise in a strip 3½" wide down center of each rectangle. Bring sides of dough to top over the mincemeat. Pinch edges together firmly to seal.
· Carefully invert loaves (sealed edge will be down) on baking sheets. Make 2" diagonal cuts, 1" apart, on top of loaves (over mincemeat). Cover and let rise in warm place until doubled, about 1 hour and 15 minutes.
· Bake in moderate oven (350°) 20 to 25 minutes. Remove from baking

sheets and place on wire racks. While still slightly warm, spread with Lemon-Orange Butter Frosting and sprinkle with nuts and slices of maraschino cherries. Makes 2 loaves.

Lemon-Orange Butter Frosting: Combine 2 tblsp. soft butter, 1½ c. sifted confectioners sugar, ⅛ tsp. salt, ¼ tsp. grated lemon peel, ¼ tsp. grated orange peel, 1 tsp. lemon juice and enough orange juice to make a frosting of spreading consistency. Beat until smooth and creamy.

ORANGE TWISTS

They'll disappear like magic at coffee time or whenever you serve them

1   portion risen dough from
        Sweet Dough Basic Mix
½ c. sugar
2   tsp. grated orange peel (1
        orange)
2   tblsp. softened butter

· Place dough on lightly floured board. Divide in half and shape in balls. Cover and let rest 20 minutes.
· Meanwhile combine sugar and grated orange peel.
· Roll each half of dough in a 12×9" rectangle. Spread center third of each rectangle with butter and sprinkle with one fourth of the sugar-orange peel mixture.
· Fold one third of dough rectangle over sugar-orange strip in center. Butter top and sprinkle with one fourth of sugar-orange mixture. Fold remaining one third of dough over sugar-orange mixture and seal dough. Repeat with other rectangle.
· Cut each rectangle into 12 strips. Twist shapes and place them on

greased baking sheets. Cover and let rise in a warm place about 40 minutes.

• Bake in moderate oven (375°) about 15 minutes. Makes 24 twists.

Christmas Bread That Pleases

This is an Americanized version of what the Greeks call Christopsomo, which means Christmas Bread.

One of the home economists who helped test readers' recipes for this cookbook gave this bread to her neighbors for a Christmas present. She baked the loaves ahead and froze them so that all she had to do the day before Christmas was to deliver them to nearby holly-decorated doors. She was pleased at the reception for the festive bread and her friends raved about it.

CHRISTMAS BREAD

A cross of dough strips adorns the top of this mildly sweet golden loaf

    ¾   c. milk
    6   tblsp. sugar
    2   tsp. salt
    ⅛   tsp. ground anise
    2   pkgs. active dry yeast
    ½   c. warm water (110 to 115°)
    ¾   c. butter, melted and cooled
    6¾   to 7¼ c. sifted all-purpose
         flour
    4   eggs
    1   beaten egg
    2   tblsp. water
    2   tsp. sesame seeds

• Scald milk; add sugar, salt and anise. Cool to lukewarm.

• Sprinkle yeast on warm water; stir to dissolve.

• Combine yeast, milk mixture, melted butter, 4 c. flour and 4 eggs. Beat until smooth. Stir in enough remaining flour, a little at a time, until dough leaves the sides of bowl. Turn onto lightly floured board. Knead until smooth and elastic, about 8 minutes.

• Place in lightly greased bowl; turn dough over to grease top. Cover and let rise in warm place until doubled, 1½ to 2 hours. Punch down.

• Turn onto board; divide in half. Cover and let rest 10 minutes. Take a piece of dough the size of a golf ball from each portion of dough. Divide each small ball of dough in half and roll each piece into a strand 5 to 6″ long. Shape remaining dough into 2 loaves and place in greased 9×5×3″ loaf pans. Place strands of dough on top of loaves to form a cross on each. Cover and let rise in warm place until doubled, 1 to 1½ hours.

• Combine beaten egg and water. Brush over tops of loaves. Sprinkle 1 tsp. sesame seeds on each loaf.

• Bake in moderate oven (350°) 40 to 45 minutes, until golden brown. Remove from pans and cool on racks. Makes 2 loaves.

Fascinating Easter Egg Bread

Almost every European country along Mediterranean shores, as well as nearby Switzerland and faraway Brazil, boasts of a traditional Easter bread festive with color-bright eggs. You see these tempting loaves during the Eastern season in the neighborhood bake shops of our great cities, like New York and San Francisco, especially where people of Italian descent live. There's no reason, though, why you can't bake this seasonal bread in your own kitchen.

One of our readers sent us a recipe for a meal-in-one breakfast. What joy either the large or individual "eggs in a bread nest" will bring the children! Grownups will enjoy them, too, if they're young at heart.

EASTER EGG BREAD

Make this traditional in your family —a memory of home

12 eggs in shell, uncooked
Easter egg coloring
½ c. milk
½ c. sugar
1 tsp. salt
½ c. shortening
Grated peel of 2 lemons
2 pkgs. active dry yeast
½ c. warm water (110 to 115°)
2 eggs (at room temperature)
4½ c. sifted all-purpose flour
    (about)
1 egg, beaten
Tiny colored candies

• Wash 12 uncooked eggs. Tint shells with egg coloring; set aside.
• Scald milk; add sugar, salt, shortening and lemon peel. Cool to lukewarm.
• Sprinkle yeast on warm water; stir to dissolve. Add to milk mixture with the 2 eggs, slightly beaten, and 2½ c. flour. Beat until smooth.
• Stir in enough remaining flour, a little at a time, to form a dough that is easy to handle. Turn onto lightly floured board and knead until smooth and elastic, 5 to 8 minutes. Place in

lightly greased bowl; turn dough over to grease top. Cover and let rise in warm place free from drafts until doubled, about 1 hour.
• Punch down; cover and let rise again until almost doubled, about 30 minutes.
• Make 2 large braided rings or 12 individual rings as follows:

Large Rings: Divide dough into 4 parts. Form each part into a 36" rope. On a greased baking sheet, shape 2 of the ropes into a very loosely braided ring, leaving space for 6 eggs (see photo elsewhere in book). Repeat with other 2 ropes of dough for second ring. Insert 6 tinted eggs in spaces in each ring.

Individual Rings: Divide dough into 12 parts. Form each part into a ring around a tinted egg.

• Cover; let rise until doubled.
• Brush evenly with beaten egg. Sprinkle with tiny decorating candies.
• Bake in moderate oven (375°) 15 minutes for individual rings, 20 minutes for large rings, or until lightly browned. Serve warm. Makes 2 large or 12 individual rings.

Note: Easter Egg Bread can be baked the day before. Refrigerate. At serving time, reheat in moderate oven (350°) 8 minutes.

Wonderfully Rich Gugelhupf

Slices of Gugelhupf (pronounced gōōǵlehŭpf), toasted and served with butter and jam, are an Austrian Christmas breakfast special. It's a cake-like bread that is also a favorite Vienna dessert. Coffee is its best accompaniment. The light, delicious bread will please your guests as much as it does Europeans. The loaf is beautiful, especially if you bake it in a fancy-shaped mold. Austrian women and bakeries use heavy tube molds similar to what we call a Turk's head, but our recipe suggests that you can use an angel food cake pan.

Perhaps you've heard of this bread by another name—Kugelhupf, for instance. Just as the bread differs in some ways from one home or country to another, its name also varies. But all the versions are delicious.

GUGELHUPF

A cake-like bread on the sweet side with a subtle lemon-almond flavor

½   c. milk
1   pkg. active dry yeast
¼   c. warm water (110 to 115°)
½   c. sugar
¼   c. butter
2   eggs
2½ c. sifted all-purpose flour
¼   tsp. salt
½   c. chopped golden raisins
1½ tsp. grated lemon peel
1   tblsp. melted butter
¼   c. finely ground almonds
15 to 18 whole blanched
    almonds (optional)

• Scald milk; cool to lukewarm.
• Sprinkle yeast on warm water; stir to dissolve.
• Cream sugar and ¼ c. butter with electric mixer until light and fluffy. Add eggs, one at a time, beating after each addition. Add yeast and milk, then flour and salt, which have been sifted together. Beat with electric mixer at medium speed until smooth, scraping bowl occasionally.
• Stir in raisins and lemon peel; cover and let rise in warm place free from drafts until doubled, about 2 hours.
• Meanwhile generously grease a heavy 1½-qt. mold with a tube, such as a Turk's head or a 10″ angel food cake pan, with 1 tblsp. melted butter. Be sure to grease tube well. Shake mold or pan to coat sides thoroughly with finely ground almonds. Arrange pattern of whole blanched almonds on bottom of pan.
• Stir down light dough. Spoon batter into mold or pan carefully to avoid disturbing almonds. Cover and let rise in warm place free from drafts until doubled, about 1 hour.
• Bake in moderate oven (350°) 25 to 30 minutes, or until cake tester inserted in bread comes out clean. (Look at bread when it has baked 15 minutes. If it has started to brown, cover loosely with aluminum foil. The bread browns easily.)
• Remove from oven and let stand in pan 10 minutes. Loosen sides and turn bread onto wire rack. Sift a little confectioners sugar over top. Makes about 12 servings.

Fruited and Frosted Stollen

Christmas morning in Germany brings Stollen to the breakfast table. The sweet, fruit-filled bread, with sugar and cinnamon between the layers and frosting on top, decorated with nuts and candied cherry rings, is an important part of the holiday. German hostesses also offer thin slices of Stollen to Yuletime callers.

Recipes for Stollen are many, but they are alike in one way. That's the folded-roll shape. Our recipe eliminates the chopping of candied fruits and citron—it calls for the convenient packaged kind. And as a step to superior flavor, we soak the mixed candied fruits and raisins in orange juice.

When you put the big roll on the baking sheet, there are two things to do to guarantee an attractive shape. One is to curve the Stollen a little to give it a shape slightly suggestive of a crescent. The other is to press the folded edge, never the open one, to encourage the bread to hold its shape when the yeast gets busy and expands the dough in the rising and baking.

Our recipe recognizes the popularity of Stollen—it makes 2 loaves.

STOLLEN

Make these big fold-over rolls for Christmas and other special occasions

1   c. raisins
1   (8 oz.) jar mixed candied
      fruits (1 c.)
¼   c. orange juice
½   c. milk
½   c. sugar
1   tsp. salt
1   c. butter or margarine (2
      sticks)
2   pkgs. active dry yeast
½   c. warm water (110 to 115°)
5   c. sifted all-purpose flour
      (about)
2   eggs
1   tsp. grated lemon peel
¼   tsp. mace
1   c. chopped blanched almonds

2   tblsp. sugar
½   tsp. cinnamon
Creamy Frosting
¼   c. slivered almonds (optional)
12 candied cherries (optional)

• Combine raisins, candied fruits and orange juice in a small bowl. Set aside.

• Scald milk; add ½ c. sugar, salt and ½ c. butter. Cool to lukewarm.

• Sprinkle yeast on warm water; stir to dissolve.

• Combine yeast, milk mixture, 2 c. flour, eggs, lemon peel and mace. Beat with electric mixer on medium speed 2 minutes, scraping the bowl occasionally, until batter is smooth. Stir in chopped almonds and fruits. Stir in enough remaining flour, a little at a time, to make a dough that leaves the sides of bowl and that you can handle easily.

• Turn onto lightly floured board; knead until smooth and satiny, about 5 minutes. Place in lightly greased bowl; turn dough over to grease top. Cover and let rise in warm place free from drafts until doubled, about 2 hours.

• Punch down dough; turn onto board, knead a few times and divide in half. Cover and let rest 5 minutes. Roll each half into a 15×9″ oval.

• Melt remaining ½ c. butter; brush part of it over each oval, saving what you do not use for frosting. Sprinkle with 2 tblsp. sugar mixed with cinnamon and sprinkle over the buttered dough.

• Fold each oval lengthwise in half to make a big Parkerhouse roll. Carefully lift folded-over rolls to a greased baking sheet and curve the ends slightly; press down the folded side slightly (not the open edges) to help the loaf keep its shape during rising and baking.

• Cover and let rise until doubled, 1 to 1½ hours.

• Bake in moderate oven (350°) 30 to 35 minutes, or until loaves are golden. While hot, brush with Creamy Frosting and decorate with slivered almonds and sliced candied cherries. Cool on racks. Makes 2 loaves.

Creamy Frosting: To 1 c. sifted confectioners sugar add 1 tblsp. cream or milk and ¼ c. melted butter. Stir until smooth.

FINNISH COFFEE BREAD

You can divide dough and make 1 coffee bread and 1 plain round loaf

2   pkgs. active dry yeast
2   c. warm water (110 to 115°)
1   egg (room temperature)
6   to 7 c. sifted all-purpose flour
½   tsp. ground cardamom
⅓   c. sugar
2   tsp. salt
¼   c. soft butter or shortening
Thin Confectioners Sugar Icing

• Sprinkle yeast on warm water; stir to dissolve.

• Blend in egg, 3 c. flour, cardamom, sugar and salt. Beat with electric mixer at medium speed about 2 minutes (or about 100 strokes by hand), until batter is smooth. Add butter and enough remaining flour, a little at a time, first with spoon and then with hand, to make a fairly soft dough that leaves the sides of bowl.

• Turn onto lightly floured board. Knead until smooth and elastic, about 8 minutes. Place in greased bowl and turn dough over to grease top. Cover and let rise in warm place until doubled, about 1 hour. Punch down dough, turn over, cover and let rest 10 minutes.

• Turn out onto board; divide in half. Cut each half into 3 equal parts.

• Roll each part under hand to make a strip 11 to 12″ long. Braid 3 strips, starting from the center and braiding to each end, pinching ends to seal. Place in greased 9×5×3″ loaf pan. Repeat with remaining 3 strips.

• Cover and let rise in warm place until doubled, about 45 minutes.

• Bake in hot oven (400°) 40 to 50 minutes, covering with sheet of foil during last 15 minutes to prevent browning too much. Remove from pans and place on wire cooling racks. After loaves are slightly cooled, brush with Thin Confectioners Sugar Icing. Makes 2 loaves.

Thin Confectioners Sugar Icing: Add 1 tblsp. plus 2 tsp. light cream to 1 c. sifted confectioners sugar, and stir until icing is smooth.

VARIATIONS

Finnish Bread—Round Loaves: Turn risen dough onto board; divide into 2 parts. Shape into 2 round loaves and place in 2 greased 9″ round layer cake pans. Make 3 or 4 slashes on tops of loaves with very sharp knife. Cover, let rise until doubled; bake and cool like Finnish Coffee Bread. Omit icing. Makes 2 round loaves.

Finnish Braids: Turn risen dough onto board; divide in half. Cut one half into 4 parts. Shape 3 parts into strands 12″ long. Place on greased baking sheet and braid, starting at center and braiding to each end. Seal ends. Cut remaining part into 3 parts; shape into strands 9" long; braid and place on top of large braid, tucking ends into large braid. Repeat with other half of dough. Cover, let rise until doubled; bake (20 to 25 minutes), cool and frost like Finnish Coffee Bread. Makes 2 braids.

Prize-winning Breads

An Oklahoma farm woman won blue ribbons at the county fair on her Classic Sweet Dough. It's a three-from-one recipe. You divide the dough in thirds and use each one to make a different bread. It might be any of the four treats for which we give recipes—Apricot Crescents, Date Braid, Swedish Tea Ring and Grecian Feast Bread. All are good.

CLASSIC SWEET DOUGH

Starting point for wonderful breads

  2 c. milk
  ½ c. butter or margarine
  ½ c. sugar
  2 tsp. salt
  2 pkgs. active dry yeast
  ½ c. warm water (110 to 115°)
  2 eggs, beaten
  9½ to 10 c. sifted all-purpose
       flour

• Scald milk; stir in butter, sugar and salt. Cool to lukewarm.
• Sprinkle yeast on warm water; stir to dissolve.
• Add milk mixture, eggs and 4½ c. flour to yeast; beat until smooth. Stir in enough remaining flour, a little at a time to make a slightly stiff dough.

(If you want to make Grecian Feast Loaf, remove one third of dough at this point.)
• Turn dough onto lightly floured board, cover and let rest 5 minutes. Knead until smooth and elastic, about 5 minutes. Put in greased bowl; turn dough over to grease top. Cover and let rise until doubled, about 1 hour.
• Punch down, turn onto board, divide into thirds and use to make the following breads.

APRICOT CRESCENTS

Twin loaves with hearts of gold

  ⅓ of Classic Sweet Dough
  2 c. Apricot Filling
  2 tblsp. melted butter
  2 tblsp. sugar

• Divide dough in half. Roll each half into a 12×8" rectangle. Spread each with 1 c. Apricot Filling. Starting at long edge, roll as for jelly roll. Seal edge.
• Place on greased baking sheet and shape in crescents. Make slashes on tops with scissors 1½" apart. Brush with butter; sprinkle with sugar.
• Cover; let rise in warm place until doubled, about 30 minutes.
• Bake in moderate oven (350°) 25 to 30 minutes. Remove to wire racks to cool. Makes 2 loaves.

Apricot Filling: Combine in a heavy saucepan 2 c. dried apricots (11 oz. pkg.) and 1 c. water. Cover and simmer until apricots are tender. Add ¼ c. butter or margarine, stir and mash until butter is melted. Add 1½ c. sugar and stir to dissolve; beat well. Cool and add 1 c. chopped walnuts. Makes 3 cups.

DATE BRAID

Filling peeks through slits in loaf

⅓ of Classic Sweet Dough
2 c. Date Filling

• Roll dough into a 14×8″ rectangle. Place on greased baking sheet.
• Reserve ¼ c. Date Filling. Spread remaining filling in 3″ strip lengthwise on center of rectangle. At each side of filling cut from edge of dough to filling at 2″ intervals. You will have 7 strips on each side.
• Bring strips from opposite sides to center, crossing them and then tucking in on sides. Spoon reserved filling into the open spaces. Cover and let rise in a warm place until doubled, 30 to 45 minutes.
• Bake in moderate oven (350°) 25 to 30 minutes. Place on wire rack to cool. Frost with Confectioners Sugar Frosting (see Index) while still warm.

Date Filling: Combine in heavy saucepan 1 (8 oz.) pkg. dates, chopped or finely cut with scissors, 1 c. chopped pecans, ¼ c. brown sugar, ⅔ c. water and 1 tblsp. lemon juice. Cook, stirring constantly, until of spreading consistency, 3 to 5 minutes. Cool before using. Makes 2 cups.

SWEDISH TEA RING

For Yuletide centerpiece put candle in center of pretty bread wreath

¼ c. soft butter or margarine
¼ c. sugar
1 tsp. grated lemon peel
½ c. ground almonds
⅓ of Classic Sweet Dough
1 c. mixed candied fruits, chopped

• Cream butter and sugar; stir in lemon peel and almonds. Mix well.
• Roll dough into a 14×10″ rectangle. Sprinkle sugar mixture evenly over dough. Arrange candied fruits evenly over the top. Roll up from the long side as for jelly roll; seal edge. Place, sealed edge down, in ring on lightly greased baking sheet. Seal ends together firmly. Snip dough with scissors from edge of circle three fourths of the way to center every 1½″. Turn cut pieces on their sides. (If you're making this bread for Christmas, place greased custard cup in center to keep hole round for non-drip candle.)
• Cover and let rise until doubled, 45 minutes to 1 hour.
• Bake in moderate oven (350°) 25 to 30 minutes. Cool on wire rack.

Note: You can frost Swedish Tea Ring with Confectioners Sugar Frosting (see Index).

Attractive Grecian Feast Bread

The world owes much to Greece for many things, including the country's festive breads. Among the great loaves is this one with three petals. It's really three small loaves baked as one. It wouldn't be Easter in many Grecian homes without this bread, which also appears in meals and refreshments on other church holidays, such as Christmas.

The three loaves represent Trinity. Grecian hostesses frequently bring the uncut bread to the table and thinly slice the small loaves. The custom is for each person to eat a slice from all three.

While Grecian Feast Bread frequently glistens with a shiny, brown glaze, as our recipe provides, sometimes it is frosted. The traditional way to add the Thin Confectioners Sugar Icing (see Index) is to pour it over each of the miniature loaves while still warm, letting it run down the sides. Flowers of three petals made of almonds and/or sliced candied cherries decorate the white tops.

GRECIAN FEAST LOAF

The 3-leaf-clover loaf is an Easter and Christmas tradition in Greece

⅓ of Classic Sweet Dough
     (before kneading)
½ c. currants
1 tsp. grated lemon peel
¼ tsp. ground mace
1 egg, beaten (for glaze)

• Remove one third of Classic Sweet Dough when mixed, before kneading. Work in the currants, lemon peel and mace; knead until dough is smooth and elastic, 3 to 5 minutes. Place in lightly greased bowl; turn dough over to grease top. Cover, let rise in warm place until doubled, about 1 hour.

• Punch down, turn onto floured board and divide into 3 equal parts. Shape each part into a smooth ball and arrange on greased baking sheet to form a 3-leaf clover. Leave ¾" between the 3 balls.

• Cover and let rise in warm place until doubled, about 1 hour. Brush each ball of dough with beaten egg.

• Bake in moderate oven (350°) about 25 minutes. Cool on wire rack.

Kulich—A Traditional Easter Bread

Kulich, the traditional Easter bread of old Russia, tastes good any time of year. We baked this dough in No. 2 (1 lb. about 4 oz.) cans in which you buy pineapple or other fruits. During the baking, the dough rises above the tops of the cans and forms a dome that resembles the domes of old Russian churches.

Most Americans like to spread the "dome" of the baked loaves with a Confectioners Sugar Frosting (see Index) and add tiny colored decorating candies or slivered nuts and sliced candied cherries. Some women omit the frosting but save out a little of the dough and shape it into four tiny short ropes. They arrange two dough strips on top of each loaf to make a cross just after they place the dough in the cans to rise. They brush the loaf tops with butter and sprinkle on sugar.

The top slice, sugared or frosted, traditionally goes to the guest of honor or to the eldest member of the family. Whipped butter is a splendid accompaniment, and Honeyed Butter also tastes wonderful on this Easter bread.

KULICH

The shape of this tasty holiday bread always promotes lots of conversation

½ c. milk
¼ c. sugar
1 tsp. salt
2 tblsp. shortening
1 pkg. active dry yeast

¼   c. warm water (110 to 115°)
2¾ to 3 c. sifted all-purpose
       flour
1   egg
¼   c. raisins
¼   c. chopped almonds
1   tsp. grated lemon peel
Snowy Frosting

• Scald milk; pour into a large bowl and add sugar, salt and shortening. Cool until lukewarm.
• Sprinkle yeast on warm water; stir to dissolve.
• Add 1 c. flour, egg and yeast to lukewarm milk mixture. Beat hard with spoon or with electric mixer at medium speed 1 minute. Stir in raisins, almonds and lemon peel. Add remaining flour, a little at a time, until you can easily handle the soft dough.
• Sprinkle about 2 tblsp. flour on board and turn out dough. Knead until dough is satiny and elastic, about 5 minutes. Shape in smooth ball and place in lightly greased bowl; turn dough over to grease top. Cover and let rise in warm place until doubled, 2 to 2½ hours. Punch down.
• Turn dough onto board and divide in half. Let rest 10 minutes. Place each half in a greased No. 2 (1 lb. about 4 oz.) can. Cover and let rise until doubled, 1 to 1¼ hours.
• Bake in moderate oven (350°) 30 to 35 minutes, or until well browned. Remove from cans at once and cool on rack before spreading tops of loaves with Snowy Frosting. Whipped butter and Honeyed Butter are excellent accompaniments. Makes 2 loaves.

Snowy Frosting: Mix ½ c. sifted confectioners sugar with 2 tsp. milk or cream to make a smooth frosting. Spread over tops of loaves. Decorate tops with tiny multi-colored decorating candies, or with 2 tblsp. slivered almonds and 2 candied cherries, sliced.

Honeyed Butter: Whip ½ c. butter (1 stick) with spoon or electric mixer until fluffy. Gradually whip in ¼ c. honey and beat until mixture is smooth. For a new note, whip 1 to 2 tsp. grated orange peel into it.

ALMOND-STREUSEL COFFEE BREAD

Almonds, lemons, sugar and butter fill bread with luscious flavors

1   pkg. active dry yeast
½   c. warm water (110 to 115°)
1¾ to 2¼ c. sifted all-purpose
       flour
1   egg
3   tblsp. sugar
½   tsp. salt
2   tblsp. soft butter
Streusel Topping (recipe follows)

• Sprinkle yeast over warm water; stir to dissolve.
• Add 1 c. flour, egg, sugar, salt and butter. Beat with spoon until smooth.
• Add enough remaining flour, a little at a time, first with spoon and then with hands, to make a dough that leaves the sides of bowl.
• Turn out onto lightly floured board. Grease fingers lightly and knead until smooth. Round up and place in greased bowl; turn dough over to grease top. Cover and let rise in warm place until doubled, 45 minutes to 1 hour. (Dent remains when finger is pressed deep into side of dough.)
• Meanwhile prepare topping.

• Punch down dough. Press evenly into greased 9" square pan. Sprinkle evenly with Streusel Topping, then with fingers make dents all over the top, pressing to the bottom of the pan to distribute topping evenly.

• Cover pan and let rise until doubled, about 45 minutes.

• Bake in moderate oven (375°) 25 to 35 minutes, or until browned. Remove from pan and cool on rack. Makes 1 (9" square) coffee bread.

STREUSEL TOPPING

Almonds give bread its superb taste

½ c. sugar
½ c. flour
2 tsp. grated lemon peel
½ tsp. vanilla
⅓ c. melted butter
⅓ c. ground unblanched almonds

• Blend together all the ingredients well, using fork. Sprinkle over dough as directed.

Election Coffee Cake

It's called a cake, but it's a yeast-leavened coffee bread. More than a century ago this fruit- and nut-studded loaf, according to legend, was the pay-off of Connecticut politicians to men who voted the straight party ticket. Today its only connection with politics is that many hostesses, especially in New England, serve it at informal parties on election day. It's a good choice if you're looking for something tasty to serve with coffee to guests in front of your television set, while listening to vote counts.

You can bake the bread days ahead and freeze it (but then omit the frosting). To use, thaw the loaf in its wrapper at room temperature for several hours; frost shortly before serving. Or if you prefer, wrap the frozen bread in aluminum foil and heat it in a hot oven (400°) 30 minutes to 1 hour. Cool slightly before you spread the frosting on top, letting it dribble temptingly down the sides of the loaf.

ELECTION DAY CAKE

Historic coffee bread as good as ever with coffee for election day parties

2   pkgs. active dry yeast
1½ c. warm water (110 to 115°)
2   tsp. sugar
4½ c. sifted all-purpose flour
¾   c. butter or margarine
1   c. sugar
1   tsp. salt
1½ tsp. cinnamon
¼   tsp. cloves
¼   tsp. mace
½   tsp. nutmeg
2   eggs
1½ c. raisins
½   c. chopped citron
¾   c. chopped nuts
Confectioners Sugar Frosting

• Sprinkle yeast on warm water; stir to dissolve. Add 2 tsp. sugar and 1½ c. flour and beat well by hand, or 2 minutes with electric mixer at medium speed. Cover and let rise in warm place until bubbly, about 30 minutes.

• Meanwhile, cream butter and 1 c. sugar until light and fluffy.

• Sift remaining 3 c. flour with salt, cinnamon, cloves, mace and nutmeg.

• When yeast mixture is bubbly, add

eggs to creamed butter and sugar and beat well. Combine yeast with creamed mixture. Add remaining dry ingredients (flour, salt and spices), a little at a time, beating with spoon after each addition. Beat until smooth. • Stir in raisins, citron and nuts. Pour into well-greased and floured 10″ tube pan. Cover and let rise in warm place until doubled, about 1½ hours. • Bake in moderate oven (375°) 1 hour. Cool in pan 5 minutes; turn out on rack to finish cooling. While faintly warm, spread with Confectioners Sugar Frosting. Makes 12 to 16 servings.

Confectioners Sugar Frosting: To 1 c. sifted confectioners sugar add enough milk or light cream to make mixture of spreading consistency. Add ½ tsp. vanilla and a dash of salt (or flavor with ½ tsp. lemon juice and ¼ tsp. grated lemon peel). Stir until smooth. Spread on coffee breads or rolls.

RICH REFRIGERATOR DOUGH

Use in the recipes that follow

¾ c. milk
½ c. sugar
2 tsp. salt
½ c. butter or margarine
2 pkgs. active dry yeast
½ c. warm water (110 to 115°)
2 eggs, beaten
6 c. sifted all-purpose flour

• Scald milk; stir in sugar, salt and butter. Cool to lukewarm.
• Sprinkle yeast on warm water; stir to dissolve.
• Add milk mixture, eggs and 3 c. flour to yeast. Beat until smooth. Stir in remaining flour to make a stiff

dough. Cover and refrigerate for several hours, or overnight. Use in the following recipes as directed.

MINIATURE PINWHEELS

Date filling is sweet and luscious

½ of Rich Refrigerator Dough
1 c. Date Filling (see Index)
½ c. mixed candied fruits
15 candied cherries, cut in halves

• Remove Rich Refrigerator Dough from refrigerator and use immediately.
• Roll to a 12×10″ rectangle. Cut in 2″ squares. Place squares on greased baking sheet. Cover and let rise in warm place 30 minutes.
• Combine Date Filling and ½ c. candied fruits. Place a teaspoonful in center of each square. Cut corners of dough three fourths way to center. Bring corners, one at a time, over filling. Press points together to form a pinwheel. Top each pinwheel with ½ candied cherry.
• Cover; let rise until doubled, about 30 minutes.
• Bake in hot oven (400°) 10 to 15 minutes. Drizzle with Confectioners Sugar Frosting (see above). Makes 30 pinwheels.

DAISY COFFEE BREAD

A tasty flower for your table—ideal to serve with coffee to company

½ of Rich Refrigerator Dough
¼ c. Apricot Filling (see Index)

• Remove dough from refrigerator and use immediately.
• Roll to a 14×7″ rectangle. Cut

crosswise into 14 strips 1" wide. Braid 2 strips together; coil into snail shape. Repeat with other strips. Arrange 1 coil in center, on greased baking sheet, and the other 6 coils around it to form a flower.
• Cover; let rise in a warm place until doubled, about 1 hour. Make a depression in the center of each coil; fill with spoonful of Apricot Filling.
• Bake in moderate oven (350°) about 25 minutes. Frost, while warm, with Confectioners Sugar Frosting (see Index). Makes 7 servings.

Flaky Danish Pastry

Delicate, flaky Danish pastry! What could taste better? No wonder recipes for it travel far and conquer in many places. The pastry, a Viennese original, captured the Danes, who call it Wienerbrød. Translated into English, it's Vienna bread.

No one can deny that it takes time to bake Danish pastry. Or that the inexperienced baker needs patience! But most women, after baking the pastries and serving them to guests, know that the time is well spent.

One of the glories of Danish pastry is the great number of different shapes you can give the dough. Another is the wide variety of luscious fillings you can use. We describe how to make several of the best-liked shapes and fillings.

And we give you two recipes for the pastry. One is made with butter, the classic style. The other, made with vegetable shortening, comes from a California woman, the wife of a walnut grower. Some women find it the easier of the two recipes, while others insist nothing but butter gives the true flavor. So try them both and decide which one is for you.

About the only trouble you might have is rolling the dough. There's a simple cure: Just chill the dough every time it gets a little hard to manage.

DANISH PASTRY (WITH BUTTER)

Quick way to chill dough: put in freezer for 10 minutes, but do not freeze

1 ½ c. butter (3 sticks)
4 ⅓ c. sifted all-purpose flour
¾ c. milk
¼ c. sugar
1 tsp. salt
2 pkgs. active dry yeast
½ c. warm water (110 to 115°)
1 egg

• Cream butter and ⅓ c. flour thoroughly. Place on sheet of waxed paper and cover with a second sheet of waxed paper. Pat out (or roll) to make a 12×6" rectangle. Chill until very cold.
• Scald milk, add sugar and salt and cool to lukewarm.
• Sprinkle yeast on warm water; stir to dissolve.
• Add yeast, egg and 1 c. flour to milk mixture; beat vigorously with spoon or electric mixer at medium speed until mixture is smooth. Stir in remaining flour, a little at a time, to make a soft dough. Turn onto lightly floured board and knead until smooth, satiny and elastic, about 5 minutes.
• Roll dough into a 14" square on lightly floured board. Lay the cold

butter-flour mixture on half the dough, fold the other half over and seal edges by pinching with fingers.

• Roll dough to make a 20×12″ rectangle. Fold in thirds to make 3 layers of dough. If the butter softens, chill dough before rolling again. Roll again to make a 20×12″ rectangle. Repeat folding and rolling 2 times more, chilling dough each time before rolling if it gets too soft.

• Chill about 45 minutes after last rolling.

• Shape and, if you like, fill pastries (directions follow). Place on ungreased baking sheets, cover and let rise in warm place until almost doubled, about 1 hour.

• Brush tops with cold water and sprinkle with sugar. Bake in a very hot oven (450°) 8 to 10 minutes. Drizzle tops of warm pastries, if you like, with Sugar Glaze (see Index). Cool on wire racks. Makes about 35 pastries.

HOW TO SHAPE DANISH PASTRY

Snails: Work with one third of pastry at a time. Roll to make a 12×7″ rectangle (dough will be about ¼″ thick). Cut in strips 6×¾″. Hold one end of strip on baking sheet and twist; then coil strips to make snails.

Knots: Tie twisted strips, as for Snails, into knots.

Rings: Shape twisted strips, as for Snails, into circles.

HOW TO FILL DANISH PASTRY

Envelopes: Cut rolled pastry (one third of it at a time) in 3 to 4″ squares. Place 1 scant tsp. Almond Filling (see Index) or thick apricot, pineapple or berry jam in center of each square. Fold 1 corner of square over filling to about 1″ from opposite corner. Press to seal.

Sheaths: Fill squares as for Envelopes. Fold 2 opposite corners to center, overlapping them slightly. Press to seal.

Packages: Fold all 4 corners of squares, as for Envelopes, over filling to center, overlapping slightly. Press to seal.

DANISH PASTRY (WITH SHORTENING)

You can make pastries of several fascinating shapes with this dough

1   c. milk
⅓ c. sugar
1   tsp. salt
¼ c. shortening
1   pkg. active dry yeast
¼ c. warm water (110 to 115°)
2   eggs
¼ tsp. nutmeg
½ tsp. vanilla
3½ to 4 c. sifted all-purpose flour
1   c. soft shortening
1   egg, beaten
Chopped nuts
Sugar Glaze
Fillings, if desired (recipes
        follow)

• Scald milk; add sugar, salt and ¼ c. shortening. Cool to lukewarm.

• Sprinkle yeast on warm water; stir to dissolve.

• Add 2 eggs, yeast, nutmeg, vanilla and 1 c. flour to milk mixture. Beat with electric mixer at medium speed, scraping the bowl occasionally, 2 minutes, or until smooth. Or beat vigorously with spoon.

• Stir in enough remaining flour, a little at a time, to make a soft dough, easy to handle. Cover with waxed paper and a clean towel; let rise in a warm place free from drafts until doubled.

• Roll dough ¼″ thick on lightly floured board. Dot with ½ c. soft shortening (softened by standing at room temperature), leaving 2″ border without shortening. Fold dough in half and seal edges. Dot dough with remaining ½ c. softened shortening; fold in half again and seal edges. Roll dough ⅓″ thick to make a square; fold in half and fold again to make a square (like a handkerchief). Repeat rolling and folding process 3 more times.

• Place dough in lightly greased bowl, cover, and let rest 20 minutes.

• Roll dough ⅓″ thick on lightly floured board. Shape and, if you like, fill (directions follow). Place on ungreased baking sheets. Cover and let rise in warm place until half doubled in size.

• Brush tops of pastries with beaten egg and sprinkle with chopped nuts. Bake in very hot oven (475°) 8 to 10 minutes. Drizzle while warm with Sugar Glaze, if you like. Cool on wire racks. Makes about 24 pastries.

Sugar Glaze: Combine 1 c. sifted confectioners sugar, 1½ tsp. melted butter and enough milk or dairy half-and-half to make a smooth frosting.

HOW TO SHAPE DANISH PASTRY

Coils or Snails, Rings and Figure 8s: Cut dough rolled ⅓″ thick into strips 8″ long and ¾″ wide. Place strips, one at a time, on ungreased baking sheet. Hold one end on baking sheet and twist. Then shape strip into desired design. (Let rise until half doubled in size, brush with beaten egg and sprinkle with nuts. After baking, while pastries are still warm, drizzle on Sugar Glaze, if you like.)

HOW TO FILL DANISH PASTRY

Foldovers: Cut dough rolled ⅓″ thick into 3″ squares. Place 1 tsp. filling in center. Fold opposite corners to center; press to seal.

Pinwheels: Make like Foldovers, only cut from each corner almost to center. Place 1 tsp. filling in center, if you like. Fold alternating points to center and press to seal.

Cockscombs: Roll half of dough at a time into a 12×8″ rectangle. Cut in 4×2″ rectangles. Place 1 tsp. Almond Filling in center of each rectangle (be sure measurement is level). Fold lengthwise in half and tightly press edges to seal. Curve rolls slightly on baking sheet and with sharp scissors snip side opposite sealed edge at 1″ intervals.

FILLINGS FOR DANISH PASTRY

Golden Apricot Filling: Cook ⅔ c. dried apricots with ⅔ c. water until apricots are very tender. Stir in 6 tblsp. sugar. Rub through strainer, or buzz in electric blender. Filling should be thick.

Prune-Spice Filling: Substitute pitted dried prunes for dried apricots in Apricot Filling and use ¼ tsp. cinnamon. Filling should be thick.

Almond Filling: Cream ¼ c. butter and ¼ c. sugar until light and fluffy. Blend in ¼ c. ground almonds. Add a few drops almond extract if you like.

Cherry Filling: Combine ½ c. canned cherry pie filling and a few drops almond extract.

Apricot Jam Filling: Combine ½ c. thick apricot jam and ½ tsp. grated orange peel.

Brioche—Light Butter Rolls

Brioche is typically French. Legend has it that the rolls originated in the district of Brie. The French serve brioche warm for breakfast. In America, we team the rolls with coffee at any time of the day. They always win applause.

There are many recipes for brioche. We give you one worked out in our FARM JOURNAL Test Kitchens. We think the rolls are extra-good and think you'll agree.

BRIOCHE

Light, delicately yeasty, golden—one of the favorite recipes from our Freezing & Canning Cookbook

1 c. milk
½ c. butter or margarine
1 tsp. salt
½ c. sugar
2 pkgs. active dry yeast
¼ c. warm water (110 to 115°)
4 eggs, beaten
1 tsp. grated lemon peel
5 c. sifted all-purpose flour
   (about)
Melted butter

• Scald milk; stir in ½ c. butter, salt and sugar. Cool to lukewarm.
• Sprinkle yeast on warm water; stir to dissolve.
• Combine eggs and lemon peel and add with yeast to milk mixture. Beat in flour, a little at a time, to make a soft dough you can handle.
• Turn onto floured board; knead lightly until dough is smooth and satiny. Place in greased bowl; turn dough over to grease top. Cover and let rise in warm place free from drafts until doubled, about 2 hours. Punch down and turn out on floured board. Knead lightly.
• Shape two thirds of the dough into smooth balls about 2″ in diameter. Shape remaining dough in 1″ balls. Place large balls in greased muffin-pan cups. Flatten balls slightly; make a deep indentation in each with finger or the handle of a wooden spoon. Shape small balls like teardrops and set one firmly in the indentation in each ball in muffin-pan cups. Brush with melted butter. Cover and let rise until doubled, about 1 hour.
• Bake in hot oven (425°) about 10 minutes. Remove from pans at once. Place on wire racks. Serve warm; or wrap cold rolls in aluminum foil and heat a few minutes in oven before serving. Makes 3 dozen rolls.

Spring's Hot Cross Buns

Shiny, brown rolls, crowned with white frosting crosses, are as English as roast beef and Yorkshire pudding. The recipes came with the early settlers and caught on from the start. Now the buns come to thousands of breakfast and luncheon tables, especially during the Easter season.

You can bake the rolls ahead and freeze them, providing you omit the frosting. It takes only a few minutes to add it the day of serving. Put the frozen rolls on a baking sheet and run them in a hot oven (400°) for 10 minutes. Cool 5 minutes, add the frosting and serve pronto.

When you bake Hot Cross Buns, you are making bread that has stood the test of time. English people first made them to honor the Goddess of Spring. When the Christian faith came to the country, bakers bowed to changing times and added the cross.

HOT CROSS BUNS

Easter buns with frosting crosses—traditionally served on Good Friday

¼ c. milk
⅓ c. sugar
¾ tsp. salt
½ c. shortening
2 pkgs. active dry yeast
½ c. warm water (110 to 115°)
3 eggs
4 c. sifted all-purpose flour
   (about)
¾ c. currants
1 egg white
1 tsp. cold water
White Frosting

• Scald milk, add sugar, salt and shortening; cool to lukewarm.
• Sprinkle yeast on warm water; stir to dissolve.
• Add eggs, yeast and 1 c. flour to milk mixture; beat with electric mixer at medium speed about 2 minutes, occasionally scraping the bowl. Stir in currants and enough remaining flour, a little at a time, to make a soft dough that is easy to handle. Beat well. Place in lightly greased bowl; turn dough over to grease top. Cover and let rise until doubled, about 1½ hours. Punch down. Turn onto lightly floured board.
• Roll or pat to ½" thickness. Cut in rounds with 2½" biscuit cutter; shape cutouts in buns. Place about 1½" apart on greased baking sheets. Cover and let rise until doubled, about 1 hour.
• With a very sharp knife, cut a shallow cross on top of each bun. Brush tops with unbeaten egg white mixed with cold water.
• Bake in moderate oven (375°) 15 minutes, or until golden brown. Cool on wire racks about 5 minutes. Then, with tip of knife or teaspoon, fill in crosses on buns with White Frosting. Best served warm. Makes about 18 buns.

White Frosting: Combine 1 c. sifted confectioners sugar, ½ tsp. vanilla and 2 tblsp. hot water. Mix until smooth.

VARIATION

Fruited Hot Cross Buns: With currants stir in 3 tblsp. finely chopped candied orange peel and 3 tblsp. finely chopped citron.

To reheat bread and rolls, wrap in aluminum foil and heat about 10 minutes in a hot oven (400°).

Bohemian Kolaches—
Fruity and Gay

If you want to collect compliments for the bread you bake, do make Kolaches. Arrange the apricot- and prune-filled rolls, dusted with confectioners sugar, on a tray for your next tea or coffee party, or pass to guests with coffee at any time of day.

Some women consider Kolaches tedious to make, but almost everyone believes they're worth the effort. Our recipe comes from a farm woman in northeastern Iowa. It came to her from her mother, as a remembrance of home, from relatives in Czechoslovakia. Frequently she fixes the fillings a day ahead and keeps them, covered, in the refrigerator ready to use.

While the rolls are simply superb when fresh-baked, you can bake them ahead and freeze. Few people can tell the difference if you warm the Kolaches before serving (dust on the confectioners sugar after warming).

BOHEMIAN KOLACHES

No European sweet bread has a more enthusiastic American following than these luscious fruit-filled rolls

½ c. milk
2 pkgs. active dry yeast
½ c. warm water (110 to 115°)
¾ c. butter or margarine (1 ½ sticks)
½ c. sugar
1 tsp. salt
4 egg yolks
4 ½ c. sifted all-purpose flour
Fillings
2 tblsp. melted butter
2 tblsp. confectioners sugar

• Scald milk; cool to lukewarm.
• Sprinkle yeast on warm water; stir to dissolve.
• Cream butter, sugar, salt and egg yolks together with electric mixer until light and fluffy. Add yeast, milk and 1½ c. flour. Beat with electric mixer at medium speed 5 minutes, scraping the bowl occasionally. Batter should be smooth.
• Stir in enough remaining flour, a little at a time, to make a soft dough that leaves the sides of bowl. Place in lightly greased bowl, turn dough over to grease top. Cover and let rise in warm place free from drafts until doubled, 1 to 1½ hours.
• Stir down; turn onto lightly floured board and divide into 24 pieces of equal size. Shape each piece into a ball. Cover and let rest 10 to 15 minutes.
• Place 2″ apart on greased baking sheets; press each piece of dough from center outward with fingers of both hands to make a hollow in center with a ½″ rim around edge. Fill each hollow with 1 level tblsp. filling (recipes follow).
• Cover and let rise in warm place until doubled, 30 to 40 minutes.

• Bake in moderate oven (350°) 15 to 18 minutes, or until browned. Brush tops of rolls lightly with melted butter and sprinkle lightly with sifted confectioners sugar. Remove from baking sheets and place on wire racks. Makes 24 kolaches.

FILLINGS FOR KOLACHES

Prune Filling: Cook 30 prunes in water to cover until tender; drain, mash with fork and stir in ¼ c. sugar and ¼ tsp. allspice. Filling should be thick. Makes enough for 14 kolaches.

Thick Apricot Filling: Cook 25 dried apricot halves in water to cover until tender; drain and press through strainer or food mill (or buzz in blender). Stir in ¼ c. sugar. Filling should be thick. Makes enough filling for 10 kolaches.

Prune-Apricot Filling: Simmer 1 c. prunes and ¾ c. dried apricot halves in water to cover until tender; drain, chop and mash with fork. Stir in ½ c. sugar, 1 tblsp. orange juice and 1 tblsp. grated orange peel. Filling should be thick. Makes enough filling for 24 kolaches.

VARIATIONS

Peek-a-boo Kolaches: Flatten balls of dough, after resting 15 minutes, to make 3½ to 4″ squares. Place about 1 tblsp. filling on center of each square. Moisten corners with milk and bring opposite corners over filling, overlapping them about 1″; press to seal. Repeat with 2 opposite corners. Place about 2″ apart on greased baking sheet; let rise and bake like Bohemian Kolaches.

Baby Bunting Kolaches: When dough is doubled, stir it down and divide in half. Let rest 15 minutes. Roll each half into a 12×9″ rectangle; cut each half in 12 (3″) squares. Place 1 tblsp. filling on center of each square. Bring one corner of dough to center over filling; repeat with opposite corner; press to seal. Place 2″ apart on greased baking sheet; let rise and bake like Bohemian Kolaches.

Flag-inspired Crescents

When the Turks, in 1683, found their siege of Vienna failing, they decided to dig tunnels by night through which they could enter the city. Bakers, hearing the digging, gave the alarm to the government officials. The city was saved. As a reward, the bakers were given permission to make rolls in the shape of the crescent, an emblem on the Mohammedan flag. From that long-ago beginning, luscious crescent rolls have captured the hearts of people in many countries— France, where people call them croissants and serve them fresh-baked for breakfast, and the United States.

This cookbook features several recipes for crescents, but none of them surpasses Butter Crescents.

BUTTER CRESCENTS

Have copies of this recipe ready— you may be sure guests will ask for it

½ c. milk
½ c. butter
⅓ c. sugar
¾ tsp. salt
1 pkg. active dry yeast

½ c. warm water (110 to 115°)
1 egg, beaten
4 c. sifted all-purpose flour
  (about)

• Scald milk and pour over butter,
sugar and salt. Cool to lukewarm.
• Sprinkle yeast on warm water; stir
to dissolve.
• Add egg, yeast and 2 c. flour to milk
mixture. Beat with electric mixer at
low speed until smooth, about 1 minute. Then beat at medium speed until
thick, about 2 minutes (or beat with
rotary beater).
• Add enough of remaining flour and
mix with spoon or hands to make a
dough that leaves the sides of bowl.
Turn onto a lightly floured board and
knead gently. Put into a greased bowl;
invert to grease top of dough. Cover
with clean towel and let rise in warm
place free from drafts until doubled,
about 1 hour.
• Turn dough onto board, divide in
half, cover and let rest 10 minutes.
Roll each half to make a 12″ circle;
cut each circle in 12 wedges. Roll up
each wedge from wide end and put,
pointed end down, on greased baking
sheets (you'll need 2). Curve ends
slightly to make crescents. Cover with
towel. Let rise until doubled, about
30 minutes.
• Bake in hot oven (400°) 15 minutes, changing position of baking
sheets in oven when half baked. Remove from baking sheets and cool on
wire racks. Makes 24 crescents.

Note: You can refrigerate the dough
overnight before you let it rise. After
kneading dough, place in lightly
greased bowl and turn dough over
to grease top. Cover with a piece of
waxed paper, brushed with salad oil,
and lay a piece of aluminum foil on
top. Place in refrigerator. In the
morning, let stand at room temperature until dough rises and is soft
enough to roll, then turn dough onto
board and proceed as with dough that
was not refrigerated.

VARIATION

Peanut Butter Crescents: Follow the
recipe for Butter Crescents, but before cutting the circles of dough and
rolling the pie-shaped pieces, spread
with this mixture: Combine ⅓ c. peanut butter and ⅓ c. honey; add ⅛
tsp. salt and ½ tsp. cinnamon. Proceed as directed for Butter Crescents.

Festive St. Lucia Buns

When it comes to yeast breads,
Swedish people know what's good.
Among their Christmas season favorites are St. Lucia Buns. Americans
also like these rolls. Choose them for
a kitchen-made gift to take to neighbors, to serve at a holiday coffee party
or to treat your family at breakfast.

The Wisconsin farm woman who
shares her recipe for this festive bread
believes one reason the rolls taste so
good is their cardamom flavor.
Scandinavian bakers favor this sweet
spice. "Some people prefer saffron to
cardamom," she says. "You can use
a pinch of it in my recipe, if you like.
Dissolve it in the hot milk and omit
the cardamom." Then she adds:
"Sometimes I omit the raisins from
the curled ends of the rolls and instead stick candied red cherries, cut
in 4 pieces, in the centers of the
coils."

The Swedish custom is for the daughters in the family, dressed in white and wearing holly crowns, to awaken their parents at dawn on St. Lucia's Day, December 13, and serve them St. Lucia Buns and hot coffee. This ceremony signals the opening of the Christmas season.

You can bake the buns ahead and freeze them to get a head start on holiday preparations. To thaw them, wrap the frozen rolls in aluminum foil and place them in a slow oven (325°) for 20 minutes, or place them unwrapped on a baking sheet and run them into a hot oven (400°) for 10 minutes. If it is easier for you, let the wrapped buns thaw at room temperature for 30 to 35 minutes.

ST. LUCIA BUNS

These breakfast buns open Sweden's Christmas season on December 13

¾   c. milk
⅓   c. sugar
2   tsp. salt
½   c. butter or margarine (1 stick)
2   pkgs. active dry yeast
½   c. warm water (110 to 115°)
1   tsp. ground cardamom
4⅓ c. sifted all-purpose flour
1   egg
Raisins
1   egg white

• Scald milk; pour into a large bowl and add sugar, salt and butter. Cool to lukewarm.
• Sprinkle yeast on warm water; stir to dissolve.
• Add cardamom, 1 c. flour, yeast and egg to milk mixture; beat with electric mixer at medium speed, scraping the bowl occasionally, 2 minutes, or until smooth. (Or beat vigorously with spoon.) Stir in enough remaining flour, a little at a time, until dough leaves the sides of bowl.
• Turn onto lightly floured board; knead until smooth and elastic, about 5 minutes.
• Place in lightly greased bowl; turn dough over to grease top. Cover and let rise in a warm place free from drafts until doubled, about 45 to 50 minutes. Punch down; cover and let rest 10 minutes.
• Pinch off balls of dough about 2½" in diameter and roll into pieces 12" long and ½" thick. Place 2 strips together, back to back, on greased baking sheets and curl or coil the ends. Stick a raisin in the center of each coil. (Or form strips of dough in the shape of an S, coiling or curling ends. Stick a raisin in the center of each coil.) Brush tops of buns with egg white beaten until foamy. Sprinkle with sugar, if you wish. Cover and let rise until doubled, about 40 minutes.
• Bake in hot oven (400°) 10 to 12 minutes, or until golden brown. Remove from baking sheet to wire racks. Serve warm or cold. Makes 18 buns.

PRUNE AND APRICOT SQUARES

This is what a Nebraska farm woman serves with coffee to morning callers

¾   c. chopped cooked, drained prunes
¾   c. chopped cooked, drained apricots
½   c. sugar
¼   c. finely chopped nuts
¼   c. milk
1   pkg. active dry yeast

¼ c. warm water (110 to 115°)
½ tsp. salt
2¼ c. sifted all-purpose flour
¼ c. shortening
1 egg
Orange Frosting

• Combine prunes, apricots, ¼ c. sugar and nuts. Set aside.
• Scald milk; cool to lukewarm.
• Sprinkle yeast on warm water; stir to dissolve.
• Combine remaining ¼ c. sugar, salt and flour; stir to mix. Cut in shortening with pastry blender as for pie crust. Add milk, yeast and egg. Stir well until blended. Place in greased bowl; turn dough over to grease top. Cover and let rise until doubled, 1 to 1½ hours.
• Turn onto board and divide in half. Cover and let rest 10 minutes. Roll out each half to make a 16×-12″ rectangle. Place 1 rectangle on greased baking sheet. Spread with prune-apricot mixture. Place other dough rectangle on top. Let rise 1 hour.
• Bake in moderate oven (350°) 30 minutes. Cool 5 to 10 minutes and frost with Orange Frosting. Cut into squares to serve. Makes 15 squares.

Orange Frosting: To 1 c. sifted confectioners sugar add ¼ tsp. grated orange peel and 1 tblsp. orange juice, or enough juice to make a frosting of spreading consistency. (If you prefer, substitute cream or milk for orange juice. Then omit orange peel.)

For Shiny Crisp Crusts

Brush yeast bread or rolls before baking with 1 egg yolk beaten with 2 tblsp. cold water.

Rolls Piquant with Sour Cream

Give a farm woman a mixing bowl, sour cream and a little time for baking and something wonderful happens. Fragrant and delicious foods come from the oven with that piquant taste that sour cream alone imparts. This holds for yeast-leavened rolls as well as for cookies and cakes.

Sugar-Crusted Rolls and Holiday Cream Twists are adequate proof. These dainty rolls are an American substitute for Danish pastries. They're a lot easier to make.

The sour cream used in most kitchens today is dairy sour cream from the grocery—the kind called for in our recipes. It has an advantage for weight watchers because the fat content is lower than that in heavy cream soured at home and its flavor is often better.

HOLIDAY CREAM TWISTS

Dainty, pretty and tasty for the holidays or any festive occasion

1 pkg. active dry yeast
½ c. warm water (110 to 115°)
4 c. sifted all-purpose flour
1 tsp. salt
1 c. shortening
1 whole egg
2 egg yolks
1 c. dairy sour cream
½ tsp. grated lemon peel
½ c. quartered candied cherries
½ c. broken walnuts
¾ c. sugar

• Sprinkle yeast on warm water; stir to dissolve.
• Sift together flour and salt; cut

shortening into flour mixture with pastry blender.

· Combine yeast, egg, egg yolks, sour cream and lemon peel; mix thoroughly into flour mixture. Stir in cherries and walnuts. Cover and place dough in refrigerator overnight (it will be stiff).

· Sprinkle sugar lightly over rolling surface. Place dough on sugared surface and sprinkle it lightly with sugar. Roll to make a 16×12″ rectangle. Fold dough from two opposite sides to make 3 layers. Sprinkle rolling surface and dough with a little sugar and roll and fold again. Sprinkle dough and rolling surface again with sugar and roll, fold and roll again. (Divide the sugar—use about 2 tblsp. at a time—so you will use no more than ¾ c. for the entire process.)

· Cut the 16×12″ sheet of dough into strips 4″ long and 1″ wide. Lift strips with both hands and twist 3 or 4 times. Place 1″ apart on ungreased baking sheets.

· Bake in moderate oven (375°) 18 to 20 minutes. Makes 48 rolls.

SUGAR-CRUSTED ROLLS

Sweet rolls that taste like Danish pastry made by a simplified method

1   pkg. active dry yeast
¼   c. warm water (110 to 115°)
3½ c. sifted all-purpose flour
1   tsp. salt
¾   c. sugar
1   c. cold butter
2   eggs, slightly beaten
¾   c. dairy sour cream
2   tsp. vanilla

· Sprinkle yeast on warm water; stir to dissolve.

· Sift flour, salt and ¼ c. sugar into large mixing bowl. Cut in firm butter with pastry blender until mixture looks like fine crumbs. Stir in yeast, eggs, sour cream and vanilla to make a smooth dough. Shape into a ball with hands.

· Wrap dough tightly in plastic wrap and refrigerate overnight. (You can keep it in refrigerator up to 3 days, or you can make the rolls after it has chilled 3 hours.)

· Divide dough in half, wrap and return one half to refrigerator. Roll out other half on lightly floured board to make an 18×12″ rectangle. Fold from 2 sides so you will have 3 layers. Roll out again on floured board to make an 18×12″ rectangle, repeat folding, then roll out again to an 18×12″ rectangle. Fold again in thirds and cut in half to make 2 (6″) squares.

· Turn in corners of 1 square of the dough to make a circle. Sprinkle the board with about 2 tblsp. of the remaining sugar. Roll dough to a 12″ circle. Cut circle into 8 equal wedges. Roll up each wedge, starting with the broad end. Place on greased baking sheet, point side down. Curve each roll slightly to make a crescent shape.

· On sugared board, roll, cut and shape crescents from the other 6″ square of dough in the same way.

· Repeat with other half of dough from the refrigerator, using the last ¼ c. sugar for the rolling of this dough.

· Cover; let rolls rise until puffy, about 45 minutes. Bake in moderate oven (375°) 12 to 15 minutes, or until golden brown. Serve warm or cold. Makes 32 crescents.

BREAKFAST CINNAMON CRISPS

One farmer's first choice of the many excellent yeast breads his wife bakes

1 ¼ c. milk
½ c. sugar
½ c. butter or margarine
1 tsp. salt
1 pkg. active dry yeast
¼ c. warm water (110 to 115°)
2 eggs
5 ½ to 6 c. sifted all-purpose flour
½ c. softened butter
1 ½ c. sugar
1 tblsp. cinnamon

• Scald milk; add ½ c. sugar, ½ c. butter and salt. Cool to lukewarm.
• Sprinkle yeast on warm water; stir to dissolve.
• Combine eggs, 2 c. flour, milk mixture and yeast in large bowl. Beat 1 minute with electric mixer at low speed, then 2 minutes at medium speed. (Or beat with spoon until mixture is smooth.)
• Mix in enough remaining flour, a little at a time, with spoon or hands to make a soft dough that is easy to handle.
• Turn onto lightly floured board; knead until smooth and elastic, about 5 minutes. Round up into ball, place in greased bowl and turn dough over to grease top. Cover and let rise in warm place until doubled, about 1½ hours.
• Turn onto board, divide in half, cover and let rest 10 minutes. Roll each half into a 20×13" rectangle.
• Make a filling by combining ½ c. butter and 1 c. sugar. Divide mixture in half, 1 portion for each rectangle of dough. Spread first rectangle with half of 1 portion butter-sugar mix-

ture (about 4 tblsp.). Fold rectangle in half; roll again to make a 20×13" rectangle; spread with remaining half portion of butter-sugar filling (about 4 tblsp.) Fold in half again and roll out to rectangle 20×13". Repeat procedure with other rectangle of dough, using remaining half of butter-sugar filling.
• Combine remaining ½ c. sugar and cinnamon. Divide in half; set aside one half for topping. Sprinkle the other half evenly over both rolled out rectangles of dough.
• Starting at wide side of rectangles, roll each one like a jelly roll. Seal well by pinching edges of each roll together. Even up rolls by stretching slightly. Cut in 1" slices. Place on greased baking sheets and flatten by pressing down and gently pulling outward with fingers from center of each slice. Sprinkle remaining sugar-cinnamon mixture evenly on tops of rolls.
• Cover and let rise in warm place about 30 minutes. Bake in hot oven (400°) 10 to 12 minutes. Cool on wire racks. Makes 40 rolls.

Peanut Butter Syrup

Mix ⅓ c. peanut butter with ⅔ c. light corn syrup until smooth. Good on pancakes.

Country Yeast Specialties

Sleepy appetites awaken quickly on wintry mornings if yeast-leavened waffles, pancakes or doughnuts come to the breakfast table. These hearty country foods never go out of style. Certainly, no bread cookbook would be complete without them.

Pizza, a supper and snack favorite, joins this group of bread specialties that have a delicate yeasty flavor. Teen-agers first promoted this Italian treat, but it quickly made friends with many grownups. More women make pizzas every year, with the help of their young folks, so that it no longer is necessary to drive to town to visit a "pizza parlor" to enjoy the food as much as the Romans do.

You will also find in this group of specialties a recipe for Sour Dough Starter, an old-time favorite that retains popularity with Western ranch people because of the tangy flavor it gives breads made with it.

YEAST WAFFLES

Change of pace and taste in waffles; recipe is reprinted from our Cooking for Company *cookbook*

2 c. milk
1 pkg. active dry yeast
½ c. warm water (110 to 115°)
⅓ c. melted butter
1 tsp. salt
1 tsp. sugar
3 c. sifted all-purpose flour
2 eggs, slightly beaten
½ tsp. baking soda

• Scald milk; cool to lukewarm.
• Sprinkle yeast on warm water in large bowl; stir to dissolve.
• Add milk, butter, salt, sugar and flour to yeast; mix thoroughly with rotary or electric mixer until batter is smooth. Cover and let stand at room temperature overnight.
• When ready to bake, add eggs and baking soda. Beat well. Bake on preheated waffle iron. Makes 6 to 8 waffles.

Yeast-leavened Flapjacks

Surprise nearby neighbors on a blustery winter day by inviting them over for a pancake supper. Make yeast-leavened cakes for a change. They're different. And they taste exceptionally good.

You let the batter stand at least an hour before baking the cakes. If you like to be an early bird when getting ready for company, you can fix the batter hours ahead. It will keep up to 24 hours if covered and stored in the refrigerator.

You can roll the flapjacks, or serve a stack of 2 or 3 on each plate. After the first few bites, guests know they are eating something different and delicious. If there is a home bread baker around the table, she will recognize that the marvelous aroma and taste come from yeast.

YEAST-LEAVENED FLAPJACKS

Easy to fix, tempting, satisfying

1¾ c. milk
2 tblsp. sugar
1 tsp. salt
1 pkg. active dry yeast
¼ c. warm water (110 to 115°)
3 tblsp. salad oil (or ¼ c. softened shortening)
3 eggs (room temperature)
2 c. sifted all-purpose flour

• Scald milk; add sugar and salt and cool to lukewarm.
• Meanwhile, sprinkle yeast on warm water; stir to dissolve. Add to cooled milk mixture. Beat in salad oil, eggs and flour with rotary beater or elec-

tric mixer on medium speed until batter is smooth.

• Cover bowl and let rise in warm place at least 1 hour before using. The batter will be light and bubbly. Use at once, or refrigerate (do not refrigerate for more than 24 hours).

• Stir down batter. Dip with a ¼-cup measure and pour onto hot griddle, greasing griddle if necessary. Turn flapjacks as soon as tops are bubbly; bake to golden brown on other side.

• Serve at once with butter or margarine and table syrup, jam or jelly Or squeeze a little lemon juice on hot cakes, sprinkle with sifted confectioners sugar and spread with canned apple pie slices or applesauce. Roll up flapjacks, sift on a little more confectioners sugar and serve at once. Makes about 18 (5″) flapjacks.

VARIATION

Spiced Yeast-leavened Flapjacks: Add ⅛ tsp. each ginger and nutmeg with the sugar and salt.

Note: You can freeze Yeast-leavened Flapjacks. Place waxed paper between cooled baked cakes and stack in a rigid freezer container. Cover, seal and label. Store up to 3 months in freezer. When ready to use flapjacks, place the frozen cakes under broiler, turning them after a few minutes to thaw and heat thoroughly.

Buckwheat Cakes for Breakfast

A stack of hot buckwheat cakes with plenty of butter and syrup often cheerfully starts a cold, wintry day for country people. These griddlecakes may be old-fashioned, but they taste as good as ever. Farmers, no matter how low the mercury goes in their thermometers, spend considerable time outdoors doing chores and errands. They know buckwheat cakes stick to the ribs and give them that well-fed feeling that defies cold.

Young women, inexperienced in making these yeast-leavened griddlecakes, will find our recipe easy to follow. They and experienced pancake makers will like the results they get with it. You do some of the fixing the night (or several hours) before you bake the cakes. With a few quick additions at mealtime, the batter is ready to bake almost before the coffee is done.

It's an old country custom to stir up enough batter to have some left over to simplify the next baking. Our recipe shows how to do it.

BUCKWHEAT CAKES

To please the men, keep the starter ready and the griddle handy to use

1	c. sifted all-purpose flour
3½	c. buckwheat flour
1	tsp. salt
1	pkg. active dry yeast
4	c. warm water (110 to 115°)
2	tsp. granulated sugar
2	tblsp. dark brown sugar
¾	tsp. baking soda
1	tblsp. salad oil

• Combine all-purpose and buckwheat flours. Stir in salt.

• Sprinkle yeast on ¼ c. warm water; stir to dissolve.

• Dissolve 2 tsp. sugar in remaining 3¾ c. warm water; cool to lukewarm.

Add lukewarm water mixture and yeast to flours. Stir to mix thoroughly. Cover and let stand overnight or several hours at room temperature. Batter should no more than half fill bowl.

• When ready to bake pancakes, stir down batter and add brown sugar, baking soda and oil. Stir to mix.

• Dip batter with ¼-cup measure; bake on lightly greased, preheated griddle (hot enough that a few drops of water dropped on it dance about). Brown on both sides, turning once. Serve hot with butter or margarine and table syrup. Makes 5 cups batter.

STARTER FOR MORE BUCKWHEAT CAKES

• The leftover batter becomes the starter. Pour it into a glass or plastic container with tight fitting lid. Fill container no more than half full of batter. Cover and place in refrigerator. It will keep several days.

HOW TO USE BUCKWHEAT CAKE STARTER

• Remove starter from refrigerator the night (or several hours) before you wish to bake cakes. Pour it into a mixing bowl and add 1 c. lukewarm water for every cup buckwheat flour you add to starter. Stir to blend, cover and let stand at room temperature.

• When ready to bake cakes, stir down batter. Add 1 tsp. salt, 2 tblsp. brown sugar, ¾ tsp. baking soda and 1 tblsp. salad oil. Stir to blend.

• Bake like Buckwheat Cakes, saving out batter to store in refrigerator to make starter for the next batch of pancakes.

Popular Pizza for Impromptu Parties

If you like a crisp pizza crust, this recipe is for you. We tried many different ones, but this one rated highest with taste-testers, among them some teen-agers.

With cans of pizza sauce in the cupboard, mozzarella cheese in the refrigerator and frozen pizza dough in the freezer, you're only minutes away from hearty refreshments that young people really like. Our youthful taste-testers rated pork sausage the most popular for pizza topping; the more highly seasoned pizza sausage, second place. But they enjoyed all the toppings we suggest. You'll almost always have at least one of these on hand.

POPULAR PIZZA

A treat for teens! Keep dough in freezer ready to fill and bake

1   pkg. active dry yeast
1 ¼ c. warm water (110 to 115°)
3 ½ to 4 c. sifted all-purpose flour
½   tsp. salt
Pizza Filling

• Sprinkle yeast on warm water; stir to dissolve. Add 2 c. flour and salt. Beat thoroughly. Stir in remaining flour. Turn onto lightly floured board and knead until smooth and elastic, about 10 minutes.

• Place in lightly greased bowl; turn dough over to grease top. Cover and let rise in warm place until doubled, about 30 minutes.

• Turn onto board and knead just long enough to force out large bubbles. Divide in half. Roll each half to make an 11″ circle. Stretch each circle to fit an oiled 12″ pizza pan. Add filling (recipes follow).

• Bake in very hot oven (450°) 20 to 25 minutes. Exchange position of pans on oven racks once during baking to brown pizzas the same. Makes 2 pizzas.

Note: If you do not have pizza pans, use baking sheets. Roll each half of dough into a 12×10″ rectangle, or one that almost fills your baking sheet. Place on oiled baking sheets and build up edges slightly. Fill and bake like pizzas in round pizza pans.

PIZZA FILLINGS

Hamburger Filling: Spread 1 (8 oz.) can pizza sauce over dough in each pizza pan (you'll use 2 [8 oz.] cans). Brown 1 lb. ground beef in skillet and drain; divide in half and sprinkle evenly over sauce in pizza dough. Then sprinkle evenly over each pizza 1½ c. shredded mozzarella cheese (about 12 oz. cheese for both pizzas). Bake as directed.

Ham and Salami Filling: Spread 1 (8 oz.) can pizza sauce over dough in each pizza pan. Alternate strips of boiled ham and salami on sauce (about 4 slices ham and 6 slices salami, cut in strips, for both pizzas). Sprinkle each pizza with 1½ c. shredded mozzarella cheese. Bake.

Sausage Filling: Spread 1 (8 oz.) can pizza sauce over dough in each pizza pan. Brown 1 lb. bulk pork sausage in skillet, drain and divide in half. Spread evenly over sauce in pizza dough. Then sprinkle 1½ c. shredded mozzarella cheese over each pizza. Bake as directed.

Choice of Pizza Fillings: Fill dough in each pizza pan with 1 (8 oz.) can pizza sauce and sprinkle on each 1½ c. shredded mozzarella cheese. Cook 1 lb. pizza sausage in skillet, drain and divide in half. Sprinkle evenly over pizza dough in pans filled with sauce and cheese. Or instead of pizza sausage, top with anchovies, mushrooms, sliced ripe olives, sardines or miniature frankfurters. Bake as directed.

To Freeze Pizza Dough: When you divide the risen dough in half, roll each into an 11″ circle. Place in oiled pizza pan with double thickness of waxed paper between circles. (Or roll each half of dough into a 12×10″ rectangle, place on oiled baking sheet with waxed paper between rectangles). Wrap and freeze. Keeps up to 1 week.

To Use Frozen Pizza Dough: Remove from freezer and let stand at room temperature 20 minutes. With fingers pull and stretch circles to cover pizza pans. (Or stretch rectangles of dough almost to edges of baking sheet and make small rim around edge.) Fill and bake as directed.

CINNAMON SWIRLS

Glazed doughnuts that look like cinnamon rolls—perfect with coffee

1 ¾ c. milk
⅓ c. sugar
¼ c. butter
2 tsp. salt
2 pkgs. active dry yeast
½ c. warm water (110 to 115°)
6 to 7 c. sifted all-purpose flour
2 tblsp. sugar
1 tblsp. cinnamon
Cinnamon Glaze

• Scald milk; add ⅓ c. sugar, butter and salt. Cool to lukewarm.

• Sprinkle yeast on warm water; stir to dissolve. Stir into lukewarm milk mixture. Add enough flour gradually to make a stiff dough. Turn onto lightly floured board; knead until smooth and satiny, about 7 minutes. Place in a lightly greased bowl and turn dough over to grease top. Cover and let rise in a warm place until doubled, 1 to 1½ hours.

• Meanwhile, combine 2 tblsp. sugar and cinnamon.

• Turn dough onto board and divide in half. Roll one half to make an 18×8″ rectangle; sprinkle half the sugar-cinnamon mixture evenly over top. Starting at long side, roll up as for jelly roll and seal edges. Cut with strong thread or sharp knife into 1″ slices. Place on ungreased baking sheets. Repeat with remaining half of dough. Do not cover. Let rise in warm place until light, 30 to 45 minutes.

• Fry in deep hot fat (375°) 1 to 2 minutes on each side; do not brown too much. Drain on paper towels. While warm, drizzle from teaspoon with Cinnamon Glaze. Makes 3 dozen.

Cinnamon Glaze: Combine 1 c. sifted confectioners sugar, ½ tsp. cinnamon and 1 tblsp. plus 2 tsp. milk. Stir until smooth.

Doughnuts on Sticks

Thread a few centers cut from doughnuts on a wooden skewer (from the meat market) and fry like doughnuts. Youngsters love them.

SPUDNUTS

Keep some of these potato doughnuts in the freezer to serve with coffee. From Cooking for Company

1 ¾ c. milk
½ c. shortening
½ c. sugar
½ c. mashed potatoes
1 pkg. active dry yeast
½ c. warm water (110 to 115°)
2 eggs, beaten
½ tsp. vanilla
6½ to 7 c. sifted all-purpose flour
1 tsp. baking powder
2 tsp. salt

• Scald milk; stir in shortening, sugar and mashed potatoes. Cool to lukewarm. Blend well.

• Sprinkle yeast over warm water and stir until yeast is dissolved. Add to milk mixture. Stir in beaten eggs and vanilla.

• Sift 6½ c. flour with baking powder and salt; add gradually to yeast mixture, mixing well after each addition. Add another ½ c. flour if needed to make a soft dough you can handle (use no more than necessary). Turn into greased bowl; turn dough over to grease top. Cover and let rise in warm place until doubled, about 1½ hours.

• Roll to ½″ thickness on floured board. Cut with floured doughnut cutter, reserving centers to make Pecan Rolls (recipe follows).

• Place cut-out doughnuts on waxed paper; cover with cloth and let rise in warm place until doubled, about 30 minutes.

• Fry a few doughnuts at a time in hot salad oil (375°). Drain on absorbent paper. Spread warm doughnuts with a thin glaze made of confectioners sugar and milk, or shake them in a bag containing sugar to coat them. Makes about 4 dozen doughnuts.

Pecan Rolls from Spudnut Centers:
Lightly grease 12 medium-size (2½") muffin-pan cups. In the bottom of each cup, place 1 tsp. brown sugar, 1 tsp. light corn syrup, ½ tsp. water, 3 pecan halves and 3 or 4 raisins. Arrange 4 doughnut centers on top, cover with cloth and let rise in warm place until doubled, about 30 minutes. Bake in moderate oven (350°) 25 to 30 minutes. Makes 12 rolls.

SOUR DOUGH STARTER

This recipe and those for Sour Dough Biscuits and Silver Dollar Hotcakes are from Cooking for Company

½ pkg. active dry yeast (1¼ tsp.)
2 c. sifted all-purpose flour
2 tblsp. sugar
2½ c. water

• Combine the ingredients in a stone crock or glass or pottery bowl. Beat well. Cover with cheesecloth and let stand 2 days in a warm place.

SOUR DOUGH BISCUITS

These biscuits are light and fluffy— they have that marvelous tangy taste

1½ c. sifted all-purpose flour
2 tsp. baking powder
¼ tsp. baking soda (½ tsp. if Starter is quite sour)
½ tsp. salt
¼ c. butter or margarine
1 c. Sour Dough Starter

• Sift dry ingredients together. Cut in butter with pastry blender. Add Starter and mix.
• Turn dough out on a lightly floured board. Knead lightly until satiny.
• Roll dough ½" thick. Cut with floured 2½" cutter. Place biscuits in well-greased 9" square baking pan. Brush with melted butter. Let rise about 1 hour in a warm place.
• Bake in hot oven (425°) 20 minutes. Makes 10 biscuits.

Note: To replenish Starter, stir in 2 c. warm (not hot) water and 2 c. flour.

SILVER DOLLAR HOTCAKES

Serve with butter and lots of "lick," the cowboy's term for sweet syrup

1 c. Sour Dough Starter
2 c. unsifted all-purpose flour
2 c. milk
1 tsp. salt
2 tsp. baking soda
2 eggs
3 tblsp. melted shortening
2 tblsp. sugar

• About 12 hours before mealtime, mix Starter, flour, milk and salt; let stand in a bowl covered with cheesecloth. Set in a warm place.
• Just before baking cakes, remove 1 c. batter to replenish Starter in crock. To the remaining batter in the bowl, add baking soda, eggs, shortening and sugar. Mix well.
• Bake cakes the size of silver dollars on a lightly greased, hot griddle. For thinner hotcakes, add more milk to the batter. Makes about 30 cakes.

Newer Ways to Bake Bread

Country people like homemade breads. We have ample proof of this in our visits with members of the FARM JOURNAL Family Test Group and other readers, and in our letters from them. One woman reflected a general attitude when she said it doesn't make too much difference what else she has for a meal if she serves bread she baked. This desire to please with food their husbands and children most enjoy is an important reason why women frequently bake yeast breads.

Time is the problem. Today's living loads women with many duties, not only in the house, but also outside on the farm and in their communities. Sometimes it takes a lot of planning to get yeast breads in the oven and out with just the right lapses for kneading and for baking.

Recognizing this situation, home economists in the test kitchens of flour milling and yeast companies work constantly to develop methods that will shorten the time needed and lessen the work in bread baking. We give you examples of their various methods—Can-Do-Quick, CoolRise, Easy Mixer, Instant Blend and Short-Cut Mixer and Rapidmix Methods.

All these newer yeast bread recipes call for unsifted all-purpose flour measured by spooning into a cup and leveling off with the straight edge of a knife (rye and whole wheat flours are measured the same way). Most specify the use of active dry yeast, which now comes in finer particles than formerly and requires no predissolving in water. The electric mixer takes over most of the work in mixing and helps develop gluten, the protein in flour that enables breads to hold their shape.

Back of these methods is the desire not only to make bread faster and more easily but also to produce loaves, rolls and coffee breads of excellent quality. We believe you will find one method (or more) that seems tailor-made for you and the minutes you have available.

The Conventional Method, featured on the preceding pages, is the basic one—the newer ways are offshoots of it. This section deals with them.

Can-Do-Quick Breads

As with all the newer methods of making yeast breads, this one is faster than the Conventional. You cut time required for making bread by one third. Developed by home economists in Betty Crocker Kitchens, the bread soon won a nickname, C.D.Q.—short for Can-Do-Quick.

Buttermilk is the liquid and you do not scald it. The electric mixer does most of the mixing, you knead the dough 5 minutes and then shape and place it in the pan for its one rising. You let the dough rise until doubled with the center of the loaf about 2" above the pan. Home economists in Betty Crocker Kitchens measure the height with a ruler (they keep rulers handy also for measuring the size of dough rectangles, circles and roll-ups —good idea for your kitchen).

The high-rise loaves that result from this method are beautiful. They brown well and the bread has an even, fine texture. The flavor is somewhat different from that of many yeast breads due to the combination of yeast and baking powder for leavening. Some of the rolls and biscuits of the early West had this same type of leavening. A Colorado rancher, eating with apparent enjoyment a buttered slice from a fresh-baked loaf of C.D.Q. bread, said: "The taste is wonderful. It reminds me of the taste of those bread-like rolls and biscuits we used to have at cattlemen's dinners and sometimes at cow camps."

An Indiana farmer's wife who has tried this method volunteers: "I do hope we'll have a good crop of tomatoes this year so we can make tomato sandwiches with C.D.Q. Cheese Bread. We like the bread for sandwiches, also for toast under creamed chicken, tuna and dried beef. But I get hungry thinking how good the bread will be with sliced, red-ripe tomatoes and curly ribbons of cooked bacon."

C.D.Q. WHITE BREAD

Tall, handsome loaf of white bread

2 pkgs. active dry yeast
¾ c. warm water (105 to 115°)
1¼ c. buttermilk
4½ to 5 c. all-purpose flour
¼ c. shortening
2 tblsp. sugar
2 tsp. baking powder
2 tsp. salt
Soft butter

• Grease a dull aluminum (anodized), glass or darkened metal 9×5×3" loaf pan (these pans encourage browning).
• Dissolve yeast in warm water in large mixer bowl. Add buttermilk, 2½ c. flour, the shortening, sugar, baking powder and salt. Blend 30 seconds with electric mixer on low speed, scraping sides and bottom of bowl. Beat 2 minutes on medium speed.
• Stir in remaining 2 to 2½ c. flour. (Dough should remain soft and and slightly sticky.) Knead 5 minutes, or about 200 turns on a generously floured board.
• Roll dough into an 18×9" rectangle. Roll up from short side as for jelly roll. With side of hand, press each end to seal. Fold ends under

loaf. Place, seam side down, in loaf pan. Brush loaf lightly with butter. Let rise in warm place (85°) until doubled, about 1 hour. (Dough in center comes about 2″ above pan.) • Heat oven to 425°. Oven rack should be in lowest position or bread will brown too quickly. Bake loaf 30 to 35 minutes. Remove from pan and brush with butter; cool on wire rack. Makes 1 loaf. (You can make 2 smaller loaves by using 2 [8½ × 4½ × 2½″] loaf pans instead of the 9×5×3″ pan. Divide the dough in half after kneading.)

Note: To make 2 large loaves C.D.Q. White Bread, double all ingredients except the yeast. Blend 1 minute with electric mixer on low speed, scraping sides and bottom of bowl. Beat 4 minutes on medium speed. Stir in remaining flour. Divide in half. Knead each half 5 minutes.

VARIATIONS

C.D.Q. Cheese Bread: Follow recipe for C.D.Q. White Bread, but omit the shortening. Stir in 1 c. shredded sharp natural Cheddar cheese with second addition of flour.

C.D.Q. Whole Wheat Bread: Follow the recipe for C.D.Q. White Bread, except substitute 1½ c. all-purpose flour and 1 c. whole wheat flour for first addition of flour; substitute 2 c. whole wheat flour for second addition of flour.

C.D.Q. Pan Rolls: Follow recipe for C.D.Q. White Bread, but roll dough into a 13×9″ rectangle. Place in greased 13×9×2″ baking pan. Score dough 1″ deep with knife to make 12 rolls. Let rise until doubled. Bake 20 to 25 minutes.

C.D.Q. SWEET DOUGH

For coffee breads and sweet rolls

2   pkgs. active dry yeast
½   c. warm water (105 to 115°)
1 ¼ c. buttermilk
2   eggs
5 ½ c. all-purpose flour
½   c. butter or margarine, softened
½   c. sugar
2   tsp. baking powder
2   tsp. salt

• Dissolve yeast in warm water in large mixer bowl. Add buttermilk, eggs, 2½ c. flour, the butter, sugar, baking powder and salt. Blend 30 seconds with mixer on low speed, scraping sides and bottom of bowl. Beat 2 minutes on medium speed.
• Stir in remaining 3 c. flour. (Dough should remain soft and slightly sticky.) Knead 5 minutes, or about 200 turns on a lightly floured board.
• Shape into coffee breads or rolls, as desired (recipes follow). Let rise in warm place (85°) until doubled, about 1 hour. (Dough is ready to bake if slight dent remains when touched with finger.)
• Heat oven to 375°.

C.D.Q. CINNAMON COFFEE BREAD

Make this for your coffee party

1   recipe for C.D.Q. Sweet Dough
½   c. butter, melted
¾   c. sugar
1   tsp. cinnamon
½   c. finely chopped nuts

• Cut dough into 1″ pieces; form each piece into a ball. Roll in butter and then in mixture of sugar, cinnamon and nuts. Place 1 layer of

balls so that they barely touch in well-greased 10″ tube pan. (If pan has removable bottom, line with aluminum foil.) Add another layer of balls.
• Let rise until doubled.
• Bake in moderate oven (375°) 1 hour. Loosen from pan. Invert pan so butter-sugar mixture runs down over loaf. To serve, break apart with 2 forks. Makes 1 loaf.

C.D.Q. CINNAMON ROLLS

Frost these rolls if you like

½ recipe for C.D.Q. Sweet Dough
1 tblsp. soft butter
¼ c. sugar
1 tsp. cinnamon

• Roll dough into a 12×7″ rectangle. Spread with butter. Sprinkle with sugar and cinnamon. Roll up, beginning at wide side. Seal well by pinching edge of dough. Cut into 12 slices.
• Place in greased 9″ round layer cake pan, leaving a small space between each slice. Let rise until doubled.
• Bake in moderate oven (375°) 25 minutes. Remove from pan to wire rack. Makes 12 rolls.

VARIATION

C.D.Q. Pecan Rolls: Make like Cinnamon Rolls, but bake slices in pan coated with ¼ c. melted butter, ¼ c. firmly packed brown sugar and ½ c. broken pecans. Bake 30 to 35 minutes.

Wrap cooled baked bread and rolls in aluminum foil for freezing and you can reheat them without unwrapping.

C.D.Q. CHEESE DIAMONDS

Unusual and distinctive—pretty, too

1 (8 oz.) pkg. cream cheese, softened
¼ c. sugar
3 tblsp. all-purpose flour
1 egg yolk
½ tsp. grated lemon peel
1 tblsp. lemon juice
½ recipe for C.D.Q. Sweet Dough
½ c. jam
Chopped nuts

• Beat cream cheese and sugar until light and fluffy. Stir in flour, egg yolk, lemon peel and juice.
• Roll dough into 15″ square. Cut in 25 (3″) squares. Place on greased baking sheets and put 1 tblsp. cheese mixture in center of each square. Bring 2 diagonally opposite corners to center of each square. Overlap them slightly; pinch together.
• Let rise until doubled.
• Bake in moderate oven (375°) 15 minutes.
• Meanwhile, heat jam until melted. Brush lightly over baked rolls while hot. Sprinkle with nuts. Makes 25 diamonds.

CoolRise Method of Bread Baking

One of the big problems of women who like to bake bread is to find time to carry the process through from start to finish. This is especially true of farm women with many outside chores and errands interrupting their days. The CoolRise Method, developed by home economists in the Robin Hood Flour Kitchens, answers the problem. It takes from 45 minutes to an hour to mix, knead, shape and place the dough in pans; you let it rise from 2 to 24 hours in the refrigerator. During the 45 minutes to an hour you have 20 minutes off while the dough rests on the board. This resting takes the place of the first rising in the Conventional Method.

With new CoolRise recipes the yeast does not need to be dissolved and hot water (hot to the touch, not scalding) is used right from the kitchen tap.

Some women tell us they like to get the dough in the refrigerator right after breakfast when they are in their kitchens attending to other duties. For instance, they say they can get the dishes in the dishwasher while it rests. After shaping the dough and placing it in pans, they refrigerate it until time to get the evening meal. If the oven is not in use, they bake the bread then. Otherwise they bake it while clearing up after dinner or supper. Several women also mentioned that they often refrigerate dough for coffee breads and rolls overnight, baking it in the morning to serve hot for breakfast.

We had good luck when we baked CoolRise breads in our Test Kitchens. We found that those baked with dough refrigerated from 2 to 8 hours had the best volume. However, the bread was acceptable even when we held the dough longer.

For success with this method, follow recipes carefully. They are designed for the CoolRise Method. Resist the temptation to improvise. By changing ingredients, you throw recipes off balance and affect your results. The ideal temperature of the refrigerator is 38 to 41°. It's also important to use the size of pans specified in recipes. Flours labeled "high protein" or "for breadmaking" are good selections for this method. Cover dough loosely when placing in refrigerator for rising—allow space for it to rise.

These breads have a tasty yeast flavor, fine and even texture and golden brown crusts. FARM JOURNAL readers tell us the CoolRise Method enables them to bake the refrigerated dough at the strategic time, just before a meal or coffee party. There's nothing like the aroma of baking yeast bread to make their families and guests hungry and eager to eat!

COOLRISE WHITE BREAD

They'll be glad to come home to this

5½ to 6½ c. all-purpose flour
2   pkgs. active dry yeast
2   tblsp. sugar
1   tblsp. salt
¼   c. soft margarine (½ stick)
2¼ c. hot tap water
Salad oil

• Combine 2 c. flour, undissolved yeast, sugar and salt in large bowl. Stir well to blend. Add soft margarine.

• Add hot tap water to ingredients in bowl all at once.

• Beat with electric mixer at medium speed 2 minutes. Scrape sides of bowl occasionally.

• Add 1 c. more flour. Beat with electric mixer at high speed 1 minute, or until thick and elastic. Scrape sides of bowl occasionally.

• Stir in just enough remaining flour to make a soft dough that leaves the sides of the bowl. Turn onto floured board. Round up into ball.

• Knead 5 to 10 minutes or until dough is smooth and elastic. Cover with plastic wrap and with towel. Let rest on board 20 minutes. Punch down.

' Divide dough into 2 equal portions. Roll each portion into an 8×12″ rectangle. Roll up tightly into loaves beginning at 8″ side. Seal lengthwise edge and ends well. Tuck ends under.

• Place in greased 8½ × 4½ × 2½″ loaf pans. (Correct pan size is important for best results.)

• Brush surface of dough with salad oil. Cover pans loosely with waxed paper, brushed with oil, and then with plastic wrap.

• Refrigerate 2 to 24 hours at moderately cold setting. When ready to bake, remove from refrigerator. Uncover.

• Let stand 10 minutes while preheating oven.

• Puncture any surface bubbles with oiled toothpick just before baking.

• Bake at 400° for 35 to 40 minutes, or until done.

• Remove from pans immediately. Brush top crust with margarine if desired. Cool on rack. Makes 2 loaves.

COOLRISE HONEY LEMON WHOLE WHEAT BREAD

You'll like the taste of lemon

3¼ to 4¼ c. all-purpose flour
2 pkgs. active dry yeast
1 tblsp. salt
¼ c. honey
3 tblsp. softened margarine
  or shortening
1 tblsp. grated lemon peel
2¼ c. hot tap water
2 c. whole wheat flour
Salad oil

• Combine 2 c. all-purpose flour, undissolved yeast and salt in large bowl. Stir well to blend.

• Add honey, margarine and lemon peel.

• Add hot tap water all at once.

• Beat with electric mixer at medium speed 2 minutes. Scrape bowl occasionally.

• Add 1 c. whole wheat flour. Beat with electric mixer at high speed for 1 minute, or until thick and elastic. Scrape bowl occasionally.

• Stir in remaining 1 c. whole wheat flour with wooden spoon. Then gradually stir in just enough remaining all-purpose flour to make a soft dough that leaves the sides of bowl. Turn onto floured board; round up into ball.

• Knead 5 to 10 minutes, or until dough is smooth and elastic. Cover with plastic wrap and then with towel. Let rest 20 minutes. Punch down.

• Divide dough into 2 equal portions.

• Roll each portion into an 8×12″ rectangle. Roll up tightly into loaves beginning at 8″ side. Seal lengthwise edge and ends. Tuck ends under.

• Place in greased 8½ × 4½ × 2½″ loaf pans. (Correct pan size is important for best results.)

• Brush surface of dough with oil. Cover pans loosely with waxed paper, and then with plastic wrap.

• Refrigerate 2 to 24 hours at moderately cold setting. When ready to bake, remove from refrigerator. Uncover.

• Let stand 10 minutes while preheating oven.

• Puncture any surface bubbles with oiled toothpick just before baking.
• Bake at 400° for 30 to 40 minutes, or until done. Bake on lower oven rack for best results.
• Remove from pans immediately. Brush top crust with margarine if desired. Cool on racks. Makes 2 loaves.

Higher than 5,000 Feet

If the recipe for CoolRise bread calls for 2 pkgs. active dry yeast, use only 1 pkg. if you live in an area with an altitude of more than 5,000 feet. In other recipes, watch the bread during the rising period. Doughs rise faster at higher elevations.

COOLRISE HEIDELBERG RYE BREAD

Cocoa adds a good flavor you can't recognize—a sandwich special

3   c. all-purpose flour
2   pkgs. active dry yeast
¼   c. cocoa
1   tblsp. sugar
1   tblsp. salt
1   tblsp. caraway seeds
⅓   c. molasses
2   tblsp. softened margarine
      or shortening
2   c. hot tap water
2½ to 3½ c. rye flour
Salad oil

• Combine 2 c. all-purpose flour, undissolved yeast, cocoa, sugar, salt and caraway seeds in large bowl. Stir well to blend. Add molasses and softened margarine.
• Add hot tap water to ingredients in bowl all at once.

• Beat with electric mixer at medium speed 2 minutes. Scrape bowl occasionally.
• Add remaining all-purpose flour. Beat with electric mixer at high speed 1 minute, or until thick and elastic. Scrape bowl occasionally.
• Gradually stir in just enough rye flour with wooden spoon to make a soft dough that leaves the sides of bowl. Turn onto floured board. Round up into ball.
• Knead 5 to 10 minutes, or until dough is smooth and elastic.
• Cover with plastic wrap, then with towel. Let rest 20 minutes. Then punch down. Divide into 2 equal parts.
• Shape each portion into round loaf, or roll each portion into an 8×15″ rectangle on lightly greased board. Roll up tightly like jelly roll, beginning with long side. Seal lengthwise edge and ends well. Tuck ends under. Taper ends by rolling gently with hands.
• Place in greased 8″ pie pans or on greased baking sheets. Brush surface of dough with oil. Cover loosely with plastic wrap.
• Refrigerate 2 to 24 hours at moderately cold setting. When ready to bake, remove from refrigerator. Uncover. Let stand 10 minutes while preheating oven.
• Slash an X in tops of round loaves with sharp knife or slash tops of long loaves diagonally at 2″ intervals just before baking.
• Bake at 400° for 30 to 35 minutes, or until done.
• Remove from pans immediately. Brush top crust with margarine if desired. Cool on racks. Makes 2 loaves.

COOLRISE FRENCH BREAD

Get it ready in the morning and bake for barbecue as guests arrive

5½ to 6½ c. all-purpose flour
2 pkgs. active dry yeast
1 tblsp. sugar
1 tblsp. salt
2 tblsp. softened margarine
   or shortening
2¼ c. hot tap water
Salad oil
Cold water

• Combine 2 c. flour, undissolved yeast, sugar and salt in large bowl. Stir well to blend. Add softened margarine.
• Add hot tap water to ingredients in bowl all at once.
• Beat with electric mixer at medium speed 2 minutes. Scrape bowl occasionally.
• Add 1 c. more flour. Beat with electric mixer at high speed 1 minute, or until thick and elastic. Scrape bowl occasionally.
• Gradually stir in just enough of remaining flour with wooden spoon to make a soft dough that leaves the sides of bowl. Turn out on floured board. Round up to make a ball.
• Cover with plastic wrap, then with towel. Let rest 20 minutes on board. Punch down.
• Divide dough into 2 equal portions.
• Roll each portion into an 8×15″ rectangle on lightly greased board. Roll up tightly like jelly roll, beginning with long side. Seal lengthwise edge and ends well. Tuck ends under. Taper ends by rolling gently with hand.
• Place, seam side down, on greased baking sheets.
• Brush lightly with oil. Cover baking sheets loosely with plastic wrap.
• Refrigerate 2 to 24 hours at moderately cold setting. When ready to bake, remove from refrigerator. Uncover.
• Let stand 10 minutes while preheating oven.
• Brush gently with cold water. Slash tops of loaves diagonally at 2″ intervals with sharp knife just before baking.
• Bake at 400° for 30 to 40 minutes, or until done.
• Remove from baking sheets immediately. Cool on racks. Makes 2 long loaves.

COOLRISE BRIOCHE

Refrigerate overnight and bake for breakfast; serve hot as the French do

6 to 7 c. all-purpose flour
2 pkgs. active dry yeast
½ c. sugar
1½ tsp. salt
½ c. softened butter or margarine
1⅓ c. hot tap water
4 eggs (at room temperature)
1 egg yolk
1 tblsp. milk

• Combine 2 c. flour, undissolved yeast, sugar and salt in large bowl. Stir well to blend. Add softened butter.
• Add hot tap water to ingredients in bowl all at once.
• Beat with electric mixer at medium speed 2 minutes. Scrape bowl occasionally.
• Add the 4 eggs and 1½ c. more flour. Beat with electric mixer at high speed 1 minute, or until thick and elastic. Scrape bowl occasionally.

• Gradually stir in enough of remaining flour with wooden spoon to make a soft dough that leaves the sides of bowl. Turn onto floured board; round up into ball.
• Knead 5 to 10 minutes, or until dough is smooth and elastic. Cover with plastic wrap, then a towel. Let rest 20 minutes; then punch down.
• Divide dough into unequal portions —one about three fourths of dough, the other about one fourth of dough.
• Cut larger portion into 30 equal pieces. Shape into smooth balls. Place in buttered muffin-pan cups; flatten slightly.
• Cut smaller portion into 30 equal pieces. Shape into smooth balls.
• Make deep indentation in center of each large ball. Press rough end of small ball into each indentation.
• Cover pans loosely with plastic wrap.
• Refrigerate 2 to 24 hours at moderately cold setting. When ready to bake remove from refrigerator. Uncover.
• Let stand 10 minutes while preheating oven.
• Bake at 350° for 15 minutes. Remove from oven and brush with egg yolk combined with milk. Return to oven immediately and bake 5 to 10 minutes longer, or until done. Bake on lower rack of oven for best results.
• Remove from pans immediately. Cool on racks. Makes 30 rolls.

Country Christmas Gift

Wrap a loaf of your best coffee bread in plastic wrap to show off its beauty. Present it in a straw basket trimmed with holly or red ribbons.

COOLRISE SWEET DOUGH

This is the start of many good things

5   to 6 c. all-purpose flour
2   pkgs. active dry yeast
½   c. sugar
1 ½ tsp. salt
½   c. softened butter or margarine
1 ½ c. hot tap water
2   eggs (at room temperature)
Salad oil

• Combine 2 c. flour, undissolved yeast, sugar and salt in large bowl. Stir well to blend. Add softened butter.
• Add hot tap water to ingredients in bowl all at once.
• Beat with electric mixer at medium speed 2 minutes. Scrape bowl occasionally.
• Add eggs and 1 c. more flour. Beat with electric mixer at high speed 1 minute, or until thick and elastic. Scrape bowl occasionally.
• Gradually stir in just enough of remaining flour with wooden spoon to make a soft dough that leaves the sides of bowl. Turn onto floured board. Round up into ball.
• Knead 5 to 10 minutes, or until dough is smooth and elastic. Cover with plastic wrap, then a towel.
• Let rest 20 minutes on board. Punch down.
• Divide and shape as desired into 2 coffee cakes or 2½ dozen rolls (recipes follow).
• Place in greased pans or on greased baking sheets. An 8″ square pan is ideal for 1 dozen pan rolls, and a 13×9×2″ pan for 1½ dozen pan rolls.
• Brush surface with oil. Cover pans loosely with plastic wrap.

• Refrigerate 2 to 24 hours at moderately cold setting. When ready to bake, remove from refrigerator. Uncover.
• Let stand 10 minutes while preheating oven.
• Puncture any surface bubbles with oiled toothpick just before baking.
• Bake in 375° oven 20 to 25 minutes, or until done. Bake on lower oven rack position for best results.
• Remove from pans or baking sheet immediately. Cool on racks.
• Brush with butter, or frost and decorate as desired. Makes 2 coffee cakes or 2½ to 3 dozen pan rolls.

COOLRISE CHERRY NUT COFFEE BREAD

Festive—looks like ribbon candy

1   recipe CoolRise Sweet Dough
¾ c. cut-up maraschino cherries, drained
1   c. chopped walnuts
Sweet Cheese Spread

• Make CoolRise Sweet Dough, but stir in cherries with wooden spoon after adding eggs and 1 c. flour and beating 1 minute at high speed.
• When ready to shape, after punching down dough, divide in half. Roll 1 portion into a 6×20″ rectangle on lightly buttered board. Cut lengthwise into 5 equal strips.
• Shape into a 6×10″ rectangle by placing first strip, cut edge down, on greased baking sheet or in a 15½×-10½″ (jelly roll) pan. Bring one end of strip around to start a second row. Join strips as you go, making rows 10″ long. Tuck loose ends under. The completed coffee bread will look like ribbon candy.

• Sprinkle with ½ c. walnuts. Press together gently to make rows of dough stand up.
• Repeat procedures with the remaining dough and walnuts.
• Cover baking sheets loosely with plastic wrap.
• Refrigerate as recipe for CoolRise Sweet Dough directs.
• Bake at 375° for 25 to 30 minutes, or until done. Bake on lower oven rack position for best results.
• Remove from baking sheets immediately. Cool on racks.
• Frost when cool with Sweet Cheese Spread. Serve remaining spread with coffee bread. Makes 2 coffee breads.

Sweet Cheese Spread: Combine 1 (8 oz.) pkg. cream cheese, softened, and ½ c. confectioners sugar. Stir until smooth.

COOLRISE APRICOT COFFEE BRAID

A beautiful braid—and the apricot-ginger taste is a luscious surprise

¾ c. dried apricots
1½ c. water
⅓ c. sugar
½ tsp. ground ginger
1   recipe CoolRise Sweet Dough

• Simmer apricots in water, uncovered, 20 to 30 minutes, or until tender. Drain; mash fruit well with fork.
• Add sugar and ginger to fruit; stir to mix well. Cool.
• When ready to shape CoolRise Sweet Dough, divide in half. Round up each portion.
• Roll 1 portion into a 9×14″ rectangle on lightly greased board. Cut lengthwise into 3 equal strips.
• Spread 2 tblsp. apricot mixture

down center of each strip. Pinch lengthwise edges of strip together to form a rope.
• Braid 3 ropes together on a lightly greased baking sheet, starting at center and braiding to each end. Tuck ends under braid.
• Repeat procedure with second half of dough and apricot mixture.
• Cover loosely with plastic wrap.
• Refrigerate as recipe for CoolRise Sweet Dough directs.
• Bake at 375° for 25 to 30 minutes, or until done. Bake on lower oven rack position for best results.
• Remove from baking sheets immediately. Cool on racks. Brush while warm with melted butter, frost when cool with Confectioners Sugar Frosting (see Index) or sprinkle with sifted confectioners sugar. Makes 2 coffee braids.

COOLRISE TWIRLS

Taste appeal—morning, noon or night

1 recipe CoolRise Sweet Dough
Confectioners Sugar Frosting
(see Index)

• Prepare CoolRise Sweet Dough as directed. When ready to shape, divide dough into 2 equal portions. Round up each portion into a ball.
• Roll each portion into a 12×15″ rectangle on a lightly greased board. Cut into 15 (1″) strips.
• Twist each strip. Hold one end of twisted strip on lightly greased baking sheet and wind strip around this point. Tuck ends under. Place rolls several inches apart.
• Cover loosely with plastic wrap.
• Refrigerate as CoolRise Sweet Dough recipe directs.

• Bake at 375° for 15 to 20 minutes, or until done.
• Remove from baking sheet immediately. Cool on racks.
• Frost while warm with Confectioners Sugar Frosting. Decorate as desired. Makes 2½ dozen rolls.

COOLRISE MEXICAN SWEET ROLLS

So good you'll want to double the recipe

½ c. sugar
½ c. flour
½ tsp. cinnamon
⅓ c. finely chopped nuts
¼ c. melted butter
1 egg white, beaten until frothy
½ recipe CoolRise Sweet Dough

• Combine sugar, flour, cinnamon, nuts, melted butter and egg white.
• Prepare CoolRise Sweet Dough as recipe directs. When ready to shape, pinch off pieces of dough of equal size and shape into balls 1½″ in diameter. Place on greased baking sheet about 3″ apart. Press each ball down to flatten slightly.
• With finger, make indentation in center of each ball. Top with spoonful of sugar-cinnamon mixture.
• Cover loosely with plastic wrap.
• Refrigerate as CoolRise Sweet Dough recipe directs.
• Bake at 375° for 15 to 20 minutes, or until done.
• Remove from baking sheet immediately. Cool on racks. Makes 18 rolls.

Note: Use 1 recipe for CoolRise Sweet Dough and double amounts of the other ingredients to make 36 rolls for a coffee party.

Easy Mixer Breads

One newer way of making yeast breads and rolls that has caught on with busy women—especially the younger, inexperienced bread bakers —is the Easy Mixer Method developed in the Ann Pillsbury Kitchens. As the name of the bread implies, the electric mixer does lots of the work. There's no milk to scald; you use instant nonfat dry milk. The fat you add is easy-to-measure salad oil.

You toss the dough on the floured board a few times and then you knead it 1 minute. You shape it next and put it in the pans to rise—it rises only once. The fast-fix bread is attractive and of good texture. It has a pleasant, delicate yeasty taste.

A FARM JOURNAL food editor first tasted Easy Mixer Bread on an irrigated farm in western Nebraska. Her young hostess baked and served with pride—the first yeast bread she ever made. Another editor tasted Sunburst Coffee Bread, made by this method, at an Iowa coffee party.

We pass along to you Ann Pillsbury recipes for these two and other Easy Mixer Breads. Do notice the dark Peasant Bread. This cereal-rich loaf is the beginning of marvelous sandwiches, and it's also especially good with cold cuts.

EASY MIXER WHITE BREAD

Correctly named—it's really easy

2½ c. warm water (110 to 115°)
2 pkgs. active dry yeast
½ c. instant nonfat dry milk
2 tblsp. sugar
1 tblsp. salt
⅓ c. salad oil
7 to 7½ c. all-purpose flour

• Pour warm water into large mixer bowl. Sprinkle yeast over top. Add dry milk, sugar, salt, oil and about 3¼ c. flour. Blend well on low speed of mixer, scraping sides and bottom of bowl. Beat 3 minutes on medium speed.

• Gradually add remaining flour by hand to make a very stiff dough. Cover and let rest 15 minutes.

• Toss dough on floured surface until no longer sticky. Knead until smooth, about 1 minute. Divide in half. With rolling pin, roll each half into a 12×6" rectangle. Roll up tightly like a jelly roll, starting with the 6" side. Seal edges and ends. Place, seam side down, in well-greased 8½×4½×3" or 9×5×3" loaf pans.

• Cover and let rise in warm place until doubled, 1 to 1½ hours.

• Bake in hot oven (400°) 30 to 35 minutes. Remove from pans immediately. Cool on wire racks. Makes 2 loaves.

VARIATIONS

Easy Mixer Herb Bread: Substitute brown sugar for white. Add ½ tsp. caraway seeds and ¼ tsp. thyme before adding flour. Shape into 2 long loaves. Place on greased baking sheets. Cover and let rise until doubled; then bake in hot oven (400°) 30 to 35 minutes.

Easy Mixer Patio Loafers: Pat half the dough in each greased 9×5×3" loaf pan. Spread each with ¼ c. barbecue sauce and sprinkle with ⅓ c. quick-cooking rolled oats and

⅓ c. chopped cashew nuts. With blunt knife, cut each loaf into 1″ strips crosswise. Cover and let rise 30 to 45 minutes. Bake in hot oven (400°) 25 to 30 minutes. Remove from pans immediately; cool on wire racks. To reheat, wrap in aluminum foil and place on barbecue grill.

EASY MIXER PEASANT BREAD

Looks like pumpernickel but contains no rye flour—a tasty cereal bread

2 ½   c. warm water (110 to 115°)
2   pkgs. active dry yeast
2   c. all-bran cereal
2   c. bite-size shredded wheat
2   tblsp. brown sugar
1   tblsp. salt
1   tblsp. salad oil
2   tblsp. bottled brown bouquet
     sauce
4 ½ to 5 ½ c. all-purpose flour
1   egg white
1   tblsp. water

• Measure warm water into large mixer bowl. Sprinkle yeast over water. Add cereals, sugar, salt, oil, bouquet sauce and 2 c. flour. Blend well. Beat 3 minutes at medium speed of electric mixer.
• By hand, gradually add enough of remaining flour to form a very stiff dough, mixing well after each addition. Cover dough with plastic wrap or waxed paper; let rest 15 minutes.
• Toss on floured surface until dough no longer is sticky. Knead until smooth, about 1 minute.
• Divide dough in half. Roll each half into an 8×15″ rectangle. Roll tightly as for jelly roll, starting with longest side. Seal edge and ends; fold under ends. Roll gently to taper ends.

• Place on greased baking sheets. Place in plastic bags and let rise in warm place about 1½ hours (or place in refrigerator overnight).
• Carefully brush dough with egg white diluted with 1 tblsp. cold water.
• Bake at 400° for 25 to 30 minutes. Remove from baking sheets at once and cool on wire racks. Makes 2 long loaves.

Note: If you wish, just after brushing dough with egg white-water mixture, sprinkle loaves with 1 tblsp. caraway seeds.

EASY-DO SWEET DOUGH

First step to coffee breads and rolls

1   c. warm water (110 to 115°)
1   pkg. active dry yeast
¼   c. instant nonfat dry milk
¼   c. sugar
¼   c. salad oil
1   egg
2   tsp. salt
3 ½ to 4 c. all-purpose flour

• Measure warm water into large mixer bowl. Sprinkle yeast over water. Add dry milk, sugar, oil, egg, salt and about 1½ c. flour. Blend well. Beat 3 minutes with electric mixer at medium speed, scraping sides and bottom of bowl.
• By hand, gradually add remaining flour to form a stiff dough, beating well after each addition. Cover; let rest 15 minutes.
• Toss dough on lightly floured board until it no longer is sticky. Knead 1 minute. Shape and bake as following recipes suggest.

Pan Rolls: Pat Easy-Do Sweet Dough into 2 well-greased 8″ square pans. Spread dough with soft butter. Using a blunt knife, cut into squares, cutting almost through dough. Let rise until doubled. Bake in hot oven (400°) 20 to 25 minutes. Remove from pans and break rolls apart. Makes about 32 rolls, 16 to a pan.

Cloverleaf Rolls: Divide Easy-Do Sweet Dough into 20 pieces of equal size. Roll quickly into balls and place in greased muffin-pan cups. Brush tops with soft butter. Using a blunt knife or kitchen scissors, cut each ball in half, or in thirds for cloverleafs. Let rise until doubled. Bake in moderate oven (375°) 15 to 20 minutes. Makes 20 rolls.

Parkerhouse Rolls: Roll out Easy-Do Sweet Dough on floured surface to make a 20×8″ rectangle. Cut in half lengthwise, making 2 (20×4″) strips. Spread lengthwise half of each strip with 1 tblsp. soft butter. With knife handle, crease each strip lengthwise, slightly off center on unbuttered side. Fold along crease. Gently pull and stretch each strip to 24″. Cut each into 12 (2″) or 8 (3″) slices. Place on greased baking sheet. Cover and let rise until doubled. Bake in moderate oven (375°) 10 to 15 minutes. Serve hot. Makes 24 or 16 rolls.

Tiny Tea Rolls: Divide Easy-Do Sweet Dough in half; roll out each half to make a 15×10″ rectangle. Spread 1 rectangle with 2 tblsp. butter; sprinkle with mixture of ¼ c. sugar, 2 tblsp. slivered almonds and 1 tsp. grated orange peel.
• Spread second rectangle with 2 tblsp. butter; sprinkle with mixture of ¼ c. firmly packed brown sugar, ¼ c. chopped walnuts and ½ tsp. cinnamon. Starting with long side, roll up each rectangle jelly-roll fashion; seal edges and ends. Place, seam side down, on greased baking sheets. Using a sharp knife, cut rolls halfway through at 1″ intervals. Let rise. Bake in moderate oven (375°) 20 to 25 minutes. Makes 30 rolls.

Note: After shaping roll dough and placing on baking sheet or in pans, you can slip pans into loose plastic bags and refrigerate several hours before baking. Bake immediately after removing from refrigerator.

EASY MIXER SUNBURST COFFEE BREAD

Crescent rolls form lovely sunburst

¾ c. shredded coconut
1 c. warm water (110 to 115°)
1 pkg. active dry yeast
¼ c. instant nonfat dry milk
¼ c. sugar
2 tsp. salt
¼ c. salad oil
1 egg
3½ to 4 c. flour
2 tblsp. soft butter
1½ tblsp. grated orange peel
½ c. sugar
Orange Glaze

• Toast coconut by spreading in shallow pan and heating in slow oven (300°) until golden brown, 15 to 18 minutes. Stir occasionally to brown evenly.
• Measure warm water into large mixer bowl. Sprinkle yeast over water. Add dry milk, ¼ c. sugar, salt, salad oil, egg and 1½ c. flour. Beat

3 minutes with electric mixer on medium speed, scraping sides and bottom of bowl.

• Gradually stir in enough remaining flour by hand to form a stiff dough. Beat well after each addition. Cover and let rest 15 minutes.

• Toss dough on lightly floured board until it no longer is sticky. Knead 1 minute. Divide dough in half. Roll each half to make a 12″ circle. Spread each circle with 1 tblsp. soft butter. Combine grated orange peel with ½ c. sugar and ½ c. toasted coconut; sprinkle half of mixture over each circle of dough.

• Cut each circle in 12 wedges. Roll up, starting at wide end and roll to the point. Arrange 12 rolls, pointed side down, on greased baking sheet in circle to make a ring or sunburst. Repeat with remaining 12 rolls. Cover and let rise in warm place until doubled, 1 to 1½ hours.

• Bake in moderate oven (350°) until golden brown, 20 to 25 minutes. Loosen rolls with a spatula and gently slide each sunburst onto wire rack. Drizzle Orange Glaze over each sunburst and sprinkle with remaining ¼ c. toasted coconut.

Orange Glaze: Combine 1 c. sifted confectioners sugar, ½ tsp. grated orange peel and 1½ tblsp. orange juice.

Test for Doneness

Tap the loaf of yeast bread with a forefinger. If you hear a hollow sound, the bread is done. If you get a "solid" sound, bake the bread a few minutes longer and test again.

Instant Blend and Short-Cut Mixer Methods

The fragrance of baking yeast bread has been filling many test kitchens recently. And there's an air of excitement akin to that when home economists were discovering you don't always have to cream butter and sugar together to make good cakes. But the emphasis now is on faster and easier ways to make good yeast breads.

Out of Red Star Yeast's Home Service Department come two ways, related to each other, Instant Blend and Short-Cut Mixer Methods. In neither of them do you dissolve the active dry yeast in water before you add it with other ingredients to the mixing bowl. The Instant Blend system enables you to use all your choice Conventional Method recipes, including the treasures of farm and ranch women in this cookbook. This is how you can adapt your recipes to it:

• Measure liquids, including the amount of water formerly used to dissolve yeast (and spices, honey, molasses or oil if these are in the ingredients), shortening, sugar and salt into a saucepan. Heat at low temperature to *warm* (120 to 130°).

• Measure the same amount of flour in cups as total liquid into mixer bowl (count each egg in a recipe as ¼ c. liquid, but do not add yet). Add undissolved yeast to flour in mixer bowl; stir to blend.

• Pour contents of saucepan into dry ingredients. If there are eggs, add now. Beat 30 seconds with electric

mixer at low speed, scraping bowl.
• Beat 3 minutes at high speed,
scraping bowl occasionally. Stop
mixer; stir in fruits, nuts, etc. and
dark flours if used.
• Stir in enough remaining flour, a
little at a time, to make a soft dough
—less flour is needed by this method.
Turn dough onto lightly floured surface. Then follow your conventional
recipe.

The Short-Cut Mixer Method and
the Instant Blend Method are the
same until you turn the dough onto
the board and knead it. Then they
part company. Our recipes from Red
Star Kitchens illustrate the Short-
Cut Mixer way—recipes must be
designed especially for this method—
but here are the highlights: After
kneading the dough, you cover it
with bowl or pan and let rest 20 minutes. Then you shape and place it in
pans or on baking sheets and let rise
until doubled. You bake the bread
after only this one rising!

When we made the first bread by
this method, we used a candy thermometer to test the temperature of
liquids heated to 120 to 130°. A few
drops on the inside of the wrist soon
taught us how to judge the temperature in other bakings without a
thermometer.

The Short-Cut Mixer breads and
rolls are quick and easy to bake,
light and even in texture. The crusts
brown beautifully. Our taste-testers
gave all of them high ratings. And our
home economists adopted the idea of
using a tent of aluminum foil over
rising bread dough instead of covering with a towel.

As the result of our testing experience, we recommend that you bake
all these fast breads the first chance
you have. We'll be surprised if you
don't get many compliments on them.

SHORT-CUT MIXER WHITE BREAD

*Smaller loaves are fine to slice and
toast, but use the pan size you have*

4½ to 5 c. all-purpose flour
2   pkgs. active dry yeast
1   c. milk
¾   c. water
2   tblsp. shortening
2   tblsp. sugar
2   tsp. salt

• Measure 1¾ c. flour into large
mixer bowl. Add yeast; stir to blend.
• Measure milk, water, shortening,
sugar and salt into saucepan. Blend;
heat until warm (120 to 130°).
• Pour into flour-yeast mixture. Beat
30 seconds with electric mixer at
low speed, scraping bowl constantly.
• Beat 3 more minutes at high speed,
scraping bowl occasionally. Stop
mixer.
• Gradually stir in more flour to form
a soft dough. Knead until smooth,
5 to 10 minutes.
• Cover dough with bowl or pan and
let rest 20 minutes. Grease 2 (8½×-
4½×2½") loaf pans or 1 (9×5×-
3") loaf pan.
• For 2 loaves, divide dough in half
and pat or roll each half into a 7×-
14" rectangle; for 1 loaf pat into
an 8×16" rectangle. Roll from narrow side, pressing dough into roll
at each turn. Press ends to seal.
Place in pans or pan. Cover with
aluminum foil tent.
• Let rise on rack over hot water until doubled, 30 to 45 minutes. Center
of small loaves will be about ½"

above pan edges, center of large loaf 2″ above pan edges.
• Bake in hot oven (400°) 35 to 40 minutes. Remove from pans to racks. Brush with butter for soft crusts. Makes 1 (2 lb.) loaf or 2 (1 lb.) loaves.

SHORT-CUT MIXER WHOLE WHEAT BREAD

So good it disappears like magic

2¾ to 3¼ c. all-purpose flour
2 pkgs. active dry yeast
¾ c. milk
¾ c. water
2 tblsp. shortening
2 tblsp. honey
2 tsp. salt
1 egg (room temperature)
1½ c. whole wheat flour

• Measure 1¾ c. all-purpose flour into large mixer bowl. Add yeast; blend.
• Measure milk, water, shortening, honey and salt into saucepan. Blend. Heat until warm (120 to 130°).
• Pour into flour-yeast mixture; add egg. Beat 30 seconds with electric mixer at low speed, scraping bowl constantly.
• Beat 3 more minutes at high speed, scraping bowl occasionally. Stop mixer.
• Add whole wheat flour, then gradually add more all-purpose flour to form a soft dough. Turn onto lightly floured board and knead until smooth, 5 to 10 minutes.
• Cover dough with bowl or pan. Let rest for 20 minutes. Grease 2 (8½×4½×2½″) loaf pans or 1 (9×5×3″) loaf pan.
• For 2 loaves, divide dough in half and roll each half into a 7×14″

rectangle; for 1 loaf roll dough into an 8×16″ rectangle. Roll from narrow side, pressing dough into roll at each turn. Press ends to seal. Place in pans. Cover with tent of aluminum foil.
• Let rise on rack over hot water until doubled, 30 to 45 minutes. Dent remains when finger is pressed gently on sides of loaves.
• Bake in moderate oven (375°) 35 to 45 minutes. Remove from pans, brush with butter for soft crusts and cool on racks. Makes 2 (1 lb.) loaves or 1 (2 lb.) loaf.

SHORT-CUT MIXER RYE BREAD

Dill-caraway flavors are delightful

2¾ to 3¼ c. all-purpose flour
2 pkgs. active dry yeast
1 c. milk
¾ c. water
2 tblsp. shortening
2 tblsp. sugar
2 tsp. salt
2 tsp. caraway seeds
2 tsp. dill weed
1½ c. rye flour

• Measure 1¾ c. all-purpose flour into large mixer bowl. Add yeast and blend.
• Measure milk, water, shortening, sugar, salt, caraway seeds and dill weed into saucepan. Blend. Heat until warm (120 to 130°).
• Pour into flour-yeast mixture. Beat 30 seconds with electric mixer at low speed, scraping bowl constantly.
• Beat 3 more minutes at high speed, scraping bowl occasionally. Stop mixer.
• Add all the rye flour, then gradually stir in more all-purpose flour to form

a fairly stiff dough. Knead until smooth, 5 to 10 minutes.
• Cover dough with bowl or pan. Let rest 20 minutes. Grease 1 (12×-15½″) baking sheet or 2 (9″) round layer cake pans.
• Divide dough in half. Round each part into a smooth ball; place on opposite corners of greased baking sheet or in round layer pans. Slash tops of loaves with sharp knife. Cover with tent of aluminum foil.
• Let rise on rack over hot water until doubled, 30 to 45 minutes. Dent remains when finger is pressed gently on sides of loaves.
• Bake in moderate oven (375°) 35 to 45 minutes. Remove from baking sheet or pans to cooling racks. Brush tops of loaves with cold water for chewy crusts. Makes 2 (1 lb.) loaves.

SHORT-CUT MIXER SWEET DOUGH

Makes superior coffee breads—fast

4½ to 5 c. all-purpose flour
2 pkgs. active dry yeast
¾ c. milk
½ c. water
½ c. shortening (part butter)
½ c. sugar
1 tsp. salt
2 eggs (room temperature)

• Measure 1¾ c. flour into large mixer bowl. Add yeast and blend.
• Measure milk, water, shortening, sugar and salt into saucepan. Blend. Heat until warm (120 to 130°).
• Pour into flour-yeast mixture. Add eggs. Beat 30 seconds with electric mixer at low speed, scraping bowl constantly.
• Beat 3 more minutes at high speed,

scraping bowl occasionally. Stop mixer.
• Gradually stir in more flour to make a soft dough. Dough will be rather sticky. Knead on lightly floured board until smooth, 5 to 10 minutes.
• Cover with bowl or pan. Let rest 20 minutes. Shape as desired (see recipes that follow). Cover with tent of aluminum foil.
• Let rise on a rack over hot water until doubled, 40 to 60 minutes. Dent remains when finger is pressed gently on sides of dough.
• Bake as directed in recipe.

SHORT-CUT MIXER STREUSEL COFFEE BREAD

Taste-testers praised this treat

1 recipe Short-Cut Mixer Sweet Dough
½ c. butter
½ c. all-purpose flour
1 c. sugar
2 tsp. cinnamon

• After dough has rested 20 minutes, divide in half. Roll or pat one half into a greased 13×9×2″ pan. Divide remaining half in 2 equal parts. Press each piece of dough into 2 greased 8 or 9″ round layer cake pans.
• Mix butter, flour, sugar and cinnamon together to make small crumbs. Sprinkle over dough in pans.
• Cover with tent of aluminum foil and let rise over warm water until doubled, 30 to 45 minutes. Dough is doubled if dent remains when finger is pressed gently on side of dough.
• Bake in moderate oven (375°) 25 to 30 minutes. Remove from pans and cool on racks. Makes 1 (13×9×2″)

and 2 (8 or 9") round coffee breads.

Note: You can bake dough in 2 greased 13×9×2" pans if you like.

SHORT-CUT MIXER DATE FILLED CRESCENTS

Interesting shape—fine to tote

1   recipe Short-Cut Mixer Sweet Dough
2   c. cut-up dates
1   c. cut-up peeled apple
1   c. water
¼   c. orange juice
½   c. chopped nuts

• While Sweet Dough rests on board, combine dates, apple, water and orange juice in saucepan. Cook over low heat, stirring often, until mixture is thickened. Add nuts; cool to lukewarm.

• After dough has rested 20 minutes on board, divide in half. Roll one half into a 12" square. Cut diagonally to make 2 triangles. Spread each with one fourth of the lukewarm date-apple filling. Roll up, starting at wide side. Seal edges well. Place, seam side down, on greased baking sheet; curve ends to make crescents. Repeat with other half of dough and filling.

• Cover with tents of foil and let rise over hot water until doubled, 40 to 60 minutes. Dent remains when finger is pressed gently on side of dough.

• Bake in moderate oven (350°) 25 to 35 minutes, or until well browned.

Remove from pans and cool on racks. Spread with Thin Confectioners Sugar Icing (see Index) or sprinkle with confectioners sugar before serving. Makes 4 crescents (about 12 servings).

SHORT-CUT MIXER SWEET WHIRLS

King-size with color-bright centers

4½ to 5 c. all-purpose flour
2   pkgs. active dry yeast
¾   c. milk
½   c. water
¼   c. butter
¼   c. shortening
½   c. sugar
1   tsp. salt
1   tsp. grated orange peel
¼   tsp. cardamom
2   eggs (room temperature)
Jam or canned fruit pieces
Quick Orange Glaze

• Measure 1¾ c. flour into large mixer bowl. Add yeast; blend.

• Measure milk, water, butter, shortening, sugar, salt, orange peel and cardamom into saucepan. Blend. Heat until warm (120 to 130°).

• Pour into flour-yeast mixture. Add eggs. Beat 30 seconds with electric mixer at low speed, scraping bowl constantly.

• Beat 3 minutes longer at high speed, scraping bowl occasionally. Stop mixer.

• Gradually stir in more flour to make a soft dough. The dough will be slightly sticky. Turn onto lightly floured board and knead until smooth, 5 to 10 minutes.

• Cover dough with bowl or pan; let rest 20 minutes. Roll into an 8×16" rectangle. Cut into 16 strips lengthwise. Roll each on board to make smooth; then twist, holding one end of strip down on greased baking sheet, winding remainder of strip round and round. Tuck end under. Cover with aluminum foil tent.

• Let rise on racks over hot water until doubled, 40 to 60 minutes. Dough is doubled if dent remains when finger is pressed gently on sides of dough. Just before baking, make a small dent in center of each whirl and fill with 1 tsp. jam or with a few pieces of drained, canned fruit, such as peaches, apples or apricots.

• Bake in moderate oven (375°) 12 minutes, or until light brown. Remove from oven and brush with Quick Orange Glaze; return to oven and bake 5 minutes longer. Remove from baking sheets and cool on racks. Makes 16 large rolls.

Quick Orange Glaze: Stir together ¼ c. orange juice and 2 tblsp. sugar.

SHORT-CUT MIXER PEPPERY CHEESE DOUGH FOR ROLLS

Serve rolls made with this dough with salads—they'll make a hit

4½ to 5 c. all-purpose flour
2 pkgs. active dry yeast
1 c. milk
½ c. water
¼ c. shortening
2 tblsp. sugar
1½ tsp. salt
2 tsp. coarse black pepper
1 egg (room temperature)
¼ lb. coarsely shredded sharp Cheddar cheese (1 c.)

• Measure 1¾ c. flour into large mixer bowl. Add yeast; stir to blend.

• Measure milk, water, shortening, sugar, salt and pepper into saucepan. Blend; heat until warm (120 to 130°).

• Pour into flour-yeast mixture; add egg. Beat 30 seconds with electric mixer at low speed, scraping bowl constantly. Beat 3 minutes at high speed. Stop mixer.

• Stir in cheese and gradually add more flour to make a soft dough. Turn onto lightly floured board and knead until smooth, 5 to 10 minutes.

• Cover dough with bowl or pan. Let rest 20 minutes. Shape the rolls (directions follow).

• Place on greased baking sheets, cover with aluminum foil tent and let rise on rack over hot water until doubled, 30 to 45 minutes. Gently press finger into side of dough; if dent remains, dough is doubled.

• Bake in moderate oven (375°) 15 to 20 minutes. Remove to rack at once, brush with butter and cool, or serve warm.

Short-Cut Mixer Peppery Cheese Twists: Roll ½ dough for Peppery Cheese Rolls into a 7×16" rectangle. Brush half the dough the long way with 2 tblsp. softened butter. Fold unbuttered side over buttered side. Cut strips 1" wide from long sides. Twist each strip several times, stretching slightly, until two ends when brought together on greased baking sheet form a figure 8. Place a little apart on baking sheet. Let rise and bake as directed in recipe for Peppery Cheese Dough for Rolls. Makes 16 twists.

Short-Cut Mixer Peppery Cheese Buns: Divide one half Peppery Cheese Dough into 10 equal pieces and shape into balls. Place on greased baking sheet and flatten. Slash an X lightly on tops. Let rise and bake as directed in recipe for Peppery Cheese Dough for Rolls. Makes 10 buns.

The Rapidmix Method

Rapidmix is a short-cut way to combine ingredients for yeast breads. This method was developed by home economists in Fleischmann's Yeast Test Kitchens. You do not dissolve the yeast in warm water. You blend it with other dry ingredients and then add the liquid. If it's more convenient for you, you can mix the dry ingredients a day ahead, or longer if kept in a cool, dry place. This is one way to get a head start on baking day.

If you are already a bread baker, you probably treasure a few recipes for bread made by the Conventional Method. You can use your own favorite recipes and convert them to this newer short-cut method. Also, you can adapt recipes from our Con-

ventional Method to Rapidmix. Here's how to do it:
• Measure all ingredients.
• Pour active dry yeast from the package into the large bowl of your electric mixer. Add one third of the flour called for in the recipe, and all the other dry ingredients. Stir to mix.
• Heat the liquid with the fat——margarine, lard, butter or shortening—until warm. (When measuring liquid, be sure to add the water called for in Conventional Method to dissolve yeast. Add it to the milk if the recipe calls for milk.)
• Add liquid to the dry ingredients in the bowl. Beat 2 minutes with electric mixer at medium speed, scraping bowl occasionally.
• Add eggs, if used in recipe, and about ½ c. more flour; beat 2 minutes at high speed, scraping bowl occasionally.
• Gradually stir in enough of remaining flour by hand to make a soft dough that leaves the sides of the bowl.
• The dough is ready to turn from the bowl. At this stage you follow the rest of the Conventional Method recipe.

When we baked breads the Rapidmix way, we found the mixing quick and easy. The dough was a joy to work with and the breads were exceptionally light. Their taste was identical to that of the bread made by the same recipe with the Conventional Method.

We tried some of the breads made by long-time popular Fleischmann recipes which their home economists have converted to the Rapidmix Method. We believe you'll like these recipes.

RAPIDMIX WHITE BREAD

This dough really is easy to handle

5½ to 6½ c. all-purpose flour
 3   tblsp. sugar
 2   tsp. salt
 1   pkg. active dry yeast
1½ c. water
 ½   c. milk
 3   tblsp. margarine

• In a large bowl thoroughly mix 2 c. flour, sugar, salt and undissolved yeast.
• Combine water, milk and margarine in saucepan. Heat over low heat until liquids are warm (margarine does not need to melt). Gradually add to dry ingredients and beat 2 minutes with electric mixer at medium speed, scraping bowl occasionally. Add ¾ c. flour, or enough to make a thick batter. Beat at high speed 2 minutes, scraping bowl occasionally.
• Stir in enough remaining flour with spoon to make a soft dough. Turn out onto lightly floured board and knead until smooth and elastic, about 8 to 10 minutes.
• Place in greased bowl; turn dough over to grease top. Cover; let rise in warm place free from draft until doubled, about 1 hour.
• Punch down dough; turn onto lightly floured board. Cover and let rest 15 minutes. Divide dough in half; shape each half into a loaf. Place in greased 8½ × 4½ × 2½″ loaf pans. Cover; let rise in warm place free from draft until doubled, about 1 hour.
• Bake in hot oven (400°) 25 to 30 minutes, or until done. Remove from pans and cool on wire racks. Makes 2 loaves.

RAPIDMIX WHOLE WHEAT BREAD

Loaves have full rich wheaty flavor

4½ c. whole wheat flour
2¾ c. all-purpose flour (about)
 3   tblsp. sugar
 4   tsp. salt
 2   pkgs. active dry yeast
1½ c. water
 ¾   c. milk
 ⅓   c. molasses
 ⅓   c. margarine

• Combine flours. In a large bowl thoroughly mix 2½ c. of the flour mixture with sugar, salt and undissolved yeast.
• Combine water, milk, molasses and margarine in a saucepan. Heat over low heat until the liquids are warm (margarine does not need to melt). Gradually add to dry ingredients and beat 2 minutes with electric mixer at medium speed, scraping sides of bowl occasionally. Add ½ c. flour mixture, or enough to make a thick batter. Beat 2 minutes at high speed, scraping bowl occasionally.
• Stir in enough remaining flour mixture to make a soft dough. (If necessary add additional all-purpose flour to obtain desired consistency.) Turn dough onto lightly floured board. Knead until smooth and elastic, about 8 to 10 minutes.
• Place in greased bowl; turn dough over to grease top. Cover; let rise in warm place free from draft until doubled, about 1 hour.
• Punch down; turn onto lightly floured board. Divide in half. Shape into loaves. Place in 2 greased 8½ × 4½ × 2½″ loaf pans. Cover; let rise in warm place free from draft until doubled, about 1 hour.

• Bake in hot oven (400°) about 25 to 30 minutes, or until done. Remove from pans and cool on wire racks. Makes 2 loaves.

RAPIDMIX RYE BREAD

Honey-sweetened loaves full of rye flavor—they're easy to make

2½ c. rye flour
2½ c. all-purpose flour (about)
1 tblsp. sugar
1 tblsp. salt
1 tblsp. caraway seeds (optional)
1 pkg. active dry yeast
1 c. milk
¾ c. water
2 tblsp. honey
1 tblsp. margarine
¼ c. cornmeal
1 egg white
2 tblsp. water

• Combine flours. In large bowl thoroughly mix 1⅔ c. flour mixture, sugar, salt, caraway seeds and undissolved yeast.
• Combine milk, ¾ c. water, honey and margarine in saucepan and heat over low heat until liquids are warm (margarine does not need to melt). Gradually add to dry ingredients and beat 2 minutes with electric mixer at high speed, scraping bowl occasionally. Add 1 c. flour mixture, or enough to make a thick batter. Beat at high speed 2 minutes, scraping bowl occasionally.
• Stir in enough flour mixture to make a soft dough. (If necessary, add additional all-purpose flour to make a soft dough.)
• Turn dough onto lightly floured board; knead until smooth and elastic, about 8 to 10 minutes. Place in greased bowl; turn dough over to grease top. Cover; let rise in warm place free from draft until doubled, about 1 hour.
• Punch down; turn out onto lightly floured board. Divide in half; form each piece into a smooth ball. Cover and let rest 10 minutes. Flatten each piece slightly. Roll lightly on board under hands to taper the ends.
• Sprinkle 2 greased baking sheets with cornmeal. Place breads on baking sheets. Combine egg white and 2 tblsp. water; brush on breads. Let rise, uncovered, in a warm place free from draft, 35 minutes.
• Bake in hot oven (400°) about 25 minutes, or until done. Remove from baking sheets and cool on wire racks. Makes 2 loaves.

RAPIDMIX FAST-NIGHT CAKES

The Pennsylvania Dutch call these holeless doughnuts Fastnachts. *They serve them on Shrove Tuesday, the night before the Lenten season begins*

3¾ to 4¼ c. all-purpose flour
⅓ c. sugar
½ tsp. salt
1 pkg. active dry yeast
¼ c. margarine, softened (½ stick)
1 c. very hot tap water
1 egg (at room temperature)
Salad oil

• In a large bowl thoroughly mix 1¼ c. flour, sugar, salt and undissolved yeast. Add softened margarine.
• Gradually add very hot tap water to dry ingredients and beat 2 minutes with electric mixer at medium speed, scraping bowl occasionally.

Add egg and ½ c. flour, or enough flour to make a thick batter. Beat at high speed 2 minutes, scraping bowl occasionally.
• Stir in enough flour to make a soft dough. Cover; let rise in warm place free from draft until doubled, about 1 hour.
• Turn dough onto lightly floured board; knead until smooth and elastic, about 8 to 10 minutes. Roll out to make an 8×16″ rectangle. Cut into 2″ squares. Cut a slit about ¼″ deep (almost through the dough) in the top of each square. Place on ungreased baking sheets. Cover; let rise in warm place free from draft until doubled, about 45 minutes.
• Fry in deep hot salad oil (375°) until golden brown on both sides. Drain on paper towels. If desired, dip warm doughnuts in sugar with a little cinnamon added. Makes 32 doughnuts.

RAPIDMIX CHERRY-GO-ROUND

Here's a pretty coffee bread for your February festivities—and it's delicious

3½ to 4½ c. all-purpose flour
½ c. granulated sugar
1 tsp. salt
1 pkg. active dry yeast
1 c. milk
¼ c. water
½ c. margarine (1 stick)
1 egg (at room temperature)
½ c. all-purpose flour
½ c. chopped pecans
½ c. light brown sugar, firmly packed
1 (1 lb.) can pitted tart cherries, well drained
Confectioners Sugar Frosting

• In a large bowl mix 1¼ c. flour, granulated sugar, salt and undissolved yeast.
• Combine milk, water and margarine in saucepan. Heat over low heat until liquids are warm (margarine does not need to melt). Gradually add to dry ingredients and beat 2 minutes with electric mixer at medium speed, scraping bowl occasionally. Add egg and ¾ c. flour, or enough flour to make a thick batter. Beat at high speed 2 minutes, scraping bowl occasionally. Stir in enough additional flour to make a stiff batter. Cover dough tightly with aluminum foil and refrigerate at least 2 hours. (Dough may be kept in refrigerator 3 days.)
• When ready to shape dough, combine ½ c. flour, pecans and brown sugar.
• Turn dough onto lightly floured board; divide in half. Roll one half the dough into a 14×7″ rectangle. Spread with ¾ c. cherries; sprinkle with half the brown sugar mixture. Roll up from long side as for jelly roll. Seal edges. Place, seam side down, in circle on greased baking sheet. Seal ends together firmly. Cut slits two thirds through ring at 1″ intervals; carefully turn each section on its side. Repeat with remaining dough, cherries and brown sugar mixture.
• Cover; let rise in warm place free from draft until doubled, about 1 hour.
• Bake in moderate oven (375°) about 20 to 25 minutes, or until done. Remove from baking sheets and cool on wire racks. Frost while warm with Confectioners Sugar Frosting (see Index). Makes 2 coffee breads.

No-Knead Batter Breads

If you look through the yellowed pages of old cookbooks, you almost always find a couple of recipes for no-knead yeast breads that require no shaping into loaves. These were the timesavers for our busy grandmothers and the forerunners of today's batter breads, which home economists developed within the last 20 years.

Beating takes the place of kneading. You do not produce loaves with the even, fine texture of well-kneaded loaves, but you do get breads with that wonderful homemade taste. They are at their best when fresh-baked.

Success with these breads depends largely on not letting the dough rise too much. Spread the batter evenly in greased pans and smooth the tops with your hand, lightly floured. You may need to push the batter into pan corners with a rubber spatula. Cover and let rise in a warm place (85°) until almost doubled—never let it rise above the top of the pan. If you do, the bread will fall in the center during baking. In case the batter gets too light, turn it back into a bowl and beat 25 vigorous strokes. Then return it to greased pan, smooth the top and let rise again.

When you take baked loaves from the oven, remove them from pans at once and cool, right side up, on wire racks away from drafts before slicing. Brush tops with softened or melted butter while loaves are warm. The crust will be a dark brown and the surface will be rather rough. Slice batter breads a little thicker than the sliced bread you buy. Slices will be neater that way and will have a tempting home-baked look.

Here are recipes for batter breads and rolls that won the approval of our taste-testers. We include a modernized recipe for a perennial favorite, Sally Lunn Supper Loaf, named for an English girl who baked and sold a similar bread 200 years ago to enthusiastic customers. It's best served warm from the oven, as for supper, with the left over cold bread sliced, toasted and buttered for breakfast. Serve this appetizing treat with plenty of butter and one of your best homemade fruit spreads. Or do as the English do, and pass orange marmalade.

ANADAMA BATTER BREAD

Easy bread to make—no kneading, only one rising—has homemade taste

¾ c. boiling water
½ c. yellow cornmeal
3 tblsp. soft shortening
¼ c. light molasses
2 tsp. salt
1 pkg. active dry yeast
¼ c. warm water (110 to 115°)
1 egg
2 ¾ c. sifted all-purpose flour

• Stir together boiling water, cornmeal, shortening, molasses and salt. Cool to lukewarm.

• Sprinkle yeast on warm water; stir to dissolve.

• Add yeast, egg and 1¼ c. flour to cornmeal mixture. Beat with electric mixer at medium speed 2 minutes, scraping sides and bottom of bowl frequently. (Or beat 300 vigorous strokes by hand.))

• With spoon, beat and stir in remaining flour, a little at a time, until batter is smooth.

• Grease an 8½ × 4½ × 2½" loaf pan and sprinkle with a little cornmeal and salt. Spread batter evenly in pan and, with floured hand, gently smooth top and shape loaf. Cover and let rise in warm place until batter just reaches the top of the pan, about 1½ hours.

• Bake in moderate oven (375°) 50 to 55 minutes, or until loaf tests done. (Tap with fingers. If there's a hollow sound, the loaf is done.) Crust will be a dark brown. Remove from pan to rack at once, brush top with melted butter. Cool in place free from drafts before slicing. Makes 1 loaf.

Note: You can bake the batter in a greased 9×5×3" loaf pan. Let batter rise to 1" from top of pan.

VARIATION

Oatmeal Batter Bread: Follow recipe for Anadama Batter Bread, but substitute ½ c. rolled oats for cornmeal. Omit sprinkling greased pan with cornmeal and salt.

PEANUT BATTER BREAD

Spread with butter and honey or jelly to treat the children

1 pkg. active dry yeast
1 ¼ c. warm water (110 to 115°)
¼ c. chunk style peanut butter
¼ c. brown sugar, firmly packed
2 tsp. salt
3 c. sifted all-purpose flour

• Sprinkle yeast on warm water; stir to dissolve. Beat in peanut butter, brown sugar, salt and 1½ c. flour. Beat 2 minutes with electric mixer at medium speed, scraping sides and bottom of bowl frequently. (Or beat 300 vigorous strokes by hand.)

• With spoon beat and stir in remaining flour, a little at a time. Stir until smooth.

• Cover, let rise in warm place free from drafts until doubled, about 45 minutes. Stir batter down by beating 25 vigorous strokes.

• Spread evenly in greased 9×5×3" loaf pan. Pat top of loaf with hand, lightly floured, to smooth surface. Cover and let rise until doubled, about 40 minutes.

• Bake in moderate oven (375°) 45 minutes. (If loaf starts to brown too fast, cover loosely with aluminum foil the last 25 minutes of baking.) Or bake until loaf has a hollow sound when tapped with a forefinger. Remove from pan at once. Cool on rack out of drafts before slicing. Makes 1 loaf.

Note: Add ¼ c. finely chopped peanuts with peanut butter for a more positive peanut flavor.

CHEESE-CARAWAY BATTER BREAD

Wonderful toasted—serve with salads

1   pkg. active dry yeast
1   c. warm water (110 to 115°)
1   c. grated Cheddar
      cheese (4 oz.)
1   tsp. caraway seeds
2   tblsp. shortening or margarine
2   tblsp. sugar
2   tsp. salt
3   c. sifted all-purpose flour

• Sprinkle yeast on warm water; stir to dissolve. Add cheese, caraway seeds, shortening, sugar, salt and 1½ c. flour. Beat with electric mixer at medium speed 2 minutes, scraping bottom and sides of bowl frequently. (Or beat 300 vigorous strokes by hand.)
• With spoon beat and stir in remaining flour, a little at a time. Stir until smooth.
• Cover, let rise in warm place free from drafts until just doubled, about 45 minutes. Stir down batter by beating 25 strokes.
• Spread evenly in greased 9×5×3″ loaf pan. Pat top of loaf gently with floured hand to smooth surface. Cover and let rise until doubled, about 40 minutes.
• Bake in moderate oven (375°) 45 minutes, or until loaf has hollow

sound when tapped with forefinger. Remove from pan at once. Cool on rack out of drafts before slicing. Makes 1 loaf.

SALLY LUNN SUPPER LOAF

Ideal hot bread for company supper

1   c. milk
1   pkg. active dry yeast
¼   c. warm water (110 to 115°)
½   c. butter
¼   c. sugar
3   eggs
4   c. sifted all-purpose flour
1   tsp. salt

• Scald milk; cool to lukewarm.
• Sprinkle yeast on warm water; stir to dissolve. Add to milk.
• Cream butter and sugar well; add eggs, one at a time, beating after each addition.
• Combine flour and salt.
• Alternately add yeast-milk mixture and flour to creamed butter and sugar, beating well after each addition. Beat until smooth. Cover and let rise in warm place until doubled, about 1 hour.
• Beat 25 vigorous strokes. Spread into a well-greased 10″ tube pan; smooth and even top with floured hand. Cover and let rise until doubled, 35 to 40 minutes.
• Bake in moderate oven (350°) about 40 minutes until crusty and brown, or until loaf tests done when tapped with fingers. Remove from pan to rack; brush top with butter. Serve warm. (Cut with electric knife if you have one.) Or slice cold bread, toast and butter. Makes 1 loaf.

DILLY CASSEROLE BREAD

A prize winner in a national baking contest—good for sandwich making

1 pkg. active dry yeast
¼ c. warm water (110 to 115°)
1 c. large curd creamed cottage
cheese
2 tblsp. sugar
1 tblsp. instant minced onion
1 tblsp. butter
2 tsp. dill seeds
1 tsp. salt
¼ tsp. baking soda
1 egg
2¼ to 2½ c. sifted all-purpose
flour

• Sprinkle yeast over warm water; stir to dissolve.
• Heat cottage cheese until lukewarm; combine in mixing bowl with sugar, onion, butter, dill seeds, salt, baking soda, egg and yeast.
• Add flour, a little at a time, to make a stiff batter, beating well after each addition. Cover and let rise in warm place until doubled, 50 to 60 minutes.
• Stir down with 25 vigorous strokes. Turn into well-greased 1½-qt. round (8") casserole. Cover and let rise in warm place until light, 30 to 40 minutes.
• Bake in moderate oven (350°) 40 to 50 minutes. Cover with foil last 15 minutes of baking if necessary to prevent excessive browning. Makes 1 loaf.

Beat—Don't Knead

In batter breads, beating takes the place of kneading. You have beaten enough when the batter leaves the sides of bowl.

DOUGH FOR BATTER ROLLS

This refrigerator dough promises good eating—just follow recipes

2 pkgs. active dry yeast
2 c. warm water (110 to 115°)
½ c. sugar
¼ c. shortening or margarine
1 egg
2 tsp. salt
6½ c. sifted all-purpose flour
(about)

• Sprinkle yeast on warm water in large mixer bowl; stir to dissolve. Add sugar, shortening, egg, salt and 3 c. flour. Beat with electric mixer at medium speed until smooth, about 2 minutes, scraping sides and bottom of bowl occasionally. Or beat by hand until smooth.
• With spoon beat in enough remaining flour, a little at a time, until soft dough is easy to handle. Place in greased bowl; turn dough over to grease top.
• Cover with aluminum foil; place in refrigerator at least 2 hours before using. Dough may be kept as long as 3 days, but punch it down occasionally as it rises. Use in the following recipes.

IRISH PAN ROLLS

Parsley-sprinkled rolls with a light taste of garlic—you'll like these

¼ Dough for Batter Rolls
¼ tsp. garlic salt
1 tblsp. melted butter or
margarine
1½ tblsp. finely snipped parsley

• Shape dough in 1" balls. Place in lightly greased 8" round layer cake pan. Cover; let rise in warm place until doubled, about 35 minutes.

• Combine garlic salt and butter. Brush lightly over tops of rolls. Sprinkle with parsley, cut fine with scissors. Cover; let rise about 5 minutes.

• Bake in hot oven (400°) 15 minutes, or until done. Remove from pan and place on rack. Makes about 18 rolls.

HERB CLAWS

Unusual shape is eye-catching—team rolls with green or tuna salad

¼ Dough for Batter Rolls
1 tblsp. soft butter or margarine
2 tsp. cheese-garlic salad dressing mix

• Roll dough into a 12×9″ rectangle. Spread with butter. Sprinkle evenly with salad dressing mix. Cut in 3″ squares. Roll up each square as for jelly roll; place on lightly greased baking sheet, seam side down.

• With sharp knife make cuts ½″ apart halfway through each roll; curve rolls slightly to separate cuts. Cover and let rise in warm place just until doubled, 25 to 30 minutes.

• Bake in hot oven (400°) 12 minutes, or until done. Makes 12 rolls.

Note: The cheese-garlic flavor is not pronounced; bake the rolls according to recipe the first time to find out if you want to sprinkle on a litle more of the salad dressing mix the next baking.

ITALIAN CRESCENTS

Excellent rolls for barbecue supper with grilled steaks or lamb chops

¼ Dough for Batter Rolls
2 tblsp. ketchup
2 tblsp. grated Parmesan cheese
1 tsp. orégano

• Roll dough into 12″ circle. (Circle will be about ¼″ thick.) Spread with ketchup; sprinkle with cheese and orégano. Cut in 12 or 16 pie-shaped pieces. Beginning at wide or rounded end, roll up. Place, point side down, on greased baking sheet. Curve ends slightly to make crescents.

• Cover and let rise in warm place until just doubled, about 30 minutes.

• Bake in hot oven (400°) 15 minutes, or until done. Makes 12 or 16 rolls.

POPPY SEED CLOVERLEAFS

Fancy looking and good tasting—serve warm to impress your guests

¼ Dough for Batter Rolls
1 egg yolk
2 tblsp. water
Poppy seeds

• Form small pieces of dough into ¾″ balls. Place 3 balls in each greased muffin-pan cup.

• Mix egg yolk and water; brush over tops of rolls. Sprinkle with poppy seeds. Cover and let rise in warm place just until doubled, about 30 minutes.

• Bake in hot oven (400°) 12 minutes, or until browned. Makes about 12 rolls.

Quick Breads for All Occasions

The two important types of bread are yeast and quick breads. So far in our cookbook we have given you descriptions of and recipes for all kinds of yeast breads. Now we'll present the versatile quick breads. Country women rely on them because they are so adaptable—fast enough to make for everyday meals and fancy enough for guests.

Fortunately, there's a quick bread for every kind of occasion. Hot biscuits, muffins, pancakes, coffee bread and waffles brighten breakfasts. They're also at home on luncheon and supper tables. Popovers, like muffins, appear at party luncheons. Waffles, once reserved for special breakfasts, now take the spotlight in guest suppers, frequently with each person pouring batter on the iron and baking his own waffle. Drop small dumplings (also a quick bread) atop the meat-vegetable stew and let everyone enjoy the transformation of an everyday dish into something distinctive.

Nut and/or fruit breads are ideal for sandwich making. Spread thin slices of these moist, luscious loaves with softened butter or cream cheese and you quickly produce appetizing open-face sandwiches.

Quick breads, like yeast breads, depend on bubbles of carbon dioxide gas for their lightness. Yeast breads rise more slowly because, as previously explained, the yeast plants manufacture the bubbles as they multiply. With quick breads, the bubbles start forming in the mixing bowl as soon as you combine the liquid with baking powder and/or baking soda and the acid (such as in molasses, sour milk or buttermilk). These bubbles expand and form tiny air pockets, which make doughs and batters light.

Another difference between the two bread types is that you handle the doughs and mix the batters for the quick varieties as little as possible. You try *not* to develop the gluten in flour, while in yeast doughs you beat, stir and knead for that very purpose. Quick breads are delightfully tender.

These breads definitely are a boon for busy women pressed for time. And baking quick breads is satisfying because you get results fast.

Piping Hot Biscuits

Pass a basket of napkin-wrapped, golden-crusted biscuits so hot that they melt butter as it's spread on them. See that, along with the butter, some honey or jam tags the hot bread around the table. You're off to a good start in serving a successful meal. It upholds an old country kitchen axiom: Hot breads make an otherwise plain-Jane meal special.

Be sure the hot biscuits you serve live up to their name—that they're hot when they reach the table. To help keep them warm, transfer them from the baking sheet to a basket or dish lined with a napkin or foil; cover loosely. Hurry biscuits to the table.

Most farm women keep a package of biscuit mix in their cupboards to use when they're in a hurry. But from-scratch biscuits are particular favorites, and many women bake them for special occasions.

If you are a make-ahead hostess, arrange the cut biscuit dough on a baking sheet and put in the refrigerator. You can hold the dough cutouts ½ to 1 hour before baking the biscuits.

Good Biscuits Every Time

Follow these directions and you'll bake tender, flaky, light biscuits:
• Sift flour, baking powder and salt into a bowl. Cut in shortening with pastry blender until mixture resembles coarse meal or crumbs.
• Make a hollow in dry ingredients and pour in the milk. Stir until dough follows a fork around the bowl.
• Turn dough onto a lightly floured board and gently round up. Knead lightly 12 to 15 strokes, unless recipe specifies otherwise.
• Pat out lightly with hands, or roll to even thickness. The thickness depends on how you like biscuits, which depends to some extent on where you live. Southerners usually prefer thin crusty biscuits. For them you pat or roll the dough about ¼" thick. Many people north of the Mason-Dixon line favor tall biscuits. For them you roll the dough ½" thick.
• Cut the dough with a biscuit cutter dipped lightly in flour. Then fit the scraps together and pat or roll them (do not knead) and cut. For biscuits with soft sides, place the dough cutouts close together on an ungreased (unless recipe specifies greased) baking sheet; for biscuits with crusty sides, arrange dough rounds 1" apart on baking sheet. For a rich brown crust, brush tops of cutouts with milk or light cream, or melted butter.
• Bake in the middle of a very hot oven (450°) 10 to 12 minutes, depending on thickness. Serve at once.

NEVER-FAIL BAKING POWDER BISCUITS

Flaky, tender biscuits—the highlight of any meal. Do try the variations

2 c. sifted all-purpose flour
1 tblsp. baking powder
1 tsp. salt
¼ c. lard or shortening
¾ c. milk (about)

• Sift together flour, baking powder and salt into bowl. Cut in lard until

mixture resembles coarse meal or crumbs.
• Make a hollow in flour-shortening mixture and stir in enough milk to make a soft dough that leaves the sides of the bowl and sticks to the mixing fork.
• Turn onto lightly floured surface and knead with heel of hand 15 times. Roll ¼ to ½" thick.
• Cut with 2" cutter; lift cutouts to ungreased baking sheet with broad spatula. Place close together for soft sides, 1" apart for crusty sides.
• Bake in very hot oven (450°) 10 to 12 minutes, or until golden brown. Serve at once. Makes 12 to 16 biscuits.

Note: If you use self-rising flour, omit baking powder and salt.

ADDITIONS TO NEVER-FAIL BAKING POWDER BISCUITS

• Before combining milk and the flour mixture, add one of the following:

Cheese Biscuits: ¼ to ½ c. grated sharp Cheddar cheese.

Blue Cheese Biscuits: ¼ to ½ c. crumbled blue cheese.

Cheese-Onion Biscuits: ¼ to ½ c. grated sharp Cheddar cheese and 1 tblsp. instant minced onion.

Orange Biscuits: Grated peel of 1 medium orange. (For serving at a salad luncheon, dip ½ cube of loaf sugar in orange juice and press into each biscuit before baking.)

Bacon Biscuits: 4 bacon slices, cooked crisp, drained and finely crumbled (You should have ⅓ c. crumbled bacon).

VARIATIONS

Drop biscuits: Use recipe for Never-Fail Baking Powder Biscuits, and increase milk to 1 c.; drop dough from teaspoon onto greased baking sheet, or into greased muffin-pan cups to fill two thirds full.

Southern Biscuits: Increase lard or shortening to ⅓ c. and reduce milk to ⅔ c. (about).

Whole Wheat Biscuits: Substitute 1 c. whole wheat flour for 1 c. all-purpose flour and add after sifting the other dry ingredients together. Stir to mix well before cutting in lard.

Buttermilk Biscuits: Add ¼ tsp. baking soda to dry ingredients and substitute buttermilk for the milk. Use ⅓ c. lard or shortening.

Cinnamon Pinwheels: Roll dough for Never-Fail Baking Powder Biscuits into a 16×6" rectangle. Combine ⅓ c. butter or margarine, 1½ tsp. cinnamon and ½ c. sugar. Spread over dough, and starting at long edge, roll up like a jelly roll. Seal edge; cut in 1" slices. Place in greased muffin-pan cups; brush tops with butter. Bake in hot oven (400°) 15 to 20 minutes. Makes 12 to 16 pinwheels.

Butterscotch Biscuits: Combine ½ c. brown sugar, firmly packed, ¼ c. melted butter or margarine and 1 tblsp. water. Spoon 2 tsp. mixture into 12 well-greased muffin-pan cups. Sprinkle pecan halves on top. Roll dough for Never-Fail Baking Powder Biscuits about ½" thick; cut with 2" cutter. Place rounds in prepared muffin-pan cups. Bake in hot oven (425°) 15 to 18 minutes. Invert at once onto waxed paper or foil; remove biscuits at once. Makes 12 biscuits.

Texas Roll-ups: Add ½ c. grated sharp Cheddar cheese to flour-shortening mixture. Roll dough into 18×9″ rectangle, ¼″ thick. Combine ½ c. grated sharp Cheddar cheese and ¾ tsp. chili powder; sprinkle over rolled out dough. Starting at long side, roll up like jelly roll. Seal edges; cut in ¾″ slices. Bake on well-greased baking sheet in very hot oven (450°) about 12 minutes. Makes about 16 biscuits. Excellent with steak.

BISCUIT FAN-TANS

Fancy biscuits that go together fast —perfect with fruit salad and coffee

2 c. sifted all-purpose flour
3 tblsp. sugar
4 tsp. baking powder
½ tsp. cream of tartar
½ tsp. salt
½ c. shortening
⅔ c. milk
2 tblsp. melted butter
¼ c. sugar
1 tblsp. cinnamon

• Sift together flour, 3 tblsp. sugar, baking powder, cream of tartar and salt into mixing bowl.
• Cut in shortening until mixture resembles coarse meal or crumbs. Add milk and stir with fork to moisten all ingredients. Turn onto lightly floured surface and knead gently 20 times.
• Roll dough into a 12×10″ rectangle. Brush with melted butter.
• Combine ¼ c. sugar and cinnamon; sprinkle evenly over dough.
• Cut lengthwise into 5 strips, 2″ wide. Stack strips, one on top of the other. Cut in 12 (1″) pieces. Place cut side down in well-greased muffin-pan cups.
• Bake in hot oven (425°) about 15 minutes. Remove carefully from pan with spatula so fan-tans will hold their shape. Serve while warm. Makes 12 fan-tans.

Biscuits Rich with Wheat Germ

Some of the good wheat taste comes from the germ, the part that grows first when you plant the grain. Flour millers extract, flatten and sift the germ; they package the golden, oily flakes for sale in supermarkets. Since wheat germ contains a bounty of wheat nutrients, baking with it gives the family a bonus. Good eating, too.

Here is a recipe for tasty biscuits made with wheat germ. (Look in the Index for other breads that contain wheat germ.)

WHEAT GERM BISCUITS

Excellent way to use wheat germ. It gives biscuits a nut-like flavor

1 ½ c. sifted all-purpose flour
½ c. wheat germ
1 tblsp. baking powder
1 tsp. salt
¼ c. shortening
¾ c. milk

• Combine flour, wheat germ, baking powder and salt in mixing bowl. Stir to blend thoroughly.
• Cut in shortening with pastry blender until mixture looks like coarse cornmeal.

• Add milk all at once and stir with a fork just until all ingredients are moistened.
• Turn onto floured board and knead lightly 15 to 20 times.
• Roll dough ½" thick. Cut with 2" floured cutter. Place on ungreased baking sheet.
• Bake in very hot oven (450°) 12 to 15 minutes. Makes 12 biscuits.

PUMPKIN BISCUITS

Bring a change to bread basket with these tasty, colorful biscuits

2 c. sifted all-purpose flour
3 tblsp. sugar
4 tsp. baking powder
½ tsp. salt
½ tsp. cinnamon
½ c. butter or margarine (1 stick)
⅓ c. chopped pecans
½ c. light cream or dairy half-and-half
⅔ c. canned pumpkin

• Sift together flour, sugar, baking powder, salt and cinnamon.
• Cut in butter with pastry blender until mixture looks like coarse meal or crumbs. Stir in pecans.
• Combine cream and pumpkin; stir into flour mixture just enough to moisten dry ingredients. You will have a stiff dough. Turn dough onto a lightly floured board and knead gently a few times.
• Roll out to ½" thickness. Cut with 2" cutter. Place 1" apart on greased baking sheet.
• Bake in hot oven (425°) until golden brown, about 20 minutes. Serve at once. Makes about 20 biscuits.

HAPPY VALLEY BISCUITS

A little cornmeal makes a difference

1 c. sifted all-purpose flour
½ tsp. salt
1 tsp. sugar
¼ tsp. baking soda
¼ tsp. baking powder
⅓ c. cornmeal
⅓ c. lard
⅓ c. buttermilk (about)
Melted butter

• Sift together flour, salt, sugar, baking soda and baking powder into mixing bowl. Add cornmeal, white or yellow, and stir to blend.
• Cut in lard with pastry blender until mixture looks like coarse meal.
• Add buttermilk to make a dough that will hold together and that is not too soft to roll. (Measurement of buttermilk varies from ⅓ to ½ c.)
• Round up dough on lightly floured board and roll about ⅓" thick. Cut with 2" cutter. Lift delicate biscuits to baking sheet with broad spatula. Place them about ½" apart. Brush tops with melted butter.
• Bake in very hot oven (450°) 12 to 15 minutes. Serve piping hot. Makes 15 biscuits.

BEATEN BISCUITS

A Southern masterpiece rarely home-made today, but you might like to try

3 c. sifted all-purpose flour
½ tsp. sugar
½ tsp. salt
3 tblsp. cold butter
3 tblsp. cold lard
½ c. cold milk
½ c. cold water

• Sift flour, sugar and salt into bowl.

• Add butter and lard; blend with pastry blender until mixture looks like coarse cornmeal.

• Add milk and water, tossing mixture with fork.

• Knead 15 minutes; then beat with rolling pin or mallet for 20 minutes, or until blistered. Or put through the coarse blade of a meat chopper several times, folding dough over frequently. Or put dough over and over through the rollers of a beaten-biscuit machine, if you have one. When ready to roll, the dough is smooth and glossy.

• Roll dough ½″ thick or a little less; cut with small floured biscuit cutter. Prick tops with fork. Place on baking sheets.

• Bake in slow oven (325°) 30 minutes. Biscuits should be pale brown. Serve cold. Makes at least 36 biscuits.

Freezer to Oven Biscuits

Place cut-out biscuit dough in pan; freeze solid. Store frozen biscuits in plastic bags. Bake as needed in very hot oven (450°) 15 to 18 minutes.

Scones—Breads for All Seasons

Scones (rhymes with on), Scottish originals, are a hot bread for all seasons, but in America they're often summer specials. An Illinois farm woman says: "When the giant sunflowers, with big yellow heads, stand tall by the garage and the morning-glory vines twining around the back fence are a cloud of heavenly blue, I know it's time to get out my electric skillet and bake scones." And a California rancher's wife writes that she bakes scones on a flat surface over coals when her family cooks supper in the yard.

In the land of heather, scones, a cousin of biscuits and of waffles, usually bake on griddles. Many American women prefer to bake them in the oven. Their choice depends on how warm the weather is.

Regardless of how you bake scones, you split, butter and serve them with honey or a fruit spread. While they're superb when freshly baked, they're almost as tasty when baked ahead or left over if split, buttered and toasted.

Here are American adaptations of Scottish recipes for excellent Summer and Winter Scones. Try them and give your family and friends a treat.

WINTER SCONES

Brighten the supper menu with these cream scones cut in pie-shaped pieces

2 c. sifted all-purpose flour
1 tblsp. baking powder
2 tblsp. sugar
½ tsp. salt
¼ c. lard or shortening
2 eggs
⅓ c. heavy cream
1 tblsp. sugar

• Sift together flour, baking powder, 2 tblsp. sugar and salt into mixing bowl. Cut in lard until mixture resembles coarse meal or crumbs. Make a hollow in the center.

• Save out 1 tblsp. egg white for topping. Beat remaining eggs; combine with cream and add all at once to hollow in flour mixture. Stir to mix —the dough will be stiff.

• Turn onto lightly floured board and knead lightly 5 or 6 times, or until dough sticks together. Divide in half. Roll each half to make a 6" circle about 1" thick. Cut each circle in 4 wedges.

• Arrange wedges about 1" apart on ungreased baking sheet. Brush tops with reserved egg white; sprinkle with 1 tblsp. sugar.

• Bake in hot oven (400°) about 15 minutes, or until golden brown. Serve at once. Makes 8 scones.

SUMMER SCONES

Serve hot for breakfast or any meal —use Sour Cream Scones (see Variations) for shortcake

2 c. sifted all-purpose flour
1 tblsp. baking powder
1 tblsp. sugar
½ tsp. salt
¼ c. lard or shortening
2 eggs
⅓ c. milk

• Sift together flour, baking powder, sugar and salt into mixing bowl. Cut in lard until mixture resembles coarse meal or crumbs. Make a hollow in center.

• Beat eggs slightly; combine with milk and stir into hollow in flour mixture with fork to moisten all ingredients. Avoid overmixing.

• Turn onto floured board and knead lightly 5 or 6 times. Roll to ½" thickness and cut with 2" biscuit cutter.

• Place on ungreased griddle or skillet preheated over medium heat; if you use your electric skillet or griddle, set heat control at 325°.

• Bake about 10 minutes, turn and bake about 10 minutes on the other side. The trick is to bake scones slowly to brown the outside delicately and to cook the inside thoroughly. Serve hot. Makes 18 scones.

VARIATIONS

Raisin Scones: Use recipe for Summer Scones and add ½ c. finely cut-up raisins (cut with scissors) to dry ingredients before cutting in lard. Bake as directed.

Currant Scones: Add ½ c. finely cut-up dried currants to dry ingredients before cutting in lard. Bake as directed.

Buttermilk Scones: Substitute ⅓ c. buttermilk for ⅓ c. milk in recipe for Summer Scones. Reduce baking powder to 2 tsp. and add ¼ tsp. baking soda. Sift baking powder and baking soda with the other dry ingredients before cutting in the lard.

Sour Cream Scones: Increase sugar to 2 tblsp. and substitute ½ c. dairy sour cream for the ⅓ c. milk. Ideal for a quick strawberry shortcake. Exciting for cookouts.

Note: Farm women who have lots of butter use it instead of the lard or shortening.

Gingerbreads

Through years of testing different kinds of gingerbreads and cakes (the dividing line between cakes and breads is not very sharp), a few stand out in food editors' memories. Here are several we call "best."

SPICY GINGERBREAD SQUARES

Serve this warm and unadorned, or serve a week after baking with a hot lemon sauce or whipped cream

2 c. sifted all-purpose flour
½ c. sugar
2 tsp. ginger
1 ½ tsp. cardamom
1 tsp. allspice
1 tsp. baking soda
½ tsp. salt
1 tblsp. grated orange peel
3 eggs
½ c. light molasses
1 c. buttermilk
½ c. melted butter

• Sift dry ingredients together into a large mixing bowl. Stir in orange peel.
• Beat eggs until thick, light and foamy; add molasses in a stream, beating constantly; gradually beat in buttermilk. Add half of the milk-molasses mixture to ingredients in large mixing bowl, and beat with a spoon until well blended. Add remaining buttermilk-molasses mixture to large bowl in two additions, beating after each until blended. Gradually add melted butter, and beat with spoon until batter is blended and smooth. Pour into a buttered 8″ square baking pan.
• Bake in moderate oven (350°) 45 to 50 minutes, or until toothpick inserted in center comes out clean. Makes about 9 servings.

WHOLE WHEAT GINGERBREAD

Serve this sturdy, fruited bread warm in 1″ slices, or cut cooled bread slightly thinner—spread with butter

½ c. butter
2 tblsp. sugar

¾ c. light molasses
1 c. sifted all-purpose flour
1 c. stirred whole wheat flour
1 tsp. ginger
¾ tsp. baking soda
½ tsp. salt
½ tsp. cinnamon
½ tsp. mace or nutmeg
½ c. chopped walnuts
½ c. raisins
3 tblsp. minced candied
      lemon peel
2 eggs
½ c. milk

• Melt butter in saucepan. Add sugar and molasses and stir to blend.
• Sift together into a large mixing bowl all-purpose flour, whole wheat flour (return chaff to sifted ingredients), ginger, baking soda, salt, cinnamon and mace. Stir in nuts, raisins and lemon peel.
• Beat eggs and milk together until blended, add to mixing bowl along with molasses mixture. Stir to moisten all ingredients. Then beat mixture with a rubber scraper or wooden spoon about 70 strokes, until well blended. Turn into a buttered 8″ square baking pan.
• Bake in moderate oven (350°) 40 minutes, or until toothpick inserted in center comes out clean. Serve warm or cool on a rack. Makes about 10 servings.

PECAN GINGER LOAF

This moist, nutted gingerbread has the tender texture of cake; slices of it broil-toast divinely for breakfast

½ c. soft butter
1 ½ c. sugar
2 eggs

1 ⅔ c. unsifted all-purpose flour
2   tsp. ginger
1   tsp. baking soda
¾   tsp. salt
½   tsp. cinnamon
½   tsp. nutmeg
¼   tsp. baking powder
¼   tsp. ground cloves
⅓   c. water
1   c. canned pumpkin
½   c. finely chopped pecans

• With electric mixer, beat butter and sugar together in mixing bowl until creamed. Add eggs, one at a time, and beat until mixture is light and fluffy.

• Sift together dry ingredients; add to creamed mixture alternately with water; beat well after each addition. Add pumpkin and beat until well blended. Stir in nuts. Turn into a buttered 9×5×3″ loaf pan and spread smooth.

• Bake in moderate oven (350°) 60 to 70 minutes, or until toothpick inserted in center comes out clean. Allow to cool in pan 10 minutes, then turn out on wire rack to cool thoroughly. Makes 1 loaf.

Hurry-up Coffee Breads

The speed with which you can bake quick coffee breads or cakes, as they are often called, has something to do with their popularity. A more important reason for their widespread acceptance is the way they go with coffee.

These are the breads farm women often bake in cold weather to serve at midmorning when the men, doing chores near the house, come to the kitchen for a few minutes to warm up and relax. Men also like to share these breads with their business callers. Farmers' coffee breaks are in friendly kitchens, not in a coffee shop around the corner. No wonder they make many business deals around the kitchen table over coffee and a delicious coffee bread.

Women say these hurry-up breads are easy to stir up and bake when neighbors stop in to exchange news on their way home from town. And these breads rate high at coffee parties. Also, farm women often bake them in summer to tote to the field for the men's midmorning break.

You leaven these breads or cakes, whichever name you prefer to call these treats, with baking powder, baking soda or a combination of the two. (You'll find recipes for yeast-leavened coffee cakes in another section of this cookbook. See the Index for them.) Many women go a step farther in simplification and use packaged biscuit mix to make them.

Try the recipes for top favorite coffee breads that follow. They come to you highly recommended.

ORANGE-CINNAMON LOAF

Fast to fix—serve warm with butter and orange or apricot marmalade

2   c. biscuit mix
1   tblsp. grated orange peel
1   tsp. cinnamon
¼   c. orange juice
¼   c. milk
2   tblsp. melted butter or margarine
Honey Glaze

• Combine biscuit mix, orange peel and cinnamon in mixing bowl. Stir

to mix and make a hollow in center.
• Combine orange juice, milk and melted butter. Add all at once to hollow in dry ingredients; stir just to moisten mixture.
• Turn dough onto lightly floured board; knead gently about 8 times. Press evenly into greased 8" square pan. With a sharp knife, make one lengthwise cut, about ½" deep, across center of top. Then make crosswise cuts across top about 1" apart. Drizzle on Honey Glaze.
• Bake in hot oven (400°) about 20 minutes, or until browned. Serve freshly baked. Makes 8 servings.

Honey Glaze: Combine 2 tblsp. honey, 2 tblsp. chopped pecans or other nuts, 1 tblsp. melted butter and ½ tsp. cinnamon.

CINNAMON-ORANGE COFFEE BREAD

Serve this warm bread at your coffee party—you'll reap many compliments

```
2    c. sifted all-purpose flour
1½  tsp. baking powder
⅛   tsp. baking soda
½   tsp. salt
½   c. sugar
1    tsp. cinnamon
½   tsp. nutmeg
⅓   c. shortening
2    tblsp. grated orange peel
⅓   c. chopped nuts
1    egg, well beaten
½   c. milk
     Cinnamon Topping
```

• Sift flour with baking powder, baking soda, salt, sugar and spices into mixing bowl.
• Cut in shortening with a pastry blender until mixture resembles fine crumbs. Add orange peel and nuts. (If made ahead, cover bowl tightly and store in refrigerator.)
• Combine egg and milk. Add to flour mixture. Mix enough to moisten flour.
• Spread batter evenly in a greased 9×9×2" pan. Sprinkle with Cinnamon Topping.
• Bake in moderate oven (375°) 25 minutes. Cut in squares. Best served warm. Makes 9 servings.

Cinnamon Topping: Combine ½ c. sugar, 2 tblsp. melted butter. Blend to make a crumbly mixture.

ORANGE-PRUNE COFFEE BREAD

Fun to make; has a tangy flavor

```
2    eggs
¼   c. brown sugar, firmly
     packed
¼   c. granulated sugar
3    tblsp. finely shredded orange
     peel
4    c. prepared biscuit mix
1½  c. chopped, pitted prunes
1    c. fresh orange juice
```

• Beat eggs; stir in sugars and orange peel.
• Place biscuit mix in a bowl. Add chopped prunes and mix well, separating prune pieces with your fingers. Stir into sugar mixture alternately with orange juice. Beat by hand 1 minute; do not overbeat.
• Pour into a greased bundt pan or 10" tube pan. Bake in moderate oven (350°) 45 minutes, or until bread tests done. Cool 10 minutes. Remove from pan and cool completely. Makes 18 to 24 medium-size servings.

SOUR CREAM COFFEE BREAD

Quick, easy-to-make and extra-good with spiced nuts on top and within

1   c. butter
2   c. sugar
2   eggs
1   c. dairy sour cream
½   tsp. vanilla
2   c. sifted all-purpose flour
1   tsp. baking powder
¼   tsp. salt
4   tsp. sugar
1   tsp. cinnamon
1   c. chopped pecans

• Cream butter and 2 c. sugar until light and fluffy. Beat in eggs, one at a time, to mix thoroughly.
• Beat in sour cream and vanilla.
• Fold in flour sifted with baking powder and salt.
• Combine 4 tsp. sugar with cinnamon and pecans; mix well.
• Spoon about one third of batter into a well-greased 9″ tube pan.
• Sprinkle with about three fourths of pecan mixture. Spoon in remaining batter and sprinkle with remaining pecan mixture.
• Bake in moderate oven (350°) 1 hour, or until done. Remove from pan and cool on wire rack. Makes 10 servings.

APPLE COFFEE CAKE

Browned cream spiral adorns top— bread is best served warm

1 ½ c. sifted all-purpose flour
½   c. sugar
2   tsp. baking powder
½   tsp. salt
½   tsp. cinnamon
½   c. chopped walnuts
1   large shredded, peeled apple
1   egg, beaten
½   c. milk
3   tblsp. melted shortening or salad oil
½   c. dairy sour cream
½   c. sugar

• Sift together flour, ½ c. sugar, baking powder, salt and cinnamon. Add nuts, saving out 2 tblsp. for topping. Stir in apple.
• Blend together egg, milk and shortening. Add to flour mixture, stirring just to mix. Turn into greased 9″ round cake pan.
• Spoon sour cream over the top in spiral fashion, leaving center uncovered. Sprinkle remaining ½ c. sugar over top; scatter on remaining 2 tblsp. nuts.
• Bake in hot oven (400°) 30 to 35 minutes. Let cool slightly before cutting into wedges. (Also makes a good dessert.) Makes 6 servings.

Luscious Blueberry Kuchen

Blueberries are one of the easiest berries to use. All you have to do is put them in a strainer, spray with cool water and drain thoroughly. There's no hulling or pitting. They do have many seeds, but these are soft and seem to vanish in the mouth. It's the blueberry taste, though, that accounts for all those blueberry fans.

The Ohio farm woman who shares with you her recipe for Blueberry Kuchen says: "The berries do sink down in the batter, but they taste just as good there as anywhere else.

Sometimes I turn the servings upside down and sift confectioners sugar over the top.

"When I have friends in for coffee or for dinner, I frequently double the recipe and bake the coffee bread in a greased 13×9×2″ pan.

"I use the grated peel of one lemon in Blueberry Kuchen. Be sure to brush the peel from the grater with a stiff-bristled brush so you get all of that good lemon flavor."

GERMAN BLUEBERRY KUCHEN

Delicate, fine-grained coffee cake for breakfast or dinner dessert

1 ½ c. sifted all-purpose flour
2   tsp. baking powder
½   tsp. salt
¾   c. sugar
¼   c. soft shortening
⅔   c. milk
1   tsp. vanilla
½   tsp. grated lemon peel
        (½ lemon)
1   egg
1   c. fresh blueberries
3   tblsp. sugar
1   tsp. grated lemon peel

• Sift together flour, baking powder, salt and ¾ c. sugar. Add shortening, milk, vanilla and ½ tsp. grated lemon peel. Beat with electric mixer on medium speed 3 minutes, or 300 strokes by hand.
• Add egg and beat with mixer 2 minutes longer (200 strokes by hand).
• Turn into greased 8×8×2″ pan.
• Lightly stir together blueberries, 3 tblsp. sugar and 1 tsp. grated lemon peel. Sprinkle over batter in pan.
• Bake in moderate oven (350°) 40 to 45 minutes, or until lightly browned.

Cool slightly in pan. Cut in squares and serve faintly warm. Makes 6 to 9 servings.

IRISH SODA BREAD

Casserole loaf borrowed from Irish kitchens—it's wonderful with tea

4   c. sifted all-purpose flour
¼   c. sugar
1   tsp. salt
1   tsp. baking powder
2   tblsp. caraway seeds
¼   c. butter or margarine
2   c. raisins
1 ⅓ c. buttermilk
1   egg
1   tsp. baking soda
1   egg yolk, beaten

• Sift flour, sugar, salt and baking powder into mixing bowl; stir in caraway seeds. Cut in butter until mixture looks like coarse meal; stir in raisins.
• Combine buttermilk, 1 egg and baking soda; stir into flour mixture just enough to moisten dry ingredients.
• Turn onto floured board and knead lightly until dough is smooth. Shape in a ball and place in a greased 2-qt. casserole. With a sharp knife, cut a 4″ cross about ½″ deep in center of dough (this makes a decorative top). Brush with egg yolk.
• Bake in moderate oven (375°) about 1 hour, or until a cake tester or wooden pick inserted in center of loaf comes out clean.
• Cool bread in casserole 10 minutes; remove. Cool on wire rack before cutting. To serve, cut down through loaf to divide in quarters; thinly slice each quarter. Makes 1 loaf.

SUGAR-TOP COFFEE CAKE

*A favorite for company breakfasts—
from our* Cooking for Company *book*

1   egg
¾   c. granulated sugar
1   tblsp. melted butter or
        margarine
1   c. dairy sour cream
1   tsp. vanilla
1½   c. sifted all-purpose flour
2   tsp. baking powder
¼   tsp. baking soda
¾   tsp. salt
½   c. brown sugar
2   tblsp. all-purpose flour
½   tsp. cinnamon
2   tblsp. softened butter

• Beat egg until frothy; beat in granulated sugar and 1 tblsp. melted butter. Cream until light and fluffy. Add sour cream and vanilla; blend well.
• Sift together 1½ c. flour, baking powder, baking soda and salt; add to sour cream mixture. Blend well. Pour into a greased 8″ square pan.
• Mix together until crumbly, brown sugar, 2 tblsp. flour, cinnamon and 2 tblsp. butter. Sprinkle over top of batter.
• Bake in moderate oven (375°) 25 to 30 minutes, or until cake tests done. Serve warm. Makes 6 servings.

Yesterday's Gems Are Today's Muffins

If you were lucky enough to have a State-of-Maine grandmother who baked graham gems, you remember how wonderful the brown beauties tasted when you broke them apart and spread on lots of butter. Children still visit their grandmothers in farm kitchens and enjoy breads hot from the oven. Instead of feasting on graham gems today, they usually eat whole wheat muffins, which are near enough the original. "Gems" is the old-fashioned name for muffins. It still makes a lot of sense, for a gem, according to Webster's dictionary, is a perfect specimen of its kind. The definition for a muffin is a little muff to keep the hands warm, which the quick bread really does if you hurry it from the oven to the table.

Packaged muffin mixes are available and convenient, but perfect muffins aren't difficult to produce from scratch. They are tender and have slightly pebbled, rounded tops, never peaked ones. Their crust is a shiny brown. If you break a perfect muffin open, you'll see no long holes, called tunnels, and you'll find that the crumb is moist. The secret in making this kind of muffin is to mix the batter just enough to moisten the dry ingredients. The batter should be lumpy, not smooth.

Two Ways to Mix Muffins

There are two ways to mix muffins successfully. One bears the muffin name, the other borrows the biscuit technique. The Muffin Method is simpler and gives a typically coarse and open texture. It is used for muffins containing a large proportion of sugar and shortening. The Biscuit Method, sometimes called the Cake Method, gives a finer, more cake-like texture. This method commonly is used for plainer type muffins. The recipes indicate which method to use.

Muffin Method: Sift the dry ingredients into a bowl and make a hollow in the center. Combine the milk or other liquid, egg and melted shortening; pour it all at once into the hollow.
• Stir just enough to moisten the dry ingredients, not to make a smooth batter.

Biscuit Method: Use a pastry blender to mix the dry ingredients with the shortening until the mixture looks like coarse meal or crumbs about the size of small peas. Make a hollow in the center.
• Beat the egg until foamy; combine it with the milk or liquid and pour it all at once into the hollow.
• Stir the dry ingredients this way: Push them with a spoon to the center of the bowl (to the hollow where you've poured liquid), slowly turning the bowl. When you go around the bowl once, chop *straight through* the center with spoon to mix ingredients.
• Now you are ready to stir. Use as few strokes as possible to moisten all the dry ingredients.

Make the muffins small or big, depending on the size of your muffin-pan cups. Fill the greased cups two thirds full. If you do not fill all the cups, partly fill empty ones with water.

If muffins must wait after you bake them, turn each muffin on its side in the pan to prevent steaming; keep in a warm place, such as a low oven. To reheat leftover muffins, split in half, butter and toast under broiler.

Here are prized muffin recipes from country kitchens. Some are such great favorites in certain areas that they bear geographical names. You will notice that you can use an astonishing variety of ingredients. Bake many kinds of muffins soon and frequently. You'll like the compliments you get.

BUTTERMILK MUFFINS

Favorites made by Muffin Method. One taste explains why they're in favor

1 ¾ c. sifted all-purpose flour
2   tblsp. sugar
1   tsp. baking powder
¼   tsp. baking soda
¾   tsp. salt
1   egg, well beaten
¾   c. buttermilk or soured milk
⅓   c. melted shortening or
      salad oil

• Sift together flour, sugar, baking powder, baking soda and salt into mixing bowl. Make a hollow in the center.
• Combine egg, milk and slightly cooled shortening. Add all at once to hollow in dry ingredients. Stir with spoon just enough to moisten dry ingredients (batter will not be smooth).
• Fill greased muffin-pan cups or paper bake cups two thirds full.
• Bake in hot oven (400°) 25 minutes, or until done. Makes about 12 muffins.

VARIATION

Sweet Milk Muffins: Omit baking soda in recipe for Buttermilk Muffins. Increase amount of baking powder to 2½ tsp. and substitute ¾ c. sweet milk for the buttermilk.

Note: You also can use the variations we suggest for Guest-Supper Muffins (recipe follows).

GUEST-SUPPER MUFFINS

Extra-special, made by the Biscuit Method. Serve plain or fancy

2 c. sifted all-purpose flour
2½ tsp. baking powder
2 tblsp. sugar
¾ tsp. salt
½ c. shortening
1 egg, well beaten
¾ c. milk

• Sift together flour, baking powder, sugar and salt into mixing bowl. Cut in shortening until crumbs are the size of small peas. Make a hollow in center.
• Combine egg and milk; add all at once to hollow in dry ingredients. Stir only until dry ingredients are just moist (batter will be lumpy).
• Fill greased muffin-pan cups two thirds full.
• Bake in hot oven (400°) 25 minutes, or until done. Makes about 12 muffins.

VARIATIONS

Blueberry Muffins: Quickly fold 1 c. blueberries into batter for Guest-Supper Muffins, and bake as directed.

Cranberry Muffins: Chop 1 c. cranberries; sprinkle with 2 tblsp. sugar. Sprinkle into batter.

Bacon Muffins: Quickly stir ½ c. finely crushed, crisp cooked bacon into dry ingredients.

Date Muffins: Add ⅔ c. coarsely cut-up dates to dry ingredients.

Raisin Muffins: Quickly fold ½ to ¾ c. seedless raisins into batter.

Pennsylvania Dutch Muffins: Sprinkle tops of batter in muffin-pan cups with cinnamon-sugar mixture, 1 tsp. cinnamon combined with ½ c. sugar. Bake as directed.

Georgia Pecan Muffins: Quickly fold ½ c. chopped pecans into batter.

Jelly Muffins: After batter is in pans, top each muffin with 1 tsp. tart jelly and bake.

CRANBERRY-RAISIN MUFFINS

Muffins that complement chicken salad—splashes of red add brightness

1 c. whole cranberries
¼ c. raisins
¼ tsp. ground cloves
½ c. sugar
2 c. sifted all-purpose flour
4 tsp. baking powder
¾ tsp. salt
1 egg, beaten
1 c. milk
3 tblsp. melted shortening
   or salad oil

• Chop cranberries and raisins. Add cloves and sugar.
• Sift flour, baking powder and salt into mixing bowl. Add cranberry mixture.
• Combine beaten egg, milk and shortening. Add to dry ingredients; stir only until blended.
• Bake in well-greased muffin-pan cups in hot oven (425°) about 25 minutes. Makes 12 medium-size muffins.

Leftover Muffins

Split and toast plain or cereal muffins and serve with chicken à la king. Serve toasted fruit muffins for dessert with ice cream or fruit topping.

CEREAL MUFFINS

The batter for these muffins takes to almost any fruit—see variations

1¼ c. milk
1½ c. whole-bran cereal
1½ c. sifted all-purpose flour
⅓ c. sugar
1 tsp. salt
3 tsp. baking powder
1 egg, beaten
¼ c. melted shortening or salad oil

• Combine milk and cereal in large mixing bowl.
• Sift flour with sugar, salt and baking powder.
• Add egg and melted shortening to the milk and cereal; add the dry ingredients. Mix only until dry ingredients are moistened (batter will be lumpy, not smooth).
• Fill greased muffin-pan cups two thirds full. (If desired, sprinkle tops with sugar-coated flakes or cereal.)
• Bake in hot oven (400°) 20 to 25 minutes. Makes 12 medium-size muffins.

Note: You can use 3 c. corn flakes or 2 c. ready-to-eat oat cereal instead of the bran cereal.

VARIATIONS

To basic Cereal Muffins recipe, add ingredients as indicated for each variation; blend these in before adding the dry ingredients.

Blueberry-Cereal Muffins: Add 1 c. fresh or unthawed frozen blueberries, or 1 c. well-drained canned blueberries.

Apple Muffins: Sprinkle 2 tblsp. sugar and ½ tsp. cinnamon over ¾ c. finely diced tart apples. Toss lightly; add as directed.

Pineapple Muffins: Add ¾ c. well-drained crushed pineapple.

Bacon-Cereal Muffins: Crumble 4 strips crisp cooked bacon; add as directed.

Cranberry-Cereal Muffins: Add 1 (7 oz.) can whole cranberry sauce.

CARAWAY PUFFINS

Nice for a women's luncheon. Biscuit mix makes these easy

2 tblsp. soft butter or margarine
½ c. creamed cottage cheese
¼ c. sugar
1 tsp. grated lemon peel
¾ tsp. caraway seeds
1 egg
1⅔ c. prepared biscuit mix
⅓ c. milk

• Cream butter, cottage cheese and sugar. Add lemon peel, caraway seeds and egg; beat with electric mixer until very smooth.
• Stir in biscuit mix alternately with milk; do not beat. Spoon batter into greased muffin-pan cups, filling two thirds full. Bake in hot oven (400°) 20 to 25 minutes, or until lightly browned. Makes 12 puffins.

Popovers Light as Air

Never underestimate miracles that take place in ovens. The popover, the bread that puffs up in a remarkable way, is a classic example. It's a pity that all women who bake this hot bread do not have glass in their oven doors so they can watch the popovers grow tall, golden and beautiful.

Contrary to the belief of many women, popovers are exceptionally easy to bake—almost child's play. This is what happens in baking. The oven heat turns the liquid in the thin batter into steam, which is responsible for the bread's lightness. You need to have the proper balance of flour, eggs and milk in the batter and to use the correct oven temperature to enable the thin, shiny, brown popover crust to hold its shape.

Country hostesses serve popovers for all meals from breakfast to dinner, but they especially like to offer them in dinners featuring steak or roast beef. Sometimes they serve only butter with the bread, but frequently they also have marmalade or jam on the table.

Here is a recipe from a reader of FARM JOURNAL who says the popovers she makes with it are so light they almost float away.

PERFECT POPOVERS

Serve the crisp, brown pockets hot with lots of butter and jelly or jam

1　c. milk
1　c. sifted all-purpose flour
½　tsp. salt
1　tblsp. melted butter or salad oil
2　large eggs

• Pour milk into small bowl of electric mixer; sift in flour and salt. Beat at medium speed until batter is smooth, about 1½ minutes, scraping bowl frequently. Add butter and eggs; beat to mix thoroughly, about 1 minute. (Avoid overbeating; it reduces volume.)

• Ladle batter into well-greased custard cups, filling cups half full. Place cups on baking sheet and place on rack in center of hot oven (400°) or moderate oven (375°). (A 400° oven gives popovers a rich brown crust, slightly moist inside, while a 375° oven produces popovers that are a lighter brown and drier inside.)

• Bake in hot oven (400°) about 40 minutes (or about 50 minutes in 375° oven). Keep oven door closed until about 5 or 10 minutes before end of baking time or popovers may collapse.

• Remove popovers from oven, prick their sides with kitchen fork or metal skewer to permit steam to escape. Lay popovers on their sides in custard cups and return to oven, heat turned off and door left ajar, for 5 minutes to dry inside (or longer to keep warm for serving). Makes 7 popovers baked in 5 oz. custard cups.

Popular Pancakes— Plain and Fancy

Pancakes, FARM JOURNAL Family Test Group members tell us, are the quick bread they make most frequently. Perhaps the attitude of men has something to do with it. One rancher expresses it this way: "Take a stack of pancakes, spread liberally with butter and pour on plenty of syrup. That's my favorite winter breakfast. Hot cakes stick to the ribs when you're outdoors in bitterly cold weather doing the chores."

While pancakes for breakfast rate high, pancake suppers, glamorous dessert pancakes and main dishes (pancakes rolled around substantial fillings) also are popular. Most farm kitchen cupboards hold packages of pancake mixes, but there are occasions when women bake them "from scratch" for their families and guests. The recipes in this cookbook are this type.

POINTERS FOR PERFECT PANCAKES

• Preheat griddle over low heat.
• Beat the batter just enough to moisten the dry ingredients. It will have lumps.
• Start baking when the griddle is at the right temperature. Portable electric griddles and skillets are ideal to use because their heat is controlled. Also because you can sit down and bake the pancakes at the table. To test the temperature of the griddle, if the heat is not electrically controlled, sprinkle a few drops of water on it. If little beads of water dance around, the griddle is ready. If you use an electric griddle or electric skillet, follow manufacturer's directions. Grease the griddle or not, as the manufacturer directs.
• You may have to grease the griddle when you bake the first batch of pancakes, but rarely for later bakings, especially if the batter contains 2 tblsp. or more fat.
• Transfer the batter to the griddle with a ¼-cup measure to get pancakes of uniform size. Use a tablespoon or soup ladle for silver-dollar-size pancakes. You can pour the batter from a pitcher (a drip-cut one is best), but it's more difficult to get pancakes of uniform size.
• Turn pancakes when the rim of each cake is full of broken bubbles and the whole top has bubbles, some

of which are broken. Turn only once. Bake until underside is golden.
• If pancakes must wait, spread them out in single layers in folded towels in a low oven—just warm enough to keep pancakes from cooling.

Here are superior pancake recipes from farm and ranch kitchens collected from one end of the United States to the other.

FAVORITE BUTTERMILK PANCAKES

Variations of this recipe make fine desserts—try them

2 c. sifted all-purpose flour
1 tsp. baking soda
1 tsp. salt
2 tblsp. sugar
2 eggs, slightly beaten
2 c. buttermilk
2 tblsp. melted butter

• Sift flour, baking soda, salt and sugar into mixing bowl.
• Combine eggs, buttermilk and melted butter. Stir into flour mixture just to moisten flour. Do not overmix. The batter will have a few lumps.
• Bake on a hot, lightly greased griddle or in an electric skillet heated to 375°.
• Dip batter with a ¼-cup measure to get pancakes of uniform size. Turn cakes when bubbles appear and break over top and around the edges; turn only once. Serve hot with butter or margarine, or with Whipped Butter (recipe follows), and syrup.

VARIATIONS

Banana Pancakes: Add ⅔ c. diced bananas to batter for Favorite Buttermilk Pancakes. Bake; sift confectioners sugar over top of pancakes. Pass Whipped Butter, honey and a tart jelly to give a choice of toppings.

Blueberry Pancakes: Drain canned blueberries well. Add ⅔ c. to batter for Favorite Buttermilk Pancakes. Bake; sift confectioners sugar on top of pancakes. Serve with Whipped Butter and maple syrup. You can fold ⅔ c. frozen or fresh blueberries into the batter instead of canned blueberries. Fold additions lightly into pancake batter just before you are ready to bake the pancakes.

Whipped Butter: Put ½ c. butter (¼ lb.) in small bowl of electric mixer. Let stand at room temperature 1 hour. Start beating at low speed; when all the big pieces of butter are beaten smooth, beat at high speed until butter is fluffy. This takes about 8 minutes. Cover and refrigerate until an hour before serving. Makes 1½ cups.

CORN GRIDDLECAKES

You can bake tiny cakes and serve with maple syrup like corn fritters— good with fried chicken or ham

1 c. sifted all-purpose flour
2 tsp. baking powder
1 tsp. sugar
½ tsp. salt
2 eggs, well beaten
¾ c. milk
2 tblsp. melted butter or
    margarine
1 c. whole kernel corn

• Sift together flour, baking powder, sugar and salt. Beat in eggs, milk and butter until batter is smooth. Stir in corn.

• Drop from ⅓-cup measure on preheated griddle and bake until golden brown on both sides. Serve hot with butter and table syrup for breakfast. Makes 9 to 10 griddlecakes.

Note: You can double this recipe. Then you'll need 1 (1 lb.) can whole kernel corn.

SOUR CREAM BLUEBERRY PANCAKES

Light, fluffy pancakes with that interesting flavor sour cream adds

1 c. sifted all-purpose flour
3 tsp. baking powder
¼ tsp. salt
1 tblsp. sugar
1 egg
1 c. milk
¼ c. dairy sour cream
2 tblsp. melted butter
½ c. blueberries

• Sift together flour, baking powder, salt and sugar.
• Beat together egg, milk and sour cream.
• Pour milk mixture over dry ingredients and blend with rotary beater until batter is just smooth. Stir in butter. Fold in blueberries.
• Pour 2 tblsp. batter onto hot griddle for each cake. (Pour 1 tblsp. batter onto hot griddle for each cake if you want silver-dollar-size pancakes. If you have the time this is a festive way to serve them.) Brown on one side until golden. Turn and brown on the other side. If cakes brown too fast, lower heat. Serve hot with butter and maple syrup or Maine Blueberry Syrup (recipe follows). Makes

12 pancakes using 2 tblsp. batter, or 24 silver-dollar-size pancakes.

VARIATION

Sour Cream Pancakes: Prepare batter for Sour Cream Blueberry Pancakes, but omit the blueberries. If you have leftover batter, cover and store in the refrigerator. It will keep 2 or 3 days, but will thicken. When you are ready to use it, add 1 to 2 tblsp. milk in which you dissolve ½ tsp. baking powder for each cup of batter. Bake as directed in recipe for Sour Cream Blueberry Pancakes.

Maine Blueberry Syrup: Simmer together 2 c. blueberries, ½ c. sugar, ½ c. water and a thin slice of lemon to make a syrup. This takes about 10 minutes. Makes about 2½ cups.

BLUE RIDGE PANCAKES

A Southern farm breakfast special worthy of adoption across country

1 c. sifted all-purpose flour
1 tsp. salt
1 tsp. sugar
1 tsp. baking soda
1 tsp. baking powder
1 c. white cornmeal (or yellow)
3 eggs, separated
2 c. buttermilk
2 tblsp. melted butter or
     margarine

• Sift together flour, salt, sugar, baking soda and baking powder into bowl. Stir in cornmeal to mix thoroughly.
• Beat egg yolks until thick and lemon-colored. Add buttermilk and butter. Beat egg whites until stiff.

• Pour buttermilk mixture into dry ingredients and stir just to blend and moisten them. Fold in egg whites.
• Drop from ⅓-cup measure onto preheated and greased griddle; bake until golden brown on both sides. Makes 16 pancakes.

DOLLAR RICE CAKES

Marvelous way to use leftover rice

¾ c. sifted all-purpose flour
1½ tsp. baking powder
¼ t. salt
½ tsp. sugar
1 egg, separated
1 c. milk
2 tblsp. melted butter or
     margarine
½ tsp. vanilla
½ c. cooked rice

• Sift together flour, baking powder, salt and sugar.
• Beat egg yolk with fork; add milk, butter and vanilla. Stir in dry ingredients and beat with rotary beater until smooth.
• Fold in rice and egg white, beaten until stiff.
• Bake tablespoons of batter on hot griddle, turning once. Serve with butter and maple or cane syrup. Makes 34 small pancakes.

BLINTZES

Serve these Russian-Jewish pancakes with butter, fruit preserves or syrup

1 c. sifted all-purpose flour
1 tblsp. sugar
¾ tsp. salt
1 c. dairy sour cream

1 c. small curd creamed
  cottage cheese
4 eggs, well beaten

• Sift together flour, sugar and salt. Combine with remaining ingredients, stirring just enough to moisten the flour.
• Drop from ¼-cup measure onto hot, greased griddle and bake until golden brown on both sides. Serve hot. Makes 14 to 16 blintzes.

French Pancakes—Crêpes

You don't need to be a juggler to bake the tender, thin pancakes the French call crêpes. They are easier to make than you may think. French cooks put on quite a show when they turn crêpes—they toss them in the air. The marvel is that they always land on the unbrowned side. You'll have better luck, unless you practice flipping them, if you use your pancake turner. In France, where omelets appear often at mealtime, the omelet pan frequently is the utensil in which cooks bake crêpes, although small, heavy skillets also fill the bill. A heavy 8″ skillet is a good choice.

It takes time to bake crêpes. The home economist and homemaker who tested the Basic French Crêpes recipe said it took about 40 minutes to bake 16 pancakes. You can bake them ahead. If you plan to use them the same day, stack them and cover with a towel. You can freeze crêpes for use days later. Here's how to do it:
• Stack 6 to 8 cool crêpes, wrap tightly in foil and put in freezer. When you want to use them, place

the packages on a rack and set in a warm place for 2 to 3 hours. To thaw faster, place packages in a very slow oven (275°) 15 to 20 minutes.

You can bake crêpes and serve them flat, or you can roll them around fascinating fillings for desserts, or around substantial fillings for main dishes to serve heated or cold. Here is the recipe for Basic French Crêpes, the way American women make them, and suggestions for how to use the thin pancakes.

BASIC FRENCH CREPES

You can make wonderful dishes with these delicate, light brown pancakes

1 c. milk
3 eggs, well beaten
¾ c. sifted all-purpose flour
1 tblsp. sugar
¼ tsp. salt

• Beat milk into well-beaten eggs. Sift together flour, sugar and salt into milk mixture. Beat with rotary beater or electric mixer until batter is smooth.
• Pour about 2 tblsp. batter into a lightly buttered 8″ skillet, preheated over medium heat. Begin at once to rotate pan to spread the batter evenly over the bottom. Turn once; bake until *light* golden brown on both sides. Repeat, buttering skillet for each baking. Makes 16 crêpes.

WAYS TO SERVE DESSERT CREPES

Strawberry Stack: Serve unrolled, in stacks of 3 pancakes, with sweetened strawberries between. Cut in wedges.

Strawberry Roll-ups: Place sweetened sliced strawberries on half of each pancake. Top with 1 scant tblsp.

whipped cream. Roll up and arrange, seam side down, on serving platter or plate, allowing 2 roll-ups to a serving. Sprinkle tops with confectioners sugar.

Hot Strawberry Crêpes: Roll crêpes around sliced, sweetened strawberries. Melt 3 tblsp. butter in chafing dish or electric skillet; place crêpes, seam side down, in butter. Heat thoroughly. Serve with sweetened whipped cream.

Crêpe Stacks with Orange-Honey Sauce: Combine ½ c. honey, ½ c. butter, ⅓ c. orange juice and 1½ tsp. grated orange peel in small saucepan. Heat, stirring to blend. Arrange 3 stacks of 5 crêpes each on heatproof platter. Pour 1 tblsp. Orange-Honey Sauce on each pancake in stacks; place in slow oven (300°) to heat, 12 to 15 minutes. Cut each stack in half for a serving and pass remaining warm sauce to pour over crêpes. Makes 6 servings.

Swedish Pancakes: Bake crêpe batter in small (3″) pancakes. If you have a Swedish griddle with indentations, by all means use it. Arrange a circle of about 6 overlapping pancakes on a dessert plate. Place a spoonful of raspberry jam or lingonberries in center of each ring and top with a puff of whipped cream.

Midwest Fish-stuffed Crêpes

Most farm women keep a few cans of salmon and tuna on hand in their cupboards. But not many have discovered teaming the fish with thin pancakes to make exciting, hearty main dishes. When taste-testers voted on Midwest Fish-stuffed Crêpes, made by a recipe contributed by a Kansas rancher's wife, they described it with one word—excellent. You'll want to try this recipe. It produces a substantial fish dish that meat-and-potato farmers praise. That's a tribute to its tastiness.

MIDWEST FISH-STUFFED CREPES

Crunchy texture of celery and water chestnuts in creamy sauce pleases

1   (7 ¾ oz.) can salmon, drained
1   (7 oz.) can tuna, drained
1   (5 oz.) can water chestnuts, drained and chopped
¼   c. finely chopped celery
1   tblsp. finely chopped onion
5   tblsp. butter or margarine
⅓   c. flour
1   tsp. salt
⅛   tsp. pepper
2 ½   c. milk
6   tblsp. grated Parmesan cheese
1   tblsp. lemon juice
16   Basic French Crêpes

• Combine salmon, tuna, water chestnuts and celery in a bowl.
• Cook onion in butter until soft (do not brown). Blend in flour, salt and pepper. Slowly add milk, stirring constantly, until mixture comes to a boil. Remove from heat and stir 2 tblsp.

cheese and lemon juice into sauce.
· Stir 1 c. sauce into salmon-tuna
mixture. Put a generous spoonful of
mixture on center of each crêpe. Roll
up; place seam side down on ovenproof platter, or in a 13×9×2″ pan.
Spread remaining sauce over crepes.
Sprinkle with remaining 4 tblsp.
cheese.
· Bake in moderate oven (350°) about
30 minutes. Serve hot. Makes 8 servings.

Company Chicken in Crêpes —Country Style

The more you experiment with
main dishes of stuffed crêpes, the
more you will appreciate why many
people, especially in Europe, are so
fond of them. Company Chicken in
Crêpes is a good example of a distinctive, delicious main dish. You can
bake the crêpes and make the chicken
filling in the morning and refrigerate
until near mealtime in the evening.
The filling may thicken too much in
the cold, but it takes only a minute
or two to reheat it.

If you plan to bake crêpes and
use them right away, it's a good idea
to roll them as you take them from
the skillet. Place them in a pan and
keep warm in a slow oven.

Turkey in Crêpes is one of the best
ways to use some of the leftover
Thanksgiving or Christmas bird.

COMPANY CHICKEN IN CREPES

*Delicate white meat and asparagus
boost this dish to the gourmet class*

3 chicken breasts
1 chicken bouillon cube, or 1
   envelope instant chicken
   broth
1 c. water
6 tblsp. butter or margarine
⅓ c. flour
1 tsp. salt
1 c. dairy half-and-half, or light
   cream
1 (8 to 10 oz.) pkg. frozen cut
   asparagus, cooked (1¼ c.
   cooked)
16 Basic French Crêpes
¼ c. toasted, slivered almonds

· Place chicken breasts, bouillon cube
and water in medium-size skillet.
Cover and simmer until chicken is
tender, about 40 minutes. Take chick-
en from broth and cool enough to
handle. If necessary, add water to
broth to make 1½ c.
· Remove skin from chicken and then
remove chicken from bones. Dice
chicken. (You should have 3 c.)
· Melt butter, stir in flour and salt.
Add broth and dairy half-and-half;
cook, stirring constantly, until sauce
thickens and is bubbly. Stir in chicken
and asparagus.
· Put spoonful of chicken mixture on
each crêpe; roll around filling. Place,
seam side down, in single layer on
ovenproof platter or in a 13×9×2″

pan. Spoon remaining chicken mixture over top. Sprinkle with almonds.
• Bake in moderate oven (350°) about 20 minutes, or until sauce is bubbly. Makes 8 servings of 2 crêpes each.

VARIATION

Turkey in Crêpes: Substitute 3 c. diced cooked turkey breast for chicken. Use canned chicken broth instead of water and chicken bouillon.

WILLAMETTE VALLEY PEAR CREPES

Oregon women combine pears and brown sugar in luscious dishes

1   (1 lb.) can pear halves
⅓ c. brown sugar, firmly packed
1   tsp. grated lemon peel
1   (3 oz.) pkg. cream cheese, softened
1   tblsp. milk
¾   tsp. brandy flavoring
1   tblsp. granulated sugar
8   Basic French Crêpes

• Drain pears; pour syrup from fruit into saucepan and add brown sugar and lemon peel. Heat, stirring occasionally, to boiling.
• Slice pear halves in lengthwise quarters.
• Blend together cream cheese, milk, brandy flavoring and white sugar. Spread over crêpes to about ¾″ from edge. Place pear slices on about one fourth section (wedge) of each crêpe. Fold crêpe in half; fold section that is not pear-topped over again to make a triangular case. Repeat with remaining crêpes.
• Place in chafing dish. Pour heated sauce, made from pear syrup, brown sugar and lemon peel, over crêpes. Place over heat at table. Makes 8 servings.

Note: You can heat this dessert in your electric skillet instead of a chafing dish.

Waffles Are Wonder Breads

Waffle bakers never had it so easy as they do today. Just think how much easier it is to plug in your heat-controlled waffle iron than it was to hold a heavy, long-handled one over fireplace coals or to judge the correct temperature of the waffle iron heating on the range. Eliminated also, along with the guesswork of obtaining the correct cooking temperature, are the mysteries of what makes waffles exceptionally good.

You want to bake waffles that are golden-crusted with a thoroughly cooked interior. And you want them light. Old-time Southern plantation cooks, to emphasize lightness, said that they could hold the good waffle on the point of a pin. You want tender waffles with a crisp crust. After all, the main difference between waffles and pancakes is the crisp, patterned crust.

HOW TO BAKE PERFECT WAFFLES

• Preheat grids to the right temperature before you pour on the batter. If your iron has no heat indicator, sprinkle a few drops of water on it. If little beads of water dance, it's time to bake the first waffle.
• Follow the manufacturer's directions for greasing or not greasing

grids. Clean the grids after use with a dry, stiff brush; never wash them with water and detergents.

• If you separate the eggs, fold the beaten whites into the batter only until little white fluffs still show. The batter has a pebbly rather than smooth look.

• Open the grids only at the end of baking to avoid pulling waffle apart and causing it to fall.

• Stir the batter, when mixing it, just enough to moisten all dry ingredients. Overmixing makes tough waffles. If you heat butter or shortening to melt it, cool slightly before stirring into the batter.

• Hold the waffle, when you take it off the grid, on the fork for a few seconds. This encourages the formation of a crisp crust. Or leave the waffle on the grid briefly after you open it. For extra crispness, go a step farther and bake the waffle a minute longer.

Waffles are a three-meal bread. Serve them for breakfast and start everyone off feeling well fed and fit. Top them with creamed chicken, turkey, ham, dried beef and other foods for a hearty, tasty main dish for luncheon or supper. Dress them up for dessert and you have inviting refreshments for evening guests.

When you have leftover waffle batter, bake it; cool the waffles thoroughly and then wrap them individually. Store in freezer. These waffles come in handy. Just drop them into electric toaster to reheat.

Here are recipes for waffles that meet the requirements—waffles that are golden, crisp, light, delicious and easy-to-make.

SUNDAY SUPPER WAFFLES

Country women vote the waffles made with four eggs a top favorite

2 c. sifted all-purpose flour
4 tsp. baking powder
1 tsp. salt
2 c. milk
4 eggs, separated
1 c. melted butter or margarine,
    or salad oil

• Start heating waffle iron.
• Sift together flour, baking powder and salt.
• Combine milk and egg yolks. Beat egg whites until stiff.
• Add milk-egg yolk mixture to dry ingredients; beat with electric mixer at high speed, or with rotary beater, just enough to moisten dry ingredients.
• Stir in slightly cooled butter. Fold in egg whites, leaving little fluffs of them showing in batter.
• Pour batter from pitcher onto center of lower grid until it spreads to about 1″ from edges. Gently close lid at once; do not open during baking.
• Bake until steaming stops or signal light shows waffle is done.
• Loosen waffle with fork and lift it from grid. Place on warm plate. Reheat waffle iron before pouring on more batter. Makes about 8 waffles.

VARIATIONS

Buttermilk Waffles: Follow recipe for Sunday Supper Waffles, but use 3 tsp. baking powder and 1 tsp. baking soda, and substitute 2 c. buttermilk for the milk. Do not separate eggs; beat them until foamy, and combine with buttermilk.

Ranch Breakfast Waffles: Reduce butter in Sunday Supper Waffles to 6 tblsp. to ½ c., or use 6 tblsp. to ½ c. bacon fat (drippings) instead of the butter. Use 2 instead of 4 eggs; do not separate eggs, beat them and combine with the milk.

Ham Waffles: Sprinkle 2 tblsp. finely chopped cooked ham over batter as soon as you pour it on waffle grid.

Corn Waffles: Add 1 c. drained, whole kernel corn (canned) to batter. This is an excellent base for creamed ham or chicken.

Cheese Waffles: Add ½ c. grated process cheese to batter.

Nut Waffles: Sprinkle 2 tblsp. coarsely chopped pecans or walnuts over batter as soon as you pour it on the grids. You can break the nuts with fingers instead of chopping them.

Bacon Waffles: Cook 6 slices bacon until crisp; drain and crumble into the batter for Sunday Supper Waffles.

Cornmeal Waffles for Sunday Supper

If you like the way cornmeal tastes, these waffles are for you. They have a true corn flavor. The Missouri farm woman who sent the following recipe features the waffles in Sunday evening suppers, especially for drop-in guests.

"I start the meal," she writes, "with chilled pineapple juice or cranberry juice cocktail. Creamed chicken tops the first round of waffles—the main course. For dessert it's another round of waffles with butter to spread and cane or other table syrup to pour on for the sweet taste."

SOUTHERN CORNMEAL WAFFLES

Crisp-crusted, feather-light waffles that truly are exceptionally good

1 ½ c. white cornmeal
¼ c. all-purpose flour
½ tsp. salt
½ tsp. baking soda
1 tsp. baking powder
2 tsp. sugar
2 eggs, beaten
2 c. buttermilk
½ c. melted lard or shortening

• Put cornmeal in mixing bowl. Add flour, salt, baking soda, baking powder and sugar. Stir to blend.

• Combine eggs and buttermilk; gradually add to cornmeal mixture, beating with a spoon until smooth. Add lard and beat again.

• Pour enough batter on preheated waffle grid to spread to about 1″ from edges. Close iron.

• Bake until steaming ceases and signal light indicates waffle is done (2 to 3 minutes). Waffle should be brown on outside and cooked within. Makes 8 large (7″) waffles.

Gingerbread Waffles for Company

When a friend telephones late in the afternoon that she and her husband are coming over to spend the evening, one of the first thoughts most women have is: What shall I serve for refreshments? It's a good time to remember waffles. There's something very sociable about them—sitting around the table, talking and watching the golden waffles come piping hot off the grids.

Even if supplies in the cupboard and freezer are at low ebb, almost always you have what it takes to make exciting Gingerbread Waffles. And if you have vanilla ice cream, heavy cream to whip or frozen whipped topping on hand, you have the trim to give waffles a festive, party look.

GINGERBREAD WAFFLES

Dice bananas into bowl of whipped cream and pass to spoon over waffles

¼ c. butter or margarine
½ c. brown sugar, firmly packed
½ c. light molasses
2 eggs, separated
1 c. milk
2 c. sifted all-purpose flour
1½ tsp. baking powder
1 tsp. cinnamon
1 tsp. ginger
¼ tsp. allspice
¾ tsp. salt

• Cream butter and brown sugar until light and fluffy; beat in molasses, egg yolks and milk.
• Sift together flour, baking powder, cinnamon, ginger, allspice and salt. Beat egg whites until they form soft peaks.
• Stir dry ingredients into creamed mixture just enough to moisten all ingredients. Fold in egg whites.
• Bake batter in preheated waffle iron until lightly browned. Serve at once with scoops of vanilla ice cream, or frozen whipped topping. Sweeten whipped cream slightly. Makes about 7 waffles.

Southern Rice Buttermilk Waffles

Ask a Southern woman what to do with cooked rice, buttermilk and eggs —she may suggest you try these Rice Buttermilk Waffles. Serve them hot off the grids with fluffs of Whipped Butter (see Index) blended with peach or other fruit preserves. You'll give your family and friends unforgettable eating pleasure. To round out the menu for supper, have sausage or bacon and a mixed fruit salad.

RICE BUTTERMILK WAFFLES

Tender delicate waffles with luscious peachy spread . . . serve with bacon

3 eggs, separated
2 c. buttermilk
6 tblsp. melted shortening
2 c. sifted all-purpose flour
½ tsp. salt
1 tblsp. baking powder
1 tsp. sugar
½ tsp. baking soda
1 c. cooked rice (cooked in salted water)
Peach Butter

• Beat egg yolks until thick and lemon-colored. Add buttermilk and shortening.
• Sift together flour, salt, baking powder, sugar and baking soda. Add to egg yolk-buttermilk mixture. Stir until smooth. Stir in rice.
• Fold in egg whites, beaten stiff.
• Bake on hot waffle iron. Serve with Peach Butter. Makes 8 (7") waffles.

Peach Butter: Beat ½ c. (1 stick) butter until fluffy. Beat in ½ c. peach preserves and a dash of nutmeg. Beat again; pass to spread on hot waffles. Vary the spread by substituting apricot or apricot-pineapple preserves for peach preserves. Makes 1 cup.

WHOLE WHEAT WAFFLES

When short of time to bake whole wheat bread, make these waffles

2 c. whole wheat flour
2 tsp. baking powder
¾ tsp. salt
3 eggs, separated
1 ½ c. milk
¼ c. melted shortening

• Combine flour, baking powder and salt; stir to mix. (Stir whole wheat flour before measuring.)
• Beat egg whites; set aside.
• Beat egg yolks, add milk and shortening. Add all at once to flour mixture and beat until dry ingredients are moistened.
• Fold in egg whites, leaving little fluffs of them showing in batter. Pour onto preheated waffle iron; bake until steaming stops or signal light indicates waffle is baked. Serve hot with butter or margarine and syrup, honey or apple butter. Makes 6 (7″) waffles.

WHEAT GERM WAFFLES

Good-to-eat and good-for-you waffles with wheat germ the star ingredient

1 ¾ c. sifted all-purpose flour
3 tblsp. sugar
2 tsp. baking powder
¾ tsp. salt
⅔ c. wheat germ
2 c. milk

⅓ c. salad oil
2 eggs, separated

• Sift together flour, sugar, baking powder and salt. Add wheat germ and stir to mix well.
• Combine milk, salad oil and egg yolks in small bowl. Beat thoroughly.
• Beat egg whites until stiff peaks form.
• Add milk-egg yolk mixture all at once to dry ingredients. Beat to make a smooth batter.
• Fold in beaten egg whites; let small flecks of egg whites show in batter.
• Bake until golden on preheated waffle iron. Makes about 9 (7″) waffles.

CHEESE-BRAN WAFFLES

These waffles are different and delicious—a good start for a busy day

2 c. sifted all-purpose flour
3 tsp. baking powder
1 tsp. salt
¾ c. bran flakes
¾ c. shredded sharp Cheddar cheese
2 eggs, separated
1 ½ c. milk
¼ c. melted shortening or salad oil

• Sift flour with baking powder and salt. Add bran flakes and cheese. Toss lightly.
• Add egg yolks, milk and shortening to flour mixture. Beat until smooth.
• Beat egg whites until stiff but not dry. Fold into batter. Let little fluffs of egg whites show.
• Bake in a hot waffle iron. Serve immediately with butter and honey or maple syrup. Makes 4 large waffles.

Note: You can use the same amount of bite-size shredded whole wheat or shredded rice biscuits (crushed with a rolling pin) instead of bran flakes.

Chocolate Waffles à la Mode

Crown warm, red-brown chocolate waffles with bright pink or green peppermint stick ice cream, or slightly sweetened whipped cream with crushed hard peppermint candy folded in, and you'll have a dessert everyone likes. Feature it as the windup for a meal or for evening refreshments for a few guests. Or suggest that the teen-agers at your house serve it when some of their friends drive by to spend the evening.

Teen-agers will think they've hit a jackpot of good eating if you set out a choice of toppings for the waffles. Provide vanilla, chocolate and other flavors of ice cream, a pitcher of chocolate sauce to pour over and a bowl of chopped nuts to sprinkle on top. And remember honey butter, for it has a big following. It's easy to whip a cup of butter or margarine until fluffy and gradually beat in ½ c. honey. Heap in a bowl.

You can serve any kind of waffles you like, even plain ones, but no kind will win greater approval than Chocolate Dessert Waffles.

CHOCOLATE DESSERT WAFFLES

Picture-pretty dessert—chocolate waffles with ice cream topping

2   c. sifted all-purpose flour
½   tsp. salt
1   tsp. baking powder
½   tsp. baking soda
¼   c. granulated sugar
½   c. butter or margarine
2   (1 oz.) squares unsweetened chocolate
3   eggs, separated
2   tblsp. brown sugar, firmly packed
1 ½   c. buttermilk
½   tsp. vanilla

• Sift together flour, salt, baking powder, baking soda and granulated sugar into mixing bowl.
• Melt butter and chocolate together over hot water.
• Beat egg whites until stiff, but still moist.
• Beat egg yolks in a second mixing bowl; add brown sugar, butter-chocolate mixture, buttermilk and vanilla. Add to dry ingredients; beat with electric mixer at high speed, or rotary beater, to make a smooth batter. Fold in egg whites, leaving little fluffs of white showing in batter.
• Pour onto greased, preheated waffle grid until batter spreads to about 1" from edges. Close lid gently and at once.
• Bake until steaming stops or signal light shows waffle is baked. Loosen waffle with fork and lift from grid to warm plate. Reheat waffle iron before pouring on more batter. Serve waffles hot, topped with ice cream or whipped cream. Makes 6 waffles, or 12 servings.

VARIATION

Cocoa Waffles: Omit chocolate and sift ½ c. cocoa with dry ingredients. Increase buttermilk to 2 c. and add 2 tblsp. more butter.

Breads You Cook in Steam

About all that dumplings and brown bread have in common is that they cook to perfection in steam and boast of many staunch devotees. Big platters of tender chicken in gravy, wreathed by plump, feather-light dumplings, continue to appear on dinner tables across the farm belt. And Saturday night suppers along New England's countryside still feature fragrant pots of baked beans and their favorite companion, hot steamed brown bread. These food teams are as American as the Fourth of July, a rich heritage too good to abandon.

For young women who are uneasy about making these great traditional dishes, we give recipes and directions that insure success. We have modernized the old-time favorites for the ingredients and appliances of today.

HOW TO MAKE
FEATHER-LIGHT DUMPLINGS

You make dumplings about the way you make drop biscuits, but cooking them in steam gives a different look and taste. The rules for producing perfect dumplings are simple. This is all you have to do:

• Drop the soft dough from a spoon onto tender chicken or meat simmering in broth, or stock, *not into the broth*. Dumplings are delicate and need support while they cook.
• Cook slowly 10 minutes with the kettle *uncovered;* then cover and cook 10 minutes longer without lifting the cover. If you have a domed cover, use it, for it helps to prevent sogginess.
• Remove dumplings and chicken or meat to a heated platter and keep warm in the oven while you make the gravy. Spoon some of the gravy over and around the dumplings; serve the remainder of it in a bowl or gravy boat.

FLUFFY DUMPLINGS
Puffs as light as thistledown

2 c. sifted all-purpose flour
3 tsp. baking powder
1 tsp. salt
¼ c. shortening
1 c. milk

• Sift flour, baking powder and salt together into a bowl.
• Cut in shortening with pastry blender until mixture resembles coarse cornmeal or crumbs.
• Lightly mix in milk with fork to make a soft dough; stir as little as possible.
• Drop tablespoonfuls of dough on top of chicken pieces or meat and vegetables in stew. Simmer 10 minutes uncovered; then cover tightly and simmer 10 minutes longer. Makes about 12 dumplings.

VARIATIONS

Chive Dumplings: Add 3 tblsp. snipped chives to sifted dry ingredients and cook as directed for Fluffy Dumplings.

Cheese Dumplings Add ¼ c. grated sharp cheese to sifted dry ingredients. Excellent for beef-vegetable stews.

Herb Dumplings: Add ¼ tsp. dried sage or dried thyme to sifted dry ingredients.

Savory Dumplings: Add ½ tsp. celery seeds to sifted dry ingredients.

Parsley Dumplings: Add ¼ c. snipped parsley to sifted dry ingredients.

SOUTHWESTERN TOMATO DUMPLINGS

Colorful complement to beef stews

1 ½ c. sifted all-purpose flour
¾ tsp. salt
2 ¼ tsp. baking powder
1 tsp. chili powder
¾ c. tomato juice

• Sift together flour, salt, baking powder and chili powder. Stir in tomato juice.
• Drop tablespoonfuls of soft dough over meat and vegetables in beef stew. Cover and simmer 15 minutes without lifting lid. Makes 8 dumplings.

Boston Brown Bread

While recipes for steamed brown bread vary, molasses sweetens and flavors them all. They may contain cornmeal, a dark flour, such as whole wheat or rye, or frequently white all-purpose flour. Today many women steam the bread in 1-lb. baking powder cans, or No. 2 (1 lb. 4 oz.) cans. A few country kitchens in New England boast of old, slender bread molds, most of which are inherited prizes. Since the owners hold onto them with pride, you rarely see the molds at auctions.

The place of brown bread, as any Yankee will tell you, is beside a pot of baked beans, but the brown circles also make delightful sandwiches with coffee, tea or milk. Many women like to steam enough bread to have at least an extra loaf to wrap and freeze for later use.

As one Massachusetts apple grower's wife says: "I try to build up a supply of several loaves of Boston brown bread in my freezer. With baked beans also in the freezer, or in cans on the cupboard shelf, I always have the makings for a fine supper for company and the family. I also can green tomato pickles and mustard pickles to bring out from the fruit closet for bean suppers. To round out the feast, I make a salad, often coleslaw, and fix a dessert, usually with apples."

STEPS TO SUCCESS

Heed these tips and you'll steam excellent brown bread:
• Grease the cans or molds and fill them ½ to ⅔ full of batter.
• Cover cans with double thickness of plastic wrap and hold in place with rubber bands; or you can lay waxed paper or foil loosely over top of each can or mold and tie with string to hold it in place. The paper prevents steam that collects on the kettle's cover from falling onto the bread.
• Place cans on a trivet in a deep kettle with tight-fitting lid. The kettle should be large enough that you do not have to add more water during the steaming. (Or use a steamer if you have one; follow the manufacturer's directions.)
• Pour in boiling water to come halfway up the sides of the cans or molds.
• Cover kettle and simmer from 3 to 3½ hours, or the time specified in the recipe.

• Take cans or molds from kettle and remove covers. Place them in a very hot oven (450°) 5 minutes. Cut out end of can with can opener and push out loaf. Slice and serve hot.

• To reheat cooled or frozen bread, place it in a colander and cover with a clean dish towel. Steam over boiling water until hot.

Here is an updated recipe for Boston Brown Bread (if you do not want to steam the bread, see Index for Oven-Baked Brown Bread):

BOSTON BROWN BREAD

New England farm supper: baked beans, this bread, ham, green tomato pickles

1 c. sifted all-purpose flour
1 tsp. baking powder
1 tsp. baking soda
1 tsp. salt
1 c. cornmeal
1 c. whole wheat flour
1 c. raisins (optional)
¾ c. molasses
2 c. buttermilk or sour milk

• Sift together all-purpose flour, baking powder, baking soda and salt into mixing bowl. Stir in cornmeal, whole wheat flour and raisins.

• Combine molasses and buttermilk. Stir into dry ingredients and mix thoroughly.

• Pour into 4 well-greased No. 2 cans (these cans usually contain 1 lb. 4 oz. fruit). Fill two thirds full or slightly less. Cover cans with double thickness of plastic wrap and fasten in place with rubber bands.

• Place on rack in kettle with tight-fitting lid. Add hot water to reach about halfway up the cans. Cover ket-

tle and steam 3 hours. Remove from kettle, uncover cans and place in very hot oven (450°) 5 minutes. Remove bread from cans (cut out the end of can with can opener and push bread out) and slice with a heavy thread drawn around the loaf, crossing ends. (Cutting hot bread with knife may make a gummy slice.) Serve hot. Makes 4 loaves.

Note: To sour milk, pour 1 tblsp. vinegar into a 1-cup measuring cup. Fill with sweet milk. Let stand a few minutes.

Breads Out of the Fry Kettle

Cake-style doughnuts, warm and sugary, and two specialties—hush puppies and sopaipillas—are excellent examples of quick breads you fry in fat. All three breads ably support the foods they accompany, such as cider or coffee with doughnuts; fried fish with hush puppies; and with sopaipillas, Spanish-American dishes seasoned with hot chili peppers or chili powder.

SUCCESS STEPS
IN FRYING BREADS

• Heat fat or salad oil 3 to 4″ deep in heavy kettle to 370° on deep-fat-frying thermometer, unless recipe specifies otherwise. Or heat fat until it browns a cube of bread in 60 seconds. Or use electric deep-fat fryer or electric skillet; follow manufacturer's directions. Correct temperature is of prime importance. If it's too high, the breads brown before they are cooked inside, and if it's too low, the bread absorbs some of the fat and becomes soggy.

• Cook only as much bread at a time as will float easily on the fat. If you fry too much, the food may cause the fat to cool down; it's also difficult to turn it to brown on all sides.

• Turn bread when it rises to the top of the hot fat, using care not to pierce it or it will absorb fat. Cook until bread is brown; the total cooking time often is brief—2 to 3 minutes.

• Lift bread with slotted spoon from fat, hold over the kettle of fat for a second and then place on folded paper towels to drain.

• When you have finished frying, save the fat for reuse: Heat 3 or 4 raw potato slices to 1 qt. fat until fat bubbles. Strain fat through sieve lined with 2 or 3 layers of cheesecloth into a can or jar; cover tightly and store in a cool, dark place.

Delicious Doughnuts

Salute the home freezer for its major role in reviving a lively interest in homemade doughnuts. Now that you can fry a big quantity of hot cakes and keep them fresh in the freezer to use as you need them, farm women frequently make a production out of frying them.

A Colorado dairyman's wife, a FARM JOURNAL Family Test Group member, describes how she does it: "I mix the dough and put it in the refrigerator to chill," she says. "Soft doughs, like those for good doughnuts, roll easier when cold. I roll out the dough and my elder daughter cuts it while I begin the frying. My younger daughter shakes the warm doughnuts, drained on paper towels, in a paper bag containing sugar. When they are cold, we package them in plastic bags, 12 to a bag.

"We like doughnuts for breakfast, so I take a bag from the freezer the first thing in the morning before we go out to do the chores. They thaw in 30 to 35 minutes. By the time we return to the house, all I have to do is take them out of the bag. If we decide to eat before we start outdoor work, I remove the doughnuts from the bag, spread them on a baking sheet and run them in a hot oven (400°). They thaw and heat in 10 to 15 minutes. The heat melts the sugar coating, but you can still enjoy its sweetness. Sometimes we freeze doughnuts without sugaring and then roll them in sugar after they thaw and warm in the oven. It's difficult to tell these doughnuts from fresh-fried ones."

Here are recipes for doughnuts from farm and ranch kitchens (see Index for yeast-leavened—or raised —doughnuts).

WONDERFUL DOUGHNUTS

Subtly spiced—increase spices if you wish. Serve plain, sugared or glazed

4   eggs, beaten
⅔ c. sugar
⅓ c. milk
⅓ c. melted shortening
3½ c. sifted all-purpose flour
3   tsp. baking powder
¾ tsp. salt
½ tsp. cinnamon
¼ tsp. nutmeg

• Combine eggs and sugar; beat until

light. Add milk and cooled shortening.

• Sift together flour, baking powder, salt, cinnamon and nutmeg. Add to egg mixture; mix until smooth. Chill soft dough thoroughly in refrigerator.

• Roll dough out gently ⅓″ thick. Cut with floured doughnut cutter; let stand 10 to 15 minutes.

• Heat fat or salad oil 3 to 4″ deep in heavy kettle or deep-fat fryer to 375°.

• Transfer doughnuts to kettle of fat on broad spatula, using care not to alter shape. (If possible, place board of doughnuts near frying kettle.) Slip into hot fat. Add only enough doughnuts at a time as can float on the fat or that can be turned easily. Turn doughnuts as they rise to the surface.

• Fry 2 to 3 minutes, or just until doughnuts are a golden brown.

• Lift doughnuts from fat with kitchen fork (tines through center holes), using care not to prick them. Drain on paper towels in a warm place. Makes 30 doughnuts.

TRIMS FOR DOUGHNUTS

To Coat with Sugar: Shake warm doughnuts, one at a time, in a paper bag containing ½ c. granulated sugar or confectioners sugar. To increase spicy flavor, stir 1 tsp. cinnamon into sugar and mix well before adding doughnuts.

To Glaze: Add ⅓ c. boiling water to 1 c. confectioners sugar. Mix well. Dip warm doughnuts, one at a time, into the warm glaze.

To Coat with Nuts and Sugar: Dip warm doughnuts, one at a time, into warm glaze. Then dip into mixture of nuts and sugar, ½ c. finely chopped nuts to ½ c. sugar. For spicy taste, add 1 tsp. cinnamon to ½ c. sugar.

GINGERBREAD DOUGHNUTS

Spicy, lemon-glazed Halloween doughnuts to serve with cider or coffee

½ c. dark brown sugar, firmly packed
1   egg, beaten
½ c. molasses
½ c. dairy sour cream
½ tsp. baking soda
2   tsp. baking powder
3   tsp. ginger
½ tsp. salt
2½ to 3 c. sifted all-purpose flour
Lemon Glaze

• Combine brown sugar and well-beaten egg. Stir in remaining ingredients, except flour and glaze. Work as quickly and lightly as possible, adding just enough flour to make a soft dough. (The dough should leave the sides of bowl and be as soft as you can have it for shaping.)

• Flour your hands and pull off 4 pieces of dough, each the size of a plum. Roll each piece quickly between the hands to make a strip and then form a ring, pinching ends together. Drop at once into hot fat (360°); cook 4 doughnuts at a time.

• When doughnuts rise to the surface, turn occasionally until they are browned on each side. (Doughnuts will be a dark brown.) Drain on paper towels. Repeat to use all of dough.

• While doughnuts are slightly warm, dip tops in Lemon Glaze. Place on racks for glaze to harden. Makes about 18 doughnuts.

Lemon Glaze: Combine 1 c. sifted confectioners sugar, 1 tblsp. light cream, 1 tsp. lemon juice and ½ tsp. grated lemon peel. Stir until smooth.

Quick Doughnuts

Cut centers from refrigerator biscuits and deep fry as for doughnuts.

Hush Puppies
Go with Fish Suppers

Fry hush puppies the next time the fishermen in your family return home with a catch. Decide to serve this corn bread with the fish and you're well on the road to a wonderful fish supper.

Fishermen named the bread, which originated around Southern camp-fires. "Hush, puppies," they called, as they tossed corncakes to whining dogs to quiet them. Now hush puppies are almost as important as fish at a Southern fish fry. The liking for this deep-fat-fried corn bread traveled across country. Packaged mixes for making it are available in many areas.

You can fry the bread in your kitchen. The trick is to cook hush puppies until they are golden all over and done inside. Success depends on using the correct temperature, measured with a deep-fat-frying thermometer, and in dropping small portions of batter into the hot fat.

Here is a recipe from a Mississippi farm woman; she uses white cornmeal, but you can use either white or yellow.

HUSH PUPPIES

Hush puppies and fish coated with cornmeal and fried—what a team!

1 ½ c. white or yellow cornmeal
½ tsp. salt
¼ tsp. baking soda
¼ c. finely chopped onion (or green onions)
¼ c. buttermilk
⅓ c. water

• Combine cornmeal, salt and baking soda; stir in onion.
• Add buttermilk and water, and stir just enough to moisten dry ingredients.
• Drop by rounded teaspoonfuls into hot fat (375°) and fry until golden brown, turning once. Remove from fat with long-handled slotted spoon. Drain on paper towels. Serve at once. Makes about 35 to 40 hush puppies.

Sopaipillas with Honey

Sopaipillas look like little sofa pillows. You fry them like doughnuts, but they come from the kettle puffed up with hollow centers. If you've visited in Old Town, Albuquerque, New Mexico, the chances are excellent that you ate this fried bread. New Mexico is its original home.

You serve the bread hot from the kettle. Natives break off a corner of the puff and fill the golden cup with honey, which is delectable and soothing to eat along with Mexican-type dishes seasoned highly with chili peppers. Sometimes, if you're under a lucky star, you encounter mesquite honey, with its own sweet, delicious flavor.

Packaged sopaipilla mixes are available in New Mexico and some adjacent communities, but not on a national scale. You can fry your own sopaipillas with this recipe from a Southwestern ranch kitchen. They'll be an exciting conversation piece with Mexican dishes.

SOPAIPILLAS

Serve this bread at your next chili supper—you'll get many compliments

1 ¾ c. sifted all-purpose flour
2   tsp. baking powder
1   tsp. salt
2   tblsp. shortening
⅔   c. cold water

• Start heating salad oil or fat.
• Combine flour, baking powder and salt. Sift into mixing bowl. Cut in shortening with pastry blender. Add enough water to make a stiff dough.
• Turn dough onto lightly floured board and knead lightly until smooth. Cover with clean dish towel and let rest 10 minutes.
• Roll dough very thin (about ⅛″ thick) into a rectangle about 15×-12″. Cut in 3″ squares.
• When oil is very hot (385 to 400° on deep-fat-frying thermometer), drop a few squares of dough into it at a time. Turn frequently so that sopaipillas will puff up evenly. Remove with a slotted spoon; drain on paper towels. Serve hot with honey. Makes 18 to 20 sopaipillas.

All-American Corn Breads

Indians taught our early European colonists how to use cornmeal that they ground between stones. Corn breads appealed to people from the start and they continue to have an important place in country meals.

Cornmeal comes in three colors— white, yellow and blue. You'll rarely find blue meal, made from calico or Indian corn, in supermarkets outside the Southwest. Some people, especially those in the South and in Rhode Island, prefer white meal, but both yellow and white meal enjoy wide acceptance.

Our grandfathers often took corn they grew to gristmills to have it ground into meal. Most of the meal today is the granulated kind made from kiln-dried corn with the germ removed. It keeps much better than water-ground meal, but many country people say that it lacks the rich flavor of the water-ground type. Some neighborhood mills still sell water-ground cornmeal. Farm women, when they can get it, package it tightly and store it in the freezer, where it keeps satisfactorily.

Southerners like little or no sugar in corn breads, which usually are on the thin, crusty side, while northerners prefer sweeter and thicker breads. You use the Muffin Method to make most of these breads—you combine the meal and leavening, add the egg and liquid and stir enough to moisten the dry ingredients.

There are exceptions to the rule. Spoon bread is one of them. You bake this Southern delicacy in a deep casserole; it comes out light, fluffy and so soft that you serve it with a spoon instead of cutting it with a knife. Spoon bread, seasoned with chopped chili peppers, is one of the great dishes of the Southwest, which includes the southern third of Colorado, New Mexico, Arizona and part of Texas.

You'll find recipes for many kinds of corn breads in this cookbook. (See Index for Anadama Batter Bread, Hush Puppies and Sopaipillas.) You can use white or yellow meal in most of them, but if a woman sharing her recipe specifies white or yellow meal, we give her preference.

MEXICAN CORN BREAD

As truly Southwestern as turquoise and silver jewelry

1 (8 oz.) can cream-style corn
1 c. yellow cornmeal
2 eggs, slightly beaten
1 tsp. salt
½ tsp. baking soda
¾ c. milk
⅓ c. melted lard or butter
1 (4 oz.) can green chilies, chopped
¾ c. grated sharp Cheddar cheese
2 tblsp. butter

• Combine corn, cornmeal, eggs, salt, baking soda, milk, lard, chilies and half the cheese.
• Meanwhile, melt 2 tblsp. butter in a 1½-qt. casserole or a 9″ skillet. Place in oven until butter is hot, but do not let brown (if skillet has a wood handle, protect it by wrapping well in aluminum foil).
• Pour the batter into the warm casserole and sprinkle top with the remaining cheese.
• Bake in hot oven (400°) 40 minutes. Serve hot with spoon. Makes 6 servings.

Note: A FARM JOURNAL Family Test Group member from Arizona pours half the batter into the casserole without adding the chilies or cheese. She sprinkles on half the chilies and cheese, then adds the remainder of the batter and sprinkles on the second half of the chilies and cheese. You can omit the chilies, but the bread would not be acceptable in the Southwest. The flavor the chilies provide makes this an unusually good corn bread.

Three Corn Bread Favorites

There are about as many favorite corn bread recipes as there are kitchens. Here are three regional specialties . . . take your pick. The chances are good that where you live will determine your selection.

If you want to bake corn sticks, grease corn stick pans very well (use about ¼ c. shortening). Heat in oven while mixing batter. Spoon batter into heated pans to fill them about three fourths full. Bake in hot oven (425°) 12 to 15 minutes. Use any of the three following recipes. You will have enough batter to make 12 to 14 corn sticks.

SOUTHERN CORN BREAD

It upholds fame of Southern cooking

2 eggs
2 c. buttermilk
1 tsp. baking soda
2 c. white cornmeal
1 tsp. salt

• Start oven heating to 450°. Gener-

ously grease a 9×9×2″ pan; heat in oven while mixing batter.
· Beat eggs; add buttermilk.
· In bowl stir together baking soda, cornmeal and salt. Add egg-buttermilk mixture all at one time; beat with rotary beater or electric mixer until smooth. Pour into heated pan.
· Bake in very hot oven (450°) 20 to 25 minutes, or just until set. Serve hot, cut in squares, with butter. Makes 9 servings.

Note: Some Southern women add 1 tsp. sugar to the other dry ingredients.

GOLDEN CORN BREAD

This is Yankee-style corn bread

1   c. sifted all-purpose flour
¼   c. sugar
4   tsp. baking powder
¾   tsp. salt
1   c. yellow cornmeal
2   eggs
1   c. milk
¼   c. soft shortening

· Sift together into bowl flour, sugar, baking powder and salt. Stir in cornmeal.
· In a small bowl beat eggs with fork; add milk and shortening. Add all at one time to cornmeal mixture. Stir with fork until flour is just moistened. Even if batter is lumpy, do not stir any more.
· Pour into well-greased 9×9×2″ pan. Bake in hot oven (425°) 20 to 25 minutes, or until done. Cut in squares and serve hot with butter. Makes 9 servings.

VARIATION

Bacon Corn Bread: Add ⅓ c. crumbled, crisp cooked bacon to batter for Golden Corn Bread just before pouring into greased baking pan.

NORTH-SOUTH CORN BREAD

A bread with many champions on both sides of the Mason-Dixon line

¼   c. sifted all-purpose flour
1 ¼ c. white or yellow cornmeal
2   tblsp. sugar
3   tsp. baking powder
1   tsp. salt
1   egg
1   c. plus 2 tblsp. milk
3   tblsp. soft shortening or
       bacon drippings

· Start oven heating to 425°. Generously grease a 9×9×2″ pan; place in oven to heat while mixing batter.
· Stir together flour, cornmeal, sugar, baking powder and salt.
· Beat egg; combine with milk; add with shortening to dry ingredients all at one time and beat with rotary beater just until smooth. Pour into heated pan.
· Bake in hot oven (425°) 20 to 25 minutes, or just until set. Serve hot, cut in squares, with butter. Makes 9 servings.

Timesaving Corn Bread Mix

Some farm women mix the dry ingredients and lard for corn breads when they have free time. This Corn Bread Mix is an example of how they "store time" to use on busy days. The mix produces tender, light breads on the sweet side in contrast to the crisp-crusted, less sweet Southern corn breads. It's at its best in coffee breads and other breakfast specialties. Try the recipes that follow and see if you don't agree.

CORN BREAD MIX

A big help when you're rushing to get a good breakfast ready on time

4¼ c. flour
2½ c. cornmeal
1½ c. nonfat dry milk
¼ c. baking powder
1 tblsp. salt
1½ c. lard or shortening

• Sift together flour, cornmeal, dry milk, baking powder and salt into a large bowl. Repeat two times.
• Cut in lard with a pastry blender to blend thoroughly.
• Place in jar or canister, cover and store in a cool place. Use mix within a month. Makes about 10 cups.

PINEAPPLE COFFEE CAKE

This will put cheer on the breakfast table, and it's quick to make

¼ c. butter
¼ c. honey
1 (8½ oz.) can crushed pineapple
¼ c. shredded coconut
2 c. Corn Bread Mix
½ c. sugar
1 egg, beaten

• Melt butter in 8×8×2" pan. Add honey and blend. Drain pineapple and reserve juice. Spread drained pineapple and coconut in pan, distributing mixture evenly.
• Combine mix and sugar in bowl.

Add water to pineapple juice to make ½ c. Combine egg and juice; add to dry mixture and stir just to blend and moisten. Pour batter evenly into prepared pan.
• Bake in hot oven (400°) about 25 minutes. Remove from oven and cool in pan 5 minutes. Invert over plate; let stand 1 minute. Remove pan and cut in rectangles or squares. Serve warm. Makes 6 or 9 servings.

CORNMEAL GRIDDLECAKES

Old-fashioned recipe, up-to-date style

2 c. Corn Bread Mix
2 eggs, beaten
½ c. water
1 tblsp. molasses

• Place mix in bowl.
• Combine eggs, water and molasses. Add to mix and stir just until moistened.
• Spoon batter on preheated griddle and bake until browned on both sides. Turn only once. If the batter thickens during the baking, thin with a little cold water.
• Serve on warm plates with butter and syrup or honey. Makes 8 large or 16 small griddlecakes.

SUGARED MUFFINS

Great with ham and eggs

1 egg, beaten
½ c. water
2 c. Corn Bread Mix
¼ c. melted butter
¼ c. sugar
½ tsp. cinnamon

• Combine egg and water; add to

Corn Bread Mix; stir just to moisten.
• Fill greased muffin-pan cups two thirds full.
• Bake in hot oven (425°) 15 to 20 minutes. Remove from pan.
• Dip tops of muffins in melted butter and then in sugar and cinnamon, mixed. Serve at once. Makes 6 muffins.

FAST-FIX CORN BREAD

Cheerful for supper on a rainy day

4½ c. Corn Bread Mix
1⅓ c. water
2 eggs, beaten

• Place mix in bowl.
• Combine water and eggs. Stir into mix just to moisten mix. Batter will not be smooth. Pour into a greased 9×9×2″ pan.
• Bake in hot oven (425°) about 25 minutes. Makes 6 servings.

FRESH CORN SPOON BREAD

Best partner fried chicken ever had

3 ears fresh corn (about)
⅓ c. cornmeal
2 c. hot milk
¼ c. butter (½ stick)
2 tsp. sugar
1½ tsp. salt
⅛ tsp. pepper
1 tblsp. minced green onion
2 eggs, separated

• Split each row of corn kernels vertically with a sharp knife. Cut off about one third of the kernels around each ear. Repeat until all are removed. Scrape the cob with a tablespoon to get the remaining pulp and juices. Measure. You should have 1½ c.

• Mix the corn with cornmeal and stir in the hot milk. Cook, stirring over medium heat, until thickened, about 5 minutes. Remove from heat and stir in butter, sugar, salt, pepper and onion.
• Beat egg yolks. Add a little of the hot corn mixture to yolks, then add yolks to hot corn mixture in saucepan.
• Beat egg whites until stiff and fold into corn mixture.
• Grease bottom of 1½-qt. casserole, but not the sides. Turn corn mixture into casserole. Set in pan of hot water.
• Bake in slow oven (325°) about 1 hour, or until knife inserted in center comes out clean. Serve at once. Makes 6 to 8 servings.

Country Kitchen Nut Breads

Fruited nut breads are giving fruitcakes a run for popularity. When FARM JOURNAL women editors visit farm homes, their hostesses frequently tell about their families' preference for loaves of these quick breads over the richer, more tedious-to-bake and more costly fruitcakes.

The moist, sweet nut breads freeze beautifully. You can make them weeks ahead for the Christmas holidays, parties and to serve on short notice when friends stop by unexpectedly. If you package a few thin slices together, they thaw much faster than a loaf—almost while you fix tea or coffee.

Nut breads make excellent sandwiches. Spread with butter or cream cheese, with or without marmalade or jelly, they are marvelous companions for tea, coffee or salads.

Nut breads are the exception to the rule that you serve quick breads hot. Cool the loaf after baking, wrap it in foil or plastic wrap, place in a cool place, such as the refrigerator, and let stand at least overnight before you slice it. Then, if you use a sharp knife, you can cut even, thin slices. You can keep the breads many days, or weeks if you put them in the freezer. Their flavors mingle and ripen and improve during storage.

"Fruited nut breads," says a Minnesota FARM JOURNAL Family Test Group member, "are something a junior cook can bake for her grandparents, aunts and uncles. Our 12-year-old daughter runs up the road to her grandparents' house on Christmas morning with a basket holding a couple of loaves of nut bread she baked, wrapped and tied with red ribbons. It's becoming a family tradition. Grandmother says she listens for her grandchild stamping snow off her boots—she's at the door in a hurry with her Christmas greeting.

"Grandmother likes the gift on several counts. She has lots of company during the holidays and nut bread comes in handy. And she especially appreciates presents her grandchildren make. Grandfather also is proud that his granddaughter gathered the nuts for the loaf in the October woods on the farm. He believes children should learn how to use the foods that are free to people who live on the land."

Take your pick of the fruit-nut bread recipes in this cookbook. And if any of the loaves have deep cracks on top, remember these are not blemishes, but the trademarks of many of the best loaves.

Honeyed Date Bread
—Extra Special

A California ranch woman mailed the recipe for this superlative date bread to her sister, who lives on an Iowa farm. When the sister made the bread, she gave it a Midwestern touch. She used ¾ c. chopped pecans, all she had in the kitchen, and ¼ c. chopped black walnuts that she gathered on the farm. The results were so pleasing to family and friends who sampled the bread that we give her version of the recipe, which also is superior when made with the kind of walnuts that grow in California and Oregon groves.

HONEYED DATE BREAD

This loaf is guaranteed to please . . . it's dark, moist and delicious

2   c. pitted fresh dates
2   tblsp. shortening
⅔   c. brown sugar, firmly packed
½   c. honey
¾   tsp. vanilla
¾   tsp. grated orange peel
¾   c. hot water
¼   c. orange juice
1   egg, beaten
2   c. sifted all-purpose flour
1   tsp. baking soda
1   tsp. salt
¾   c. coarsely chopped pecans
¼   c. chopped black walnuts

• Cut the dates in small pieces with scissors. Put dates, shortening, brown sugar, honey, vanilla, orange peel, hot water and orange juice into a mixing bowl. Stir to mix; set aside for 15 minutes.

• Add egg and mix well. Sift in flour, baking soda and salt; stir just enough to moisten dry ingredients. Fold in nuts. Turn into a greased 9×5×3″ loaf pan.

• Bake in slow oven (325°) 1 hour, or until bread tests done with cake tester inserted in center of loaf. Let stand in pan 10 minutes; turn onto wire rack to cool. Wrap in foil or plastic wrap and store in cool place, or freeze, overnight or longer before slicing. Makes 1 loaf.

PINEAPPLE-DATE LOAF

Tastes like a mellow fruitcake—improves after standing overnight

¼   c. soft butter or margarine
½   c. sugar
1   egg
¼   tsp. lemon extract
1   (8½ oz.) can crushed
       pineapple
¼   c. chopped nuts
2½ c. sifted all-purpose flour
2½ tsp. baking powder
¼   tsp. baking soda
1   tsp. salt
½   c. finely chopped, pitted
       dates
¼   c. water
¼   c. chopped maraschino
       cherries, well drained

• Cream butter and sugar; add egg and lemon extract. Drain pineapple, reserving liquid. Add crushed pineapple and nuts to creamed mixture.

• Sift dry ingredients together. Add dates and mix well, separating date pieces with your fingers. Stir dry ingredients into creamed mixture alternately with reserved pineapple juice plus ¼ c. water. Fold in the chopped maraschino cherries.

• Pour into a greased 9×5×3″ loaf pan. Bake in moderate oven (375°) about 55 minutes. Cool in pan 10 minutes. Remove from pan; cool completely. Makes 1 loaf.

CRANBERRY BREAD

A Merry Christmas loaf dotted with berries—makes elegant sandwiches

1½ c. chopped raw cranberries
4   tsp. grated orange peel
3   tblsp. sugar
3   c. sifted all-purpose flour
3   tsp. baking powder
½   tsp. baking soda
¾   tsp. salt
¾   tsp. nutmeg
1¼ c. sugar
2   eggs, beaten
¾   c. orange juice
¾   c. water
½   c. melted shortening
1   c. chopped walnuts

• Combine cranberries, orange peel and 3 tblsp. sugar. Stir to mix and set aside.

• Sift together flour, baking powder, baking soda, salt, nutmeg and 1¼ c. sugar.

• Add eggs to orange juice and water; mix well. Add with cranberry mixture and shortening to dry ingredients. Stir just enough to blend and moisten all dry ingredients. Fold in nuts.

• Turn into a greased 9×5×3″ loaf pan.

• Bake in moderate oven (350°) 1½ hours, or until cake tester or wooden pick inserted in center comes out clean. Set pan on wire rack; cool 20 minutes. Turn bread out on wire rack and cool completely. Wrap in aluminum foil or plastic wrap; store in refrigerator or other cool place, or freeze. Do not cut for 24 hours. Makes 1 loaf.

MIDGET RAISIN LOAVES

Christmas gift for neighbors—a loaf for every member of the family

⅓ c. shortening
¾ c. sugar
1 tblsp. grated orange peel
1 egg
3 c. sifted all-purpose flour
3½ tsp. baking powder
1½ tsp. salt
1 c. milk
⅓ c. orange juice
1 c. chopped pecans
½ c. snipped raisins
Orange Topping

• Cream shortening, sugar, orange peel and egg together until mixture is light and fluffy.
• Sift together flour, baking powder and salt. Add to the creamed mixture alternately with milk and orange juice. Fold in pecans and raisins, snipped into pieces with scissors.
• Turn into 7 greased 4½×2¾×2¼" loaf pans. (These midget loaf pans can be found in the housewares section of many stores.)
• Bake in moderate oven (350°) about 40 minutes, or until cake tester inserted in center of loaf comes out clean. Let stand in pan 10 minutes.

• Turn onto wire rack to cool. While slightly warm, spread with Orange Topping. Makes 7 individual loaves.

Note: You can bake the batter in a 9×5×3" greased loaf pan. Bake in moderate oven (350°) about 1 hour and 15 minutes, or until bread tests done. Makes 1 loaf.

Orange Topping: Combine 1 c. sifted confectioners sugar, 1½ tblsp. orange juice and ½ tsp. grated orange peel. Stir until smooth.

ORANGE-FIG NUT BREAD

Just the bread to serve to afternoon callers with a cup of tea or coffee

¾ c. boiling water
1 c. finely chopped figs
2 tblsp. butter or margarine
1½ c. sifted all-purpose flour
½ c. sugar
1 tsp. salt
3 tsp. baking powder
1 tsp. vanilla
1 egg, beaten
4 tsp. grated orange peel
⅓ c. orange juice
¾ c. whole-bran cereal
½ c. chopped walnuts

• Pour boiling water over figs and butter; let stand for 10 minutes.
• Sift together flour, sugar, salt and baking powder.
• Add vanilla, egg, orange peel and juice to figs. Beat well.
• Add sifted dry ingredients and cereal to fig mixture. Beat well. Fold in chopped nuts.
• Pour into a greased 8½×4½×2½" loaf pan; push batter into corners.
• Bake in moderate oven (350°) 45 to 50 minutes, or until a cake tester

or wooden pick inserted in center comes out clean. (For ovenproof glass loaf pan reduce oven temperature to 325°.)
• Let stand in pan 10 minutes. Loosen sides of loaf with knife; turn onto wire rack to cool. Wrap in foil or plastic wrap and store in a cool place, or freeze. Let stand overnight before slicing. Makes 1 loaf.

BANANA BREAD

One of the most popular nut breads —chop nuts fine for easy slicing

3 ½   c. sifted all-purpose flour
3   tsp. baking powder
1   tsp. salt
1   tsp. baking soda
2   c. mashed, ripe bananas
        (4 to 6)
2   tblsp. lemon juice
¾   c. shortening
1 ½   c. sugar
3   eggs
¾   c. milk
½   c. chopped pecans or walnuts

• Sift together flour, baking powder, salt and baking soda.
• Mash bananas with rotary beater or fork. Add lemon juice and mix.
• Cream shortening and sugar with electric mixer at medium speed, or with spoon. Add eggs and beat thoroughly until very light and fluffy (4 minutes' beating in all). Add sifted dry ingredients alternately with milk; fold in bananas and nuts. Beat after each addition.
• Pour into 2 greased 8½ ×4½ ×2½″ loaf pans.
• Bake in moderate oven (350°) 1 hour, or until cake tester or wooden

pick inserted in center of loaf comes out clean. Cool in pans 10 minutes. Remove from pans and cool on wire rack. Wrap in foil or plastic wrap and let stand in cool place overnight before slicing, or freeze. Makes 2 loaves.

PEACHY OATMEAL BREAD

You'll enjoy this as a dessert or a coffee cake. Eat it with a fork

1 ¾   c. sifted all-purpose flour
¾   c. granulated sugar
4 ½   tsp. baking powder
¾   tsp. salt
1 ½   tsp. cinnamon
¾   tsp. nutmeg
¼   tsp. cloves
1 ½   c. quick-cooking rolled oats,
        uncooked
½   c. chopped nuts
⅔   c. milk
1   egg, slightly beaten
½   c. melted butter or margarine
1   (1 lb. 14 oz.) can cling
        peaches, well drained
⅓   c. brown sugar, firmly
        packed
3   tblsp. melted butter or
        margarine

• Sift together flour, granulated sugar, baking powder, salt and spices. Stir in oats and nuts.
• Combine milk, egg and ½ c. melted butter. Stir into dry ingredients until moistened. Do not beat.
• Pour batter into a greased 8×8×-2″ baking pan. Bake in moderate oven (375°) 40 to 45 minutes. Cool in pan.
• Chop or slice peaches. Arrange on cooled bread. Sprinkle with brown sugar and dribble 3 tblsp. melted but-

ter on top. Broil 4" from broiler unit until topping bubbles and tops of peaches begin to brown. Makes about 9 servings.

Note: You can freeze this bread if you wish. Defrost and add topping just before serving.

To Cut Nut Breads

Cool the bread several hours or overnight before slicing. If in a hurry, partly freeze bread; it will slice without crumbling.

GLAZED LEMON BREAD

So good we reprint it from Freezing & Canning Cookbook—*make butter sandwiches to serve with fruit salads*

⅓   c. melted butter
1 ¼ c. sugar
2   eggs
¼   tsp. almond extract
1 ½ c. sifted all-purpose flour
1   tsp. baking powder
1   tsp. salt
½   c. milk
1   tblsp. grated lemon peel
½   c. chopped nuts
3   tblsp. fresh lemon juice

• Blend well the butter and 1 c. sugar; beat in eggs, one at a time. Add almond extract.
• Sift together dry ingredients; add to egg mixture alternately with milk. Blend just to mix. Fold in peel and nuts.
• Turn into a greased 8½ × 4½ × 2¾" ovenproof glass loaf pan. Bake in slow oven (325°) about 70 minutes, or until loaf tests done in center.

• Mix lemon juice and ¼ c. sugar; immediately spoon over hot loaf. Cool 10 minutes. Remove from pan; cool on rack. Do not cut for 24 hours (it will slice easily). Makes 1 loaf.

Note: If you bake this bread in a metal 8½ × 4½ × 2½" loaf pan, use a moderate oven (350°).

SWEET POTATO NUT BREAD

Sweet and moist, extra light. This big recipe makes loaves and muffins

½   c. soft butter or margarine
½   c. shortening
2 ⅔ c. sugar
4   eggs
2   c. cold, mashed sweet
       potatoes
3 ½ c. sifted all-purpose flour
1   tsp. salt
1   tsp. cinnamon
1 ½ tsp. nutmeg
2   tsp. baking soda
1   c. chopped walnuts
⅔   c. cold, strong black coffee

• Cream butter, shortening and sugar. Add eggs, one at a time, mixing well after each addition. Blend in sweet potatoes.
• Sift together dry ingredients; add nuts. Stir into creamed mixture alternately with cold coffee.
• Pour batter into 2 greased 9×5×3" loaf pans and 8 greased muffin-pan cups. Bake in moderate oven (375°) 1 hour for loaves and 25 minutes for muffins, or until they test done in center.
• Cool 10 minutes; remove from pans and cool completely. Makes 2 loaves plus 8 muffins.

CARROT SANDWICH BREAD

Sliced thin, this nut bread makes marvelous sandwiches. Do try it

1 c. finely grated raw carrots
1 c. brown sugar
1 tsp. baking soda
1 tblsp. melted shortening
1 c. boiling water
2 eggs
2½ tsp. baking powder
1 tsp. salt
1½ c. sifted all-purpose flour
1 c. whole wheat flour
1 c. chopped walnuts

• Combine carrots, sugar, baking soda and shortening in a large bowl. Pour on boiling water and stir just to mix. Set aside until cool.

• Beat eggs with a fork and add to cooled carrot mixture. Sift in the baking powder, salt and all-purpose flour. Stir in whole wheat flour. Fold in walnuts.

• Pour into a greased 8½ × 4½ × 2½" loaf pan. Let stand 5 minutes.

• Bake in moderate oven (350°) 1 hour. Remove from pan and cool on wire rack. Bread slices better if allowed to stand, wrapped in aluminum foil or plastic wrap, in a cold place overnight. Makes 1 loaf.

OVEN-BAKED BROWN BREAD

Molasses-flavored nut bread for sandwiches—fine escort for baked beans

1½ c. sifted all-purpose flour
1½ c. rye flour
1 c. yellow cornmeal
1 tsp. baking soda
1 tsp. salt
½ c. seedless raisins
⅔ c. chopped walnuts
2 c. buttermilk
½ c. dark molasses
Butter

• Stir together flour, rye flour, cornmeal, baking soda and salt to mix thoroughly. Stir in raisins and nuts.

• Slowly add buttermilk and molasses alternately to dry ingredients; beat after each addition.

• Pour batter into a greased 9×5×-3" loaf pan.

• Bake in moderate oven (375°) 50 minutes, or until cake tester or wooden pick inserted in center of loaf comes out clean.

• Remove from oven and let stand in pan 5 minutes; loosen sides with knife and turn out on wire rack. While still warm, brush top with butter. Serve warm with baked beans. (Make bread and butter sandwiches with cool loaf.) Makes 1 loaf.

Index

K

L

J

P

Q

R

T

V

W

Y

Z